THE STORY OF
THE WEST

THE STORY OF
THE WEST

A HISTORY OF THE AMERICAN
WEST AND ITS PEOPLE

ROBERT M. UTLEY, GENERAL EDITOR

LONDON, NEW YORK, MUNICH,
MELBOURNE AND DELHI

Managing Art Editor Louise Dick
Managing Editor Debra Clapson
Production Wendy Penn
Digital Maps Created by
John Plumer, JP Graphics

Editorial Direction Andrew Heritage
Art Direction Bryn Walls

Produced for Dorling Kindersley by

Hydra Publishing LLC
Publisher Sean Moore
50 Mallard Rise, Irvington, New York 10533
Editor George Ochoa
Art Editor Claire Legemah
Imaging & Photo-Retouching Nick Harris
Design Assistance Rebecca Painter
Commissioned Photography Karen Prince

Smithsonian Project Coordinator
Ellen Nanney
Photo Researcher
Amy Pastan

First American Edition, 2003
10 9 8 7 6 5 4 3 2 1

Published in the United States by
DK Publishing, Inc.
375 Hudson Street
New York, New York 10014

ISBN 978-0-7894-9660-7
ISBN 0-7894-9660-7

Color reproduction by GRB, Italy
Printed and bound in China by
Hung Hing offset printing Co Ltd.

For our complete catalog visit
www.dk.com

CONTENTS

INTRODUCTION

THE AMERICAN WEST, especially the "Old West" of frontier times, continues to fascinate not only Americans but people around the world. The western movie is far from extinct. Cable television, especially the History Channel, commands a wide audience for western documentaries. Books good and bad, fiction and nonfiction, yearly roll off the presses. Magazines featuring the Old West enjoy wide circulation. Reenactment groups—cowboys, Indians, soldiers, mountain men, covered-wagon migrants—flourish in every western state, and some in the East and South as well. They have sprung up in Europe too: "Texas Rangers" assemble in England, and a meticulously adorned band of "Lakota Sioux" gathers each year in the Bulgarian mountains that these make-believe Indians call their "Black Hills."

For decades, from New York and Washington to Seattle and Los Angeles, Westerner corrals have brought together in monthly meetings men and women of every profession who share a love of western history. All over the West, state, county, and local historical societies evoke and celebrate their western heritage. The Western History Association joins scholars and buffs in yearly conventions and quarterly publications. The Western Writers of America unite historians and novelists to promote and respond to the public's zest for the Old West. And as the new century begins, Internet search engines can call up information and displays on virtually every aspect of western American history.

Of course, much that the public regards as western history is really western legend. Hardly any realm of our national past so readily lends itself to mythology as the western past. The Indian; the man on horseback; the six-shooter practitioner; the covered-wagon pioneer heeding the call of Manifest Destiny to carve out a new home in the wilderness; the wilderness itself, whether mountain, plain, or desert—all lend themselves to sagas that stir the public imagination even while distorting or substituting for reality. Buffalo Bill Cody's Wild West Show and like circuses nourished the western legend and then fed on it. Both print and visual media still peddle it.

Yet, when properly presented, the West claims a history as solid and appealing as the legend. After years of neglect, in the past decade and a half academia has rediscovered a West full of interest, significance, and ample scope for scholarly debate.

"Traditionalists" no longer pay homage to Frederick Jackson Turner, once the doyen of all westernists, but cling to elements of his largely discredited "frontier thesis." They tell the story of successive waves of migrating peoples, European colonials and then Americans, and appraise their successes and failures in exploiting western resources or establishing new civilizations.

Champions of the so-called "New Western History" discard the frontier concept altogether. They emphasize continuities that transcend frontiers and chronological units. They portray westering Americans as failures, and Indians, minorities, women, and the environment as victims. Race, gender, and ethnicity are rallying cries of a generation of scholars seeking fresh interpretations at the expense of traditionalists who still labor in the shadow of Turner. The different ways of viewing the Old West have kindled tensions in the scholarly world, but also brought vibrant new life to western studies. Entering the twenty-first century, westernists have grown increasingly aware that the history of the American West is not solely the Old West history of fur trappers, cowboys, Indians, gunmen, and other traditional players. It is also a West of families, women, and children, as well as a West no longer to be labeled "old." Whether or not Turner's frontier thesis ever had interpretive meaning, the frontier of settlement had indeed vanished by the end of the nineteenth century. The twentieth century transformed the West more substantively and radically than all the preceding centuries combined. More and more historians specialize in a modern West that almost entirely eclipsed the Old West of earlier centuries.

When the Smithsonian Institution asked me to assemble a panel of historians to tell the story of the American West, we set several goals. For one, we intended to target the general reader, not the academic specialist. For another, we wanted distinguished historians who could write narrative prose that the general reader would find interesting and informative, and that the scholarly community would applaud. We sought sound history untainted by Buffalo Bill legendry, but we also sought history unencumbered by scholarly controversy. We aimed for the complete western story, beginning with the peoples of pre-Columbian times and extending beyond the era of the Old West through the twentieth century to the present.

The historians who agreed to participate in this undertaking are among the most distinguished in their respective fields. They bring to the task not only the insights of long study and reflection but the ability to communicate beyond the classroom. They have enabled the Smithsonian to meet all the goals we set at the beginning of this project.

CHAPTER 1: THE WEST BEFORE COLUMBUS, PREHISTORY TO A.D. 1500. Before Columbus made landfall, humans had roamed the New World for millennia. In the American West, their story is one of shifting demography, varied means of subsistence, warfare, ingenuity, and ultimately either extinction or evolution into a succeeding people. As the precursors of later inhabitants of the West, and as manipulators of the western environment in lasting and long-unappreciated ways, they are a large element of the story of the West. W. Raymond Wood's impressive contributions to the literature of this time make him ideal to relate this story.

CHAPTER 2: SPAIN IN THE WEST, 1500–1800. Columbus launched nearly three centuries of colonial history. For the American West, the imperial rivals mostly contested the fringes of the region while struggling for possession of less daunting environments elsewhere in the Americas. French, British, and Russians nibbled at the edges, but Spain dominated the colonial era in what later became the American Southwest and California. Rarely has the story of Spanish conquest and colonization been told with more insight and narrative appeal than by John Kessell, who has devoted a long career to understanding what these colonial invaders gained and then lost.

CHAPTER 3: THE WINDS OF CHANGE, 1800–1840. Except for some lingering rivalries, the American Revolution ended the colonial era in eastern North America. For the American West, however, the end came with the Louisiana Purchase of 1803. For the next four decades, Americans devoted themselves to finding out and exploiting the resources of what they had bought. Government exploring expeditions such as that of Lewis and Clark helped translate fanciful theory into the beginnings of reality. But fur trappers, traders, and other opportunists seeking financial reward contributed even more to geographical knowledge and laid the groundwork for settlement. The history of this period has been immeasurably enriched by the work of James Ronda, who applies his acumen to these formative decades.

CHAPTER 4: THE EAGLE SCREAMS, 1840–1865. Change on a massive scale abruptly followed the first tentative probes. Overland immigrants headed for California and Oregon, even while the one belonged to Mexico and the other remained disputed with Great Britain. Settlement of the Oregon boundary dispute in 1846 and the Mexican War of 1846-48 transformed the United States into a continental nation, with the West both linking and dividing the eastern states and the Pacific possessions. These huge territorial acquisitions confronted the nation with daunting challenges, not least Indians and slavery. The distinguished John Logan Allen tells how the eagle screamed through a civil war that crushed slavery but not its ugly legacy.

CHAPTER 5: THE WEST SUBDUED, 1865–1900. Not even a screaming eagle, however, could subdue the Indians. More than two decades of war, diplomacy, and a cultural gulf that doomed mutual understanding traced the relations of the two peoples after Appomattox . Tribal identity and continuity ignored the vanishing frontier, and Indian-white relations persisted as a continuing theme throughout the twentieth century. Other themes traditionally identified with the Old West also endured in changing incarnations. Even so, the stereotypical cowboys, Indians, ranchers, sod-busters, traders, miners, town-builders, and others identified with the decades between the Civil War and the close of Turner's frontier in 1890 lived on only in the public imagination. But for a time, the stereotypes were real, or almost real, and their experience forms a significant chapter in the chronicle of millennia of human occupation. Glenda Riley, of high reputation in all aspects of western history, relates the story of the close of the Old West.

CHAPTER 6: THE CONTEMPORARY WEST, 1900 TO PRESENT. The late Gerald Nash was the preeminent authority on the West in the twentieth century. The perspectives of time permit the patterns of a century's evolution to emerge more clearly afterward than during it, as Nash's narrative, ably completed by Richard Etulain, demonstrates. The harnessing of river systems with great dams; electrification; urbanization; industrialization; the exploitation of reservoirs of oil and gas; the blossoming of agribusiness; the mass migration to the Sunbelt and high-mountain retreats; the proliferation of air corridors; the explosion in motor transport and highways; and the role of all these developments in degrading the land, water, air, flora, and fauna—such are some of the motifs that are unique to the twentieth century or legacies of earlier centuries. Thus comes to a close our history of the American West from its human beginnings to the present.

Taken together, the contributions of these esteemed scholars, supplemented by informative maps and stunning images, add up to a new kind of western history: one that is historically sound while satisfying our perennial fascination with the West.

Robert M. Utley

PINE RIDGE, SOUTH DAKOTA
Indian-white relations were a major part of the story of the West. In 1891, Sioux gather around two white men on horseback.

CHAPTER 1

THE WEST BEFORE COLUMBUS

PREHISTORY TO A.D. 1500

AGES BEFORE EUROPEANS REACHED
THE WEST, NATIVE AMERICANS HAD SETTLED
IN EVERY PART OF THE REGION. THE STORY OF THESE
FIRST WESTERNERS BEGINS THOUSANDS OF YEARS AGO
WITH THE EPIC MIGRATION OF THEIR ANCESTORS FROM
ASIA ACROSS THE BERING STRAIT, AND CONTINUES TO
1500 WITH THE DEVELOPMENT OF PREHISTORIC
WESTERN CULTURES. FROM THE PACIFIC COAST TO
THE GREAT PLAINS, THESE SOCIETIES WERE AS
RICHLY VARIED AS THE TERRAINS IN
WHICH THEY DEVELOPED.

No written records are available about life in the West before Columbus. A timeline of this period must rely on archaeological, linguistic, and biological evidence and tribal folklore. From this record emerges a story of migration and cultural development: one in which Paleo-Indians, the ancestors of present-day Native Americans, entered North America from Asia, colonized the West, and developed complex societies.

38,000–10,000 B.C.
Asian hunters arrive in North America from Siberia, possibly by crossing the Bering Strait.

9500–8000 B.C.
Clovis culture spreads throughout North America. Also active in the West is the Folsom culture.

8000–4500 B.C.
Plano cultures flourish in the Great Plains.

7500 B.C.
Desert culture produces the earliest baskets in North America at Danger Cave, Utah.

5000–1000 B.C.
Archaic or Foraging period: people in North America develop greater variety in their diet and cultures. Most of the big game animals they had previously hunted have become extinct.

3500 B.C.
At a settlement of the Cochise culture at Bat Cave, New Mexico, maize (corn), introduced from Mexico, is cultivated.

1500 B.C.–A.D. 1500
Formative or Postarchaic period: agriculture spreads, along with villages, weaving, and pottery.

300 B.C.–A.D. 1500
In Arizona and New Mexico, the Mogollon and Hohokam cultures practice corn cultivation.

100 B.C.–A.D. 1300
Anasazi culture flourishes in the Four Corners region where Colorado, Utah, Arizona, and New Mexico meet. They pass first through the Basket Maker period, and later through the Pueblo period, during which they live in multi-floored buildings.

A.D. 300
Bow and arrow appear in the Great Plains.

A.D. 900
*•The Inuit of Alaska split into two groups, Inupiat and Yupik.
•Agricultural peoples from the Northeast migrate into the Great Plains.*

A.D. 1000
In the Northwest Coast region, Native Americans build totem poles.

A.D. 1025–1400
Navajo and Apache ancestors reach the Southwest.

A.D. 1300
Paiute, Ute, and Shoshone migrate from California across the Great Basin.

A.D. 1400
Middle Missouri culture develops in the Dakotas.

NATIVE AMERICANS ARRIVE

DESPITE THE CULTURAL AND LINGUISTIC DIVERSITY THEY LATER DEVELOPED, NATIVE AMERICANS ARE A SINGLE RACE WHOSE ANCESTORS FIRST ENTERED THE NEW WORLD 12,000 YEARS AGO OR EARLIER. THEIR PRINCIPAL MIGRATION ROUTE WAS FROM EASTERN SIBERIA ACROSS THE BERING LAND BRIDGE. BY 11,000 YEARS AGO, THEY WERE IN WHAT IS NOW THE AMERICAN WEST.

PERHAPS THE GREATEST migration in human history was the slow filtering of immigrants across the Bering Strait into North America during the waning of the last glacial era. No one yet knows when the first people crossed into the New World, but it was the beginning of a slow southward movement that eventually took them to the very tip of South America, an airline distance of more than 10,000 miles, and forty percent of the world's circumference.

The people that Columbus found in the New World were never formally named. The term "Indian" that came to be used for all Native Americans—at least those living south of the Inuit, or Eskimo—was based on a letter in which Columbus offhandedly called them *los indios*. The misconception that they were natives of India, although soon corrected, did not stop Europeans from applying the term "Indian" to Native Americans wherever they lived, despite their innumerable languages and cultural differences.

PEOPLING OF THE AMERICAS

The first human settlers reached the Americas by crossing the Bering land bridge (Beringia) from Siberia about 25,000 years ago, but their progress south was blocked by the vast Cordillerian and Laurentide ice sheets. The melting of the ice over the next few millennia isolated the settlers from Asia, as Beringia was flooded by seawater, while opening land passages for them to travel south and permitting them to settle the North American landmass and reach southern South America by c. 12,000 B.C. The big-game hunters of North America developed large, sharp stone points (Clovis points) capable of piercing mammoth hide; by about 9000 B.C. herds of mammoth had been hunted to extinction.

Migration into North America, across the Bering land bridge created by lower sea levels during the last Ice Age, possibly as early as 25,000 years ago

Ice corridor opened from 11,300 B.C.

Arctic Circle

Beringia

Bluefish Cave

Dry Creek

Cordillerian Ice Sheet

Mackenzie

Laurentide Ice Sheet

Arctic Circle

NORTH AMERICA

ROCKY MOUNTAINS

Lake Agassiz

Lake Minong

Lake Missoula

Lake Chippewa

Great Lakes

St. Lawrence

Wilson Butte Cave

Lake Bonneville

GREAT PLAINS

Missouri

Meadowcroft

APPALACHIAN MOUNTAINS

Lake Lahontan

Lamb Spring

Kimmswoci

Clovis

Mississippi

San Diego

120

30

Rio Grande

Gulf of Mexico

Early human settlers extinguish North American megafauna (mastodons and mammoths) c.8000 B.C.

30

Tropic of Cancer

COLONIZATION OF THE AMERICAS

→ probable colonization route
◆ major human settlement site, 25,000–12,000 B.C.
⬚ extent of ice sheet 18,000 B.C.
⬚ extent of ice sheet 10,000 B.C.
⋯ coastline c.18,000 B.C.
⬬ ancient lake

Valsequillo

El Bosque

WEST INDIES

Caribbean Sea

Taimataima

80

Orinoco

GUIANA HIGHLANDS

El Inga

ANDES

Equator

Equator

AMAZON BASIN

Amazon

Pedra Furada early classical settlement

ALASKAN COAST RANGE

Probably the first part of the New World to be settled, Alaska is home to mountains of forbidding height. While many of the mountains remained heavily glaciated even after the last Ice Age, Alaska's coastal areas developed a moderate climate.

Guitarrero Cave

SOUTH AMERICA

Pikimachay

São Francisco

Tropic of Capricorn

Alice Böer

Parana

30

Querero

There was a reasonable explanation for this generalization: the residents of the New World were a single race despite their diversity in biology, language, and culture. Few people would confuse a Cheyenne Indian with a Hopi, for there are conspicuous differences in physical characteristics as one crosses the continents. Nevertheless, there is perhaps less biological variation in the Indians of North and South America than there is in the far smaller confines of Europe.

As opposed to their biology, there was incredible diversity in their languages: about 550 different languages were spoken in North America, perhaps 150 of them in the American West—an area that was far more complex linguistically than all of Europe. Some languages might differ in vocabulary and grammar as little as English and German, but more often the languages were as incomprehensible as English and Chinese might be to a Malay or a Samoan speaker. The splintering of language groups was most

Monte Verde

PATAGONIA

Patagonia settled by 11,000 B.C.

Fell's Cave

⟡FROM LAND BRIDGE TO STRAIT⟡

THOUGH it is a commonplace that at least some of the ancestors of Native Americans crossed into the New World across the "Bering land bridge," that term may conjure a false image of a narrow, rickety structure barely able to support its migrants. In fact, the Bering land bridge, or Beringia, a corridor of land that most recently joined Siberia and Alaska from about 25,000 to 14,000 years ago, was at times 1,000 miles wide—about one-third the distance across the present-day United States. Those traveling across it would not have known they were on a bridge, or that they were migrating from one continent to another. The climate and terrain—that of steppe and tundra—would have been the same as in adjacent areas, as would the herds of grass-eating mammals—mammoths, mastodons, giant bison, musk ox, horses, and others—that they hunted for food and whose movements they were following.

As the last Ice Age came to an end, sea levels rose, flooding the Bering land bridge and creating the 51-mile wide Bering Strait. Nevertheless, the region did not become uninhabited, nor did traffic across the Bering Strait become completely impossible. From about 2500 to 1000 B.C., humans crossed the Bering Sea (which extends from the Bering Strait to the Aleutian Islands) from Siberia to North America, using boats made of skin and wood. These were the ancestors of the Inuit, or Eskimo, and Aleut peoples who still live in Alaska and the Aleutian Islands. The Inuits continued to migrate eastward, forming a distinct cultural group with a remarkably wide range, living in coastal areas within and near the Arctic Circle from Siberia to Alaska to Canada to Greenland.

The cultures of the Bering Sea traditionally lived by hunting and fishing, with sea mammals (such as seal, whale, and walrus) and caribou as preferred game. The animals provided not only food but oil for heat and light, and bone and hides for tools and weapons.

The Bering Strait remained the preserve of the Inuits and Aleuts until 1648, when Russian navigator Semyon Ivanov Dezhnyov sailed through it. However, Dezhnyov's discovery was not publicized, and Danish navigator Vitus Bering, sailing for Russia, rediscovered it in 1728. This time the discovery was publicized, and to this day the strait—and the land bridge that preceded it—go by the name of Bering.

INHABITANT OF KOTZEBUE SOUND
Inuit culture was remarkably well adapted to life in the frigid Arctic Circle. Caribou and other animal hides provided warm clothing for people like this man, a resident of the Kotzebue Sound region near the Bering Strait whose image was captured in 1821.

HARPOONS AND SPEARS
The natives of Alaska obtained much of their food by hunting sea animals. Hunters used harpoons (such as those at top and middle) to kill large seals and beluga whales. They hunted small game, such as waterfowl, with spears (such as the one at bottom).

pronounced among the small tribes of the Columbia Plateau and in California, with the Great Basin showing the least diversity.

Perhaps their biological similarities are the result of limited physical variation in the populations that crossed the Bering Strait, coupled with the relative recency of their arrival. But when did they arrive? Many questions remain concerning the peopling of the New World despite more than a century of archaeological and other investigations. Estimates of antiquity range up to 40,000 years ago, though there are more conservative and generally accepted estimates of between 28,000 and 12,000 years. The matter will not be resolved soon, but this much is clear: the ancestors of Native Americans entered the New World from eastern Siberia, a conclusion supported by DNA studies and by many other lines of biological evidence.

Several means of crossing the Bering Strait were practical. First, during the last Ice Age, sea levels dropped nearly 370 feet because of the vast amount of water that had been absorbed in the glaciers that covered much of Canada and northern Europe. The depressed sea level created a 1,000-mile-wide land corridor that joined Siberia and Alaska, providing a land bridge that many archaeologists think was probably the principal means for crossing into North America from Asia. The most recent such bridge existed between about 25,000 to 14,000 years ago. Crossing the frozen sea ice in winter also would have been practical, if hazardous, especially if the ocean level was lower and Bering Strait was narrower than today. A final means of entry was by some form of watercraft, although this is considered the least likely possibility because of the heavy, dangerous tides in the strait. Still, people reached Australia more than 40,000 years ago by sea, so the possibility of immigration by this means should remain open.

Inuit ivory amulet

ALEUT HUNTING VISOR
Hunters from the Aleutian Islands used kayaks to navigate the surrounding waters. To shield their eyes from glare, they often wore visors while on the hunt. This visor is decorated with ivory carvings of gull and walrus heads.

INUIT COUPLE
Living in one of the most inhospitable areas in the world, the Inuits, such as this Kaviagmiut man and wife, depended on close familial bonds for their very survival. Extended families—often including grandparents, aunts, uncles, and cousins—frequently lived together under one roof.

"IN THE BEGINNING THERE WAS NO SUN, NO MOON, NO STARS...EVERYWHERE THERE WAS ONLY WATER. A RAFT CAME FLOATING ON THE WATER. IT CAME FROM THE NORTH."

—MAIDU MYTH, ON THE RAFT THAT CARRIED THE CREATOR OF PEOPLE

PAWNEE CHIEF
American artist George Catlin's unfinished portrait of Pawnee leader Te-ah'-ke-ra-lée-re-coo, from 1832. The chief holds a calumet and wears a silver peace medal. The paint on the subject's face and shoulders shows that he is prepared for war.

OCCUPYING THE NEW WORLD

After entering what is now Alaska, immigrants faced the mile-thick sheets of ice that covered most of Canada. People could have moved south by one of two routes: along the glacier-rimmed, mountainous northwestern coast to the present-day United States, or along the "ice-free corridor" that at times marked the boundary between the glaciers covering the Rocky Mountains of western Canada and the continental mantle of ice to the east. Either route would have been hazardous, and neither has been proved to be the route: perhaps both were used. We may never be sure how the people migrated, for glacial advances and erosion undoubtedly have erased some of their campsites, and still others now lie beneath the waters of the Pacific Ocean, submerged as the ice sheets melted and sea levels rose.

Archaeologists have pieced together a detailed history of the human occupation of the western United States beginning more than 11,000 years ago. There may have been earlier settlers, but the first people in the West about which archaeologists can talk with assurance is the Clovis culture. These "first westerners" occupied much of the western United States beginning about 11,200 years ago, hunting mammoths, giant ground sloths, camels, and other large animals that are now extinct. The horses that Clovis hunters killed also became extinct, and these animals did not become part of Native American life again until the Spaniards reintroduced them.

Humans eventually spread across all of North and South America and the Caribbean islands. They occupied every part of the New World, from the deserts of the American Southwest to the chilly wastes of the Arctic and Patagonia. In the American West they adapted to and lived, at least seasonally, in every microenvironment from arid deserts to grassy steppes to alpine tundra. Some areas, such as the parched wastelands of Nevada, were once more heavily populated than they were at European contact. By A.D. 1500 every part of the continent was being used by these first inhabitants either for living space or hunting. No part of the New World was a *terrae nullis*, or "empty land."

⇥HOW THE KIOWAS GOT HERE⇤

MANY NATIVE AMERICANS look skeptically on scientific accounts of their origins. They find more truth in their tribal myths and legends, which typically claim that their people originated in America, rather than coming from some other continent.

One such legend is that of the Kiowas, a Plains nation. According to their folklore, Saynday, a superhuman hero, discovered his people trapped under a hollow cottonwood tree. The people cried to get out, and Saynday complied, sticking his hand through an opening in the tree and under the ground. Feeling in the dark, he grabbed the hand of the nearest person and told everyone underground to do the same, so that they formed a human chain. Then Saynday pulled the first person out, and the others followed, pouring out of the hole like ants. Their rescuer declared, "I will teach you how to live in this world, how to find food to eat, and how to be happy. I will be your Uncle Saynday, and you will be my people."

The people, who became known as Kiowas, kept pouring out from underground until a pregnant woman got stuck in the hole and blocked it so that the rest couldn't get out. That, says the legend, is why the Kiowas "have always been a small tribe."

KIOWA CEREMONIAL FAN
Resplendent with eagle feathers and beads, this fan was used by the Kiowas during peyote ceremonies. The mind-altering drug peyote was used as a sacred substance by Mexican and southwestern tribes since before Columbus, and later spread to Great Plains tribes such as the Kiowas.

INUIT HUNTERS
Photographed in the Bering Sea in 1877, two Inuits travel the Arctic waters in kayaks while on the hunt for seals. The hunter on the left wears a sun visor and holds a harpoon.

BLUFFS ABOVE THE MISSOURI
Painted in 1832, this view overlooking the Missouri River shows the region before the mass migration of white settlers.

"HO! YE HILLS, VALLEYS, RIVERS, LAKES, TREES, GRASSES, ALL YE OF THE EARTH, I BID YOU HEAR ME! INTO YOUR MIDST HAS COME A NEW LIFE."

—OMAHA SONG INTRODUCING A NEWBORN CHILD TO THE UNIVERSE

THE LAND AND ITS RESOURCES

THE WEST BEFORE COLUMBUS WAS ONE OF DIVERSE ENVIRONMENTS: FROM LUSH FORESTS TO HARSH DESERTS; FROM ROLLING GRASSLANDS TO ARCTIC SNOWS. AS NATIVE AMERICANS ADAPTED TO USE THE RESOURCES OF THE DIFFERENT SETTINGS IN WHICH THEY LIVED, DISTINCT CULTURE AREAS DEVELOPED, EACH MARKED BY A UNIQUE WAY OF LIFE.

NATIVE NORTH AMERICA at the time of Columbus can be divided into two great cultural provinces along a sinuous boundary that extended from the St. Lawrence River to the mouth of the Colorado River in southern California. North and west of this irregular line, most of the groups depended for their living on hunting, fishing, and gathering wild foods; to the south and east, peoples' economies relied to varying degrees on supplementing these wild foods with garden crops—principally corn (or maize), beans, squash, and sunflowers.

The Pueblo Indians and many of their neighbors in the Southwest, as well as the village-dwelling Plains Indians along the Missouri and Arkansas rivers, had this dual hunting and gathering/ gardening economy. Food crops were especially important in the Southwest, where men were the farmers, and less so in the Great Plains, where women gardened to supplement a diet dominated by buffalo and other game. But despite the importance of crops among a few groups, nowhere in the West could people ignore the wild plants and animals surrounding them. The only domesticated

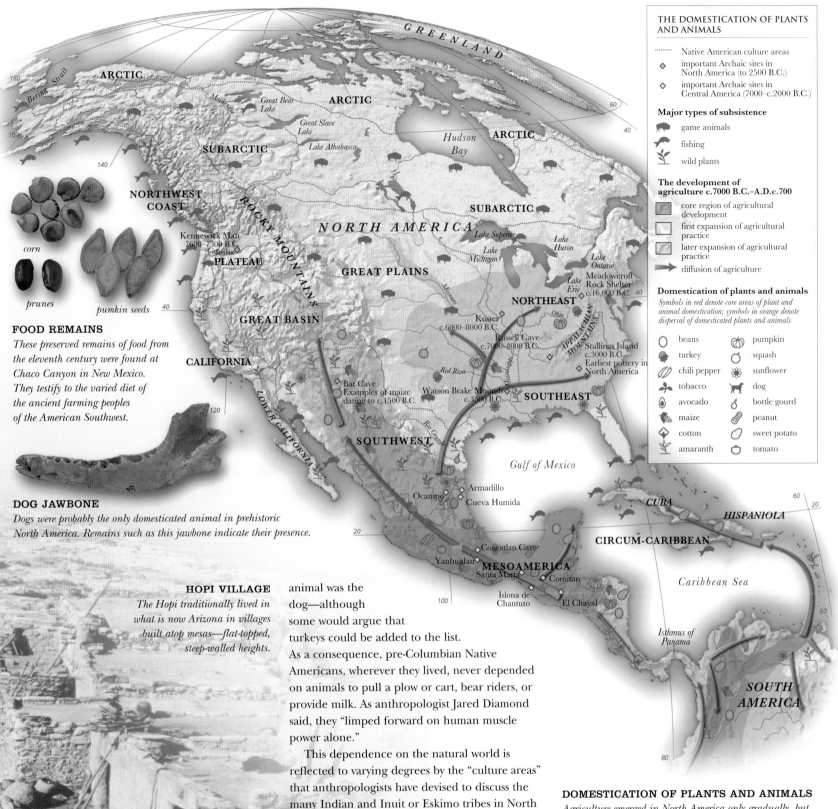

THE DOMESTICATION OF PLANTS AND ANIMALS

---------- Native American culture areas

◇ important Archaic sites in North America (to 2500 B.C.)

◇ important Archaic sites in Central America (7000–c.2000 B.C.)

Major types of subsistence

🐂 game animals

🐟 fishing

🌱 wild plants

The development of agriculture c.7000 B.C.–A.D.c.700

▨ core region of agricultural development

▢ first expansion of agricultural practice

▨ later expansion of agricultural practice

→ diffusion of agriculture

Domestication of plants and animals

Symbols in red denote core areas of plant and animal domestication; symbols in orange denote dispersal of domesticated plants and animals

○ beans   pumpkin

turkey   squash

chili pepper   sunflower

tobacco   dog

avocado   bottle gourd

maize   peanut

cotton   sweet potato

amaranth   tomato

FOOD REMAINS

These preserved remains of food from the eleventh century were found at Chaco Canyon in New Mexico. They testify to the varied diet of the ancient farming peoples of the American Southwest.

corn

prunes

pumpkin seeds

DOG JAWBONE

Dogs were probably the only domesticated animal in prehistoric North America. Remains such as this jawbone indicate their presence.

HOPI VILLAGE

The Hopi traditionally lived in what is now Arizona in villages built atop mesas—flat-topped, steep-walled heights.

animal was the dog—although some would argue that turkeys could be added to the list. As a consequence, pre-Columbian Native Americans, wherever they lived, never depended on animals to pull a plow or cart, bear riders, or provide milk. As anthropologist Jared Diamond said, they "limped forward on human muscle power alone."

This dependence on the natural world is reflected to varying degrees by the "culture areas" that anthropologists have devised to discuss the many Indian and Inuit or Eskimo tribes in North America. Tribes are grouped into culture areas depending largely on the way in which they made their living and on elements of culture that imply related histories. Geographers such as Fenneman and Hunt have divided the western United States into physiographic provinces that correspond in many ways to these culture areas. The parallels are all the more understandable since all human groups must closely adapt to their immediate surroundings or they will not survive.

DOMESTICATION OF PLANTS AND ANIMALS

Agriculture emerged in North America only gradually, but proved revolutionary in its impact. Animal husbandry was almost absent. In Central America, a few plants were cultivated as a supplement to hunting as early as 5000 B.C. New plants—especially corn (maize), beans, and squash—were brought under cultivation, and Central America came to be dominated by settled horticultural villages. Further north, the first crops served initially as supplements rather than staples. Agriculture became more important throughout the first millennium A.D., with many villagers in the Southwest and Southeast becoming largely agricultural by the beginning of the second millennium A.D.

THE GREAT PLAINS

For many people the Great Plains—the great interior grasslands of the United States—are the quintessential West, perhaps because the feathered headdresses and tipis that characterize their residents have become part of the stereotypical image of the American Indian for more than a century. The Great Plains comprise the western two-thirds of the Interior Plains province, a semiarid plain that rises gradually from elevations of about 2,000 feet west of the Mississippi valley to nearly 5,000 feet at the Rocky Mountain front. Extending from southern Canada to south Texas, this "sea of grass," later scorned for a time as the "Great American Desert," teemed with human activity for millennia. Great Plains streams, predominantly flowing to the east, cut deeply into the grassy mantle of this gentle incline, were lined by narrow floodplain forests, and provided water and other resources for its inhabitants.

Game was plentiful if unequally distributed, the principal food animal being the buffalo. According to many estimates, some 60 million of these huge shaggy beasts ranged the area. Smaller game included pronghorn antelopes, white-tailed and mule deer, wildfowl (present seasonally by the millions along the many midcontinent flyways), and fish for those tribes along major streams. Rainfall was low, most of the area receiving less than 20 inches annually. The Great Plains is bounded on the west by the Rocky Mountains and their outliers. Like the Black Hills and other upland "islands" that rise above this rolling grassland, these mountain environments provided many resources: plant and animal food, raw material such as obsidian for stone tools, and straight young lodgepole pine trees for tipi poles. In the North, bitterly cold winters alternated with scorching summers.

THE SOUTHWEST

The Southwest at the time of Columbus was a farming area, and it is best known today for its prehistoric cliff dwellings and magnificent

TIPIS ON THE PLAINS
Tipis were the perfect dwellings for the nomadic Plains tribes. Quick to put up and take down, tipis were easy to carry from place to place as these peoples followed the great herds of buffalo that roamed the Plains.

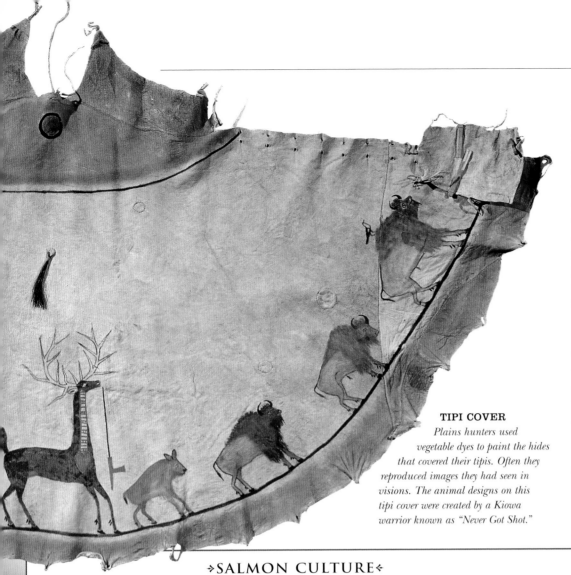

TIPI COVER

Plains hunters used vegetable dyes to paint the hides that covered their tipis. Often they reproduced images they had seen in visions. The animal designs on this tipi cover were created by a Kiowa warrior known as "Never Got Shot."

polychrome pottery. Its heartland was the semiarid Colorado Plateau, the highest plateau in the West, much of it—like the rim of the Grand Canyon—more than a mile above sea level. The most celebrated of its many prehistoric pueblos (or towns) cluster in the southern part of the plateau, encircling the Four Corners area where Utah, Colorado, Arizona, and New Mexico have a common junction. Many other prehistoric and historic pueblos were in the mountainous provinces to the south and east, including those along the upper reaches of the Rio Grande River in New Mexico.

The Southwest is undoubtedly the most colorful part of the West. Streams have eroded deeply into the flat-lying sedimentary rocks, creating brightly colored and steep-walled canyons. The divides between streams have little vegetation; often they consist of bare rock, some of it composed of sheets of lava surrounding now-dormant volcanoes. The mountainous areas are heavily timbered with Ponderosa pine, Douglas fir, and spruce.

The south margin of the Colorado Plateau is bordered by deserts, and the Chihuahan Desert of south-central New Mexico and the Sonoran

⋄SALMON CULTURE⋄

SALMON FISHING was central to many of the peoples who lived in the Columbia Plateau and the Northwest Coast before the arrival of Europeans. The salmon of the North Pacific spend their mature lives in the salt water of the open sea, but return to spawn in the fresh-water streams in which they were hatched, only to die once they have laid their eggs. In prehistoric times, as the salmon made these annual upriver runs, Native Americans waited for them at eddies, rapids, and side streams, ready to spear them or catch them in nets and traps. In the Columbia Plateau, tribes that depended heavily on salmon included the Coeur d'Alene, Kalispel, Klamath, Nez Percé, Spokan, and Umatilla. In the Northwest Coast, they include the Chinook, Nisqually, Sliammon, Suquamish, and Wasco.

The salmon runs took place at roughly the same time each year, allowing residents of the region to plan for the harvest. Often they built villages alongside the river and prepared elaborate traps to catch the fish, including seines, or weighted nets that hang vertically in the water

with floats at the top; and weirs, or fences placed in streams. Fishers thrust their spears into the water from canoes or from platforms built in the water at regular fishing spots. By such means, the tribes of the region annually harvested huge numbers of salmon, drying the surplus on racks and storing it for later use and for trade.

But salmon was not just a matter of food or technology. It influenced many aspects of northwestern culture, including myths, legends, and spiritual practices. Each spring, many Northwest Coast tribes held First Salmon Ceremonies, in which the bones of the first salmon caught that year were returned to the river. Known as the Chief Salmon, this salmon was the object of prayer and song, conducted to ensure the return of the fish the following year.

One Northwest Coast tribe, the Chinooks, gave its name to the area's best-known species of salmon. Before the coming of Europeans, they parlayed their own surpluses of dried salmon, coveted by distant tribes, into a dominant position in regional trade, and gave their name to the region's trade jargon. Not surprisingly, the tribal logo they adopted in modern times represents a salmon.

STONE WEIGHT

On the Northwest Coast, Native American fishermen held down their nets with weights, such as this one found in Oregon.

Hupa man watching for salmon

⊰SOUTHWESTERN POTTERY⊱

THE ART OF POTTERY began to flourish in the Southwest about A.D. 200. It was associated with the spread of farming and of sedentary villages among such cultures as the Mogollon and Patayan. After 400, southwestern pottery became increasingly common, with a dizzying variety of styles replacing the unpainted brown clay plots of earlier times. The Hohokams, for example, made two-color, red-on-buff pots, at first decorated with simple line patterns and later with figures of animals, humans, and gods. The Mimbres, related to the Mogollons, made black-on-white pottery that mixed geometric patterns and human and animal figures.

Among the most impressive potters were the Anasazi of the Four Corners region where present-day Colorado, Utah, Arizona, and New Mexico intersect. From 700 to 1100 they developed many specialized styles of pottery,

often indented and corrugated and typically painted with black-on-white geometric designs. This art reached its peak from 1100 to 1300.

Around 1300, Anasazi civilization came to an end, but many of their traditions were inherited by the Pueblo peoples, descendants who migrated to new locations, such as southeastern Arizona and the Rio Grande Valley. From 1300 to the arrival of the Spanish about 1540, the Pueblos kept developing new styles of pottery, usually decorated in red, black, and white, with both geometric and representational designs. The Hopis introduced unglazed polychrome (many-colored) pottery, known as Sikyatki Polychrome. Among other Pueblo groups, lead glaze paint was used on pottery. Women were the principal makers of pottery.

The Southwestern pottery tradition has continued to the present, and Pueblo pottery is still in demand.

MIMBRES BOWL
The Mogollon of the Mimbres Valley were accomplished makers of black-on-white pottery.

ZUNI WATER JAR
This jar features a rainbird design, which was a favorite of Zuni Pueblo potters in the early nineteenth century.

CLIFF DWELLINGS
Colorado's Mesa Verde National Park is home to the dramatic ruins of a large Anasazi cliff dwelling. The Anasazis probably built cliff dwellings to protect them from their enemies, because it was nearly impossible for intruders to attack these structures without being seen.

Desert of southern Arizona and California extend deep into Mexico. The warm desert climate and low rainfall—three to sixteen inches—support creosote bushes, mesquite, and yuccas. The climate is moderated by altitude, with great variation in temperatures and plant and animal life.

THE GREAT BASIN AND COLUMBIA PLATEAU

The streams in virtually all of the state of Nevada, and in substantial parts of adjoining states, have no outlet to the ocean. Very large lakes developed in this great interior basin during the last glaciation, when rainfall was greater and when Death Valley became a deep, ninety-mile-long lake. Much of western Utah was covered by Lake Bonneville, of which Great Salt Lake is a shrunken remnant. West of Great Salt Lake is the Basin and Range province, an area where one north-south-trending mountain range succeeds another, separated by narrow valleys that, from space,

CANYON DE CHELLY
Ancient Anasazis once lived in Canyon de Chelly in present-day Arizona. Its steep stone walls rose up to 1,200 feet.

THROWING STICKS

Native American hunters in what is now Utah and Arizona used these boomerang-shaped throwing sticks to kill rabbits, which provided them with an important source of protein.

resemble giant ripples. Rainfall, game, and resources are sparse everywhere, and the people lived principally on seeds, nuts, and rodents. Except in "oasis" areas such as around Great Salt Lake, the people were among the most impoverished in North America.

West of the Rocky Mountains and north of the Great Basin, the deserts rise onto the Columbia Plateau. This semiarid upland is drained by two great waterways, the Columbia River and its principal tributary, the Snake. Both streams provided its inhabitants with a bountiful harvest of salmon every fall. Secondary foods were land animals and roots. The plateau is a land of great diversity, its natural bounty augmented to the east, north, and west by the high mountain ranges that enclose it.

CALIFORNIA AND THE NORTHWEST COAST

The western rim of the United States consists of the Pacific Coastal and Mountain region, a 100- to 200-mile-wide band that expands to greater width as one moves north into Canada. The arid valleys in southern California become increasingly moist and vegetated as one goes north, and in coastal Oregon and Washington they are mantled by lush

rain forests of spruce and fir that flourish under 200 inches of rainfall annually on the Olympic peninsula. Acorns provided the principal food for inland residents throughout much of California. Deer and, to a lesser extent, elk were the major source of game. Salmon was another important resource, especially in the northern streams.

The climate of the northwestern coast of the continent is moderated by the Japan Current, so there are no extremes of temperature. The warm offshore current provides water vapor that, blown inland, creates heavy rainfall in the mountains and fast-running streams pouring through the deep valleys. The heavily forested and rugged topography produces spectacular scenery but makes it difficult to travel on foot, so people tended to live in small enclaves, traveling principally by dugout canoes. There was heavy reliance along the coast on the abundant fish, especially salmon, halibut, cod, and herring, and on marine mammals. The most spectacular cultures of the Northwest Coast were in the panhandle of Alaska and along the coast of British Columbia; those in coastal Oregon and Washington blended into the less elaborate tribes of northern California.

CHIEF WITH A CALUMET
*Coo-coo-coo was a chief of the Menominee tribe.
He was supposedly more than 100 years old
when he posed for this George Catlin portrait.*

"THE HOME WAS
THE CENTER
OF LAKOTA
SOCIETY—THE
PLACE WHERE
GOOD SOCIAL
MEMBERS WERE
FORMED AND THE
PLACE WHENCE
FLOWED THE
STRENGTH OF
THE TRIBE."

—LUTHER STANDING BEAR,
LAKOTA SIOUX

THE PEOPLE

MOST WESTERN NATIVE AMERICANS SHARED CERTAIN CULTURAL TRAITS
IN COMMON. STRONGLY INDIVIDUALIST, THEY ORGANIZED THEMSELVES
LOOSELY INTO BANDS OR TRIBES. THEY FOLLOWED HEADMEN WHO
EARNED THEIR CLAIM TO AUTHORITY BY PERSONAL CHARISMA RATHER
THAN FORCE. THEY BELIEVED STRONGLY IN A SUPERNATURAL REALM
TIGHTLY LINKED TO NATURE AND ACCESSIBLE THROUGH RITUAL.

THE MANY TRIBES of the western United
States were most often divided by language,
for nearly every tribe spoke a dialect that
was either not intelligible or was poorly understood
by its neighbors. They did, however, share many
cultural features.

One element especially augured ill for Native
Americans—the fact that, for the most part, they
were incurable individualists. The rights of the
individual were so strongly held and the rights of
those in the community were so strongly valued
that Indians rarely found it possible to effectively
combine into multi-tribal units to fight the white
invaders. The Battle of the Little Big Horn was a
hollow exception, for the coalition of Sioux and

Cheyenne that destroyed General Custer came
too late to provide anything more than a
temporary victory. Instances where such coalitions
did take place consistently led to unions that were
"too little and too late."

Native American tribes were not static bodies
but were constantly undergoing change. Novel
elements came into tribal culture through trade
and other contacts—and added to those
innovations devised by tribal members. Nor did
tribes remain politically changeless: they often
broke in two when a conservative faction decided
to go off on its own, or when a group divided
because of an argument. In the Great Plains, a
debate over the division of slain buffalo was a

common reason given for breaking away. The Crows are said to have separated from the Hidatsas, and the Assiniboins from the Sioux after such disputes.

The loose and highly individualistic political organization of the Indians of the West can be described as either "bands" or "tribes." Nothing resembling the complex centralized civilizations of Central or South America was known. Most groups, rather, were characterized as bands, or units that consisted of small numbers of related families that simply camped together. Bands were nomadic hunters and gatherers that changed their camp locations seasonally as food resources were depleted or in response to seasonal changes in plant and animal life, particularly where resources were too sparse to make it possible to remain very long in one area or for very many people to live together. A variant of the band was found in California, where its tiny tribes, called "tribelets," consisted of self-governing villages that sometimes exploited areas of no more than 100 square miles.

Tribes were larger than bands and were more formal unions of a number of villages that were integrated by the common possession of a number

HIDATSA VILLAGE
Painted by George Catlin in 1832, the Hidatsas' largest village was located on the Knife River, North Dakota. Five years later, the tribe was devastated by a smallpox epidemic.

✦NATIVE AMERICAN LANGUAGES✦

By 1500, the native peoples of North America were speaking about 550 different languages. Many of these tongues are now extinct, but others are still spoken, including more than 100 in the United States. Although scholars differ about how the Native American languages of the United States and Canada are related (or unrelated), here is one commonly accepted system for classifying them into phyla, or superstocks. All the languages within each phylum are believed to be descendants of an original mother tongue. Phyla, in turn, can be divided into language families in which the languages are even more closely related.

AMERICAN ARCTIC-PALEOSIBERIAN
Includes the Eskimaleut family of languages spoken in the Arctic, such as Inuit, Eastern Aleut, and Western Aleut. The word "Alaska" comes from the Aleut word for the Alaskan peninsula.

NA-DENE
Includes the Athapascan family of languages, which spread from western Canada and Alaska to the Southwest. Northwestern examples of Athapascan languages include Kutchin and Beaver; southwestern ones include Navajo and the various Apache tongues.

MACRO-ALGONQUAIN
Includes two large families of languages: Algonquian and Muskogean. Algonquian languages are widely spread across North America; western examples include Arapaho, Blackfoot, Cheyenne, Gros Ventre, and Ojibwa. Muskogean languages originated in the Southeast but are spoken today in Oklahoma and Texas by tribes that migrated there, such as the Chickasaws, Choctaws, and Creeks. The name "Oklahoma" was coined from the Choctaw words for "red" and "people."

MACRO-SIOUAN
Includes two language families widely spoken in the west: Siouan and Caddoan. Siouan tongues include Crow, Hidatsa, Mandan, Ponca, and Sioux. Caddoan languages include Arikara, Caddo, Pawnee, and Wichita. Iroquoian languages are spoken in Oklahoma and other western states by tribes that migrated there from the east, including the Cherokees, Cayugas, and Senecas. "Tipi," for a conical tent dwelling, comes from a Sioux word.

HOKAN
Includes the Yuman family of the Southwest, with such languages as Upland Yuman and Upriver Yuman. Also includes the Pomo family of California, with such examples as Coast Pomo and Northeast Pomo.

PENUTIAN
Includes several language families of the Northwest Pacific Coast and Columbia Plateau, such as Chinookian and Sahaptian. Upper Chinook is a Chinookian language; Nez Percé and Walla Walla are Sahaptian ones. Also includes several California language families, such as Yokuts and Maidu. North Foothill Yokuts is an example of a Yokuts language, Southern Maidu an example of a Maidu one.

AZTEC-TANOAN
Includes two language families spoken in many parts of the West and Mexico. The Kiowa-Tanoan family includes Kiowa in the southern Plains and Tewa in New Mexico. The Uto-Aztecan family includes languages spoken in California, the Great Basin, the Plains, and the Southwest, such as Comanche, Hopi, Northern Paiute, Southern Paiute, and Ute. It also includes several Mexican languages, most notably Aztec, the tongue of Mexico's ancient empire. The word "kachina," for an ancestral spirit or the doll that represents it, is a Hopi word.

UNCLASSIFIED
Includes the Zuni language, which has no close relative, and several language families whose affiliations are undetermined. Examples are the Yukian Family of California, whose members include Wappo and Yuki, and the Salishan family, whose members include Coeur d'Alene, Flathead, and Squamish.

Cherokee syllabary

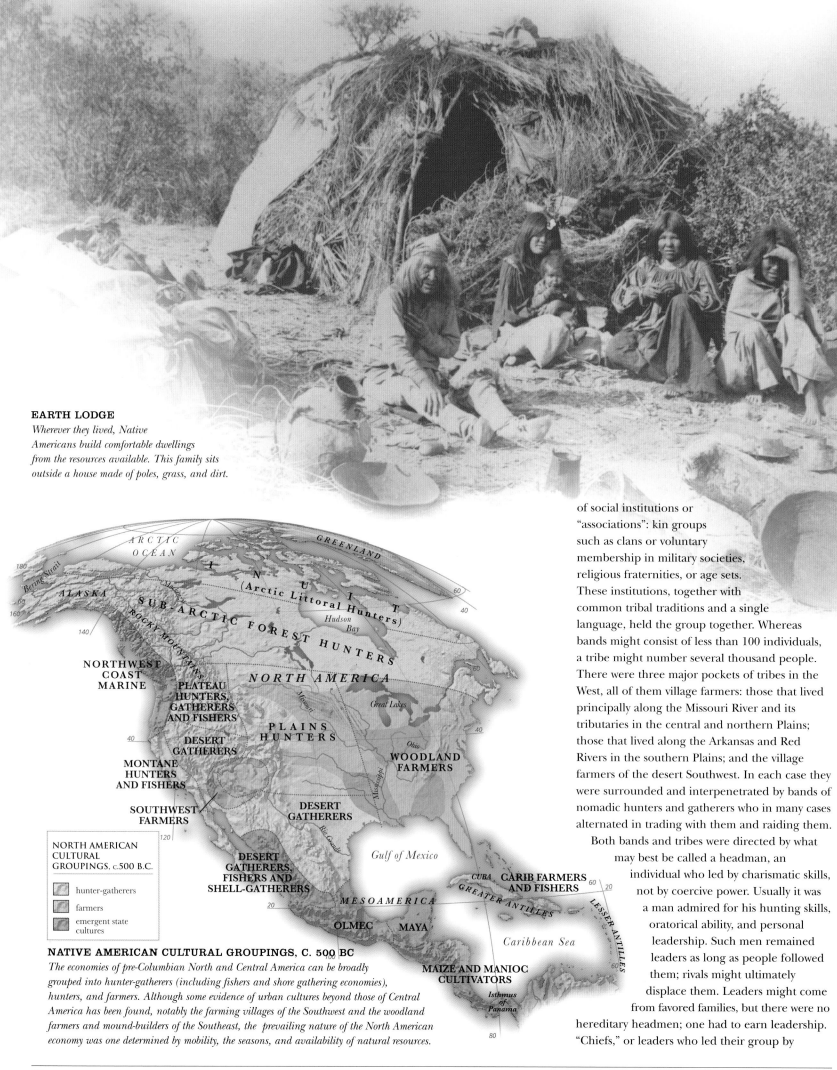

EARTH LODGE

Wherever they lived, Native Americans build comfortable dwellings from the resources available. This family sits outside a house made of poles, grass, and dirt.

NORTH AMERICAN CULTURAL GROUPINGS, c.500 B.C.

- hunter-gatherers
- farmers
- emergent state cultures

NATIVE AMERICAN CULTURAL GROUPINGS, C. 500 BC

The economies of pre-Columbian North and Central America can be broadly grouped into hunter-gatherers (including fishers and shore gathering economies), hunters, and farmers. Although some evidence of urban cultures beyond those of Central America has been found, notably the farming villages of the Southwest and the woodland farmers and mound-builders of the Southeast, the prevailing nature of the North American economy was one determined by mobility, the seasons, and availability of natural resources.

of social institutions or "associations": kin groups such as clans or voluntary membership in military societies, religious fraternities, or age sets. These institutions, together with common tribal traditions and a single language, held the group together. Whereas bands might consist of less than 100 individuals, a tribe might number several thousand people. There were three major pockets of tribes in the West, all of them village farmers: those that lived principally along the Missouri River and its tributaries in the central and northern Plains; those that lived along the Arkansas and Red Rivers in the southern Plains; and the village farmers of the desert Southwest. In each case they were surrounded and interpenetrated by bands of nomadic hunters and gatherers who in many cases alternated in trading with them and raiding them.

Both bands and tribes were directed by what may best be called a headman, an individual who led by charismatic skills, not by coercive power. Usually it was a man admired for his hunting skills, oratorical ability, and personal leadership. Such men remained leaders as long as people followed them; rivals might ultimately displace them. Leaders might come from favored families, but there were no hereditary headmen; one had to earn leadership. "Chiefs," or leaders who led their group by coercive means, did not exist before they were created by historic white traders and Indian agents who "appointed" individuals to speak for the very individualistic tribal members, most of whom had about equal social rank. In this way Europeans could control the Indians through these men, chosen because of their close ties with the newcomers.

Throughout most of the continent, the largest permanent group was the family, and the largest effective social group was the band or community, not—as one might expect—the tribe. Even communities that had a strong sense of identity tended to be weak and fluid. If a family had a dispute with village leaders, they were free to move to another village where they would align themselves with their clan members. This fluid state of affairs encouraged the development of tribal factions and divisions. Band or tribal boundaries might be vague to an outsider, but how a group handled a case of murder said much about its loyalties. Homicide within the group was a matter for arbitration; if the murderer was outside the group, it was a matter for war and revenge.

Matters were different among the Pueblo dwellers in the Southwest. Religious and political power in their towns was in the hands of groups of priests and officers—a priestly hierarchy that determined community affairs and intertribal relations. These village theocracies did have coercive power. The council of priests at Zuni, for example, appointed officers who ran the pueblo but acted in accordance with the wishes of the priests.

SPIRITUAL BELIEFS

A central concern of all Native Americans was their belief in a supernatural realm harmoniously related to the natural realm, a world that was heavily populated by gods in the Southwest and Plains and by ghosts and spirit beings in every part of the continent. This awareness of another and incorporeal world was embodied in a variety of concepts as, for example, the Siouan *wakan* (the idea of the holy), though the word was different and its meaning varied across the continent.

Nature was alive with spirits. Individual animals possessed them, as did mountains, streams, trees, and even rocks. One prayed for the blessing of these spirits or asked their forgiveness every hour of the day. This outlook on nature was given deeper expression by the host of ceremonials in which the community participated, many of them

SKIN BAG
Animal skins provided Native Americans with materials for shelters, clothing, and containers.

of great length and complexity. The Sun Dance of the Plains Indians requires a long book to describe its four-day ritual, one that involved self-torture. While the rituals of many California Indians were not excessively long or complex, their sheer number meant there was constant daily preparation for or participation in them. Ghosts and spirit beings were believed to be very powerful but have very human characteristics; they were intelligent and had emotions similar to those of humans. They could be pleased, become angry, experience joy or fear, and act in beneficial or malevolent ways. More important, they could affect the outcome of events by intervening in human activities, and they could reward or punish people for their actions. It was necessary, for example, to take these emotions into account in hunting, for it was important not to anger the spirit of an animal one had killed. Spirits of slain animals would listen to prayers offered to them and accept sacrifices and other offerings. Neglecting such prayers might lead all animals of its kind to avoid

being killed for food, and the entire community would suffer. The supernatural world was a very powerful one, and every group had some religious specialist, or shaman, to help deal with it.

Shamans or medicine men were believed to be capable of manipulating the powerful spirits for the benefit of the community by performing rain dances or curing ceremonies, although some shamans also performed malevolent magic. In some groups these men or women were renowned for their magic acts and sleight-of-hand performances, in which individuals were violently beheaded yet later returned intact, or in which a full ear of corn was drawn from someone's mouth. Such acts were extremely realistic, and early explorers marveled at the skill of the performers. Among some groups with band organization, shamans were allied with the head man if they themselves were not leaders, the two jointly exercising great power in the community.

A personal guardian spirit was acquired by fasting, a practice that was universal across the Great Plains, Plateau, and Northwest Coast, though it was absent among the Pueblos. In such vision quests a young man—or less often a young woman—went alone to an isolated place to fast and pray until a representative of the spirit world came to him. Typically, a young man would go to a mountain top or other secluded area, disrobe,

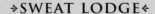

⇒SWEAT LODGE⇐

THE SWEAT LODGE was believed to bring purification through exposure to heat. Common to many Native American nations across the continent, the lodges were of two main types: small wigwams with shallow fire pits for pouring water onto heated rocks for steam sweating; or large, communal lodges sunk into the earth, with deep pits for direct fire-heat sweating. Topped with a dome, usually of cut branches covered with hides, sweat lodges often served as clubhouses or for ceremonial meetings.

The sweat lodge ceremony has several purposes and meanings for Native Americans who have practiced it for centuries. It remains an important part of the vision quest, in addition to its role in physical and spiritual purification. Lasting approximately two

hours, the sweat lodge ceremony, which includes prayers and songs, is presided over by a sweat leader. He is assisted by a fire keeper, who maintains the fire and opens and closes the door at specific times during the ceremony. Afterwards, participants exit in a clockwise direction and lie on the grass.

PURIFICATION RITES
Sitting around a steaming fire pit, Native American men often gathered in sweat lodges to purify their bodies and minds.

"THE GOD...ADORED AT THAT TIME WAS THE SUN AND THE FIRE."

—PABLO TAC, LUISEÑO

and pray to the spirit world while going without food, water, or sleep. After a few days of such deprivation and exposure to the cold of night, the supplicant would be visited by an animal spirit, or a spirit in animal form.

The spirit would provide the supplicant with a degree of supernatural power, or "medicine," in some aspect of life—hunting, say—teach its client a dance and a song, and tell him what objects representing the vision he was to include in a medicine bundle. Such a bundle was a concrete symbol of the individual's contact with the supernatural and enhanced his ability to draw on that source of power. It provided the individual with a deep sense of security in a turbulent life: no one could be a warrior without such assurance. If one was not successful in life, it was common to go seek another vision.

THE SWEAT LODGE

In much of the West, and especially in the Plains, a spiritual and physical purification rite was undertaken before seeking a vision, going on a war party, or taking part in a religious ceremony. A number of men would gather in a small, covered, dome-shaped structure to conduct the Sweat Lodge ceremony, in which water was sprinkled over hot rocks that were handed in from the outside. The heat from the resulting steam filled the lodge, andthe men were bathed in sweat, even as they flagellated themselves with pine branches or buffalo tails. A plunge into water concluded the ceremony.

The religious aspect of the Sweat Lodge ceremony was enhanced by smoking a pipe, for everywhere tobacco smoking was a spiritual event undertaken with much ceremony. Tobacco was grown everywhere in Native North America except in Alaska and northern Canada. The modern word "tobacco" comes from an Arawak term for the cigars they smoked in the Caribbean area, but elsewhere on the continent pipe smoking was the preferred means of enjoying nicotine. Most groups diluted the strength of tobacco by adding sumac leaves, the bark of dogwood trees, or other substances to produce a mixture known as *kinnikinnik*.

⟡ SPIRITUAL DANCES ⟡

FOR NATIVE AMERICANS, the supernatural was part of everyday life, and spiritual practices brought them closer to the forces that governed the world. All important decisions and activities were preceded by some ritual—prayer, sacrifice, or dance. In the hunting nations of the North, the emphasis was on animal spirits. In the agrarian South, ceremonies centered on planting and harvesting. As these traditions mixed, so did dance rituals that ensured success in hunting and farming.

SNAKE DANCE

The desert-dwelling Hopis conducted ceremonies throughout the year to ensure sufficient rainfall. The main summertime festival lasted sixteen days, culminating in the Snake Dance. Dancers, painted red-brown, wrapped live snakes around themselves and held them in their mouths. The snakes were later thrown on a bed of corn meal and released outside the pueblo.

KACHINA DOLL
Traditionally, the Pueblos made dolls to help teach their children about the kachina spirits.

The Hopi Snake Dancers wore elaborate masks representing kachinas, supernatural beings who inhabited a separate world. The Hopis and Zunis believed that kachinas entered human bodies at the winter solstice and remained until mid-summer. Some kachina masks, with long teeth and protruding eyes, were intended to frighten naughty children.

Hopi and Zuni children learned the characteristics of different kachinas from the small, elaborate figures their fathers carved for them. Often called kachina dolls, they were treasured as religious artifacts to be handed down to one's own children.

CORN DANCE

This was performed in many places, though not in California or the Northwest Coast, where corn was not grown. Some cultures performed it at harvest time, while others, on the West Coast, celebrated at planting time to guarantee the earth's renewal. In all Corn Dances, specific movements and gestures symbolized elements of earth and sky to attract the Corn Mother.

The Hidatsas and Mandans shared the Corn Dance Feast of the Women. It was believed the Old Woman Who Never Dies sent them springtime waterfowl as a symbol of the seed corn they planted. To acknowledge their debt, older women hung dried meat on poles as a sacrifice, then performed a dance while younger women fed them meat and received in return grains of sanctified corn to be included in the planting.

SNAKE DANCE
Performed by the Hopis as part of a sixteen-day ceremony, the Snake Dance was a prayer to the spirits for a plentiful harvest.

GHOST DANCE

The Ghost Dance of the late nineteenth century was rooted in movements against white incursion that sought the revitalization of native religion and culture through purification. Its immediate forerunner was the Dreamer Religion of the 1850s, in which music and dancing induced visions of a world without white men. In 1889 Wovoka, a Northern Paiute, had a vision in which the earth came to life in its former state, with no white men but many buffalo. He preached that this ideal world could be realized by

CORN DANCERS
With the Corn Dance, many tribes celebrated the renewal of the earth at harvest time.

rejecting the white man's ways, including alcohol, and by meditation, prayer, chanting, and dancing—specifically, the Ghost Dance, which was, in essence, a resurrection of the dead and their previous way of life.

The basic dance, over four to five days, combined singing and chanting with slow, shuffling movements that followed the sun's course. Many nations adopted it and created their own versions. Federal authorities confused the Ghost Dance with war dances and banned Sioux Ghost Dance gatherings. In 1890, prior to one gathering, some 200 Sioux were massacred by the American army at Wounded Knee, South Dakota, a tragedy that effectively ended the movement.

DEERSKIN DANCE

This autumn rite of California's Hupas sought to renew the world and ensure good fortune. After a shaman's secret rituals, dancers performed the White Deerskin Dance wearing animal-skin aprons and feather headdresses, and carrying poles draped in deer hides. The skin of the rare white deer brought much prestige to the dancer who wore it.

GHOST DANCE DRESS
Ceremonial Ghost Dance shirts and dresses were thought to protect dancers from the bullets of their enemies.

DEERSKIN DANCE
The Hupas of California considered it a great honor to wear the skin of a rare white deer during the annual Deerskin Dance.

NATIVE FARMERS
This sixteenth-century engraving shows Florida natives preparing and planting farmland.

"MY CORN IS

ARISING

MY CORN IS

CONTINUALLY

ARISING

IN THE MIDDLE

OF THE WIDE

FIELD MY CORN

IS ARISING."

**—NAVAJO SONG TO
HELP THE CORN GROW**

THE CHANGING WEST

THOUGH THERE ARE NO WRITTEN RECORDS OF THE MILLENNIA THAT PASSED IN THE WEST BEFORE COLUMBUS, ARCHAEOLOGICAL EVIDENCE REVEALS A LONG SUCCESSION OF CHANGES: FROM THE CLOVIS HUNTERS, WITH THEIR DISTINCTIVE STONE SPEAR POINTS TO THE AGRICULTURAL REVOLUTION IN THE SOUTHWEST AND THE DEVELOPMENT OF LARGE COMMUNITIES IN CALIFORNIA AND THE NORTHWEST.

THE CLOVIS PEOPLE who lived in the western United States at the close of the escendants remained hunters and gatherers for thousands of years. Their spears were tipped with lanceolate-shaped, chipped stone points that carried a flute on both sides of the base. The Folsom hunters who followed the Clovis hunted essentially modern game, although the buffalo they killed were larger than present-day forms. They, too, used fluted points, but theirs were smaller and more delicate.

Hunting techniques evolved over the millennia, but some techniques are very ancient. One especially spectacular event was the buffalo jump, in which large numbers of buffalo were stampeded along drive lanes and over cliffs. The animals either died in the fall or were so badly injured they could easily be slain. In another variant, they were driven into enclosed spaces. Sometimes the trap was a dead-end gully, sand dune, or other natural feature, but sometimes the Indians built corrals into which the animals

WINTER CHASE
George Catlin's 1832–33 painting depicts Indians on snowshoes hunting buffalo in winter. Snow made buffalo easier to track and slowed their escape. Wood-framed snowshoes with rawhide webs kept wearers from sinking into deep snow.

were driven and then killed by the hunters that converged on them. Surplus meat would be dried and made into jerky.

Stone tool technology changed as the centuries passed, and the western hunters beginning about 9,000 years ago produced exquisitely chipped stone tips for their darts or spears. These weapon tips are among the finest chipped stone tools in the world, and Eden and Scottsbluff points especially are products of highly skilled craftsmen. These Plano hunters sought out buffalo that were like those of today, augmenting their diet with a wide range of wild plants and smaller game.

THE CORN REVOLUTION

It was not until about the time of Christ that a major change in lifeways took place in the West. A revolution in how people lived came about with the introduction of corn from Mexico into the American Southwest. Corn was known in the Southwest 2,500 years ago, but people did not become dependent on it there until the first centuries before Christ. Corn-growing slowly spread east and north, and became important after A.D. 700 in the eastern United States,

and perhaps a century later on the Great Plains. Growing corn provided a food surplus that led to rapid population growth, although there was a downside to its cultivation: its consumers had a shorter life span than their hunter-gatherer ancestors, for reliance on these carbohydrates (especially if fed to children) led to nutritional imbalance, disease, and biological stress. Dental health also rapidly deteriorated because the carbohydrates in corn were transformed into sugars in the mouth. Tooth decay, previously an insignificant problem, now appeared, and many people developed massive caries and abscesses that must have been excruciatingly painful.

Cornfields—invariably containing a mix of beans and squash—also spread west into southern California and the southern Great Basin, and in the Great Plains farming spread up the Platte and Missouri River valleys to the northernmost effective

✦CLOVIS POINTS✦

CLOVIS, a small town in New Mexico named after the medieval Frankish king, was the site of one of the West's most important archaeological discoveries. In the 1930s, in a bed of mammoth fossils located near Clovis, archaeologist Edgar Billings Howard discovered stone spear points that were older than any previously known tools in the Americas. The points had a lanceolate (lance-like) shape, tapering up from a concave base, and distinctive fluting, or lengthwise channels, on both sides of the base. Intended to be mounted at the tip of wooden spears, the points were made by pressure-flaking, a technique in which antler or bone was used to chip away at the stone.

In time, a picture emerged of the Clovis culture as late Pleistocene big-game hunters with an assortment of stone and bone tools, including scrapers for defleshing hides; gravers for incising wood and bone; hammerstones; choppers; and knives. They cooked their meat over hearths and left much debris, including flint flakes (from making tools) and charred animal bones. They hunted mammoths and other species, many of them now extinct. Dominant about 11,200 years ago, at the end of the Pleistocene Epoch, the culture was so widespread that Clovis points have been found in every mainland U.S. state.

Clovis point, showing lanceolate shape

CORNFIELD
Navajos in Arizona in 1889 watch over their growing cornfield. Their subsistence farming methods were rooted in the prehistoric past.

ZUNI ARCHITECTURE
The Zuni constructed large adobe dwellings with several stories that receded like stairsteps. Tall ladders allowed residents to reach the upper stories and the roof, which provided an additional work space.

limits of horticulture on this continent, in southern Canada. It was corn that made it possible for large populations to settle into permanent villages, both in the desert Southwest and in the Great Plains. People remained hunters and gatherers in those areas beyond the limits of corn growing. Quite different agricultural practices developed in the Southwest and in the Plains. Special techniques were developed for the high, dry southwestern plateaus. The prehistoric Hohokams and Anasazis dug irrigation canals; in the more rugged uplands, small check dams were built across small drainages. These dams trapped sediment and resulted in small terraces, or *trincheras*, each of which supported a few stalks of corn and bean plants. Much of the gardening was in small plots of this sort scattered across the countryside, some of them many miles from the pueblo.

In the Great Plains, women cultivated large gardens in the river bottomlands. Their hoes, made from buffalo shoulder blades, and their rakes of deer antler, were not capable of tilling the tough

prairie sod, but were sufficient to turn and weed the soft, highly productive floodplain soil after trees were removed to permit the entry of sunlight. Trees were killed by ringing their bark, the smaller ones were removed, and rows of corn were mingled with beans in two- to six-acre garden plots. In good years harvests were generous and provided food during the winters when buffalo were scarce.

Communities grew to large size in the Plains and the Southwest. In both areas enemy raiders, probably nomadic hunters and gatherers, periodically forced many of them into fortified towns. On the upper Missouri River, communities of 2,000 or more individuals built ditched,

palisaded redoubts (fenced, protected places); while in the Southwest, people retreated into inaccessible alcoves on cliff faces.

Other areas of high population developed for quite different reasons. California had one of the highest population densities in pre-Columbian America, since the richness of its resources permitted large numbers of people to live in small areas. Similarly, the abundance of fish along the coasts of Oregon, Washington, British Columbia, and south Alaska encouraged the building of villages whose residents "harvested" this inexhaustible natural resource. The population of the West varied according to the availability of its food

resources, and according to the techniques developed to grow crops in often difficult environments. How many Indians, then, lived in the West? Early in the twentieth century, the number of Native Americans living in the United States as a whole was estimated to have been about one million people. Recent studies, however, have shown this figure to be false, for the early estimates did not properly take into account the massive population losses that resulted from diseases after the arrival of Europeans.

Native Americans had no immunity to the diseases brought to the New World by Europeans. In the Old World, centuries of exposure had led

⊹ORIGINS OF CORN GROWING⊹

DESPITE THE POPULAR image of prehistoric Indians as hunter-gatherers, cultivation of food crops was widespread in North America long before written history. In Mexico, pumpkins and gourds began to be cultivated about 7000 B.C. By 4000 B.C., in the same region, farmers in the region were growing corn, or maize. By the end of the B.C. era, corn provided a staple crop for the rising civilizations of Mesoamerica and had spread into what is now the U.S. Southwest.

Evidence of corn cultivation in the Southwest has been dated by some experts to as early as 3500 B.C., at Bat Cave, New Mexico, a site occupied by the Cochise culture, which subsisted mainly by gathering wild foods and trapping and hunting small game. However, agriculture did not catch on quickly, perhaps in part because the available strains of corn were not adapted to the dry southwestern environment. By the end of the B.C. era, a more productive, drought-resistant strain had been introduced, permitting

agriculture to take hold. It was especially suited to the high, mountainous region along the southern boundary between Arizona and New Mexico. From there it spread elsewhere across the Southwest.

By A.D. 500, corn provided the basis for three civilizations in the region: the Hohokams, Mogollons, and Anasazis. It supported settled village life, greater population, and more extensive material culture. Social, economic, and religious life became organized around the planting and harvesting of corn. In the words of Sevenka Qoyawayma, a member of the Hopi people, descendants of the Anasazi: "Mother Corn has fed you, as she has fed all Hopi people, since long, long ago when she was no larger than my thumb."

HIDATSA RAKE
A Hidatsa farmer made this weeding tool by tying antler horns to a wooden handle.

GRINDING CORN
Native American women grinding corn into meal. Cultivation of corn often gave native populations a surplus of food, allowing their numbers to increase.

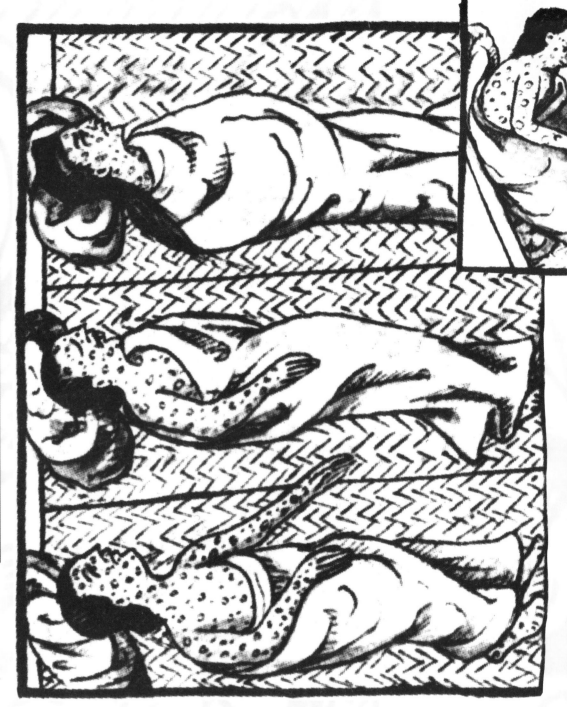

⋄GEORGE CATLIN⋄

MUCH of what is known about Native American cultures at the time of contact is due to men like George Catlin (1796–1872). Born in Wilkes-Barre, Pennsylvania, Catlin practiced law until 1821, when he began working as a portrait painter. In 1828, after seeing a delegation of Native Americans in Philadelphia, he resolved to record "the looks and customs of the vanishing races of native man in America." He traveled west to produce some of the earliest—and best—pictorial records of Plains Indians and other nations. From 1830 to 1838, he painted Native Americans, their villages, games, religious ceremonies, and occupations, collecting some 600 paintings into his "North American Indian Gallery." Catlin provided the best record of the Mandan nation, virtually destroyed by smallpox in 1837. In 1841 he published *Letters and Notes on the Manners, Customs, and Conditions of the North American Indians,* illustrated with 300 engravings. Other works followed over the next 26 years. In 1879 Catlin's gallery was donated to the Smithsonian.

to a degree of immunity to many diseases common there that once were thought of as "childhood diseases." But to American Indians, a case of smallpox or measles was a death sentence, for a person often would die within twenty-four hours after showing the first symptoms of smallpox.

New World epidemics began when Spanish ships arrived in the Caribbean carrying infected passengers. A smallpox epidemic of lethal proportions began to ravage Mexico in 1520. Spanish documents report that one-half of the native population there died—an estimate that is almost certainly too low. Repeated epidemics across North America over two and a half centuries eventually led to a reduction by about 97 percent of the nearly 25 million Native Americans who were living in central Mexico on the eve of the Spanish conquest.

Smallpox is very infectious, and it rapidly moved north from Mexico between 1520 and 1524, when the disease is believed to have spread across most of North America far in advance of any European contact. The possibility of a continent-wide epidemic is made plausible by how rapidly this disease spread across the West in the early

1780s. In those years a smallpox epidemic moved from the American Southwest into the Great Plains, then to western Canada and into Alaska in a matter of a few years, leaving a trail of death in its wake.

Some villages were all but extinguished by disease, and survivors joined other villages simply to maintain numbers large enough to protect and perpetuate themselves. In 1795 fur trader J. B. Truteau said of the Arikara Indians that "in ancient times" they were reduced from thirty-two "populous villages" to two villages. Only a few families had escaped from each village. Disasters of this sort also led small tribes to ally themselves with others equally devastated. Certainly diseases were present in numbers enough to accomplish this; these included smallpox (perhaps the most

lethal), measles, diphtheria, cholera, and scarlet fever, along with afflictions such as whooping cough that could be fatal to someone in a weakened condition. Ninety-three epidemics of these diseases are documented beginning in 1520, a serious one taking place about every four years, not to mention the ones that went unrecorded.

People in the New World did not often die from these kinds of illnesses before Columbus. In a sense, Native North America was "a disease-free paradise," however they may have suffered from lesser ailments. Estimates of some pre-Columbian populations suggest that Native Americans suffered a population reduction of more than 90 percent from the time these diseases first appeared. For example, estimates for the pre-

EPIDEMIC DISEASE
A sixteenth-century drawing of native peoples suffering from smallpox. This and other Old World diseases killed millions of Native Americans during the early years of contact with Europeans.

epidemic Mandans, Hidatsas, and Arikaras suggest a population of about 19,000 people—a figure that was reduced to less than 6,000 at the time of Lewis and Clark, or a loss of 13,000 people and a mortality rate of 68 percent. During the famous 1837 epidemic that ravaged the Mandans, only about 125 people remained alive of a village of perhaps 1,600 people, a mortality of 78 percent. Even higher percentages of deaths are recorded. Diseases in North America were as devastating to Native Americans as the Black Death that scourged Europe in the 1300s, when "half the world died" of bubonic plague, a disease imported from Asia.

The history of the West would not be written as it is had this massive depopulation not taken place. The United States alone may have been reduced from perhaps 18 million people to the post-epidemic figure of about one million. How would the white settlement of North and South Dakota have differed, for example, had there been 50,000 Native Americans living in that territory instead of the handful of survivors that remained after disease had taken its toll?

The homelands and culture of Native Americans at the time of Columbus were strikingly different than they had been a few centuries earlier—and than they would be a few centuries later, when white settlement began moving west across the Mississippi River into the West. Homelands differed in part because, as whites moved inland from the Atlantic coast, tribes were displaced westward. As an extreme example, the Kickapoo Indians, who once lived in southern Michigan, first moved to central Illinois, then to Missouri, Kansas, and Texas, ultimately to settle in Oklahoma and northern Mexico.

As tribes moved west, or in other directions, in response to pressures from new neighbors, people who had once been strangers came into contact, and fresh intertribal rivalries developed. Matters were worsened by European trade for furs that led to economic rivalries over diminishing resources. Moving into new environments meant even further changes in everyday life as people adjusted to unfamiliar factors.

☀ THE BOW AND ARROW ☀

O NE OF THE MOST IMPORTANT new inventions in the prehistoric West was the bow and arrow. Though there is some controversy about its origins, the most common view is that Arctic peoples imported this weapon from northeast Asia, and that it spread to what are now the lower forty-eight states during the first millennium A.D. For the hunter or warrior, its advantages over the old-fashioned spear and atlatl, or spear-thrower, were higher accuracy, greater power, and improved ability to shoot from a hidden position. Its power derived from the sudden, concentrated release of energy slowly stored by the tightening of the bowstring.

Indian arrows were usually short, as were the bows: three to four feet long, depending on the tribe. Even so, Native Americans used the weapon with great speed and accuracy.

QUIVER WITH ARROWS
Native American hunters and warriors were highly skilled bowmen. While riding horseback, they could fire several arrows in only a few seconds.

"THIS MAN MADE THE FIRST BOW AND ARROWS...HE MADE THE FIRST ARROW POINT FROM THE SHORT RIB OF A BUFFALO...WHEN A BUFFALO CAME ALONG THE PATH, HE SHOT; THE ARROW DISAPPEARED IN THE BODY AND THE ANIMAL FELL DEAD."

—ARAPAHO LEGEND

APACHE WARRIOR
This Apache man holds a bow and arrow, traditionally his people's weapon of choice. After contact with whites, however, guns obtained through trade were increasingly used in warfare and on the hunt.

LAND OF THE MANDAN
The Mandans who lived in this village of earth lodges, painted by George Catlin in 1837–39, lived by hunting and gardening.

"I WAS BORN UPON THE PRAIRIE WHERE THE WIND BLEW FREE AND THERE WAS NOTHING TO BREAK THE LIGHT OF THE SUN."

—TEN BEARS, COMANCHE

PEOPLES OF THE WEST IN 1500

ON THE EVE OF EUROPEAN CONTACT, THE WEST CONTAINED GREAT CULTURAL VARIETY. ON THE GREAT PLAINS, BUFFALO HUNTERS LIVED IN TIPIS. IN THE SOUTHWEST, THE CORN-GROWING ANASAZIS LEFT BEHIND SPECTACULAR CLIFF DWELLINGS. THE GREAT BASIN, COLUMBIA PLATEAU, AND PACIFIC COAST AND MOUNTAINS EXHIBITED STILL OTHER WAYS OF LIVING, FROM GATHERING SEEDS TO HARPOONING WHALES.

THE DIVERSITY IN LANGUAGE and culture in the West was so great that only vague generalizations can be made about the area. It is more practical to describe the major groups that lived in each of the culture areas, realizing that even such localized descriptions neglect much of the variation that existed.

THE GREAT PLAINS

Two strikingly contrasting lifeways existed on the Plains about 1500. Along its eastern rim, clustered along the banks of its major streams, were the semipermanent villages of the gardening tribes. To the west were the scattered camps of the nomadic hunting and gathering bands. The two groups were sometimes in conflict and sometimes interacted peacefully, as when they exchanged goods.

The village tribes consisted of the ancestors of the historic Mandans, Hidatsas, and Arikaras who lived along the Missouri River in the northern Plains; and the Pawnees, Wichitas, and Caddoan-speaking groups who lived along the Arkansas and Red Rivers and their principal tributaries in the southern Plains. These people, for the most part, had lived in or near their historic territory for hundreds of years. Archaeologists have unearthed many of their villages, some of them built 600 years before Columbus.

There was a good deal of variation in housing. In the northern Plains, the ancestors of the Mandans and Hidatsas lived in rectangular homes with gabled roofs, probably mantled by earth. The Arikaras and Pawnees lived in circular earth lodges, covered by earth, and built over a foundation of four or more posts. Their rafters were first covered with small branches, then grass,

TOY TIPI
Native American children enjoyed playing with toy tipis such as this one created by a Lakota Sioux parent from hide, wood, porcupine quills, tin cones, and feathers.

WICHITA LODGE
Like many tribes of the Southern Plains, the Wichita built houses from dome-shaped frames of saplings covered by tight bunches of prairie grass.

and finally earth and sod. In central Kansas, the Wichitas occupied villages of beehive-shaped grass houses. Further south, houses with walls of interwoven branches plastered with mud and thatched with grass were home to many of the Caddoans. Villages along the Missouri River often were heavily fortified by deep, bastioned ditches reinforced by log palisades. Further south, the open villages testify to less concern with enemies.

The villagers built their homes along streams having floodplains large enough to support the gardens necessary for their crops. Their harvests supplemented the buffalo that provided the major part of their diet. The Mandans, who lived near present-day Bismarck, North Dakota, provide a good example of these village peoples. Some Mandan women planted

SIOUX HEADDRESS
Only men who had proven their bravery in battle could wear the beautiful eagle-feather headdresses made by Plains craftspeople for special occasions.

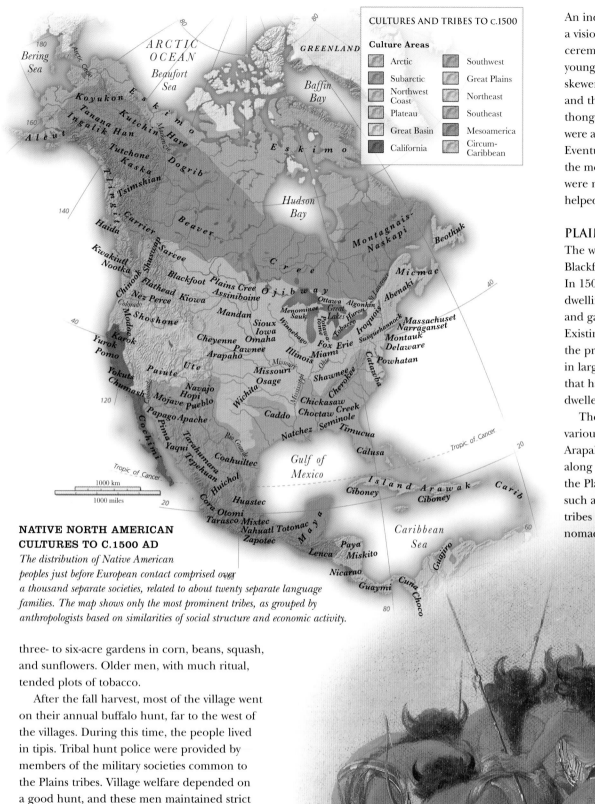

NATIVE NORTH AMERICAN CULTURES TO C.1500 AD
The distribution of Native American peoples just before European contact comprised over a thousand separate societies, related to about twenty separate language families. The map shows only the most prominent tribes, as grouped by anthropologists based on similarities of social structure and economic activity.

CULTURES AND TRIBES TO C.1500
Culture Areas
Arctic
Subarctic
Northwest Coast
Plateau
Great Basin
California
Southwest
Great Plains
Northeast
Southeast
Mesoamerica
Circum-Caribbean

An individual sponsored the Okipa in response to a vision. The ritual itself was held in the village ceremonial lodge, where the sponsor and other young men underwent severe self-torture. Wooden skewers were threaded through cuts in the skin and the participants were lifted above the floor by thongs attached to them; sometimes buffalo skulls were attached to their bodies as they hung in midair. Eventually the skewers tore through the flesh and the men fell to the ground. Scars from these events were marks of great prestige, for these men had helped renew the history and power of their society.

PLAINS NOMADS

The western nomads were the ancestors of the Blackfeet, Wind River Shoshones, and other tribes. In 1500, before the arrival of horses, these tipi-dwelling nomads lived much as their hunting and gathering ancestors had lived for millennia. Existing in small bands, moving in response to the presence of the buffalo, they came together in larger groups only rarely. It was a way of life that had been inherited largely from Plains dwellers harking back to Clovis times.

The well-publicized historic nomads—the various Sioux or Dakota bands, the Cheyennes, Arapahos, Crows, and others—were once residents along the Plains margins. Some of them entered the Plains from the northeast, although others, such as the Crows, broke away from the village tribes and became nomads. A visitor to a Plains nomad camp in 1500 would have found a scene

three- to six-acre gardens in corn, beans, squash, and sunflowers. Older men, with much ritual, tended plots of tobacco.

After the fall harvest, most of the village went on their annual buffalo hunt, far to the west of the villages. During this time, the people lived in tipis. Tribal hunt police were provided by members of the military societies common to the Plains tribes. Village welfare depended on a good hunt, and these men maintained strict discipline on these excursions.

The peak of the rich ceremonial life of the Mandans took place annually. Known as the "Okipa," this four-day ceremony recapitulated their creation myth and helped ensure their welfare. It was the Mandan version of the Sun Dance, a ritual historically practiced everywhere on the Plains. It is not known how old either the Sun Dance or the Okipa might be, but their roots certainly reach deep into the prehistoric past.

✦THE BUFFALO✦

ALTHOUGH THE IMAGE of the Plains Indian warrior on horseback hunting buffalo suggests great antiquity, the truth is that the people of the Great Plains had no horses until the Spanish brought them from Europe in the sixteenth century. Before that, Plains hunters had to chase the buffalo on foot and rely on such devices as stampeding them over cliffs. Even so, the American bison, commonly called a buffalo (even though that term is more accurately restricted to certain African and Asian animals), has been central to the way of life of the Great Plains for thousands of years. These magnificent beasts, each weighing up to 2,500 pounds, were perfectly suited to the dry grasslands of the Plains and provided an abundant source of meat for its people.

After contact with Europeans, the adoption of the horse made hunting far easier, strengthening the existing connection between the Plains tribes and the buffalo. For peoples such as the Arapahos, Cheyennes, Comanches, and Sioux (some of whom only entered the region after contact with Europeans), the buffalo provided not only food but clothing, housing, tools, and a religious focus. From the animal's hide came the walls of the portable dwelling places called tipis; from its hair, thread for sewing; from its sinew, bow strings; from its bones, sled runners; from its dried feces, fuel for fires; and from its horns, ceremonial items to be used in rites to honor the buffalo and ensure a good hunt.

Despite the antiquity of the relationship between buffalo and buffalo hunters, it came to an end with dizzying speed. At the beginning of the nineteenth century, more than sixty million buffalo roamed the Great Plains. By century's end, there were only a few hundred, the rest killed off by advancing U.S. settlers. Their numbers have since climbed back into the tens of thousands.

BUFFALO SKULL
The lives of Plains people revolved around the buffalo, which provided them everything they needed to live.

BUFFALO HUNT
After Plains natives obtained horses from the Spanish, mounted hunters rode among buffalo herds, armed first with bows and arrows and later with rifles. The buffalo hunt was a thrilling experience. Boys looked forward to their first hunt as a means of proving their manhood.

BUFFALO DANCE
The buffalo was central to the culture of Plains Indians, including the Mandans, painted here by George Catlin engaging in a buffalo dance.

strikingly different from those viewed by the later explorers. Because only dogs were available to carry burdens, their tipis were smaller and they could carry fewer household goods as they traveled. Camps were smaller and the area over which they hunted was limited, since people did not have the mobility that horses provided to range over large tracts of land.

Warfare was a way of life on the Plains, and small-scale raiding often erupted in savage conflicts that destroyed entire villages, but it was muted to some degree by the Calumet Ceremony in the eastern Plains. In this ceremony, as the Pawnee Indians practiced it, members of one band, village, or tribe "adopted" or were adopted by members of another amidst much ceremonial exchange of goods. The ceremonial relationships thus established meant that meetings between groups could take place

peacefully because members of the other group were viewed as kinsmen. The Calumet Ceremony encouraged peaceful intertribal trade and relations. War parties, for example, would not attack a party traveling with the calumet pipe. Such pipes often were made of catlinite, a soft red shale that was quarried at the Pipestone quarries in southwestern Minnesota and made famous by the artist George Catlin.

TRADE ON THE PLAINS

Intertribal trade was important in the Plains; indeed, it was important everywhere on the continent. Some of the trade was in "needed" goods: high-quality stone for making tools, for example. Other items obtained through trade were luxuries, such as seashells used for beads and other ornaments. Different localities provided different resources that people either needed or wanted, and a continent-wide trade network developed to accommodate these wants.

Dentalium shells from the Pacific Coast, conch shells from the Gulf of Mexico, Anculosa snail shells from rivers in the Southeast, and native copper from the Great Lakes area all found their way to prehistoric villages along the Missouri River in South Dakota. By this means goods were spread across half the continent, and knowledge of distant events traveled far in advance of Europeans when they arrived. American Indians were more cosmopolitan in their outlook than has been imagined.

THE SOUTHWEST

As in the Great Plains, the Southwest was the home of two contrasting lifeways. The ancestors of the crop-growing, pueblo-dwelling Indians had lived on the scene for generations, but sometime before 1500 the Southwest was invaded by newcomers: the ancestors of modern-day Navajos and Apaches. Moving south through the Rocky Mountains and Plains from a homeland somewhere in western Canada, these people spread across much of the Southwest, around and between the pueblos.

The Pueblo Indians were well adapted to the harsh Southwestern environment and had devised means to grow crops in a land that was hostile to agriculture. That they succeeded, and prospered, is a tribute to their ingenuity and perseverance.

The farming communities of the Southwest developed about the time of Christ from hunter-gatherer ancestors, in part in response to influences from Mexico. Three principal prehistoric cultures developed in different parts of the area: Hohokam, Mogollon, and Anasazi.

The descendants of the Hohokams in historic times are the Pimas and Papagos. A modern tourist in Arizona may visit what is perhaps the best-known Hohokam ruin at Casa Grande National Monument, Arizona. Mogollon culture disappeared about A.D. 1100 when it was incorporated into the Western Pueblos. Their more modest ruins are not well known to tourists, but examples can be viewed at Casa Malpais, near Springerville, Arizona.

THE ANASAZIS

The Anasazi culture left the spectacular cliff dwellings in Mesa Verde National Park, Colorado, in Canyon de Chelly National Monument, Arizona, and many other sites. Their historic descendants

ADORNMENTS
Clam shell beads (left) and engraved bone disks (right). Prehistoric artisans used stone tools to make these decorative objects in about 8000 B.C.

are the Western and the Rio Grande (or Eastern) Pueblos. Sites like those at Mesa Verde, however, are the end product of a long development, going back to Basketmaker culture sites dating to about the time of Christ, camps and small villages that presaged later developments. Circular houses were made of horizontally laid logs set in mud mortar,

> "THE BEST PART OF MY LIFE, AND ALL MY EARTHLY MEANS HAVE BEEN EXPENDED IN THUS RECORDING THE LOOKS AND CUSTOMS OF THESE VANISHING RACES."
>
> —GEORGE CATLIN, ARTIST OF INDIAN LIFE, 1852

✦CALUMET✦

THE WORD "CALUMET," from the French, means reed or tube. Originally a symbolic shaft between eighteen and forty-eight inches long, it eventually developed into a tube, typically made of ash or sumac, with a pipe bowl usually made of catlinite, or pipestone. While tobacco was commonly smoked in pipes made of wood, animal horns, and other materials, the long-stemmed, sacred calumet had a more significant purpose. In addition to using it in religious ceremonies, some nations made calumets for trade, while others used them as a diplomatic accessory. Since the smoking of tobacco (and other plants) was common across the continent, calumets were universally recognized as signs of peace and as a form of bonding. Thus, smoking ceremonies played an important part in formal occasions, including diplomatic councils and declarations of war.

Calumets, which could have stems up to five feet long, were decorated by carvings, feathers, fur, horsehair, drawings, or paintings that identified their origins. Sometimes the feathers strung along a calumet indicated the occasion being marked: white feathers meant peace; red feathers indicated war. Trade calumets possessed lesser significance and were often used in dances and other social events rather than ceremonial occasions. Lewis and Clark made detailed observations of the Plains Indians' smoking ceremonies, noting how the sacred pipe was offered to the heavens, to the four quarters of the earth, and to the earth itself before being passed around. This ritual emphasized the spiritual bond created by the act of smoking.

smoking pipe

⋆ALFRED VINCENT KIDDER⋆

TO CONSTRUCT a prehistoric chronology for the West, historians depend on the work of archaeologists, who piece together the past of cultures from their buried artifacts. One of the most influential archaeologists of the West was Alfred Vincent Kidder (1886–1963). Born in Marquette, Michigan, he earned a Ph.D. in archaeology from Harvard (1914) and, from 1915 to 1929, was director of excavations for the Phillips Academy, Andover, Massachusetts, at Pueblo ruins at Pecos, New Mexico. There he conducted the first large-scale, systematic archaeological excavation in North America based on the principles of stratigraphy, the study of strata. In 1927, he proposed the Pecos Classification, a sequence of cultural periods for the Anasazi area. He later excavated Mayan ruins in Mexico and Central America and worked at the Carnegie Institution in Washington, D.C., and the Peabody Museum, Harvard.

PUEBLO BONITA

In the heart of Chaco Canyon, the Anasazis constructed Pueblo Bonita, an enormous multi-storied dwelling with more than 800 rooms.

and their inhabitants grew both com and squash. Later villages of the Basketmaker and of the Pueblo I through IV periods consisted of houses built first in pits and later above ground using carefully laid stone walls.

The kiva, a subterranean religious structure common in pueblo sites, closely resembles the circular pit houses of late Basketmaker times, an example of the use of an older architectural pattern in a religious setting. It was centrally located and always circular, even when other houses in the village were rectangular. Members of religious societies met in them to fast and make offerings. Masked dancers impersonating kachina rainmakers, the ancestral spirits, often gave public performances. Kachinas are best known today as the elaboratelycostumed dolls sold as souvenirs to tourists.

AFTER THE ANASAZIS

The Anasazi people, for reasons that are still debated, abandoned much of their territory —including Mesa Verde in the Four Corners region—perhaps 200 years before Columbus. Before about 1500 the Pueblo people had most of the Southwest to themselves, but the arrival of the Athapascan-speaking Navajos and Apaches led to sweeping changes in the Southwest. These new immigrants not only moved into areas now abandoned by the Pueblos, but aggressively began raiding their remaining settlements. The Navajos took women and food, and they actively borrowed Pueblo gardening, weaving, and religious practices, soon becoming as dependent on their gardens as their neighbors. Some of the Apaches—such as the Western Apaches and Jicarillas—also borrowed ceremonies and garden practices from the Pueblos. The Navajos' reputation as pastoral sheepherders came much later, after the Spanish introduced that Old World animal.

The historic descendants of the Western Pueblos include the Hopis and Zunis, while the Rio Grande or Eastern Pueblos include Taos and others on the upper Rio Grande River, plus Acomas and Lagunas. Only about thirty pueblos remain today of the eighty that were occupied at the time of Spanish contact. Many of them were abandoned because of Navajo, Apache, and Ute raids, and still others were deserted after the abortive Pueblo Revolt against the Spanish in 1680.

HOPI CEREMONY

Hopi dancers gathering for a bean-planting ceremony at Walpi Pueblo in present-day Arizona, photographed in the 1890s. The masked figures represent kachinas. These spirit beings were thought to watch over the Hopis.

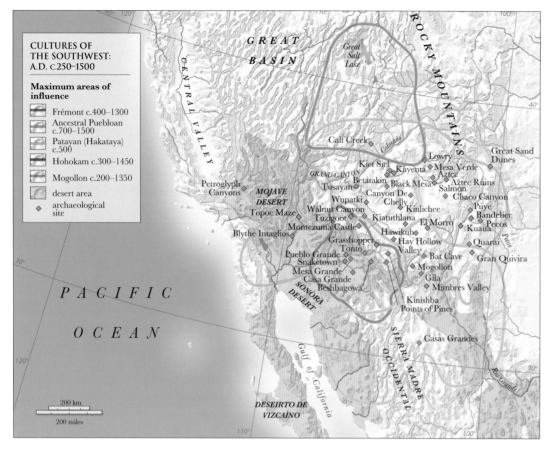

CULTURES OF THE SOUTHWEST: A.D. c.250–1500

Maximum areas of influence

- Frémont c.400–1300
- Ancestral Puebloan c.700–1500
- Patayan (Hakataya) c.500
- Hohokam c.300–1450
- Mogollon c.200–1350
- desert area
- ◆ archaeological site

Pueblos were compact communities of stone and adobe buildings, often set on the flat tops of steep-walled mesas for protection against attack. Some of the towns consisted of multistoried apartment dwellings clustered around kivas set in a central plaza. In place of stairs, ladders provided access to rooms on the upper levels. Crops were crucial to life, and a cycle of ceremonies throughout the year was devoted to bringing rain and ensuring a good harvest.

The culturally conservative Pueblo people adopted less from the nomads than the latter did of Pueblo lifeways. The village farmers in the Southwest have retained more of their traditional culture than in any other peoples in the West. Pueblo daily life was under the direction of religious specialists who had a vested interest in retaining the old ways, and they were very successful in resisting change, except that they had to respond first to the raiding pressures by the aggressive nomads, then to Spanish and, later, Anglo-American demands. Among the Pueblo, the individual was everywhere subordinate to the group.

Descendants of the Apaches, such as the Jicarilla Apaches in the Texas panhandle, later would pose equally difficult, if different, problems for the Anglo-American settlement of the Southwest and southern Plains. The Comanches did not yet exist: these Shoshonean Numic-speaking people from the Great Basin assumed their historic character in the eighteenth century only after obtaining Spanish horses.

CULTURES OF THE SOUTHWEST

In the Southwest, sedentary ways of life developed through the first millennium, producing villages and cliff dwellings such as those of the Hohokams of Arizona, and regional polities such as Chaco Canyon and Casa Grandes. The Hohokams developed irrigation systems to allow corn to grow in the semiarid climate, and built multistory pueblos, including storehouses and dwellings. The Anasazi and Mogollon peoples left evidence of pueblos constructed for defensive purposes, probably to counter hostile groups who moved into the area from c. 1300. Population pressure and increasing acidity caused decline in the region after c. 1250.

TURQUOISE ORNAMENTS

Two combs (left) and two ear pendants (right) found at the site of the ancient Zuni town of Hawikku. Turquoise was a valuable trade item among the native peoples of the Southwest.

THE GREAT BASIN

A first view of the Great Basin landscape suggests that no one could or would want to live there without the benefit of modern technology. Prehistorically, however, people occupied every part of it, albeit in small and widely scattered groups. In the least productive areas, perhaps only one person could extract a living from 50 or 100 square miles, although in more productive regions one person could subsist in a five-square-mile area. Its arid nature belies the availability of food, which was accessible everywhere to those knowledgeable about desert resources, although finding enough to eat might require much of one's waking hours. Most of the Great Basin was occupied by Numic-speaking bands of Shoshones, Utes, and Paiutes, distant linguistic relatives of the Aztecs of Mexico.

The Numic people who inhabited the Great Basin were desert dwellers who depended entirely on natural products, for no crops were grown. There was no staple food, for there was too much annual fluctuation in the abundance of natural resources. Many animals were locally important, like rabbits, but there were cycles when they were abundant and others when they were scarce. Antelope were hunted, but it might be years between a drive that netted animals enough for more than a small group. Piñon nuts were gathered everywhere, and although people might collect enough for the winter, an exceptional harvest took place only every three to seven years. They principally ate plant foods, of which the environment produced many varieties, but each of limited quantity.

The people might best be described as seed-gatherers, but who neglected no other resource. Much of the area was mantled by grass and sagebrush, but there were scattered, miniature oases in the form of spring-fed lakes and marshes. Resources varied also

ZUNI PUEBLO

Zuni Pueblo, here seen in the 1870s, is the only Zuni town still in existence. Before contact with whites, the Zunis lived in six villages located along the Zuni River in present-day New Mexico.

✦ THE ANASAZIS ✦

THE NAME "ANASAZI" means ancient ones or ancient enemies in Navajo, and the people we know by that name were indeed of great antiquity. Living in the Four Corners region, they began their development around the time of Christ and left descendants in today's Pueblo peoples. Their first stages of development, lasting until a.d. 750, are known as Basketmaker because of the skill they showed as weavers of baskets, sandals, and other goods constructed from vegetable fibers. The Basketmakers lived exclusively in pit houses quite different from the pueblos of later times.

From 750 to 1300, the Anasazis were in their Pueblo period, which was their golden age. During this time, they used stone and adobe to build multifamily "apartment house" towns with many rooms and several levels connected by ladders. The levels were stepped back to form terraces, so that the roof of one floor could provide a front yard for another. Usually built on top of mesas or in canyons, these pueblos (Spanish for towns) were marked by distinctive underground ceremonial chambers called kivas.

A notable example of an Anasazi site was Chaco Canyon. Located in northwestern New Mexico, this complex of pueblos was first occupied around 900 and was abandoned by 1150. In its heyday, Chaco Canyon was a major trading center served by a network of stone roads that connected it to outlying towns. Irrigation supported agricultural production for a large population. Its largest building, Pueblo Bonito, had 800 rooms and was home to at least a thousand people, and perhaps many more. It contained thirty-seven kivas, the largest of which, known as a great kiva, was forty-five feet in diameter. At Chaco and throughout their territory, the Anasazis used sophisticated craft techniques to make many objects, including pottery, mosaics, jewelry, and cotton clothing adorned with feathers.

From 1000 to 1300, perhaps as a defense against enemies, the Anasazis abandoned their above-ground dwellings and built houses in canyon recesses, such as the cliff dwellings at Mesa Verde, Colorado. In the late 12th century, they were increasingly plagued by drought and attacks from invading Athapascan peoples, ancestors of sthe Apaches and Navajos who gave the Anasazis their name. About 1300, some of the Anasazis abandoned their cliff dwellings, leaving them as ruins over which later generations would marvel. Some moved south to the Rio Grande Valley, where the Pueblo peoples inherited many of their traditions.

polychrome bowl

frog-shaped ornament with turquoise eyes

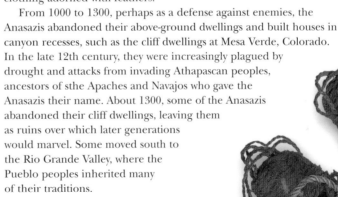

snare for catching birds

ANASAZI CRAFTS

A wide variety of goods made by Anasazi artisans were available at their trading center in Chaco Canyon.

sandals woven from wicker

✦MARK TWAIN ON THE GOSHUTES✦

MARK TWAIN's satirical tongue lacerated many people, including the rich and famous, but some of his severest words were reserved for a group that was poor and little known: the Goshute Indians, a subgroup of the Shoshone people of the Great Basin. He encountered them during a trip through Utah and Nevada in the 1860s, recorded in *Roughing It* (1872). *"It was along in this wild country somewhere,"* wrote Twain, *"and far from any habitation of white men...that we came across the wretchedest type of mankind I have ever seen...I refer to the Goshoot Indians."* Exhibiting the racial attitudes of his day, he described them as more *"inferior"* and *"degraded"* than any *"savage tribe"* except possibly the *"bushmen"* of South Africa. The Goshutes, Twain asserted, were small, scrawny, and desperately poor, living with barely any shelter, making their way by begging, treachery, and eating crickets, grasshoppers, and carrion. Their habits made him question, he said, his belief in the romantic notion of the *"Noble Red Man."*

What Twain didn't report was the resourcefulness and endurance that had allowed the Goshutes, like other Great Basin peoples, to survive for millennia in a forbidding desert environment. Nor did he note that their condition in his day had been considerably worsened by the degradation of that environment by white men.

At least Twain did find one group he considered more base than the Goshutes: the employees of the Baltimore and Washington Railroad Company. Although the two groups were frequently confused, he said, this was unfair to the Goshutes.

most immigrants began passing through the area, the original environment and native way of life had been vastly altered and the Indians further impoverished. What the Forty-Niners saw and recorded of them, including Mark Twain's harsh judgment, was a catastrophically altered version of what once had been an austere but rewarding life.

THE COLUMBIA PLATEAU

The mountains and deserts of the Columbia Plateau are deeply incised by four great rivers: the Columbia, the Snake, the Okanogan, and, in Canada, the Fraser. There was great diversity in landforms and in the natural resources they supported. Population was concentrated along streams where fish, especially salmon, were abundant, and this permitted village life to blossom. The late prehistoric way of life was

SHOSHONE FALLS
The Shoshone Falls are the largest and most spectacular waterfalls on Snake River in Idaho. Traditionally, the Shoshones gathered at the foot of the falls to fish during the springtime salmon run.

with altitude, for as one climbs the innumerable mountain ranges, plants and animals change from those that prefer a shrub desert setting to those living in aspen and fir forests. The small groups that occupied the basin before the arrival of horses lived in small bands and hunted and foraged over a small area, but one that did not remain the same over the years, for erratic harvests forced them to move about a great deal to take advantage of the best available resources.

Hence, the people of the Great Basin lived in a hostile environment in impoverished groups. The adaptation of these people to the desert was the end product of a long development of perhaps 10,000 years, as the desert West continued to become more arid in the post-glacial era. Small groups lived either in simple structures with bark or grass beds, or in caves and rock overhangs, their lives dominated by the problems of everyday

life. Their campsites are marked by milling stones on which they ground seeds and nuts, later to be cooked as mush or cake. Quids, or pieces of vegetation that were chewed to extract moisture or nutrients, are common in caves, as are woven sandals and basketry. Realistic duck decoys made from tule reeds and duck feathers were found in Lovelock Cave. Other items include grass-cutting tools, bone whistles, and a variety of chipped stone cutting tools and arrowpoints.

The Great Basin people were not seen by most Euro-Americans in their heyday. Destruction of their habitat began in the early nineteenth century as first horses and then livestock began to compete with them for grasses, and as timber was stripped for use in mines and towns. By the time little altered when the first Americans—Lewis and Clark—passed through the Columbia gorge in 1805. Towns are recorded where salmon were easily caught, and many such localities were inhabited for thousands of years.

Villages usually consisted of houses dug into the earth, their roofs supported by poles. Towns of thirty to fifty or more houses, sometimes set in rows, were built on level terraces along the river and were home to several hundred people. In the fall, when salmon were running, there was constant commotion as fish by the ton were caught, gutted, and hung up to dry. Salmon provided not only a staple food but surplus for trade to their less fortunate neighbors.

Other people occupied the deserts and mountains, and still others lived, like the Klamaths, along smaller streams and around Klamath Lake. Most of the lakes in the Great Basin and Plateau vanished as rainfall decreased in post-glacial times, but Klamath Lake remained, and as time passed, its residents adapted to a more arid setting. The Klamath lived in

permanent villages, their homes built in deep pits, with each house supported by four center posts set around a central hearth. The inhabitants entered and left by a notched log that served as a ladder. Their lives changed little as time passed, the lifeways of thousands of years persisting to the historic period.

The Klamaths lived on the resources of the river and swamps around the lake, for little use was made of the open lake itself. Rivers provided staples, including salmon, trout, and suckers. Wildfowl were important seasonally, and hunting large game was secondary. Wocas (or water lily) seeds, gathered from dugout canoes, were the most important plant food; the roots of the camas plant were also widely eaten. Camas Prairie is a common place-name in the Plateau, for the plant grew in such abundance that its blue flowers often made a distant prairie resemble a lake. The permanent food supply, however, was fish, as it was through most of the Plateau.

Many changes were introduced into some Plateau cultures when horses arrived in the eighteenth century, especially in those areas that were ideal for their rearing.

Thanks to the horse, the Nez Percés, for example, imported buffalo robes and parfleches—the skin storage container of the Plains Indians—in great quantities, so their lives changed considerably in advance of American settlement. Other groups did not take to horses, and their way of life remained more like that of their late prehistoric ancestors, living in small, isolated villages that did not aggregate into tribes until historic times. In this sense they were much like their neighbors in modern California.

PACIFIC COASTS AND MOUNTAINS

In late prehistoric times, California was heavily populated, as it is now, especially in contrast to neighboring areas. The state had a density as much as four times that of the rest of the continent north of Mexico. The area was blanketed by a host of "tribelets" that consisted of a main village and a number of smaller outlying ones. There were some 500 tribelets, usually numbering about 100 to 500 people. The Pomo Indians, for instance, though thought of as a tribe, consisted of some thirty-four tribelets, made up of families related through the male line. Each tribelet

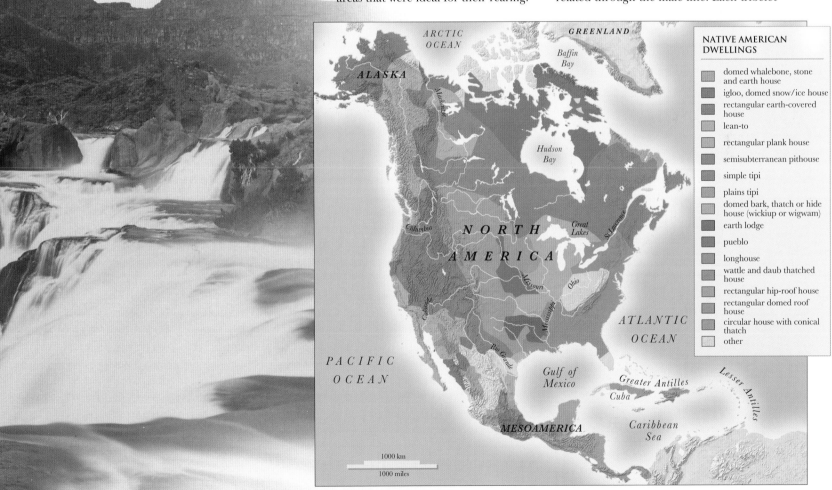

	NATIVE AMERICAN DWELLINGS
	domed whalebone, stone and earth house
	igloo, domed snow/ice house
	rectangular earth-covered house
	lean-to
	rectangular plank house
	semisubterranean pithouse
	simple tipi
	plains tipi
	domed bark, thatch or hide house (wickiup or wigwam)
	earth lodge
	pueblo
	longhouse
	wattle and daub thatched house
	rectangular hip-roof house
	rectangular domed roof house
	circular house with conical thatch
	other

NATIVE AMERICAN DWELLINGS

Native Americans constructed a wide variety of shelters and dwellings, often reflecting the availability of raw materials. Some peoples lived in different shelters according to the season: some permanent, some temporary or movable. Characteristic shelters in the West ranged from the rectangular plank houses of the Northwest Coast to the tipis of the Great Plains.

acknowledged the leadership of a headman in its central village. Political atomization in California was further emphasized by their many languages; there were perhaps eighty mutually unintelligible dialects in the area, some of them spoken by only a few groups.

Most houses in California were dome-shaped dwellings thatched with grass or other plants, supported by poles bent to the desired shape, but the Miwok and others lived in a tipi-shaped structure covered with thatch or bark. During

⟡POMO BASKETS⟡

THE BASKETS made by the California and Northwest Coast cultures were so tightly woven that some could hold water and be used as cooking vessels. Superlative among skilled Native American weavers were the Pomo Indians of Upper California, who created not only baskets but also waterproof headwear, cradles, traps, and even boats, using grasses, reeds, bark, and roots. In the late 1800s, a growing interest in "art baskets" meant a lucrative market for the Pomo's unique handiwork.

Among the Pomos, men weave as well as women, making them an exception among traditional Indian cultures. They use two main methods: twining, with two or more horizontal strands twisted around each other and woven in and out of vertical warp strands; and coiling, employing thin strips of grasses, reeds, or other material wrapped in a bundle and coiled to produce a continuous spiral. Some of the baskets the Pomos produce are so fine that the stitches need magnification to be counted. Typically decorated with feathers and shells, they are colored in ornate patterns with specific meanings. Baskets can range in size from as large as three feet in diameter to as small as a fingernail.

THE SPIRIT DOOR
The maker of this Pomo basket purposely created a gap between two rectangles in the design. This intentional irregularity was called a dau, *or spirit door. It allowed good spirits to enter the basket.*

winters earth-covered pit houses sometimes were used, though such structures usually were community assembly houses. Each tribelet occupied and owned a specific territory with well-marked boundaries.

California was a mosaic of many hundreds of tiny, independent, and sometimes feuding groups, each differing from its neighbors in minute ways. Some groups lived in an area of no more than about 100 square miles, and as a consequence, many people never went more than ten to fifteen miles in any direction from home. Furthermore, some of them probably did not speak to more than about 100 people in a lifetime. Feasts and ceremonies were a prominent part of life, and some groups had one such activity or another every few days, honoring a birth, marriage, the chief's birthday, and even the appearance of the first rattlesnake in the spring. It was a small, safe, and familiar world.

The environmental diversity in California necessitated many different responses by people in order to wrest a living from its land. In the southern deserts, such tribes as the Cahuillas lived primarily on plant seeds and small game. Along the coast, peoples' economies were based on ocean resources, some depending heavily on shellfish, as in San Francisco Bay, and others on sea mammals. Inland, there was great emphasis on acorns, with lesser parts of the diet consisting of salmon, birds, deer, and elk. There is great time depth to these varying patterns, and in some areas much the same pattern persisted for at least 4,000 years or more. Technology was not complex, but California Indians are known as among the finest basket makers in the world. Baskets were used as containers for every purpose.

HOUSE ON NOOTKA SOUND
Smoked fish hang from the ceiling of this Pacific Coast house. Natives of the region learned to preserve fish, which guaranteed they would have plenty of food year-round.

Some tightly woven baskets would hold water; others were used as hats.

For much of the state, acorns provided the staple food. Great numbers of these nuts were harvested every fall and stored for winter use. A favorite acorn was from the tan oak; these nuts were gathered in large baskets and carried to camp for processing. Depending on their species, acorns contain varying amounts of bitter tannic acid that must be removed to make them palatable. The nut meats were removed and ground on a milling stone into a fine flour, which was placed in a fine-woven basket. Water was poured through the paste until the meal lost its bitter taste and was then ready to cook. It was served as a thin mush, heated by dropping hot stones into it, or was baked into cakes on a hot stone.

BURNING THE HILLS
In today's coastal and mountain California, fires often rage across the chaparral hills, destroying both homes and utilities. Fires were less destructive in native times, for the Indians burned the hills each fall after the grasses had matured and were harvested. New shoots quickly appeared, as did fire species (those that are rare or absent when land is overgrown). Old chaparral was useless as food for people or animals, but the new shoots and plants provided more foods for humans and more browse for deer. The Indians thus turned fires—which, sooner or later, are inevitable in chaparral settings—into agents that greatly increased their ability to make a living from the

land. Suppressing fires today until they have an unquenchable fuel makes them a deadly enemy.

The generally mild climate of California, and the ease of obtaining a living there, permitted its peoples to maintain a high, and relatively constant, standard of living, despite the fact that they were hunters and gatherers. But the epitome of hunting and gathering life on the continent was among the Northwest Coast Indians along the Pacific shore between northern California and southern Alaska. No other group of people on earth with a similar mode of existence had a more complex and comfortable way of life.

The northwestern margin of the continent is ringed by high mountains, many of which, especially in south Alaska, are heavily glaciated. The coastal areas, however, have a moderate climate, and there is no extreme cold, even in the north, because of the warm offshore Japan Current. The agreeable climate, abundant water, and astonishing richness of the fish population combined to accommodate a sedentary lifeway that permitted the accumulation of great wealth, even though they depended entirely and directly on natural products—there was no agriculture. The most complex cultures were on the Alaska panhandle and coastal British Columbia, with those of coastal Washington and Oregon blending slowly into those of northwestern California.

PACIFIC COAST SEAFARING
The peoples of the Pacific Northwest crafted canoes from the trunks of giant cedar trees. In these vessels, they traveled up and down the coast to the villages of neighboring tribes to visit and to trade.

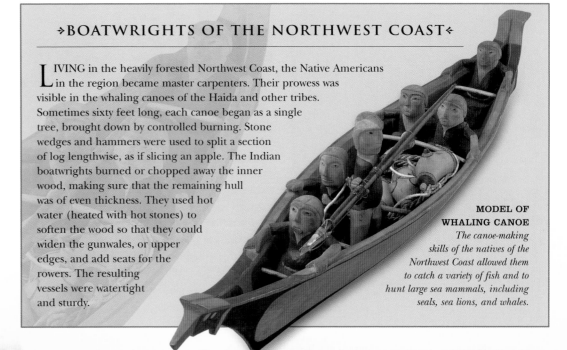

✦BOATWRIGHTS OF THE NORTHWEST COAST✦

LIVING in the heavily forested Northwest Coast, the Native Americans in the region became master carpenters. Their prowess was visible in the whaling canoes of the Haida and other tribes. Sometimes sixty feet long, each canoe began as a single tree, brought down by controlled burning. Stone wedges and hammers were used to split a section of log lengthwise, as if slicing an apple. The Indian boatwrights burned or chopped away the inner wood, making sure that the remaining hull was of even thickness. They used hot water (heated with hot stones) to soften the wood so that they could widen the gunwales, or upper edges, and add seats for the rowers. The resulting vessels were watertight and sturdy.

MODEL OF WHALING CANOE
The canoe-making skills of the natives of the Northwest Coast allowed them to catch a variety of fish and to hunt large sea mammals, including seals, sea lions, and whales.

"GATHER UP THE CLOUDS, WET, BLACK, UNDER THY ARMS—THAT THE RAINS MAY CEASE TO FALL. BECAUSE THY FRIENDS ARE ALL HERE ON THE BEACH READY TO GO FISHING—READY FOR THE HUNT."

—HAIDA SONG TO THE SUN

✦FRANZ BOAS✦

SINCE there are no written records about western Native American cultures before Columbus, scholars trying to reconstruct them have depended heavily on observation of cultures since then. In this they have been indebted to the work of Franz Boas (1858–1942), the father of modern anthropology. Born in Germany, Boas came to America in 1886 and spent years studying Native Americans in the field. He was particularly known for his investigations of the Inuits (Eskimos) and the Northwest Coast tribes of British Columbia, though he also researched the Pueblos of the Southwest and the pre-Columbian peoples of Mexico. As a teacher at Columbia University from 1896 and curator of anthropology at the American Museum of Natural History (1896–1905), Boas shaped the future of anthropology by emphasizing precise methodology and stressing the role of culture rather than race on human behavior. His writings include *The Mind of Primitive Man* (1911). His influence was felt partly through such illustrious students as Margaret Mead and Alfred Kroeber, the latter himself an expert on the Indians of California.

Plank houses were usually built in a row facing the water. The doorway was an oval hole cut into the central plank or pole. These large rectangular dwellings, often built in pits, were supported by interior vertical posts and usually floored by planks, providing a large, comfortable living space. Each home was occupied by an extended family made up of several individual families. Each component family had its own living space and did its own cooking. Their possessions were kept in large wooden boxes, each carved from a single piece of wood and steamed to shape.

The dense forests surrounding them provided many kinds of wood for carving and building. Boats large enough to carry many men were cut from single trees. Whales were hunted from such canoes using harpoons and sealskin floats. Dishes, spoons, hooks for catching halibut, and most other tools and weapons were of wood, including slat armor closely resembling that found in northeast Asia—all laboriously carved using stone tools.

These coastal, riverine people developed distinctive and complex tools and weapons that were perishable, as they were made of wood. The surplus of food was so great that this dense population had considerable leisure to devote to elaborating their culture. This elaboration is especially visible in their art, for virtually everything they used was robustly carved or painted. Their

BASKETRY HAT
Using strips of cedar, expert basket makers of the Northwest Coast wove waterproof hats as protection from the seasonal rains.

art was all the more distinctive because the areas surrounding them did not share this artistic tradition but produced rather simple geometric designs. This art was functional and deeply ingrained in their lives. It was always decorative, but however elaborate, design was always subordinate to function. Each lineage had a crest identifying its owner or maker, a crest analogous to the coats of arms in medieval Europe. The designs included killer whales, beavers, and mythological animals. Archaeology reveals that the foundation for this art is very old, but the popular view of Northwest Coast villages as abounding in totem poles is a misconception.

COASTAL CULTURES

People did not live in the high mountains that hugged the coast, but dwelt in villages perched on the rims of cliffs or benches along the coast, or on the lower reaches of its rivers. The cultures were oriented to water by the great volume of the many salmon species that live in the sea but breed in fresh water. Herring and smelt also were present in large numbers. Oil was obtained from the amazing oulachon, or candlefish, so rich in oil that a thread passed through it will burn like a candle. A few groups hunted whales, seals, and sea otters that augmented the already abundant food supply. Inland hunting was limited.

PEOPLES OF THE FAR NORTH

The harsh landscapes of the Arctic and sub-Arctic were sparsely populated by resourceful nomadic hunters, including the Aleuts and Inuits (Eskimos) of the Arctic and the Athapascan groups of the sub-Arctic. From c. A.D. 1000 the Thule Inuits migrated eastward. By then the furs, copper, and animal oils produced by the northern peoples had become valuable currency throughout much of the continent.

PEOPLES OF THE FAR NORTH

Aleut indigenous people	**Inuit migration routes**
◇ Aleut site	➤ from 1000
◆ Inuit site	➤ 1000–1200
● Norse settlement	➤ 1200–1500
▢ core region of the Inuit people	▢ subarctic culture area

Captain James Cook, the first visitor to the Northwest Coast, did not mention totem poles, and it was not until the mid-nineteenth century that they became common—because only a few such immense carved poles would have been possible before iron tools were generally available from European traders. There were many reasons for erecting totem poles: they might celebrate the building of a new house, contain the cremated remains of the dead, or memorialize someone who had died. The ease of sculpting with iron tools permitted each village to erect dozens of such memorials.

Two areas of North America saw an initial elaboration of culture following the arrival of Europeans: the Great Plains and the Northwest Coast. In both areas, later events, principally the arrival of disease epidemics, were to help destroy those cultures. But in the Great Plains, the arrival of horses created wealth and prosperity for the hunters who formerly pursued buffalo on foot. On the Northwest Coast, the arrival of Europeans brought great wealth from the fur trade—a business in which the Northwest Coast peoples often acted as intermediaries for inland tribes. It was the historic fur trade that led to the wealth that fueled the explosive elaboration of their carved art and architecture, and led to social institutions such as the potlatch that today provide us with our stereotype of these people.

ALASKA AND HAWAII

Alaska north and west of its panhandle consisted of two provinces. The land-locked Athapascan-speaking peoples hunted and fished in the interior coniferous forests. Their linguistic relatives continued into the lowlands of western Canada east to Hudson Bay. The coastal Inuits, or Eskimos, and the Aleut inhabitants of the Aleutian Islands surrounded them, practicing open-water hunting and fishing. Relatives of the Inuits occupied the entire northern coast of North America, east to Labrador. Both the Inuits and Athapascans had occupied and survived the continent's most environmentally hostile lands for thousands of years. Of the two groups, the Inuits lived the most prosperous lives. Fishing, whaling, and sealing, abetted by caribou hunting, provided a more dependable food source than the fully inland resources available to the Athapascans.

The native peoples of Hawaii have a history entirely separate from those living in North America. They are members of the great Polynesian family that expanded across the Pacific, and whose

WHALE HUNTING
In this English illustration, natives in canoes and Europeans in a sailing ship are shown hunting whales side by side along the Pacific Coast.

"WHERE WILL YOU AND I SLEEP? AT THE DOWN-TURNED JAGGED RIM OF THE SKY YOU AND I WILL SLEEP."

—WINTU DREAM SONG

ultimate home was southeast Asia. Migrants from Melanesia first settled Micronesia, then sailed across the Pacific to Hawaii and Easter Island. Hawaii was first settled about A.D. 600 by migrants from eastern Polynesia, probably the Marquesas Islands. Accomplished navigators, Polynesians were capable of crossing great reaches of ocean in their outrigger canoes to reach even small islands, using their knowledge of the stars, ocean currents, wave patterns, and the flight of birds. The first settlers brought with them food crops, dogs, pigs, and fowls, and in the fertile Hawaiian setting, their population grew rapidly. It was not long before a powerful hierarchy of chiefs and nobles developed by controlling and redistributing food, a hierarchy found by the first European explorers.

TOTEM POLE
The carvings on totem poles celebrated spirits associated with families of high status.

ENCAMPMENT ON THE PLAINS
A Native American man looks out over an encampment of Bloods, Blackfeet, Sarcees, and Assiniboines in Alberta, Canada.

"I WOULD NOT CRY IF I WERE TO HEAR THAT YOU HAD BEEN KILLED IN BATTLE. THAT IS WHAT MAKES A MAN: TO FIGHT AND TO BE BRAVE."

—PAWNEE MOTHER'S ADVICE TO HER SON, LONE CHIEF

TRIBAL RELATIONS IN 1500

CONFLICT WAS A FACT OF LIFE IN THE WEST BEFORE COLUMBUS. TRIBES OFTEN CLASHED VIOLENTLY, MOST OFTEN IN HIT-AND-RUN RAIDS. IN MUCH OF THE WEST, WARRIORS GAINED PRESTIGE BY KILLING AND SCALPING ENEMIES. BUT TRIBES ALSO INTERACTED PEACEFULLY THROUGH A CONTINENT-WIDE NETWORK OF TRADE.

INTERTRIBAL RIVALRY and violence was an important part of life through much of the West for thousands of years. These conflicts grew as white settlement displaced eastern Indians toward the west and onto the lands of the tribes living there. Later, competition for fur-bearing animals intensified existing problems.

WARFARE

Intertribal conflicts did not often lead to warfare in the usual sense, because formal military encounters between two political groups were rare. Culturally sanctioned and institutionalized raiding is a better definition for their activities.

Conflict rarely involved fielding large groups of men, the general practice being to ambush enemies in a surprise attack. The widespread practice of hit-and-run raiding by small parties of warriors led to innumerable deaths. Probably more people died in such raids than did of disease in pre-European times, for endemic warfare was a permanent cultural fact across most of the United States. Small-scale attacks nevertheless sometimes escalated into serious affairs in which entire villages were destroyed. The destruction of the prehistoric Crow Creek village in South Dakota, and the massacre, mutilation, or dismemberment of all or most of its inhabitants testify to the level of savagery that could be reached.

From the Atlantic seaboard to the Rocky Mountains there was a highly developed "war

☀SCALPING☀

SCALPING was not peculiar to North America but performed worldwide. Within North America, research indicates that it was originally limited to the eastern United States and Canada's lower St. Lawrence region and only later spread to cultures further west. The normal victory trophy was the head itself, but this was cumbersome to carry. Scalps were easier, and scalp-taking undoubtedly increased with the granting of scalp bounties by colonial and later governments. Hair was a symbol of strength among many Native American nations, and this probably led to further spread of the practice.

The part of the scalp taken was usually a small patch of skin just behind the crown. Sometimes all of the head's skin was taken with hair attached and later divided among warriors. Some Plains Indians stretched scalps on hoops, displaying them on poles and carrying them in ceremonial scalp dances.

Scalping, while painful, was not always lethal. A Plains warrior might try to scalp his enemy before killing him, in order to cause greater pain. Prisoners were sometimes scalped and then returned to their own people as a symbol of defeat.

TAKING A SCALP
A Mandan scalps an enemy in battle. Many Plains warriors took scalps as treasured war trophies.

SIOUX WAR CLUB

Indian weapons were often carefully fashioned, such as this war club carved from elkhorn in the shape of a water bird. Its eyes are copper.

complex" involving the prestige of warriors; economic gain was secondary. A young man attained adulthood by virtue of killing an enemy and obtaining a scalp. Without such status as a warrior, a man could not marry well or advance socially or politically. Prestige was the objective of warfare, not plunder, though horses as booty became important later on the Plains and in the Basin and Plateau.

Anyone could assemble a raiding party, sometimes under the aegis of a war chief, but peace chiefs (themselves formerly noted warriors) discouraged such raids in the interest of maintaining good relations with their neighbors. Since prestige was linked to success in conflict, the advice of their elders to forego raids generally was ignored by aspiring warriors. How else could a young man be successful in life? Individualism thus overrode the welfare of the community, and "irresponsible young men" often provoked major problems with their neighbors, especially those that spoke different languages. Historic Indian-white relations often were strained by such raids, for whites blamed the tribe or its leaders for actions over which they had no control.

An integral part of warfare was scalping, a firmly established practice across most of the United States. The taking of trophy heads from the slain was common throughout the West, and often all or part of the hair from such prizes was removed. In the Great Plains especially, scalps consisted of small circles or patches of hair removed from a dead (or living) enemy that were used as decorative war honors. Being scalped was a painful experience but not necessarily fatal, and if one was not killed the major problem was avoiding infection.

Scalping was an old custom, and the marks left on skulls by the victor's knives testify to an antiquity of no less than 2,000 years. Scalps had supernatural or religious significance in many tribes, and an Arikara Indian who

survived scalping was regarded as no longer quite human, and went off to live away from the village. The practice of scalping was so widespread it may have entered North America when people first settled in the New World, but the historic white practice of offering bounties for Indian scalps clearly led to its intensification.

Taking an enemy's life or scalp, however, often was a lesser honor than the equally hazardous act of "counting coup" in which one simply touched an enemy (an act called a coup) without injuring him. In the Plains, a man who killed an enemy after another man had touched him was given a lower grade in that combat. "Coups" ranked the men in war honors, and the stories of how they were made were repeatedly told publicly to reinforce one's warrior status.

Sometimes war parties traveled great distances for booty or captives. The Hidatsa Indians, for instance, often raided the Shoshone Indians along the Rocky Mountain front from their villages on the Missouri River—an airline distance of 500 miles. It was on such a raid that they captured Sacagawea, the young Shoshone girl who was purchased by

PLAINS WARRIORS

Warriors stand and sit on rock croppings at St. Mary Lake, Montana. The Blackfeet believed spirits called the Suyitapis (the Underwater People) dwelled in bodies of water.

Toussaint Charbonneau and who accompanied Lewis and Clark back to her home near the headwaters of the Missouri River. Iroquois war parties also traveled nearly twice that distance to attack Pawnee villages in present-day Nebraska. Across most of the United States, captives taken on war parties might become slaves or bartered to other groups, but they often became a member of their captor's group by adoption or marriage.

BEYOND THE PLAINS

West of the Great Plains, prestige as a warrior often was a less important motive for war than slaves and other plunder, adventure, or revenge. On the Northwest Coast, slaves were stigmatized and often were not ransomed after capture because of the disgrace they had brought to their family. They could be cruelly treated and were often sacrificed. Children of slaves also became slaves, the only instance in North America where slavery could be hereditary.

The Indians of California were the most peaceful groups in North America. Tribelets sometimes clashed in formal battles, but bloodshed was not a goal, and the battle ended when someone important was killed. However, the level, organization, and intensity of violence varied widely. Raids by the Yuman Indians in the desert Southwest were small and timid in contrast to the aggressiveness of the Navajo and Apache warriors who often struck the pueblos. The Pima Indians of northern Mexico had the largest "armies" in the West and provide an exception to the usual kind of small-group conflicts. Groups of as many as 1,000 men, divided into "squadrons" led by commanders, would march and fight in formation.

The reputation of the "peaceful Pueblos" is misleading. They were peaceful principally by contrast to their nomadic Navajo and Apache neighbors, whom they periodically had to hold at bay. All pueblos had a war chief, and it is often forgotten that the pueblos all united under Popé, a Tewa medicine man of the San Juan Pueblo, to violently expel the Spanish from the Southwest in 1680. There is good evidence that prehistoric pueblos fought not only defensively but with other Pueblos. The Pueblo peoples, like the Plains village farmers, were at a disadvantage in conflicts, for their enemies always knew where to find loot and prisoners—at the towns where they lived year-round. Their nomadic neighbors were harder to find and could be anywhere in an area of several thousand square miles.

"IN THIS HARSH AND DIFFICULT ENVIRONMENT PUEBLO CULTURE REACHED ITS HIGHEST DEVELOPMENT."

—ARCHAEOLOGIST ALFRED VINCENT KIDDER
ON CHACO CANYON, 1924

CHACO RUINS

Chaco Canyon, New Mexico, the site of impressive ruins, was an important trade center when it was occupied by the Anasazis.

Plains village tribes were the common targets of the Plains nomads, although traditional hostility between these two groups was seasonally muted by mutual interests—trade. There was a symbiotic relationship between them despite their traditional hostility and the fact that the villagers regarded the Sioux as equivalent to locusts and disease.

Most traditional examples of rivalries and alliances, however, probably date to the historic period. Because so many tribes changed locations in the post-Columbian era, few groups were living historically in the same localities when Europeans arrived to report their practices. The Plains provide an extreme example of tribal movement, for it was a more fluid area than the rest of the West. So many people flowed into the Great Plains about the time the horse arrived that some early anthropologists believed the core of that great grassland originally had been uninhabited, or at least very lightly populated. To the contrary, the Great Plains has been continuously inhabited since Clovis times. But more than half of the important tribes that lived there came from beyond its borders in early historic times—the Cheyennes, Arapahos, and some of the Sioux from Minnesota; the Plains Crees and Ojibways from the northeast; and the Sarsis from the north, among others—so it is hardly surprising that the myth developed that it had been vacant.

INTERTRIBAL TRADE

Trade has always been an important component in human affairs, for no area contains all of the resources that people come to prize as necessities or luxuries. Prehistoric North America was in fact united by a continent-wide trade network that tied every tribe to one or more of its neighbors in an exchange network. Goods flowed along these trade routes in a system that fostered close intertribal relations using two artificial languages to communicate.

Trade took place between neighboring Indian tribes, but the cumulative effect of repeated transactions meant that goods could travel for hundreds if not thousands of miles from their origin. Marine dentalium shells from the West Coast found their way into the Missouri valley, and Gulf Coast conch shells have been found in the northern Plains near the Rocky Mountains. Major trade centers developed at various times near The Dalles on the Columbia River; at the Mandan, Hidatsa, and Arikara villages on the upper Missouri; at Chaco Canyon, Casas Grandes, and Snaketown in the Southwest; and in the Opita villages in northwestern Mexico. These major centers were linked by secondary centers scattered across the West. Goods from the

California coast reached the pueblo dwellers and people in the Great Basin, and objects originating in the Northwest Coast spread across the Columbia Plateau to the upper Missouri River.

The latter example illustrates how complex the system could be. The village-dwelling Mandans, Hidatsas, and Arikaras who lived on the upper Missouri River were the focus of a far-flung trading network. Every fall in the early historic era, neighboring nomadic tribes came, individually, to their villages to trade products of the hunt for their garden produce. The Crows came from the west; the Assiniboins from the north; the Sioux from the east and south; and numerous tribes, but principally the Cheyennes, from the south. The nomadic tribes were fond of corn but grew none themselves, and they brought items not locally available along the Missouri. During these visits the women exchanged articles of skin clothing and food, and in historic times the men exchanged horses and guns.

The tribes involved in this exchange spoke very different languages, and communication would have been impossible except for the Plains Indian sign language. This system of hand gestures was so highly developed that individuals could transmit any everyday message across language barriers. It was, coincidentally or not, most highly developed in the Plains among the

SIOUX BEADWORK
Plains artists used small glass beads they obtained from white traders to decorate animal skins with colorful, geometric patterns.

very tribes most heavily involved in this trade. Another feature that prompted ready exchange was the network of fictive "fathers" and "sons" that were established through the Calumet Ceremony. A man in one tribe "adopted" as his "son" a man in another, and the two men placed their interaction on a kin basis. This ceremony served two purposes: it helped cement friendly relations between tribes, and it drew the men together as trading partners.

The Plains sign language and the adoption ceremony together bound many tribes into close partnerships but did not prevent warfare. Even permanently hostile relations were set aside in the fall when the trading season opened. Men who would have slain one another on the prairie one day could mix with their enemies in safety when they went to trade with a village—a kind of "market peace." Once out of sight of the village or trading ground, however, both host and visitor could fall upon one another in bitter fighting.

SIOUX DEERSKIN ROBE
The hard-working women of the Plains tribes cleaned and tanned the hides of animals killed by hunters and sewed the processed skins into clothing.

✦FAVORITE TRADE GOODS✦

WOODPECKER SCALPS and mollusk shells may not seem valuable to us, but to pre-Columbian Native Americans on the Pacific coast, they were as good as money. The bird scalps were a way of representing value and measuring personal wealth, as were dentalia, the remains of a kind of marine mollusk. Such currency was actively traded, along with items of more obvious value, such as meat and arrows.

The following chart, based on analysis of ethnographic literature, compares twenty different trade goods by how often they are mentioned as being imported or exported in accounts of California's Indians. Though these accounts necessarily date from the period after contact with Europeans, they give an indication of the scope of goods traded among western Native Americans before contact.

TRADE GOOD	NUMBER OF TIMES MENTIONED
Salt	79
Basketry	76
Hides and pelts	68
Dentalia	45
Clam disc beads	44
Fish	37
Obsidian	35
Pigments and paint	29
Sinew-backed bows	20
Rabbit-skin blankets	18
Arrows	18
Miscellaneous seeds and nuts	16
Animal meat	11
Tobacco	11
Woodpecker scalps	10
Dugout canoes	10
Basketry raw materials	8
Horn for spoons	6
Dogs	4
Human slaves	2

ITEMS FOR TRADE
To make trade items, Native American artisans worked with a variety of locally available materials, from copper to bone, from shell to turquoise.

copper bells

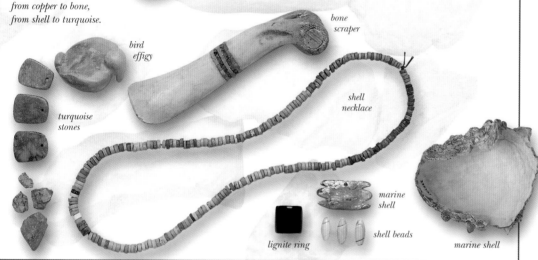

bird effigy

bone scraper

turquoise stones

shell necklace

marine shell

lignite ring

shell beads

marine shell

NORTHERN PLAINS GIRL'S DRESS
Sewn from two deer hides, this dress is decorated with beadwork and displays deer tails on the front and back of its yoke.

These trade fairs, or rendezvous, were not simply a means of exchanging goods. They were important in many other ways: the haggling, visiting, and dances that took place were a perfect medium for exchanging information. It was through such contacts that the Mandans learned of the Spanish Southwest. Plains Indians had a number of games of chance, and through betting on their outcome, the stakes could exchange hands, so that anything the visitors brought to the trade fair could well be left behind together with what they had formally traded. By these means all manner of things passed between tribes: dances, songs, stories, and material goods, large and small.

They were a perfect means for homogenizing the cultures of the northern Great Plains.

A similar system was present in the Columbia Plateau. In the fall, after the salmon harvest, tribes from all over the plateau would meet along the Columbia River in another great trade fair. They assembled at the villages of the Wishram and Wasco tribes that lived near the renowned Celilo Falls at a point on the river known as The Dalles. These great cascades were perfect places to catch countless salmon as they migrated upriver to spawn. Lewis and Clark observed literally tons of dried fish in these villages in 1805, and conditions along the river had not changed

for centuries. Further upriver the salmon lost weight and food value, but at Celilo Falls they were still in prime condition.

The Columbia Plateau is one of the most linguistically complex parts of North America north of Mexico. Few of the many small tribes were capable of understanding the language of another, but this difficulty was overcome by an artificial language—Chinook jargon—with a simple grammar and words borrowed from tribes between northern California and central British Columbia. Some people think the jargon grew up in response to the need to communicate with white traders in historic times, but its integration into the trading network in the plateau suggests it is an ancient system, one that was perhaps elaborated with the arrival of European traders along the coast.

Men did not "adopt" one another in the plateau, but a system of establishing "trading partners" with whom one would trade exclusively led to much the same circumstance. Intertribal relations often were strengthened when the children of partners would marry. So prevalent was this practice that the entire Columbia Plateau has been said to constitute one giant social system—one in which exchange at The Dalles and smaller markets had muted tribal differences so that everyone used virtually the same kinds of household goods and weapons.

THE SHOSHONE RENDEZVOUS

The fall trading fairs at The Dalles and the Missouri River villages were linked by intermediate tribes who met at a spring rendezvous in the area northeast of Great Salt Lake. Crow Indians who had been to the Missouri villages came to this fair, as did the Shoshones and others who had traded at the Dalles. The Shoshone rendezvous, as it is now called, provided the means for dentalium shells from the Pacific Coast to reach the Mandan villages, and goods from those villages to reach the Columbia Plateau.

An item traded at The Dalles one fall might be exchanged at the Shoshone rendezvous the following spring and in the fall become the property of someone on the Missouri River. Such trade routes historically provided the means by which horses spread from the Spanish Southwest to the northern Plains and to the Columbia Plateau.

The trade between the Pacific Northwest and the village tribes in the heartland of the continent illustrates how elaborate the trade networks could be and how they affected Native American lives. The exchange of luxury and necessary goods simultaneously enriched their lives, reinforced their way of life, and spread new and old ideas far and wide.

A net of real and fictive kinsmen accompanied this exchange and fostered goodwill between tribes. Languages developed that made this trade practical. Knowledge and goods from half a continent away united groups of people across the West.

European traders infiltrated these systems to obtain wealth and information. The experiences of the La Vérendrye family is instructive. Hoping to reap benefits from the beaver trade, the Sieur de la Vérendrye and his sons built forts west of Lake Superior and explored to the southwest in the mid-1700s, eventually reaching the Mandan villages in present North Dakota. At those villages they saw Spanish goods, including a cotton shirt embroidered with silk, and heard very accurate stories of how the Spanish lived in Santa Fe, nearly 1,800 miles away. No Mandan had been there, but goods and tales had reached them by way of the Indian intermediaries that carried goods north from the Spanish Southwest.

Trade did more than satisfy the wants and needs of its participants, for there were important cultural byproducts of this exchange. Two contrasting effects are immediately obvious. First, because a group needed to spend additional time to accumulate a tradable surplus of resources by hunting, gathering, or growing, its existing lifeway was reinforced and made more dependent on local products. On the other hand, trade spread all manner of cultural elements over very broad areas. The Columbia Plateau is a prime example, so intimately were the people related and so closely did their tools and weapons resemble one another. Trade relations thereby helped cement tribes living in similar settings into culture areas, and may have had less desirable consequences: epidemics may have followed the same routes.

THE POWWOW CIRCUIT

The pre-Columbian-trading network that spanned North America was destroyed by the arrival of Europeans, who first insinuated themselves into this system and then replaced it by trading directly with the Indians. The trade system nevertheless survives today in spirit in a very different form: the powwow circuit. Virtually every Indian reservation holds a dance sometime during the summer, and the larger events may be attended by members of dozens of other reservations, some of them from hundreds of miles distant. The timing of the powwows is staggered so that a family can spend the greater part of the summer moving from one event to another. Members of different reservations come to know one another, and they invariably exchange dance steps and songs, but more important, they exchange information as they camp together. The powwows fulfill much the same function the pre-Columbian and later trade centers did in spreading both news and other cultural features among widely separated peoples.

⇥THE POWWOW CIRCUIT⇤

POWWOWS are social gatherings of Native Americans at which they perform traditional dances and celebrate their heritage. They are particularly important in the Great Plains, where many powwows are held once a year, for example in Iowa, Kansas, Minnesota, and Nebraska. Indian food and crafts are available and prize money may be awarded in dance competitions. In a given summer, families can move from powwow to powwow, enjoying the social interaction and keeping Native American traditions alive.

Despite the powwow's importance to western Indian life, the term itself is not western, but eastern—from Connecticut, to be exact. It originated in the Narragansett word *"powwow,"* which meant literally "one who has visions," and was applied to a shaman or medicine man, or to a ceremony in which a shaman was involved.

POWWOW DANCERS
A large crowd gathers on the Mall in Washington, D.C., in 2002 to watch a Plains-style powwow.

CHAPTER 2

SPAIN IN THE WEST

1500–1800

FOR NEARLY THREE CENTURIES, THE GREATEST
EUROPEAN POWER IN THE AMERICAN WEST WAS
SPAIN. FOLLOWING THE INITIAL EXPLORATIONS OF
CABEZA DE VACA AND CORONADO, SPAIN COLONIZED
NEW MEXICO, TEXAS, ARIZONA, AND CALIFORNIA,
AND MADE CLAIMS FARTHER NORTH. DESPITE
DETERMINED EFFORTS TO PROTECT ITS EMPIRE
AGAINST RIVALS SUCH AS FRANCE AND ENGLAND,
SPAIN DECLINED IN POWER. IN THE NINETEENTH
CENTURY, ITS WESTERN LANDS BECAME
PART OF MEXICO, THEN FELL TO THE
EXPANDING UNITED STATES.

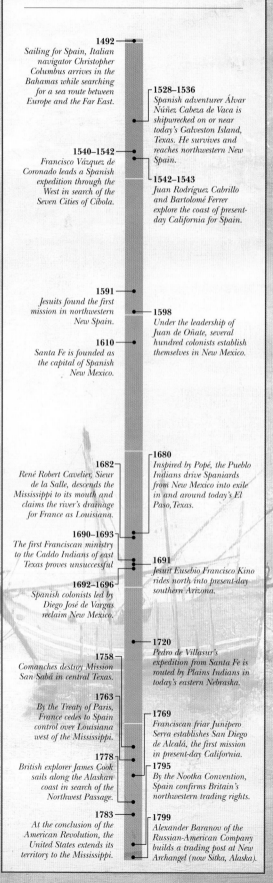

✦TIMELINE✦
1500–1800

In the three centuries after the arrival of Columbus, the Spanish secured a vast empire in North America, including much of the American West. Holding this area with small bands of soldiers, missionaries, and settlers proved to be a constant struggle—one that pitted them against the Indian peoples of the region as well as European rivals intent on establishing their own colonies in the West.

1492
Sailing for Spain, Italian navigator Christopher Columbus arrives in the Bahamas while searching for a sea route between Europe and the Far East.

1528–1536
Spanish adventurer Álvar Núñez Cabeza de Vaca is shipwrecked on or near today's Galveston Island, Texas. He survives and reaches northwestern New Spain.

1540–1542
Francisco Vázquez de Coronado leads a Spanish expedition through the West in search of the Seven Cities of Cíbola.

1542–1543
Juan Rodríguez Cabrillo and Bartolomé Ferrer explore the coast of present-day California for Spain.

1591
Jesuits found the first mission in northwestern New Spain.

1598
Under the leadership of Juan de Oñate, several hundred colonists establish themselves in New Mexico.

1610
Santa Fe is founded as the capital of Spanish New Mexico.

1682
René Robert Cavelier, Sieur de la Salle, descends the Mississippi to its mouth and claims the river's drainage for France as Louisiana.

1680
Inspired by Popé, the Pueblo Indians drive Spaniards from New Mexico into exile in and around today's El Paso, Texas.

1690–1693
The first Franciscan ministry to the Caddo Indians of east Texas proves unsuccessful

1691
Jesuit Eusebio Francisco Kino rides north into present-day southern Arizona.

1692–1696
Spanish colonists led by Diego José de Vargas reclaim New Mexico.

1720
Pedro de Villasur's expedition from Santa Fe is routed by Plains Indians in today's eastern Nebraska.

1758
Comanches destroy Mission San Sabá in central Texas.

1763
By the Treaty of Paris, France cedes to Spain control over Louisiana west of the Mississippi.

1769
Franciscan friar Junípero Serra establishes San Diego de Alcalá, the first mission in present-day California.

1778
British explorer James Cook sails along the Alaskan coast in search of the Northwest Passage.

1795
By the Nootka Convention, Spain confirms Britain's northwestern trading rights.

1783
At the conclusion of the American Revolution, the United States extends its territory to the Mississippi.

1799
Alexander Baranov of the Russian-American Company builds a trading post at New Archangel (now Sitka, Alaska).

SPAIN ENCOUNTERS THE WEST

THROUGHOUT THE SIXTEENTH CENTURY, SPANISH EXPLORERS AND CONQUISTADORS SOUGHT NEW LANDS IN NORTH AMERICA TO CLAIM FOR THEIR EMPIRE. THEIR QUEST REPEATEDLY BROUGHT THEM INTO CONTACT WITH THE REGION'S NATIVE INHABITANTS, WHO WERE UNDERSTANDABLY SUSPICIOUS OF THESE STEEL-AGE INTRUDERS.

TO SPAIN, the American West was always north. Ever a distant frontier, the West's alluring vastness kept Spaniards guessing for nearly three centuries, from the middle 1500s to the early 1800s. First, it appeared as a shimmering mirage where anything seemed possible but virtually nothing panned out. New Mexico led the way. Then, during generations of imperial rivalry, most notably with France and England, Spaniards set out further preemptive colonies in present-day Texas, Arizona, and California, and broadcast sweeping claims across western North America from the Gulf of Mexico to the ice floes of Alaska. Finally, with the nineteenth-century erosion of Spain's global power, its colonies in the West became vulnerable northern provinces of an independent Mexico and easy picking for *los americanos* of the westward-surging United States.

CORONADO'S MARCH

Francisco Vázquez de Coronado led an expedition through the American West in search of elusive riches. Near the end of his mission, he wrote to the King of Spain, "And what I am sure of is that there is not any gold nor other metal in all that country."

THE FIRST EUROPEAN CONTACTS

Norse Expeditions
- Bjarni Herjolfsson 985–86
- Leif Eriksson 1003
- Thorvald Eriksson 1005–12

Spanish and Portuguese Expeditions
- Christopher Columbus 1492–1503
- Miguel Corte-Real 1501, 1502
- Christopher Columbus 1502–4
- Hernán Cortés 1519–21
- Juan Ponce de León 1513
- Panfilo de Narváez and Alvar Núñez Cabeza de Vaca 1528–36
- Francisco de Ulloa 1539–40
- Hernando de Soto 1539–43
- Francisco Vázquez de Coronado and Garcia Lopez de Cardeñas 1540–42
- Sebastián Vizcaíno 1602–3

English Expeditions
- John Cabot 1497
- Martin Frobisher 1576–77
- Francis Drake 1579
- John Davis 1585–87
- Henry Hudson 1610–11

French Expeditions
- Giovanni da Verrazano 1524
- Jacques Cartier 1535–36
- Samuel de Champlain 1604–7
- European settlement and date of foundation 1608

Map labels:

ARCTIC CIRCLE
ICELAND
BRITISH ISLES
GREENLAND
Baffin Bay
LABRADOR
985: Bjarni Herjolfsson sights land west and south of Greenland
1610: Hudson reaches a "spacious sea" Hudson Bay
L'Anse aux Meadows c.1000
1535: Cartier starts expedition into St. Lawrence River
NEWFOUNDLAND
NOVA SCOTIA
Quebec 1608
Lake Winnipeg
Lake Superior
Lake Huron
Lake Michigan
Lake Ontario
Lake Erie
St. Lawrence
1524: Verrazano anchors close to present-day New York and is met by friendly native peoples
1542: Coronado's expedition sees vast herd of buffalo on Great Plains
Missouri
Ohio
APPALACHIAN MOUNTAINS
Chesapeake Bay
Jamestown 1607
1579: Drake sails north after raiding ports in Pacific South America. On landing near San Francisco Bay, he names the land New Albion
Santa Fe 1609
Arkansas
Red River
Mississippi
San Agustín 1565
1513: de León's ships land at Florida, believing it to be an island
1541: Mississippi crossed for the first time by Europeans
1492: Christopher Columbus sights land now thought to be one of the Bahamian Islands
COLUMBIA
LOWER CALIFORNIA
SIERRA MADRE OCCIDENTAL
SIERRA MADRE ORIENTAL
Rio Grande
Gulf of Mexico
BAHAMAS
CUBA
HISPANIOLA
San Juan 1509
Santo Domingo 1496
LESSER ANTILLES
Tropic of Cancer
La Paz 1535
Tampico 1528
Guadalajara 1531
Tenochtitlan (Mexico City)
Vera Cruz 1519
Santiago de Cuba 1514
GREATER ANTILLES
Caribbean Sea
1529–34: Cabeza de Vaca and three men including the African Estebán are only survivors of Narváez expedition after living among coastal Indians
Acapulco 1565
1521: Cortés destroys Aztec capital Tenochtitlan
1513: Vasco Núñez de Balboa is first explorer to sight Pacific Ocean
ISTHMUS OF PANAMA
SOUTH AMERICA
1000 km
1000 miles

The Spaniards' earliest line of approach ran from the Caribbean. In 1492 Genoese mariner and mystic Christopher Columbus, sailing for Spain in search of an oceanic trade route from Europe to the riches of the Far East, had landed on islands unknown to him and his crews. Two decades later, robust Juan Ponce de León navigated what he mistook for a very long island, naming it La Florida. His subsequent colonizing enterprise in 1521—the first by Europeans within today's United State—met determined resistance from Florida Indians and ended with Ponce de León's death from a festering arrow wound.

By the pivotal year 1521, Spaniards had charted the Gulf of Mexico's entire north coast, noted the mighty discharge of the Mississippi

THE FIRST EUROPEAN CONTACTS

Though the first Europeans to visit North America were Norsemen in the tenth century, European exploration only began during the fifteenth century, when developments in shipping made the longer exploratory voyages of Columbus and Cabot viable. These voyages and those of the sixteenth century were driven by population pressure, land hunger, and the search for new sources of wealth.

River, and founded a coastal municipality at Veracruz on the Mexican mainland. From that base, Hernán Cortés and several hundred Spanish soldiers, aided by a few horses, gunpowder, and thousands of Indian allies, launched the stunning conquest of the Aztec capital, upon whose ruins rose Mexico City. Grandly, Cortés named his colony New Spain. After his time, it grew to twice the size of modern Mexico and many times the size of Spain. Hence, from the 1520s onward, the Spanish advance toward the American West, or northern mystery, flowed up from the south, with a single notable exception.

Álvar Núñez Cabeza de Vaca's bizarre odyssey across the North American continent from east to west through parts of present-day Texas and northern Mexico happened wholly by chance. A Spanish gentleman seeking adventure, Cabeza de Vaca had signed on as second-in-command of an expedition from Spain to Florida under hell-bent Pánfilo de Narváez. In 1528, despite hurricanes and heavy desertion, and over Cabeza de Vaca's objections, Narváez plunged inland from the vicinity of Tampa Bay.

LIP ORNAMENT
This Aztec labret, or lip ornament, is made of gold and fashioned in the shape of an eagle's head.

A ghastly summer campaign brought him and some 250 emaciated survivors to coastal marshes southwest of today's Tallahassee, where no ships awaited them. Driven by desperation, the men fashioned five shallow-draft boats, dragged them to the gulf, and put out. Most perished. Only the wreck of Cabeza de Vaca's boat, washed ashore on or near Galveston Island, Texas, is known.

When he finally published it in 1542, Cabeza de Vaca's tale ranked him earliest in a number of categories dealing with any part of the present-day United States: Hispanic literature, captivity narrative, and firsthand travel account describing Native Americans, the environment, and buffalo. Stripped for eight years of every cultural advantage–high position in a European imperialist state, firearms, long-range sailing capability, use of his literacy, horsemanship, and manufactured trade goods—except what he retained in his memory and spirit, Cabeza de Vaca stayed alive

MAP OF TENOCHTITLAN
This map of Mexico's ancient Aztec capital was included in a letter from Hernán Cortés to Holy Roman Emperor Charles V. The city, built on an islet in salty Lake Texcoco, was conquered by Cortés in 1521.

among native peoples by making himself useful or amusing. As slave, oddity, trader, and healer, he got to know them as fellow human beings, cruel and tender, deceptive and loyal, hateful and loving, not unlike his own kind. Emerging from the ordeal with an unshaken belief in European superiority, Cabeza de Vaca nonetheless joined other Spanish advocates of human rights, recommending to the king of Spain that conquest of the Americas proceed with kindness. It did not.

THE QUEST OF FRANCISCO VÁZQUEZ DE CORONADO

The castaways' arrival in Mexico City in the summer of 1536—Cabeza de Vaca, two white companions, and the black Moroccan slave Estebanico—caused a sensation. Conqueror Hernán Cortés and Antonio de Mendoza, the king's recently appointed viceroy of New Spain, competed to entertain them. In the prevailing climate of wonder, even the wanderers' veiled references to distant northern cities excited keen

→CABEZA DE VACA←

AMONG HIS accomplishments, Spanish explorer Álvar Núñez Cabeza de Vaca (c. 1492–c. 1559) is best remembered today for his detailed descriptions of the Native Americans he encountered during his unplanned, eight-year residence among them. From the wreck of his boat on the Texas coast to his eventual appearance in the Spanish settlements of western Mexico, he observed the cultures of a variety of Indian peoples.

Of the Karankawas he first met in Texas, for example, Cabeza de Vaca recalled that they were "tall and well formed." He and his companions feared slaughter, but instead the Indians fed and housed the strangers. The Karankawas were "most dexterous" with bows and arrows, dwelled in lodges made of matting, and lived by fishing and foraging for roots, oysters, and berries. The men were notable for their body-piercings. The women, he wrote, "do the hard work." To please his hosts, Cabeza de Vaca treated the sick by reciting Christian prayers and breathing on them. The method satisfied his patients, and he used his reputation as a healer to gain the friendship of other tribes.

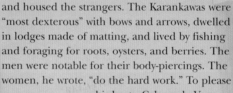

CABEZA DE VACA'S BOOK
The Relation de (Narrative of) Álvar Núñez Cabeza de Vaca was published in 1542.

CHRISTOPHER COLUMBUS
The explorer's first American landing occurred at Watling Island, or San Salvador, in the Bahamas in 1492. Columbus went on to found a colony in what is now the Dominican Republic on nearby Hispaniola.

interest. The viceroy, purchasing the services of Estebanico, dispatched him in the company of well-traveled Franciscan fray Marcos de Niza on a northern reconnaissance up the Pacific slope in 1539. Beyond the last Spanish settlement, the black man swaggered ahead. News of his death at the hands of Zuni Pueblo Indians in New Mexico stunned fray Marcos, who claimed to have pressed on fearfully to within sight of a town larger than Mexico City.

This supposed eyewitness report, reinforced by European and Native American myth, set off a delirious quest for the golden Seven Cities of

Cíbola. Viceroy Mendoza invested a small fortune, as did his thirty-year-old protégé, Francisco Vázquez de Coronado, who had married a rich widow. The expeditionary force of more than 300 armed Spaniards and their train, trailing north after review by the viceroy in February 1540, looked as though they had marched off a medieval European tapestry. Elegantly mounted, Coronado, the ideal warrior-knight in gilded

COURT OF MONTEZUMA
Aztec emperor Montezuma (or Moctezuma) received Cortés and his delegation at court in hopes of assuaging them. The effort failed. Montezuma was made a puppet governor for the Spanish and was later killed by his own people in the struggle for control of the empire.

armor, hand on the hilt of his Toledo-steel blade, led a cavalcade of officers astride Spanish barb stallions, followed by footmen in coats of mail and pot helmets, wielding matchlock harquebus or crossbow. Heavy gray habits and sandals distinguished a knot of tonsured Franciscan friars. Decorative detail revealed the officers' pavilion tents, mastiffs and greyhounds, and a few light, swivel-mounted, breech-loading bronze guns hauled on mules and capable of hurling a one- to two-inch ball. Evident in the background, but uncounted, came muleteers, cooks, and other support people; Africans and women; and droves of animals, including sheep.

SPANISH COLONIZATION OF THE NEW WORLD 1492–c.1600

Spanish settlement

- Spanish town
- fort
- Jesuit mission
- silver mine

Yuma Native American people

1632 date of foundation

SPANISH COLONIZATION OF THE NEW WORLD
The first Spanish visits to the Caribbean and the Gulf of Mexico, in the late 1400s and early 1500s, were followed by the conquest of the Aztec empire on the Mexican mainland, exploration of much of Central America, and colonization of the Southwest.

✦FRANCISCO VÁZQUEZ DE CORONADO✦

BORN in Salamanca, Spain, Francisco Vázquez de Coronado (1510–54) emigrated to New Spain with Viceroy Antonio de Mendoza in 1535. Marriage two years later to heiress Beatriz de Estrada brought him considerable wealth. Office followed in 1538 when the viceroy appointed Coronado governor of Nueva Galicia in present-day Mexico. From there he led the privately financed expedition of 1540 through a corner of today's Arizona into New Mexico. The sudden appearance of an invading force 2,000 strong temporarily upset the balance of power among Pueblo Indian communities.

From near present-day Albuquerque, Coronado's cavalcade ventured eastward in April 1541, drawn by the mirage of great riches, traversing the Texas panhandle, veering north across Oklahoma, and fording the Arkansas River into central Kansas. Empty-handed, the expedition returned to Mexico in 1542. Subjected to investigation and removed from his governorship, Coronado continued serving as a Mexico City councilman until just before his death.

Yet, on closer examination, this tapestry revealed more New World features than Old. The points of the crossbow darts, manufactured in iron-deficient New Spain, were copper. Many Spaniards wore padded cotton armor, as did some of the horses. The expedition's weaponry was overwhelmingly Mexican Indian: wooden, obsidian-edged swords, or *macanas*; lances with obsidian points; and slings. Even more conspicuous was the formidable contingent of a thousand Indian footmen from central Mexico with their elaborate insignias of feathered headdresses, pennants, and shields. From this time forward, on campaign, native auxiliaries regularly outnumbered Spaniards two or three to one, which explains in large part how relatively few Europeans would hold sway in so vast a region for almost 300 years.

Coronado's two-year, 4,000-mile trek up and across western North America, along with the various side expeditions he sent out, brought these bearded, iron-clad invaders face-to-face with the inhabitants of interconnected native worlds stretching from the arid delta of the Colorado River in the west to the plains of central Kansas. Impressions of their first encounters varied. Among gatherers and hunters, Spaniards reported haughtily that these primitive peoples took them for sons of the sun who had dropped from the sky. But when the town-dwelling Pueblo Indians of New Mexico put up a spirited fight or offered them foodstuffs, European expeditionaries saw in Native Americans human traits they understood.

A sharp clash between Coronado's hungry vanguard and defenders of the first multistoried,

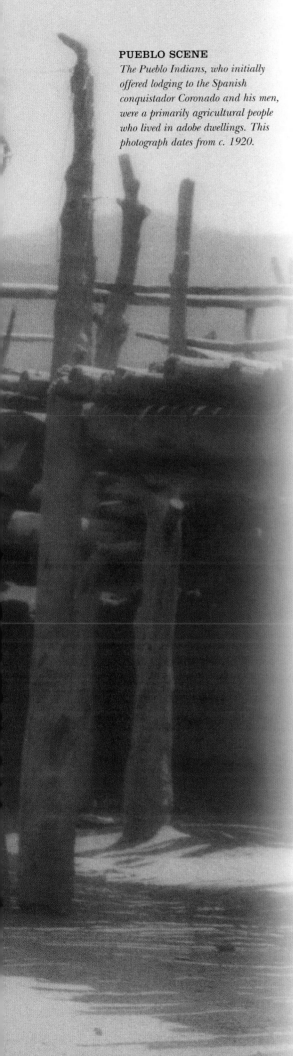

PUEBLO SCENE
The Pueblo Indians, who initially offered lodging to the Spanish conquistador Coronado and his men, were a primarily agricultural people who lived in adobe dwellings. This photograph dates from c. 1920.

mud-and-stone Zuni town, which nearly cost the Spanish general his life, put the intruders in possession. Soldiers, who had gambled everything on the prospect of princely returns, now cursed fray Marcos. Still, for two years, the Spaniards stayed among the Pueblo Indians, upsetting the latter's balance of power. Altogether sixty thousand people more or less, in a hundred little city-states scattered along the Rio Grande and its tributaries and on high, broken plateaus to the west, the natives possessed no tradition of common defense. During the Spaniards' brutal winter fight with the southern Tiwa-speaking Pueblos on the middle Rio Grande, Keresan Pueblos to the north supplied food to the Spanish invaders.

Meantime, the half-dozen Franciscans persuaded residents of Pueblo communities to erect in their plazas tall, free-standing crosses. When the Indians hung feathered prayer plumes on them and sprinkled sacred cornmeal nearby, the friars imagined that they were venerating them, not taming for themselves whatever power such symbols might possess. Because these expeditionary chaplains expected to move on to new and greater discoveries, they did not ask the natives to build churches. That would come later.

Coronado's summer dash in 1541 across the Great Plains to the east in search of an illusory kingdom of Quivira revealed structures no more substantial than the Wichita Indians' houses of grass. Try as they might, the Europeans found no exploitable resource, nothing of profit to put native peoples to extracting, planting, or assembling. There appeared no way to make their discoveries pay: the Grand Canyon; the Continental Divide; the endless, moving dark sea of buffalo on the plains. So, at the command of their despondent leader, in the spring of 1542 they withdrew. Among the Pueblo Indians, there remained hardly a trace. They absorbed easily the few Mexican natives left by the expedition and the babies born of foreign fathers to Pueblo women. They ate the sheep. But they remained anxious. They had endured an army of Europeans, watched it break camp and vanish from sight, but they sensed the inevitable.

OTHER COSTLY EXPEDITIONS

As the failed Coronado expedition disbanded in 1542 and Viceroy Mendoza set about recouping his losses, three other far-ranging Spanish journeys of exploration were underway. Two had the viceroy's backing; the third represented competition. Each proved fatal to its commander.

Up the Pacific coast of New Spain, Mendoza sent merchant and shipbuilder Juan Rodríguez Cabrillo with 250 men aboard a tiny armada of three ships: the slim, 200-ton, 100-foot galleon

---

⇸SPANISH ARMOR⇷

SPANISH EXPLORERS and settlers arrived in the New World in the mid-1500s heavily armored. Infantrymen likely wore shirts called hauberks that were made of chain mail, metal rings tightly linked together. They also probably wore cuishes, plates that protected the thighs and knees.

Cavalrymen, meanwhile, wore more complete suits of plate armor. Their horses were protected as well, often with armor made of ox hide.

Standard in Europe for centuries prior to the Middle Ages, chain mail was rendered less effective by advances in weaponry such as the longbow and crossbow. By the late 1200s–early 1300s, plate armor was being used to reinforce exposed areas of the bod such as the chest and shoulders. The full suit of steel-plate armor, including breastplate and gauntlets (gloves) appeared in the early 1400s, only to be proven ineffective with the advent of gunpowder weapons during the sixteenth century.

Inspired by native armor, some Spaniards chose escaupiles, canvas garments stuffed with cotton. Lightweight, more comfortable to wear, and affordable, well-made escaupiles deflected Indian arrows. Spaniards also carried shields (targets or bucklers), commonly round or oval in shape and made of metal or leather-covered wood.

Popular helmets included the chapel de fer ("iron hat"), the morion, and the basset, a Spanish version of the morion. The morion-cabasset of the late 1500s combined the former's peaked brim and the latter's keeled bowl. The popular burgonet, or Burgundian helmet, featured a comb or brim over the eyes, hinged earpieces, and optional facial protection.

HELMET
A conquistador's helmet, such as this one, was essential protection on the field of battle.

San Salvador, square-rigged with high sterncastle; the smaller, round-bellied carrack *Victoria*; and another carrack or a bergantine, the *San Miguel*. The Ipai, Chumash, and other coastal California Indians who paddled canoes out to these strange floating houses or met shore parties of Cabrillo's Spanish, African, and Indian crewmen had already heard of Coronado's intrusion inland.

Like other native peoples, the painted coastal Indians, dressed in skins and adorned with bone, shell, and feathers, traded with the Spaniards: sardines, nuts, and acorns for bits of cloth, beads, and metal objects. They sensed quickly how acquisitive these aliens were. Eagerly the Indians agreed by gesture to whatever the white men sought, but always it lay farther on, always beyond the horizon. Surely seven days up the coast, the Spaniards would find a great river across the continent emptying into the sea. More important, the California coast was thought to veer westward toward Asia. So, bucking contrary currents, winds, and endless swells, the three little ships sailed northward along the rugged coastline, while Cabrillo claimed in the king's name every point, inlet, and island en route.

When howling storms drove them back, their crews prayed for divine protection. Anchored at last in the shelter of Santa Catalina Island, sailors who went ashore now found the native residents unwilling to share. Cabrillo, hastening to aid his men in a fight with Indians at Christmastime in 1542, jumped awkwardly from a launch, shattering

his leg. Soon gangrene gripped him. In a few days their leader was dead. Second-in-command Bartolomé Ferrer set course north again. Before doubling back, he sighted a rockbound shore near the California-Oregon border at about 42°, but no waterway or passage across North America, no land bridge to China, no rich cities.

CHOLOVONI HUNTERS

Spanish explorers dubbed the native Californians costeños, *or "coastal people." These San Francisco bay hunters were depicted in 1822 in a book by Russian naval officer Otto von Kotzebue.*

The second of Viceroy Mendoza's seaborne enterprises of 1542 ventured far out into the Pacific in search of spices and gold. Sailing among the islands of an extensive archipelago, its members bestowed the name "Philippines" in honor of Spain's young prince, later Philip II. Unable to navigate back against prevailing westerly winds, however, the frustrated Spaniards succumbed to mutinies, sickness, and the Portuguese.

At about the same time, half a world away in the present-day southeastern United States, Hernando de Soto's men were tying weights to their leader's makeshift coffin to sink it in the Mississippi River so Indians would not find and desecrate the body. The rapacious don Hernando, a rival of Viceroy Mendoza, had launched from Cuba in 1539 intent on exploring westward from

Florida toward New Spain. Unknowingly, at one point in July 1541, he and Coronado came within 300 miles of each other, the former in today's Arkansas, the latter in Kansas. De Soto's reckless, zigzag course through Mississipian chiefdoms had subjected the Indians of the Southeast to disease, pitched battles, rapes, and service as burden bearers, often fatal. Yet barely half of his 600 men survived.

Taken together, these costly, wide-ranging explorations of the 1540s offered Spaniards little incentive to settle. Geographic realities, however, had begun to take shape. Spanish mapmakers now possessed a fair idea of North America's width and the endlessness of the Pacific Ocean. Colonies would follow in due course for a variety of reasons.

SAILING THE NORTHWEST

For years, ships traversed the waterways of upper North America searching for the Northwest Passage. An easy ocean pathway to China and untold riches was never found, but the exploration led to the settlement of Canada.

RIO GRANDE

In 1540 Coronado arrived at the banks of the Rio Grande, where he stayed through the winter. The Pueblo Indians lived in city-states scattered along the Rio Grande and its tributaries and on plateaus to the west.

✦THE NORTHWEST PASSAGE✦

THE EARLIEST CIRCUMNAVIGATION of the globe, accomplished in 1519–22 by Ferdinand Magellan and Juan Sebastián del Cano, demonstrated not only the extent of the Americas but also the vastness of the south Pacific Ocean. While hope for a westward sea route from Europe to Asia still resided in the north, the California coastal exploration of Juan Rodríguez Cabrillo and Bartolomé Ferrer in 1542–43 failed to confirm that America was joined to China. By the 1560s and 1570s, European mapmakers (taking the name from Marco Polo's Kingdom of Anian) featured a Stretto di Anian, or Strait of Anián, separating North America and Asia.

Later, as Spaniards and their European rivals quickened the search for a navigable waterway across North America connecting the Atlantic and Pacific Oceans, the illusory Strait of Anián shifted its locale. After publication of Sir Humphrey Gilbert's *Discourse* in 1576,

THE PERILS OF EXPLORATION
Like Hernando de Soto in Florida, depicted below, explorers searching for the Northwest Passage risked death from Indian battles, disease, and starvation.

Englishmen called it the Northwest Passage. Sir Francis Drake, plundering the Pacific coast of Spanish America in 1578–79, returned to England so swiftly, completing the second around-the-world circumnavigation, that Spaniards thought mistakenly that he must have found and sailed back through the Strait of Anián.

The quest for the legendary strait spurred the northern explorations of Sebastián Vizcaíno, Henry Hudson, William Baffin, Captain James Cook, Juan Francisco de la Bodega y Quadra, Alexander MacKenzie, and dozens of others. Gradually, as the northern expanse of the continent became known, the lure of discovery drew Arctic explorers. In 1905 Norwegian Roald Amundsen completed an all-water crossing. The American nuclear submarine *Seadragon* slid through arctic waters from the Atlantic to the Pacific in 1960, accomplishing the first underwater crossing of the Northwest Passage.

TEWA GIRL
New Mexico founder Juan de Oñate encountered Tewas, a Pueblo tribe to which this girl, photographed in 1906, belonged.

THE FOUNDING OF NEW MEXICO

IN 1598 JUAN DE OÑATE LED HUNDREDS OF SETTLERS INTO PUEBLO INDIAN TERRITORY, INITIATING THE SPANISH COLONIZATION OF THE WEST. RECHRISTENING THE AREA NEW MEXICO, OÑATE DEALT OUT HARSH PUNISHMENTS TO PUEBLOS WHO DEFIED HIS AUTHORITY. BUT HIS COLONISTS FACED THE EVEN GREATER CHALLENGE OF SURVIVING DAY TO DAY IN AN UNFAMILIAR AND UNWELCOMING ENVIRONMENT.

"OTHERS IN GROUPS DID GIVE AID TO THE FIRE SO THAT IT MIGHT LEAP UP WITH MORE VIGOR CONSUME THE PUEBLO AND DESTROY IT ALL."

—POET-CAPTAIN GASPAR PÉREZ DE VILLAGRÁ, 1610, ON THE CONQUEST OF THE ACOMAS

AFTER CORONADO, the northward advance of New Spain fell back on itself. Silver got it moving again, if in a slower, more purposeful way. A rich bonanza unearthed in the late 1540s at Zacatecas, in today's Mexico some 300 miles northwest of Mexico City, drew hordes of miners into a high-desert world of cactus, jagged sierras, and shimmering desolation known as the Gran Chichimeca. To exist in so hostile an environment, settlers learned new ways of coping: cattle ranching on a huge scale to provide meat and hides to the mines; long-range freighting and supply; and perennial war against mobile bands of Chichimeca Indians, superb bowmen and masters of ambush. Spanish presidios, or garrisons of salaried armed men and their families placed along a defensive cordon, proved more visually reassuring than effective. When the Spaniards' offensive warfare failed to quell the Chichimecas, welfare eventually did. A shift in policy in the late 1580s, from search-and-destroy campaigns to treaties and peace by purchase, turned the tide. Such lessons served as precedents for succeeding frontiers in New Mexico, Texas, and California.

While this motley mining frontier lurched from strike to strike, memory of Coronado's Tierra Nueva, the new land far to the north,

INDIANS CARRYING EQUIPMENT
Indians from Mexico accompanied Oñate's colonizing venture as servants. Spanish expeditions frequently employed Indians to carry equipment.

reawakened. In 1561 fray Jacinto de San Francisco, a Franciscan lay brother, wrote to Philip II about a project to peacefully convert the Chichimecas as well as the inhabitants of another, or new, Mexico thought to exist beyond. Had fray Jacinto's plan prevailed, the rediscovery of the Pueblo Indians would have been gentler.

Instead, in the early 1580s, two rough, fast-moving parties, each led by veteran Indian fighters and prospectors, penetrated the Pueblo world looking for mines. So promising did the region appear to their eyes that they began promoting la Nueva México, the New Mexico. Now Philip II responded. The Spanish king, his treasury heavily burdened by European wars, called in 1583 for pacification of this New Mexico by a God-fearing gentleman of sufficient private means. Putting Coronado's fiasco out of mind, moguls of the silver frontier competed for the honor and profit of colonizing New Mexico. One eager individual, hoping to erase technicalities by his accomplishment, invaded the area without royal license. Down on his luck, Gaspar Castaño de Sosa, lieutenant governor of Nuevo León southeast of New Mexico, transported some 200 men, women, and children with all their belongings up the Rio Grande and Pecos rivers and into the midst of the Pueblo

✦PHILIP II✦

THE SON OF Holy Roman Emperor Charles V, Spain's King Philip II (1527–1598) married four times, in 1543 to Mary of Portugal, who died two years later. In 1554 he married England's Mary Tudor in hopes of strengthening Catholicism in the British Isles and forming a union of England, Spain, and the Netherlands against France. Mary died childless in 1558, after which Philip married Elizabeth of Valois (1560) and then Anne of Austria, mother of Philip III (1570).

In 1556 Charles abdicated, making Philip ruler of Spain; its territories in America; the Netherlands; and Naples, Sicily, and Milan in Italy. His policies, dominated by a rigid Catholicism, led to conflict with Protestant princes. He looked upon the Americas not only as a source of wealth to pay for his European armies but also as an opportunity to bring Native Americans to the Catholic faith. Philip's *Ordinances for New Discoveries* (1573) addressed these goals. His long reign (1556–98) spanned the first settlements in Florida (1565) and the founding of New Mexico (1598).

DOUBLOON
Plentiful gold and silver from New World mines were used to mint Spanish coins like this one from Philip II's reign.

TULAROSA BASIN
Spanish settlers survived in many environments, but parts of New Mexico were too harsh even for them. Their name for southern New Mexico, which includes the gypsum sands of the Tularosa Basin, was Las Salinas, *or the "Salt Lands."*

Indians. But because they found no treasure to share with the crown, the law was enforced. The viceroy dispatched an armed party to remove them, and the hapless don Gaspar, punished by exile to the Philippines, died in a mutiny of Chinese galley slaves on a voyage to the Moluccas.

JUAN DE OÑATE

In 1595 Juan de Oñate, silver-rich son of a Zacatecas developer, seized the prize. Contracting with the king's viceroy of New Spain, don Juan at age forty-five had all the right credentials: experience as a mine developer and military leader, an impressive New World lineage, the viceroy's confidence, and, most important, great personal wealth. For concessions he and his consortium deemed worth the risk, Oñate gambled on New Mexico. He would be the colony's first governor and captain general and its only *adelantado*, or founding proprietor. That proud title promised him an income out of revenues from the territory, tax exemptions, possible

monopolies, and a large landed estate. For his part, Oñate guaranteed to recruit, transport, and settle in New Mexico at his expense 200 armed colonists and their families.

To attract such people, he was authorized to grant them lands (*mercedes*); the privilege of collecting as personal income the tribute owed by a specified number of native households (*encomienda*); and, finally, title as members of the Spanish gentry (*hidalgo*). To qualify, a settler had to reside in the colony for five years. Escaping pressures in Mexico City, certain of Oñate's recruits were probably crypto-Jews, descendants of Jews expelled from Spain or converted to Christianity who still practiced Jewish ways in secret.

On the last day of April 1598, don Juan took possession of New Mexico at a camp on the Rio Grande downriver from today's El Paso, Texas. No one mistook this for Coronado's army. Oñate's colonists had come to stay. They ranged in status from doña Francisca Galindo, a Spanish captain's wife who had packed in chests nine stylish court dresses of velvet, taffeta, and satin, to mulatto muleteers with hardly a change of shirt. The Mexican Indians among them came not as a fighting force but as servants. Freight wagons stood lashed high with everything from horseshoe nails to laxatives. Boys and girls scampered underfoot. Among the thousands of milling cattle, horses, and sheep, herders tended breeding mares, not just stallions of war.

Because proprietor Oñate had fallen seventy-one colonists short of the 200 agreed upon, he was required under bond to provide them in the

⇒JUAN DE OÑATE⇐

JUAN DE OÑATE'S father, a wealthy Mexican mine owner, hailed from the Basque country of northeastern Spain. Hence, Juan (c. 1550–1626), a native of Zacatecas, was a criollo, that is, a European born in the Americas. In his late thirties, don Juan married Isabel de Tolosa Cortés Moctezuma, a high-born mestiza, a woman of Spanish and American Indian blood descended from Hernán Cortés and a daughter of the Aztec emperor. While the prestige of his lineage no doubt aided Oñate in securing the royal contract to colonize New Mexico, there is no evidence that doña Isabel ever joined her husband during his long residence in the far north. Their young son, Cristóbal, about age eight in 1598, did accompany his father and share the hard experience. They left the colony early in 1610. Neither doña Isabel nor Cristóbal lived to share in Oñate's exoneration of cruelty charges in Spain during the 1620s.

CELEBRATING MASS
This sixteenth-century manuscript illustration by Lienzo de Tlaxcala shows Spanish priests celebrating Mass for the Mexican locals, who receive communion. Catholic traditions intermingled with Indian rituals over the years.

SPREADING CHRISTIANITY
Father Narcisco Durán offers an apple to a young Indian at a California mission in 1841. At crown expense, ten Franciscan friars accompanied Oñate's expedition to spread Christianity to New Mexico's natives.

future. The crown's only major expense had been the complete outfitting of ten Franciscan friars and their Mexican Indian catechists and interpreters.

SAN JUAN BAUTISTA

A colony on the move, Oñate's migration labored up the Rio Grande to a Tewa-speaking pueblo they renamed San Juan Bautista, still known as San Juan Pueblo today. The intruders set local Indians to digging irrigation ditches and building a Christian church. On September 8, 1598, the feast of the Nativity of the Blessed Virgin Mary, they dedicated their sacred structure and celebrated. After displays of bullbaiting and horsemanship, these culturally Hispanic but racially mixed Spaniards regaled the assembled Indians with a thoroughly Castilian ceremonial, a rousing sham battle between Moors and Christians, the latter on foot firing harquebuses without ball, the former on horseback with shields and lances. As always, the Christians won. The vanquished Moors, after a time, got up laughing and brushed themselves off, causing some of the native spectators to wonder if the effect of Spanish firearms was only temporary.

The people of Ácoma soon found out. Two days' ride west of the Rio Grande, that seemingly impregnable pueblo rested atop an isolated mesa rising 350 feet above the surrounding valley. In October 1598, Governor Oñate and his entourage camped below and put several Ácoma leaders through a ritual act of obedience. This made the

✦CRYPTO-JEWS✦

EARLY IN THE 1480s, Spain's Queen Isabella and King Ferdinand received the pope's blessing to establish the Spanish Inquisition as a special government tribunal to bring to trial alleged heretics and sentence those found guilty. When, in 1492, the Spanish monarchs decreed that all Jews within their realms must convert to Christianity or face expulsion, more than half converted, becoming conversos, or New Christians; the rest, some 150,000, were expelled. Of those who converted, a number continued to practice Judaism in secret, becoming crypto-Jews. The Spanish Inquisition made the persecution of these Jewish pseudo-converts to Catholicism a high priority.

Because the Spanish Indies appeared to many crypto-Jews as a relatively safe haven, they spread throughout the empire. In 1571 Philip II authorized the Mexican Holy Office of the Inquisition, and, during the 1580s and 1590s, its agents sought to eradicate the crypto-Jews of New Spain. The celebrated case of Luis de Carvajal (1566–96) struck fear into the hearts of many. Carvajal was burned at the stake in the century's largest auto-da-fé, or public display of sentencing and punishing of the convicted.

There is little doubt that some settlers of New Mexico were crypto-Jews, escaping Inquisition pressures in urban areas. Eventually, those pressures ended: in 1820, the Spanish Inquisition ceased to exist.

FLAGELLANT
Religious fervor took violent forms during the time of the Spanish Inquisition. Flagellants, like the one depicted here walking with a Spanish gentleman, were part of a movement that promoted scourging oneself for one's sins.

Ácomas, in an utterly foreign sense, vassals of the Spanish crown. As a result, Oñate tried to explain through an interpreter, they would henceforth enjoy royal justice, peace with their neighbors, and orderly development of their commerce and industries—specious but consistent justifications for European conquest. Yet later that fall, when Oñate's brash young nephew and second-in-command, Juan de Zaldívar, climbed the mesa and demanded food, the Ácomas refused, killing him and most of his party. Word spread. The Ácomas had defied the invaders.

This was the test. Oñate, leader of a colony of six or seven hundred nervous foreigners in the midst of tens of thousands of unwelcoming natives, knew the odds. Back at San Juan Bautista, he first secured the Franciscans' opinion that this was open rebellion against a Christian prince. Hence, just war could be waged and slaves taken. Vicente, the fallen commander's brother, volunteered. Among Oñate's instructions to him was a standard admonition to show mercy.

ÁCOMA ROADWAY
Twentieth-century Ácoma women carry pottery and navigate a stone path between rock formations. The people of the Ácoma pueblo rebelled and received harsh treatment at the hands of Juan de Oñate's forces.

Don Vicente, while maintaining his stern countenance, must make it appear, however, that the chaplain had interceded. "In this manner," wrote Oñate, the Ácomas "will recognize the friars as their benefactors…and come to love and esteem them, and to fear us."

Thus, with seventy armed men, their support column, and a few small cannon, Vicente de Zaldívar rode out in the brittle cold of January 1599 to humble the defiant Ácomas. Incredibly, in a well-planned, bloody, several-day assault, he did

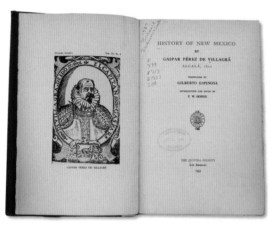

GASPAR PÉREZ DE VILLAGRÁ
An account of the Spanish conquest of the Ácoma people is given in Gaspar Pérez de Villagra's Historia de la Nueva México (History of New Mexico), *published in 1610 and primarily written in verse. Written by a captain of Oñate's, the epic casts the grisly combat in a noble light.*

just that, scaling the pale cliffs and laying waste the pueblo on top. By the Spaniards' count, more than 1,000 Ácomas died or were rounded up as captives. The Indians had refused to identify or turn over the instigators of Juan de Zaldívar's murder. Hence, in the Spaniards' eyes, there had been no opportunity to show mercy.

News of the outcome shook the Pueblo world. Delegations hastened to San Juan Bautista to reaffirm their obedience. Now that he had their attention, Oñate sought to teach his Pueblo subjects a lesson in European justice. Marching the rebel Ácoma captives to centrally located Santo Domingo Pueblo, the Spanish governor put them on trial, found them guilty, and pronounced cruel punishment. Two dozen men over twenty-five, the age of full adulthood under Spanish law, were to have one foot cut off. Younger males and all the women received sentences of twenty years of personal servitude. Children under twelve Oñate entrusted to Spaniards to bring up as Christians. Since no subsequent mention of one-footed Ácoma slaves appears in the record, it may be that Oñate himself showed mercy, allowing the friars to appeal his harsh sentence.

While it mattered little to the affected Ácomas, years later in Mexico City, Oñate would be tried

for a variety of excesses, found guilty, and fined on a dozen counts. His poet-captain, Gaspar Pérez de Villagrá, whose epic, 11,877-line *Historia de la Nueva México* was published in 1610, omitted the trial of Ácoma prisoners. Instead, he dwelt on the battle, etailing severed limbs and spilt entrails and endowing Ácoma warriors with noble European characteristics, if only to make them worthy adversaries for the nobler Spaniards to vanquish or convert.

SAN GABRIEL AND DEFEAT

With so many Ácoma servants and the reinforcements who arrived in a supply caravan just before Christmas in 1600, Oñate saw fit to move his colony's headquarters across the river to a site he called San Gabriel. Regardless, the colonists complained. They had enlisted in the hope that New Mexico, like Zacatecas, would yield silver or other mineral wealth, but sample after sample proved discouraging. Their women and children, weakened by harsh weather and poor living conditions, hated this place. They feared the sullen Pueblo Indians, who, they knew, resented the levies of corn, forced sexual encounters, and other outrages.

TERESA OF AVILA
Missionaries in New Mexico helped keep the colony alive. Spanish saint, author, and mystic Teresa of Avila was treated with special honor in New Mexican iconography, where she was usually depicted with a book and pen.

In 1601 Oñate returned from a bootless exploration far out onto the plains to find that a majority of his colonists had deserted. Hard-pressed to sustain the remnant colony, the proprietor despaired. Appeals to Mexico City and Madrid went mostly unheeded.

A last-ditch effort to discover a harbor on the Pacific late in 1604 provided no more than a long and plodding look at some very difficult terrain. In August 1607, the same year John Smith's sickly Englishmen dug in at Jamestown, Virginia, more than half a continent away, Juan de Oñate gave up on New Mexico. Writing from San Gabriel, he resigned his post. He could no longer maintain the wretched colonists. His fortune was spent, more than 600,000 pesos.

In the end, the decision not to abandon New Mexico turned on the number of Pueblo Indian baptisms claimed by the Franciscans: more than 7,000. Inflated or not, no one challenged the friars' accounting. Converted from proprietorship to royal colony, New Mexico became, in effect, a government-subsidized Franciscan ministry to the native peoples. Its remnant colonists were bound

FIRST BAPTISM
Franciscan friars minister to Native Americans in an illustration from the book
The American Indian (Uh-nish-in-na-ba) *by Elijah Middlebrook Haines.*
The occasion portrayed is the first baptism in Upper California, July 22, 1769.

"I CANNOT HELP BUT TO INFORM YOUR MAJESTY THAT THIS CONQUEST IS BECOMING A FAIRY TALE. LESS SUBSTANCE IS BEING REVEALED EVERY DAY."

—VICEROY MARQUIS DE MONTESCLAROS,
REQUESTING JUAN DE OÑATE'S DISMISSAL

by decree to stay on. Only by written permission of the new governor, who arrived with the supply caravan late in 1609, could anyone leave.

Oñate and his staff, their families, and servants were the exceptions. Dejected and almost sixty, the undone proprietor would suffer successively the loss of his only son, a lengthy trial for alleged abuses committed in New Mexico, and his wife's death, only to carry an appeal to court in Spain. There, exonerated, he finished his days as inspector general of mines, dying in 1626 in his mid-seventies on duty underground in a mine shaft.

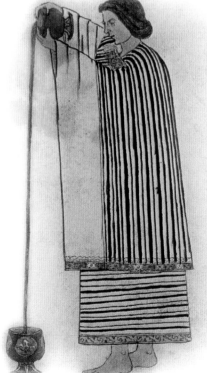

MAKING CHOCOLATE
Indians in Mexico and the Southwest introduced many cultural elements to the Spanish, including chocolate. Here a Mexican Indian woman pours liquid chocolate foam, the most prized part of the drink, from one container into another.

ST. FRANCIS OF ASSISI
The founder of the order to which Franciscan missionaries belonged is represented here in a seventeenth-century Mexican statue.

"WE CAME TO HER
AND BOARDED
HER, AND...
FOUND IN HER
GREAT RICHES,
AS JEWELS AND
PRECIOUS
STONES."

—FRANCIS PRETTY, SIR FRANCIS
DRAKE'S GENTLEMAN-AT-ARMS,
ON SACKING A SPANISH SHIP, 1579

MARINERS AND MISSIONARIES

THROUGHOUT THE SEVENTEENTH CENTURY, SPAIN HAD TO DEFEND ITS GROWING WESTERN EMPIRE. ON THE SEA, SPANISH MARINERS BATTLED FOREIGN PIRATES, WHO THREATENED SPANISH HOLDINGS ALONG EVEN THE PACIFIC COAST. ELSEWHERE, THE COUNTRY'S CLAIMS WERE PROTECTED BY FRANCISCAN AND JESUIT MISSIONARIES, WHO ATTEMPTED TO SPREAD SPANISH CULTURE AND RELIGION AMONG THE NATIVES.

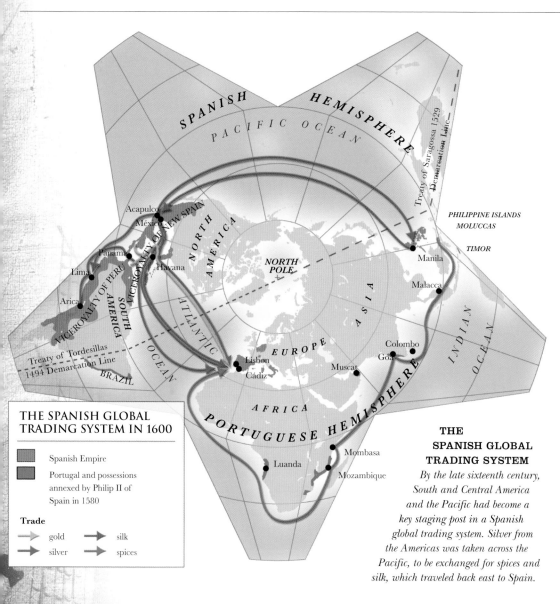

SPANISH HEMISPHERE

PACIFIC OCEAN

Treaty of Saragossa 1529
Demarcation Line

PHILIPPINE ISLANDS
MOLUCCAS

TIMOR

Acapulco
México
VICEROYALTY OF NEW SPAIN
NORTH AMERICA
Panama
Havana
NORTH POLE
Manila
Lima
VICEROYALTY OF PERU
Arica
SOUTH AMERICA
ATLANTIC OCEAN
EUROPE
ASIA
Malacca
Treaty of Tordesillas
1494 Demarcation Line
BRAZIL
Lisbon
Cádiz
AFRICA
Muscat
Goa
Colombo
INDIAN OCEAN

PORTUGUESE HEMISPHERE

Mombasa
Luanda
Mozambique

THE SPANISH GLOBAL TRADING SYSTEM IN 1600

- ▢ Spanish Empire
- ▢ Portugal and possessions annexed by Philip II of Spain in 1580

Trade
- → gold
- → silver
- → silk
- → spices

THE SPANISH GLOBAL TRADING SYSTEM

By the late sixteenth century, South and Central America and the Pacific had become a key staging post in a Spanish global trading system. Silver from the Americas was taken across the Pacific, to be exchanged for spices and silk, which traveled back east to Spain.

EVEN BEFORE the disenchanted Oñate handed over New Mexico, Spain moved to rid the eastern and western shores of North America of European rivals. On the Straits of Florida, route of silver fleets to Spain, mariner Pedro Menéndez de Avilés in 1565 founded St. Augustine, earliest permanent European settlement in the present-day United States, while annihilating a nearby colony of French Huguenots. That same year, another daring Spanish seaman, Basque navigator and Augustinian friar Andrés de Urdaneta, charted a course north from the Philippines, picked up the Japan Current, and navigated back across the Pacific and down North America's west coast to Acapulco. At last Spain, by transhipment across Mexico, had gained access to the ivory, jade, porcelains, silks, and spices of the Orient.

MISSIONARIES

Like merchants and pirates, missionaries depended on the sea to make their way to the New World and throughout the far-flung Spanish dominions. In this detail from an eighteenth-century painting, a ship transports a group of missionaries.

The Manila trade, however, demanded a voyage described as "the longest and most dreadful of any in the World." Outbound, at least annually from the 1560s until 1815, galleons bore westward sundry European goods and a few American products like chocolate, but mostly silver from New Spain and Peru, enough to transform the economies of the Far East. Returning eastward was a horror: six or seven months of deadly tediousness, putrid food, scurvy, and terrifying storms. Nevertheless, thanks to the Manila galleon, New Mexico's governors ate oysters on fine China service.

A pirate's prize to die for, the lumbering Manila galleon bulged with exotic goods worth on average 2 million pesos. Late in the 1570s, as English privateer Francis Drake set a course of pillage up the west coast of New Spain, Spaniards feared the worst. God, warned one Franciscan chronicler, was using the Protestant Drake and the barbarous Chichimecas as twin scourges to punish them for their mistreatment of other Indians.

It was not Drake, however, but fellow Englishman Thomas Cavendish who scored

the greater coup, capturing in 1587 the virtually unarmed, 600-ton Manila galleon *Santa Ana* off the tip of Baja California. Hanging a priest and putting ashore 190 passengers, Cavendish ordered the choicest spoils transferred to his two small ships. He then had the galleon set afire, provided food and wine to the castaways, and sailed off. As wind and tide moved the smoldering hull toward shore, quick-witted survivors put out the fire and made Acapulco.

SEBASTIÁN VIZCAÍNO

An especially enterprising merchant seaman, Sebastián Vizcaíno, now availed himself of renewed interest in the Pacific Coast. Offering in 1595 to pacify Baja California in return for mining and pearl-fishing concessions, he signed a contract with the viceroy in the same year as Oñate. The two simultaneous enterprises reflected the Spanish resolve to defend both the Pacific and the northern perimeters of New Spain. With luck, Vizcaíno would also claim the Pacific entrance of an illusory waterway believed to traverse North America between the South and North seas, the Pacific and the Atlantic. Referred to since the 1560s as the Strait of Anián (or the Northwest

→SIR FRANCIS DRAKE←

AS THEIR two nations vied for naval supremacy, the English privateer Sir Francis Drake (ca. 1540–1596) spent a large part of his life raiding Spanish shipping. In 1567, commanding one of John Hawkins's ships on a slave-trading venture to the Spanish Indies, Drake barely averted capture. His plundering along the Isthmus of Panama in 1572 brought fame and wealth.

In December 1577 Drake set out on his greatest feat, sailing south through the Straits of Magellan and raiding along the Pacific coast of the Americas. With his vessel *The Golden Hind* full of booty from a Peruvian treasure ship, Drake put in for repairs at or near Drake's Bay on the California coast. After claiming the region for Elizabeth I as Nova Albion, he sailed out across the Pacific, dropping anchor at Plymouth in September 1580, the first Englishman to circumnavigate the world. A vice admiral in the fleet that defeated the Spanish Armada in 1588, Drake died during an ill-fated voyage to the Caribbean. He was buried at sea.

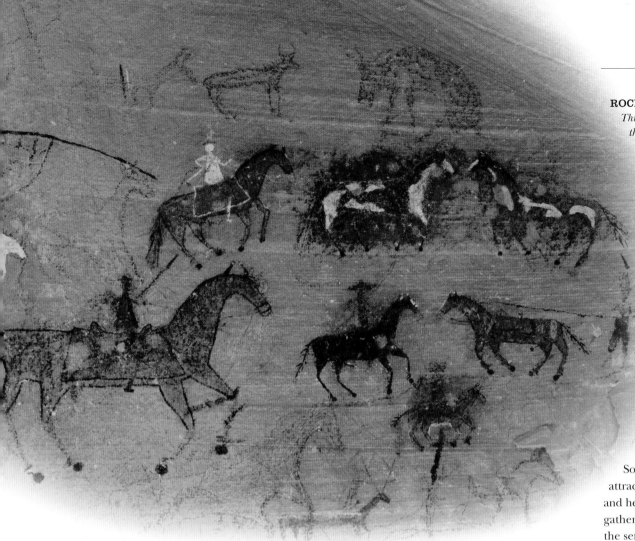

This nineteenth-century Navajo artwork, painted in the caves of Arizona's Canyon de Chelly National Monument, depicts Spanish troops early in that century, but the Spanish presence in Arizona dates back to Spanish Jesuit missionaries who ministered there in the seventeenth century.

Passage by Englishmen), Oñate too was encouraged to search for it beyond New Mexico. Finally, Spanish strategists proposed a port of haven for returning Manila galleons high on the northern California coast.

Vizcaíno's colonizing venture aborted in 1596, but a half-dozen years later, in command of three ships, he mapped the outer coast of the Californias northward from Cabo San Lucas to Cape Mendocino, a seemingly endless shoreline of some 1,700 miles. On November 12, 1602, the feast of San Diego, the fleet entered and named the bay still known as San Diego. A month later, up the coast, Vizcaíno

LACQUER STAND
This eighteenth-century stand for a Catholic missal was made for members of the elite Jesuit religious order.

anchored in another large but unprotected bay, which he praised unduly and called Monterrey in honor of his patron, the viceroy. But because the pirate threat dissipated in the Pacific and priorities shifted, Spain would not occupy San Diego or Monterrey for another 167 years, not until 1769.

THE JESUITS' NORTHWEST MISSIONARY EMPIRE

In the closing years of the sixteenth century, maps of New Spain exhibited a notable void in the far northwest corner, where lie today's Mexican states of Sinaloa and Sonora. The need for missionaries to the region had come to the attention of Jesuits, members of the new, elite, intensely trained Society of Jesus. Founded by a repentant Basque soldier, Ignacio de Loyola, and sanctioned by the pope in 1540, the order had gained swift prominence throughout the Spanish empire. Because they wore black cassocks instead of

distinctive habits, people called the Jesuits black robes. The first of them had arrived in New Spain in 1572 and for two decades dedicated themselves to teaching the sons of the wealthy. More than a few, however, yearned to work among heathens.

In 1591 resolute Jesuit Father Gonzalo de Tapia crossed Mexico's western sierra and established himself among the village, or ranchería, peoples on the Río Sinaloa, 400 miles south of the present U.S.-Mexican border. Soon he and a companion—holding out attractive aspects of their Christianity, new foods and healing methods, and marvels like telescopes—gathered in mission communities hundreds of the semisedentary Sinaloa Indians. Many died of measles and smallpox. After three years, in 1594, a native medicine man, resentful of the Jesuits' spreading influence, bashed Tapia's head in with a war club.

Spurred on, dozens of fellow Jesuits conveyed their engaging material benefits, faith, and demands northward from river valley to river valley, as if climbing a ladder. By the mid-1640s they lived with Lower Tarahumaras on the east side of the mountains and on the west among the Mayos, Yaquis, and Lower Pimas. Just then, Franciscan friars from New Mexico entered the Sonora Valley and began ministering to the

⊹ IGNACIO DE LOYOLA ⊹

BORN Iñigo López de Oñez y Loyola in Guipúzcoa, Spain, Ignacio de Loyola (1491–1556)—the future St. Ignatius of Loyola—served as page to a Spanish courtier before becoming a soldier. Badly wounded in battle, he spent his convalescence in 1521 studying religious works and reading lives of Christ and saints, whom he vowed to imitate. Determined to adopt the spiritual life, he practiced extreme asceticism, spending up to seven hours a day in prayer.

In 1534, with five associates, Loyola founded the Society of Jesus (the Jesuits), whose members took vows of poverty and chastity. They were ordained in 1537 by Pope Paul III, who recognized the Society in 1540. As founder and first father general, Loyola set the priorities of the order: foreign missions, schools, and study in the sciences and humanities. Loyola was canonized in 1622, sixty-six years after his death. His famous *Book of the Spiritual Exercises* applies the precepts of the Gospels to the individual soul.

SOUTHWESTERN INDIANS

This photograph, c. 1875, shows two women in traditional dress, surrounded by pieces of pottery as they stand in front of an adobe dwelling. The lives and cultures of southwestern Indians were intertwined with those of Spaniards from the sixteenth century.

Ópatas, crossing the Jesuits' path. Superiors of the rival orders met. Under a negotiated agreement, the friars withdrew, and the black robes kept coming north. Precisely 100 years after Tapia, they crossed into present-day southern Arizona.

SEVENTEENTH-CENTURY NEW MEXICO

Until the last decades of the seventeenth century, the only European colonial presence in the hugeness of the American West was New Mexico, upon which Spain hung claim to half a continent. Yet the colony itself was puny. From Oñate's several hundreds, the sum of everyone living in a manner more Spanish than Indian scarcely reached 2,500 at any time before 1680. Attracting little immigration, New Mexico became a colony of cousins. Santa Fe, founded as capital and seat of royal authority in1610, remained until the 1690s the colony's only chartered municipality.

Most of the colonists lived on subsistence agriculture (mainly corn, with some wheat), stock raising (predominantly rangy little churro sheep), and Indian tribute and trade. A few prospered: the Spanish governor, his household, and fifteen or twenty interrelated leading families. Exports included animal hides and skins, simple woven items of wool and cotton, piñon nuts, salt, and

SANTA FE MISSION

This painting by Diego Correa of Santa Fe Mission in the Valley of Mexico was completed around the beginning of the eighteenth century. By then Spanish mission culture was well established in the Southwest.

non-Pueblo Indian slaves, mostly Apaches, Navajos, and Plains captives acquired in battle or trade.

Despite the contrary aspirations of its settlers, New Mexico's reason for being was missionary, and that gave the Franciscans the upper hand. Economically, the friars' twenty or twenty-five missions in or near Pueblo Indian communities, taken together, ran larger flocks and harvested more corn than any single colonist. Franciscans also controlled the colony's only regular supply service, the caravan of heavy, mule-drawn freight wagons that rumbled north from Mexico City every third year. Moreover, in the spiritual realm they exercised an extraordinary monopoly. They were New Mexico's only Roman Catholic priests. To have their way, on occasion, they threatened to withhold the sacraments of the Church, and the faithful either went along or risked doing without.

CONFLICTS

Wanting to isolate their mission communities, the friars clashed repeatedly with royal governors over Pueblo Indian labor, land, and loyalty. In 1613 fiery fray Isidro Ordóñez schemed to confine Governor Pedro de Peralta for months in a cell at one of the missions. Turning the tables a half-century later, brash and blaspheming Governor Diego de Peñalosa in 1663 arrested Franciscan superior Alonso de Posada and hustled him at night under guard to the governor's palace in Santa Fe. Bystanders, notably property owners and officeholders, found themselves caught between facing, on the one hand, denial of royal justice

FRANCISCAN FRIARS

Franciscan missionaries Juan Díaz and José Moreno were killed by Yuma Indians in the Yuma Massacre of 1781 as they prepared for Mass. Despite such setbacks, the Franciscans remained influential in the Southwest for many years.

and favors and, on the other, excommunication. Although they occurred only intermittently, such open conflicts fostered distrust not only among the colonists but also among the Pueblo Indians they sought to exploit.

Most days, however, Spaniards and Pueblos got along. Influenced culturally by the dense Indian communities with whom they coexisted, seventeenth-century New Mexicans assumed an identity of their own.

On farm and ranch, they learned from Pueblo neighbors and domestic servants to substitute animal skins and homespun for Spanish Golden Age frills; buffalo jerky for beef; local wares for imported dishes and bowls; and native cures, curses, and love potions for European ones. On occasion, employment of Indians inside or outside a Spanish home; negotiations between Pueblo and Spanish officials; or barter of beans, chile, or firewood resulted in mortal combat or rape, but typically such daily encounters did not.

PIECES OF EIGHT

The designs on these silver pieces of eight were struck by hand around 1630. Mints in both Spain and Spanish America were stocked with silver discovered in the New World.

Dealings between Pueblo Indians and the foreign missionaries who moved in with them varied considerably. Most of the 250 Franciscans who served in New Mexico before 1680 were devout and dedicated, if at times clumsy and insensitive. A few were deviants by any standard, men like fray Nicolás Hidalgo, who brutally punished or sexually abused the people in his care. At outlying communities among the Jemez, Zunis, and Hopis, and at Taos, traditional Pueblo leaders periodically incited their people to kill a missionary. But sooner or later another always took his place.

The Franciscans labored to replace Pueblo culture with Spanish Catholic culture. Although unworkable, this ideal found its most eager expression in the *Memorial* of fray Alonso de Benavides, published at government expense in Madrid in 1630. The observant Benavides, Franciscan superior and first agent of the Inquisition in New Mexico, came with the supply caravan of 1625. Fray Alonso convinced himself that Christian churches of stone or adobe were winning the Pueblo Indians away from kivas, their traditional, often-subterranean sacred chambers.

But Benavides was wrong. Some Pueblo Indians, to be sure, especially boys in the

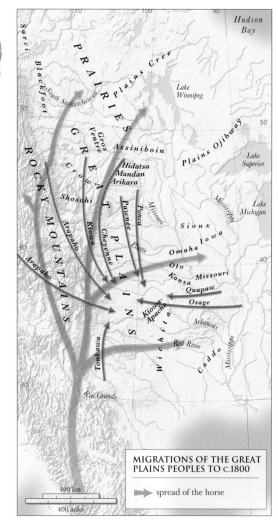

MIGRATIONS OF GREAT PLAINS PEOPLES
Several Native American peoples migrated into the Great Plains after European contact, adopting a hunting and gathering way of life. Their success was made possible in part by Spain's introduction of the horse to the continent.

friars' service, learned to read, write, and act Spanish. Most, however, never advanced far enough in their understanding of the imported religion to receive Communion meaningfully. While adopting certain elements of Catholic ceremonialism, the Pueblos took their old ways underground.

ALTARPIECE, SAN ESTEBAN DEL REY
Construction of the San Esteban del Rey mission at the pueblo of Ácoma in New Mexico began in 1629 and continued for about fourteen years. The mission complex was built with the labor of Ácoma Indians under the direction of the Spanish. It was one of the few Spanish missions to survive the Pueblo Revolt of 1680.

"HOLD ON TO WHAT IS GOOD EVEN IF IT IS A HANDFUL OF EARTH...HOLD ON TO WHAT YOU BELIEVE."

—TRADITIONAL PUEBLO BLESSING

KACHINAS
Ancestral spirits, also called "katsinas," are symbolized by Pueblo dolls like this one, given to Hopi girls as they reach marrying age.

"FOR THIS PURPOSE I SHALL NOT SPARE ANY MEANS IN THE SERVICE OF GOD AND OF HIS MAJESTY, LOSING A THOUSAND LIVES IF I HAD THEM...AND SHEDDING MY BLOOD FOR GOD."

—NEW MEXICO GOVERNOR DON ANTONIO DE OTERMÍN, ON SAVING THE COLONY, SEPTEMBER 1680

THE PUEBLO REVOLT AND FRENCH RIVALS

IN 1680, AFTER YEARS OF SPANISH RULE AND A LONG DROUGHT, PUEBLO WARRIORS LED BY POPÉ DROVE SPANISH COLONISTS FROM NEW MEXICO. TO THE EAST, SPANIARDS FACED ANOTHER THREAT AS FRENCHMEN BEGAN CHALLENGING SPAIN'S CLAIMS TO THE GULF COAST OF PRESENT-DAY TEXAS. SPAIN ALSO EXPERIENCED RISING PRESSURE FROM TWO SOURCES FARTHER EAST: FRENCH LOUISIANA AND ENGLAND'S ATLANTIC COLONIES.

AS THE SEVENTEENTH CENTURY wore on, tensions mounted in New Mexico. A searing dry cycle set in during the 1660s. Crops withered, and people went hungry. Apaches and Navajos, who earlier in the century had taken to Spanish horses, intensified their raids on Pueblo and Hispanic settlements, absconding with livestock and captives and inviting similar strikes on their camps. Disenchanted and keen to fix blame, Pueblo Indians in the Salinas area, southeast of today's Albuquerque, began plotting to rid the land of Spaniards.

Pueblos had conspired before, but always the Spaniards found out, whipping, imprisoning, or executing the alleged instigators. This time they were shocked by the identity of the chief conspirator. Esteban Clemente, a thoroughly Hispanicized Indian leader, or *indio ladino*, spoke, read, and wrote Spanish. In 1660, at the urging of a missionary, Clemente had denounced kachinas, traditional Pueblo spirit beings. Later, for whatever reasons, he experienced a change of heart and tried to overthrow the colonial regime. When he was hanged for treason, about 1670, officials "found in his house a great quantity of idols and whole pots of idolatrous powdered herbs, feathers, and other disgusting things."

By the mid-1670s, beset by adverse weather, Apache and Navajo raiding, and Pueblo unrest,

CHURCH ENTRANCE
The original church of Taos Pueblo was built in 1619 and destroyed in the chaos of 1680. The Taos Pueblo church shown here was built in the nineteenth century.

the Hispanic community had begun to pull together. In 1675 an aging and superstitious Franciscan reported to Governor Juan Francisco de Treviño that Tewa Pueblo medicine men had bewitched him. Straightaway the governor rounded up forty-seven Tewa headmen. Three he ordered hanged, each in a different pueblo; one hanged himself; and the rest were whipped. The Franciscan superior, fray Francisco de Ayeta, appealed to the viceroy. Without substantial aid, New Mexico was lost. In response, the royal treasury paid to transport fifty convict soldiers, a thousand horses, and a hundred harquebuses, which reached the colony in the caravan of 1677. A new governor, don Antonio de Otermín, came too.

UPRISING

A heavy-handed administrator, Otermín heard how his predecessor had punished alleged Pueblo troublemakers. In August 1680, when two Tewa messengers confessed that a general uprising was imminent, the governor sent word to his district officers: stay alert. Whipped in 1675, Popé, the alleged mastermind, since then had formed a network of sacred leaders and war chiefs that cut across the half-dozen different Pueblo languages. So secretive were his operations that no Spaniard knew his Christian name. Supposedly, in a Taos kiva he had drawn inspiration from Pueblo supernaturals and a mysterious "very tall, black

PUEBLO BONITO RUINS
The Chaco Canyon complex in what is now northwestern New Mexico, including Pueblo Bonito, was built by the Anasazi, ancestors of the Pueblos who revolted against the Spaniards in 1680.

man with very large yellow eyes." Learning that word of the uprising had been leaked to Otermín, Popé advanced the day. Whatever his motives, the aggrieved Tewa leader had succeeded in uniting the Pueblo world in what Spaniards would later perceive as genocide against them and obliteration of everything Spanish.

The effect was stunning. On the feast of San Lorenzo, August 10, 1680, grim-faced Pueblo fighting men erupted out of dozens of kivas, catching missionaries and colonists by surprise. Twenty-one Franciscans died at their posts, mutilated and mocked by the adults they had treated as children. Nearly 400 culturally Hispanic New Mexicans,

EL PASO

This illustration of a church and surrounding plaza in El Paso, Texas, was made by William Emory, a member of a nineteenth-century U.S. Army boundary survey team. One thousand Spanish survivors of the Pueblo Revolt fled to El Paso with New Mexican governor Don Antonio de Otermín.

ÁCOMA MAN

This 1904 photograph shows an Ácoma Pueblo man in typical blanket dress. Ácoma resistance was violently suppressed in 1599, but the Ácomas joined other Pueblo groups in the revolt against the Spanish in 1680.

entire families, dazed by the sudden madness of their Pueblo neighbors, also perished or were taken captive. Governor Otermín, besieged in Santa Fe with a thousand survivors, finally broke out, abandoning the place and retreating downriver. Six weeks later, with the refugees huddled in the vicinity of El Paso, the governor took count. Spanish New Mexico had been reduced to a pathetic colony-in-exile of fewer than 2,000 souls.

Upriver, the Pueblos celebrated, then fell to quarreling. Once their common enemy had been driven out, the cause that united them evaporated. Popé could no more eradicate generations of Spanish cultural conditioning, or bind up traditional Pueblo divisions, than he could bring about the better times he promised. Even his swagger was more Spanish than Pueblo. So he was deposed. Some Pueblos, remembering the security and more bountiful trade provided by their former masters, made it known that they would not oppose the Spaniards' return. Meanwhile, life for the New Mexican exiles was wretched. Half-housed in hastily constructed shelters of poles, adobes, and brush, suffering drought and flood, poverty and profiteering, dozens of families deserted. Others

✦PUEBLO REVOLT✦

THE UPRISING OF 15,000 or 20,000 Pueblo Indians, skilfully planned and fiercely executed in late summer of 1680, plunged New Mexico into a three-phase Pueblo-Spanish war lasting sixteen years. Although Pueblo Indians had conspired previously against Spanish colonial oppression in New Mexico, two conditions explain their success in 1680. A withering dry cycle had fastened upon the colony a decade earlier, causing extreme hardship in an environment of limited resources, and, at long last, a Pueblo Indian leader, Popé, emerged to unite the diverse Pueblo communities. Their hope of annihilating everything Spanish, following upon three generations of cultural coexistence, proved impossible.

Vicious but brief, the opening phase of the uprising claimed the lives of an unrecorded number of Pueblo fighting men and at least 400 Spanish colonists, among them twenty-one Franciscan missionaries. Later, Governor Antonio de Otermín recalled a night under siege in Santa Fe: "the most horrible that could be thought of or imagined, because the whole villa was a torch and everywhere were war chants and shouts." Vastly outnumbered, the surviving 2,000 Spaniards had fled as refugees down the Rio Grande Valley to the El Paso district (in today's west Texas).

Between 1681 and 1691, the exiled Spanish colonials endured a mean existence in a half-dozen makeshift communities, while upriver the Pueblo Indian union dissolved. Both peoples suffered during this second phase, and delegations from each visited the other. During the final phase, from 1691 through 1696, Spaniards reestablished themselves by force of arms among the Pueblo peoples, some of whom welcomed them back, while others resisted to the death.

A slow but steady increase in New Mexico's Hispanic population, along with a rising tide of Apache, Navajo, Ute, and Comanche raiding, encouraged the reconciliation of Spanish and Pueblo farmers and herders during the succeeding century. They traded all manner of goods, became compadres, and fought shoulder to shoulder on countless campaigns against common enemies of the colony. Never again did Pueblos and Spaniards resort to war against each other.

HOPI INDIAN
The Hopis joined other Pueblo tribes in the 1680 revolt against Spanish rule. Spanish laws before the Pueblo Revolt forbade Indians from owning horses, but after the uprising, the horses left behind were taken up by the Pueblos. This photograph of a Hopi on horseback dates from the 1880s.

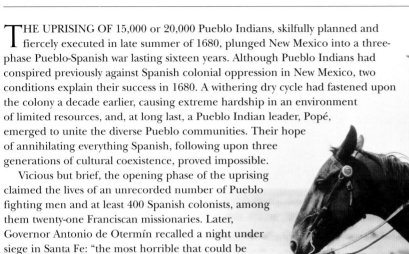

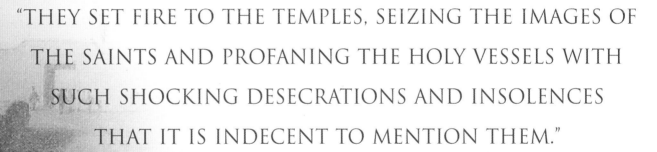

"THEY SET FIRE TO THE TEMPLES, SEIZING THE IMAGES OF THE SAINTS AND PROFANING THE HOLY VESSELS WITH SUCH SHOCKING DESECRATIONS AND INSOLENCES THAT IT IS INDECENT TO MENTION THEM."

—CONDE DE PAREDES, VICEROY OF NEW SPAIN, 1681, ON THE PUEBLO REVOLT

petitioned to relocate in Nueva Vizcaya to the south. Imperial strategists consulting maps in Mexico City and Madrid, however, refused to consider abandonment. Rude as they might be, El Paso and the refugee settlements strung out down the Rio Grande were critical to the defense of the northern frontier. Without them, the rich mines farther south would lie exposed.

Besides, if the Pueblo Indians were not punished for their affront to Spanish arms, every subject tribe in the north would be similarly emboldened. Spain also bore the obligation, Franciscans said, to ransom these apostate Pueblo souls from slavery to the devil. Then, coincidentally in the mid-1680s, there arose a more compelling reason to restore Spanish New Mexico: a colony of lost Frenchmen had planted a settlement on the Texas gulf coast.

FRENCHMEN IN TEXAS

Far to the northeast, in present-day Canada, French colonizers had built a post at Quebec in 1608 as headquarters for New France. Footloose French

NEW FRANCE NATIVES
The French maintained relatively good relations with Native Americans in their empire. This engraving of Canadian tribesmen was published in 1633.

fur traders with liquor in their packs and disapproving Jesuit missionaries had ranged through the woodlands as far as the Great Lakes. In 1682 René Robert Cavelier, Sieur de la Salle, descended the Mississippi, claiming for France its immense drainage as Louisiana. Because of confusing twists in the multiple channels through the delta, La Salle miscalculated the location of the river's mouth, where he envisioned a French colony.

Later, in 1684, setting course from France with several hundred ill-suited settlers, he made for where he thought the Mississippi was, but overshot it far to the west. Sick and confused, La Salle disembarked late in February 1685 on the bleak, windswept shores of Matagorda Bay, Texas, in Karankawa Indian territory. Aroused, Spanish authorities restated their claim to the Texas gulf coast with a series of sea and land expeditions

designed, as they put it, "to pluck out the thorn which has been thrust into the heart of America." When at last, on a gray and rainy day in April 1689, Governor Alonso de León of Coahuila and his party came upon the depressing ruins of La Salle's Fort St. Louis, there were no signs of life. Instead they found, strewn within the crude stockade, three skeletons, one seemingly of a woman shot in the back with an arrow; torn and scattered pages from French books; dead pigs; and broken boxes, wine casks, bottles, and furniture. From the absence of other human remains, the onlookers surmised that attacking Karankawas had thrown the bodies into the creek, where they had been eaten by alligators. Inland, among the Hasinai people, Spaniards ransomed a few survivors. Dressed in skins, these Frenchmen revealed La Salle's fate. Striking out overland for New France in desperation, the mean-spirited explorer had been killed in 1687 by his own men.

At the close of the 1680s, Spain stood by its exclusive claim to the American West. Yet the prospect of French Louisiana at mid-continent threatened to rupture Spanish command of the entire gulf coast from Florida to Texas. Moreover, since founding Jamestown in 1607, England had strung the Atlantic seaboard with colonies whose swelling population, coupled with the expanding French empire, cast ominous shadows westward. In geopolitical terms, such shadows would orient Spain's moves and countermoves in the West in the eighteenth century.

⇥JACQUES MARQUETTE⇤

JESUIT missionary, linguist, and explorer, Jacques Marquette (1637–1775), born in Laon, France, joined the Indian Missions at Three Rivers on the St. Lawrence in 1666. He founded a mission at Sault St. Marie in 1668 and another at Point St. Ignace, near Mackinac on Lake Superior. There he

MARQUETTE THE EXPLORER
This U.S. stamp, issued in 1968, shows Jacques Marquette accompanied by guides.

received a delegation of Illinois Indians who told of a mighty river that flowed south from their land. Marquette imagined the river, the Mississippi, must cross the continent and empty into the Gulf of California. With permission from his superiors, Marquette joined Louis Joliet and five other Frenchmen to find out. The party reached the Mississippi on June 17, 1673, and Marquette mapped and recorded their journey as far south as the mouth of the Arkansas River, where they learned that the river flowed instead into the Gulf of Mexico. Fearing arrest by Spaniards, they turned back. On a subsequent journey to the Illinois Indians, Marquette fell ill and died.

⇥NEW FRANCE⇤

IN 1524–25, GIOVANNI da Verrazano sailed up the east coast of North America, claiming the territory for France as "New France." Later, Jacques Cartier explored the St. Lawrence River and brought back to France Huron Indians whose seeming confirmation of gold and silver persuaded King Francis I to establish a colony. The furs acquired by French fishermen trading with coastal Indians stimulated companies to seek settlement grants. Port Royal in Nova Scotia was settled in 1605 and Quebec in 1608.

For some years, Quebec's founder Samuel de Champlain downplayed colonization, envisioning New France as a network of trading posts. By 1635 there were fewer than 300 Frenchmen in the colony and immigration remained sparse because of rigid control by the French Catholic Church. Attempts to develop farming foundered, and the fur trade continued to dominate the economy. From the continent's interior, fur traders carried prized beaver furs down the St. Lawrence and its tributaries. The Comte de Frontenac, governor from 1672 to 1682 and again in the 1690s,

described his business as the conversion of souls and the conversion of beaver, an accurate depiction of the colony for over a century.

French missionaries often found favor among Native American nations because, in contrast to English settlers, they did not seek to dispossess Indians of their land. Protected by that favor, the missionaries traveled far, as did French fur traders, who became the first Europeans to reach the Great Lakes and beyond.

René Robert Cavelier, Sieur de la Salle, explored the Mississippi River to the Gulf of Mexico in 1682 and claimed the whole Mississippi Valley for France, naming it Louisiana. Although Spaniards and Englishmen resisted the claim, French traders soon built posts along the lower reaches of the river. In 1718 Jean Baptiste le Moyne, Sieur de Bienville, founded New Orleans and began to encourage a plantation economy. To the north, Frenchmen reached today's Dakotas, Montana, and Saskatchewan. Imperial rivalry intensified as English settlers pressed westward from the Thirteen Colonies. The French and

Indian War (1754–63) halted French expansion in North America. At the war's end, the Treaty of Paris (1763) ceded New France to England and split Louisiana between England and Spain.

DIVIDED LOYALTIES
This 1758 woodcut symbolizes the European struggle for the loyalties of Indian tribes. A Native American stands midway between an Englishman, left, and a Frenchman, right.

THE EUROPEAN COLONIZATION OF NORTH AMERICA 1603—1750

- British control and settlement
- Spanish control and settlement
- French control and settlement
- French influence
- approximate western limit of French claim
- Dutch control and settlement
- migration from Britain
- migration from France
- migration from Spain
- movement of slaves
- 1682   date of foundation
- conflict with native Americans
- Russian exploratory navigation
- *Houma*   indigenous people

THE EUROPEAN COLONIZATION OF NORTH AMERICA

European settlers and their laborers, combined with trading and missionary activity, permitted a European claims map to be drawn up that covered the entire continent. It notably avoided the issue of Native American rights.

EUROPEAN AND NATIVE CONFLICTS

①	Jamestown	1622, 1644
②	Pequot War	1636–37
③	New Haven	1637
④	Kieft's War	1643–46
⑤	King Philip's War	1675–76
⑥	Bacon's Rebellion	1676
⑦	Deerfield	1676
⑧	Boston	1676
⑨	Montreal	1689
⑩	Tuscarora War	1711–13
⑪	Yamasee War	1715–28

500 km
500 miles

81

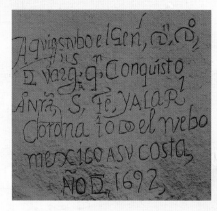

INSCRIPTION

This inscription at the New Mexican rock formation El Morro, translated below, was made by Governor Don Diego de Vargas.

"HERE WAS
THE GENERAL
DON DIEGO
DE VARGAS, WHO
CONQUERED FOR
OUR HOLY FAITH
AND FOR THE
ROYAL CROWN
ALL OF NEW
MEXICO AT HIS
OWN EXPENSE."

—INSCRIPTION AT EL MORRO, 1692

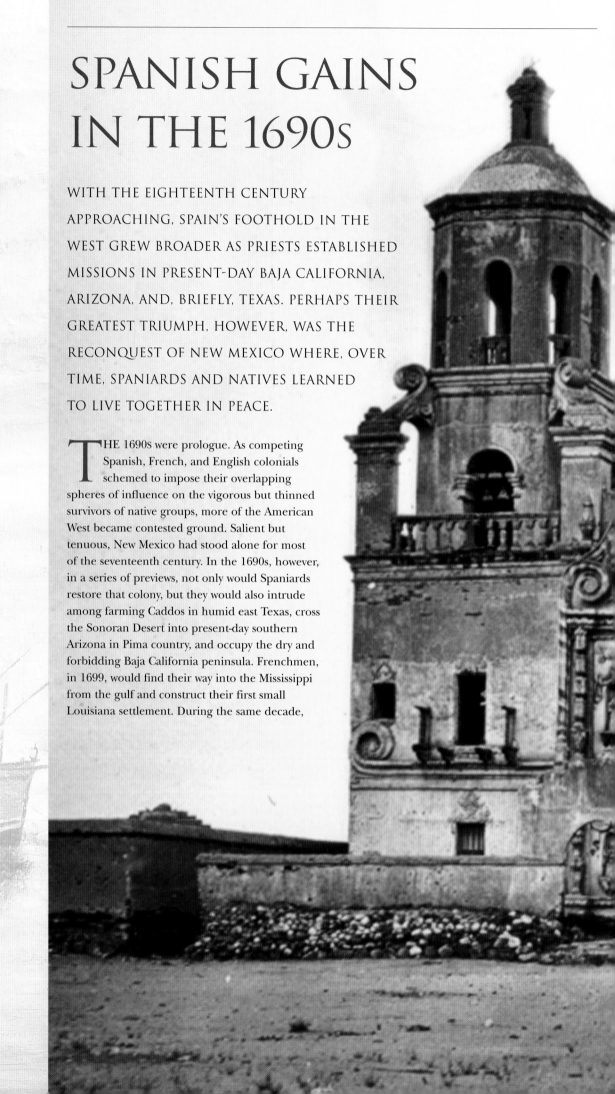

SPANISH GAINS IN THE 1690s

WITH THE EIGHTEENTH CENTURY APPROACHING, SPAIN'S FOOTHOLD IN THE WEST GREW BROADER AS PRIESTS ESTABLISHED MISSIONS IN PRESENT-DAY BAJA CALIFORNIA, ARIZONA, AND, BRIEFLY, TEXAS. PERHAPS THEIR GREATEST TRIUMPH, HOWEVER, WAS THE RECONQUEST OF NEW MEXICO WHERE, OVER TIME, SPANIARDS AND NATIVES LEARNED TO LIVE TOGETHER IN PEACE.

THE 1690s were prologue. As competing Spanish, French, and English colonials schemed to impose their overlapping spheres of influence on the vigorous but thinned survivors of native groups, more of the American West became contested ground. Salient but tenuous, New Mexico had stood alone for most of the seventeenth century. In the 1690s, however, in a series of previews, not only would Spaniards restore that colony, but they would also intrude among farming Caddos in humid east Texas, cross the Sonoran Desert into present-day southern Arizona in Pima country, and occupy the dry and forbidding Baja California peninsula. Frenchmen, in 1699, would find their way into the Mississippi from the gulf and construct their first small Louisiana settlement. During the same decade, for their own good reasons, some natives collaborated. Others, not surprisingly, took up arms to resist. Yet the outsiders kept coming.

The restoration of New Mexico had become a priority. To avenge that colony's loss in the Pueblo Revolt of 1680, redeem the Pueblo Indians for God and king, and repair northern defenses called for a latter-day conquistador.

MISSION

Jesuit priest Eusebio Kino first visited Pima Indian country in 1692, but the church for which he laid the foundation was never built. Franciscan friars later constructed this church, Mission San Xavier del Bac, in the same village.

DIEGO DE VARGAS AND THE RESTORATION OF NEW MEXICO

Son of an illustrious but indebted noble family of Madrid, Diego José de Vargas Zapata Luján Ponce de León y Contreras had come to New Spain in 1673, proven himself a tough and able administrator, and in 1688 bought the governorship of New Mexico in exile. He reached El Paso in 1691. "This kingdom," he boasted to his son-in-law in Madrid, lay "at the ends of the earth…remote beyond compare." Yet here lay the challenge.

Late in 1692, partly at his own expense, Governor Vargas led a couple of hundred armed men—government-salaried presidial soldiers, Pueblo Indian auxiliaries, and citizen militiamen— north from the El Paso refugee settlements on a bold, four-month reconnaissance of the Pueblo world. At Santa Fe, which Vargas found occupied by Pueblo rebels, his bravado carried the day. After tense negotiations, the Indians deferred without a fight to the Spanish governor's theatrics. With shouts of "*Viva el Rey*" ("Long Live the King"), don Diego presided over a purely ceremonial repossession, then rode on.

Repeating the ritual in twenty-two other Pueblo communities, Vargas played on the Indians' factionalism and uncertainties. He assured them that he sought not vengeance, only their renewed loyalty. For confirmation, he called often on Bartolomé de Ojeda. A Spanish-speaking Pueblo war captain, Ojeda had once fought valiantly against the Spaniards but had since changed his allegiance. As leader of Vargas's Indian auxiliaries, interpreter, and negotiator, he may have believed that he was better serving his people by easing their inevitable reconquest.

While Franciscan chaplains absolved assembly after assembly and baptized children born since 1680, the glamorous Vargas stood as godfather to the sons and daughters of their leaders, making himself, in Hispanic Catholic terms, their *compadre*, or ritual co-parent. Halfway through the tour, he paused to write again to his son-in-law in Spain. He wanted to know firsthand how the court reacted to news of his triumphal campaign so that, in his words, "I can consider my possibilities for advancement."

Word that Vargas had restored the lost colony set off celebrations in Mexico City. His friend and patron, the Conde de Galve, viceroy of New Spain, offered congratulations and funds from the royal treasury to recruit, transport, and resettle colonists in New Mexico. Vargas, meanwhile, counted the people available in the El Paso district, many of them survivors of the 1680 revolt: 73 married couples; 115 widows, widowers, and sundry single people; 448 boys and girls; and 250 other dependents. Then he rode south with an escort to buy cattle and other provisions, put pressure on treasury officials, and enlist men for a Santa Fe presidial garrison.

GOVERNOR VARGAS

This portrait of the governor of New Mexico is found in a published version of his own account, First Expedition of Vargas into New Mexico, *1692. Citizens of Santa Fe celebrate his memory with a yearly festival.*

Vargas rarely missed an opportunity. At Zacatecas in May 1693, he dictated a lengthy memorial to the king, recounting his heroics in New Mexico and suggesting as reward a noble title of Castile and "the post of governor and captain general and president of the kingdom of Guatemala," or the Philippines, Chile, or Buenos Aires and the Río de la Plata. He knew that delivery of a petition to Madrid, action by the bureaucracy, and response regularly took two years. Meanwhile, he had to have more colonists—500 families, he reckoned.

Ever impatient, Vargas could not wait. Unwisely, he set out in October 1693 for Santa Fe with perhaps 1,000 colonists, counting children and servants. After a slow-moving, wretched trip from El Paso, the families huddled outside New Mexico's former capital in blowing snow, only to be refused entry by the Pueblo occupants. Negotiations failed, and infants died of exposure. There remained no alternative. The Spaniards'

BARTERING

This illustration depicts Mexicans going to the market with goods for barter. Trade markets that used both coins and goods for currency were widespread throughout the Southwest.

murderous, room-by-room assault during the last days of December might not have succeeded but for the support of 140 Pecos Pueblo fighting men. As an example to Indians who had disavowed the allegiance sworn the year before, Governor Vargas ordered seventy of the defenders shot. Once again Spaniards hoisted the royal banner over Santa Fe.

Beyond, the countryside was unsafe. From fortified sites on mesatops, Pueblo resisters struck at the colonists' livestock, until they had almost no cattle or sheep. They had been unable to plant crops. Only their raids for foodstuffs stored in temporarily abandoned pueblos kept them alive. Gradually, however, Vargas gained ground, relying on tough diplomacy and the aid of Pueblo Indian allies. Combined Spanish-Pueblo columns assailed the dissidents' strongholds, captured women and children, and held them until their leaders agreed to reoccupy their former communities.

NEW COLONISTS

In Mexico City, meanwhile, officials debated Vargas's repeated requests for more colonists. Before resorting to prisoners or vagabonds, the viceroy agreed to open the rolls to good people, artisans and the like, preferably *españoles*, individuals perceived as Spaniards, rather than *castas*, or people of mixed race. By early September 1693, only 250 such men, women, and children had responded to the prospect of free transportation; subsidies of land, tools, and animals; and the privileged status of *hidalgos* accorded new settlers. For this they would endure the long and perilous journey to New Mexico, sixteen per heavy freight wagon. The men's occupations varied almost as much as their looks: barber, blacksmith, cabinetmaker, cartwright, chandler, filigree maker, coppersmith, cutler, miller, mining

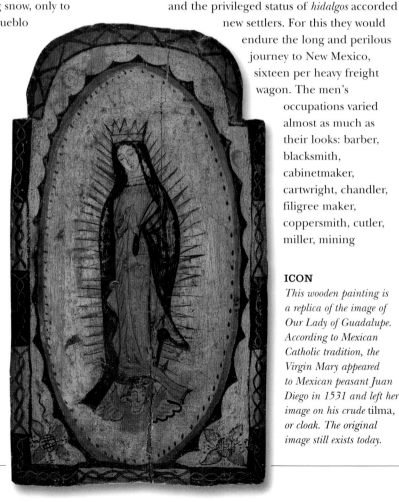

ICON

This wooden painting is a replica of the image of Our Lady of Guadalupe. According to Mexican Catholic tradition, the Virgin Mary appeared to Mexican peasant Juan Diego in 1531 and left her image on his crude tilma, or cloak. The original image still exists today.

"THERE, I SHALL FEED THEM MEAT AND MAIZE, WHEAT, AND OTHER CEREALS AND SHALL MYSELF DO WITHOUT BEFORE THEY DO."

—DON DIEGO DE VARGAS, ON TAKING COLONISTS BACK TO SANTA FE, 1693

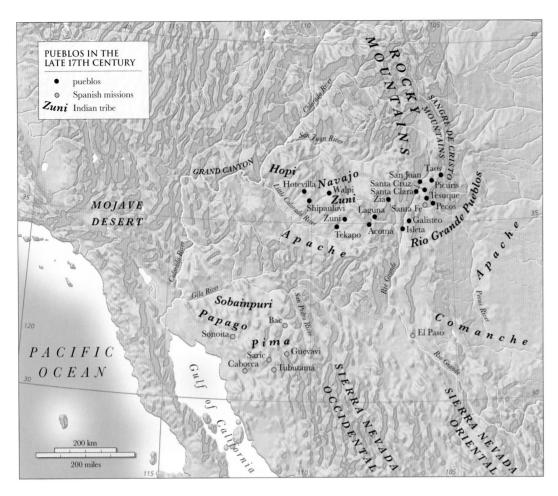

PUEBLOS IN THE LATE 17TH CENTURY
- pueblos
- ○ Spanish missions
- *Zuni* Indian tribe

PUEBLOS IN THE SOUTHWEST

The sedentary, farming Pueblos of the Southwest presented Spanish colonists with a robust and resistant urban culture that required more than sheer military strength to subdue. The establishment of Catholic missions in the region did as much as military garrisons to reinforce Spanish control.

amalgamator, musician, painter, paver, stone- and brickmason, and weaver. Most were from urban Mexico City and Puebla, and many were related by family ties or membership in craft guilds or religious lay brotherhoods. For generations in New Mexico, these people would stick together, intermarry, and maintain their social networks.

Instead of the hundreds of better families Governor Vargas and the viceroy were counting on, fewer than seventy made the journey north. At that, in the spring of 1695, when he relocated them to Santa Cruz de la Cañada twenty miles north of Santa Fe, Vargas upset adjacent Pueblo Indians. Everyone suffered during the terrible winter of 1695–96. Vargas almost died, seemingly of recurring typhus. Fierce weather, food shortages, an unnamed epidemic, and rumors of Pueblo Indian plotting contributed to peoples' fears. Franciscan missionaries complained of the Indians' insolence and debated whether it was noble or stupid to die at the hands of mockers. A second Pueblo uprising broke out in early June 1696. Five friars and twenty-one colonists died at

the hands of Pueblo Indians. This time, however, the Pueblo world was not of one mind, and after six more months of intermittent fighting and parlays, the long Pueblo-Spanish war stretching from 1680 to 1696 ended. Pueblo and Hispano neighbors resumed bartering corn, firewood, and favors. Increasingly in the coming century, their very survival depended on accommodation. And while the two peoples maintained their reassuring cultural identities, the men would find themselves shoulder to shoulder in pursuit of Gila Apaches, Navajos, or Comanches, sharing the casualties and spoils of a hundred campaigns against *los indios bárbaros*, or non-Christian, "barbarian" Indians.

As for Diego de Vargas, reconqueror of New Mexico, he fell on unexpected hard times. After allegedly obstructing the succession of Pedro Rodríguez Cubero as

FRANCISCAN CHURCH

The Church of the Santa Cruz is located in Querétaro, Mexico, a village founded by the Spanish in 1531. The Franciscans founded the first in a series of missionary colleges at Querétaro in 1683. This photograph was taken in the late nineteenth century.

governor in 1697, the disdainful don Diego languished as a prisoner in Santa Fe for nearly three years. Charges against him ranged from misuse of government funds to gross immorality. Unrepentant, he characterized his accusers, members of Santa Fe's town council, as men "of very low class and menial offices—tailors, a shoemaker, and a lackey—poor and base people."

His eventual exoneration in Mexico City allowed the fatigued, sixty-year-old aristocrat to exercise his reappointment as governor of New Mexico. Reaching Santa Fe for a second term late in 1703, Diego de Vargas lasted only four months. He died the following April on campaign against Faraón Apaches, not from an enemy arrow but, apparently, from dysentery.

FRAY DAMIÁN MASSANET

The seventeenth century's growing demand for missionaries to Spanish America had put pressure on the rival religious orders. The Society of Jesus responded by securing royal permission to import non-Spanish Jesuit priests from Europe. The Franciscans countered by founding a series of missionary colleges, the first at Querétaro, northwest of Mexico City, in 1683. Members of both orders simultaneously nudged New Spain's frontier northward on its flanks, far to the east of restored New Mexico and far to the west.

As Franciscan chaplain to Alonso de León, fray Damián Massanet of the Querétaro college had already been to Texas in 1689. What had interested him more than La Salle's desolate fort was word that a beautiful white woman, a Spanish nun, had miraculously visited the Hasinai Indians a generation before, instilling in these industrious village farming folk a desire for Christian baptism. Curiously, a thousand miles west near the confluence of the Gila and Colorado rivers, Massanet's Jesuit contemporary, the science-minded, northern Italian Eusebio Francisco Kino would hear a similar story.

⊹CADDO INDIANS⊹

THE CADDO INDIANS of present-day Louisiana and Texas first met Spaniards when survivors of Hernando de Soto's party, minus their deceased leader, spent several months among them in 1542. By the time the next Europeans appeared, nearly a century and a half later, the greatly thinned Caddo population, perhaps 10,000 in all, had coalesced into three loose confederations: the Kadohadachos near the common borders of today's Arkansas, Texas, and Oklahoma; the Natchitoches in Louisiana; and the Hasinais in east Texas. A highly developed communal society, led by chiefs and subchiefs, the Caddos cultivated maize, beans, and squash; ate fish and game; hunted buffalo; and lived in villages of pole-framed grass houses. They were noted for their settled agrarian communities and social unity.

In 1686 Hasinais greeted French explorer René Robert de La Salle with great ceremony, distinguishing him from Spaniards they knew only through indirect trade. La Salle's expedition wrote of the Caddo people's fine cabins reaching forty or fifty feet high. Several of La Salle's party deserted to live with the Hasinais. In March 1687 La Salle was murdered by some of his own men; then they too enjoyed Hasinai hospitality en route back to New France.

Spanish efforts to establish missionary settlements among the Caddos in the early 1690s failed miserably. Another attempt beginning in 1716 had only limited success. On two sides, the Caddos faced the competing colonial systems of France and Spain. Clearly, French trade and alliance, when combined with the Caddos' strong traditions and their agricultural self-sufficiency, won out over the Spanish missionary program. By the end of the eighteenth century, disease, alcoholism, and the incursion of white settlers had caused the Caddos to decline. Forced from their lands after the Texas Cherokee War (1839), the Hasinais moved several times and were finally settled in Indian Territory (Oklahoma) in 1859.

CLAY VESSEL
The Caddos were known for their sophistication in manufacturing items out of clay, wood, stone, and other materials. This figural vessel was sculpted around 1300.

In 1690 Massanet and León were back in east Texas, this time on the upper Neches River with authorization to found missions among the favorably disposed Hasinais, one of three Caddo-speaking confederacies. The Caddo greeting, which to Spanish ears sounded like "Tejas, Tejas, Tejas," had given rise to the name "Texas." Spaniards sought also to enlist Caddos against Frenchmen from neighboring Louisiana. This sudden entry of Christian evangelists into the world of the Hasinais, accompanied by misunderstanding, disease, resistance, and depopulation, foreshadowed similar Spanish missionary *entradas* among semisedentary peoples from Texas to California.

Not that these at-first-willing Native Americans enjoyed an idyllic existence before the coming of white men. They, too, had long fought and tortured each other, known internal conflict, and suffered periodic hard times. Yet by concentrating them in artificial mission communities, where stress, sickness, and unsanitary conditions resulted in high mortality rates, particularly for women and children, and by rounding up others for several generations to replace those who died, Spaniards hastened their demise. That thousands received baptism before death, earning them Christian salvation, was reward enough, said the missionaries.

Well-intentioned or not, the styles of these foreign evangelists differed notably. The impetuous Father Massanet proved as unrealistic in the field as his coworker, fray Francisco de Jesús María Casañas, proved clumsy. Massanet thought the Hasinais would convert eagerly to Christianity, noting the orderly manner in which they governed themselves. Their circular houses of wooden poles and thatch were neat if dispersed, and their harvests of corn, beans, squash, sunflower seeds, and tobacco plentiful. Besides, they appeared already to believe in a creator god. With studied respect and gifts of fancy clothing, Massanet tried ingratiating himself with Hasinai leaders. He rejoiced in early summer 1690 as the Indians joined enthusiastically in putting up the first crude mission church, San Francisco de los Tejas. When Alonso de León suggested leaving fifty armed Spaniards to protect the missionaries, fray Damián objected, arguing that they would surely abuse Hasinai women.

> "THEY GAVE THANKS TO GOD FOR HAVING MERITED SUCH A GRACE AS TO BE CALLED TO SAVE THE SOULS OF THE HEATHEN."
>
> —FRAY DAMIÁN MASSANET, ON HIS FELLOW MISSIONARIES, 1690

So only three soldiers were left, along with Father Casañas, two other Franciscan priests, a lay brother, cows, farm equipment, sugar, and chocolate. Once Massanet had departed with León for Coahuila to collect more missionaries and supplies for his Hasinai ministry, Casañas decided to whip the natives into shape. To begin, the haughty thirty-four-year-old from Barcelona founded a second mission, Santísimo Nombre de María, where he made himself thoroughly hated. He ridiculed Hasinai medicine men, showed open contempt for the overall Hasinai chief, and performed an exorcism that resulted in an Indian's death.

That winter of 1690–91, when smallpox ravaged Hasinai settlements, killing hundreds, Casañas told a fearful delegation of survivors that the disease was God's holy will. Later, the insensitive and unpopular Casañas, while serving in New Mexico on loan from the missionary college of Querétaro, met a cruel end. Pueblo Indians at San Diego de los Jemez, in the uprising of 1696, mocked and tortured him, eventually throwing his broken corpse out in the brush, where wild animals ate his flesh. Ill-suited though he may have been, fray Francisco de Jesús María won a coveted place in his order's book of martyrs.

As promised, fray Damián Massanet returned to the Hasinais in 1691 with twenty-one more friars, escorted by Domingo Terán de los Ríos, first governor of Spanish Texas. But their ministry went sour, and almost everyone withdrew. Only Massanet and a couple of other friars, with nine soldiers, stuck it out. A flood washed away mission Santísimo Nombre. More distressing to fray Damián was the Hasinais' stubborn refusal to give up belief in their own principal god. Finally, the Indians' death threats convinced the Spaniards to bury what they could, set fire to San Francisco de los Tejas to prevent its desecration, and flee. Although some twenty years would elapse before Spaniards in numbers again appeared among the diminished Hasinais, they would be driven by the same motives: Christian missionary zeal and defense against French intrusion from Louisiana.

Far to the west, at the very end of 1690, two Jesuit missionaries in black cassocks had ridden north at the head of an impressive pack train.

✦HACIENDAS✦

IN SIXTEENTH-CENTURY Mexico, a system was established to repay conquistadors and other Spanish notables for their services with land grants. Often comprising hundreds or thousands of acres, such private estates, or haciendas, expanded northward with the mining frontier. The classic north-Mexican hacienda included mining, crop production, and ranching. Such large, diverse operations were rare in the Southwest because of the threat of Indian raids and the failure of Spaniards to discover significant mineral resources. The hacienda of San Antonio de Padua near present-day El Paso, Texas, was one exception.

Inspired by similar estates on the earlier Moorish frontier of semiarid southern Spain, the Mexican hacienda featured a fortified great house, or *casa fuerte*, built around an open inner patio. Thick adobe walls, often with defensive towers, enclosed the entire complex. Virtually self-sufficient, haciendas resembled small towns, with stores, workshops, granary, stables, guest accommodations, and a chapel. Most also produced for a market. The *hacendado* (owner) and his wife presided over every aspect of hacienda life, including the celebration of weddings, baptisms, saints' days, and other fiestas.

Hacienda workers, whether Indians or of mixed blood, received minimal wages, if any. Yet their basic needs were met, frequently on credit at the hacienda store, where they often fell into debt.

MANZANILLA
A 1787 map by D. Joaquín Oronsoro shows Manzanilla, a San Diego hacienda. Haciendas resembled small towns, complete with stores and workshops.

The winter sun was pleasantly warm, the air dry. They chatted in Italian. Their course led across the Sonoran Desert, a little-known, basin-and-range landscape of creosote bush and mesquite, an expanse already labeled on Spanish maps Pimería Alta, land of the Upper Pima Indians, today's southern Arizona south of the Gila and northern Sonora, Mexico. They were on business.

FATHERS KINO AND SALVATIERRA

The slightly younger man, big, heavy-jowled Juan María de Salvatierra, was the Jesuit field inspector. The order's superior in Mexico City had asked Salvatierra to look into the ministry of Eusebio Francisco Kino. Self-interested ranch and mine owners in the province of Sonora, who wished the Pima Indians to remain as a heathen labor pool, had complained that these thieving natives despised Christianity and ran from Father Kino.

As tough as they came, Kino was more than equal to the dare. Born near Trent in the Tyrolean Alps, he had excelled in science and mathematics,

TUMACÁCORI
This Franciscan mission at Tumacácori was built in the nineteenth century on a site visited by Father Kino in 1691.

but vowed to serve in foreign missions. China had been his choice, New Spain his destiny. Because the group with which he sailed included more than the quota of non-Spanish Jesuits, his name had appeared on the passenger list as Eusebio de Chávez. Kino had gained his first missionary experience among the nomadic foraging, hunting, and fishing peoples of Baja California in the mid-1680s during a failed, three-year effort to occupy that daunting ecological niche. He hated failure and always wanted to go back.

Of muscular build and intense countenance, with a prominent, bushy brow, Kino took full advantage of his physical and cultural attributes. The Pimas came to view the charismatic black robe as a strange but wonderful giver of gifts: glass beads, cloth, knives, cattle, hard sugar candy. Early in 1691 the two Jesuits' approach caused a stir at the ranchería of Tumacácori, a loose cluster of forty or so conical, pole-and-brush huts on the

shallow Santa Cruz River in present-day southern Arizona. Giant, leafless cottonwoods traced the river's meandering course. Directed by Kino's Indian helpers who regularly arrived ahead of him, the Pimas of Tumacácori had built three ramadas: "one in which to say Mass, another in which to sleep, and a third for a kitchen." As missionary contact man and creator of demand for European goods, Kino excelled.

BAJA CALIFORNIA

The tour more than convinced Father Juan María. He lauded not only Kino's labors in Pimería Alta but also his desire that surpluses from these mainland missions supply a Jesuit return to the abandoned Indians of Baja California. Kino planned to build a boat in the desert and roll it on logs to the coast. Salvatierra took up the appeal. When government officials repeatedly refused to underwrite another California venture,

the resourceful Salvatierra devised an endowment that, three centuries later, still exists: the famous Pious Fund for the Californias.

By financing the enterprise themselves, the Jesuits, under license from the Spanish crown, gained near-absolute control of Baja California. But the beginning was shaky. Kino had permission to join Salvatierra, but violence broke out when some of the western Pimas rose in 1695 and shot dead with arrows a newly arrived young Sicilian Jesuit. Soldiers from Sonora retaliated, but it was Father Kino's influence that stemmed the violence. This one Jesuit, swore Governor Domingo Jironza, was worth more than an entire presidio; he must stay in Pimería Alta. Therefore, in 1697, Salvatierra crossed over by ship to Baja California without Kino.

The dozen members of this tiny Jesuit expedition put in to shore a third of the way up Baja California's long inside coast and dragged their gear across the beach onto a rise, the future

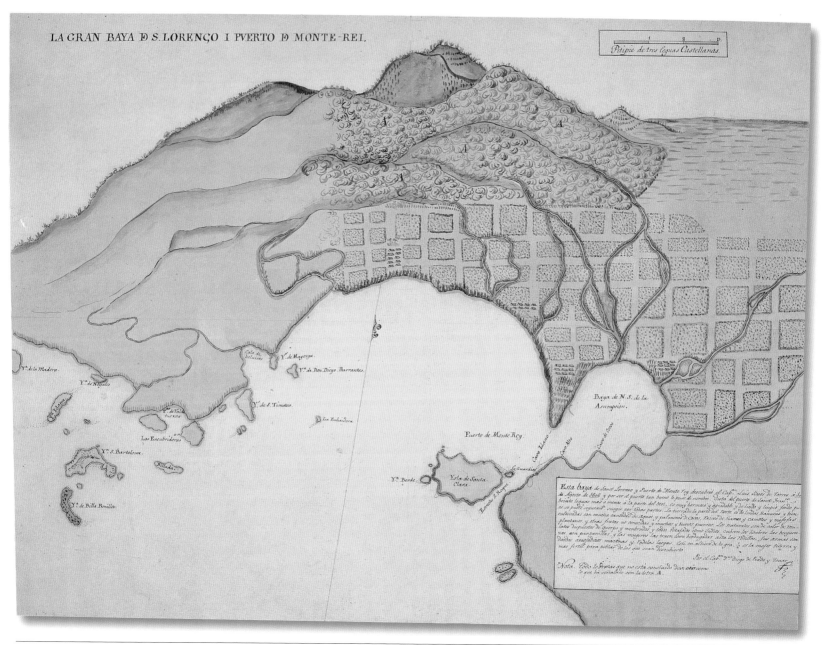

site of the presidio and community of Loreto. The natives were curious. Word spread. The strangers had food. For several weeks the crowd grew, until one day Salvatierra and his helpers found themselves fighting off several hundred arrow-shooting and rock-throwing California Indians. Failing to overrun the makeshift compound and the two swivel guns that guarded it, the Indian attackers faded away at sunset. So began the Jesuits' tenacious, seventy-year-long occupation of Baja California.

KINO AS CARTOGRAPHER: THE QUESTION OF CALIFORNIA

Father Kino, in the meantime, puzzled over the geographical nature of California. Named for a mythical island in a sixteenth-century Spanish romance of chivalry, the real place, known by navigators since the 1530s to be connected to the continent, kept reverting to an island in people's minds. Although Kino, a skilled cartographer, had been taught in Europe that California was a peninsula, he began to wonder, after having crossed it himself, if it really were a huge island. In 1695–96, on his busy map of Jesuit missions in northwestern New Spain, he drew California as an island stretching northward past the bays of San Diego and Monterey but encircled by the sea beyond Cape Mendocino. Still, he wanted proof.

Kino always justified exploration in terms of Christian ministry. At the same time, during dozens of journeys to every part of Pimería Alta, he gathered data for his maps. On one such expedition, squinting from the summit of a desert sierra in March 1701, he and Salvatierra made out what had to be, given the convergence of distant mountains, the head of the Gulf of California. Later that year, Yuman-speaking Quíquima Indian swimmers pushed Father Kino in a big basket on a raft across the lower Colorado River, and he hiked down on the west side to a point below the gulf's head to watch the sun rise across the water. How much proof did he need? Hence, on the maps he drew between 1701 and 1710, Baja California reattached itself

BAY OF MONTEREY

This eighteenth-century Spanish map depicts the Bay of Monterey, California. In 1776, Spain named Monterey the capital of both Baja (Lower) and Alta (Upper) California.

to the mainland. Although skeptics remained unconvinced, Kino had answered the question. California was not an island.

Geography aside, Baja California required of the Jesuits a keen balancing act. As their gift to the Spanish crown, they must laud the potential of the colony, but not to the point of exciting rival interests. To survive, even Salvatierra conceded that they had to beg for limited government appropriations, but not so large as to invite surrender of their control. While spreading the Christian faith among natives whose very lowliness in their eyes suggested heavenly rewards, they had to stress the worldly benefits of their ministry. They promised to provide a supply port for returning Manila galleons, which eventually they did, founding mission San José del Cabo in 1734 near the peninsula's very tip. And, they suggested, the colony could serve as a base from which to occupy

"WE ARRIVED AT A SETTLEMENT CALLED TUCSONI MOO [THAT HAD] A GREAT MOUND OF WILD SHEEP HORNS...THE HEATHEN INDIANS WELCOMED US PROFUSELY, SHARING WITH THE SOLDIERS SOME OF THEIR SUPPLIES. WE COUNTED 200 COURTEOUS AND PEACEFUL PEOPLE."

—JUAN MATEO MANJE, FATHER KINO'S TRAVELING COMPANION

San Diego and Monterey in Alta California. Ironically, just before realizing the latter project in the late 1760s, Spain's king would expel the Jesuits from all his dominions.

Long before that, in 1711, Kino, relentless apostle to the Pimas, had died. While none of Kino's Jesuit successors ever saw as much of the desert as he did, they persevered at up to eight Pima missions, waging the daily struggle to keep a few hundred neophytes alive, fed, and occupied. Because Kino spent so much time on the trail, he avoided the nasty confrontations that his successors had with Pima traditionalists over ceremonial drunkenness, orgies, or transvestites. Routinely, the missionaries recorded more burials than baptisms. To replace river Pimas who died, the black robes invited desert-dwelling Pápagos to move in. More and more came each winter, worked for food, let their children be baptized,

then left in the summer, thereby incorporating a stay at the missions in their seasonal migrations.

Not until 1732 did resident Jesuits venture to live in the Santa Cruz Valley of southern Arizona: the Austrian Juan Bautista Grazhoffer at Guevavi, not far from present-day Nogales, and the Swiss Felipe Segesser von Brunegg at San Xavier del Bac, near Tucson. Installed by veteran Basque captain Juan Bautista de Anza, the black robes brought their cows and goats and Hispanicized native herders with them. A few Hispanic ranchers, too, began building adobe homes and running livestock in the valley, among them Anza himself. Sporadic mining strikes to the south spawned more prospectors and more pack mules. In 1736 the astonishing discovery of slabs of virgin silver just south of the present U.S.-Mexican border near a property called Arizona (in Basque, "the good oak") gave rise ultimately to the state's name.

VIOLENCE IN PIMERÍA ALTA

As surrounding Apaches intensified the competition for resources—animals, captives, food—Pimería Alta saw more violence. In 1740 an Apache war party ambushed and scalped Captain Anza, orphaning his four-year-old namesake. Twenty years later, in 1760, the second Anza assumed command of the presidio at Tubac on the Santa Cruz River. Created to police Pimas who had risen against the Jesuits in 1751, the Tubac garrison, joined by Pima auxiliaries, sallied forth instead against elusive Apaches. In that war, no one earned greater respect from his enemies than Juan Bautista de Anza the younger.

Thanks to the fervor of Jesuit Fathers Kino and Salvatierra, Spain had achieved a tenuous, mainly missionary occupation of Pimería Alta and Baja California. The missions of restored New Mexico also returned slowly to a familiar routine. Most Pueblo Indians again accepted Franciscan missionaries, though the relationship was often wary. In contrast, the isolated, mesatop Hopis served vicious notice in 1701 that they had no intention of returning to the Christian fold. When it appeared that their own people at Awatovi were wavering, they destroyed that community. From then on, while Franciscans and Jesuits bid in vain for the honor of winning these apostates back, the Hopis preserved their independence.

"THE SECURITY AND LIBERTYS OF EUROPE COULD BY NO MEANS BEAR THE UNION OF THE KINGDOMS OF FRANCE AND SPAIN UNDER ONE AND THE SAME KING."

—TREATY OF UTRECHT ENDING THE WAR OF THE SPANISH SUCCESSION, APRIL 12, 1713

IMPERIAL RIVALRY: FRANCE AND SPAIN

ECHOING THE RIVALRY BETWEEN THEIR MOTHER COUNTRIES, FRENCH AND SPANISH COLONIALS CONTINUALLY JOCKEYED FOR POWER IN THE FIRST DECADES OF THE EIGHTEENTH CENTURY. TO GAIN AN ADVANTAGE, OFFICIALS FROM EACH NATION TRIED TO EXPAND THEIR CLAIMS BY ESTABLISHING NEW SETTLEMENTS, SENDING OUT EXPLORATORY PARTIES, AND COURTING THE ALLEGIANCE OF NATIVE PEOPLES. ONE RESULT WAS SPAIN'S ESTABLISHMENT OF SAN ANTONIO, TEXAS, IN 1718.

SPAIN'S LUSTER as Europe's super power had faded in the seventeenth century. In 1643 French forces at Rocroi near today's Belgian border shattered the lingering illusion of Spanish invincibility. The weak Hapsburg successors of Philip II, archpatron of imperial expansion in the previous century, lost ground at home and abroad. Beset by monetary crises, natural disasters, regional revolts against Madrid, and the listless leadership of court favorites, Spain's future seemed uncertain. France, at the same time, grew stronger under Louis XIV, the Bourbon king whose reign began in 1643 and did not end until his death in 1715. Louis schemed openly to bring Spain under French sway.

When the Spanish Hapsburg Charles II died childless in 1700, Louis moved swiftly to put his Bourbon grandson on the throne in Madrid as Philip V. The prospect of Philip eventually inheriting the French crown as well, thereby uniting Spain and France and overturning Europe's balance of power, triggered the War of the Spanish Succession (1701–14). England, leading an alliance against France and Spain, forced the Bourbons at war's end to concede that the French and Spanish crowns would never be united. Yet Philip V was left to rule Spain, and throughout the eighteenth century, an on-again-off-again Bourbon family compact against England drew Spain and France together now as allies, now as enemies. As a consequence, neither Spanish nor French colonials in North America could ever be sure.

In 1718, when France joined with England, Holland, and Austria in the Quadruple Alliance to thwart Philip V's grab of Sicily and Sardinia,

CHARLES II OF SPAIN
Charles (reigned 1665–1700), descended from Philip II, was the last Spanish Hapsburg. The lack of a clear successor enabled French monarch Louis XIV to enthrone his own grandson as Philip V, king of Spain.

Frenchmen and Spaniards found themselves enemies again. That suited Antonio Valverde y Cosío, governor of New Mexico between 1717 and 1722. A wily politician, Valverde had emerged from the half-dozen of Diego de Vargas's lieutenants who jockeyed for control of the colony after the reconqueror's death. In 1719 he led a large expeditionary probe northeast

⇢VILLASUR'S LAST STAND⇠

WHAT IS MOST noteworthy today about Pedro de Villasur's last stand in 1719 is that a colorful contemporary painting survives, seventeen feet long by four and a half feet high, on buffalo or elk hides sewn together. The unknown artist, perhaps mission-trained in New Mexico, must have interviewed survivors of the battle between Spaniards and Native Americans in present-day Nebraska. The action depicted is frantic: a knot of presidial soldiers, dressed in their protective, sleeveless, thigh-length, multi-ply leather jackets and flat, broad-brimmed hats, is encircled by Indians wielding bows, tomahawks, and swords. Nearby lies Villasur in bright red officer's uniform jacket. Fray Juan Mínguez, the chaplain, with cross in hand, runs toward him.

French accounts of the Spanish defeat did not identify any Frenchman who took part. Survivors agreed that their attackers had firearms but disagreed about the presence of French technical advisers. Regardless, the artist painted in the French advisers, arming them with unrealistically long muskets to display the advantage taken by people the artist saw as cowards.

Somehow the rolled-up mural came into the possession of Jesuit missionary Felipe Segesser von Brunegg in Sonora, who shipped it in 1760 to his brother in Switzerland. To bring it back home to New Mexico, state officials in 1988 purchased it from descendants of the Jesuit's family. This telling artifact is now on exhibit in the Palace of the Governors at Santa Fe.

PHILIP V OF SPAIN
The ascension of Philip (reigned 1700–24, 1724–46) to the throne triggered the War of the Spanish Succession (1701–14). Despite Philip's family tie to France, the relationship between Spain and France remained uneasy.

Obviously the Cuartelejo Apaches wanted Spaniards as allies, and it worked. The Marques de Valero, viceroy of New Spain, ordered a reconnaissance. Valverde passed it on to his lieutenant governor, Pedro de Villasur, who commanded a force of forty-two presidial veterans, chief of scouts José Naranjo, some sixty Pueblo auxiliaries, a few volunteer civilians, chaplain fray Juan Mínguez, and, as interpreter, expatriate Frenchman Juan de Archibeque. Unknowingly, all were being drawn into a Spanish preview of Custer's Last Stand.

Spying on the Spaniards' camp in tall grass near the confluence of the Platte and Loup rivers in present-day eastern Nebraska, a numerous combined force of Pawnees, Otos, and others waited through the dawn, when the intruders might have

suspected an attack. Then, after sunrise, the Indians fell on the Spaniards with full fury. Villasur died just outside his tent. Of the soldiers, only those guarding the horse herd escaped— about a dozen—along with most of the Pueblo auxiliaries, who as usual had camped separately. Naranjo, Mínguez, and Archibeque all perished in the onslaught.

FRENCH LOUISIANA AND SPANISH TEXAS

While France and Spain maneuvered for position in Europe, colonists in French Louisiana and Spanish Texas tried to use each other, not only to gain immediate advantage, but also to attract the attention of their respective governments. Frenchman Louis Juchereau de Saint-Denis and Spanish fray Francisco Hidalgo personified such gamesmanship.

of Santa Fe to investigate French influence among Plains Indians. On the Arkansas River, Valverde heard excited reports from Cuartelejo Apaches. Frenchmen had built two towns larger than Taos on the plains and were providing long guns and pistols to the Apaches' enemies. They mocked Spaniards, calling them weak and despicable whores.

⇢LOUIS XIV⇠

SUCCEEDING to the French throne at the age of five, Louis XIV (1638–1715) assumed control of the government in 1661 and for the next fifty years sought to expand France's frontiers worldwide. Louis's placing of a French Bourbon prince on the Spanish throne sparked the European War of Spanish Succession (1701–14).

Louisiana, Louis's sprawling colonial claim since 1682, although long of dubious value, greatly interested the king. When, in 1685, Louis revoked the Edict of Nantes, which had guaranteed toleration of French Protestants, many Frenchmen emigrated to America. In 1712 Louis granted a monopoly of commercial privileges in Louisiana to Antoine Crozat, who ceded these rights to Frenchman John Law's "Western Company."

Louis's constant campaigns in Europe eventually weakened his country. Although the Treaty of Utrecht (1713) secured the Spanish throne for his grandson as Philip V, its provisions disallowed any claims to the French crown and required ceding several valuable colonies. Louis's death signaled an end to French expansion and the subsequent rise of the British Empire.

→THE FRENCH AND INDIAN WARS←

THE FRENCH AND INDIAN WARS—mostly pitting Frenchmen and their Indian allies against British colonials and their allies among the Iroquois nations—were four conflicts fought between 1689 and 1763 for control of eastern North America. From the colonial viewpoint, they can be seen as a single conflict with interruptions. Sometimes grouped as the Imperial Wars, the corresponding wars in Europe between coalitions formed to preserve the balance of power all had repercussions in Spanish North America.

KING WILLIAM'S WAR
(1689–1697)

France invaded the Holy Roman Empire, expecting support from England's Catholic James II, who had been overthrown by William of Orange and wanted to be restored to the throne. This French intervention aroused England's allies, including Spain, and brought on the European War of the Grand Alliance (1688–97).

In America, King William's War centered on the area north of New England. A series of raids and counter-raids by French and British colonials, each with their Indian allies, produced no clear victor. The Treaty of Ryswick (1697) officially ended the war in Europe but settled nothing on the contested ground between New France and New England. In the South, Spaniards found and destroyed the ruins of La Salle's Fort St. Louis on the Texas coast and tried unsuccessfully to establish a mission among nearby Caddo Indians.

QUEEN ANNE'S WAR
(1702–1713)

Known in Europe as the War of the Spanish Succession (1701–14), hostilities this time saw France and Spain allied against England, Holland, and Austria. In New England, a French raid in 1704 devastated Deerfield, Massachusetts. English forces again failed to take Quebec but did capture Port Royal, Nova Scotia, in 1710.

In the South, British colonists from Carolina in 1702 plundered the Spanish coastal town of St. Augustine, Florida, but failed to take the fort. They and their Indian auxiliaries later devastated the Apalachee missions of western Florida. English defenders repulsed a combined French and Spanish fleet at

Charleston in 1706. The war ended with the Treaty of Utrecht (1713), which ceded Hudson Bay, Newfoundland, and Acadia to the British.

KING GEORGE'S WAR
(1744–1748)

Following upon the so-called War of Jenkins' Ear (1739–41) over Spanish exclusion of English trade in the Americas, the War of the Austrian Succession (1740–48) again made allies of France and Spain against England. Earlier, England's founding of Georgia in 1733 spurred Spain to counter in the 1740s with the occupation of territory on the western Gulf of Mexico.

In 1745 Englishmen from Massachusetts captured the French coastal fortress of Louisburg, later traded back to France by the Treaty of Aix-la-Chapelle (1748). Sir William Johnson's growing influence among the Iroquois nations and the intense rivalry of French and British interests in the upper Ohio River Valley foreshadowed a fourth and final war.

FRENCH AND INDIAN WAR
(1754–1763)

The most consequential of the four colonial wars, this conflict, part of the wider Great War for Empire or Seven Years' War (1756–63), flared as British settlers moved into the French-claimed Ohio River Valley. At first Frenchmen had more success. The tide of war turned, however, in 1758, when the elder William Pitt, England's prime minister, ordered the Royal Navy to blockade the St. Lawrence River, halting reinforcements and supplies from France. That same year, Louisburg and Fort Duquesne fell to British forces, and the brilliant capture of Quebec in 1759 by General James Wolfe foretold English victory. Montreal surrendered the following year.

By the Peace of Paris (1763), England gained New France as Canada, along with islands in the West Indies. As France's ally, Spain had to cede East and West Florida to England. To compensate, France turned over to Spain Louisiana west of the Mississippi.

DEATH OF MONTCALM
The French were defeated in 1759 at Quebec and their general, the Marquis de Montcalm, was killed, but victorious British commander General Wolfe also lost his life in the fighting.

The lanky charmer Saint-Denis, born in the vicinity of Quebec and schooled in Paris, had come to Louisiana in 1700, only a year after his countrymen had established Biloxi in what is now Mississippi. Hidalgo, a seemingly guileless young Spanish Franciscan from the missionary college of Querétaro, had been in east Texas with Father Massanet, ministering among the Hasinai Indians. In 1693 Hidalgo had fled against his will, vowing to return. At mission San Juan Bautista, on the Coahuila frontier just below the Rio Grande, Hidalgo drafted letters to the governor of French Louisiana between 1711 and 1713, begging his assistance in restoring missions among the Hasinais. That got things moving.

As he studied Hidalgo's letters in 1713, newly arrived Governor Antoine de la Mothe, Sieur de Cadillac, smiled. Here was an opening. Cadillac and the proprietor for whom he worked agreed that their best chance to turn a profit in Louisiana was to encourage contraband markets for French goods in silver-rich New Spain and New Mexico. Defying Spanish mercantilism, which restricted colonial economic activity and sought to prevent the drain of precious metals, Cadillac called on Saint-Denis, outfitted him, and issued a passport.

The Frenchman and his small party reached San Juan Bautista in July 1714. Caught off guard, the captain of the local presidio sent for instructions from the viceroy. Saint-Denis, meanwhile, wooed Manuela Sánchez, the captain's lovely granddaughter. Escorted to Mexico City, the Frenchman won over the viceroy, who appointed him supply officer of a Spanish expedition to reoccupy Texas in 1716. Passing back through San Juan Bautista en route, Saint-Denis married Manuela, who was soon with child.

NEW ORLEANS AND SAN ANTONIO

By this time Father Hidalgo had begun to distrust all Frenchmen. Writing to the viceroy from a second mission San Francisco de los Tejas, the friar admitted that "they are slipping in behind our backs in silence, but God sees their intentions." So did strategists on both sides, consulting ever more precise maps, like players of an international chess game. Their countermoves in 1718 were hardly coincidental. That year, French planners laid out a new capital at New Orleans, Louisiana, and Spaniards founded a way-station at San Antonio, Texas. By then only a dozen miles separated their pawns: the French post at Natchitoches on the Red River and the Spanish

GLORIETA MESA
New Spain's northern frontier, including this New Mexican mesa southeast of Santa Fe, was a focus for rivalry between France and Spain.

mission of San Miguel de los Adaes, near today's Robeline, Louisiana. Soon the presidial town of Los Adaes sprang up, serving as the capital of Texas until 1773.

In geographical and cultural terms, Spanish Texas was two provinces. The first, east Texas—where the cunning Frenchman Saint-Denis, his Spanish wife, and his Indian trade partners managed an uneasy alliance—looked toward Louisiana, with its mossy woods and swamps. San Antonio, in contrast, on the camino real from Coahuila, was situated in prairie and rolling brush country, a natural extension of northeastern New Spain.

In 1721–22 the Marques de Aguayo, governor of Coahuila and Texas, reinforced both Texases. And nothing gave him greater satisfaction than marking off the foundations of a new Spanish presidio at La Bahía, precisely on top of debris from La Salle's long-abandoned Fort St. Louis.

Even after a European treaty ended the war of the Quadruple Alliance in 1720, French colonials showed no sign of slackening their commercial offensive toward Spaniards in the American West. Louisiana's Governor Jean-Baptiste Le Moyne de

Bienville dispatched explorer Jean-Baptiste Bénard de La Harpe to find out if the Arkansas River were navigable to New Mexico. Explorer Étienne Véniard de Bourgmont received a royal contract to make peace "among all the Indian tribes between Louisiana and New Mexico in order to open a safe trade route" and to establish "a post, which will shield the mines of the Illinois from the Spaniards."

Results varied. During times when the Bourbon kings of Spain and France, reacting to England's growing power, joined in family compacts, Frenchmen tested porous Spanish colonial borders. In 1739 French traders Pierre and Paul Mallet and their companions showed up in Santa Fe and caroused with Spaniards. Two married daughters of their local hosts and stayed to raise families. Though the Mallets' bid to open regular trade between Louisiana and New Mexico failed, now and again a French deserter or trader would survive the plains crossing to Santa Fe, but never could he be sure of his reception. If he knew a useful trade—carpentry, tailoring, or barbering— he might be forced to remain. If his timing was bad, as was Pierre Mallet's return in 1750, he might see his goods confiscated and his person escorted under guard to Mexico City.

PEDRO DE RIVERA'S INSPECTION OF THE NORTHERN FRONTIER

Philip V, Spain's Bourbon king, seemed more intent on economy than parrying such French thrusts. As the king's advisers saw it, improved efficiency and an end to graft in military supply along New Spain's entire northern frontier could save the treasury tens of thousands of pesos.

Hence, in the mid-1720s, on the king's orders, veteran Brigadier Pedro de Rivera carried out a scrupulous inspection of twenty-three presidial garrisons in the near and far north. Baja California's presidio at Loreto, managed by the

Jesuits, was the sole exception. The inspector liked Santa Fe. He stayed there all summer in 1726, looking into alleged corruption, nepotism, and proliferation of military titles under the previous governor, Antonio de Valverde, and the incumbent, Valverde's nephew and son-in-law, Juan Domingo de Bustamante.

Ignoring local outcries, Rivera cut the hundred-man garrison by twenty and reduced the soldiers' annual pay from 450 to 400 pesos. He assured them that they and their families would be better off, since he was eliminating former deductions and standardizing prices. Even at that, most of the soldiers who had signed on for one or more ten-year enlistments would remain debtors to the company store.

Evidently the inspector did not like Los Adaes, the humid capital of Texas, which he visited in September 1727 and where his inspection lasted only eleven days. The presidio, surrounded by a log stockade, and the neighboring mission, which had no resident Indians, marked the extent of Spanish territory. The French fort, with twenty-five men, lay only an hour's ride through the woods to the east, where Spaniards went regularly to trade for corn, beans, and other goods. Since France and Spain were again at peace, Rivera reduced the hundred-man roster at Los Adaes to sixty.

✧SAN ANTONIO, TEXAS✧

AFTER FORDING the Rio Grande about thirty miles downriver from today's Eagle Pass, Texas, Spaniards en route to east Texas still had 500 miles to travel. As early as 1691, they had named a campsite along the way San Antonio de Padua. In 1718, with Spain moving to occupy east Texas as a buffer to French Louisiana, a Spanish captain, a band of colonists, and a Franciscan priest founded the military "villa de Béxar" and Mission San Antonio de Valero (later the famed Alamo). The town, presidio, and eventual five missions remained a way station for two generations, while far to the east the capital of Spanish Texas resided at Los Adaes.

Following the transfer of Louisiana to Spain in 1762, Spanish strategists called for a withdrawal from east Texas and, in 1773, named San Antonio the provincial capital. Its racially mixed community of herders and farm laborers by 1790 had stabilized at about 2,000, including mission Indians, Europeans, mestizos, and some black slaves.

An unsympathetic governor in 1794 ascribed the San Antonio area's lack of agricultural production to the people's "laziness and their having given all their attention to the capture of wild livestock."

San Antonio suffered siege and capture during the struggle for Mexican independence (1813) and again during the Texas Revolution, when in March 1836 Mexican troops overran the outnumbered defenders of the Alamo. By 1846 population was down to around 800. A considerable influx of Germans made San Antonio the largest settlement in Texas by 1860, with a population exceeding 8,200. After the Civil War and the arrival of the first railroad in 1877, it thrived as a cow town and regional center with a distinctly Hispanic, German, and southern Anglo-American flavor. Not until 1940 did the community expand beyond the limits of its original Spanish charter. Today, after Houston and Dallas, San Antonio ranks as the third largest city in Texas.

MILITARY PLAZA
This illustration of San Antonio, Texas, was made by topographer William Emory in his survey of the Mexican border in the 1850s.

"MANY ANIMALS ARE FOUND IN THE COUNTRYSIDE, SUCH AS THE BISON (A SPECIES SIMILAR TO CATTLE)...BIRDS ARE PLENTIFUL, IN PARTICULAR THE TURKEYS, WHICH ARE FOUND IN FLOCKS."

—DESCRIPTION OF TEXAS FROM THE DIARY OF PEDRO DE RIVERA, 1727

NIAGARA FALLS

The journeys of Franciscan friar Louis Hennepin, the first European to describe Niagara Falls, helped to establish the French empire in North America. His account of the "vast country" of Louisiana, from which this illustration comes, helped to publicize the discovery.

Doubling back to the southwest, Inspector Rivera praised the location of San Antonio, noting the rich irrigable land and the potential for stock raising, even while he pared the garrison from fifty-four to forty-four men. He wanted at least twenty-five civilian families brought in to colonize the lands around the presidio and the two missions nearby on the San Antonio River. Because of the expense, however, he opposed an earlier plan to recruit hundreds of Canary Islanders for Texas. Nevertheless, fifteen such farm families, fifty-some people in all, were already in transit, arriving at San Antonio in 1731. That summer they laid out the plaza, house lots, and pasture lands of a chartered municipality. Three more missions relocated on the river. That completed greater San Antonio's presidio of Béjar, villa of San Fernando, and five Franciscan missions.

The published military regulations resulting from Rivera's inspection were all but ignored. His suggested reforms brought little relief to the far northern frontier, as the people of San Antonio attested. While they quarreled among themselves during the 1730s, trying to learn to live together, Lipán Apaches struck at will. Colonists who had lived in San Antonio before 1731 resented the inept Canary Islanders who arrived with *hidalgo* status and claims on the offices of the villa. Local non-mission stock growers damned the Franciscans, whose hired foremen, free Indian herders, and extensive outlying ranches gave them an unfair advantage. Tempers also flared over crop lands along the river, Indian laborers, and soldier guards for the missions. What finally drove the community to cooperate was defense.

Rivera had underestimated the threat posed by hard-riding Native American hunting peoples. When next, forty years later, another inspector took the measure of the far north, there was no question. Bands of Apaches, Navajos, Utes, and especially Comanches had taken the offensive. They, not rival Europeans, were the more immediate enemy. While that realization was dawning, a large-scale, government-sponsored colonization scheme attracted hundreds of settlers to the lower Rio Grande Valley, and a rich man's experiment to provide Franciscan missions for Lipán Apaches in central Texas went up in well-publicized flames.

NATIVE AMERICANS

For both French and Spanish colonists, poor relations with Native Americans could spell disaster. At left is a native hunter from the 1796 Travel Encyclopaedia; above, an Indian with a peace pipe, or calumet, from Hennepin's 1698 account of Louisiana.

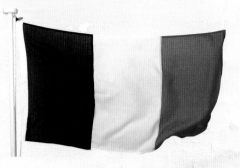

COLONIAL RIVAL
Competition with France (symbolized above by the present-day French flag) drove Spain to increase its colonial presence in the West.

"THE STATE IN WHICH WE HAVE FOUND THE APACHES IS SO DIFFERENT FROM WHAT I EXPECTED THAT I ASSURE YOU THE METHOD OF THEIR PACIFICATION IS A MAJOR CONCERN TO ME."

—LETTER FROM COLONEL DIEGO ORTIZ PARRILLA TO PEDRO ROMERO DE TERREROS, 1757

DEFENSE OF THE FAR NORTH

BY THE MID-EIGHTEENTH CENTURY, EUROPEAN GOODS HAD CHANGED MANY NATIVE CULTURES. PERHAPS NO PEOPLE WAS MORE DRAMATICALLY TRANSFORMED THAN THE COMANCHES. AFTER OBTAINING GUNS AND HORSES, THIS FORMIDABLE WARRIOR SOCIETY EFFECTIVELY MAINTAINED SUPREMACY ON THE SOUTHERN PLAINS AGAINST ALL CONTENDERS.

BY THE LATE 1740s, a large-scale, closely regimented migration from north-central New Spain to the upper gulf coast plain and the lower Rio Grande Valley was underway. Spanish strategists had noted that the 400-mile-long arc of coastline bending eastward from Pánuco in New Spain as far as La Bahía, Texas, lay unsettled and vulnerable to foreign encroachment. The colony of Nuevo Santander materialized almost overnight. In 1755 its population stood at 6,200 people, mostly families of *castas* willing to risk the move for a 100-peso bonus, land, and tax exemptions. Plotted on a map, most of the new communities, like beads on a rosary, dotted the inland road from San Luis Potosí all the way to the Rio Grande at Reynosa. From there, a traveler could strike northwest along the river's left bank through Camargo, Mier, Revilla, and on to the good livestock ford across the shallow, brown water to Laredo, then double back into central and east Texas.

While Nuevo Santander prospered, another contemporary effort, smaller in scale and farther north, came to notable grief. In the summer of 1756, Pedro Romero de Terreros, mine owner, philanthropist, and cousin of Franciscan missionary fray Alonso Giraldo de Terreros, contracted to underwrite missions for Apaches in Texas. That winter in San Antonio, where the venture's diverse components came together, fray Alonso

quarreled with the project's military commander, Colonel Diego Ortiz Parrilla, accusing him of intentional delays. For his part, Ortiz Parrilla expressed his distrust of the smiling Lipan Apaches who were showing up at San Antonio for gifts of corn, tobacco, and sugar candy.

A few months later, overseeing construction of a log presidio on the north bank of the Río San Sabá, in hill country more than 100 miles northwest of San Antonio, the colonel remained skeptical. Three miles downstream on the opposite bank, the Franciscans and their helpers labored to build mission Santa Cruz. The missionaries' spirits rose in June 1757 when they looked out over a colorful sea of Apache tepees. But, just as Ortiz Parrilla suspected, these Apaches had not come to stay. They were moving after buffalo, hoping at the same time to attract Spanish allies against their Comanche enemies.

A fortuitous union of innate boldness, Spanish horses, and French guns had lifted the Comanches in two generations to fierce prominence on the south plains. Late arrivals, this Shoshonean-speaking, Great Basin people had, about

COMANCHES MOVING CAMP
This George Catlin painting from 1834–35 shows a dogfight erupting as Comanches saddle up and prepare to move camp. The Comanches were accomplished horsemen and warriors who killed many enemies, particularly in proportion to their own modest numbers.

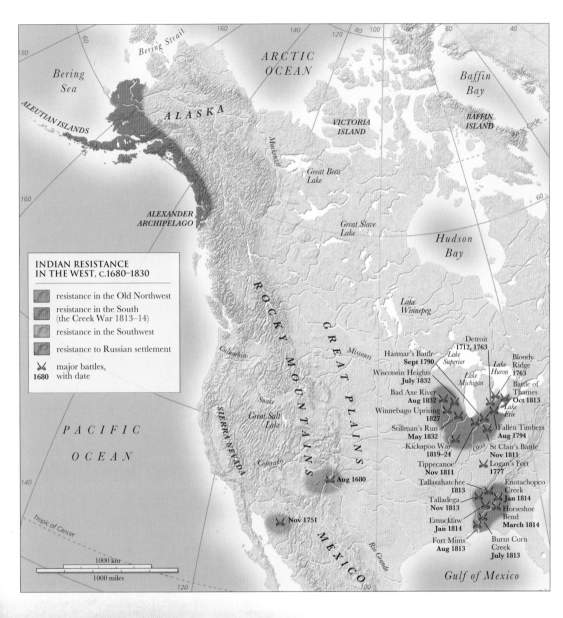

INDIAN RESISTANCE IN THE WEST

As European settlement in North America began to forge westward, pockets of violent resistance broke out among Native Americans. Tribal uprisings, often provoked by minor differences or misinterpretations, were quelled, but at considerable cost to both sides. These resulted in a general movement westwards of the native peoples in the face of a developing settler frontier in the East.

1700, ventured with kindred Utes out onto the grassy expanses where they took to horse and hunt with a vengeance. Turning on the Utes and scattering the Plains Apaches, the Comanches had pushed their rivals south against Spanish Texas and west against New Mexico, alternately raiding and trading as they willed.

In March 1758 leaders of a reported 2,000 armed and mounted Comanches, Bidais, Tejas, and Tonkawas requested entry into the San Sabá presidio to parley. Ortiz Parrilla refused. That made them mad. Despite signs of this anti-Apache confederation's hostile intent, Father Terreros spurned the colonel's warning to take refuge in the presidio. Without hesitation, the Indians swarmed the mission. Terreros and another Franciscan died in the attack; a third, fray Miguel de Molina, miraculously escaped. "I saw nothing but Indians on every hand," Molina recalled, "arrayed in the most horrible attire. Besides the paint on their faces, red and black, they were adorned with the pelts and tails of wild beasts, wrapped around them or hanging down from their heads, as well as deer horns." They killed even the mission cats.

Trailing northwest from San Antonio via the presidio of San Sabá in late summer 1759, Ortiz Parrilla led a column of several hundred soldiers, armed cowboys, and other assorted irregulars to avenge the mission's destruction. Too easily, they surprised a Tonkawa camp just beyond the Brazos River, where they claimed to kill 55, capture 149, and recover recently stolen horses and mules and a piece of one of the friar's vestments.

Unfortunately, they kept on. None of them predicted the scene of their next encounter: a large Taovaya village where Comanches and other allied peoples had come together in defiance, erected a European-style stockade, dug a moat, and put up a French flag. Worse, all these Indians seemed to have muskets. In repeated Spanish assaults, Ortiz Parrilla was grazed twice and had a horse shot out from under him. Yet the Indian fort held. When the attackers brought up a couple of small swivel-mounted cannon, the defenders greeted each shot with a gale of laughter. After hours of fighting, heavy casualties, and numerous desertions, Ortiz Parrilla gave up, blaming the inferior caliber of his men. A decade later, Spaniards abandoned the San Sabá presidio.

FRAY SERRA
By founding missions in California, Father Junípero Serra advanced the expansionist aims of Inspector General José de Gálvez.

THE AGE OF GÁLVEZ

ALARMED BY THE APPEARANCE OF RUSSIAN TRADERS AND ENGLISH EXPLORERS ON THE PACIFIC COAST, JOSÉ DE GÁLVEZ, INSPECTOR GENERAL OF NEW SPAIN, LAUNCHED AN AMBITIOUS PROGRAM TO ESTABLISH SETTLEMENTS AND MISSIONS NORTHWARD INTO ALTA CALIFORNIA. ALSO DURING GÁLVEZ'S WATCH, SPAIN FURTHER EXTENDED ITS INFLUENCE THROUGH A SERIES OF EXPLORATORY ADVENTURES ON BOTH LAND AND SEA.

"BUT I ASSURE YOU BEFORE GOD, AND WITH ALL SINCERITY, THAT I HAVE NOT UPON MY CONSCIENCE THE SLIGHTEST SCRUPLE OF HAVING EXCEEDED THE LIMITS OF JUSTICE."

—JOSE DE GÁLVEZ, ON HIS STERN PUNISHMENT OF REBELLIOUS INDIANS, 1767

B Y THE TREATY OF PARIS in 1763, European diplomats redrew the imperial map of North America. The Great War for Empire (1756–63), better known to Americans as the French and Indian War, concluded with a British victory that erased French sovereignty from the continent. Britain took over New France (now Canada) as well as Louisiana east of the Mississippi River. Reluctantly, Spain assumed responsibility for Louisiana west of the river, from New Orleans in the south to St. Louis in the north. French families already living in the territory stayed on during the Spanish occupation, preserving the cultural flavor of the colony and influencing how the new governors did things.

In Europe, too, French ways influenced Spain, particularly during the long reign of the Spanish king Charles III (1759–88). Bourbon reformers embraced the more optimistic, professional, and secular approach to government championed by the eighteenth-century French political philosophers. As first servant of the state, the king justified his enlightened despotism as necessary for the prosperity and happiness of the Spanish people. The pervasive spirit of reform reached out even to the northern frontier of New Spain. There, one man and one act set the tone. The man was José de Gálvez—driven, egotistical inspector

general to New Spain between 1765 and 1771— and the act the summary expulsion of the Jesuits from Spain and the empire.

EXPULSION OF THE JESUITS

Gálvez, whose rise to high office reflected a new emphasis on merit, threw himself into administrative reforms in New Spain, all intended in one way or another to increase revenue from the colony. While the banishment of the Jesuits in 1767 had little to do with their performance as missionaries in the Spanish empire and everything to do with their conservatism, influence, and allegiance to Rome over Madrid, it staggered Pimería Alta and Baja California. In those colonies, Jesuits administered the sacraments of the Church, engaged actively in economic enterprise, and served as the principal purveyors of health, education, and welfare. The efficiency of their expulsion greatly pleased Gálvez.

Deliberately planned for the night of a holiday, the feast of St. John the Baptist, the government take-over of the order's main house in Mexico City proceeded flawlessly. To justify the operation and head off popular reaction in favor of the Jesuits, Gálvez used propaganda.

The Society of Jesus, he charged, was a parasite on the social body. Jesuits had profited mercilessly from the sweat of hacienda workers and mission Indians. In a vain effort to display ill-gotten Jesuit treasure, Gálvez ordered even the cesspool probed, yielding, one Jesuit recalled, no more than "an unbearable smell in the house and raging

SANTA BARBARA, CALIFORNIA
Known as the "Queen of the Missions," Santa Barbara was founded in 1782. The twin bell towers, eighty-seven feet tall, are the only ones to be found among the California missions. Its facade is patterned after a Roman temple.

THE TREATY OF PARIS 1783

- United States (13 colonies)
- Spanish territory
- British territory
- Russian territory
- Disputed territory
- Unclaimed territory

THE TREATY OF PARIS, 1783

The Treaty of Paris in 1763, which ended the Seven Years' War, resulted in France ceding most of its claims in Canada to Britain. Twenty years later, in 1783, the Revolutionary War officially ended with a further Treaty of Paris, which recognized the independence of Britain's Thirteen Colonies as the United States, and extended their territories to the Mississippi.

Indians "will not stay put in their pueblos, look after their families, cultivate their lands, or take care of their goods, if left to their own devices."

After a disastrous year-long experiment, during which mission managers took every advantage to profit personally and Indians came and went as they pleased, Gálvez had to agree. By fiat, he returned administration of mission properties and discipline to the friars. No one had to tell him how to correct lazy or uncooperative neophytes: twenty-five lashes for the first offense, fifty for the second. Although he disliked traditional missions, Gálvez could not argue with their cost-effectiveness for controlling native peoples and occupying new territory. Therefore, despite the muttering of reformers, missionaries other than Jesuits continued to figure prominently, nowhere more so than in the belated occupation of Alta California.

ALTA CALIFORNIA

The Jesuits had fully expected to carry their California ministry northward. They had long urged a settlement on Monterey Bay. The need was obvious. By the 1760s, sea otter and fur seal hunters in Russian employ were harvesting their way down the Pacific coast from the Aleutian Islands and Alaska. Englishmen, bent on discovery of the Northwest Passage, also challenged Spanish claims. Now, with the Jesuits gone, José de Gálvez leapt into the breach.

The California project suited his vanity. First, he provided that a naval department and supply base be founded amid clouds

SAN CARLOS

Supply problems hampered settlement of Alta California. In 1769, the supply ship San Carlos, assigned to bring provisions to San Diego, took fifty-five days to complete the difficult, scurvy-ridden sea journey from Baja California.

dispositions on the part of the commissioners." Later in the summer of 1767, after the rainy season had begun in Pimería Alta, soldiers from the Altar presidio appeared unannounced at the Jesuit mission village of Guevavi, a few miles northeast of today's Nogales, Arizona. They asked for the missionary, tall, young Custodio Ximeno. They demanded that he surrender his keys. He was to speak to no one. Church valuables, they told him, would be safe in the sacristy. During his absence, the mission foreman would distribute daily rations to the Indians.

The same day, all over northwestern New Spain, similar scenes unfolded. Shaken, Captain Juan Bautista de Anza of neighboring Tubac, baptized and married by a Jesuit he considered his dear friend and mentor, nonetheless took the rude expulsion in stride. "After all," he wrote, "the king commands it and there may be more to it than we realize. The thoughts of men differ as much as the distance from earth to heaven."

Jose de Gálvez had an alternate vision. Instead of paternalistic mission concentration camps, where Indians labored under a stern regimen, Gálvez would substitute productive communal farms managed by enlightened civilian agents. As for missionaries, no longer burdened by economics or discipline, they could devote themselves exclusively to spiritual ministry. Laughable but sad, agreed the veteran Franciscan friars of the missionary college at Querétaro. What did Gálvez know of Indians? Under this new system, reckoned the superior of Franciscan replacements destined for Pimería Alta, the

⇒SPANISH MISSIONS IN CALIFORNIA⇐

WHEN FRANCISCAN missionary Junípero Serra established a mission at San Diego in 1769, an estimated 300,000 Native Americans lived within the artificial boundaries of today's California. Half a century later, in 1821, when Mexico declared its independence from Spain, 200,000 survived. That the eventual twenty-one California missions, through disease, overwork, and other causes, contributed to Indian population decline is certainly true. When compared, however, with the disastrous eighty-percent collapse during the Gold Rush decade of the 1850s—from about 150,000 to 30,000—the impact of the missions is put in perspective.

While the Franciscans' sincerity was rarely in doubt, their methods of conversion intentionally disrupted Native American life. Spanish soldiers routinely rounded up families from scattered Native villages and relocated them at or near a mission. The friars sought to teach their

"neophytes," or new converts, to speak Spanish; gave them Catholic instruction; and taught them farming and trades as ways of making them useful—if lowly and segregated—members of a Spanish colonial society. Mission runaways, alleged shamans, and native leaders accused of conspiring to revolt faced whipping or time in shackles.

European diseases—measles, smallpox, influenza, syphilis, and others—accounted for numerous deaths. Infant mortality was especially high. Psychological stress also resulted from the suppression of native religious practices, mixing of peoples from numerous tribes, unfamiliar and unhealthy living conditions, and the upsetting of traditional male and female roles. On occasion, Spanish soldiers raped Indian women. Yet some natives, especially those favored by individual friars, adapted to life in the missions, came to admire Catholic ceremonialism while practicing some of their customs in secret, and endured. Others protested passively, dragging their feet at work, ignoring orders, and making fun of the missionaries behind their backs. Fewer joined open rebellions. Late in 1775, some 800 Indians rose up in arms, burned the mission buildings at San Diego,

CARMEL BAY
The settlement at Carmel Bay, California, was the site of the San Carlos Mission. It is depicted here in an engraving from an 1839 book by Alexander Forbes.

and put to death fray Luis Jayme. Another plot a decade later, involving a woman shaman, Toypurina, centered on Mission San Gabriel. When Spanish soldiers found out, they arrested the leaders and put them on trial. Eight men suffered public flogging, while Toypurina, after baptism, was deported to another mission.

Sporadic resistance continued under Mexican rule. When a large-scale armed revolt among the Chumash Indians of Santa Inés, La Purísima, and Santa Barbara ultimately failed in 1824, a native official led 453 Indians into California's interior, where they set up a community that embraced ways from both native and Hispanic cultures.

What disease and the mission system left intact of the Indians' traditional lifeways, the Gold Rush and California statehood all but obliterated.

SAN CARLOS MISSION
This mission on the sea is one of only four stone missions in California. Father Serra is buried under the altar here.

---

of mosquitos at swampy San Blas on the west coast of New Spain well south of the tip of Baja California. In July 1768 the inspector general himself crossed over to the peninsula and worked himself into a frenzy. "So infinite is my business, so many are the things to be seen to by me at one time," the harried Gálvez complained, "that even though my ardor rises with my difficulties, my

days not merely are consumed, but in great part my nights!" The all-male occupation force was to move north in stages by sea and land, join up at San Diego, and press on to Monterey.

Franciscans from the missionary college of San Fernando in Mexico City would participate. No less ardent or irascible than Gálvez, fray Junípero Serra, their asthmatic superior, vied with

Governor Gaspar de Portolá to bring off this quixotic venture. Somehow, with enormous suffering and hardship, they did.

For the first half-dozen years, the tenuous colony endured a starving time. Frustrated survivors raped Indian women, and the friars protested. Serra founded a makeshift mission among hesitant Ipais at San Diego in 1769, only to have it burned by the Indians in 1775 and later rebuilt. At long last, on the shores of Monterey Bay in 1770, a rough-hewn presidio and mission within a palisade betokened Spanish possession. Still, by 1774, counting soldier-colonists, missionaries, and the first Hispanic women who appeared with reinforcements, the new colony's nonnative population stood at fewer than 200. Alta California had been occupied, but as yet it seemed not worth the cost.

Supply from San Blas by ship, exposed to heavy seas, adverse winds and currents, and terrible loss of life from scurvy, held little hope for the future. An overland route from Pimería Alta, first proposed by the Jesuit Kino, might still serve. Fray Francisco Garcés, the Franciscan replacement at San Xavier del Bac near present-day Tucson, had already retraced the Gila River route to the Colorado River. An earthy, intrepid, but unassuming sort who treated Indians as fellow

human beings, Garcés once embarrassed his superiors by reporting that curious natives had lifted the skirt of his habit to determine whether he was man or woman. "In short," wrote a more urbane friar, "God has created him, as I see it, solely for the purpose of seeking out these unhappy, ignorant, and rustic people."

Juan Bautista de Anza, captain of the nearby presidio at Tubac, thought Father Garcés a fool to wander alone in the desert. Anza also thought, as his father had before him, that he could open a road overland to California. Singled out as an exemplary officer by the Marqués de Rubí, first general inspector of the northern frontier in forty years, Anza dutifully endorsed Rubí's recommendations, codified in the *Reglamento* of 1772. These new regulations offered little innovation—a realigned cordon of fifteen presidios stretching some 1,800 miles from the Gulf of Mexico to the Gulf of California, unified

military command, and a war of extermination against unyielding native nations. Captain Anza, a member of Sonora's tight Basque landowning, mercantile, and military elite, also commanded the respect of his men and of Apache, Pima, and Seri leaders he engaged in battle. Hand-to-hand combat, wounds, and numerous campaigns filled Anza's service record.

Joining in a union of convenience with Father Garcés, Captain Anza secured the viceroy's permission and in 1774 led an exploratory expedition via the Yuma crossing of the Colorado River through the deserts and mountain of southern California to mission San Gabriel. That earned him a promotion and a hero's welcome in Mexico City. Next, during the fall and winter of 1775–76, Anza headed a migration over the same route: seven officers and friars, including Garcés; ten Tubac troopers making the trip a second time but expecting to return home; dozens of other

⋆THE GRAND CANYON⋆

THE GRAND CANYON is the gorge cut by the Colorado River through the high plateau of northern Arizona. Although it extends 280 miles from Marble Gorge to Grand Wash Cliffs near the Nevada border and comprises several canyons within a larger one, its best-known section is the 105-mile long stretch lying within today's Grand Canyon National Park.

The canyon's width varies from five to fifteen miles, and at some points it is over a mile deep. Its walls, cut relentlessly by the churning river, are mainly a dull red interspersed with parallel beds of

multicolored rocks. Fading pictographs painted by prehistoric peoples are still to be seen on the canyon's walls.

The first European of record to view the Grand Canyon was Captain García López de Cárdenas, a member of Coronado's expedition. Led to the south rim by Hopi Indians in 1540, Cárdenas ordered three of his men over the edge with the intent of reaching the river. The trio returned later that afternoon having climbed no more than a third of the way down. Not until 1776 did other Spaniards approach the chasm. That year,

descending from the north, the small Domínguez-Escalante party scrambled down into Glen Canyon, upriver from today's Grand Canyon National Park, while fray Francisco Garcés visited Havasupai Indians downriver.

In 1826 fur trapper James Ohio Pattie claimed to be the first Anglo-American to see the Grand Canyon. Eventually, in 1869 Major John Wesley Powell and nine companions traveled down the entire canyon in four small wooden boats. Fifty years later, in 1919, Congress established the Grand Canyon National Park.

THE GRAND CANYON
The Colorado River winds through the Grand Canyon in northern Arizona. First viewed by Spaniard García López de Cárdenas in 1540, the canyon became one of America's best known national parks.

soldiers, settlers, muleteers, wranglers, and servants; and 165 wives and children—nearly 300 people in all, mostly families who meant to stay. One woman died giving birth early in the journey, but her baby and two other newborns, along with everyone else, survived to reach California.

Again Anza was the toast of Mexico City. This time he took with him Olleyquotequiebe, the wheezing principal leader of the Yuma Indians, by whose grace travelers crossed the Colorado River. The Indian's lavish reception by Viceroy Antonio María Bucareli and his baptism as Salvador Palma in the yawning, candle-lit cathedral were meant to impress him for life. Settlers Anza had shepherded by land to Monterey, meantime, moved north. At a site he had chosen, they built the first flat-roofed log houses of San Francisco's presidio on the best natural harbor in the world. The year was 1776.

HEROIC EXPLORATIONS

That same year, José de Gálvez, now Minister of the Indies in Spain, implemented his grandest reform. The General Command of the Interior Provinces would become almost but not quite a northern viceroyalty. Henceforth, frontier governors from Texas to California reported to the commandant general, who eventually came to reside in Chihuahua. Binding the North administratively, Gálvez knew, would prove easier than binding it physically. All the same, his initiatives called forth some of the most heroic explorations since the sixteenth century.

In 1775 doughty Juan Francisco de la Bodega y Quadra, commanding a cramped schooner scarcely 36 feet long, had navigated up the Pacific Coast to 58° 30' of northern latitude. In the watery maze of inlets, bays, and straits west of today's Juneau, Alaska, even though he spied no foreigners, he hastened to take symbolic possession for Spain. Bleeding gums and aching, swollen joints, the symptoms of scurvy, tormented every hand. Back at Monterey, Bodega and his second-in-command had to be carried ashore. Only after nursing by Father Serra and his friars were they fit to sail on southward back to San Blas.

FATHER GARCÉS
The intrepid explorer and founder of Tucson met his final fate at the mission settlement of La Purisima Concepcion, where Yuma Indians massacred the priests, soldiers, and citizens in 1781.

On land, no explorer excelled Father Garcés. Thinking he could close the gap between Monterey and Santa Fe, the footloose Franciscan set out in 1776 from San Gabriel, near present-day Los Angeles. With a succession of Indian guides, he rode his mule into the interior valley of California, across the Tehachapi Mountains, Mojave Desert, and Colorado River; and eastward into a kaleidoscope of canyon lands as far as the Hopi pueblo of Oraibi, where his appearance interrupted a summer ceremonial. The Hopis wanted no part of him. So, calling for his mule, on July 4, 1776, he rode back west.

Later that month, Franciscan friars Francisco Atanasio Domínguez and Silvestre Vélez de Escalante struck northwest from Santa Fe. Instead of reaching Monterey, they and their small party got as far as Utah Lake. From there, with no sign that they were on the right track and winter approaching, they swung south and east toward the Grand Canyon and with great difficulty lowered themselves, their animals, and gear down the slick rock to the so-called Crossing of

FREEDOM SUIT
On July 4, 1776, even as Father Garcés explored the Southwest, England's Thirteen Colonies declared their independence. This freedom suit from one of those colonies, Rhode Island, was intended to be used by an indentured servant after his servitude was over.

the Fathers, submerged today by Lake Powell. The Hopis at Oraibi tolerated them overnight. Finally, back in Santa Fe on January 2, 1777, they closed their valiant, up-and-down, 1,800-mile loop through the Great Basin.

Although single-minded risk takers like Bodega y Quadra, Garcés, and Domínguez and Escalante filed notable diaries and contributed to geographical knowledge about the American West, their feats of exploration remained precisely that. Colonization did not follow. Simply holding the existing line all but consumed spit-and-polish Teodoro de Croix, Gálvez's choice as first commandant general. When Croix learned in 1779 that Spain had declared war on England, which meant a shift of military resources to the Mississippi Valley and Gulf Coast theaters, he patriotically dropped his request for an additional 2,000 men.

"OH! WHAT LANDS SO SUITABLE FOR MISSIONS! OH! WHAT A HEATHENDOM SO DOCILE! HOW FINE IT WOULD BE IF THE WISE AND PIOUS DON CARLOS III MIGHT SEE THESE LANDS!"

—DIARY OF FATHER GARCÉS, 1774

CONTINENTAL ARMY COAT
Spain took sides against Great Britain in the American Revolution, aiding the rebels represented by this uniform coat from 1777.

"I RECOGNIZED FROM HIS PENNANTS AND INSIGNIAS THE FAMOUS CHIEF CUERNO VERDE... AND HIS HAUGHTY AND ARROGANT MANNER CAUSED ME TO RESOLVE TO DEPRIVE HIM OF HIS LIFE."

—DIARY OF NEW MEXICO GOVERNOR JUAN BAUTISTA DE ANZA, 1779

THE WEST DURING THE AMERICAN REVOLUTION

AS SPAIN JOINED THE WAR AGAINST GREAT BRITAIN, FINANCIAL SUPPORT FOR THE SPANISH COLONIES IN THE WEST DWINDLED, FORCING OFFICIALS IN NEW SPAIN TO DEVELOP NEW WAYS OF DEALING WITH NATIVE PEOPLES—FROM MAKING STRATEGIC MILITARY ALLIANCES WITH FORMER ENEMIES TO ENSURING PEACEFUL RELATIONS THROUGH FREQUENT AND LIBERAL GIFTS OF EUROPEAN TRADE GOODS.

AN ABSOLUTE MONARCHY, Spain had no love for the thirteen British North American colonies that had declared their independence from England in 1776. Yet by joining with France to aid in the fight, Spain stood not only to harm a hereditary enemy but also to regain Florida, lost in the previous war. Thus, while presidial captains on New Spain's northern frontier collected donations from their men toward the war effort, Commandant General Croix cut back on defense projects in the American West.

THE YUMA MASSACRE
Original plans had called for a full-strength garrison and missions to hold the strategic Colorado River crossing on the road to California. But Croix economized, providing instead for two low-budget settlements that took irregular shape on the west bank in 1780. Each housed two Franciscans and twenty-five colonist families. So many intruders, humans and animals, quickly strained the fragile riverside environment. The Yuma Indians grew resentful, and in the airless heat of mid-July 1781, they erupted, killing even fray Francisco Garcés, whom no Spaniard thought they would harm.

Unaware of their good fortune, a train of emigrant families had just departed westward for

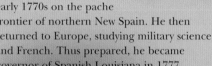

California, bound to settle Los Angeles that year. Most of their military escort, however, doubled back for horses and mules that had been too weak to swim the river. These jaded men and their commander died in the massacre. Later, the ransomed widow of Lieutenant Santiago Islas lamented that she could never forget "the night my heart was broken, when my beloved husband was clubbed to death before my very eyes." The Yumas, unrepentant, had cut the overland way to California.

That colony, having survived its early years, was by the 1780s well on its way to self-sufficiency. Benign climate and rich soils rewarded the efforts of those colonists already settled in its coastal valleys. Cattle and horses did phenomenally well. So did wheat. With a stable food supply, the missions grew to house far larger populations than any previous such establishments on the northern frontier. Despite the mission Indians' high death and runaway rates, syphilis, unsanitary quarters, and altered gender roles, the Franciscans baptized thousands and produced surpluses of foodstuffs for sale to presidios and civil settlements.

Recruiting schemes to reinforce California's small non-Indian population resulted in passage by ship of no more than a few dozen artisans, whores, orphans, and convicts and their wives. Some served their time and left. Yet Hispanic *californios*, like Texans or New Mexicans, produced large families and multiplied steadily, until by 1790 they

AMERICAN REVOLUTION RIFLE

The Pennsylvania or Kentucky rifle, a muzzleloader, originated around 1720. Also known as the "long rifle," it was slim, lightweight, and highly accurate, requiring less powder than its predecessors. Popular with frontiersmen and wielded in the American Revolution, the rifle remained in use into the nineteenth century.

YUMA INDIANS

The Yuma people, numbering around 3,000 by the mid-1800s, made their home throughout southwest Arizona. This illustration, made in the mid-nineteenth century, shows Yumas who have learned to combine native and European traditions.

numbered 1,000. Favored by their pastoral environment and the absence of Apaches, the Hispanic residents of California had it relatively easy. Too easy, thought American ship captains out of Salem, Massachusetts, and other American ports, who in the 1790s began putting in at San Diego and Monterey for provisions.

BERNARDO DE GÁLVEZ

A hero of Spanish action against England during the American Revolution, Bernardo de Gálvez governed Louisiana between 1777 and 1783. The only nephew of Jose de Gálvez, don Bernardo convinced his uncle that the French method of dealing with non-Christian native peoples —making them dependent trade partners and allies—could work in the western provinces as

CALIFORNIAN NATIVES DANCING

This scene at the San Francisco Mission is drawn from Picturesque Travels Around the World, 1822, *by Otto von Kotzebue. Kotzebue was a Russian naval officer who commanded two voyages around the world and traveled on a third.*

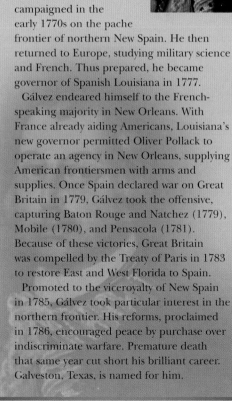

⇥ BERNARDO DE GÁLVEZ ⇤

BORN IN Spain, Bernardo de Gálvez (1746–86), who greatly admired France, became an easy ally and hero of American patriots during the American Revolution. Nephew and protégé of Spanish colonial administrator José de Gálvez, Bernardo campaigned in the early 1770s on the pache frontier of northern New Spain. He then returned to Europe, studying military science and French. Thus prepared, he became governor of Spanish Louisiana in 1777.

Gálvez endeared himself to the French-speaking majority in New Orleans. With France already aiding Americans, Louisiana's new governor permitted Oliver Pollack to operate an agency in New Orleans, supplying American frontiersmen with arms and supplies. Once Spain declared war on Great Britain in 1779, Gálvez took the offensive, capturing Baton Rouge and Natchez (1779), Mobile (1780), and Pensacola (1781). Because of these victories, Great Britain was compelled by the Treaty of Paris in 1783 to restore East and West Florida to Spain.

Promoted to the viceroyalty of New Spain in 1785, Gálvez took particular interest in the northern frontier. His reforms, proclaimed in 1786, encouraged peace by purchase over indiscriminate warfare. Premature death that same year cut short his brilliant career. Galveston, Texas, is named for him.

well. In 1779 Jose de Gálvez, admitting the hopelessness of defeating Apaches militarily, urged Commandant General Croix to offer gifts, alliance, and commerce, even firearms. Then, in 1785, when Bernardo de Gálvez became viceroy of New Spain, he subordinated the command structure of the Interior Provinces to himself and promulgated his *Instructions* of 1786, in effect a program of cultural genocide.

Victory over the *indios bárbaros*, Bernardo de Gálvez believed, would be won only by "obliging them to destroy one another." He ordered commanders to accept any peace overture. That gave enemy bands a choice. They could keep on raiding and risk Spanish retaliation, symbolized by the sun-shriveled Apache heads stuck on the

wall of the Tucson presidio, or they could opt for treaties, firearms, gifts, and land if they chose. Dependency was the goal. Bound to Spanish suppliers for powder and repair of purposely inferior trade guns, native fighting men would war not against Spaniards but against the latter's enemies.

Gálvez also wanted to get them drunk. According to him, the so-called Nations of the North, the tribes beyond San Antonio, already had a fondness for liquor. Now, if only he could addict the Apaches. "The supplying of drink to the Indians," Gálvez reasoned, "will be a means of gaining their good will, discovering their secrets, calming them so that they will think less often of conceiving and executing their hostilities,

and creating for them a new necessity which will oblige them to recognize their dependence upon us more directly." Evidently, however, owing to the thirst of Hispanic colonists and short supply, liquor dealers on the frontier had little to offer.

ANZA AND THE COMANCHES

Juan Bautista de Anza, acceding to the governorship of New Mexico in 1778, carried specific orders to divert the Comanches, scourge of the colony. Previous governors had tried to enlist Comanches against Apaches. Negotiations with headmen from one or another band among the Comanche nation's several divisions had proven all but useless. Anza had to get the attention of them all. He wasted no time. At the head of 600 Hispanos and Indians, he ventured northwest into present-day Colorado, scoring an unexpected victory in August 1779 over the notorious Comanche war leader Cuerno Verde. Word of the feat spread like grass fire. Almost

before he could package his trophy—Cuerno Verde's boastful headdress with its single green buffalo horne—for shipment to the commandant general, every Comanche fighting man knew who Anza was.

Yet alliance waited. Efforts to sway drought-stricken Hopis, open a road between New Mexico and Sonora, and capture elk live for the royal zoo in Madrid occupied the governor. In 1780–81 the worst smallpox epidemic of the century descended on much of North America. In New Mexico, thousands of Pueblo Indians and hundreds of Hispanos succumbed. So, evidently, did many Comanches. More survived, *caripicados*, with pock-marked faces.

Finally, in 1786 Comanches, for their own good reasons, chose to pursue an alliance with Anza. For the emissaries on both sides, the process of peacemaking was almost fun. Participants in the culmination at Pecos, a pueblo decimated by previous Comanche raids, could not have been

more demonstrative, exchanging speeches, gifts, and affectionate gestures. Anza the diplomat submitted to countless embraces. The Comanches' principal leader, Ecueracapa, bedecked in the regalia of a native captain general, presided with dignity. By the terms of the treaty, Comanches were free to move closer to New Mexico, call on the governor in Santa Fe, and trade at Pecos. They swore, for their part, to keep the peace with New Mexicans and carry war to the camps of eastern Apaches. And the treaty held.

Instead of reports of killings and abductions by Comanches, Anza now received tally sheets neatly filled out by these former enemies indicating with marks the casualties they had inflicted on Apaches. Each spring when the annual trade caravan returned from Chihuahua, delegations of these non-Christian allies, along with Utes, Navajos, and Jicarilla Apaches—New Mexico's four allied tribes—lined up at the government warehouse for gifts. Considered a military expense, Spaniards

furnished bolts of bright cloth, hats, shoes, knives, mirrors, rope, strings of beads, coral, vermillion, indigo, bars of soap, cigarettes, and *piloncillos*, rock-hard cones of raw sugar. For peace, this was a small enough price to pay.

The Comanche treaty also opened the Pecos drainage to Hispanic settlement and the Plains to travel. Pedro Vial, a gunsmith from Lyon, France, who became the consummate Plains Indian agent and traveler, tested Comanche commitment when he rode with only one companion from San Antonio, Texas, to Santa Fe in 1786–87. His next excursion, in 1788–89, took him 2,400 miles, from Santa Fe to Natchitoches in Louisiana, then back via San Antonio to Santa Fe. Finally, in 1792–93, he traced what would become the Santa Fe Trail, from Santa Fe to St. Louis in today's Missouri and back. By that time, aggressive, westward-moving *americanos* of the United States gazed eagerly across the Mississippi at the increasingly peaceful and economically inviting northern colonies of Spain.

OLD MESILLA PLAZA
Mesilla, shown here in the nineteenth century, is testimony to the westward-moving nature of Americans. The town was founded on the Mexican side of the border c. 1848 by nuevomexicanos who did not want to be part of the U.S. takeover of the Southwest. Even so, Mesilla was acquired by the United States with the Gadsden Purchase in 1853.

JOSEPH BONAPARTE
This eldest surviving brother of Napoleon was awarded the Spanish throne in 1808. An unsuccessful king, he abdicated in 1813.

"I WANT YOUR CHILDREN'S CHILDREN TO PRESERVE MY MEMORY AND SAY: HE IS THE REGENERATOR OF OUR FATHERLAND."

—NAPOLEON BONAPARTE, PROCLAMATION TO SPAIN, MAY 25, 1808

SPAIN AND THE UNITED STATES

THE FINAL YEARS OF THE EIGHTEENTH CENTURY SAW SPAIN'S HOLD ON ITS WESTERN TERRITORIES WEAKENING. EMBROILED IN POLITICAL TURMOIL IN EUROPE, THE MOTHER COUNTRY COULD PAY ONLY SCANT ATTENTION TO NEW SPAIN. ALL THE WHILE, THREATS POSED BY THE NEWLY FORMED UNITED STATES GREW AS AMERICANS, HUNGRY FOR LAND AND WEALTH, BEGAN EYEING THE SPANISH COLONIES.

ANOTHER TREATY signed at Paris in 1783 brought an end to the American Revolution. Spain recovered east and west Florida but gained another formidable rival. The newly independent and expansionist United States took over the former British territory stretching west to the Mississippi River, while England retained Canada.

The American West, for Spain, became a paradox. While peace with the Comanches and other native nations promised growth and security in the Interior Province, these conditions also made Spanish territory more appealing to imperial rivals. Ever bolder and more numerous, they seemed to come from all sides. Few Americans at this stage dreamed of manifest destiny, the later doctrine justifying their expansion as far as the Pacific. Instead they were out for personal gain: supply contracts, furs, horses, hides and tallow, free land, and whatever else beckoned. If the

ARRIVING IN CANADA
Missionaries and other Europeans land in eighteenth-century Canada in this engraving by J. M. Dumesnil.

Spanish general staff stuck colored pins in a great map of North America to represent foreign penetration, three clusters began taking shape. Along the California and North Pacific coast, English, American, and Russian pins intermingled. From the lower Mississippi Valley into Texas, they were mostly American. And westward from the Great Lakes and upper Mississippi Valley, again English and American pins vied.

Such a profusion of threats would have caused alarm in any period. But these were also years of unprecedented turmoil in Europe. First, the French Revolution (1789–99) toppled the French monarchy, and several European nations, including Spain, went to war against republican France. Emerging as France's dictatorial leader, Napoleon Bonaparte set about dominating Europe in the Napoleonic Wars (1799–1815). Spain, under Charles III's weak successors, struggled to maintain its national identity, then became a satellite of France. Napoleon forced Spain to cede Louisiana back to France in 1800, then sold it to the United States in 1803, vaulting Americans westward. In a final indignity, in 1808, Napoleon placed his brother, Joseph Bonaparte, on the Spanish throne, prompting revolts in Spain and Spanish America. Bloody but abortive, the revolution for independence that engulfed central New Spain in 1810 invited U.S. intervention. Against this chaotic backdrop, Spain's less-than-vigorous defense of its colonial empire becomes readily understandable.

FALL OF THE BASTILLE
This Parisian fortress and prison was stormed by a crowd of rebels on July 14, 1789, marking the start of the French Revolution. Through this period of bloody unrest, the French monarchy was overthrown and Napoleon emerged to seek domination of Europe.

PALACE OF THE GOVERNORS
This adobe building in Santa Fe, shown in a twentieth-century photograph, was built in the early seventeenth century as the seat of administration for Spanish rule of the Southwest. It now serves as a history museum for the state of New Mexico.

THE PACIFIC NORTHWEST

In 1789, when the feisty Esteban José Martínez sailed the frigate *Princesa* into Nootka Sound on the seaward side of present-day Vancouver Island with plans for a Spanish settlement, ships from other nations already rode at anchor. American skippers like Robert Gray of the sloop *Lady Washington* were too busy to care, trading hardware and dry goods to coastal natives for lustrous otter furs. An Englishman, James Colnett of the *Argonaut*, however, took issue with Martínez. Colnett, representing a London commercial firm, proposed to build a trading post ashore. After both had drunk heartily, the debate degenerated. "God damn Spain!" Colnett blurted. Never one to ignore an insult, Martínez arrested the British captain and seized his vessel. As the operetta played on, the Spaniards captured another British ship, put prize crews aboard both, and sailed them to San Blas. During the resulting international crisis, which ran its course between 1790 and 1795, Spanish negotiators backed down, formally allowing the right of other nations to frequent the north coast.

TEXAS AND CALIFORNIA

At mid-continent, too, by treaty with the United States in 1795, Spain made other concessions, allowing a boundary for west Florida generously far south and permitting free navigation of the

109

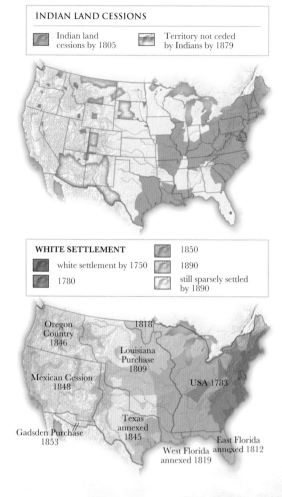

INDIAN LAND CESSIONS

Indian land cessions by 1805	Territory not ceded by Indians by 1879

WHITE SETTLEMENT

white settlement by 1750		1850
1780		1890
		still sparsely settled by 1890

Oregon Country 1846

1818

Louisiana Purchase 1809

Mexican Cession 1848

USA 1783

Gadsden Purchase 1853

Texas annexed 1845

West Florida annexed 1819

East Florida annexed 1812

INDIAN LAND CESSIONS AND WHITE SETTLEMENT

Confronted by successive waves of European settlers, Native Americans signed successive treaties by which they eventually ceded their lands, traditional or otherwise. By the end of the nineteenth century, in legal terms, over eighty percent of the coterminous United States was legally in white settler hands.

Mississippi, something Americans had been doing illegally for years. Upriver, Spain was more concerned about Englishmen. North of St. Louis, British companies in Canada controlled the Indian trade. Spaniards feared that English wilderness agents would work westward, then drop down to Santa Fe. Competition intensified in the 1790s, as Spanish officials at St. Louis encouraged local trading companies to challenge British dealers and redirect the flow of furs southward from the Mandan-Hidatsa-Arikara trade centers on the Missouri River.

Former British subjects, now citizens of the United States, pressed against the full length of the Mississippi boundary from St. Louis to New Orleans. Many crossed over, especially into lower Louisiana and Texas: adventurers, land seekers, mustangers, and traders. Louisiana's prophetic Governor Manuel Gayoso de

Lemos in 1798 likened their influx to an infestation of destructive insects. "They introduce themselves in the thickness of the forests, like the Indians…They are settled in sufficient numbers so that they will establish their customs, laws, and religion. They will form independent states, aggregating themselves to the Federal Union, which will not refuse to receive them, and progressively they will go as far as the Pacific Ocean."

Unbridled Philip Nolan epitomized such intruders. An Irishman from Kentucky, he took dubious oaths to Spain and engaged in questionable ventures with Gayoso. He dealt in wild Texas horses and kept a place and mistress at Nacogdoches, a community founded in 1779 deep in the woods of east Texas and home to a rowdy bunch of traders, hunters, and smugglers. During the 1790s, Spanish officials alternately issued passports to Nolan and ordered his arrest. He, at the same time, gathered information for his scheming former employer, General James Wilkinson, who passed it on to then-Vice President Thomas Jefferson.

Late in 1800, when Nolan led a couple of dozen formidably armed men into central Texas, Commandant General Pedro de Nava called for his arrest. Strangely, Nolan and his band hunkered down and built shelters on

THE BRITISH IN CANADA
British companies in Canada controlled the fur trade north of St. Louis in the late eighteenth century. Although the British acquired Canada only in 1763, they had briefly captured Quebec in 1629, as shown in this illustration.

"THESE LAST WERE UNFORTUNATE MEN WHO PUT CONFIDENCE IN SPANISH PROMISES. THESE ARE A PEOPLE IN WHOM YOU SHOULD PUT NO TRUST OR CONFIDENCE WHATEVER."

—ELLIS P. BEAN OF PHILIP NOLAN'S PARTY, ON BEING IMPRISONED BY SPANISH FORCES

THE LAUNCH OF THE NORTH WEST AMERICA
The British sloop North West America *was built on Nootka Sound in 1788. The first of its kind to be built in the Pacific Northwest, the ship reinforced Britain's territorial claim, which Spain contested by sending an expedition led by Esteban José Martínez. In 1789, Martínez seized the* North West America *and another British ship, the* Argonaut, *sparking a crisis that ended in 1795 with Spain permitting other nations to frequent the region.*

the Brazos River near today's Waco, where they wintered and collected horses. In March, surrounded by a much larger force from the Nacogdoches garrison, Nolan chose to die fighting.

To seaborne Americans who visited it, California held even greater promise than Texas. In 1803, William Shaler of the *Lelia Byrd* from Salem, Massachusetts, noted covetously how easy it would be to capture California. "For several years past," he wrote in an account published in 1808, "the American trading ships have frequented this coast in search of furs, for which they have left in the country about 25,000 dollars annually, in specie and merchandize…At present, a person acquainted with the coast may always produce abundant supplies of provisions. All these circumstances prove that, under a good government, the Californias would soon rise to ease and affluence."

SANTE FE

In most respects, Santa Fe, New Mexico, typified Spanish communities in the American West. When Pedro Vial rode out of town in 1804 with orders to arrest Lewis and Clark, he left behind a European municipality founded in 1610, 194 years earlier.

With a population of nearly 5,000, Santa Fe in 1804 boasted no cathedral, printing press, or university. But there was an adobe-built governor's palace fronting on the town plaza, with military barracks behind; a well-attended primary school attached to the presidio; three churches, soon to be four; several active religious confraternities; and no beggars. Santa Fe had a doctor, don Cristóbal de Larrañaga, surgeon of the garrison, who in 1804 vaccinated children against smallpox with vaccine that had arrived in the arms of inoculated boys.

⊹SANTA FE⊹

TO MARK THE CHANGE from proprietary to crown colony, New Mexico's second governor, Pedro de Peralta, formally founded Santa Fe (Holy Faith) in 1610. Designated a villa, or chartered municipality second only to a ciudad, or city, the community served as the capital of Spanish New Mexico until the Pueblo Revolt of 1680, when its residents fled down the Rio Grande and occupying Pueblo Indians built a multistoried tenement right over the former governors' palace. Not until late 1693 did Governor Diego de Vargas recapture Santa Fe.

Despite its relative isolation and the influence of surrounding Pueblo Indians, New Mexico's mud-built capital, crude though it was, remained essentially Spanish. Its religion, language, food, architecture, and art, including music and dance, were all firmly rooted in Spanish tradition. Somewhat awkwardly, Santa Fe's several thousand residents celebrated Mexican independence early in 1822, ending Spanish rule. With the simultaneous opening of the Santa Fe Trail, a traders' route between the Missouri frontier of the United States and Mexican Santa Fe, a great variety of relatively cheap manufactured goods flooded the community. The U.S. flag followed in 1846, when American troops under Brigadier General Stephen Watts Kearny occupied Santa Fe. Two years later, New Mexico was ceded to the United States, and Santa Fe's enduring Spanish traditions became part of the culture of the American Southwest.

SANTA FE
By the time this late nineteenth-century photograph was taken of a dirt road in front of a row of stores, Santa Fe belonged to the United States.

The wealthier families of Santa Fe—Ortiz, Pino, Archuleta, Sena, and Delgado—enjoyed putting on airs, dressing up, and strutting. Based more on their social position than blood, they considered themselves *españoles* and everyone else beneath them.

Because so many *santafecinos* were related, church officials routinely conducted prenuptial investigations. Judging from these records, as well as civil and criminal proceedings filling the archive, the populace of Santa Fe rarely lacked deviant behavior to gossip about. Not ncommonly, women accused priests of soliciting sex in the confessional. And so it was in San Antonio, Tucson, and Monterey.

Because farming land around Santa Fe had filled up, Lorenzo Márquez and fifty-one heads of family petitioned for a community land grant about fifty miles southeast at the uninhabited ford of the Pecos River. They called their settlement San Miguel del Bado.

To earn title, the law required that they make improvements and occupy the land for five years. In 1803 don Pedro Bautista Pino, Santa Fe's

district officer, put the families in final possession of their land and ditch frontage. When he finished, Pino recalled, "upon taking leave of them (having refused the fee they were going to give me for my labor), my heart, at that moment as never before, was overcome with joy. Parents and little children surrounded me, all of them expressing, even to the point of tears, their gratitude to me for having given them lands for their subsistence."

By that time, however, Spanish sovereignty on New Spain's far northern frontier was growing precarious. Just how far did the Louisiana Purchase of 1803 extend to the west?

In 1821, the year of Mexican independence, William Becknell, a gritty, semiliterate Missouri trader, predicted he could get wagons through to Mexican Santa Fe, crossing the Pecos River at San Miguel del Bado. Mountain men who bothered could now obtain licenses to trap beaver on the Rio Grande and Gila. Why not a whiskey distillery at Taos? Meanwhile in Mexican

Texas, empresario Stephen F. Austin had begun relocating hundreds of American Catholic families to new homes on the Brazos River. On the West Coast, arriving by sea, American agents in the hide-and-tallow trade were taking up comfortable residence in Mexican California.

Plainly, the American West had begun to overlay the Spanish North. And that, as time would tell, was Mexico's problem.

⇒AN INDIAN-SPANISH PRAYER BOARD⇐

A RECENTLY rediscovered prayer board provides a glimpse into one of the places where Spaniards and Native Americans interacted: Spanish mission schools. The prayer board, about eight inches wide by twelve inches high, was apparently used as a kind of textbook by teachers who held it up before the Indian children who were their students. The text is written in ink on paper and pasted on both sides of a wood board equipped with a handle at the bottom. On one side are prayers and songs in Spanish, Latin, and the Salinan Indian language of southern California; on the other are Acts of Faith, Hope, and Charity in Spanish and Salinan. Collected in 1817, the prayer board was evidently the work of two Franciscan missionaries, Father Miguel Pieras and Father Bonaventura Sitjar. The former died in 1795, the latter in 1808. Although the Salinan language is long dead, the prayer board commemorates a time when it was still alive and in close contact with Spanish.

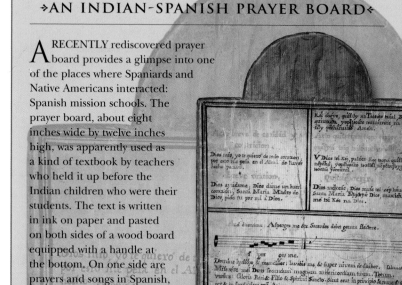

RARE FIND
This prayer board is one of only two of its kind in existence. Its text is in Spanish, Latin, and Salinan.

SUNSET AT SANTA BARBARA
Evening light colors the stone façade of mission Santa Barbara, founded in 1786. Still used for church services, Santa Barbara is the only California mission under the continuous control of Franciscan priests since the day it was founded.

"THE GENIAL INFLUENCES OF
CULTIVATED SOCIETY WILL BE
LIKE THE SUN SHEDDING LIGHT,
FRAGRANCE, AND BEAUTY."

—STEPHEN F. AUSTIN, REFLECTING ON
HIS AIMS IN COLONIZING TEXAS, 1832

CHAPTER 3

THE WINDS OF CHANGE

1800–1840

WITH THE BIRTH OF THE UNITED STATES, WINDS OF CHANGE BEGAN TO BLOW ACROSS THE WEST. IN THE LATE EIGHTEENTH CENTURY, THE REGION REMAINED LARGELY THE IMPERIAL PRESERVE OF SPAIN, BRITAIN, AND RUSSIA, BUT THE LOUISIANA PURCHASE IN 1803 BROUGHT THE UNITED STATES DIRECTLY INTO THE CONTEST. LEWIS AND CLARK'S JOURNEY OF DISCOVERY OPENED UP NEW REGIONS WEST OF THE MISSISSIPPI RIVER TO AMERICAN EXPLORERS AND MOUNTAIN MEN, WHO PREPARED THE WAY FOR THEIR NATION'S EXPANSION ACROSS THE CONTINENT.

THE IMPERIAL WEST

THE END OF THE EIGHTEENTH CENTURY SAW DRAMATIC SHIFTS IN THE CONTINUING BATTLE FOR CONTROL OF THE WEST. EXCITED BY VISIONS OF TERRITORIAL EXPANSION, ENGLAND, RUSSIA, AND THE UNITED STATES SENT TRADERS TO STAKE OUT CLAIMS IN THE NORTHWEST, ENDANGERING SPAIN'S ONCE SEEMINGLY UNSHAKABLE HOLD ON ITS WESTERN LANDS.

SOUTH CAROLINA PLANTER, politician, and jurist William Henry Drayton never saw the West over the Alleghenies and hardly imagined regions beyond the Mississippi, but he knew the meaning of American independence for those lands and the people who called them home. Writing in 1776, the year of independence, Drayton proclaimed an American nation of continental sweep. "The Almighty," he boasted, "has made choice of this present generation to erect the American empire." That claim hardly squared with the real power and immediate circumstances of the first U.S. states during the American Revolution.

WILLIAM DRAYTON
Even before U.S. independence, Drayton predicted the nation's westward expansion.

But in the largest sense, Drayton was right. The Revolution created a nation rooted in an imperial ideology, with an economic and political system well-suited to what historical geographer D. W. Meinig has called "the Outward Movement."

The implications of American independence and the creation of an expansion-minded nation were not lost on policy makers in London, Madrid, Montreal, or Mexico City. Spanish officials, long suspicious of English designs on the lands south and west of St. Louis, were especially alert to the moves of the American republic. In 1783, the year the Revolution ended, Spanish colonial official Juan Gassiot took

YELLOWSTONE FALLS

Spectacular scenery, such as that seen in this 1885 photograph of the falls of the Yellowstone River, filled early western travelers with awe.

DECLARATION OF INDEPENDENCE

After declaring and winning independence, the United States emerged as a rival to European powers for control of the West.

the measure of his neighbors. "A new and independent power has now arisen on our continent. Its people are active, industrious, and aggressive. It would be culpable negligence on our part not to thwart their schemes of conquest." Those "schemes of conquest" seemed even more threatening five years later when Manuel Antonio Florez, viceroy of New Spain, surveyed the western scene from Mexico City. American settlers and merchants were fully established in Kentucky, tensions over passage rights on the Mississippi were increasing, and American traders were ever more visible on the Northwest coast. The viceroy shrewdly calculated the western consequences of American independence and found that "we ought not to be surprised that the English colonies of America, being now an independent Republic, should carry out the design of finding a safe port on the Pacific and of attempting to sustain it by crossing the immense country of the continent above our possessions of Texas, New Mexico, and California." Twenty years before John Jacob Astor laid plans for an American commercial empire in the Northwest and more than half a century before

THE EARLY AMERICAN ECONOMY TO C. 1820

The colonial "Triangular Trade" system set the pattern for the overseas trading system of the independent United States. High-value products such as furs proved cash earners; crops such as tobacco and cotton provided a stable basis for European trade.

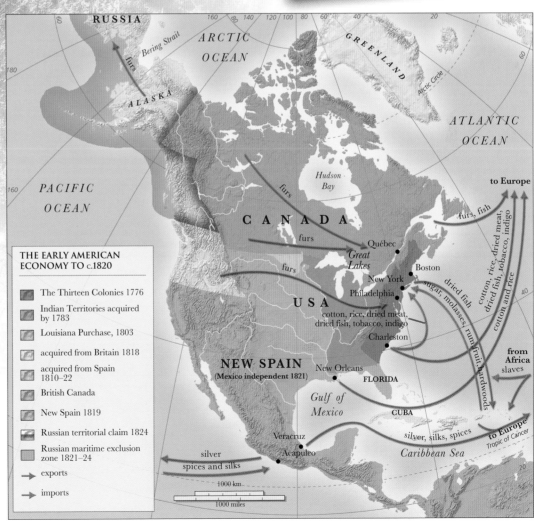

THE EARLY AMERICAN ECONOMY TO c.1820

- The Thirteen Colonies 1776
- Indian Territories acquired by 1783
- Louisiana Purchase, 1803
- acquired from Britain 1818
- acquired from Spain 1810–22
- British Canada
- New Spain 1819
- Russian territorial claim 1824
- Russian maritime exclusion zone 1821–24
- → exports
- → imports

117

the Oregon Trail migrations, Florez had an inkling about what 1776 had set in motion. Another Spanish official was far less diplomatic. Captain Jose Vidal branded Americans as "ambitious, restless, lawless, conniving, changeable, and turbulent."

FUR TRADE STRATEGISTS

In 1800 Canadian explorers, traders, and adventurers were on the edge of securing the West for the British empire. Having lost the Atlantic colonies, Britain seemed ready to fashion a second empire from Lake Winnipeg in what is now Manitoba to the Northwest coast. These imperialist energies were charged by two powerful forces. The fur trade had long been a stimulus for territorial expansion. As representatives of the North West Company, Canada's most aggressive fur-trading firm, explained: "It is the peculiar nature of the Fur Trade to require a continual extension of its limits, into new Countries." Competition between the more established Hudson's Bay Company and the younger North West Company sparked a widening search for new trapping and trading territories. That quest was guided by one of the oldest and most durable ideas in the European exploration of North America. From the sixteenth century on, explorers looked in vain for the Northwest Passage, a fabled water route connecting the Atlantic and Pacific Oceans. For Canadian fur- trade strategists, finding the Northwest Passage meant connecting Montreal, Lake Winnipeg, the Athabasca trading grounds, and the Northwest coast to the China

✦THE CANADIAN FUR TRADE✦

THE fur trade in Canada had its roots in the sixteenth century, when French fishermen sailed to the Grand Banks, landing on Newfoundland and Cape Breton Island. The furs they brought back from trading with the local natives aroused interest in France, and King Henry IV granted charters to fur-trading companies with the double aim of competing with English colonial ambitions and providing a profitable industry for France.

Young Frenchmen who wanted excitement or challenge took to trading goods with Native Americans for the furs France wanted. Meanwhile, although the French claimed Canada, the British had given a charter to the Hudson's Bay Company in 1670, and this soon controlled the fur trade in northern areas. When Canada became a British possession in 1763, the Hudson's Bay Company became the dominant fur-trading organization, though many French trappers continued on an individual basis. They were joined by Scotsmen who brought in new ideas of trading. While the Hudson's Bay Company had established posts to which Native Americans brought furs, the Scots and French went out and transacted business directly with the Indians. This resulted in their expanding the trade westward and south, into the Louisiana Territory. In fact, French traders had reached the Dakotas by 1738, before English settlers to the south had crossed the Alleghenies.

Competition among the French and Scots traders was fierce, but in 1779 they agreed to consolidate their interests. This was formalized in the winter of 1783–84, and the North West Company was born. For nearly four decades, North West and Hudson's Bay fought for control of the fur trade. The Nor'Westers created an efficient system of transporting furs whereby trappers and traders from the West met supply canoes from Montreal at Fort William, on the western edge of Lake Superior, and exchanged furs for trade goods and supplies. (The later mountain men used the same system with their annual rendezvous.)

The bitter rivalry between Hudson's Bay and North West led to violent clashes, and in 1821 the British government forced the two companies to amalgamate. In any event, the fur trade was in serious decline by this time due to over-trapping and the clearing of land for farming. By the 1870s it had all but ended.

HUDSON'S BAY TRAPPERS
During the height of the fur trade, the motley employees of the Hudson's Bay Company explored much of present-day Canada in a search for new lands where they could trap and trade.

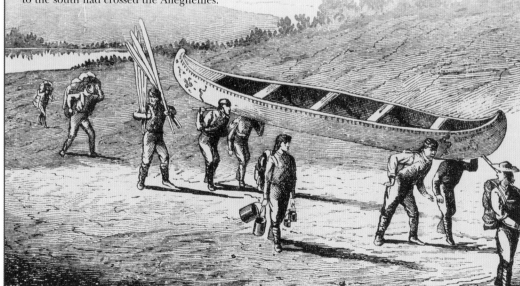

market in Canton. The West would become part of a large-scale British economic system with unmistakable political and cultural consequences for North America.

Such dreams were the result of efforts made by a small group of ambitious and sometimes ruthless visionaries. While no single individual could claim leadership, Peter Pond came closer than most to being its intellectual godfather. Born in Milford, Connecticut, in 1740, Pond left his apprenticeship as a cobbler, joined the Connecticut provincial militia, and eventually sailed to the West Indies on a merchant voyage. With the French gone from the Great Lakes, many English traders headed to the lakes hoping to make profit in the expanding fur business. Pond soon became part of that trading world. But he and other "pedlars from Quebec" as they were called, knew that the richest pelts came from beyond Lake Winnipeg. By the mid-1770s Pond and fellow traders Alexander Henry the Elder and Joseph Frobisher were doing business with native trappers west of Winnipeg.

The widening fur business and competition with the Hudson's Bay Company drew Pond and his sometime-partner Henry deeper into the Northwest. There they collected more than pelts and profits. They gathered information and formulated strategies that put the Canadians at the forefront of the race for empire in the West. In 1776, the same year Drayton proclaimed the American empire, Henry heard Indians describe a river and lake system that supposedly led directly to the Pacific. Two years later Pond took his canoes up the Churchill River, over Methye Portage, and into the fur-rich Athabasca country.

At the same time, more than a thousand miles to the west, British explorer Captain James Cook probed the Alaska coast in search of the Northwest Passage. Cook was persuaded that an inlet later called Cook's River led deep in the interior, perhaps even connecting to the lakes Pond and Henry knew so well. By the 1780s Pond and Henry had taken these fragments and constructed a geography of empire. As they imagined it, the Canadian West was ribboned by a series of water

COAST OF ALASKA

In 1778, British captain James Cook explored the Pacific Coast while looking for the Northwest Passage.

→JAMES COOK←

AMONG the greatest of British maritime explorers, James Cook (1728–79) joined the Royal Navy in 1755. He charted the St. Lawrence River in 1759 and the coast of Newfoundland in 1762. In 1768–71 he circumnavigated New Zealand, charting the coastline as he went, and surveyed Australia's east coast. On his second expedition (1772–75), Cook sailed to the Antarctic and explored the South Pacific, returning home via Easter Island, Tonga, and Cape Horn. His third and last mission, begun in June 1776, was to look for the Northwest Passage. He sailed to Tasmania and New Zealand, reaching the Sandwich Islands (now the Hawaiian Islands) in February 1778. He went on to the west coast of America, sailing north to the Bering Straits. Along the way, he became the first European to land on Vancouver Island and discovered what is now Nootka Sound. On his return journey, in February 1779, he was killed by Hawaiian natives.

NOOTKA SOUND
Though tranquil-looking, Nootka Sound on Vancouver Island became the center of an international crisis between England and Spain in 1795.

its boundaries, Louisiana was a Spanish possession. California marked the western edge of Spain in America. Important military events on the Gulf Coast, often ignored in standard accounts of the American Revolution, firmly established Spanish influence in that region, and both East and West Florida were under Spanish administration. With powerful Indian allies, a corps of energetic officials, and a professional army, Spain seemed secure in the West.

But Spanish strength was more apparent than real. The decade of the 1790s saw one storm after another. The winds of change first blew along the northern reaches of the Pacific Northwest coast. Spain had paid little attention to the coast of what is now Oregon, Washington, and British Columbia until the dramatic expansion of the sea otter trade with China. Once European and American merchants heard about the market for furs at Canton, ships flying many flags raced to the north Pacific. And there was the increased presence of the Russians, thanks to the leadership of Russian-American Company general manager Alexander Baranov. The same Viceroy Manuel Antonio Florez who predicted American expansion across the continent to the Pacific now worried about a combined British-American-Russian threat on the Northwest coast. The viceroy

highways: Great Slave Lake and Cook's River were the fabled Northwest Passage; and the Rocky Mountains, envisioned as a series of low ridges with many gaps and passes, would be no obstacle to the Canadian course of empire.

Throughout the 1780s both Pond and Henry promoted exploration schemes aimed at finding routes to the Pacific. No one paid more attention to those ideas than Alexander Mackenzie, a young trader in the employ of the North West Company. During the winter of 1787–88, Mackenzie wintered with Pond at Athabasca. That season was Mackenzie's education in fur-trade geography and imperial strategy. From his mentor, Mackenzie learned about river systems, the promise of the Pacific, and the belief that Cook's River was the true Northwest Passage.

Pond's ideas, now carried by Mackenzie, found a home in the North West Company. The Nor'westers were determined to out-trade, out-smart, and out-flank the Hudson's Bay Company. Mackenzie's journey from Atlantic to Pacific waters in 1793 was far more than simply the first crossing of the continent north of Mexico by a party of European explorers. The expedition put Anglo-Canadians and the British Empire in an unparalleled position to determine the geopolitical

destiny of the Rockies and the Pacific Northwest. Mackenzie made that point with unmistakable clarity when he concluded his *Voyages from Montreal* (1801) with a compelling plan to advance British influence in the West. Mackenzie called for the union of the North West Company and the Hudson's Bay Company, royal support of a new and powerful trading company, and the construction of a chain of trading posts from Lake Winnipeg to the mouth of the Columbia River. Mackenzie had in mind not only the fur business but permanent settlement. Drawing on his own experience and the ideas of Pond and Henry, Mackenzie fashioned a comprehensive strategy for empire. That strategy, called by some "the Columbian Enterprise," guided Canadian expansion and goaded Thomas Jefferson into launching the Lewis and Clark expedition.

THE SPANISH EMPIRE
The Canadians were filled with dreams about what might be. In 1800 Spanish soldiers, bureaucrats, missionaries, and settlers surveyed an empire that already was. At the end of the American Revolution, Spain was the premier European power in the American West. Whatever

ALEUT BASKET
In the mid-eighteenth century, Russian explorers first encountered the natives of the Aleutian Islands. Russian traders later enlisted Aleut men to hunt sea otters, whose furs brought high prices in China.

responded in 1789 by sending Captain Esteban Jose Martinez to fend off the interlopers. Nootka Sound on the west coast of Vancouver Island had emerged as the principal trade center. At Nootka, Martinez found several ships, including one commanded by English Captain James Colnett. After angry exchanges, Martinez arrested Colnett, seized two English ships and crews, and sent his prisoners down the coast to the Spanish naval base at San Blas.

This outburst might have been overlooked except for larger issues of European politics and diplomacy. Eager to gain commercial advantage at Spanish expense, British politicians and merchants stirred up public outrage over Colnett's fate. The result was a full-blown international crisis. At least for the moment, the Nootka Sound Controversy drove Britain and Spain to the brink of war. Once tempers cooled, diplomats on both sides began to do their work. Those negotiations, culminating in the Nootka Convention of 1790, significantly lessened Spanish strength in the north Pacific. Spain was forced to accept the notion of shared sovereignty on the Northwest Coast. Although Spanish officials did not abandon efforts to secure power and place along the coast, the initiative clearly slipped to the British and the Americans. Five years later Spain formally relinquished all claims to exclusive sovereignty. This retreat was on the margins of the continent, but its meaning was a sign of things to come.

The year 1795 signaled Spain's withdrawal from the Northwest. It also marked a second retreat, this one on the other side of the continent. The border between Spanish West Florida and the United States was a source of tension as were Spanish claims to the lower portion of the Ohio country. Equally troublesome were arguments over American transit rights on the Mississippi. In 1794 American ambassador to Great Britain Thomas Pinckney was sent to Spain to negotiate a treaty resolving these difficulties. The Treaty of San Lorenzo, or Pinckney's Treaty as it is sometimes known, was another diplomatic defeat for Spain in America. Fearing renewed hostilities with England, Spanish diplomats virtually surrendered as a way to gain American support. Taken together, the troubles at Nootka and in the Southeast were sure signs that Spain's western empire was crumbling at the edges.

LOUISIANA

Having lost on both ends of the West in the 1790s, Spain began the new century with a devastating loss at the very center of the continent. Louisiana was a region of vast size and undetermined borders. European diplomats looking to fix it on the imperial map were sure of only one thing: Louisiana had major strategic value in the battle for America. As Joseph Xavier Delfau de Pontalba later explained, "Louisiana is the key to America." In 1762, at the end of the Seven Years' War,

MAJOR GENERAL THOMAS PINCKNEY
In 1795 Spain guaranteed American transit rights on the Mississippi River in the Treaty of San Lorenzo, also known as Pinckney's Treaty after negotiator Thomas Pinckney.

"ALEXANDER MACKENZIE, FROM CANADA, BY LAND, THE TWENTY-SECOND OF JULY, ONE THOUSAND SEVEN HUNDRED AND NINETY-THREE."

—ROCK INSCRIPTION MARKING MACKENZIE'S ARRIVAL, FROM THE EAST, AT THE PACIFIC OCEAN

VANCOUVER ISLAND
Artist John Webber, who accompanied British explorer James Cook on his final voyage, sketched a Nootka village on Vancouver Island in 1778.

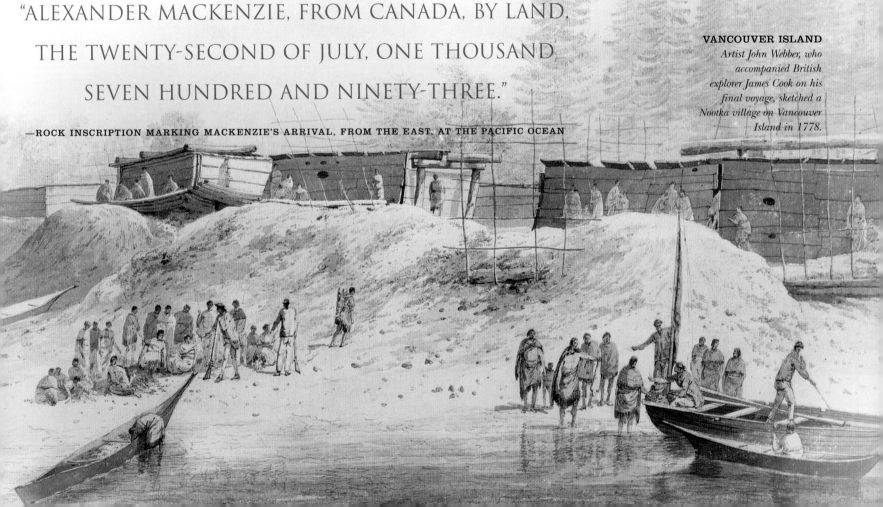

✦TLINGIT WARS✦

THE TLINGITS LIVED along the coastal strip and islands of today's southern Alaska and northern British Columbia. When the explorer Vitus Bering claimed Alaska for Russia in 1741, he was soon followed by Russian traders who sought to exploit the fur-bearing resources of the region. After establishing themselves in the Aleutian Islands and savagely putting down an Aleut rebellion, the Russians decided to compete with British and American traders in the area by establishing a permanent settlement on Kodiak Island in the Gulf of Alaska in 1784.

The Tlingits gave trading preference to British and American traders, whose goods they felt were better than those the Russians offered. They were, however, willing to grant permission to the Russians to hunt over tribal lands. After the Czar granted a monopoly to the Russian American Company in 1799, more Russian hunters arrived and built a fort at New Archangel (now Sitka, Alaska) on Baranov Island. The Tlingits grew alarmed at the vast numbers of furs being taken and determined to resist increasing Russian encroachment.

In 1802 Katlian, chief of the Sitka Tlingits, led an attack on the fort at New Archangel, destroying the town, killing some 20 Russians and 130 Aleut, and recovering the pelts taken on Tlingit land. Katlian held the post for two years until Alexander Baranov returned with ships and bombarded the Tlingits with cannon fire, forcing them to withdraw.

In 1805 the Tlingits attacked and captured the Russian post at Yakutat, and in 1806 they launched another assault on New Archangel with 400 war canoes and 2,000 warriors. The Russians bought them off with feasts and presents, but further Tlingit attacks followed in 1809 and 1813, leading the Russians to send a warship to patrol the area. The Tlingits, now armed with British and American firearms, continued to resist Russian incursions and were an important factor in Russia's decision to sell Alaska to the United States in 1867.

BOX DRUM
This ceremonial drum is painted with images of a Tlingit family's spirit ancestors.

BIRD-EFFIGY RATTLE
Tlingit shamans used rattles during rituals to cure illness and combat evil spirits.

SHAMAN'S MASK
The eyes of this Tlingit mask were made from Chinese bronze disks. Its creator probably found the disks in junk cast along the shore or obtained them through trade with Russians.

France secretly ceded Louisiana to Spain. Over the following years, soldiers, explorers, and merchants reached out from New Orleans and St. Louis to secure Louisiana for Spain. Administrators like François Luis Hector Carondelet, governor-general of Louisiana, saw the province as a barrier to halt American invaders and a country rich in fur and other resources. The shortsighted Manuel de Godoy, Spanish first minister of state, placed much less value on Louisiana. His strategy was to offer the country to France, reasoning that a French Louisiana would serve the same buffer function in the face of the restless Americans and at far less cost.

Spanish offers went unanswered until 1799, when the vision of Louisiana and a greater France captured Napoleon's imagination. At the Treaty of San Ildefonso (1800), Spain's American fortunes suffered a third setback. Nemesio Salcedo, Commandant of the Interior Provinces, despaired about the growing power of Spain's rivals. These foreigners, he wrote, are "crows to pick out our eyes." Spain was still a power to be reckoned with in 1800. Yet the shape and outcome of the reckoning was less and less in the hands of Madrid, Mexico City, and Santa Fe.

RUSSIAN AMERICA

When Canadians measured the West in 1800, they saw challenge and promise. Spanish officers could imagine only an endless series of defensive moves and strategic retreats. Far to the north, at the Russian trading post called New Archangel (present-day Sitka), established in 1799, Alexander Baranov faced the new century intent on extending Russian commercial and political influence down the Northwest coast and perhaps even into the interior. Like his American contemporary John Jacob Astor, Baranov believed that corporate enterprise and imperial expansion marched together. In 1799 Emperor Paul I issued a decree uniting the various Russian fur companies then trading in Alaska. The Russian American Company was not only a commercial venture but an agent for Russian territorial ambitions. Baranov, its general manager, had great plans for Russian America, but the news from New Archangel in 1800 was anything but encouraging.

Baranov's schemes depended on a prosperous fur trade with China. Without those profits, the company would be hard-pressed to fund its designs. Unlike its American and British rivals, the Russian American Company did not have permission to sell furs in the Canton market.

Russian furs, including those from America, could enter China only at the remote border post of Kyakhta. But marketing difficulties were the least of Baranov's troubles. The establishment of New Archangel on Baranov Island made good commercial sense yet the region's native people—especially the Tlingits–saw this as a direct challenge to their position. Well-armed by American traders, the Tlingits launched effective raids against Russian establishments. New Archangel briefly fell to a spirited attack in 1802. There were raids against St. Paul's Harbor in 1809 and 1813, and as late as 1855 Tlingits succeeded in destroying that post and Ozyorsk Redoubt. The company's fortunes were checked not only by native resistance but by scarcity of food and provisions. Nikolai Rezanov, leader of an important coastal expedition to Spanish California in 1806, put it bluntly: "The shortage of foodstuffs causes diseases, starvation and death among the people." The tyranny of time and distance, a demanding and often

ALEXANDER BARANOV
As general manager of the Russian-American Company, Baranov oversaw the Russian fur trade from New Archangel, a trading post on the site of what is now Sitka, Alaska.

unforgiving environment, steadfast native resistance, and an unpredictable world fur market—all these faced Baranov and the Russian American Company in 1800.

> "AT ANCHOR...WAS A BRIG UNDER RUSSIAN COLORS, FROM SITKA... SHE HAD...A CREW OF BETWEEN TWENTY AND THIRTY; AND SUCH A STUPID AND GREASY-LOOKING SET, I NEVER SAW BEFORE."
>
> —RICHARD HENRY DANA, ON ENCOUNTERING RUSSIAN TRADERS, 1834

RUSSIAN SETTLEMENT
This drawing from the early nineteenth century depicts a Russian outpost on the Aleutian Islands.

CROW ENCAMPMENT
As the nineteenth century began, the Crow were among the largest and most powerful tribes in what is now Montana.

"IF THE[SE] ACCURATE SURVEYS...PROVE INSTRUCTIVE AND BENEFICIAL TO MY COUNTRY, I SHALL ESTEEM MYSELF AMPLY REPAID."

—GEOGRAPHER THOMAS HUTCHINS, 1784

MAPPING THE WEST: 1800

FOR AMERICANS LOOKING WEST, LOUISIANA WAS THE PRIZE MOST CLEARLY IN SIGHT. AS THE YEAR 1800 BEGAN, THIS VAST EXPANSE OF LAND WAS CONTROLLED BY SPAIN. NEVERTHELESS, LAND-HUNGRY AMERICANS, INTRIGUED BY CARTOGRAPHERS' DESCRIPTIONS OF THIS TERRITORY, INCREASINGLY GAZED WITH LONGING TO THE WORLD BEYOND THE MISSISSIPPI.

WHEN THE GIFTED Spanish geographer Isidro de Antillón y Marzo published his comprehensive map of North America in 1802, he struggled to portray the continent's imperial complexity. On the eastern edge of the continent, Antillón sketched the new American republic, now reaching from the Atlantic to the east bank of the Mississippi and from somewhere in the western Great Lakes to the southern boundary set by Pinckney's Treaty.

Antillon's grasp of the extent of Russian America was strangely uncertain. He surely knew about the Russian presence in Alaska, but the place names up the coast to the Bering Strait are all defiantly Spanish and English. British North America arched across the top of Antillón's continental map. Drawing on recent maps published by Aaron Arrowsmith, the Spanish geographer marked important lakes and rivers first explored by Alexander Mackenzie and David Thompson.

Perhaps still unwilling to acknowledge the growing power of English-speaking peoples in North America, Antillon insisted on labeling British North America as "Canada or New France."

THE UNITED STATES IN 1800

No matter how accurate his cartography, there was something missing from Antillon's map. When English traveler Henry Wansey toured the American states in the mid-1790s, he reported feeling that the country had "the appearance everywhere of a vast outline, with much to fill up." Modern geographers might draft a different map of the West in 1800, one that takes account of cultural values, expansionist energies, and national institutions.

On such a map the United States looms far larger than its 900,000 square miles of territory in 1800. Capitalist institutions and an aggressive, acquisitive mentality shaped an enterprising people always looking for the main chance. The passion for land directed much of American life. It was a hunger that reached back to the first days at Jamestown and Plymouth, prompting long-time British colonial Indian agent Sir William Johnson to describe it as a "pestilential thirst for land, so epidemic thro' the provinces." The drive for land was supported by state and national government policies that encouraged expansion. Even more

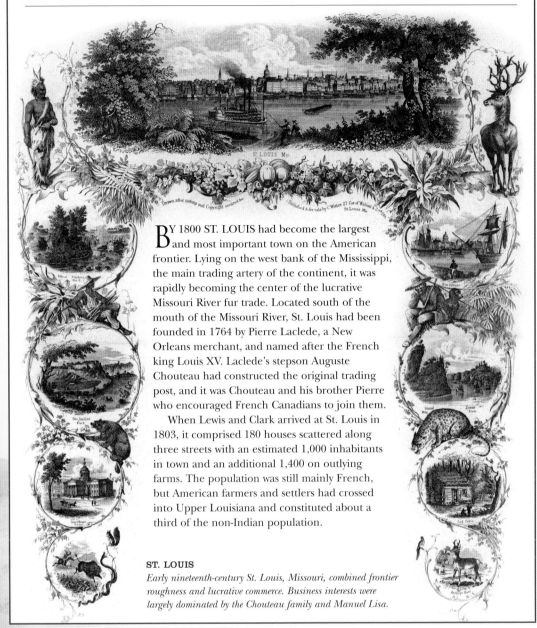

✦SAINT LOUIS C. 1800✦

BY 1800 ST. LOUIS had become the largest and most important town on the American frontier. Lying on the west bank of the Mississippi, the main trading artery of the continent, it was rapidly becoming the center of the lucrative Missouri River fur trade. Located south of the mouth of the Missouri River, St. Louis had been founded in 1764 by Pierre Laclede, a New Orleans merchant, and named after the French king Louis XV. Laclede's stepson Auguste Chouteau had constructed the original trading post, and it was Chouteau and his brother Pierre who encouraged French Canadians to join them.

When Lewis and Clark arrived at St. Louis in 1803, it comprised 180 houses scattered along three streets with an estimated 1,000 inhabitants in town and an additional 1,400 on outlying farms. The population was still mainly French, but American farmers and settlers had crossed into Upper Louisiana and constituted about a third of the non-Indian population.

ST. LOUIS
Early nineteenth-century St. Louis, Missouri, combined frontier roughness and lucrative commerce. Business interests were largely dominated by the Chouteau family and Manuel Lisa.

important, federal legislation like the Land Ordinances of 1784 and 1785 established ways to incorporate new territories into the republic. And as the Ohio Indian Wars of the 1780s made plain, the government was prepared to use force against native peoples. But nothing made the United States expand so large on this mental map as the growing belief in the moral rightness and inevitable growth of the American empire. Few put that conviction better than Thomas Hutchins, first Geographer to the United States. After estimating the habitable land of North America

BLUFFS ABOVE THE MISSOURI
Centuries before Americans began exploring the Missouri River Valley, tribes such as the Hidatsas and the Mandans lived in the region, depicted here by George Catlin.

at about three and a half million square miles, Hutchins simply remarked, "If we want it, I warrant it will soon be ours."

By whatever map or calculation we imagine the West in 1800, it is Louisiana that dominates the landscape. Louisiana in 1800 was not so much a place as a statement of imperial ambition. Its very name linked it to the swirl of wars and rivalries that had locked France, Spain, and Britain in generations of bloody conflict. Louisiana in 1800 was an expression of power that can best be comprehended by looking from two very different places.

When Antoine Soulard drafted his map of western North America in 1794–95, St. Louis was barely thirty years old and already a principal gateway to the western country. Founded in 1764

CHEYENNE SHIRT
Much of Louisiana was the hunting territory of the Cheyennes, Sioux, Shoshones, Crows, and other Great Plains tribes. This shirt belonged to Northern Cheyenne leader Little Chief.

⇢GUNS AND THE WEST⇠

GUNS OF many kinds were used and traded in the early nineteenth-century West, but some were especially well-suited to the region. The guns that European immigrants brought to America proved too heavy and inaccurate for life on the Western frontier. With long-distance accuracy a necessity, the lighter-weight Kentucky Rifle of the early 1800s was introduced. A similar weapon, the Tennessee Rifle, was less ornate. The Plains Rifle, introduced in 1840, offered even better long-distance accuracy and, along with the Mountain Rifle, was popular with settlers and trappers throughout the West. The 1841 Mississippi Rifle proved attractive to both the military and civilians, with more than 60,000 produced between the early 1840s and the end of its production run in 1852.

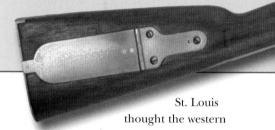

by Pierre de Laclede Liguest and Auguste Chouteau, the settlement quickly emerged as a trading and administrative center. Despite the international troubles of the 1790s and increased competition from Canadian traders up the Mississippi and on the northern Great Plains, St. Louis remained Louisiana's opening to the West.

SOULARD'S LOUSIANA

Soulard's map, drafted at the request of Governor Carondelet and based on recent Spanish explorations up the Missouri, recognized St. Louis's place of power. From St. Louis, Soulard struggled to comprehend and set boundaries for a vast Louisiana. Soulard's Louisiana had two distinct faces. Its first face was outlined by the sweeping arc of the Missouri River. Smaller tributaries like the Platte and the Kansas wrinkled

out of Louisiana's face. On the western edge of the continent, Soulard took notice of the River of the West, here called the Oregan. The Rockies, unnamed on Soulard's map, were the Missouri's counterpoint. Like other European cartographers, Soulard had no notion about either the complex character of the Rockies or their vast continental range. His western mountains were like eastern hills, isolated bumps and ridges on the farthest edge of Louisiana's face. Between the river and the mountains, Soulard imagined a well-watered garden of the world. There was no hint of a great American desert here, no endless, empty plains. From St. Louis, Louisiana stretched out like a featureless paradise with river highways and perhaps even the promise of a passage to India.

Soulard's Louisiana had few terrain features other than a lacy network of rivers, but no one in

St. Louis thought the western country an empty place. Soulard filled Louisiana's second face with Native American names. Thinking largely in economic terms, the geographer divided Indians into two broad categories, employing circles to represent village sites occupied by farming peoples like the Mandans and Arikaras, while triangles indicated the hunting territories of the Sioux, Cheyennes, Crows and Shoshones. Soulard clearly depicted the presence of horses, guns, and trading posts on native life. What was more difficult to

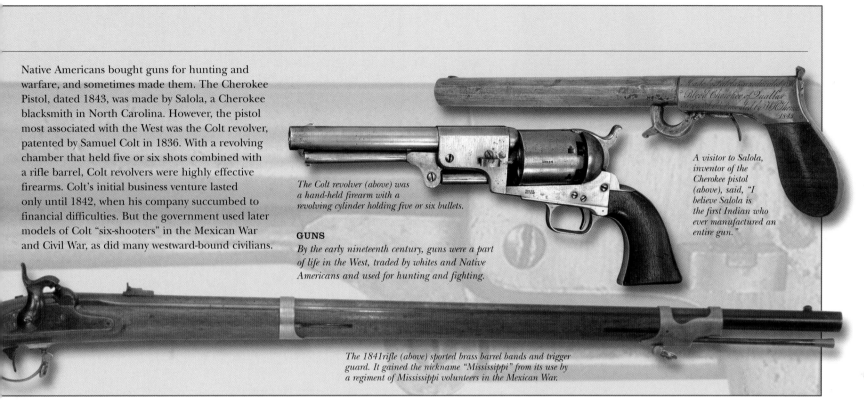

Native Americans bought guns for hunting and warfare, and sometimes made them. The Cherokee Pistol, dated 1843, was made by Salola, a Cherokee blacksmith in North Carolina. However, the pistol most associated with the West was the Colt revolver, patented by Samuel Colt in 1836. With a revolving chamber that held five or six shots combined with a rifle barrel, Colt revolvers were highly effective firearms. Colt's initial business venture lasted only until 1842, when his company succumbed to financial difficulties. But the government used later models of Colt "six-shooters" in the Mexican War and Civil War, as did many westward-bound civilians.

The Colt revolver (above) was a hand-held firearm with a revolving cylinder holding five or six bullets.

GUNS

By the early nineteenth century, guns were a part of life in the West, traded by whites and Native Americans and used for hunting and fighting.

A visitor to Salola, inventor of the Cherokee pistol (above), said, "I believe Salola is the first Indian who ever manufactured an entire gun."

The 1841 rifle (above) sported brass barrel bands and trigger guard. It gained the nickname "Mississippi" from its use by a regiment of Mississippi volunteers in the Mexican War.

portray—and in fact was invisible—were the diseases that had transformed a large part of upper Louisiana. Beginning in the 1780s, smallpox raced up the Missouri, killing thousands of Indians. The western pandemic of 1780–81 took the lives of perhaps 75 percent of the Arikara Indians. Writing early in the century, St. Louis trader and explorer Pierre-Antoine Tabeau found that "of the eighteen fairly large villages, situated upon the Missouri at some distance from each other, the Ricaras are reduced to three very mediocre ones." Soulard's map could not show that sort of devastation. For many native peoples, the winds of change were already roaring like a Great Plains tornado.

CAMEAHWAIT AND CLARK

Antoine Soulard was not the only mapmaker trying to portray the western country; St. Louis was not the only vantage point to survey Louisiana. In late August 1805, Lemhi Shoshone headman Cameahwait met with explorer William Clark at a camp along the Lemhi River in present-day Idaho. When Clark asked Cameahwait to instruct him "with respect to the geography of his country," the headman knelt down and prepared,

BLACKFOOT HUNTING CAMP

After acquiring horses and guns from Europeans, the native peoples of the Plains developed a culture focused on hunting buffalo from horseback.

CHEYENNE BOOKLET OF BEADS

Early American explorers in the West developed friendships with native peoples by offering gifts of beads and other trade goods.

with lines in the dirt, a complex terrain map. While no drawing from that map survives, Clark did compose a detailed summary for his journal. Cameahwait had a comprehensive understanding of large parts of present-day Idaho, Montana, and the Dakotas. Because Clark was interested in possible southern routes to the Pacific, Cameahwait and an elderly man the explorers called Old Toby began by sketching the course of the Salmon River. The Indian cartographers made it plain that the Salmon could not be safely navigated. Using "heeps of sand," Cameahwait depicted the mountain ranges of central Idaho as a desolate and dangerous place. After listening to a description of the Snake River plains, Clark was convinced that his passage to the Pacific was up north, over what came to be called the Lolo Trail. Old Toby reported that the Nez Perce people used the route each year as they crossed over the Continental Divide to hunt buffalo.

Cameahwait and Old Toby understood much about the Rocky Mountains from northern Idaho to the Snake River plains. But their grasp of the land and its peoples was much greater when they looked east to the northern plains. Lemhi Shoshones divided their year between fishing west of the Continental Divide and buffalo hunting east of the Divide in what is now west-central Montana. From the Great Falls of the Missouri south to the Three Forks country and on to the Yellowstone River, Cameahwait knew the landscape. And what shaped that landscape were not terrain features but the promise of buffalo and the presence of well-armed enemies. In one of Clark's most vivid journal entries, he recalled Cameahwait's "fierce eyes and lank jaws grown meager for the want of food," as the headman talked about guns and survival.

Cameahwait's Louisiana was a dangerous place where the balance of power had shifted against the Shoshones. Blackfeet and Hidatsa warriors and hunters, armed by Canadian traders, made every venture onto the plains a hazardous enterprise. Cameahwait's sister Sacagawea had been kidnapped as a child when Hidatsa raiders caught a Shoshone party at the Three Forks. Shoshones had horses but no guns. What remade the plains landscape was the convergence of horses and guns. Cameahwait's mental map took the measure of that unstable world. "If we had guns," he told Clark, "we would then live in the country of the buffaloe and eat as our enemies do and not be compelled to hide ourselves in the mountains and live on roots and berries as the bear do."

MONTICELLO
At his Virginia home, Thomas Jefferson amassed an extensive library of books about the exploration of the West.

"FROM THIS DAY THE UNITED STATES TAKE THEIR PLACE AMONG THE POWERS OF THE FIRST RANK."

—AMBASSADOR ROBERT R. LIVINGSTON, ON THE LOUISIANA PURCHASE OF 1803

SO FAIR A COUNTRY: THE CONTEST FOR LOUISIANA

UNDER THE WEAK RULE OF SPAIN, LOUISIANA NEVER FLOURISHED AS A COLONY. BUT, IN A TREATY IN 1800, FRANCE ACQUIRED THE REGION, PLACING AMERICA'S DREAMS OF WESTWARD EXPANSION IN JEOPARDY. SENSING THE COUNTRY'S DESTINY LAY IN THE WEST, PRESIDENT THOMAS JEFFERSON SET ABOUT DETERMINING WHAT ROLE THE UNITED STATES WOULD PLAY IN LOUISIANA'S FUTURE.

ONE OF THE MOST enduring myths in American history involves Louisiana, Thomas Jefferson, and the Lewis and Clark expedition. The myth has no name, but its powerful attraction lies in the ability to offer a simple explanation for complex events. Filled with national self-congratulation, the myth goes like this. Thomas Jefferson, muscular son of the Virginia frontier, had long been fascinated by the West. He even built his house to look west over the Blue Ridge Mountains. Jefferson's lifelong fascination with the West and his scientific interest in Native Americans set him on the road to be an ardent expansionist. Once seated in the presidency (1801-9), so the story goes, he skillfully engineered the Louisiana Purchase and then sent Lewis and Clark to explore the new territory. Historians hostile to Jefferson sometimes put a slightly different spin on the story, suggesting that the purchase fell into the president's lap as a happy accident. In either case this textbook wisdom not only confuses the chronology of events but lessens the

JEFFERSON'S LAP DESK
Jefferson wrote the Declaration of Independence on this portable desk, which he designed himself. It features a hinged writing board and a drawer for paper, pens, and inkwell.

meaning of American expansion in the West. The purchase and the expedition were shaped by a powerful imperialist tradition that reached back to the colonial beginnings of the American republic and had profound consequences for the future of the West.

THE AGE OF JEFFERSON
While the first years of the nineteenth century were filled with memorable characters all vying for power and place in the West, the time properly belongs to Thomas Jefferson. It was the Age of Jefferson in the West, but not because his ideas about geography, Indians, and empire were original. Nor could the president assert that he was the only national leader with dreams of western empire. Rather, by the convergence of ideas, political determination, and circumstances, he thrust the American republic into the West. American soldiers, bureaucrats, merchants, farmers, and fur traders were Jefferson's agents of empire. From St. Louis to the mouth of the Columbia, Jefferson made the United States a western contender.

Jefferson did not become what historian Donald Jackson called "the most towering westerner of them all" quickly or by birth. His road west had more twists and turns than many explorers' trails. By education and temperament, Jefferson was attracted to Atlantic cultures. It was the talk of Williamsburg, Philadelphia, London, and Paris that appealed to him. There was a Virginia exploration tradition, a tradition that conjured up images of fertile lands beyond the

NEGOTIATING FOR LAND

Thomas Jefferson contemplated buying not only Louisiana but West Florida. This political cartoon satirizes the covert negotiations of Thomas Jefferson (pictured as a dog coughing up money) to purchase West Florida in 1804. A hornet with Napoleon's head stings him.

somewhere along the Pacific Coast. Such disturbing news came at the very time Jefferson was busy with additional writing and research for *Notes on the State of Virginia*. Jefferson's Virginia had boundaries far larger than those of the present-day state. His Virginia had an imperial, almost continental sweep, running to the east bank of the Mississippi. Thinking about the West as he pondered a greater Virginia, Jefferson wrote a hurried letter to the one Virginian who most fully embodied the state's western ambitions: George Rogers Clark, the frontiersman and adventurer, who had led Virginia militiamen in the 1778 invasion of the Illinois country. While Jefferson doubted that an expedition could be mustered in time, he asked Clark to consider leading such a party. Already deep in debt and sliding toward alcoholism, Clark politely but firmly declined. Jefferson pressed no further, but he had signaled an interest in the West. Equally important, he began to grasp the significance of Anglo-Canadian ambitions.

JEFFERSON IN PARIS

Circumstance and opportunity turned Jefferson westward again during his time as ambassador in Paris. In the mid-1780s French political and scientific circles were challenged by the accomplishments of Captain James Cook. Cook's three voyages (1768–71, 1772–75, 1776–79) to explore the Pacific Ocean gave Great Britain a Pacific presence and commanding authority in scientific discovery. The French answer to Cook was an expedition led by Jean Francois de Laperouse. In early August 1785 Jefferson heard about the expedition and worried that it marked a renewal of French imperialism. Determined to know more, the ambassador

Ohio, western rivers, and the passage to the Pacific. Jefferson undoubtedly heard about such geographic speculations from his gifted tutor, James Maury. And there was the example of his father, Peter Jefferson, a talented cartographer and traveler. But none of these influences made Jefferson either a western visionary or a determined imperialist. Perhaps French diplomat Charles-Maurice de Talleyrand-Périgord was right when he sarcastically named the American republic an "empire of circumstances." Circumstances outside Jefferson's own life increasingly drew his attention westward. Jefferson did not create those circumstances, but he did choose to act on them, and the actions slowly began to accumulate and take more formal shape.

In the 1780s the most comprehensive plans for expansion came from Canadian traders like Peter Pond and Alexander Henry the Elder. Jefferson got wind of these plans late in 1783, probably hearing a garbled account of Pond's ideas. This report led Jefferson to believe that an English expedition was preparing to explore and settle

⟡ THOMAS JEFFERSON ⟡

THOMAS JEFFERSON (1743-1826), third president of the United States, combined the roles of lawyer and statesman with those of scientist and architect. A leading figure of the Enlightenment, he graduated from William & Mary College in 1762 and served in the Virginia House of Burgesses from 1769 to 1775. As a delegate to the Continental Congress, he drafted the Declaration of Independence. He later served as governor of Virginia before becoming ambassador to France and then secretary of state under George Washington. Vice president under John Adams and leader of the Democratic-Republican Party, he became president in 1801, serving two terms.

Important events of Jefferson's presidency included the Tripolitan War (1801-5); the Louisiana Purchase (1803); the Lewis and Clark Expedition (1804-6); and the Embargo Act (1807), by which Jefferson struggled to maintain America's neutrality in the Napoleonic Wars. After his retirement from political life, he devoted himself to intellectual activities at his home, Monticello. At the age of 76, he founded the University of Virginia. He died on July 4, 1826, within hours of John Adams.

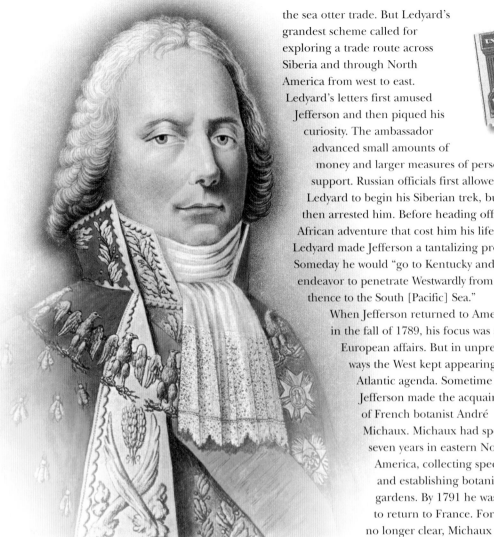

the sea otter trade. But Ledyard's grandest scheme called for exploring a trade route across Siberia and through North America from west to east. Ledyard's letters first amused Jefferson and then piqued his curiosity. The ambassador advanced small amounts of money and larger measures of personal support. Russian officials first allowed Ledyard to begin his Siberian trek, but then arrested him. Before heading off to an African adventure that cost him his life, Ledyard made Jefferson a tantalizing promise. Someday he would "go to Kentucky and endeavor to penetrate Westwardly from thence to the South [Pacific] Sea."

When Jefferson returned to America in the fall of 1789, his focus was still on European affairs. But in unpredictable ways the West kept appearing on his Atlantic agenda. Sometime in 1791 Jefferson made the acquaintance of French botanist André Michaux. Michaux had spent seven years in eastern North America, collecting specimens and establishing botanical gardens. By 1791 he was ready to return to France. For reasons no longer clear, Michaux stayed

LOUISIANA PURCHASE STAMP

This stamp was issued in honor of the one hundredth anniversary of the Louisiana Purchase.

in the United States and began to consider an expedition to the Pacific. Sometime in 1792 he brought his idea to the American Philosophical Society. In the 1790s most European geographers believed that there were two possible routes across the continent. The northern track advanced by Pond and the North West Company was being tested by Alexander Mackenzie. The older strategy for the passage to India, the one that captured Michaux's attention, proposed using the Missouri River as a western highway. Conventional wisdom had it that the Missouri ran up to the base of the Rockies. Travelers could make an easy portage over the mountains and then come upon the River of the West and a path to the Ocean. The Missouri as the gateway to the Pacific had been a feature of exploration geography since the Marquette and Jolliet expedition first commented on the possibility in 1673–74. Jefferson accepted that notion and advanced it in his Notes on the State of Virginia. Now Michaux proposed giving the idea a real test.

As vice president of the American Philosophical Society, Jefferson took responsibility for raising expedition funds. But far more important than

TALLEYRAND

As Napoleon's minister of foreign affairs, Charles-Maurice de Talleyrand-Périgord participated in negotiations over Louisiana.

detailed John Paul Jones to snoop around the docks at Brest. Jones' tardy report—it came two months after the expedition sailed—at least partially reassured Jefferson. French ambitions aimed at the south Pacific. North America's coast was not to be part of any greater France overseas.

No sooner had these worries subsided than the West again intruded on Jefferson. John Ledyard, restless Connecticut Yankee and one-time corporal in the Royal Marines on Cook's third voyage, was a whirlwind of energy and ambition. Projects, enterprises, and speculations flew from his mind at dizzying speed. By the time Jefferson met him in late 1786, Ledyard had already published his *Journal of Captain Cook's Last Voyage to the Pacific Ocean* (1783) and was enmeshed in half a dozen projects involving

BOTANICAL DRAWINGS

André Michaux published these drawings of (left to right) the American larch, the pistacia tree, and the white pine.

"SEARCH FOR & PURSUE...THE SHORTEST & MOST CONVENIENT [ROUTE] BETWEEN THE HIGHER PARTS OF THE MISSOURI & THE PACIFIC OCEAN."

—THOMAS JEFFERSON
TO ANDRÉ MICHAUX, 1793

the begging letters he sent fellow society members was his role as Michaux's key planner and consultant. From his wide reading in expedition literature, Jefferson understood that exploration was a carefully planned, highly organized enterprise. By the end of April 1793 he had prepared an exploration master plan, one that might be read as a first draft for the later and even more comprehensive directions sent to Lewis and Clark. Jefferson instructed Michaux to study plants, animals, terrain features, and Native American cultures. He raised money for Michaux, wrote exploration instructions, and used whatever personal influence he could to advance the cause. But Michaux's own interests changed, and by 1796 he was no longer committed to a Pacific journey.

Correspondence with Clark, conversations with Ledyard, and a role as consultant for Michaux all pointed Jefferson toward the farthest western edge of the continent. But in the mid-1790s diplomatic and domestic events forced him to confront the destiny of a nearer West—the world of New Orleans, the Mississippi River, and Louisiana.

North America was always an empire of rivers. The St. Lawrence, the Columbia, the Missouri, and the Arkansas shaped the lives of natives and newcomers alike. But in the two decades after American independence no river played a larger role in the clash of empires than the Mississippi.

Boom times in Kentucky and Tennessee depended on river traffic down the Mississippi to New Orleans. Without secure transit privileges on the river, and without the right of deposit (the right to place American agricultural products, bound for other ports, in New Orleans warehouses free of high customs duties), the trans-Appalachian economy would collapse. And equally dangerous, western settlers might abandon the new nation for the security promised by a Spanish embrace.

SPAIN AND LOUISIANA

Confronted by the swelling tide of American settlers, Spanish officials found it difficult to know what policy to pursue. Some officers conspired with disaffected western politicians hoping to stir storms of resentment and secession, while others argued that Americans should be kept out of Louisiana at all costs. A third group of policy makers accepted American settlement as inevitable. The Spanish crown and colonial bureaucracy wrestled with the Louisiana question and in the process adopted policies that many Americans thought capricious and unjust. In 1784 the lower Mississippi was closed to all foreigners. Four years later, after intense negotiations, New Orleans was opened for American traders.

Throughout the 1790s, as rumors spread that Spain might return Louisiana to French control, American concern deepened. And there was genuine reason for worry. During the 1790s the French government had laid plans for the recovery of its North American empire lost at the end of the Seven Years' War. When Napoleon Bonaparte seized power in 1799, he and Talleyrand made common cause to reassert French domain in America. Canada might be beyond Napoleon's grasp; Louisiana was not.

In October 1800 France and Spain agreed on the terms of the Treaty of San Ildefonso, setting in motion the process of transferring Louisiana from Spanish to French rule. Textbook wisdom often has it that Napoleon bullied Spain into handing Louisiana over to France. But many

✦RIVERBOATS✦

IN THE early nineteenth century, Americans used inland rivers and man-made canals to transport goods and people. At first, flatboats and keelboats dominated the waterways. The flatboat included a small shelter for travelers and open deck space for livestock. Not durable enough for a return trip against the river's current, flatboats were taken apart and used as lumber when they reached their destination. Keelboats were sturdier and more versatile, relying on the current to bring them downriver and brute human strength for the return trip. The crew used poles to push the vessel along, also relying at times on towlines pulled from the shore. The steam engine changed the face of the river. Able to travel both up and down the river with relative ease, the steamboat offered more options and amenities, such as bars, barbershops, and entertainment, for travelers. Less fortunate passengers traveled economically on the lower deck with the livestock and other cargo.

Robert Fulton is credited with navigating the first steamboat on New York's Hudson River in 1807. But it was later in the century that the vessel increased tremendously in popularity, from sixty steamboats traversing the rivers in 1820 to 740 in 1850.

RIVERBOATS
Magnificent paddle-wheel riverboats use steam power to travel on the Mississippi.

CESSION OF LOUISIANA

The Louisiana Purchase is negotiated by (left to right) French representative the Marquis Barbé-Marbois and American diplomats Robert Livingston and James Monroe.

Spanish diplomats, increasingly apprehensive about tensions with the Americans, were eager to abandon Louisiana. As Spanish Secretary of State for Foreign Affairs Mariano Luis de Urquijo bluntly put it, "Louisiana costs us more than it is worth." Louisiana did carry a high price. For the Spanish it was constant trouble with the restless Americans. Napoleon and Talleyrand recognized that a French Louisiana might exact an even higher price in shattered relations with both the United States and Great Britain. But no nation would pay more dearly for a French Louisiana than the American republic. Whatever their political allegiance—whether Republican or Federalist—Americans knew that a revitalized French Louisiana doomed the nation to being little more than a collection of Atlantic states. As geographer Jedediah Morse taught his readers years before, "We cannot but anticipate the period, as not far distant, when the AMERICAN EMPIRE will comprehend millions of souls, west of the Mississippi." That vision of a transcontinental republic now collided with an equally expansive dream of a French empire in North America.

Thomas Jefferson had been president no more than three months when he learned that rumors about a secret Louisiana treaty were true. Jefferson understood that once France occupied Louisiana, the crisis over the river, its trade, and

the entire political future of the central part of North America suddenly became far more dangerous and complex. Dealing with a weak Spanish nation was one thing; facing Napoleonic France was entirely another matter. Likening the French occupation of Louisiana to a "speck which now appears as an almost invisible point in the horizon," he told friend and advisor Pierre Samuel Du Pont de Nemours that the "speck" was "the embryo of a tornado which will burst on the countries on both sides of the Atlantic, and involve in its effects their highest destinies."

JEFFERSON TAKES ACTION

Jefferson's options were many but his powers of choice were severely limited. He could do nothing, a course that violated his own expansionist commitments. A second option involved purchases—buying West Florida or the Isle of New Orleans, or both. A third option was a war against France requiring an alliance with Great Britain. In the first months of 1802, Napoleon's strategy became clearer. General Charles Le Clerc's forces landed in Santo Domingo in January and prepared to smash the rebellion mounted by Toussaint L'Ouverture. In April the French government set in motion plans for the military occupation of New Orleans. The tornado seemed ready to spin through Louisiana.

JEFFERSON'S YEAR

This box dates from Thomas Jefferson's election as president in 1800—the year that France regained Louisiana from Spain, setting in motion the events that would result in Jefferson's purchase of the territory for the United States.

NAPOLEON
While conducting wars of conquest in Europe, Napoleon regained control of Louisiana from Spain. The prospect of a French Louisiana alarmed American officials, who feared it would present an insurmountable obstacle to westward expansion.

"YOU HAVE MADE A NOBLE BARGAIN FOR YOURSELVES. AND I SUPPOSE YOU WILL MAKE THE MOST OF IT."

—FRENCH FOREIGN MINISTER
CHARLES DE TALLEYRAND, 1803

TOUSSAINT L'OUVERTURE
The Haitian slave rebellion led by Toussaint L'Ouverture dampened Napoleon's enthusiasm for building French colonies in North America.

On April 12, 1802, Jefferson wrote a carefully worded letter to Robert R. Livingston. The ambassador had been in France since November 1801, trying to get reliable information about Napoleon's American ambitions. Drafting a letter he was sure French agents would see and copy for Talleyrand and Napoleon, Jefferson struck his most belligerent pose.

The Spanish cession of Louisiana and the Floridas to France "works most sorely on the United States," he told Livingston. "It completely reverses all the political relations of the United States and will form a new epoch in our political course." Jefferson appreciated the larger consequences of the crisis at hand, but his deepest concern focused on one place. Louisiana was just a name; New Orleans spelled power and profit. It was a place worth rattling sabers and even unsheathing them. "There is on the globe," the president asserted, "one single spot, the possessor of which is our natural and habitual enemy." Spain had been unwilling to pay the price exacted by playing the enemy. Would France also count the cost? Just to make sure Napoleon and Talleyrand toted up the full bill, Jefferson predicted that once France took New Orleans, the United States would "marry ourselves to the British fleet and nation." All this trouble could be averted if France would only sell New Orleans and West Florida to the United States. Having done what he could to warn France of the dangers in its Louisiana policy, Jefferson took himself to summer at Monticello.

FORT CLATSOP REPLICA
In Oregon in December 1805, Lewis and Clark built Fort Clatsop, depicted in this replica, as a winter post for their expedition.

"YOUR OBSERVATIONS ARE TO BE TAKEN WITH GREAT PAINS & ACCURACY, TO BE ENTERED DISTINCTLY, & INTELLIGIBLY FOR OTHERS AS WELL AS YOURSELF."

—THOMAS JEFFERSON TO LEWIS AND CLARK, 1803

AMERICAN ODYSSEY: THE LEWIS AND CLARK EXPEDITION

EVEN BEFORE THE UNITED STATES ACQUIRED LOUISIANA, THOMAS JEFFERSON BEGAN ORGANIZING AN EXPEDITION THROUGH THE REGION. SETTING OFF IN 1804, MERIWETHER LEWIS AND WILLIAM CLARK JOURNEYED FROM THE MISSOURI RIVER TO THE PACIFIC OCEAN, STUDYING THE GEOGRAPHY AND PEOPLE OF THIS LARGELY UNCHARTED TERRITORY.

JEFFERSON TOLD LIVINGSTON that "every eye in the United States is now fixed on this affair of Louisiana." But in the summer of 1802 Jefferson's own eyes were elsewhere. Always a reader with wide-ranging interests, Jefferson was keenly interested in books dealing with North America. Exploration accounts, travel narratives, descriptions of native peoples, and general histories of the continent—all enjoyed a place in his Monticello library. In late June Jefferson ordered a volume that was the exploration bestseller of its day—Alexander Mackenzie's *Voyages from Montreal.* Even by eighteenth-century standards *Voyages* was not especially lively. But its concluding pages blew up a storm equal to the Louisiana tornado. One sentence was enough to jolt the president: "By opening this intercourse between the Atlantic and Pacific Oceans, and forming regular establishments through the interior, and at both extremes, as well as along the coasts and islands, the entire command of the fur trade of North America might be obtained." And by emphasizing that lands along the Columbia River were ideal for settlement, Mackenzie could have easily rewritten the sentence to read "the entire command of western North America."

Jefferson had considered French Louisiana the principal barrier to American expansion. Suddenly Great Britain seemed ready to thrust its power through Canada across the continent and down the Pacific coast. William Henry Drayton's generation had feared encirclement by Bourbon France. Now the American republic faced a far tighter imperial circle, one that nearly ringed North America. This made the view of the West from Monticello far more menacing.

RESPONSE TO MACKENZIE

Jefferson's forceful response to Mackenzie came in early December 1802. By then Congress and the President were fully focused on New Orleans, or so it seemed. When the Spanish decision to deny right of deposit in New Orleans reached Washington, D.C., in November, New England Federalists and western Democratic-Republicans called for direct American intervention in Louisiana. In the midst of all this bellicose talk, Jefferson took Spanish ambassador Carlos Martinez de Irujo aside for a private talk. What he told Irujo was the first inkling of an American response to Mackenzie. As the diplomat recalled it, "The President asked me the other day in a frank and confident tone, if our Court would take it badly, that the Congress decree the formation of a group of travelers, who would form a small caravan and go and explore the course of the Missouri River." Both Irujo and Jefferson knew that such a journey would cross lands claimed by Spain. The diplomat's protest meant little, and, in Irujo's words, Jefferson seemed intent on extending American population "up to the coasts of the South Sea." The Lewis and Clark expedition had its initial expression in that confidential talk with the Spanish ambassador.

In the first week of December 1802 Thomas Jefferson balanced two powerful western initiatives—the bid to buy New Orleans and a thrust across the continent to the Pacific coast. Jefferson accomplished that delicate balancing act because he now had a theory about expansion and the American empire. That theory combined territorial acquisition and an American version of republicanism.

SACAGAWEA'S HOMECOMING

Sacagawea, Shoshone interpreter and guide on the Lewis and Clark expedition, is shown here being returned to her people.

Republican virtues—industry, frugality, personal independence, and minimal government—fit Jefferson's own conception of himself and his world. A republic, a small state with a homogenous population, was the best repository for those values. Republics that expanded became empires, losing their true character. And Jefferson foresaw additional problems as he contemplated the future of an expanding republic. Many eighteenth-century thinkers believed that human societies were like organic beings, having predictable life cycles from birth to death. The most common conception envisioned four stages of social evolution as human communities moved from hunting and herding to farming and finally toward more urban ways. Jefferson saw this development in terms of progress toward civilization. And the most civilized and republican societies were agricultural. While he later tempered his anti-urban bias, in 1803 Jefferson was persuaded that cities spelled social stagnation and political ruin. Simply put, how could the republic be kept at the agricultural stage, especially when the taste for commerce and luxury was already deep in the nation's being?

›ALEXANDER MACKENZIE'S‹ VOYAGES FROM MONTREAL

THE FIRST NON-INDIAN to cross north of the Spanish possessions, Scottish-born Alexander Mackenzie (1764–1820), began work as a fifteen-year-old with a Montreal fur-trading company. In 1787 the North West Company posted him to northern Alberta, and two years later he led a party looking for a water route to the Pacific. Unsuccessful, he set out again in 1793, traveling westward along the Peace River, crossing the Continental Divide, following the Fraser River south, and then marching overland to reach the western coast, where he wrote his name and the date (July 22, 1793) on a rock near today's Vancouver Island.

Mackenzie subsequently returned to Scotland, where he began writing about his journey. It took eight years

to convert his journals into book form, with the help of ghostwriter William Combe. *Voyages from Montreal, on the River St. Lawrence, Through the Continent of North America to the Frozen and Pacific Oceans* was published in England in 1801 and became a best-seller. It contained vivid descriptions of Mackenzie's expedition across the continent, including encounters with Native Americans. However, it was his prophecy that his route would secure the lucrative fur trade for the British that excited public interest—and galvanized Thomas Jefferson into action, setting in motion the first stages of the Lewis and Clark expedition.

FROM

MONTREAL,

ON THE RIVER ST. LAURENCE,

THROUGH THE

CONTINENT OF NORTH AMERICA,

TO THE

FROZEN AND PACIFIC OCEANS:

IN THE YEARS 1789 AND 1793.

WITH A PRELIMINARY ACCOUNT OF

THE RISE, PROGRESS, AND PRESENT STATE OF

THE FUR TRADE

OF

THAT COUNTRY.

ILLUSTRATED WITH A MAP.

BY ALEXANDER MACKENZIE, ESQ.

FIRST AMERICAN EDITION

VOYAGES FROM MONTREAL

Alexander Mackenzie's 1801 bestseller told of his westward journeys through North America and gave an account "of the fur trade of that country."

⊹LEWIS AND CLARK⊹

MERIWETHER Lewis (1774–1809) was born in Albemarle County, Virginia, to a wealthy family of planters. As a young man, he excelled in the study of natural history. He joined the Virginia militia in 1794 and the regular army in 1795, where he eventually rose to the rank of captain. As an army officer, he served in the Indian wars in the Ohio Valley, where he met his future partner in exploration, William Clark.

In 1801, President Thomas Jefferson chose Lewis to be his personal secretary, and, in 1803, to head an expedition westward across the Louisiana Territory to the Pacific Ocean. Lewis chose Clark as co-leader, and the two set out from St. Louis, Missouri, in the spring of 1804. They returned in the fall of 1806 with a wealth of information about the region and a lasting place as heroes in the history of exploration.

After the expedition, Lewis served as governor of Louisiana Territory (1807-9), but he was unsuited for the administrative role and unhappy over his lack of progress in writing a report about the expedition. Always prone to depression and hounded by critics of his governorship, he died of gunshot wounds in October 1809, probably a suicide.

YOUNGER brother of Revolutionary War hero George Rogers Clark, William Clark (1770–1838) was born in Caroline County, Virginia. He was commissioned a lieutenant in 1792 and fought against Indians in the Ohio Valley to 1795. After resigning from the army, he managed his family's plantation in Kentucky (1796–1803) until Meriwether Lewis invited him to co-lead an expedition to the Pacific.

Though their names were forever afterward joined as "Lewis and Clark," the two men had somewhat different duties during their 1804-6 journey, with Clark concentrating on mapmaking and Indian negotiation, Lewis on natural history and expansionist opportunities. After the expedition, Clark served in several western posts, including brigadier general of militia and superintendent of Indian Affairs for Lousiana Territory, and, from 1813 to 1821, governor of Missouri Territory. After Lewis's death in 1809, Clark selected writer Nicholas Biddle to complete the expedition report Lewis had been unable to finish.

Louisiana. It is not only New Orleans that I will cede, it is the whole colony without any reservation." The following day, Madison reached Paris and soon learned from Talleyrand that all of Louisiana was available. Negotiations began on April 14, and both sides quickly agreed on a draft treaty of cession. Circumstances played their part, but the Louisiana Purchase came to pass because Jefferson made it clear what would happen if Louisiana was not part of the United States.

PLANNING THE EXPEDITION

Meriwether Lewis once called the journey to the Pacific his "darling project." Jefferson might not have used just those words, but in the late winter and early spring of 1803 the president put all his energies into planning the expedition. For guidance he turned to recent English experience—especially the three voyages made by Captain James Cook. Those expeditions were official in character, representing British ambitions in the Pacific. The explorers and their ships came from the Royal Navy. Sir Joseph Banks, president of the Royal Society, was the key planner. This approach tied government and private institutions to a program of scientific and imperial exploration. No one was better suited to play the Banks role in North America than the president of the United States and president of the American Philosophical Society.

For an expedition leader, Jefferson turned to his young private secretary, Captain Meriwether

EMPIRE FOR LIBERTY

The answer came in Jefferson's notion of an empire for liberty, what one historian has pointedly called "pious imperialism." By the end of the eighteenth century the American economy was fully commercial and completely a part of the larger Atlantic marketplace. For Americans to remain farmers and planters, there had to be an expanding supply of arable land and a reliable farm-to-market transport system. The West was the republican garden of the world, and Lewis and Clark were to join the garden to the market.

The quiet talk with Irujo marked the private beginnings of the Lewis and Clark expedition. Public events culminating in the Louisiana Purchase now moved with astonishing speed. In January 1803, just a week before secretly asking Congress for funds to prepare the Pacific expedition, Jefferson secured James Monroe's appointment as special envoy

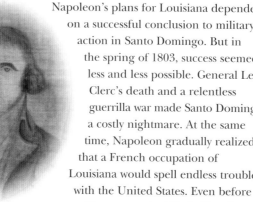

THOMAS JEFFERSON

The task he set for Lewis and Clark went far beyond anything previously attempted by European explorers in North America.

to France. By the time Monroe reached France in early April, the Mississippi crisis had taken two unexpected twists, one widely reported and the other a closely guarded secret. In March, Spain restored the right of deposit at New Orleans. When word of that decision reached Washington in mid-April, it was welcome news, but fears of a French occupation were still at fever pitch.

Napoleon's plans for Louisiana depended on a successful conclusion to military action in Santo Domingo. But in the spring of 1803, success seemed less and less possible. General Le Clerc's death and a relentless guerrilla war made Santo Domingo a costly nightmare. At the same time, Napoleon gradually realized that a French occupation of Louisiana would spell endless troubles with the United States. Even before Monroe reached Paris, Napoleon was determined to offer Louisiana for sale. On April 11 he told Minister of the Treasury Francois de Marbe-Marbois, "I renounce

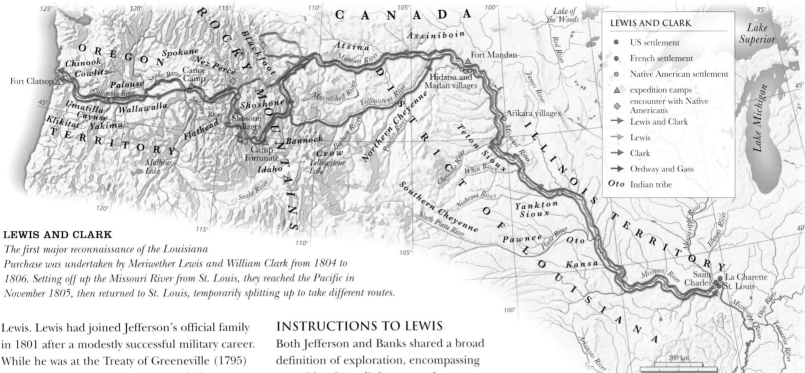

LEWIS AND CLARK

The first major reconnaissance of the Louisiana Purchase was undertaken by Meriwether Lewis and William Clark from 1804 to 1806. Setting off up the Missouri River from St. Louis, they reached the Pacific in November 1805, then returned to St. Louis, temporarily splitting up to take different routes.

Lewis. Lewis had joined Jefferson's official family in 1801 after a modestly successful military career. While he was at the Treaty of Greeneville (1795) that ended Indian resistance in the Ohio country, he took no part in armed actions during those campaigns. Lewis's real skills were as a woodsman and naturalist. As Jefferson later wrote, Lewis had "a talent for observation" that gave him "an accurate knowledge of the plants and animals of his own country." For all his abilities, Lewis had serious problems. He was quick-tempered, impulsive, and suffered from the kind of mood swings that contemporaries called "melancholia." Jefferson recognized those difficulties, describing them as "depressions of the mind."

Given a single task or goal, Lewis pursued it relentlessly. What he could not accept was ambiguity or defeat.

INSTRUCTIONS TO LEWIS

Both Jefferson and Banks shared a broad definition of exploration, encompassing everything from diplomacy and commerce to botany and ethnography. Nothing better illustrates that vision than Jefferson's June 20, 1803, letter to Lewis. That document reflected not only the president's own reading, but the talents of many scientists and cabinet members. Throughout the spring of 1803 Jefferson sought advice from Benjamin Smith Barton, Benjamin Rush, and other members of the Philadelphia scientific community. He also turned to cabinet officers, getting suggestions from Secretary of State James Madison, Secretary of the Treasury Albert Gallatin, and Attorney General Levi Lincoln. What Jefferson fashioned became not only the intellectual center of the Lewis and Clark expedition, but the charter for federal exploration throughout the remainder of the century.

When Jefferson sent James Monroe to France, the instructions and vision behind that initiative were surprisingly narrow. The Lewis and Clark mission, and the conception of

AN UNEXPECTED OBSTACLE

A canoe runs into a tree in this drawing from the journal of Lewis and Clark expedition member Patrick Gass.

continental geography informing it, was far grander. The president instructed Lewis "to explore the Missouri river, and such principal stream of it, as, by it's course and communication with the waters of the Pacific ocean, whether the Columbia, Oregan, Colorado or any other river may offer the most direct and practicable communication across this continent for the purposes of commerce."

Those few words expressed not only the expedition's central purpose, but Jefferson's geographic understanding of the West and the role of the region in national economic and political growth. The president never allowed his explorers to stray from the task at hand—finding a useful trade route across the continent. As Jefferson imagined it, the Missouri River could take the explorers to the edge of the Rockies. An easy portage over a narrow ridge of mountains and the party would find the River of the West and a route to the Pacific. The president envisioned a geographic system designed to insure the agricultural growth of the republic. The "communication across this continent for the purposes of commerce" was a way to link the garden of the West to markets in Europe and Asia.

For all his focus on that task, Jefferson devoted most of the instructions to other things. His western landscape was never an empty place. The garden was spacious, but it already had some settled places. Native people loomed large in the instructions, both as objects of scientific inquiry and as partners—albeit junior ones—in trade and

⇢THE JOURNEY OF LEWIS AND CLARK⇠

ON MAY 14, 1804, approximately forty-five men, led by Meriwether Lewis and William Clark, set out in a keelboat and two pirogues from Camp Dubois, near St. Louis. Following instructions from Thomas Jefferson, they were to travel up the Missouri River as far as possible, then look for a passage by water to the Pacific. Their journey, with all its twists and turns, became one of the best- known episodes in the history of exploration.

Navigating against the strong Missouri current, the Corps of Discovery reached the Mandan Indian villages (near modern Bismarck, North Dakota), 1,600 miles upstream, in late October 1804. Along the way Sergeant Charles Floyd died of a ruptured appendix, the only member of the Corps of Discovery to die on the expedition. After wintering with the Mandans and the nearby Hidatsas, Lewis and Clark sent the keelboat downriver with boxes of artifacts, specimens, and papers.

Leaving Fort Mandan on April 7, 1805, the party of thirty-three included Toussaint Charbonneau, a French-Canadian trader hired as interpreter; his young Shoshone wife Sacagawea; and their two-month-old baby, Pomp. They continued upriver in two pirogues and six dugout canoes. Their laborious portage around the Great Falls of the Missouri took a month to complete, and it was not until August that they reached the Continental Divide and met the Shoshone Indians. In one of the most dramatic moments of the expedition, Sacagawea recognized the Shoshone chief, Cameahwait, as her brother. To the captains' chagrin, there was no passable water route through the Rockies, but the Shoshone sold

them horses and provided a guide to help them traverse the forbidding Bitterroot Mountains.

After an arduous and dangerous crossing, the explorers met the Nez Percé Indians, who helped them build canoes and provided guidance down the Clearwater and Snake rivers to the Columbia River. When the expedition reached the Columbia's mouth on November 7, 1805, Clark reckoned they had traveled 4,162 miles; he was only forty miles off in his estimate.

After a rainy winter camped near the Clatsop Indians, the party began their return journey in March 1806, but deep mountain snows delayed their crossing until June. The captains then split their party into two (and later into five) groups, a potentially disastrous decision. While Lewis took one party east, Clark and the remainder turned south to explore the Yellowstone River. At Great Falls, Lewis and three men went off to explore the Marias River.

Journal of expedition member Patrick Gass, published 1808

HEATH COCK
William Clark drew this image of a heath cock, also known as a sage grouse or cock of the plains.

William Clark's compass, with leather case

CLARK SHOOTING BEARS
On the Lewis and Clark expedition, hunting was a way of collecting both food and specimens for study. This drawing from Patrick Gass's journal shows "Captin Clark and his men shooting Bears."

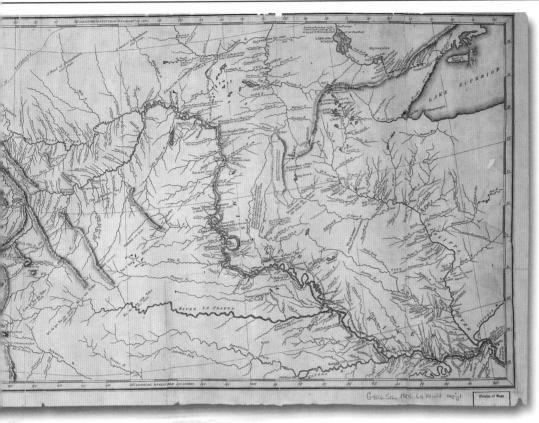

MAPPING THE JOURNEY

Geographer Samuel Lewis copied this map of Lewis and Clark's track across western North America from an original drawing published by Clark in 1814.

diplomacy. Jefferson presented Lewis a detailed list of questions about Indian cultures, ranging from tribal boundaries and politics to languages and clothing. The president's interest in things Indian stemmed from two concerns, one scientific and the other commercial. He was persuaded that native cultures represented an earlier stage in the evolution of human societies. Europeans might study Native Americans as a means to understand another time. At the same time, Jefferson knew that Indians were a vital part of an expanding fur trade.

As Jefferson and Lewis watched the Pacific expedition grow in complexity, they must have known that the original conception of the party as eight or ten men and one officer was no longer realistic. On June 19, a day before the president finished the instructions, Lewis moved to make the expedition much larger. His first move was to recruit a second officer, a co-commander for what became an infantry company on the move. Lewis had known William Clark since the time of the Ohio Indian campaigns. While the two were not close friends, they had stayed in touch over the years. Born in 1770 and four years older than Lewis, Clark came from a distinguished Virginia military family. The most powerful influence on William Clark was his older brother, George Rogers Clark. George Rogers represented personal courage, dedication to duty, and perseverance in the face of adversity. But William also knew that his older brother had flirted with Spanish agents advocating western secession, had slid deep in debt, and was troubled by alcoholism. The example of George Rogers made William Clark both courageous and prudent, a man ready to march to the Pacific, but also intent on protecting personal and family fortunes.

THE EXPEDITION

No story of western exploration is more familiar than the journey made by the Lewis and Clark expedition from St. Louis to the Pacific and back in 1804-6. That story has been memorialized on highway signs, at roadside markers, and in many museums. While never overlooking moments of drama and danger, it makes more sense to imagine the expedition as one human community moving through the lands and lives of other human communities.

In the fall of 1804 more people lived in the Mandan and Hidatsa villages along the Missouri in present-day North Dakota than called St. Louis home. These five earth-lodge villages were at the crossroads of the northern plains. Long before an American exploring party headed up the Missouri, Mandans and Hidatsas were used to welcoming all sorts of strangers. When the expedition built winter quarters at Fort Mandan, their native

Meanwhile, four men from Clark's party set off across the Great Plains with horses, later stolen by Indians. The resourceful men walked to the Yellowstone and made bull boats to carry them downriver. Two Blackfeet were killed in a violent encounter with Lewis's group, while Clark's trip down the Yellowstone was made in two dugouts. Although the corps had been scattered across hundreds of miles, they all reassembled on the Missouri, returning to St. Louis in triumph on September 23, 1806. While they had not found an all-water passage to the Pacific, the expedition had succeeded in many other respects. Lewis and Clark showed America what the West had to offer and set an enduring example of courage and leadership.

neighbors faced a challenge quite unlike any before. Years of experience had taught them to expect certain kinds of behavior from strangers. Looking north to the Canadian trading posts and down the river toward St. Louis, Mandans and Hidatsas were accustomed to visits by small parties of traders. These men always came in small numbers; the largest recorded European trading expedition before Lewis and Clark had ten men. They came for short periods and while a few stayed to join native families, most left after completing trade transactions. Like native merchants who came to exchange horses and fancy leather goods for Mandan corn, the white traders moved easily in and out of the earth-lodge world.

But from the moment Mandans first saw the American expedition in October 1804, they recognized this party as something new under the sun. As Jefferson's explorers built their post and made their observations, native people began to explore the explorers. What happened over the next six months was mutual discovery, the tentative and sometimes confusing process of understanding other peoples and other ways. Just as Lewis and Clark followed the Enlightenment exploration strategies of observation, collection, description, and classification, earth-lodge people pursued their own ways to name the unknown.

The Mandan winter represented an extended time of mutual discovery. Near the end of the expedition, in late July 1806, there was a very different kind of exploration encounter—one that ended in violence and death.

THE MARIAS RIVER

Jefferson believed that all lands drained by the Missouri and its tributaries were included in the Louisiana Purchase. Such an expansive view meant that the United States had claims in the fur-rich countries north of the present-day U. S.-Canadian border. Lewis and Clark decided that on the return journey there had to be a side excursion to examine the upper reaches of the Marias River. Taking along the brothers Joseph and Reubin

HIDE PAINTING
Traveling through the Upper Missouri River country, source of this painting of a battle scene, Lewis and Clark had both peaceful and hostile encounters with Indians.

Field and interpreter George Drouillard, Lewis struck out from the Great Falls of the Missouri to trace the course of the Marias. Lewis soon found that the river did not run as far north as he had hoped. Geographic disappointment was one thing; an encounter with hostile Indians was something else. And there had been plenty of signs that the party was not alone on the shortgrass plains. When the explorers found even more evidence that Indians were around, Lewis confessed that he was "extreemly fortunate in not having met these people."

That good fortune came to a sudden stop the next day. During the afternoon of July 26, Lewis saw what he pointedly described as a "very unpleasant sight." Several Indians were carefully watching George Drouillard as he scouted the Two Medicine River valley in present-day Pondera County, Montana. At that moment Lewis decided he could not hide from these Indians. He did not know that the Indians were Piegan Blackfeet. After cautiously circling each other, the explorers and the Indians settled in to an evening camp by three solitary cottonwoods along the Two Medicine River.

Around the fire that night, Lewis used Drouillard's signs to make "much conversation" with the young Piegans. In that talk there was one troubling piece of news: the Piegans had at least one white trader in their camp. Pressing for more details, Lewis learned what Jefferson feared.

Traders from the North West Company and the Hudson's Bay Company were active in the Northern Rockies. From posts like Rocky Mountain House and Buckingham House, the Blackfeet exchanged beaver and wolf pelts for guns, ammunition, and alcohol. While this was bad news for American traders, what Lewis told the Blackfeet darkened the native future. The American blandly announced there would be an alliance of Nez Percés, Shoshones, and Kutenais—traditional Blackfeet enemies—secured by American arms and supplies. Here was news of a profound geopolitical shift. It promised a new order in the Rockies, one where the Blackfeet no longer held full sway.

VIOLENCE BREAKS OUT

But matters of politics and imperial power were not on the minds of these young Indians in the early morning hours of July 27. They were thinking about taking horses and guns, acts that would win them personal honor. When Joseph Field dozed off, one Piegan grabbed his gun while others moved quickly to take weapons from Drouillard and Lewis. In the confusion and fighting that followed, Reubin Field chased down

and killed Side Hill Calf. Having failed to get guns, the surviving Piegans turned their attention to horses. Lewis knew at once that this was the greatest threat. His party could survive without guns, but robbed of horses they would be stranded in a dangerous country. In a moment of fury, Lewis pursued one Piegan and shot him. As quickly as the violence exploded, it vanished. But to make sure the Piegans knew they were up against a new enemy, Lewis put a peace medal—one of those medals carried by the expedition to give to Indian leaders as a sign of American sovereignty—around the neck of one dead Indian. As the explorer later explained, the medal was there that "they might be informed who we were." The medals were calling cards of empire; they promised the storm to come.

PEACE MEDAL
During their expedition, Lewis and Clark gave these peace medals to tribal chiefs as signs of American sovereignty.

ELK HERD IN MONTANA
Some of the territory through which Lewis and Clark passed has been preserved in a state they would have found familiar. Here elks run through the Sun River Game Preserve, Bob Marshall Wilderness Area, Montana.

GRAND CANYON
With the West laid open by Lewis and Clark, Americans were soon to become familiar with such vistas as Arizona's Grand Canyon.

"[AMERICAN]
TRAPPERS...
[ARE] PEOPLE OF
THE WORST
CHARACTER...
THIS
'MOTLEY CREW'
ACKNOWLEDGE
NO MASTER,
WILL CONFORM
TO NO RULES."

—SIR GEORGE SIMPSON
OF THE HUDSON'S BAY
COMPANY, 1829

THE FIRST AMERICAN EMPIRE IN THE WEST

ENTREPRENEURS SUCH AS MANUEL LISA SOON SENT FUR TRADERS WEST TO CAPITALIZE ON LEWIS AND CLARK'S DISCOVERIES. ONE OF THESE MERCHANTS WAS JOHN JACOB ASTOR, WHOSE PACIFIC FUR COMPANY ATTEMPTED TO WREST CONTROL OF THE FUR TRADE FROM CANADIAN RIVALS WHILE SECURING AN AMERICAN CLAIM TO THE NORTHWEST.

LEWIS AND CLARK never met North West Company employee Peter Corney. But writing more than a decade after the expedition returned to St. Louis, Corney grasped the larger significance of the Lewis and Clark journey. "The whole of that western country," he wrote, "is now laid open." The American explorers had been involved in an opening on a continental scale. As Lewis and Clark unpacked their journals, maps, and botanical specimens, the character of that opening became clear. There were plants and animals new to European science. Journal entries described a whole range of landscapes and climates. Maps gave visual and spatial definition to those written descriptions. And in everything there were signs of native people. Even the most casual observer now knew that Jefferson's garden was Indian country.

Lewis and Clark pried open the western country for the eyes of science. But Corney meant something more than intellectual discovery when he used the phrase "laid open." From his vantage point in the early 1820s, he understood that the expedition was the opening shot in an imperial war for the West. The expedition was not the legal foundation for American claims in the Northwest. Those assertions, as Jefferson explained to geographer John Melish in 1816, were based on Astoria as a permanent settlement at the mouth of the Columbia River. Lewis and Clark's Fort Clatsop, built in December 1805 near the mouth of the Columbia as the expedition's winter post, might not satisfy diplomats wrangling about the future of the Oregon country, but it did represent the American intention to play the imperial game on the whole western field.

LEWIS REPORTS TO JEFFERSON

Corney's confidence was not completely shared by Lewis and Clark. For them the meaning of their "tour" was far more confused and uncertain. No sooner had the Corps of Discovery reached St. Louis than Lewis was busy explaining away the expedition's failure to accomplish its central

UPPER MISSOURI RIVER

Inspired by the findings of the Lewis and Clark expedition, entrepreneurs such as Manuel Lisa saw the upper Missouri River, depicted in this 1832 painting by George Catlin, as a royal road to a fur-trading empire.

purpose. Jefferson had defined that mission in unequivocal terms. His captains were charged to find the passage through the garden, the "communication" bridging the continent from Atlantic to Pacific waters. Lewis and Clark had not found the president's hopeful geography. Instead, they found hazardous rivers, boiling rapids, and "tremendious" mountains.

Lewis's letter to Jefferson, dated September 23, 1806, was a sleight-of-hand masterpiece. Lewis told the president that the expedition had found "the most practicable route which does exist across the continent by means of the navigable branches of the Missouri and Columbia Rivers." Having announced the passage as the mainline across the West, Lewis promptly downgraded it to a bumpy branchline. "We view this passage across the Continent as affording immence advantages to the fur trade, but fear that the advantages which it offers as a communication for the productions of the East Indies to the United States and thence to Europe will never be found equal on an extensive scale to that by way of the Cape of Good Hope." The passage might be fine for goods "not bulky, brittle, nor of a very perishable nature." Furs, yes; agricultural goods from the republican garden, no. This was not what Jefferson had in mind. Unless the garden joined the market, Americans would abandon republican ways for the lure of cities and the tyrannies of monarchy. A joyful president welcomed his explorers home. A more sober Jefferson must have wondered what the journey had revealed after all.

MANUEL LISA AND THE FUR TRADE

If Jefferson was uncertain about the expedition's meaning, merchants and traders in St. Louis quickly understood its commercial consequences. The fur trade up the Missouri was already growing well before Lewis and Clark. Expedition reports expanded that enterprise, giving it new energy and direction. No St. Louis entrepreneur responded more quickly and with more determination than Manuel Lisa. Coming to St. Louis in 1798 from New Orleans, Lisa soon established a reputation as a feisty trader with expansive ambitions. He ran afoul of many rivals; Lewis once angrily called him "damn Manuel." Kept out of the Osage trade by the Chouteau monopoly and outmaneuvered for a place in the Santa Fe trade by General James Wilkinson, Lisa was eager to act on new possibilities. As he later told Clark, "I put into my operations great activity; I go a great distance while some are considering whether they will start today or tomorrow."

Other St. Louis fur trade planners had plotted grand schemes for empires up the Missouri and

MISSOURI RIVER FALLS AND PORTAGE

The Lewis and Clark expedition brought back a wealth of geographic information useful to fur traders, including this map, drawn by William Clark, of falls and portage on the Missouri River.

toward the mountains. Thanks to Lewis and Clark, the energetic Lisa now had reliable knowledge about both the Yellowstone country and the fur-rich Three Forks region of present-day western Montana. That information came in large part from George Drouillard, Lewis and Clark's ablest hunter and scout. By the spring of 1807 Drouillard had joined Lisa along with expedition veterans John Colter, Peter Wiser, and John Potts. Using their connections, Lisa and Drouillard recruited a party of fifty or sixty men—the first organized trading and trapping expedition up the Missouri after Lewis and Clark.

After considerable trouble on the river, Lisa's expedition reached the junction of the Yellowstone and the Bighorn rivers in the fall of 1807 and built Fort Raymond. It was one thing to build a post and something quite different to announce its presence to potential Indian partners. That task fell to John Colter.

From an undisciplined rowdy when he first joined Lewis and Clark's Corps of Discovery, Colter had matured

in a few years to become a frontiersman of exceptional ability. In the winter of 1807–8, Colter made a solitary reconnaissance of present-day northwestern Wyoming, a journey that soon grew to legendary status. Manuel Lisa was not interested in legends. Pelts and profits were what counted. And after doing some counting, Lisa was persuaded that the western fur business was worth the price.

Back in St. Louis during the winter of 1808–9, Lisa began laying plans for a full-fledged fur company. With backing from William Clark, Auguste Chouteau, Jr., and Andrew Henry, Lisa established the Missouri Fur Company. The company's first move was to plan a large expedition, scheduled for the spring of 1809.

Some 160 men, many of them wholly inexperienced, signed on for the journey. It should have come as no surprise that many deserted on the way up river. While those desertions lessened the Missouri Company's labor force, they did not diminish Lisa's determination. In the spring of 1810 some eighty fur hunters,

CANADIAN TRADER

American fur merchant John Jacob Astor preferred to hire Canadian fur trappers and traders for the expertise they had gained through long experience in the field. This image of a "Canadian half-breed trapper" was engraved in 1871.

"THE VETERAN TRAPPERS...OF [MANUEL] LISA'S PARTY SHOOK THEIR HEADS AS THEIR COMRADES SET OUT, AND TOOK LEAVE OF THEM AS OF DOOMED MEN."

—WASHINGTON IRVING, 1836, ON WILSON PRICE HUNT'S 1811 EXPEDITION TO THE PACIFIC

✦CANOES✦

UNTIL THE ARRIVAL of the horse, travel tended to follow water routes. To navigate North America's rivers and lakes, some Native Americans became skilled at building canoes, vessels pointed on each end and propelled by paddles, which were later adopted by American frontiersmen and explorers.

Canoes were of five main types. The most familiar today is the slim, portable birch-bark canoe, used by nations of the Northeast. Other types included the kayaks and umiaks of the northern peoples and the crude balsa boats used by nations in California and the Southwest. The Arikara, Hidatsa, and Mandan nations were noted for their small, circular boats made by stretching a bull

buffalo skin around a willow framework. These clumsy "bull boats," or skin canoes, were used for short river trips, and the Lewis and Clark expedition made them at least twice during their journey.

The most common type of canoe in North America was the dugout. Made from hollowed-out logs, dugouts were usually worked and shaped with adzes, gouges, wedges, and knives. From the Nez Percé Indians, Lewis and Clark learned to use fire to burn out the log's center. Ranging from crude, simple craft to elaborate boats superbly carved and painted, dugouts were strong enough to withstand rocks and rapids and could carry significant quantities of goods and equipment.

and danger in unequal measures. What Lisa wanted was profit and when that goal eluded him, the company dissolved in January 1812.

JOHN JACOB ASTOR

Manuel Lisa was not the only fur trade entrepreneur who saw empire in both personal and national terms. No merchant adventurer more fully linked the fur trade to American expansion than John Jacob Astor. By the time of the Louisiana Purchase, Astor was an established New York City fur merchant, buying pelts each year at the Montreal trading market. Those connections made Astor something more than a provincial businessman with a regional focus. In Montreal the sociable Astor enjoyed invitations from some of the most influential Nor'westers. In private homes and at gala meetings of the Beaver Club, Astor heard about the plans laid by Pond and Mackenzie. And Astor's Montreal agent and mentor was none other than Alexander Henry the Elder, one of the foremost fur-trade geographers. News of the Lewis and Clark expedition simply repeated the lessons learned from such Canadian tutors.

In late January 1808, at the very time Lisa was struggling to define his own fur trade empire, John Astor wrote New York politician DeWitt Clinton, spelling out a remarkable scheme for western expansion. In cautious but unmistakable terms, Astor laid out plans "on the Subject of a company for carrying on the furr trade in the United States even more extensive than it is done by the companys in Canada." Borrowing liberally from his Canadian teachers, Astor sketched an ambitious strategy for American domain from the Great Lakes to the Pacific. As he elaborated it over the next two years, the plan called for a series of trading posts up the Missouri and across

DEWITT CLINTON
In 1808 New York politician DeWitt Clinton received a letter from John Jacob Astor proposing a fur-trading empire based in New York. Later the state's governor, Clinton is best known for supporting the building of the Erie Canal.

including Colter, Drouillard, and Meriwether Lewis's brother Reuben left Fort Raymond for the Three Forks country. Three Forks was anything but kind to Lisa's men. They met fierce resistance from the Blackfeet, who saw them as both commercial rivals and allies to traditional enemies. A number of trappers, including Drouillard and Potts, were killed, and Colter barely escaped with his life.

Andrew Henry's party was more fortunate. Taking an Indian trail over Bannock Pass, the trappers crossed the Continental Divide into present-day Idaho and briefly established a trading post on Henry's Fork of the Green River. Lisa's men got adventure, geographical information,

⟶JOHN JACOB ASTOR⟵

BORN TO A BUTCHER in Waldorf, Germany, John Jacob Astor (1763–1848) had $25 when he came to the United States in 1783. An uneducated man of amazing financial vision, he quickly became successful in the fur business, employing agents to buy directly from Native Americans and shipping the furs to China and Europe, where they brought high prices. In 1808 he set up the American Fur Company to trade along the Missouri and across to the Pacific; subsidiaries included the Pacific Fur Company. Astor's proposed trading post at the mouth of the Columbia river had the dual advantage of establishing an American presence in the region and providing a depot from which to ship furs direct to China. Astoria, founded in 1811, became the first permanent settlement in the Pacific Northwest but was sold to Canadian rivals during the War of 1812. Astor nonetheless profited from the war, raising funds in the first U.S. bond issue. He continued to dominate the fur trade until he sold out his interests in 1834 and concentrated on buying real estate in New York. At his death he was worth more than $20 million—and, reportedly, regretful that he had not bought all of Manhattan.

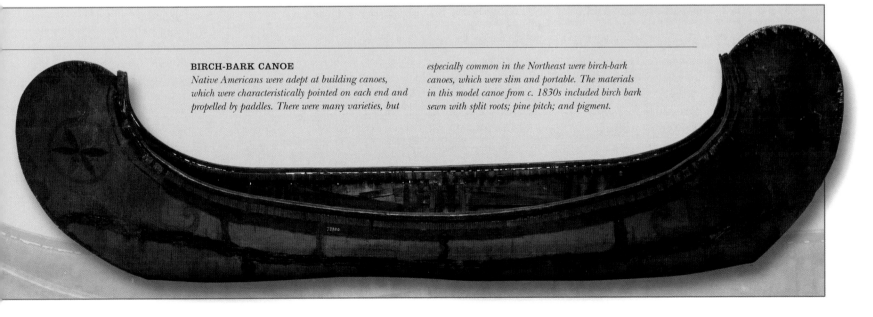

BIRCH-BARK CANOE
Native Americans were adept at building canoes, which were characteristically pointed on each end and propelled by paddles. There were many varieties, but especially common in the Northeast were birch-bark canoes, which were slim and portable. The materials in this model canoe from c. 1830s included birch bark sewn with split roots; pine pitch; and pigment.

❖YELLOWSTONE❖

ALTHOUGH NATIVE AMERICANS had explored the Yellowstone region countless years, the first white man to pass through the area was beaver trapper John Colter, a member of the Lewis and Clark expedition, in 1807. In the early 1800s, trappers such as Jim Bridger and Joe Meek wandered through the region, later regaling others with virtually unbelievable tales of steaming springs, spouting geysers, and petrified trees.

Significant exploration, however, did not occur until 1869, when David E. Folsom, Charles W. Cook, and William Peterson, all from Montana, journeyed through Yellowstone. The following year, Henry Washburn, surveyor general of Montana, led a six-week expedition that included a U.S. Cavalry escort. In 1871, scientist Ferdinand V. Hayden led a larger party that included photographer William H. Jackson and artist Thomas Moran.

With Jackson's photos and Moran's sketches of the wonders of Yellowstone, Congress had sufficient evidence to set aside the region "as a public park or pleasuring-ground." On March 1, 1872, the United States Congress passed the Yellowstone Act of 1872, preserving 2,221,773 acres of pristine land—primarily in northwestern Wyoming but also including areas of eastern Idaho and southern Montana—for public use and protecting it from commercial exploitation, thereby creating the world's first national park.

YELLOWSTONE
Thomas Moran's images helped bring Yellowstone to America's attention. This painting depicts the Grand Canyon of the Yellowstone River.

the continent. The commercial network would be anchored in New York, with field offices in St. Louis and at the mouth of the Columbia. Such a vast system required an extensive transportation and communication network. Astor envisioned two distinct connections between the western trapping grounds and markets in Europe and China. Experience with the Northwest coast fur trade suggested shipping routes from New York to the Columbia around the Cape of Good Hope via Hawaii. The heaviest goods and items of low priority could use that seaborne system. Company dispatches, new employees, and some furs might travel overland on routes pioneered by Astor's men. Most of Astor's plan had been talked about in Montreal for two decades. What he gave it was personal energy, unrelenting determination, and financial resources.

Like his rivals in the North West Company, Astor wanted his Pacific Fur Company to be wrapped in the flag of national interest. His traders were not merely employees, but agents of a political enterprise. As Astor smoothly explained to Albert Gallatin, the Pacific Fur Company would "act as much as possible with its [the United States's] wishes." The security Astor wanted was official "approbation," a slippery word if ever there was one. By 1810 he thought he had it, only to see that security slip away in times of crisis.

Astor's quest for protection extended to the employees he recruited. Years of experience taught him that Canadian traders and voyageurs were essential for success. At the same time, Astor knew his company had to have the appearance of an American enterprise. The Pacific Fur Company's ablest employees were recruited around Montreal,

and the company's roster was filled with Canadian and French-Canadian names—men like Donald Mackenzie, Guillaume Le Roux, and Jean-Baptiste Prevost. However, Astor's choice for chief field agent was made on the basis of citizenship, not travel skills or organizational abilities. Wilson Price Hunt, born in New Jersey and a St. Louis merchant since 1803, had no direct fur trade experience. No matter how interested he was in the possibilities of the West for personal fortune or national expansion, Hunt was an inexperienced expedition leader.

HUNT'S EXPEDITIONS

Bernard DeVoto once said that the stars danced for Lewis and Clark. The first American crossing of the continent was remarkably well organized, enjoyed endless turns of good fortune, and delivered much of what Jefferson demanded. Lewis and Clark did not find the Northwest Passage, but there were plenty of consolation prizes. The second American continental crossing, as headed by Hunt, was poorly organized, badly led, and had one piece of wretched luck after another.

Hunt's original plan was to follow the Lewis and Clark track up the Missouri and over the Rockies to the Pacific. But talks with Clark and Colter persuaded him that the Yellowstone route was quicker and safer. That revised plan was abandoned in late May 1811 when Hunt's party was about to leave the Ponca village just below the mouth of the Niobrara River. There Hunt met Jacob Reznor, Edward Robinson, and John Hoback, members of Andrew Henry's 1809–10 expedition. Their travels had taken them over the Continental Divide to the Snake River country, across the Teton Range to present-day Jackson Hole, and along the Wind River. From these mountain men Hunt made a third travel plan, one that called for leaving the Missouri at the Arikara villages and striking southwest through present-day South Dakota and Wyoming. The trappers persuaded Hunt that somewhere around present-day Shoshone, Wyoming, the party could follow the Wind River to a narrow ridge of mountains. Once across, the travelers would soon find the Columbia. Henry's men did have a good grasp of the Wind River country, but they knew nothing about the hazards of the Snake River.

The overland Astorians barely survived their Snake River ordeal. Starvation, terrible weather, and raging waters were their constant companions. What they found at the mouth of the Columbia was a modest trading post, built in the spring of 1811 by Pacific Fur Company employees who had come on the ship *Tonquin*. Astoria was hardly the impressive imperial and commercial entrepot Astor had imagined. Further, because Astor played on the world stage, his plans were hostage to forces largely beyond his control. No matter how cunning, Astor could not escape the swirl of events that surrounded the War of 1812.

Because of that war, Astoria became a strategic target, albeit a minor one. Most of Astor's employees, certainly influential partners like Duncan McDougall and Donald Mackenzie, were subjects of the British crown. When news of the war reached Astoria on January 16, 1813, Astor's partners decided to cut their losses and abandon the enterprise. They were convinced that a British naval force was on the way to destroy Astoria. As it turned out, the Royal Navy did not reach the Columbia until the first week of December 1813. By that time Astoria had been sold to agents of Astor's rival, the North West Company.

THE WAR OF 1812
Astor's trading post Astoria was sold in 1813 when his partners became convinced that a British naval force was on its way to destroy it during the War of 1812. Here the USS Chesapeake *confronts the HMS* Shannon.

BEAVER
The fur-trading empire of the 1820s and 1830s was founded on international demand for beaver felt used in making men's hats.

"TO ENTERPRISING YOUNG MEN: THE SUBSCRIBER WISHES TO ENGAGE ONE HUNDRED MEN, TO ASCEND THE RIVER MISSOURI TO ITS SOURCES."

—ADVERTISEMENT TAKEN OUT BY FUR TRADER WILLIAM H. ASHLEY, 1822

THE EMPIRE REBORN

DURING THE 1820s, THE ASHLEY-HENRY EXPLORATIONS BREATHED NEW LIFE INTO THE AMERICAN FUR TRADE. KEY TO THE SUCCESS OF WILLIAM H. ASHLEY AND ANDREW HENRY'S FUR-TRADING ENTERPRISE WERE THE FAMED MOUNTAIN MEN. THESE ADVENTUROUS TRAPPERS AND TRADERS HELPED BLAZE NEW TRAILS THROUGH THE WEST THAT THOUSANDS OF AMERICANS WOULD FOLLOW IN THE DECADES TO COME.

ANYONE SURVEYING the West in 1814 would have recognized that Jefferson's bold initiative was stopped dead in its tracks. Astoria, now renamed Fort George, was in the hands of the Canadians. American traders had been driven out of the upper Missouri country. Native American leaders from the Great Lakes to the northern Rockies saw Canadians as the most reliable partners. The fur trade, the

principal incentive for American expansion, was in deep depression. The West in 1814 was still an imperial battleground, but at least one of the armies seemed in full retreat.

Soon after Lewis and Clark returned from their epic journey, Jefferson expressed the hope that some "enterprizing mercantile Americans" would take up the commercial challenge set out by the Corps of Discovery. Astor undoubtedly saw

SMITH IN THE DESERT
*Mountain man Jedediah Strong Smith
made many extraordinary journeys across the
West. In one of his most celebrated, depicted in this
painting by Frederic Remington, he led a party across
the inhospitable Mojave Desert during his 1826–27
overland trek to California.*

During the spring and summer of 1822, Henry established a post on the Yellowstone, but the venture suffered a painful reversal when valuable goods were lost in a river accident. Persuaded that there was still money in fur, Ashley and Henry spent the winter of 1822–23 recruiting additional employees. The partners now envisioned a more complex fur trade strategy, one that involved both Indians and company trappers. To make that approach pay off, Ashley and Henry hired an extraordinary band of frontiersmen. Thomas Fitzpatrick, William L. Sublette, James Clyman, David E. Jackson, and Edward Rose joined Jedediah Strong Smith and James Bridger. Together they made up the American mountain man elite.

Spring 1823 found Ashley's forces heading up the Missouri toward the Yellowstone country. But in April their plans collapsed in gunfire and sudden death. The Arikaras had welcomed Lewis and Clark in 1804, but now they were increasingly hostile to St. Louis traders. That hostility sprang from careful calculations of economic advantage and political influence. Like their Teton Sioux neighbors, the Arikaras enjoyed power as brokers and merchant intermediaries. The St. Louis traders threatened that position and Ashley's men

himself in that role. The fates and furies of war and diplomacy kept him from that destiny. Manuel Lisa's death in 1820 meant that he was no longer a candidate for fur trade leadership.

Between 1820 and 1822 no single individual dominated the St. Louis fur trade. Instead, five small companies fought for the fur wealth of the northern plains and the Rockies. As the global fur business gradually recovered, the stage was set for an entrepreneur with Lisa's energy and Astor's grasp of strategy and geography. William H. Ashley, Missouri businessman and politician, hoped he could play that part. Ashley and his partner, the redoubtable Andrew Henry, now launched the second American invasion of the West.

In mid-February 1822 Ashley and Henry began to advertise in St. Louis newspapers for 100 "Enterprizing Young Men." The partners initially had in mind the traditional fur trade strategy, one that made native people the trappers while company employees stayed at trading stations. Yet the implication was that Ashley's men might do something more than remain behind log walls.

⇥JAMES BRIDGER & JEDEDIAH STRONG SMITH⇤

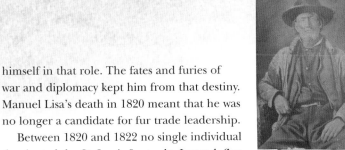

BORN in Virginia, mountain man Jim Bridger (1804–1881) went to St. Louis with his family around 1812 and was orphaned some five years later. In 1822 he volunteered to join William H. Ashley's fur-trapping party on the upper Missouri, and for the next 20 years his trapping took him into areas previously unexplored in today's Wyoming, Idaho, Utah, and Colorado. During the winter of 1824–25, he became the first non-Indian to reach the Great Salt Lake, which he initially assumed to be an arm of the Pacific Ocean. In 1843 he established Fort Bridger in southern Wyoming, running it as a supply post for the next ten years. He discovered Bridger's Pass through the Rockies (now part of Interstate 80) in 1850. The following year he was an interpreter for the Shoshones in the great Treaty Council. After the Mormons drove him from Utah in 1853, he returned in 1857 to guide General Johnston's invasion party. He later served as guide in the Yellowstone expedition of 1859–60 and the Powder River expedition of 1865–66. He retired in 1868, having led more wagon trains west than all other guides.

MOUNTAIN man Jedediah Strong Smith (1799-1831) was born near Binghamton, New York. In 1822 he enlisted with William H. Ashley to trap furs along the upper Missouri River and northern Rockies. In 1824 he led a group that crossed the central Rockies westward via South Pass, then traveled north to southern Idaho. Although South Pass had been discovered earlier, Smith opened it up as a regular route through the Rockies.

During his short life, Smith traveled through more unexplored territory than any other non-Indian. On his most famous journey, in 1826–27, he led a party to the Great Basin and Great Salt Lake, west across the Mojave Desert towards Los Angeles, and then north and east through the Sierra Nevada. He was the first non-Indian to explore the Great Basin and the first American to travel to and from California overland.

In 1830 Smith turned to trading along the Santa Fe trail from Missouri to New Mexico. He died the following year in a Comanche ambush.

paid the price. Pinned down by withering fire, the adventurers lost fourteen of their number before escaping the ambush.

In the aftermath of the Arikara disaster, Ashley was forced into an innovative strategy. Born of desperation and daring, the plan called for company men to strike west away from the river to find trapping grounds far from Arikara or Blackfoot warriors. Ashley sent Henry, Fitzpatrick, Smith, and Clyman riding into the Wind River country. Smith's journey had remarkable and enduring consequences. In February or March 1824, this group crossed the Continental Divide from east to west over what is now called South Pass. A broad saddle straddling the divide, South Pass was the key not only to fur trade expansion but also to later overland emigration to Oregon and California.

Jedediah Smith's trappers were not the first Americans through the pass. Pacific Fur Company agent Robert Stuart had led a group of eastbound Astorians over the divide in late October 1812, but the demise of Astor's company and the disruptions caused by the War of 1812 made

it difficult to follow up on this discovery. Ashley, however, immediately understood the meaning of South Pass as part of a larger transportation system linking St. Louis to trapping grounds in the Rockies. By September 1824 he applied to Indian Superintendent William Clark for a license to trade with Indians beyond the Continental Divide. Smith's rediscovery of South Pass and Ashley's license from Clark marked the renewal of American commercial ambitions in the West.

THE MOUNTAIN MAN SYSTEM

The story of the Rocky Mountain trapping system is often told as a series of colorful anecdotes featuring the exploits of daring mountain men. But the meaning of the mountain man decade from 1825 to 1835 has less to do with drama and adventure, although there was plenty of that. Ashley knew the system was all about profit and organization. And like Astor, he recognized that commerce and empire marched together. The Rocky Mountain trapping system was just that: a system for hunting animals, managing labor, accumulating wealth, and advancing national ambitions. The principal

ARIKARA MAN

In 1823 an attack by Arikara Indians forced fur merchant William H. Ashley to seek fur-trapping lands far from Arikara country. The result was the development of the mountain man system for trapping furs. This Arikara man was photographed in the early twentieth century.

ARIKARA BATTLE

The Arikaras enjoyed a position of power and influence as merchant intermediaries. In this George Catlin painting, they do battle with the Mandans, a rival tribe.

"THERE WAS A TIME WHEN OUR PEOPLE COVERED THE LAND AS THE WAVES OF A WIND-RUFFLED SEA COVER ITS SHELL-PAVED FLOOR ADD MORE TO QUOTE TEXT ADD MORE TO."

—SEATTLE (SEALTH), DUWAMISH-SUQUAMISH CHIEF, 1855

trappers were Americans, not native people. Indians might bring pelts to the annual rendezvous and exchange them for manufactured goods, but those bargains were incidental to the real fur business as Ashley imagined it.

The system depended on three kinds of non-native laborers. Company employees were called *engagés*, a reminder of the French heritage in fur trade culture. Skin trappers were "fur trade share croppers," working on credit advanced by employers. Finally there were the free trappers, independent entrepreneurs who traveled alone or in small groups, showing up at rendezvous times to sell furs at the best price. What modern eyes see as a romantic and colorful mountain man society was in fact an occupational culture. The work of trapping and trading fashioned a language, a clothing style, and a set of social customs. Mountain men, whether they stayed in the fur business for a year or a lifetime, were part of a world made by the demands of work. Nathaniel J. Wyeth, an enterprising fur merchant, was not far wrong when he called the trappers "mere slaves to catch beavers for others."

The fur business in North America had long been tied to the whims of male fashion. Beaver felt provided the fabric for men's hats. And no respectable Euro-American man, whether in a civilian occupation or in the military, neglected to wear a hat as a sign of status and prestige. But when silk replaced beaver felt, the fur market experienced a dramatic collapse, bringing the mountain man decade to an end.

✦THE MOUNTAIN MAN CULTURE✦

SETH KINMAN
This mountain man sports buckskins and is seated in a bearskin chair.

EVEN BEFORE Lewis and Clark returned from their epic exploration of 1804–6, frontiersmen had begun venturing westward to trap beavers and trade with Native Americans. Some discovered unexplored territory and blazed new trails to the Pacific. These were the mountain men, whose heyday lasted less than two decades, but whose role in the opening of the West has become the stuff of legend.

In 1822 William H. Ashley, a St. Louis businessman, started advertising for men to take part in a trapping expedition up the Missouri river. Until then, the usual practice had been to trade goods for furs trapped by Native Americans. Alternatively, semipermanent trading posts were built upcountry. After initial failures, Ashley introduced a new system of "free trappers," who would operate in small brigades over a wide area. In 1825 he initiated the annual rendezvous, where trappers gathered in July at a prespecified location, meeting with traders and selling their furs for cash and supplies to take them through another year's trapping. The rendezvous continued until 1840, and over time they evolved into a form of carnival where the mountain men engaged in raucous singing, dancing, drinking, gambling, and racing.

The mountain man wore clothes made from animal skins; his equipment included a horse and saddlery, beaver traps and bait, a gun and ammunition, a knife, tobacco, and fire-making tools. Trapping began in the spring and lasted until the quality of the beaver pelts deteriorated

in the warmer weather, then began again in the fall. The calendar, the weather, and the environment prescribed the mountain man's way of life. Winters were long and tedious, so the summer rendezvous provided a rare opportunity to relax and enjoy the company of one's fellows.

As increasing numbers participated in the lucrative trade, the more adventurous mountain men moved even further west, into and across the mountains, seeking new, virgin areas to trap. Though some were killed by hostile Indians, they posed little or no threat to Native Americans whose territories they entered. Some even became members of local tribes; the African American Jim Beckwourth, for example, was made a chief of the Crow nation. Many took Indian wives and adopted the way of life of the tribe among whom they lived.

Some mountain men were employed by fur-trading companies; others contracted a fixed percentage of their furs for supplies. The aristocrats of the trade, the free trappers, went and trapped where they liked, selling their furs to the highest bidder. Many became explorers and guides who surveyed new territory and led parties into the West. The best known included Jedediah Strong Smith, Jim Bridger, Thomas Fitzpatrick, Kit Carson, and William L. Sublette. As the fur trade went into decline in the 1830s, the mountain man culture died out, leaving behind legends that never died.

SUDDEN HALT
In this 1866 lithograph, fur trappers on horseback halt behind a hill as Indians are observed. One trapper holds pack mules in the background.

ESKIMO FUR TRADING
Fur traders collected much geographic knowledge of remote places. This trader buys white fox furs and other skins from an Eskimo.

"THE GREEN CARPETED BLUFFS INVITED ME TO RECLINE...I WAS AT ONCE LOST IN CONTEMPLATION. SOUL MELTING SCENERY...WAS ABOUT ME!"

—PAINTER GEORGE CATLIN, 1841

EMPIRES OF THE MIND: ART AND SCIENCE IN THE EARLY WEST

IN THE EARLY NINETEENTH CENTURY, WRITERS, ARTISTS, AND MAPMAKERS FOUND A LARGE AUDIENCE FOR WORDS AND IMAGES DESCRIBING THE WEST. FROM THE JOURNALS OF MERIWETHER LEWIS AND WILLIAM CLARK TO THE PAINTINGS OF GEORGE CATLIN AND KARL BODMER, THESE DOCUMENTS THRILLED A PUBLIC CURIOUS ABOUT THE CONTINENT'S WESTERN REACHES.

WHEN THOMAS JEFFERSON presented his annual message to Congress in late December 1806, he reported that Lewis and Clark had "learnt the character of the country." But the president knew that learning the country meant little unless that knowledge was available to a wider audience. Jefferson expected that Lewis would quickly begin preparing the expedition's formal report, a narrative much like those produced by the Cook and Vancouver expeditions. No one expected that the explorers' unedited notes and journals would appear before the public.

Lewis went to his formidable task with commendable energy. He engaged a publisher, gathered additional material, and warned off potential competitors. But in the years after the expedition's return, Lewis slipped into a morass of difficulties as governor of the Louisiana Territory. Those political troubles were compounded by personal confusions. The expedition report was an early victim of those problems. When Lewis showed no progress withthe narrative, Jefferson testily wrote that "every body is impatient" for the volumes. After Lewis's suicide in 1809, his publisher told Jefferson that the press had not received a single line from the would-be author.

Lewis's failure as an author did not mean that the expedition's accomplishments were kept from the public. Many newspapers reprinted William Clark's letter of September 23, 1806, outlining the expedition's route to the Pacific and some of its notable discoveries. As fortune had it, the first published expedition journal came not from Lewis but from Patrick Gass, one of the party's sergeants. Gass kept a diary throughout the trip and handed it over to Pittsburgh printer David McKeehan. While modern scholars have often been critical of McKeehan for rewriting and sanitizing Gass's journal, what the printer did was wholly acceptable by nineteenth-century standards. McKeehan produced a colorful story, short on science but with enough adventure to satisfy generations of readers.

BIDDLE AND CLARK

After Lewis's death, Clark began the long process of finding a suitable author for the expedition's report. He finally settled on Nicholas Biddle, writer and member of an influential Philadelphia family. Biddle reviewed the Lewis and

PATRICK GASS
Last survivor of the Lewis and Clark expedition, Gass reported his experiences in a published diary.

EXPLORERS AT WORK
Government-sponsored exploration was important in mapping the West. The Army engineers in this illustration from 1852 are exploring the valley of the Great Salt Lake in Utah.

Clark journals, studied Sgt. John Ordway's richly detailed diary, and carried on an extensive correspondence with Clark. After endless delays, *The History of the Expedition under the Command of Captains Lewis and Clark* was published in two volumes in 1814. Biddle fashioned a superb story, but what was missing was science—the botany, zoology, and ethnography that Jefferson now touted as the expedition's chief accomplishment.

If the consequences of Biddle's *History* were hard to judge at the time of its publication, the map of the West that accompanied the report had far greater impact. In 1810 Clark sent Biddle a highly detailed map he had been preparing for some time. That map reflected not only the Lewis and Clark journey but the southwestern expedition of American army explorer Lt. Zebulon Montgomery Pike (1806–7) and several fur trade adventurers. The map published in 1814 offered a blend of new information and old ideas. The image of western mountains reveals how

⇞ZEBULON PIKE⇞

THE FRONTIER explorations of Army officer Zebulon Montgomery Pike (1779–1813) rivaled those of Lewis and Clark. Born in Lamberton, New Jersey, the son of a veteran of the American Revolution, he enlisted in the army at age fifteen. In 1805–6 he led a party to find the headwaters of the Mississippi, which he erroneously concluded was Leech Lake in northern Minnesota. (The real source is Lake Itasca.) Later that year Pike was sent to explore the Red and Arkansas rivers in the Southwest, then Spanish territory. His journey took him due west from St. Louis to the Rocky Mountains, where he wintered before turning south and reaching the Rio Grande. It was in November 1806 that he sighted the mountain peak in Colorado named after him, Pikes Peak. Pike and his party were captured by the Spanish and eventually released, but his papers and maps were confiscated. His subsequent record of the journey, which was written partly from memory, reported possible routes across areas hitherto unknown to Americans.

During the War of 1812, Pike was promoted to brigadier general. He led the successful assault in the Battle of York (today's Toronto) but died when a powder magazine exploded.

⹂SACAGAWEA⹊

AS THE STORY of Lewis and Clark became part of American lore, it became embroidered with legends, particularly those surrounding Sacagawea (c. 1789–1812). The idea became entrenched that this Native American woman guided Lewis and Clark to the Pacific and back. This legend is unfounded, although she did contribute to their success.

The daughter of a Lemhi Shoshone chief in what is now Idaho, Sacagawea (sometimes spelled Sacajawea or Sakakawea) was ten or twelve years old when she was kidnapped by a Hidatsa war party. The trapper Toussaint Charbonneau later bought her for his wife. They were living with the Hidatsas in today's North Dakota when Lewis and Clark arrived in late 1804. The explorers engaged Charbonneau as interpreter and, appreciating how useful Sacagawea would be, requested she accompany them. When they resumed their journey in April 1805, she and her newborn baby, Pomp, left with them.

Although primarily an interpreter with the Shoshone, Sacagawea played a far more important role. Her presence reassured Native Americans that the expedition was peaceful, since women did not accompany war parties. Her recognition of the Shoshone chief Cameahwait as her brother proved fortunate for the expedition. In addition, she found edible plants and roots for the men to eat when little else was available, and she acted as guide on William Clark's return journey through Shoshone territory down to the Yellowstone River in 1806.

Controversy surrounds Sacagawea's death. While most historians agree that she died in 1812 at Fort Manuel (South Dakota), Shoshone legend has it that she died in 1884 at the Wind River Indian Reservation in Wyoming.

SACAGAWEA
The legend of Sacagawea was still strong in 1954 when she was pictured in this commemorative stamp.

of Discovery and in many cases far outstripped official explorers in learning the country. Because fur trade adventurers like George Drouillard, John Colter, Jim Bridger, and Jedediah Smith did not produce the volume of maps, journals, and reports that government surveys yielded, it is often assumed that only fragments of fur-trade knowledge reached the public. But new research shows that discoveries made by mountain men had considerable impact on the emerging image of the West.

Fur-trade geography reached a wider audience through three channels. Newspapers were eager to print news from the mountains, and no editor was better placed to do that than Joseph Charless, proprietor of St. Louis's *Louisiana Gazette*, sometimes known as the *Missouri Gazette*. As early as 1811 Charless printed information gleaned from Andrew Henry about passes over the Rocky Mountains. When Robert Stuart reached St. Louis in April 1813 with word about South Pass, Charless gave his readers a full account of the discovery. He set the pattern among Missouri editors, and in the 1820s and 1830s newspapers were the best source for information about the travels of the Ashley men and other fur-trade explorers. On the national scene, Hezekiah Niles's *Weekly Register* reprinted every bit of information about the West and the fur trade. Twenty years before emigrant wagons rolled along the Oregon Trail, newspapers speculated on the route and the pioneering efforts of fur-trade trailblazers.

It is often said that mountain men had maps in their heads but drew only a few for others to see. But a close look at the surviving maps suggests a different story. George Drouillard gave Clark vital

much had changed in a decade. When geographer Samuel Lewis sketched his idea of the Rockies in 1804, they appeared as a single, narrow ridge with the promise of an easy portage to Pacific waters. Clark's map charted not one but two great mountain ranges—the Rockies and the Cascades. And in a twisted tangle of range after range, any notion that western mountains were mirror images of eastern ones was quickly lost. Lost as well was the dream of an easy portage over the northern Rockies to the Pacific. For the first time the idea of a Continental Divide, a high ridge from each side of which the continent's rivers flow in different directions, was given realistic shape and location.

Rivers also received fresh and more accurate treatment. Samuel Lewis had the Missouri and the Platte wandering to the Shining Mountains; his Columbia made a tentative thrust eastward from the coast. The 1814 map presented a remarkably accurate picture of the principal western rivers. Clark understood the course and direction of the Missouri and the lower Columbia. But no matter how precisely he drew those waterways, he could not escape the power of the Northwest Passage. If the Missouri and the Columbia were not the water highway to the Pacific, another river system must exist to fulfill the dream. The ghost river Multnomah was Clark's new candidate. Part Willamette River and part pure fantasy, Clark's Multnomah strikes across present-day Oregon and northern Utah to what the cartographer thought was a common source area for the Arkansas, Rio

Grande, and Platte rivers. Here was a revived passage, proof that the dream could survive even the strongest dose of exploration reality.

Geographers like Samuel Lewis and Thomas Jefferson envisioned the West as a single region. It was the Garden of the World, a place of remarkable fertility and unbounded promise. Biddle's *History* and Clark's map began the long process of educating Americans about regional boundaries and western diversity. After 1814 a careful reader might begin to appreciate differences in regional soils, climates, plants, animals, and native cultures. The lands of the Missouri Valley were not like those of the Great Columbia Plain. Fort Clatsop's climate was dramatically different from the one experienced on the northern plains at Fort Mandan. The peoples of the lower Columbia were unlike those encountered living along the Lemhi River or on the Missouri. After 1814, the American image of the West had more texture, more complexity.

FUR TRADE GEOGRAPHERS

Lewis and Clark and other government explorers were not the only ones learning the western country. Fur traders made up their own Corps

FUR TRADERS

Fur traders made their living doing business with Native Americans. The traders also created new maps and provided accounts of frontier life for newspaper reporters. Here traders offer European goods in exchange for Indian furs.

THE FUR TRADE

Valued in Europe as luxury goods, furs were among the first commodities to be traded between Native North Americans and white settlers. The search for more product drove European and American fur trappers and traders ever westward.

information in 1809, information that Clark used to prepare a map of the Yellowstone country and later in his 1810 master map. Fur trader John Dougherty drew a map of the upper Missouri as it was understood in 1810–12. Warren Angus Ferris, a trader in the employ of the American Fur Company, prepared a highly detailed map of the Rocky Mountain fur country in 1835. And when David Burr prepared his massive atlas of the United States in 1839, he relied on fur trade information from Jedediah Smith and William H. Ashley. By many means this geography made its impact felt on maps and in the public mind. Diplomats in distant capitals, busy waging the war for the West, laid their plans and marked maps in part based on fur-trade geography.

Newspaper accounts and maps testified to the enduring accomplishments of fur-trade geographers. But the traders themselves passed along what experience had taught them. As the beaver trade declined in the 1830s, mountain men sought other employment. Some, like Kit Carson and Pierre Beatte, worked as guides for government explorers. Jim Clyman, one of the most widely-traveled fur men, offered his services to both explorers and California-bound emigrants,

THE FUR TRADE
● major fur station

BOTANICALS

Scientists and artists satisfied public interest in all things western, such as flora mountain hemlock (left) and Cholla Opuntia Whipplei (right).

as did Moses Harris and Joseph R. Walker. Jim Bridger and Louis Vasquez ran Fort Bridger, a key supply post located on Blacks Fork of the Green River, from 1843 to 1853. These adventurers had studied the country and now taught lessons to others.

SCIENTISTS AND ARTISTS

Eastern audiences learned about the West from a growing number of teachers. Among those teachers was a remarkable company of scientists and artists. Thomas Jefferson once lamented the fact that scholars could not be lured from their comfortable "closets" to face the hazards of western exploration. But as early as 1811 two experienced naturalists—Thomas Nuttall and John Bradbury—ventured up the Missouri to collect plant specimens.

Nuttall's career as an explorer-scientist covered the entire period from 1811 to 1836 and spanned the continent from the Missouri to the Columbia by way of Arkansas, California, and Hawaii. Born in England and trained as a printer, Nuttall came to Philadelphia in 1807 or 1808 and was soon hired by Benjamin Smith Barton. Paid to do botanical field work, Nuttall headed to St. Louis, where he joined the Astoria expedition led by Wilson Price Hunt. Along with Bradbury, he was part of Hunt's voyage up the Missouri. When the Astorians left the river at the Arikara villages and headed west, Nuttall and Bradbury continued on

to the Mandan villages. With tensions between the United States and Great Britain ready to explode into the War of 1812, Nuttall hurried back to England with his notes and seed samples. In 1818, just before returning to the United States, Nuttall published his important *Genera of North American Plants.*

Nuttall's second scientific venture (1818–20) took him into Arkansas Territory and present-day eastern Oklahoma. That trip produced a classic account of frontier life, *A Journal of Travels into the Arkansas Territory.* Nuttall's last expedition (1834–1836) was his most ambitious. Taking up with fur trade entrepreneur Nathaniel J. Wyeth, Nuttall and ornithologist John Kirk Townshend traveled the Oregon Trail to the Columbia River. Nuttall continued his botanizing with two trips to Hawaii and a brief excursion to California before leaving the West in 1836.

Perhaps no other naturalist saw as much of the West before 1840 as Thomas Nuttall. Eccentric

FLOWERING DOGWOOD

Exemplary naturalist/explorer Thomas Nuttall canvassed the West from the Missouri River to Hawaii from the 1810s through the 1830s. He drew specimens of plants like the flowering dogwood, encountered in Oregon. He and other naturalists compiled early surveys of western plant life.

in his ways and not always the most careful specimen collector, Nuttall was an inveterate traveler. From the Missouri to the Columbia, from Arkansas to Hawaii, he studied a world new to European science. Nuttall counted many miles, but his contributions are difficult to measure. Most of his notes, journals, and plant specimens have not survived. Publishing opportunities were few, and although he was appointed Lecturer on Natural History at Harvard, Nuttall's influence was less than it might have been. Despite such limitations, Nuttall represents the first wave of American professional scientific exploration in the West.

CATLIN AND BODMER

In the 1830s two extraordinary artists went up the Missouri to portray native people, plants and animals, and the western landscape. Both George Catlin and Karl Bodmer painted with a clear mission in mind. When Catlin reached St. Louis in the summer of 1830 and paid a call on William Clark, the artist knew at least the outlines of that mission. Catlin began his career as a history painter in Philadelpha and New York. Legend has it that after seeing a delegation of western Indians in Philadephia, he decided to go West to paint these memorable people. Catlin's motives were always more complex than this charming story. His life mixed personal ambition, the pursuit of financial reward, and a growing commitment to the connection between art and scientific investigation. Portraits of native people and paintings of landscapes and animals were his testimony to cultures he was certain were vanishing. Catlin saw his mission as the preservation of a scientifically accurate record of cultures on the brink of disaster. His travels took him up the Missouri as far as Fort Union in present-day North Dakota and into the Wichita Mountains of southern Oklahoma. In traveling exhibitions, countless paintings, and *Letters and Notes on the Manners, Customs, and Conditions of the North American Indians* (1844), Catlin sought to reveal the West before it was forever lost.

Karl Bodmer, artist for Prince Maximilian's scientific expedition up the Missouri in 1833–34, had all Catlin's dedication to the link between art and science and an even larger measure of artistic ability. Professionally trained and an able draftsman, Bodmer brought to his western paintings a keen eye for color and detail. His principal mission was to make visual records to supplement ethnological observations made by Maximilian. But Bodmer went well beyond scientific illustration. In his landscapes and portraits Bodmer captured a vast country and the faces of compelling people.

MOUTH OF THE PLATTE RIVER
Artists such as George Catlin traveled along the Missouri River and in the surrounding mountains to paint. The western vistas he recorded included this one, from 1832, of the mouth of the Platte River.

"I THINK I NEVER BEFORE SAW SO GREAT A VARIETY OF BIRDS WITHIN THE SAME SPACE. ALL WERE BEAUTIFUL."

—ORNITHOLOGIST JOHN KIRK TOWNSEND ON THOMAS NUTTALL'S 1834 EXPEDITION

MEXICAN GENTLEMEN
By easing trade and immigration restrictions, Mexico inadvertently threatened the culture represented by these courtly riders.

"SCARCELY A DAY PASSES WITHOUT... REGRET THAT I AM NOT NOW ROVING AT LARGE UPON THOSE WESTERN PLAINS."

—TRADER JOSIAH GREGG RECALLING LIFE ON THE SANTA FE TRAIL, 1844

COMMOTION IN THE SOUTHWEST

WHEN MEXICO DECLARED ITS INDEPENDENCE IN 1821, LANDS FORMERLY HELD BY SPAIN BECAME MORE WELCOMING TO AMERICANS. ALMOST OVERNIGHT, TRADE BETWEEN THE UNITED STATES AND MEXICO BLOSSOMED ALONG THE SANTA FE TRAIL. WITH MEXICO'S BLESSING, AMERICANS ALSO ARRIVED IN TEXAS—ALTHOUGH THERE THE CLASH OF CULTURES QUICKLY SPARKED REBELLION.

CATLIN AND BODMER were sure they were recording the consequences of change in the lives of native people. But if the artists had looked to Texas and New Mexico, they might have seen an equally dramatic set of transformations. The fragmentation of the Spanish empire and the independence of Mexico marked the end of one imperial age and the beginning of another. When Augustin de Iturbide proclaimed Mexican independence in early 1821, there was little reason to think the new republic might enjoy quiet times. Many Mexican officials argued that the former frontier territories could be protected and made prosperous by opening

them to outside contact. Spain had long closed its colonial borders to all foreigners. Opening those borders to traders and settlers was a calculated risk some Mexican politicians were willing to take.

Throughout the eighteenth century, Spanish New Mexico was a market hungry for manufactured goods. The long trail from Chihuahua was the only merchant route since legal restrictions kept foreign traders out of Santa Fe. At the end of the century, Pedro Vial, a Frenchman in Spanish service, pioneered trails from Santa Fe to San Antonio and St. Louis. But strangers were still banned from Santa Fe. After the Louisiana Purchase and Zebulon Montgomery Pike's travels

in the Southwest, St. Louis merchants began to venture trips to Santa Fe. Those trading expeditions all ended up the same way—traders arrested and goods confiscated.

With Mexican independence, trade policies changed. American merchants once hustled to jail were now greeted as business partners. The first American to enjoy that change was William Becknell, a Missouri trader and entrepreneur. In late summer 1821 Becknell organized a large trading party. While scholars have long debated where Becknell planned to travel and what his goals really were, the results of his expedition are beyond question. In mid-November the Becknell party was in northeastern New Mexico when it met a party of Mexican troops. Instead of being arrested, the Missourians were escorted to Santa Fe and warmly embraced by Governor Facundo Melgares. By January 1822 Becknell was back in Franklin, Missouri, busy organizing his next Santa Fe trading venture.

THE SANTA FE TRADE

Becknell's 1822 journey was the real beginning of the overland Santa Fe trade. He quickly understood the need for an efficient transportation system linking Missouri suppliers with Santa Fe consumers. Simply put, it meant wagons moving in large caravans. Such caravans provided both security and efficiency. Only wagons could carry the heavy goods (textiles, iron ware, and foodstuffs) essential for the trade. Over the next several years the Santa Fe trade fell into a predictable pattern.

✦THE SANTA FE TRAIL✦

PRIOR TO MEXICAN INDEPENDENCE in 1821, the Spanish zealously guarded their territory in the Southwest, and Americans who ventured over the border risked arrest and imprisonment. Nevertheless, in the summer of that year, William Becknell, a trader from Franklin, Missouri, organized an expedition to the Southern Plains. His purported intention was to trade goods with the Comanche Indians for horses and mules, which were in short supply in the U.S.-occupied West. Becknell and his party took a train of pack animals due west from Franklin to the great bend of the Arkansas River before turning southwest into New Mexico. Expecting to be arrested by the Spanish, they found instead that they were welcomed, Mexico having achieved independence in September. On November 16, 1821, the pack train reached Santa Fe, where they sold all their goods at an excellent profit. The 870-mile journey back to Franklin was made in 48 days.

The following year Becknell and another party repeated the expedition, carrying their cargo in wagons, the first time a wagon train had traveled west of the Missouri River. This proved equally profitable, and the trail thereafter became the standard route from Missouri to the Southwest, crucial for trade between the United States and Mexico. In 1825, in a treaty with the Osage Indians, the U.S. government obtained the right of way for the highway, now called the Santa Fe Trail. In 1827 Fort Leavenworth was built, and military escorts against raiding Comanche were instituted in 1829. In 1831 Charles and William Bent established Bent's Fort, a trading post along the route on the Arkansas River.

Several separate branches of the Santa Fe Trail were blazed over the years, and its termini at either end also varied. While the trail produced profits for the traders who used it, its real significance lay in its becoming the regular route to the Southwest and in the establishment of new settlements along it. With the completion of the Santa Fe Railroad in 1872, the trail ceased to be used as a major travel artery.

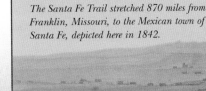

VIEW OF SANTA FE
The Santa Fe Trail stretched 870 miles from Franklin, Missouri, to the Mexican town of Santa Fe, depicted here in 1842.

Caravans shuttled between Missouri and New Mexico, sometimes by way of Bent's Fort. No one more fully captured the color and meaning of the trade in its first years than Josiah Gregg. Traveling the trail between 1831 and 1839, Gregg carefully recorded all aspects of life along the route. In 1844 he published *Commerce of the Prairies*, the classic account of days on the Santa Fe Trail.

Like the Oregon Trail, the road to Santa Fe was far more than a set of deeply rutted wagon tracks. The trail was a highway for diplomacy, war, and, most important, economic and cultural change. The trail brought the goods of the industrial revolution to the Southwest. In turn, Missouri's economy was enriched by New Mexican silver and mules. Well before the Mexican War, the Santa Fe Trail made the Southwest part of the American commercial empire.

TEXAS

An early visitor to Texas once pronounced it not a place but a commotion. And most of the commotions were about the cultural and political future of Texas. Although the Adams-Onis Treaty (1819) kept Texas first Spanish and then Mexican, East Texas was the scene of endless adventures by enterprising and sometimes lawless Americans and their Mexican allies. By the time of Mexican independence, officials in Mexico City were ready to try almost anything to stabilize Texas and secure it as a prosperous province for the new republic.

CARAVANS AT SANTA FE
Josiah Gregg's Commerce of the Prairies *(1844) is the classic account of life along the Santa Fe trail. This illustration from his book depicts the arrival of trade caravans at Santa Fe.*

✦THE TEXAS REVOLUTION✦

THE ROOTS of the Texas Revolution lay in the 1820s, when Americans began immigrating to Texas, then part of Mexico. In 1830, fearful of growing unrest among the newcomers, Mexico banned further American immigration, but the influx of settlers from the United States continued. In 1833 Stephen Austin, who had brought the first American families to Texas, went to Mexico City to seek a degree of autonomy for the American settlements but was imprisoned when he was found to have written a letter favoring Texas independence. He did not return to Texas until July 1835, by which time General Antonio Lopez de Santa Anna had declared himself dictator, revoked the 1824 Mexican constitution, and announced his intention to bring the various regions of Mexico under centralized control. Santa Anna had already begun reinstating garrisons in Texas that had earlier been withdrawn.

The first troops had arrived at Anahuac in January 1835, only to be expelled a few months later by a Texan force under William B. Travis.

On October 2, 1835, the Texas Revolution began at the Battle of Gonzalez, where

DAVY CROCKETT

Trapper Davy Crockett, Jim Bowie, and others fought and died for Texas independence at the Alamo.

a small force successfully repelled a Mexican effort to retrieve a cannon. Thereafter there were a series of defeats for Santa Anna's son-in-law, General Martín Perfecto de Cos, as the Texans took control of Goliad, Concepción, and San Antonio. On November 3, 1835, at San Felipe de Austin, a convention of Texans met and voted for separate statehood under the 1824 Mexican constitution. Shortly after the new year, Santa Anna crossed the Rio Grande with 6,000 soldiers; joined by Cos and a force of 2,000, he proceeded to march on San Antonio. The outnumbered Texans withdrew to a mission building on the edge of town called the Alamo.

The siege of the Alamo lasted twelve days, from February 23 to March 6, 1836. Six hundred Mexicans died in the attack, but the 187 Texans—who included Travis, Jim Bowie, and Davy Crockett—were finally overpowered in hand-to-hand combat. Five survivors were executed on Santa Anna's orders, but women, children, and blacks were spared.

While heroic, the wisdom of the stand at the Alamo is questionable, since there was little prospect of other Texans coming to provide reinforcement. Not until March 2, when the siege was nearing its end, did the Texan leaders declare independence at Washington-on-the-Brazos, naming David Burnet as provisional president and Sam Houston as commander of the Texan forces. Even then, Santa Anna's advance caused the provisional government and many colonists to flee north and east (known as the "Runaway Scrape"). Three weeks after the Alamo, a force of more than 300 Texans under the command of James Fannin surrendered to

SAM HOUSTON

Texan commander Sam Houston led a surprise attack in 1836 against Mexican troops at San Jacinto. The decisive battle won Texas its independence.

General José de Urrea at Goliad. Although Urrea had promised they would be treated as prisoners of war, Santa Anna ordered them executed.

Texan fury over the Alamo and the Goliad massacre combined with Santa Anna's over-confidence to turn the tide. Convinced the rebels were on the defensive, he took insufficient precautions, and his 1,300 troops were resting when Houston launched a surprise attack on April 21, 1836, at the San Jacinto River. With cries of "Remember the Alamo!", 900 Americans and Tejanos under Sam Houston and Juan Nepomuceno Seguin defeated the Mexican army in a battle that lasted less than 20 minutes. Santa Anna was captured, but Houston spared his life conditional on his formal recognition of the independence of Texas. Santa Anna agreed but later reneged on his promise.

The war that won Texas its freedom from Mexico had lasted just six months. In March 1837 President Andrew Jackson formally recognized the Republic of Texas, which entered the Union as the 28th state on December 29, 1845.

THE ALAMO

The twelve-day battle at the mission called the Alamo galvanized Texan resolve to fight Mexican forces and win independence. The Republic of Texas lasted from 1836 until 1845, when it was annexed as a U.S. state.

Filling East Texas with enterprising American settlers loyal to Mexico seemed a promising solution. Moses Austin, sometime merchant and full-time dreamer, promoted such a scheme for American settlement in Texas. When Austin died in June 1821, leadership for that venture fell to his son Stephen. The younger Austin surveyed available lands and prepared plans for a large colony. By the end of 1823 those efforts began to pay off as nearly 300 families settled in rich bottom lands along the Bernard, Colorado, and Brazos rivers. Austin established his own headquarters at the village of San Felipe de Austin.

THE ROAD TO REBELLION

Despite good intentions and careful planning, American emigration to Texas caused troubles far beyond Mexico City's ability to manage. Time, distance, and differing cultural values all worked to increase such troubles. As early as 1825, Mexican officials expressed alarm about the persistence of American loyalties among the Texas settlers. Alarm bells rang louder when Haden and Benjamin Edwards launched an abortive revolution in 1826, proclaiming the Republic of Fredonia. Although Austin worked to defeat the rebellion, officials in Mexico City were increasingly persuaded that the very presence of Americans was a threat to Mexico's internal security.

For all these tensions, it was the twists and turns of Mexican politics that finally set Texas on the road to rebellion and independence. For more than two decades Mexican politics had been dominated by two rival ideologies. Federalists looked to the United States for inspiration in building a society based on social reform, liberal democracy, and local autonomy. Federalist politicians had close ties to Austin and other Americans in Texas. So long as Federalists remained in power there was the possibility of compromise on divisive issues. The Centralists embraced a far different vision of the republic, opposing social reform and urging that power be centralized in Mexico City. They also argued that American immigration to Texas had to be halted. When President, and one-time Federalist, Antonio Lopez de Santa Anna purged liberals in his government in 1834 and joined the conservative Centralists, it was plain that policies toward Texas were about to change.

THE TEXAS REVOLUTION

The events of 1835 and 1836 are a now-familiar story, beginning with Santa Anna's decision to use military force in Texas and the response of both American and Mexican settlers. That response was violent but, like the first year of the American Revolution in 1775, not necessarily revolutionary. Texas independence, like the independence of the English colonies, was not inevitable. When Texas politicial leaders met in November 1835, delegates affirmed their allegiance to the Republic of Mexico and the Constitution of 1824. But by March 1836, events had overtaken old loyalties and at the Washington-on-the-Brazos convention, Texas representatives declared independence from Mexico.

TEXAS $100 BILL

Between 1836 and 1845, the Republic of Texas operated as an independent nation. It established a government, headed first by Sam Houston, and printed its own currency, such as this 1839 bill.

PIKE'S SOUTHWESTERN EXPEDITION

American knowledge of the Southwest was advanced by Zebulon Pike's 1806-7 expedition across the Sangre de Cristo Mountains, during which a Spanish patrol arrested him in Spanish territory and took him to Santa Fe.

The Texas Revolution was always more than the actions of spirited leaders like Sam Houston, William Travis, the tejano leader Colonel Juan Nepomuceno Seguin, and Austin himself. And the revolution meant more than legendary battles like the Alamo, Goliad, and San Jacinto. No sooner had Texas declared independence than a delegation was on its way to Washington to test the waters for annexation to the United States.

If the Texas Revolution revealed the fragmentation of one empire and the rise of another, it also showed the nearly irreducible ethnic and racial tensions that pervaded the region. Colonel Seguin was just one of many tejanos who actively supported Texas independence. Yet once the Republic of Texas came into being, Americans came to doubt Seguin's loyalty, forcing him to leave Texas for Mexico. Seguin's lament, that he had become "a foreigner in my own land," made plain the real price of the revolution.

WHITMAN MISSION
Founded by Marcus and Narcissa Whitman in Oregon in the 1830s, the Waiilatpu Mission aimed to convert the Cayuse to Christianity.

THE WEST IN 1840

BY 1840 DECADES OF EXPLORATION HAD PRODUCED A ROUGH MAP OF THE ENTIRE WEST. KNOWLEDGE OF THE REGION AND ITS RESOURCES INSPIRED A THIRST IN BOTH POLITICIANS AND THE GENERAL PUBLIC FOR CONTROL OVER THE REGION. JOINED TO THIS HUNGER WAS A GROWING CONVICTION THAT IT WAS THE DESTINY OF THE UNITED STATES TO EXPAND ACROSS THE CONTINENT.

WHEN SAMUEL LEWIS drafted his map of Louisiana in 1804 he portrayed a nearly empty West. Thirty-five years later, in 1839, government cartographer David H. Burr prepared a landmark atlas for the United States Post Office. The western portion of Burr's map stands in stunning contrast to Lewis's effort. Through William H. Ashley, then a member of the House of Representatives from Missouri, Burr had access to knowledge gathered by Jedediah Smith. Many scholars believe that Burr had at least one Smith map to examine as he prepared his own work. Seeing the West through Smith's eyes gave Burr an unparalleled vision of the lands beyond the Missouri.

Once again it was the depiction of mountains and rivers that measured changes in understanding the western landscape. Burr accurately sketched the extent, if not the complexity, of the Rockies and the Cascades. Gone was Samuel Lewis's narrow chain of mountains. In its place was the image of western mountains quite unlike any in eastern North America. Burr also used fur-trade information to chart the course of western rivers. The key rivers of the West—the Missouri and the Columbia—found their correct channels. Burr also paid close attention to Smith's southwestern and California journeys. And Burr was able to note what John Charles Frémont later termed "the Great Basin."

THE SMALLPOX PANDEMIC

Samuel Lewis had scattered a few tribal names on his western landscape, more by whim than knowledge. Burr could be much more accurate. What he could not depict were the profound changes overtaking native people throughout the West. Burr gave the Mandan, Hidatsa, and Arikara Indians what he thought were their territories, lands located in present-day North and South Dakota. But by 1839 these native peoples barely existed as tribal societies. In 1837 the earth-lodge people had suffered a smallpox pandemic of almost unprecedented intensity. Accidently brought up the Missouri by the American Fur Company steamboat *St. Peter*, the disease roared through the villages, eventually killing thousands. Perhaps the best commentary on Burr's map is the letter Indian Agent Joshua Pilcher wrote in late February 1838: "It appears that the effects of the Small pox among most of the Indian tribes of the Upper Missouri Surpass all former Scourges, and that the country through which it has pass'd is literally depopulated and converted into one great grave yard."

INDIAN REMOVAL

Burr's map was silent on the disease disaster of 1837. It was harder to ignore the geographic consequences of the federal government's Indian Removal policy. By 1839 that policy was fully underway. Burr carefully noted lands allocated to Creeks, Cherokees, and other southeastern tribes in what is now eastern Oklahoma. What was more difficult to judge was the struggle of the "emigrant Indians" to rebuild lives in new places. Burr's map did not make plain the pioneering aspects of those native people who survived the Trail of Tears. They carried with them cultural, political, and religious institutions usually identified with Euro-American settlers. In the 1830s, Protestant Christianity, formal schooling, national governments, and written constitutions moved into the West at the hands of Indian pioneer families.

The three and a half decades between the Samuel Lewis and David Burr maps were years of intense imperial conflict. They were years when American diplomats

→THE TRAIL OF TEARS←

IN 1838–39 MORE THAN 4,000 Cherokee Indians died as a result of a forced march from their lands in Georgia to Indian Territory (present-day Oklahoma). The Cherokees called their route "Nunna dual Tsuny" ("The Trail Where They Cried"). The term "Trail of Tears" now refers to the forced removal of the Cherokee, Chickasaw, Choctaw, Creek, and Seminole nations (later known as the Five Civilized Tribes) as a result of the 1830 Indian Removal Act. President Andrew Jackson had signed the act to remove Native Americans living east of the Mississippi River to Indian Territory, making their tribal lands available to white settlers.

The first to be moved were the Choctaws of southern Alabama and Mississippi. From 1831 to 1834 they were rounded up and marched hundreds of miles to today's Oklahoma. An estimated one-quarter of the Choctaws died en route due to insufficient food, blankets, and wagons. In 1836 the Creek nation of Alabama, already weakened by intertribal warfare, were subjected to the same forcible removal, and 3,500 out of 15,000 died from hunger, exposure, and disease along the journey. Many Chickasaws from northern Mississippi, western Tennessee, and western Kentucky had already moved before the act came into force, and their journey's comparative shortness in 1837 meant that they suffered less on the march. Nevertheless, many died from cholera and food poisoning after their arrival in Indian Territory.

While some 3,000 Seminole traveled west, those remaining in the Florida swamps put up a fierce resistance in the Second and Third Seminole Wars (1835–42 and 1855–58). The third war ended in a stalemate, and although some Seminoles agreed to move, the nation never signed a treaty, and many stayed in Florida, where they still live today.

Of the five nations dispossessed of their tribal lands, probably the saddest case is that of the Cherokees, who lived in small villages in an area stretching from West Virginia to northern Alabama. American allies in the Creek War of 1813, they had adapted to white ways, become successful farmers and businessmen, evolved a written language, had a written constitution, and, from 1828, produced their own newspaper. Despite all this, the discovery of gold near Dahlonega, Georgia, was enough to seal their fate. The Cherokees took their case to the Supreme Court and won it, but Jackson simply ignored the decision.

The roundup of more than 15,000 Cherokees began on May 23, 1838. In July some 13,000 were imprisoned in military stockades to await the break of a drought, during which time approximately 1,500 died. The first of two journeys began in October, and thirteen Cherokee contingents marched through Tennessee, Kentucky, and Illinois. Ice floes on the Mississippi prevented their crossing, and many died as they waited out the harsh winter. Chief John Ross received permission to lead the second march westward in December 1838. Yet despite the

numerous precautions he had taken, disease, a shortage of blankets and food, and inadequate protection from the U.S. Army meant the loss of more Cherokee lives, including that of his own wife.

The first Cherokee contingent arrived at Fort Gibson in January 1839; the last, led by Ross, arrived in March. In addition to the thousands who had already died, 800 more died of disease and starvation in Oklahoma. In all, over one-quarter of the Cherokee Nation was lost.

The Cherokees and other Native Americans, including nations from the Great Plains and Old Northwest, soon began to rebuild their lives in Indian Territory, which at that time stretched from the Red River in northern Texas to the Missouri River in Nebraska. But as more white settlers moved west, the Indians were repeatedly forced to sell or cede their lands as new states were created. Following the formation of Oklahoma Territory in 1890, the Cherokees and Choctaws sued in the federal courts to retain their lands, but the Curtis Act of 1898 dissolved their tribal governments and imposed land allotment policies on them. Oklahoma became a state in 1907.

Following the Trail of Tears, widespread indignation throughout the country and charges of fraud resulted in a government inquiry carried out by Major Ethan Hitchcock. However, his report of "bribery, perjury forgery…and every conceivable subterfuge" was not made public at the time.

TRAIL OF TEARS
The 1830 Indian Removal Act authorized the forced resettlement of Native American peoples to Indian Territory in modern-day Oklahoma. Between 1838 and 1839, thousands of Cherokees took the bitter journey later called the Trail of Tears.

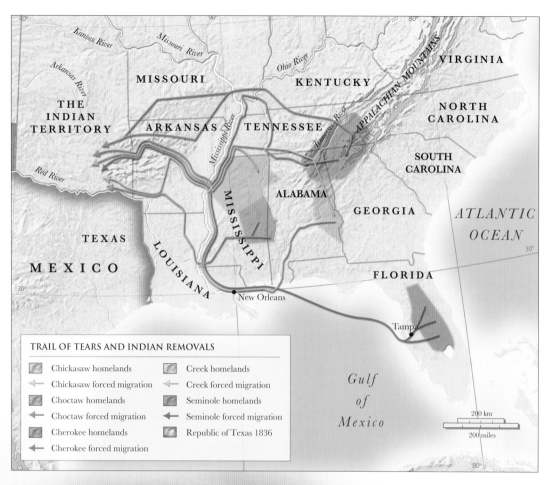

TRAIL OF TEARS AND INDIAN REMOVALS

The forced migration of major groups of Native Americans from their homelands in the east to the relatively barren country of Indian Territory (present-day Oklahoma) not only imposed great hardships on the reluctantly migrant peoples, but placed enormous demands on their traditional ways of life. The name "Trail of Tears" came to refer to the removal of the Cherokee, Chickasaw, Choctaw, Creek, and Seminole nations—known as the Five Civilized Tribes—as a result of the 1830 Indian Removal Act.

and empire builders like Thomas Jefferson and John Quincy Adams redrew the boundaries of empire in the West. And no one was more direct in his imperialism than Adams. As Secretary of State in the administration of James Monroe, Adams relentlessly pursued a policy of territorial expansion. In 1819, well before the phrase "manifest destiny" entered the political vocabulary, Adams made plain the western ambitions of the United States. "The world," he wrote, "shall be familiarized with the idea of considering our proper dominion to be the continent of North America. Europe shall find it a settled geographic element that the United States and North America are identical."

No place in the West was Adams' assertion more contentious than in the region contemporaries called the Oregon Country. At the conclusion of the War of 1812, the Treaty of Ghent stipulated that territories occupied during the hostilities be returned to their original owners. It was widely believed that Fort Astoria had been seized by British naval forces during the war. Astor himself promoted that myth, doing his best to conceal the facts surrounding Astoria's sale to the North West Company. While an American official finally reasserted federal authority over the post, the larger question of boundaries and territorial claims in the Pacific Northwest became a hotly debated issue between the United States and Great Britain. A compromise of sorts was reached in 1818 with the Joint Occupation Treaty. That treaty, and subsequent ones, gave citizens of both nations

CALIFORNIA VISIONS

While Texas and the Oregon Country dominated U.S. expansionist interest in the 1830s, the natural riches of California beckoned. By the time of this 1864 image, California would be a U.S. state.

JOHN QUINCY ADAMS
As James Monroe's secretary of state, John Quincy Adams argued that the proper dominion of the United States stretched across the continent of North America.

symbolic power that Oregon had taken on for many Americans. Like Texas, Oregon had become more a cause than a place.

When William Henry Drayton claimed that "the Almighty has made choice of the present generation to erect the American empire," he presumed too much on the national loyalties of the divinity. And Drayton was probably off by a generation or two in his calculations. But in the long run he was right. For fifty years the forces of global markets, imperial rivalries, epidemic diseases, and personal ambition assaulted the countries beyond the Missouri and made them part of an empire.

Thomas Jefferson likened the Mississippi Crisis to the "embryo of a tornado." That American tornado roared through the West, changing lives and rearranging landscapes. Jefferson would not have used the word *tornado* to describe his "empire for liberty." He was always more comfortable using the image of the garden where every day promised peace and virtue. But the decades from American independence to the end of the 1830s were anything but peaceful and virtuous. No matter what Jefferson hoped, it was stormy weather. William Henry Drayton and Thomas Jefferson talked boldly about American empire. From the thunder in their words came the winds of change.

equal access to the Oregon country for settlement and commerce. Such a diplomatic solution might have pleased negotiators, but for many Americans Oregon became a symbol of national, religious, and personal ambitions in the West.

In the 1830s the Oregon Question attracted a remarkable company of visionaries, zealots, and propagandists. Politicians like John Floyd and Thomas Hart Benton were linked in common cause with schemers and promoters like Nathaniel J. Wyeth and Hall Jackson Kelley. Missionaries like Marcus and Narcissa Whitman and Father Jean Pierre DeSmet added their evangelical passion. David Burr confidently lettered the word OREGON on his map. What he could not show was the

> ## "IT IS THAT I MAY BE ABLE TO HELP THOSE WHO STAND IN NEED THAT I FACE EVERY DANGER...FOR THIS... I TRAVERSE THE MOUNTAINS... [AND] PASS OVER THE SANDY PLAINS."

—MOUNTAIN MAN
JEDEDIAH STRONG SMITH, 1829

✦MISSIONARIES IN THE NORTHWEST✦

IN THE EARLY 1800S, virtually every denomination sent missionaries out West with the intent of converting Native Americans to Christianity. The American Board of Commissioners of Foreign Missions (ABCFM) alone represented Congregationalists, Presbyterians, and the Dutch Reformed Church. Most missions provided schooling, religious services, and farming or small business opportunities for Native Americans, but often failed to convert local natives to Christianity. Belgian Jesuit Jean De Smet founded Catholic missions throughout the Northwest, and inspired hundreds of European Jesuits to follow in his footsteps. A skilled negotiator and peacekeeper, De Smet earned the respect of many Indian leaders.

Other missionaries did not fare as well. In 1836 ABCFM missionaries Marcus and Narcissa Whitman, along with Henry and Eliza Spalding, began the long journey to Oregon, during which the two wives became the first white women to traverse the Rocky Mountains. The Presbyterian Whitmans established the Waiilatpu Mission in the Walla Walla Valley near the Cayuse tribe, building a school, sawmill, gristmill, and blacksmith shop. A physician, Marcus Whitman also offered medical services to white settlers.

Unfortunately, large numbers of Cayuses died from the diseases that settlers brought with them to the mission. A measles epidemic, coupled with the Whitmans' advocacy of a complete break from Native American culture, prompted the Cayuses, in 1847, to attack the mission and massacre the Whitmans and twelve others, as well as seize fifty hostages. Although the hostages were released and five Cayuses were hanged for the massacre, violence continued for the next two years as the militia sought to punish the Cayuses. An era of Indian wars in the Northwest followed. Threats of death persuaded the Spaldings to abandon their mission among the Nez Percés, and De Smet's successors among the Flatheads temporarily withdrew from that tribe.

WHITMAN MISSION
Christian missionaries like Marcus and Narcissa Whitman, whose mission is depicted here, helped prepare Oregon for more extensive settlement by Americans.

THE EAGLE SCREAMS

1840–1865

FROM 1840 TO THE TIME OF THE CIVIL WAR,
THE UNITED STATES EXPANDED ACROSS THE WEST
LIKE AN EAGLE SCREAMING ACROSS THE SKY.
AMERICAN EXPLORERS FILLED IN THE EMPTY SPACES
ON WESTERN MAPS. WAR WITH MEXICO AND
SETTLEMENT OF THE OREGON DISPUTE ADDED NEW
TERRITORIES TO THE NATION AND TRANSFORMED
IT INTO A CONTINENTAL POWER. MIGRANTS POURED
INTO OREGON, THE CALIFORNIA GOLD FIELDS,
AND MORMON UTAH, BUILDING NEW ECONOMIC
CENTERS AND A NEW CULTURE. THE WEST TOOK
SHAPE IN THE AMERICAN MIND AS A PLACE
OF GRANDEUR AND OPPORTUNITY.

DEFINING THE WEST

FROM 1840 TO 1865, THE WEST BECAME DEFINED AS A DISTINCT REGION IN THE MINDS OF AMERICANS. EXPLORERS MAPPED AND MIGRANTS COLONIZED THE LAND, EVEN AS THE UNITED STATES ACQUIRED MORE TERRITORY THROUGH WAR AND DIPLOMACY, THE REGION'S NATURAL ABUNDANCE FUELED ECONOMIC GROWTH AND CULTURAL CHANGE.

DURING THE PIVOTAL quarter century between the end of the fur trade, circa 1840, and the end of the Civil War in 1865, the West came to have meaning as a distinct region with known qualities. In the American mind, the West metamorphosed from a vast, vague territory through which wandered fur trappers and wild Indians into a discrete area defined in geographical, political, economic, and cultural terms. Geographical definition of the region came about as the process of scientific exploration finally filled in nearly all of the empty spaces on maps of the West by identifying and naming rivers, lakes, mountains, and passes. Political definition of the American West also occurred by 1865 as the American governmental system, with its federal structure and organization of states and territories, spread from the

Mississippi Valley to the Pacific Ocean. That spread was accomplished by several means: a great folk migration to Oregon, an even greater migration to the gold fields of California, the Mormon colonization of the Great Basin, the first hesitant agricultural occupations of the Great Plains, the annexation of the Republic of Texas, the imperial urges that culminated in the military conquest of the Southwest during the Mexican War, and the resolution of the great sectional conflict of the Civil War. With political definition came political demarcation and the surveying and marking of the boundary lines between the western United States and its neighbors to the north and south.

Economic definition of the West came about through the creation of centers of western economic

activity. These centers owed their existence to many of the same processes that created political definition during this period. The movement of an American population into the vast spaces of the West, and that population's rapid use of mineral deposits and timber, grazing, and crop lands, established the economic importance of the region. The sites at which wealth-producing activities developed often became the centers of later regional development and growth. Finally, cultural definition of the West as a region quite different from other regions of the United States followed the displacement of native peoples and Hispanics by Yankees, Texans, Knickerbockers, Hoosiers, Mormons, or folks from the Middle Border—all of whom, in one way or another, came to consider themselves "Westerners."

LOOKING WESTWARD

Emanuel Gottlieb Leutze's 1861 mural study Westward the Course of Empire Takes Its Way *captures the pioneers' sense of divine mission.*

→TEXAS JOINS THE UNION←

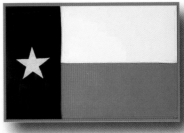
Texas state flag

EVEN BEFORE Texas won its independence from Mexico in 1836, many of its settlers wanted annexation by the United States. Following their victory at the Battle of San Jacinto, Texans ratified a new constitution, legalized slavery, elected Sam Houston president, and sent an envoy to Washington to request annexation. Failing that, Texas sought American recognition as an independent republic, which President Andrew Jackson granted on March 3, 1837.

The chain of events leading to statehood eight years later was a complicated one. At first many in both North and South were against annexation. Some northerners felt it would mean war with Mexico or the addition of another slave state to the Union. Some southerners feared the size and potential importance of the new territory, while others wanted Texas admitted to counter the admission of Wisconsin, Iowa, and Minnesota as free states. In 1841 Texans attempted unsuccessfully to annex New Mexico.

Still hoping for U.S. annexation, Houston nevertheless asked France and Britain for a guarantee of Texas's independence. Both countries were willing, but such an international guarantee depended on Mexico's agreement, which was not forthcoming. A rumor then reached Washington that Britain would guarantee Texan independence if slavery were abolished. This led to alarm in both the North, which saw American territory being lost, and the South, which saw a slave state being lost.

Britain firmly denied the abolition rumor, but the fear remained. While many in the North saw no reason why Texas should not remain independent, other Americans saw annexation as vital. When it became part of James K. Polk's platform in the 1844 presidential race, John Tyler, accepting public opinion, spent his last months as president working to admit Texas as a state. After Congress failed to ratify two treaties, he suggested that Texas could join the Union though a joint resolution of both houses. This was achieved on February 28, 1845.

Texas entered the Union as the 28th state on December 29, 1845. As many had feared, Mexico saw this as a hostile act, and the stage was set for the Mexican War (1846–48).

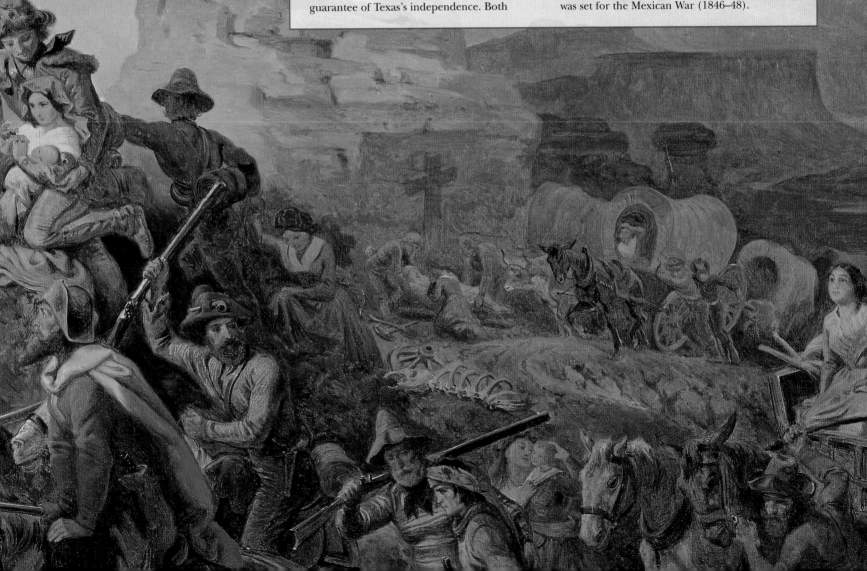

UPPER CATARACT CREEK
From the 1840s onward, more of the West became known, such as this area visited by the Colorado Exploring Expedition in 1864.

DECADE OF DECISION: THE 1840s

THE DECADE OF THE 1840S BROUGHT GREAT CHANGES TO THE WEST, SPEARHEADED BY THE EXPLORATIONS OF JOHN CHARLES FRÉMONT, WHICH PROVIDED A MORE COMPLETE PICTURE OF THE REGION. EXAMINING FRÉMONT'S DETAILED MAPS AND RECORDS, AMERICANS GREW MORE EAGER TO SEE THIS RICH LANDSCAPE FOR THEMSELVES.

"THE NERVOUS, ROCKY WEST IS INTRUDING A NEW AND CONTINENTAL ELEMENT INTO THE NATIONAL MIND."

—POET AND PHILOSOPHER
RALPH WALDO EMERSON, 1844

THE GEOGRAPHICAL, political, economic, and cultural definition of the West began in 1840 and continued through the decade of the 1840s. During this watershed decade, the imperial reach of the United States neared its political and spatial zenith. The nation annexed the Republic of Texas, and the Mexican War, partially the consequence of that annexation, culminated in American victory and an enormous land cession from the vanquished Mexico. That cession added to the Union all or parts of what would become the states of New Mexico, Colorado, Arizona, Utah, Nevada, Wyoming, and California. North of the 42nd parallel, the "Oregon Question," the

1848 QUARTER
This coin was minted in California and contains real gold.

issue of the legal boundary between land then under Mexican jurisdiction and territory jointly occupied by the United States and Great Britain, was resolved by treaty with Great Britain, making what would eventually comprise the states of Idaho, Oregon, and Washington into solely American territory. For all practical purposes, the end of the decade saw the final establishment of the United States as a continental nation.

During the 1840s, the Rocky Mountain beaver trade, the premier economic activity in the West prior to then, virtually disappeared. Fur-trade exploration gave way to government exploration as John Charles Frémont filled in most of the

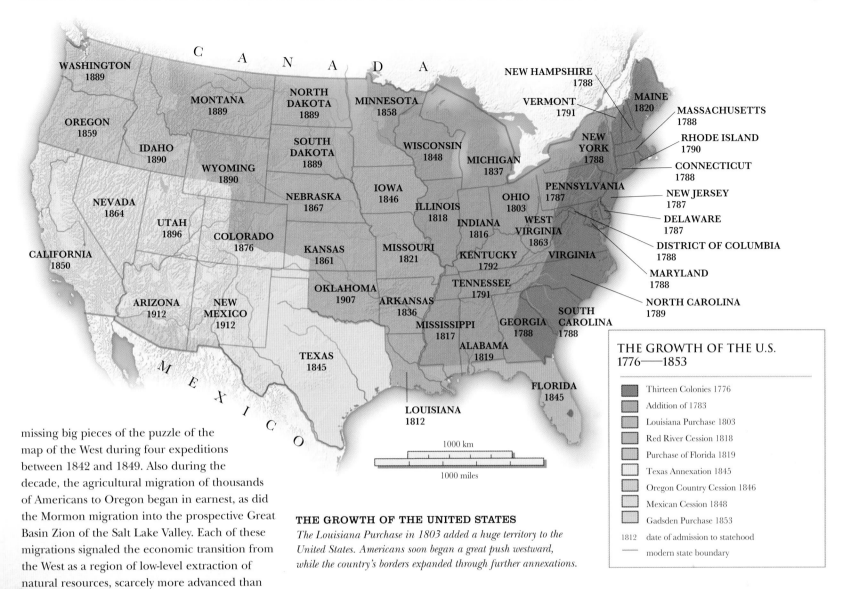

THE GROWTH OF THE U.S.
1776——1853

- Thirteen Colonies 1776
- Addition of 1783
- Louisiana Purchase 1803
- Red River Cession 1818
- Purchase of Florida 1819
- Texas Annexation 1845
- Oregon Country Cession 1846
- Mexican Cession 1848
- Gadsden Purchase 1853

1812   date of admission to statehood

——   modern state boundary

1000 km

1000 miles

THE GROWTH OF THE UNITED STATES

The Louisiana Purchase in 1803 added a huge territory to the United States. Americans soon began a great push westward, while the country's borders expanded through further annexations.

missing big pieces of the puzzle of the map of the West during four expeditions between 1842 and 1849. Also during the decade, the agricultural migration of thousands of Americans to Oregon began in earnest, as did the Mormon migration into the prospective Great Basin Zion of the Salt Lake Valley. Each of these migrations signaled the economic transition from the West as a region of low-level extraction of natural resources, scarcely more advanced than hunting-gathering even though it supplied furs for a world market, to the West as a locus of agricultural production with enormous potential for wealth in grain and livestock. Finally, at the end of the 1840s, gold was discovered in California. The discovery was followed by the California Gold Rush, a massive migration and the first great mineral exploitation of the western environment. The Gold Rush set patterns of exploitation that produced

new landscapes of extraction throughout much of the remainder of the farther West by the end of the Civil War. Accompanying the development of the California gold fields was the agricultural development of adjacent regions. The transition of the California agricultural landscape from pastoralism to American-style cropping systems was as important as the development of the mining regions for the later character of this portion of the West.

EXPLORATION AND EMPIRE: FRÉMONT EXPLORES THE WEST

One of the nineteenth century's most successful explorers opened a new wave of exploration in the American West in the early 1840s. Army lieutenant John Charles Frémont began his expeditions in 1838 as part of a survey team charged with the responsibility of developing a map of the hydrographical basin of the upper Mississippi. From this modest beginning Frémont rose meteorically to become the premier explorer of the mid-nineteenth century.

In 1841 Frémont came in contact with the powerful Senator from Missouri, Thomas Hart Benton. He soon became a frequent visitor at Benton's Washington residence, entranced perhaps by the aura of power surrounding the Missouri senator, and entranced certainly by Benton's daughter, Jessie, to whom Frémont was married in October 1841. With Benton as a father-in-law and Secretary of War Joel Poinsett as a personal friend, young Lieutenant Frémont was virtually assured of being handed important exploratory assignments. With Jessie Benton Frémont as his wife, he was also assured that fame would follow the completion of those assignments, for Jessie was a skilled writer, capable of tapping the mainstream of American opinion and framing her husband's field reports in ways certain to

MORMON FAMILY

In 1846, Mormons journeyed to Utah to escape religious persecution. This family is equipped for pioneer life with log cabin and spinning wheel.

FIVE-CENT STAMP

Over 7.5 million of these stamps depicting explorer John C. Frémont in the Rocky Mountains were issued in 1898.

appeal to a nation eager to learn of things western. From the very earliest days of their marriage, Jessie edited the explorer's field journals. At least in part, it is the result of her skillful handling of the literary motifs of the time that those journals, when published, reached unparalleled levels of popularity.

Frémont's first major expedition as commander of his own party left St. Louis in the spring of 1842, bound for the Sweetwater River, the western tributary of the Platte with a source in the region of South Pass. This first exploration was almost purely symbolic, since Frémont covered the trail from St. Louis to South Pass that was already well-worn by the rendezvous-bound caravans of the St. Louis fur trade and, by 1841, was carrying migrants to Oregon. Frémont's ostensible commander (it is never certain whether Frémont viewed his Army superiors or his Senator father-in-law as his actual commander), J. J. Abert, chief of the U.S. Army Corps of Topographical Engineers, gave him instructions to survey and map the country as far as the Sweetwater River. As was his wont, once in the field Frémont enlarged those orders to include a survey that extended as far as South Pass and even incorporated an

WIND RIVER RANGE

This Wyoming mountain range, explored by John C. Frémont in 1842, remains a largely roadless wilderness area today. Frémont was moved by the beauty of the area's rocky crags and abundant lakes and wildflowers.

investigation of the Wind River Range north of South Pass. In the Wind Rivers, Frémont climbed a peak that he mistakenly believed to be the highest in the chain, indeed the highest in all of North America, and while at the top of the mountain now known as Frémont Peak, the symbolism of the first expedition was made manifest. As he surveyed the surrounding terrain and reflected on the grandeur of the West and the importance of the South Pass—in view on the southern horizon—as the key to the American migration to the Pacific, a "bumblebee" landed on Frémont's knee. This was not a common honeybee of the Rocky Mountains but a honeybee of the domestic variety. In Frémont's mind it was a harbinger of the wave of migrants that would

soon burst through the wide gap in the Rocky Mountain chain that was called South Pass and flow to Oregon, the Great Basin, and California.

There is no way of knowing whether a bee actually lit on the young explorer's knee on the top of a high peak in the Rockies. But his published account of his first expedition, as edited by his wife, carried the story, and it is quite likely that the symbolism was lost on no one. Symbolism aside, Frémont's first field command produced a report and map that provided western-bound migrants with their first accurate account of the Oregon Trail as far as South Pass.

FRÉMONT'S SECOND EXPEDITION

Frémont's second expedition of 1843–44 was a great deal more significant, and had he done nothing more than complete the "great circuit" of these two years, his fame as an explorer would have been guaranteed. His instructions from

---

⇥THE FRÉMONT-BENTON CLAN⇤

BORN in Savannah, Georgia, John Charles Frémont (1813–1890) joined the army, taking part in surveys of the Upper Mississippi (1837–38) and the Des Moines River. In 1841 he married Jessie Benton. The following year he led his first expedition west, across the Great Plains and through the Rockies' South Pass. He became known as The Pathfinder.

In 1843–44 and 1845 Frémont explored the Columbia River south to the territories on both sides of the Sierra Nevada. In California in 1846 he instigated the Bear Flag Revolt. His later career included a court-martial for insubordination and resignation from the army; further western expeditions; election as U.S. senator (1850); a presidential candidacy (1856); and brief, unsuccessful service in the Civil War. Thereafter his reputation rested on his wife's written accounts of his explorations.

THE daughter of Senator Thomas Hart Benton, Jessie Benton Frémont (1824–1902) was seventeen when she eloped with John Charles Frémont, causing a temporary break with her father. Although undoubtedly the stronger partner, she was always her husband's staunchest supporter. Her connections brought Frémont into contact with political and financial leaders, while her literary skill in helping her husband write about his expeditions successfully publicized them.

Jessie Benton Frémont supported her husband financially for the last twenty years of his life, writing for magazines. In addition to helping her husband with his memoirs (1887), she wrote several books, principally about her own experiences. They included *The Story of the Guard: A Chronicle of the War* (1863), *A Year of American Travel* (1878), *Souvenirs of My Time* (1887), *Far West Sketches* (1890), and *The Will and the Way Stories* (1891).

BORN in North Carolina, Thomas Hart Benton (1782–1858) fought in the War of 1812. After practicing as a lawyer in St. Louis, in 1820 he was elected to the U.S. Senate, where he served for thirty years. A strong supporter of his son-in-law, Frémont, Benton favored settlement of the West. In 1836 he sponsored a bill that public lands should be paid for with hard currency (gold and silver), earning Benton his nickname of "Old Bullion."

Despite Benton's expansionist policies, he was against annexing Texas but nonetheless supported the government in the Mexican War. Although his views on slavery were conservative, he believed it hindered western settlement and therefore favored gradual abolition. His opposition to the Compromise of 1850 led to his defeat in the next Senate election, but he was later returned briefly to the House of Representatives. Following his retirement, Benton wrote his autobiography, *Thirty Years' View* (1854–56).

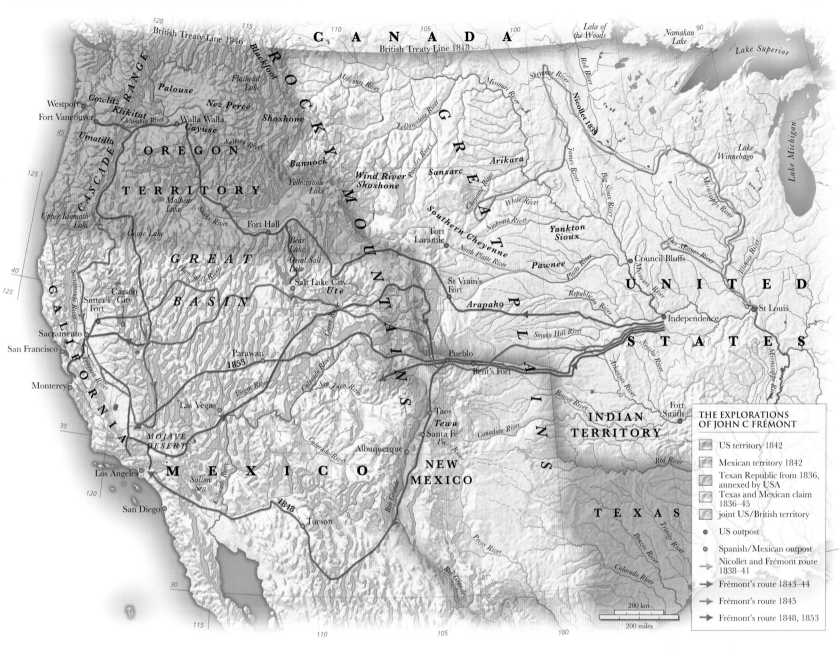

THE EXPLORATIONS OF JOHN C FRÉMONT

Legend	
	US territory 1842
	Mexican territory 1842
	Texan Republic from 1836, annexed by USA
	Texas and Mexican claim 1836–45
	joint US/British territory
●	US outpost
●	Spanish/Mexican outpost
→	Nicollet and Frémont route 1838–41
→	Frémont's route 1843–44
→	Frémont's route 1845
→	Frémont's route 1848, 1853

200 km
200 miles

Abert (quite probably actually written by Benton) directed him to proceed to the ending point of his earlier trek—South Pass—and from there to link his 1842 travels with the "U.S. Exploring Expedition, "a U.S. Navy survey of the Pacific basin (including the west coast of North America) led by Lieutenant Charles Wilkes. Although this was a seemingly direct objective, hidden within the instructions was an injunction to resolve the two greatest riddles that yet remained about the greater geography of the West. Did there exist somewhere in the region of South Pass a central source area from which all major western rivers flowed? If so, could the westernmost of these rivers—the "Rio San Buenaventura" on many maps of the West, presumably entering the Pacific Ocean near San Francisco Bay—be used to reach the Pacific more directly and easily than the circuitous route via the Snake and Columbia Rivers followed by the Oregon-bound

migrants or the treacherous mountain crossings required to reach California?

During two years of brilliant exploration, Frémont answered not only those two questions but many others as well. Accompanied by a sizeable party—including two legends of the fur trade, "Kit" Carson and Thomas "Broken Hand" Fitzpatrick, and the skilled German cartographer, Charles Preuss, who had been on the first Frémont expedition—Frémont traveled west following well-known routes to South Pass. From the western side of the pass, he followed the Green River (the upper Colorado) south to Fort Bridger in southwestern Wyoming and then turned northwest to Bear Lake and Fort Hall in southern Idaho, with a brief detour to Great Salt Lake. From Fort Hall, astride the migrant route to Oregon, Frémont and his command traveled through the Snake River Plain to the lower end of Hells Canyon and thence across the Blue Mountains west of the Snake's great

THE EXPLORATIONS OF FRÉMONT

The expeditions led by Lieutenant John C Frémont to survey the Far West consolidated American knowledge of these territories, and opened the way to a number of important trails for settlers.

and impassable gorge to the Whitman mission near present-day Walla Walla, Washington, and near the junction of the Snake and Columbia rivers. The party followed the Columbia downstream to the Hudson's Bay Company post of Fort Vancouver, across the Columbia River from the entry of the Willamette River into the larger stream. At Fort Vancouver, Frémont was entertained by the Company's factor, Dr. John McLoughlin, a man who was unfailingly hospitable, cordial, and helpful to the Americans—whether migrants or Army explorers—who would (as he probably well knew) tip the scales of ownership of Oregon Territory in favor of the United States.

✦ THE WILKES EXPEDITION ✦

ON AUGUST 18, 1838, Navy Lieutenant Charles Wilkes and his men left Norfolk, Virginia, and began an expedition to the Pacific Ocean that would last three years and ten months. With six ships and more than 400 men, the U.S. Exploring Expedition was a huge undertaking that ultimately confirmed that Antarctica was a continent and provided a wealth of scientific information. Its eminent scientists included the geologist and naturalist James Dwight Dana.

The voyage to Antarctica was particularly arduous because the expedition was ill equipped for it. The ships were not fitted to deal with ice, and the men lacked appropriate clothes for the climate. In fact, only half of the men completed the expedition. One ship, the *Sea Gull* and its crew, was lost at sea. The deteriorating *Relief* and *Flying Fish* both left the expedition in 1839.

On January 14, 1840, the *Vincennes*, the *Porpoise*, and the *Peacock* encountered the dazzling vision of sixty icebergs, and on

January 16 Wilkes sighted land. In fact, land was evident from all three ships for the next few days, establishing the existence of a continent. On January 24, the *Peacock* suffered extreme ice damage and returned to Australia, while the *Porpoise* left for New Zealand on February 24. The *Vincennes*, with Wilkes at the helm, continued on and sighted land along 1,500 miles of coast.

Until returning to New York in 1842, various contingents of the expedition explored and charted the South Pacific, the Hawaiian Islands, Singapore, and the Philippines. After entering the Strait of Juan de Fuca in present-day Washington in 1841, the expedition also explored the Pacific Northwest, with Wilkes noting Puget Sound's potential as a port. Wilkes himself was a controversial figure who was twice court-martialed. Wilkes Land in Antarctica is named in his honor.

JAMES DWIGHT DANA
Dana, a Yale-educated geologist and zoologist, accompanied the Wilkes Expedition as a scientific expert.

LT. CHARLES WILKES
The expedition commander's intelligence and strong will compensated for his lack of sea experience.

DISAPPOINTMENT BAY
Although six ships were originally assigned to the expedition, only the flagship USS Vincennes, *shown here, finished the Antarctic mission.*

ACROSS THE SIERRA NEVADA

The trek from South Pass west and north to Fort Vancouver had linked Frémont's survey with that of the Navy, and his formal objective, as written by Abert (or Benton) was achieved. But he had discovered no great westward-flowing stream, and the idea of a common source region for all major western rivers was becoming less viable in Frémont's developing geographical understanding of the West beyond South Pass. Still, a final testing had to be made, and, departing from his official orders, Frémont backtracked eastward from Fort Vancouver, up the Columbia and through the gorge that mighty stream makes through the Cascade Range, to the eastern flank of the Cascades. From a point near The Dalles of the Columbia, he and his command turned south

up the Deschutes River and, following the eastern front of the Cascade range, trekked southward to Klamath Lake and thence eastward and south again through the desert country of southern Oregon and northern Nevada. After traveling past the Pyramid Lake region to the Carson Valley (in the vicinity of Reno), Frémont decided that the Rio San Buenaventura was only a figment of cartographers' imaginations, and he crossed the Sierra Nevada to the California Great Valley.

This crossing demonstrated several components of Frémont's personality and character as an explorer. Undertaken in the dead of winter, the Sierra crossing revealed great personal courage and the ability to lead men in a direction they would probably rather not have gone. It also revealed foolishness and a trace of

vainglory. As hazardous and foolhardy as the mountain crossing was, it was accomplished successfully, and Frémont and his men recuperated in California at the small trading post on the American River established by the Swiss emigrant John Sutter in 1838. From Sutter's Fort the expedition traveled south through California's Great Valley, with the Sierra Nevada on the east and the coastal ranges on the west. Reaching the southern end of the valley, they recrossed the Sierras eastward into the Mojave Desert. Crossing the Mojave into southern Nevada, Frémont turned northeast toward Great Salt Lake and, once in the vicinity of that key landmark, veered eastward across the Wasatch Range to the Green River valley. Beyond the Green another major mountain transit was made across the Colorado

Rockies and through the "parks" between the western Colorado Rockies and the Front Range in the neighborhood of Pike's Peak. From there Frémont turned eastward to the Arkansas River and across the central Great Plains to the Missouri River at St. Louis, and home in July, 1845.

Frémont's circuit had achieved a great deal. The mythical Rio San Buenaventura was removed from the map of the West once and for all. The old concept of a central source area for all western streams was clarified and refined and Frémont's map showed—properly—two core source regions: one in northwestern Wyoming where the waters of the Green (Colorado), Snake, North Platte, and Yellowstone had their rise; a second in central Colorado from which flowed the Colorado proper, the Rio Grande, the Arkansas, and the South Platte. The concept of the Great Basin—a vast region of interior drainage with no outlet to any ocean—was introduced to science and added to American maps of the West. The Great Salt Lake valley

was described as an oasis in the desert, a characterization that would induce Brigham Young to settle on the Wasatch oasis as the site for his Kingdom of Deseret. The Great Plains were assessed as a region of enormous agricultural potential, the first such assessment by a major American explorer since Meriwether Lewis in 1805.

There were still holes to fill in the American view of the West, and much exploration–some of it by Frémont himself—remained to be accomplished. But Frémont's great expedition of 1843–44 was the high-water mark of the nineteenth-century exploration of the West, and after the publication of his accounts (as rendered by Jessie Benton Frémont) and maps (as beautifully drawn by Charles Preuss), Americans would view the West in a different way. They would see it as a region not of uniformity but of diversity: the great pasturelands of the Plains, the grandeur of the Rockies and Sierra Nevada, the deserts of the Great Basin, the rich valleys and mighty forests of the Pacific Northwest. The glorious literary passages and the detailed maps produced by the Frémonts and Preuss provided western migrants and prospective settlers with their first reliable views of the West. The light from Frémont's countless campfires during two years in the field illumined the way west, and the explorer himself was a symbol of his age.

"[WE STOOD] WHERE NEVER HUMAN FOOT HAD STOOD BEFORE."

—EXPLORER JOHN C. FRÉMONT
ON HIS TRAVELS

MOVING CAMP
John C. Frémont's first expedition, which took him through the Platte River Valley (shown here), saw both hardship and exhilaration.

BIRTH OF OREGON
This is a detail from William H. Jackson's painting Birth of Oregon. *Jackson was the last notable Oregon Trail journalist.*

"OUR JOURNEY IS ENDED, OUR TOILS ARE OVER, BUT...NO TONGUE CAN TELL, NOR PEN DESCRIBE THE HEART RENDING SCENES THROUGH WHICH WE PASSED."

—OREGON TRAIL PIONEER
A.H. GARRISON, 1846

THE GREAT WESTWARD MIGRATION BEGINS

THE MID-1840S SAW THOUSANDS OF SETTLERS HEADING WEST ALONG THE OREGON AND CALIFORNIA TRAILS. LURED BY LUSH FARMLAND, THESE IMMIGRANTS TRAVELED BY WAGON OVER 2,000 MILES OF WILDERNESS— ENDURING BAD FOOD, WORSE WEATHER, DISEASE, AND FATIGUE, ALL FOR A CHANCE AT A NEW LIFE. JOHN CHARLES FRÉMONT WENT EVEN FURTHER, RAISING A REVOLT TO SEIZE CALIFORNIA FROM MEXICO.

ALTHOUGH THE GREAT MIGRATIONS to Oregon, California, and the Great Basin were lent impetus by the reports of Frémont's journeys in 1842 and 1843–44, the migrations themselves were already underway as he and his exploratory force were wandering the West during his first two expeditions.

THE OREGON TRAIL
The efforts of advocates of Oregon settlement were successful in stirring up fervor for American occupation of the Pacific Northwest. The cause of migration was aided and abetted by expansionist politicians like Thomas Hart Benton. Prepared for the rigors of the trail by emigrant "guide books" that began to appear in the early 1840s, armed with the journals and maps of Frémont, and frequently guided westward by former fur trappers who knew the country like the backs

of their hands, the folk migrations began in the late 1830s and continued without interruption through the 1840s.

The route to Oregon Country—the Oregon Trail—was essentially that used by the fur trade and popularized by Frémont's 1843 trek westward. Departing from Independence, Missouri, migrant wagons followed the Kansas River west to its tributary, the Big Blue. Turning north up the Big Blue to the low drainage divide between that stream and the Platte, the Trail finally reached

CHICAGO WAGONS
In the Black Hills, the pioneer wagons of choice were manufactured by Chicago's Peter Schuttler Wagon Company. This advertising image depicts both flat-bottomed farm wagons and, on the lower right, a spring wagon.

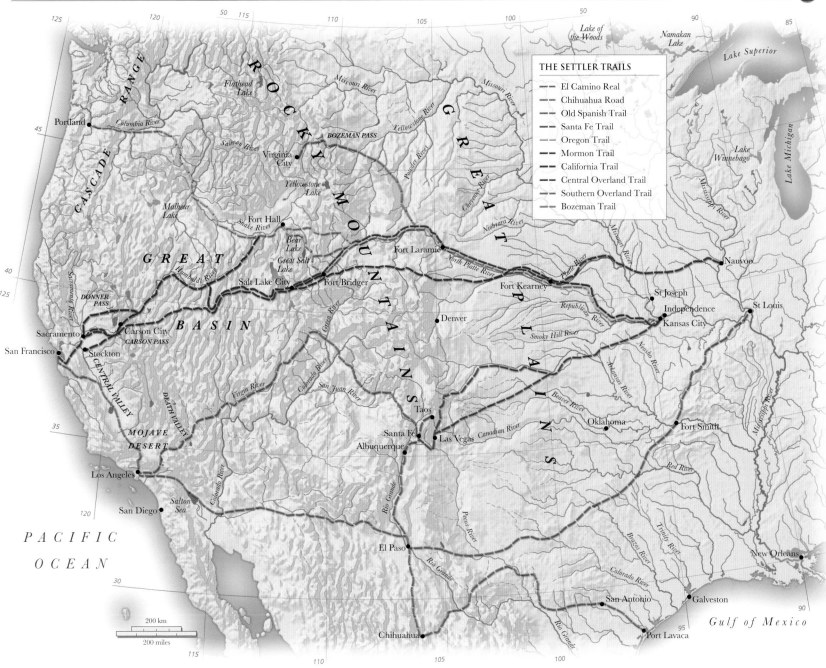

THE SETTLER TRAILS

- El Camino Real
- Chihuahua Road
- Old Spanish Trail
- Santa Fe Trail
- Oregon Trail
- Mormon Trail
- California Trail
- Central Overland Trail
- Southern Overland Trail
- Bozeman Trail

THE SETTLER TRAILS

Given the hardships confronting them, it is astonishing that the westward progress of settlers, following trails mapped by John C. Frémont and Jedediah Smith, was so successful. The Oregon-California Trail and the Old Spanish Trail were the most used routes.

the meridian river of the West and thence upstream to the division of the river into a northern and southern fork. The favored route followed the North Platte past many of the most famous landmarks of the trail in western Nebraska—Courthouse Rock, Chimney Rock, Scotts Bluff—and through the treacherous Ash Hollow. There a deep defile leading to a crossing of the Platte made travel dangerous and often costly, with the price paid in the form of a broken wheel, downed oxen, or overturned wagons. Beyond Ash Hollow and the bluffs country lay

Fort Laramie in eastern Wyoming, a frontier outpost of the fur trade since the 1830s and maintained by the U.S. Army after 1849.

Up to this point, travel had been relatively easy through a country that most migrants viewed as having considerable agricultural potential. The claims on the part of some historians that migrants avoided settling the Plains east of Fort Laramie because they viewed it as part of "the Great American Desert" simply do not hold up to scrutiny. It was not so much avoidance of the Plains as it was the attraction and lure of Oregon that drew settlers across what would later become one of the world's greatest agricultural regions without even pausing to break ground.

At Fort Laramie migrants often halted to rest their stock and, if possible, refurbish their supplies. The stop at Fort Laramie also provided the Oregon-bound pioneers with what for many was their first and only contact with native peoples, particularly the Sioux, Cheyennes, and Arapahos who frequented the trading post. Attacks on the Oregon Trail wagon trains by mounted Indians, as popularized by movies and television, were a great rarity. Most travelers along the Oregon Trail saw native peoples only at a distance;

CHIMNEY ROCK

Chimney Rock, located in what is now Bayard, Nebraska, was a popular landmark for migrants on the Oregon, California, and Mormon Trails. The rock formation stands 325 feet tall.

where contacts did take place, they were more frequently helpful to the migrants than otherwise. Indians provided information on routes and helped to locate key landmarks; they instructed whites unfamiliar with the western flora and fauna as to what was and was not edible. Indeed, along the Platte in particular, the Indians often provided crucial assistance in getting wagons and livestock across the river during the several required fordings of the Platte. When contact between migrant and native did result in tragedy, more often than not it was a tragedy for Indians rather than whites: many more Indians were killed by white migrants during the Great Migrations than the reverse.

Beyond Fort Laramie, the journey westward became increasingly difficult, west and north through the rugged hills south of the North Platte, through broken country covered with buffalo grass and sagebrush, to the junction of the North Platte with the Sweetwater, just west of present-day Casper, Wyoming. The Sweetwater, a lengthy stream but never a large one, led westward past two more famous landmarks of the Trail: Independence Rock, where most migrants hoped to be by July 4, and where they left the record of their passing by carving their names into the granite dome rising above the plains; and Devil's Gate, where the Sweetwater cut a dramatic gorge through an enormous granite outcrop. Beyond lay the fabled South Pass, not a mountain pass at all but a broad break in the Rocky Mountain chain. To the north of South Pass is the Wind River Range, and to the south the Wyoming or Great Divide Basin that extends to the resumption of high mountain country near the Wyoming-Colorado border. The ascent and descent of the Continental Divide is so gentle that many migrants were never aware of having crossed the backbone of the continent until the few small streams on the Pacific side were encountered, flowing not east but west to the Green River.

THE TRAIL DIVIDES

Since leaving Fort Laramie, the migrants had found the country increasingly dry, and beyond South Pass it became even drier. But a water supply existed in the form of the Big Sandy and other small feeder streams of the Green River, and these were followed westward. Before reaching the Green River, the trail separated, with some migrants moving south to Fort Bridger and then northwest to the Bear River. Here they rejoined those travelers who had taken "Sublette's Cutoff"—a deviation from the more southerly Fort Bridger route and named for the mountain man who had first pioneered this more direct route from South Pass to the Bear River. The Bear River was followed northwest to Soda Springs, where the stream veers to enter Great Salt Lake. From Soda Springs the trail split again, with some migrants moving overland in a slightly northwestern direction to Fort Hall on the Snake River, and others following the Hudspeth Cutoff (pioneered by an early Oregon immigrant) slightly southwest to the Raft River, a tributary of the Snake. From there, the route was either down the Raft to the Snake to rejoin the main trail, or across the drainage divide between the Raft River and the Humboldt River, which was followed across Nevada to the Sierras and California.

FORT LARAMIE

The first trading post by this name was constructed in 1834 in a spot where hunting and trading routes of the Cheyenne, Sioux, and Arapaho tribes converged. Later, it was replaced with a second fort.

✦THE CONESTOGA WAGON✦

ORIGINALLY DEVELOPED around 1750 by settlers of German descent in Pennsylvania, the Conestoga wagon served for over 100 years as Americans' main form of freight transport. Large (up to twenty-eight feet long) and heavy, the Conestoga had an unusual, boat-like shape, with a floor that dipped towards the middle and up at each end, ensuring barrels and bales would not tip out when going up or down hills. Another distinctive feature was the canvas bonnet, the frame of which sloped forward and over the wagon's rear, protecting its goods from rain. Carrying up to five tons of cargo, the Conestoga was pulled by teams of up to eight large draft horses.

The Conestoga wagon's robust build made it popular for settlers moving west in the early nineteenth century and for traders along the Santa Fe Trail. Even when the railroads crossed the continent, the Conestoga and other covered wagons remained the standard rural freight carrier until the internal combustion engine revolutionized transport.

Because the Conestoga proved too cumbersome for the Oregon Trail, a derivative, the so-called Prairie Schooner, evolved. Less than half the size of the Conestoga, the Prairie Schooner was about twelve feet long and four to five feet wide, and could be easily dismantled.

COVERED WAGON

This Conestoga wagon, built in eastern Pennsylvania in the 1760s, was used by homesteaders for seventy years.

Throughout nearly all its course from Fort Hall across Idaho, the Snake carves a gorge through a vast lava plateau. Although the trail followed the Snake, it did not approach the river closely but stayed well above the stream in the Snake River Plains, a rocky but level area where grass was available for the livestock, but where sharp volcanic rocks cut the feet of oxen and horses and mules and greatly diminished what small comforts there might have been to wagon travel.

The trail stayed south of the Snake as far as Glenns Ferry and then north across the river to the junction of the Snake and the Boise River. Near this point is Farewell Bend, Idaho, where the Snake enters its vast Grand Canyon (Hells Canyon), the deepest in North America. Following the Snake River beyond this point was impossible, and the trail cut overland in a northwestern direction, across the Blue Mountains of northeastern Oregon and down to the Columbia River at the major falls and cascade of The Dalles. Here many migrants chose to abandon land travel for water travel and, placing their wagons on large flatboats, floated downstream through the Columbia's gorge across the Cascades, to the mouth of the Willamette and the core of American settlement in the Northwest. Some few migrants chose to cross the Cascades by wagon, but most favored the river trip. For those who did use the river route, the passage of the Blue Mountains was the only major mountain crossing of the entire voyage, fulfilling the promise

made in St. Louis newspapers as early as 1814 that "there is no part of the track that cannot be successfully completed by waggon." It was, of course, not as easy as it sounds—over 2,000 miles of unsettled wilderness territory subject to violent extremes of climate; food shortages and their accompanying syndromes of weakness and of diseases like scurvy; the dreaded cholera and dysentery, acquired mostly from fouled water supplies; draft animals that died of overwork, bad water, and inadequate forage; and wagons that disintegrated from the rough road and the dry air, which shrunk wood like leather and popped loose iron bolts, rivets, and wagon wheel rims. But the lure of Oregon was greater than the perceived hardship, and although the folk saying "the cowards never started and the weak died on the way" may have been true, the fact is that more women and children traveled the Oregon Trail than did men. It was in the nature of the family migration that the Oregon settlement found its particular strength and staying power.

The numbers of Oregon migrants who made this epochal journey in the forties were never enormous: nowhere near the numbers of those who traveled to California as part of the Forty-Niner experience. But although small in number, the Oregon migrants made a great impact on international affairs and imperial ambition.

A party of approximately 125 persons arrived in the Willamette Valley in 1842 (having traveled by wagon as far as Fort Hall) and were, like earlier and later migrants, hosted by Dr. John McLoughlin until they could find their farmlands. Some of these migrants actually were disappointed and moved on to California, but St. Louis newspapers reported that larger migrations were being organized and that the Oregon fever" was raging all along the American settlement frontier of the Mississippi Valley.

In 1843, 875 migrants made the crossing, nearly all of them making it by wagon to The Dalles of the Columbia, whence they floated on flatboats down the Columbia to Fort Vancouver and the Willamette. A total of 1,475 more migrants arrived

BLUE MOUNTAINS

Wagon trains crossing the Blue Mountains on the Oregon Trail had to endure steep grades and poor roads, but in their writings pioneers expressed delight at the fabulous scenery. From here, the trail led to the Columbia River. When gold was later discovered in these mountains, emigrants settled in the rich surrounding farmland.

✦CLIPPER SHIPS✦

SINCE BEFORE the Revolutionary War, American shipbuilders had been turning out ships with a slimmer, faster profile than the British, their main rivals. Following the War of 1812 and the Napoleonic Wars, heavy armament on merchant ships was no longer necessary, and in 1816 the Black Ball Line began sailing between New York City and Liverpool, England. Their ships carried fewer passengers and less freight than the bulkier British ships, but the Americans' speed soon brought them much business carrying mail, cargo, and passengers.

The first true clipper ship is usually accepted to be the *Ann McKim*, built at Baltimore in 1832. Square-rigged, with yacht-like lines and raked masts, she was 143 feet long and 31 feet broad, with the sharp bows that became the trademark of the "Yankee clippers," as the American ships were called. In 1845 the New York-built *Rainbow*

became the first of the "extreme" clippers, with even sharper bows and less cargo space.

On the *Rainbow's* maiden voyage, she sailed to China and back to New York in seven months and seventeen days. Thereafter Yankee clippers continued to set records across the world. The most famous builder, Donald McKay of Boston, produced ships that achieved speeds of twenty-one knots and made runs of 420 nautical miles in a day. In 1849 the appearance of American clippers in Britain caused a sensation, but the British were slow in copying the design.

After the 1848 California gold discovery, clippers were prized for their speed in carrying passengers westward around Cape Horn to the California gold fields. Clippers were driven so hard and were built so lightly that few lasted many years. After 1860, clippers were gradually put out of business by the steamship.

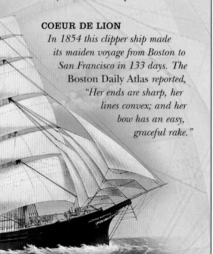

COEUR DE LION
In 1854 this clipper ship made its maiden voyage from Boston to San Francisco in 133 days. The Boston Daily Atlas *reported, "Her ends are sharp, her lines convex; and her bow has an easy, graceful rake."*

In 1846 international negotiations with Great Britain resulted in the cession of Oregon (meaning the territory west of the Continental Divide and south of the 49th parallel) to the United States. The first phase of Manifest Destiny, the geopolitical concept that held it was America's divine right to settle and control the continent from Atlantic to Pacific, was complete. The United States of America now legally extended from sea to sea, American control over Oregon was secured, and Americans were on their way to becoming a continental people.

CALIFORNIA

The second phase of Manifest Destiny was being played out to the south, in the Mexican province of Alta (Upper) California, now the present-day state of California. Independence from Spain had brought abandonment of the mission settlement system that had been the bulwark of California when the Spanish held it. Since California was too removed from the centers of Mexican population and economy to be attractive as a region for Mexican settlers, secular settlement of mission lands was no solution. The few secular settlers were either members of the old Spanish aristocracy holding enormous land grants or were Mexican convicts sent to California to eke out a meager and punitive subsistence from the land. Economically, California was dominated by a pattern of livestock raising in which the chief products were cattle hides and tallow traded with English and American merchant ships making landfalls along the California coast. The growing commerce in hides and tallow was accompanied by increasing contact between California and American merchant vessels, forging links between California

MODEL OF MCCORMICK'S REAPER
Patented in 1834, Cyrus McCormick's ingenious farm tool revolutionized American agriculture. It won the top prize at the 1851 London World's Fair.

in the following year and nearly 2,500 in 1845, at least some of them successfully getting their wagons across the Cascades. By 1845 American farmers occupied attractive farm sites in the Willamette Valley, extending as far as sixty miles above the Falls of the Willamette. As Americans were accustomed to doing, they formed a government, drew up a constitution and legal code, demarcated counties for the country south of the Columbia (north of the river was still viewed by most Oregon settlers as British territory), created the office of territorial governor, and established a capital at Oregon City at the Falls of the Willamette.

and the United States that were stronger than the links between California and Mexico.

Into this isolated region, beginning shortly after Mexican independence, there slowly began to trickle migrants from Europe; from the Atlantic Seaboard of the United States (particularly New England and the Middle Atlantic states, where maritime activity was a dominant part of the economy); and from the Rocky Mountain

region, from which came former fur trappers seeking a more stable or less adventurous way of life. Nearly all of these migrants were males who took Indian wives or married into the families of the *californios* or wealthy livestock ranchers. Few settlers attempted the creation of European or American patterns of agricultural settlement. California before the 1840s remained largely a Spanish-style pastoral region, dominated by livestock raising.

This began to change in 1841 with the arrival of the first emigrant train from the United States. The party was led by a wealthy Missouri farmer, John Bartleson, and a frontier schoolteacher, John Bidwell, who also served as the party's chronicler, producing the first of the California overland accounts. The Bidwell-Bartleson party is remembered as the first emigrant group to travel to the Pacific without experienced members of the fur-trade brigades as guides during the entire trip. The migrants did travel the Oregon Trail as far as Soda Springs in the company of Thomas "Broken Hand" Fitzpatrick, who would, two years later, accompany Frémont on the great circuit of the West. But from Soda Springs, Fitzpatrick waved a hand in a vaguely southwestern direction, pointing out probable routes to California, and from that point on, the small party, including five women and ten children, was on its own.

CRADLE SCYTHE

This tool, made obsolete by the introduction of the McCormick reaper, lopped off stalks of grain and held them in a "cradle," keeping overripe seeds from falling out.

BEAR HUNT

This lithograph shows three native Californians on horseback, armed with rifles, attempting to lasso a bear. Black bears still roam the state.

From Soda Springs, the Bidwell-Bartleson wagon train followed the Bear River south nearly to its entry into Great Salt Lake. North of the lake, they turned west across the Salt Lake Desert and, relying on information obtained from Indians, swung south near the Idaho-Utah border to Rabbit Spring and Pilot Peak. This southern track caused them to miss the headwaters of the river called "Ogden's River" that Fitzpatrick had told them about. Having missed the upper part of the river that would shortly be renamed "Humboldt" by Frémont, in honor of the great German geographer Alexander von Humboldt, the Bidwell-Bartleson group was forced to strike out across the desert to the southwest, aiming for the Ruby Mountains visible on the southwestern horizon. By the time the party reached the Ruby range, in northeastern Nevada, they had abandoned their wagons and loaded their remaining supplies on pack mules. From the Ruby Mountains, the party traveled westward until finally striking the Humboldt and following it to the Sinks, where the river simply disappears into the sands of the Great Basin some forty miles east of the Sierra Nevada Range. The Sierras were crossed via Sonora Pass, which drops into the headwaters region of the Stanislaus River, a major tributary of the Sacramento River system, which they followed down into the Sacramento Valley, the northern end of the Great Valley of California.

Thirty-four Americans had reached California from the east, traveling overland. Their arrival was more important than the fact that they had done so without their wagons, abandoned in the desert country of the Great Basin. The members of the Bidwell-Bartleson party represented a farm-family migration, different in kind from the previous American arrivals: individual sailors jumping ship to stay in California or worn-out mountain men seeking refuge from the snows of the Rockies. This migration signaled the beginning of an influx that, although never large during the decade of the forties, placed enough Americans in California by 1846 to provide a nucleus of settlement that could help to wrest control of

YERBA BUENA
San Francisco was still known as Yerba Buena when this drawing was completed in 1837. The name was changed in 1846.

the area from Mexico. It also established a center of agricultural production that supplied at least some of the food demands of the early mineral exploitation of the California gold fields.

The arrival of the Bidwell-Bartleson party in the Great Valley was a momentous event, made even more so by the fact that one of the party's members, J. B. Chiles, headed back east to bring

another party to California in 1843. Also in 1843, the veteran mountain man Joseph Walker led an emigrant party across the Great Basin via the Humboldt, then crossed the Sierras through Owens Valley and across Walker Pass to the San Joaquin Valley (the southern portion of the California Great Valley). The total number of migrants in the two parties of 1843 was thirty-eight. In 1844, fifty-three more would follow in what was perhaps the most significant of the early migrations, the Stevens-Murphy party. This party departed Council Bluffs, Iowa, in the spring of 1844 and laid out what became the California Trail.

THE CALIFORNIA TRAIL

The Stevens-Murphy party was named for Missouri farmer Patrick Murphy, whose family comprised more than half of the group's complement of forty-six persons (twenty-three men, eight women, and fifteen children), and for Elisha Stevens, an experienced mountain man who served as the party's field commander. They followed the known track of the Oregon Trail west to South Pass. From South Pass, Stevens (who knew a great deal about this part of the country) recommended striking out directly west for the Green River and, once across the Green, nearly due west again to pick up the Oregon Trail on the Bear River, using the "Sublette's Cutoff" route pioneered by William Sublette of the Rocky Mountain fur trade. The Sublette's Cutoff route was thereafter a fixture of both the Oregon and California trails. Stevens and his party followed the Oregon road as far as Fort Hall and from that key landmark they followed the route of Joseph Walker the year before, south to the Humboldt River, which they followed across Nevada to the Sinks. Following Indian directions, they trekked westward over a good pass across the Sierra Nevada. This was Donner Pass, named later after the ill-fated migrant parry of 1846, and it represented the major emigrant entry to California. The Stevens-Murphy party succeeded in getting their wagons across the pass and down the western slopes of the Sierras to Sutter's Fort.

The emigrant trail to California—the one to be used by thousands of Forty-Niners bound for the gold fields—was now a fact, and 260 migrants used it to get to California in 1845. The route became even more fixed in the American

---

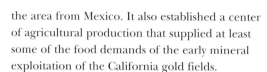

⇥THE DONNER PARTY⇤

IN 1845 Lansford Hastings, a California promoter, published *The Emigrants' Guide to Oregon and California,* recommending a quicker route for California-bound emigrants, one that turned directly west from Fort Bridger rather than following the established trail. Hastings, however, had never traveled his recommended route himself.

In April 1846 the brothers George and Jacob Donner and their large families left Independence, Missouri, and joined other travelers on the Oregon Trail. They decided to follow Hastings's recommended cutoff, despite warnings of snows closing the passes through the Sierra Nevada. The Donner party, comprising eighty-seven people in twenty-three wagons, found the route from Fort Bridger difficult to follow and did not reach the Great Salt Lake valley until the end of August. By then supplies of food and water were running low, and many animals had been lost crossing the desert.

It was not until mid-October that the party, now numbering eighty-two, reached the eastern slopes of the Sierra Nevada, where they found the Truckee Pass (today's Donner Pass) impassable with snow. With their animals lost to blizzards, some emigrants abandoned their wagons and camped in an abandoned cabin at Truckee Lake (now Donner Lake). Five miles down the trail, at Alder Creek, the remainder improvised shelters from branches and wagon canvas.

In mid-December a group of fifteen men and women—"the Forlorn Hope"—left Truckee Lake in an

Eliza Donner   *Georgia Ann Donner*   *Frances Donner*

attempt to cross the mountains and secure help from Sutter's Fort. Four died, and the survivors used their dead bodies for food. More died during the month-long journey, and only two men and five women reached a settlement in Sacramento.

Although several attempts were made to rescue the party, it was not until February that the survivors at Alder Creek were found and not until April that the remainder were rescued at Truckee Lake. They too had had to resort to cannibalism. In the six months spent in the Sierra Nevada, thirty-five had died, including both Donner brothers. A survivor later advised other pioneers: *"Never take no cut ofs, and hury along as fast you can."*

TREE STUMPS
Travelers later found tree stumps cut by the Donner Party at heights of twenty feet or more, indicating the depth of the snow they endured.

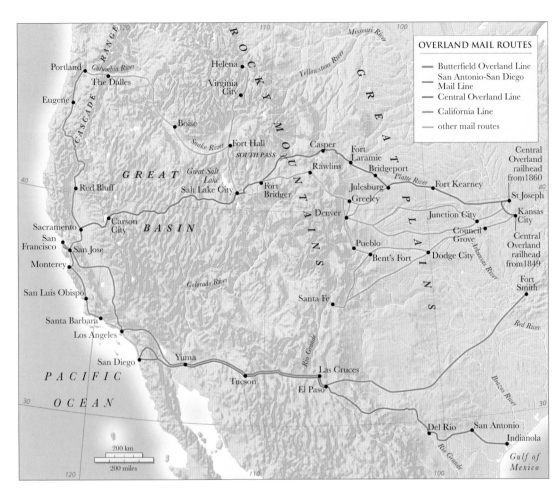

OVERLAND MAIL ROUTES

— Butterfield Overland Line
— San Antonio-San Diego Mail Line
— Central Overland Line
— California Line
— other mail routes

FRÉMONT'S THIRD EXPEDITION

In the spring of 1845, Frémont was in Washington busily preparing for a third western expedition. His written orders from Colonel Abert were to travel from Bent's Fort, a trading post on the Arkansas River, into the Rocky Mountains of Colorado to survey the headwaters of the Arkansas, Rio Grande, and Colorado rivers. As with his previous expeditions, however, the true objectives of Frémont's third expedition were probably known only to Senator Benton and himself, and Frémont later noted that his instructions included a completion of the survey of Great Salt Lake and the regions west and southwest to the Cascade Mountains and the Sierra Nevada. It may well be that, even at this early date, Benton and Frémont were thinking of a route suitable for railroad construction across the Rockies to California, particularly in the light of Frémont's failure to locate a central river route to the Pacific via the apocryphal San Buenaventura during his second expedition. In any event, during his third expedition into the West, Frémont certainly had no qualms in departing from his official orders in what he (and probably Benton) perceived as the interests of international politics, economics, or science.

OVERLAND MAIL ROUTES

By 1847 the first properly subsidized mail route across the continent was established. This pack animal service was replaced by a stagecoach system in 1850, and several companies soon competed for control of overland mail.

consciousness in that year as one of the emigrant groups was led by Lansford Hastings, author of the most famous of all emigrant guide books: *The Emigrants' Guide to Oregon and California.* In the following year, 1,500 emigrants arrived in California by the overland route.

By this time conditions in California were in a state of political flux and confusion. While a state of near anarchy in terms of government organization had existed for years, since the arrival of the first overland American emigrants in 1841, conditions of formal government had worsened. The *californios,* or Mexican land owners, neither wanted nor needed government interfering in their livestock-hide-tallow trade with English and American ships. Entrepreneurs who had received large

grants of land from the Mexican government, such as the Swiss John (Johann Augustus) Sutter, were more interested in building their own empires free from government control than they were in consolidating formal and institutionalized political systems. And the independent American farmers, such as those accompanying the Bidwell-Bartleson, Stevens-Murphy, and other emigrant parties, were used to frontier governmental systems in which laws were loosely defined. By 1846 California was a volatile mix of native *californios,* wealthy landed merchants like Sutter, and American frontier farmers and fur trappers. Thrown into this mix, and again playing a major role in the decade of the forties, was John Charles Frémont.

RAT SNAKE

This Great Plains rat snake, once known as Scotophis emoryi, *was sketched by U.S. Army surveyor William Emory on a trip to the Mexican border in 1846.*

GIANT TREE

A hunter is dwarfed by the "Grizzly Giant," a sequoia in California's Mariposa Grove, in this 1861 photograph.

By June 1845 Frémont had assembled his command and begun a rapid march from St. Louis to Bent's Fort on the Arkansas River, which they reached in August. From Bent's Fort, Frémont and his company of about sixty well armed men—including Kit Carson and Philadelphia artist Edward Kern—proceeded westward along the Arkansas River. Regardless of his official orders to explore the Colorado Rockies, Frémont and his men were headed straight for California, and there seems little doubt that his intent had ever been otherwise. His course to the west took Frémont around the Royal Gorge of the Arkansas, across the Continental Divide, and over the Grand (upper Colorado) River to the plateau country of western Colorado and eastern Utah. Great Salt Lake was reached in October 1845, and Frémont remained in this vicinity long enough to make detailed surveys and collect plant and animal specimens. The course west from Salt Lake carried Frémont's party to Pilot Peak and the Humboldt Mountains via the route that later came to be called the Hastings Cutoff of the California Trail. At the Humboldt, Frémont divided his command: one party under Kern to follow the Humboldt to the Sinks and then to Walker Lake; one party under himself to travel due west across the Great Basin and then south to Walker Lake to rendezvous with Kern. At the rendezvous on Walker Lake, Frémont split the command again, ordering Walker to take part of the command south to a southern pass across the Sierras, while Frémont would cross the mountains (probably via Donner Pass or Truckee Pass) directly to Sutter's Fort in the Sacramento Valley, where he would be joined by Walker.

From this point on the tale is one of subterfuge, political intrigue, and bombast—with a dose of comic opera thrown in besides. To simplify a long

MIRROR LAKE

In 1864 President Abraham Lincoln granted California 39,000 acres of land in the Yosemite Valley for public use, including this lake that reflects Mount Watkins and other natural landmarks. Mount Watkins is named for Carleton E. Watkins, an early photographer of Yosemite.

and very complex series of events: Frémont and Walker rejoined forces in northern California, and the Mexican authorities were concerned about the presence of a sizable American military force in a vulnerable region. They asked Frémont to depart; he refused and erected fortifications, announcing that he would die fighting. Perhaps thinking better of this bellicose behavior, Frémont finally did turn his command north for the Klamath Lake area of Oregon. Here he was intercepted on May 9, 1846, by messages from Washington informing him that war between the United States and Mexico was imminent and to behave accordingly. Exactly what this suggested to Frémont is difficult to say, but he was obviously disturbed enough that he forgot to post a guard around his Klamath Lake camp and was attacked by Indians during the night, with loss of life on both sides.

THE BEAR FLAG

The following day, after a retaliatory raid against the Indians that was mostly one-sided in favor of the better armed Americans, Frémont once again turned toward California. Back in the northern part of the Great Valley, he learned that rumors abounded to the effect that the Mexicans had ordered all Americans out of the province, or that a large Mexican force was heading toward the American farming settlement in the Sacramento Valley to drive out the foreigners, or that Mexico and the United States were at war, or that a British naval vessel loaded with marines was in San Francisco Bay preparing to launch an attack on California and secure it for Great Britain. In retrospect, Frémont did about the only thing he could. He wrote to Benton resigning his commission, leaving his father-in-law with the decision as to whether to forward the letter to the secretary of war. Frémont informed American settlers in northern California that their best interests lay in exerting control over their own destiny and taking over the reins of government, and he incited them to take over control of Sonoma, north of San Francisco. The result of this action, known as the "Bear Flag Revolt," was a victory for rough American frontier farmers against poorly trained and equipped Mexican

WAR BEGINS

This lithograph depicts popular reaction upon hearing news of the war with Mexico in 1846. The men at center excitedly reads the Richmond Inquirer Extra *outside a hotel, while others read over his shoulder.*

❖THE BEAR FLAG REVOLT❖

WHEN TEXAS gained independence from Mexico in 1836, Mexican leaders saw this as a U.S. move to expand its territory. They were further alarmed by President Andrew Jackson's offer to buy part of California and turned down similar offers during the Tyler administration. President James Polk, a proponent of America's Manifest Destiny, feared that Mexico would sell California to Britain to keep it out of American hands, increasing the number of British possessions in the Pacific.

In 1845 John Charles Frémont reached California on his third expedition. Expelled by Mexican authorities, he went north to Oregon, where it is believed he received secret orders to prepare for a war with Mexico. Frémont subsequently returned south to help the growing resistance. On June 14, 1846, American settlers at Sonoma, south of Monterey, took General Mariano Vallejo prisoner and declared independence. Frémont joined them, and on July 5 he was made leader of the "Bear Flag Republic." The name derived from the rebels' adopted flag, showing a grizzly bear and a star on a white background; it was designed by William L. Todd, a nephew of Mary Todd Lincoln.

On July 7, 1846, Commodore John Sloat landed at Monterey, raising the American flag, and Frémont organized forces to assist U.S. troops in the conquest of California. By August 13 they had taken Los Angeles, and most of California was under American control. A counter-revolution by Mexican Californians was defeated by reinforcements from the U.S. Navy and an overland force led by General Stephen Kearny. On January 13, 1847, Frémont formally accepted Mexico's cession of California. Ironically, he was subsequently court-martialed for his "unauthorized actions," even though the United States had officially been at war with Mexico since May 13, 1846.

irregulars. In Sonoma the Americans proclaimed the California Republic and ran up a homemade flag with an image of a California grizzly bear, giving a name to the revolt. Frémont himself entered Sonoma at the head of his troops, the only actual American military presence in California. Shortly thereafter, in early July 1846, Frémont learned that war had been declared between his country and Mexico.

DAUGHTER OF LONE WOLF
Land acquired through the Mexican War sowed the seeds of conflict with the region's Indians, such as the Kiowas led by Lone Wolf.

MIGRATION TO THE SOUTHWEST

U.S. ANNEXATION OF TEXAS IN 1845 WORSENED RELATIONS WITH MEXICO. THE DISPUTE LED TO THE MEXICAN WAR, THROUGH WHICH THE UNITED STATES ACQUIRED MORE THAN HALF A MILLION SQUARE MILES OF MEXICAN LAND. WITHIN THIS AREA WAS THE GREAT SALT LAKE VALLEY, WHICH IN THE LATE 1840S BECAME THE PROMISED LAND TO MORMON MIGRANTS FLEEING RELIGIOUS PERSECUTION.

"[IT IS] OUR MANIFEST DESTINY TO OVERSPREAD THE CONTINENT ALLOTTED BY PROVIDENCE FOR THE FREE DEVELOPMENT OF OUR YEARLY MULTIPLYING MILLIONS."

—JOHN LOUIS O'SULLIVAN, MAGAZINE EDITOR, 1845

THE MEXICAN WAR had its origins, at least in part, in the political doctrine of Manifest Destiny, the electric phrase first printed in 1845 to give meaning to the inexorable and inevitable surge of the United States toward the Pacific. The more immediate cause of the war was the American annexation of Texas in 1845 and Polk's dispatching of American troops under General Zachary Taylor to the east bank of the Rio Grande near Matamoros. Recognizing the Nueces River to the north as the boundary between Texas and Mexico, the Mexicans responded to what they perceived as an American invasion of their territory by crossing the Rio Grande and destroying a small American contingent.

Using this incident as a provocation, the president read his war message to Congress on May 11, 1846. Although the Congress declared

CAMPAIGN FLAG
Democrat James K. Polk and running mate George Dallas supported admitting Texas to the Union.

war, there was considerable hesitancy. Even an outspoken advocate of American expansion like Thomas Hart Benton was unsure of the motives or morality of the war. There was also considerable concern among the northern representatives and senators that the war would culminate in an expansion of slavery into new territories in the Southwest. These objections were cast aside in favor of overwhelming public support for the war, and the United States embarked upon a conflict that, in terms of territorial gain, would add over half a million square miles to its territory.

THE MEXICAN CESSION
In February 1848 the Treaty of Guadalupe Hidalgo ending the war was signed, and the United States received a massive territory ceded from Mexico by the treaty. The Mexican-American border was specified as the Rio Grande River as

✦THE MEXICAN WAR✦

UNEASY RELATIONS BETWEEN MEXICO and the United States worsened after Texas won its independence in 1836. Already suspicious of U.S. intentions, Mexican authorities were outraged when Texas was annexed in 1845 and further infuriated when the American government raised the matter of the state's southern borders. The Mexicans claimed the Texas boundary was the Nueces River, while the United States held it to be the Rio Grande, further west. Furthermore, an international commission had decided Mexico owed American settlers millions of dollars in damages resulting from past political crises—money that Mexico refused to pay.

On April 24, 1846, Mexican cavalry attacked American outposts on the Rio Grande. On May 8–9, though outnumbered, General Zachary Taylor forced the Mexican troops back across the Rio Grande. In August, after Congress had formally declared war, Taylor advanced into Mexico, taking Monterrey on September 25 and Saltillo in mid-November. To the north, General Stephen Kearny had taken New Mexico with little difficulty and then marched west, where John Charles Frémont and the Bear Flag Revolt had already begun the conquest of California.

The news that General Antonio Lopez de Santa Anna, returned from exile, was advancing with large forces led Taylor to withdraw to Buena Vista, where, in February 1847, he repelled the larger Mexican

force. Meanwhile, a force of Missouri volunteers led by Colonel Alexander W. Doniphan, dubbed "Doniphan's Thousand," marched south from New Mexico, capturing El Paso and Chihuahua along the way and joining Taylor at Monterrey in May 1847.

By this time Polk had decided that only the invasion of Mexico City would force the enemy to accept terms. On March 9, 1847, General Winfield Scott and 12,000 men landed on Mexico's east coast near Vera Cruz, which surrendered on March 27 after a fierce siege. Scott then marched westward along the same road Hernán Cortés had marched 300 years earlier. Despite having only half the troops he had asked for and insufficient supplies and ammunition, he outflanked the Mexican army at the fortified pass of Cerro Gordo. On August 20, after a three-month wait for troop replacements, Scott won a decisive battle at Churubusco in which he lost a seventh of his force.

After Santa Anna refused an armistice, another battle was fought at Molina del Rey on September 8, followed by a final battle at Chapultepec on September 13. On September 17, 1847, Mexico City surrendered, ending the fighting. Under the Treaty of Guadalupe Hidalgo, signed on February 2, 1848, Mexico agreed to the Rio Grande as the Texan border and ceded California and New Mexico to the United States for $15 million. The United States assumed responsibility for claims of $3.25 million against Mexico.

U.S. FORCES AT CHURUBUSCO
An 1847 battle is commemorated in a detail from artwork by James Walker, who recorded major episodes of the Mexican War in nine paintings.

far upstream as El Paso, then west from the Rio Grande to the Gila River and down that stream to its junction with the Colorado. From the Colorado-Gila confluence, the border ran straight west across the deserts and mountains to just south of the mission of San Diego. As a result of this cession the United States nearly reached the full continental configuration of what would

BROWNSVILLE, TEXAS
Fort Taylor was established here in 1846. Following the first major battle of the Mexican War, in which Major Jacob Brown died defending the fort, it was renamed Fort Brown in his honor.

become the "lower 48" states, excepting only a small strip of territory south of the Gila, the southernmost portions of New Mexico and Arizona, that would be added by purchase from Mexico five years later (the Gadsden Purchase, 1853). In this massive "Mexican Cession" were all of the present states of California, Nevada, and Utah, most of Arizona and New Mexico, portions of Wyoming and Colorado, and the "disputed" region of Texas between the Nueces River and the Rio Grande.

The Mexican Cession was significant for several reasons. Over half a million square miles in area, it increased the size of the United States by nearly 20 percent. Because it added such a large piece of land to the southern regions of the United States, it helped to sow the seeds for the great sectional conflict of the Civil War by extending the territory that was potentially open to slavery. The cession brought into cultural conflict, along a zone some thousand miles long, the two dominant nonindigenous North American cultures—Anglo and Hispanic—and created a region of cultural conflict when Anglo-Americans moved into territory that had been occupied by Hispanics since the late 1500s. Finally, the cession removed the concept from American political geography of a "permanent Indian frontier," paving the way for the acquisition of Indian lands throughout the region of the cession and beyond. Before the Mexican War, many politicians had thought of the farther West as a huge, permanent Indian reservation, perhaps cut in two by the lands adjacent to the overland route via South Pass. After the acquisition of New Mexico and California, such thinking was no longer possible. The entire West would provide a destination for American settlement from North, South, and Midlands. In this sense, the Mexican War sowed the seeds of not only the Civil War but also many of the Indian Wars, including those between the United States and the Comanches

and Kiowas on the southern Plains; the Apaches in the desert and mountain country of the Southwest; and the horse nations (the Sioux, Cheyennes, and Arapahos) of the central and northern Plains.

GREAT BASIN KINGDOM

As the Mexican War was being settled, another great and pivotal event that would shape the face of the later West was taking place to the north: the migration of the adherents of the Church of Jesus Christ of Latter Day Saints, popularly known as "Mormons," into the Wasatch Oasis or Salt Lake Valley on the eastern edge of the Great Basin. Founded by Joseph Smith in upstate New

GUNNISON'S ISLAND

Howard Stansbury and John Gunnison of the U.S. Army's Corps of Topographical Engineers surveyed Utah's Great Salt Lake Valley, including this island. Stansbury reported on the expedition in 1852.

York earlier in the century, the Mormons had wandered about the Middle West for nearly two decades, continually at odds with their "Gentile" or non-Mormon neighbors. In 1844 Smith was murdered in Illinois, and the new church leader, Brigham Young, determined that if the church were to survive it needed breathing space, a location far removed from a Gentile population. There was perhaps no location on the continent more suited for Young's preferred condition of isolation than the valley of the Great Salt Lake.

Although assumed by many Americans to be virtual desert country and therefore worthless, this region had been evaluated by Frémont as one of great agricultural potential. While Mormon tradition has long held that Young and other leaders of the church fled westward to the Great Basin because they knew the land was so harsh and barren that it would be unattractive to competing Gentile populations, and that the

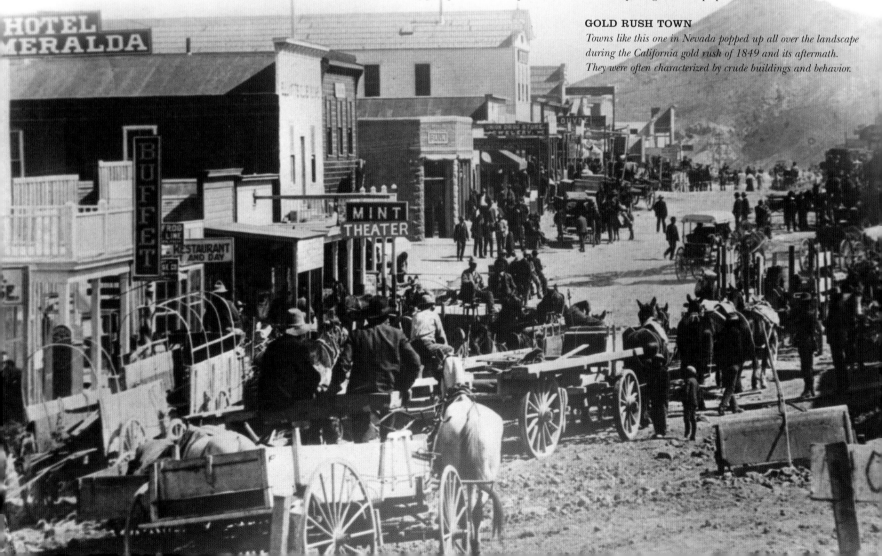

GOLD RUSH TOWN

Towns like this one in Nevada popped up all over the landscape during the California gold rush of 1849 and its aftermath. They were often characterized by crude buildings and behavior.

rigors of the desolate environment would help them weld their followers into a cohesive unit, in fact nothing could be farther from the truth. In selecting the Wasatch Oasis as the site of the New City of Zion, Young was responding to the extremely favorable reports on that region appearing in Frémont's accounts of his 1843–44 expedition, published early in 1845 and already enormously popular.

MORMON MIGRATIONS

While the bulk of the Mormon population moved across the Mississippi and up the Missouri to the "Camp of Israel" just north of present Omaha, Nebraska, Young led a small advance party of about 130 men west along the Oregon Trail early in 1847 to South Pass, then south to Fort Bridger and due west across the Wasatch Mountains via Echo and Emigrant canyons to the Salt Lake Valley. Here they planted wheat and potatoes in the West's first irrigated lands since the disappearance of the irrigation civilization of the Southwestern native peoples in the thirteenth century. Later that year a larger party of over 1,500 men, women, and children arrived at the Salt Lake settlement. By the end of the decade the population of the developing Mormon region in the Wasatch Oasis numbered well over 10,000.

The Mormon migrations to the kingdom of Zion were little different from those of other emigrants bound for Oregon and California. They followed essentially the same route to South Pass (although often staying on the opposite side of the Platte River to avoid conflicts with Gentiles) and met with the same hardships and difficulties. What made the Mormon migration different was that by the time the migrants had crossed South Pass and traveled about 200 miles further to the Salt Lake Valley, they were "home"; Oregon- and California-bound migrants still had a thousand miles to travel before reaching their final destination.

In part, it was the shortened nature of the migrant route west that contributed to the early success of the Mormon settlement. Also important was the organization and communalism practiced by the Mormons, a degree of cooperation that allowed them to develop systems of irrigation that were more feasible in the theocratic and nearly autocratic political structure of the early Mormon settlements than in the loosely-organized typical American frontier settlement. The rapid emergence of the Wasatch region as the thriving economic

center of a culture area was also attributable to Brigham Young's foresight and planning. Desiring to develop a corridor to the Pacific—either westward to San Francisco or southwestward to San Diego—Young directed the establishment of lines of small agricultural settlements in coordinated and planned fashion, radiating outward with Salt Lake City itself at the hub of a growing network. In ten short years after their arrival at Salt Lake, the Mormons had founded ninety-six separate

> ## "NATURE IS THE GLASS REFLECTING GOD, AS BY THE SEA REFLECTED IS THE SUN, TOO GLORIOUS TO BE GAZED ON IN HIS SPHERE."
>
> —MORMON LEADER BRIGHAM YOUNG

settlements, most of them based on irrigation agriculture. Most were directed either to the Oregon Trail to the north or, via the "Mormon Corridor," to the all-weather route to southern California that ran through southwestern Utah and thence across Nevada to the low passes providing entry into the coastal region.

Finally, in one of the greatest ironies in the history of the West, the growth of the Salt Lake region as one of the West's earliest economic and

GREAT SALT LAKE CITY

Army engineers Howard Stansbury and John Gunnison wintered in this Mormon city in 1849–50, documenting Mormon customs and buildings such as the bowery, mint, and president's house shown here.

urban centers was the consequence of just what Young had claimed he was trying to avoid: contact with Gentile populations. Less than a year after the Mormons harvested their first crops in the Salt Lake Valley, and shortly after their horses, cattle, and sheep had foaled, calved, and lambed for the first time in the Wasatch Oasis, gold was discovered in the foothills of the Sierra Nevada Mountains in January 1848, setting in motion the great California Gold Rush. Before 1849, approximately 2,750 Americans had settled in all of California. During the first year following the discovery, approximately 25,000 "Forty-Niners" traveled to the gold region. In the largest single year of the gold-rush migration, 1852 nearly 80,000 people crossed the plains, mountains, and deserts, or took ship for the new El Dorado. By the end of the decade of the 1850s, the total number of migrants to California is estimated to have been slightly more than half a million persons. Many of these migrants to the California gold fields chose to pass through Salt Lake City, providing the market for Mormon agriculture and industry that allowed the Great Basin Mormon region to prosper. Brigham Young's "Deseret," as he called the Mormon domain, would become a reality as a culture region.

TRAIN OF FREIGHTERS
Long lines of ox-driven carts, wheelbarrows, and pioneers on foot left telltale furrows in the western prairie.

THE REGIONALIZATION OF THE WEST: THE 1850s

BEGINNING WITH THE CALIFORNIA GOLD RUSH, A SERIES OF MINERAL STRIKES HELPED TRANSFORM THE WEST. EACH DISCOVERY BROUGHT MIGRATION, WHICH SPURRED THE GROWTH OF TOWNS, ACCELERATED THE FORMATION OF STATES AND TERRITORIES, AND ENCOURAGED DEMAND FOR TRANSPORTATION SYSTEMS TO SEND WESTERN GOODS EAST.

"THE HAND OF PROVIDENCE SO PLAINLY SEEN IN THE DISCOVERY OF GOLD IS NO LESS MANIFEST IN THE TIME CHOSEN FOR ITS ACCOMPLISHMENT."

—CALIFORNIA PIONEER JOHN BIDWELL ON GOLD'S ROLE IN STABILIZING THE U.S. ECONOMY

WHERE THE DECADE of the 1840s had been one of dramatic opening events, that of the 1850s was one of consolidation and organization. The vast western territory that had become American during the previous ten years took more definite shape, as the American public and American science understood more clearly just what the nation had acquired via the cession of Oregon Territory and the Mexican Cession. More important, perhaps, the West—long viewed as an area without internal regional boundaries or, indeed, much regional variety—began to develop economically, organized around several core areas.

Economic development in the West proceeded along lines quite different from the traditional farm-to-market orientation of American landscapes from the Mississippi Valley eastward to the Atlantic Seaboard. By the end of the decade of the 1850s there were the beginnings

of established regional centers at San Francisco, Denver, Portland (and the Puget Sound lowlands), and the upper Rio Grande Valley, based on economic systems oriented to largely non-agricultural activities, the extractive economics of mining and forestry. Only in the Wasatch oasis of the Salt Lake Valley did an economic region that was primarily agricultural exist.

Economic organization of the region and continued immigration toward the regional centers—particularly in California and other mineral-rich areas—stimulated the popular demand for increased exploration directed toward "scientific understanding," which primarily meant resource evaluations, including knowledge of the location of mineral deposits. The West was developing as a resource-extractive region, and most Americans knew that the future of the region lay in rapid exploitation of what was believed to be almost limitless raw materials. "Scientific understanding" also came to refer to a knowledge of the location of the

LABORING IN THE WEST
This sketch is the work of George Horatio Derby, one of the first humorists to address the hardships of the West.

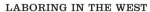

most feasible routes for transportation lines to convey the extracted resources to the industrializing East and Midwest. The most favored transportation technology for the West was a railroad that would link the Mississippi Valley with the resource-rich areas of the West. The consequent "Great Reconnaissance" to increase scientific understanding had two primary elements. One was a federal attempt—in the form of the U.S. Army Corps of Topographical Engineers, aided and encouraged by learned societies such as the Smithsonian Institution—to develop a total geographic inventory of the trans-Mississippi area. The other was the effort, also primarily by the Topographical Engineers, to undertake the Pacific Railroad Surveys to determine the most appropriate route for a transcontinental rail line.

WESTERN TOWN
This photograph, c. 1870, shows the layout typical of western cities as they emerged in the second half of the nineteenth century. The wide central road is flanked by businesses like saloons, post offices, and mercantiles.

✣COMPROMISE OF 1850✣

THE 1848 TREATY ending the Mexican War added 500,000 square miles to the United States. This provoked immediate debate over the vexed question of slavery. Many southerners wanted to extend the Missouri Compromise line of 1820 to the Pacific and allow slavery south of 36°20', while northern abolitionists urged that slavery should be banned in the Mexican Cession.

The increase in California's population as a result of the 1848 Gold Rush gave a new urgency to the matter. Since 1840, four new states—Florida, Texas, Iowa, and Wisconsin—had joined the Union, maintaining the balance between free and slave states. A decision either way on California would upset that balance. In January 1850 Kentucky senator Henry Clay proposed a compromise in hopes of appeasing both North and South, defending it in a speech that lasted two days.

DANIEL WEBSTER
The orator's brilliant speech to the U.S. Senate regarding the Compromise of 1850 is considered one of his finest moments.

Although South Carolina's John C. Calhoun vilified the proposal as an attack on the South and slavery, Clay's old opponent, Daniel Webster of Massachusetts, provided support for the compromise with a superb oration putting the Union before factional interests. After intense debate, the Senate defeated an omnibus bill, but Illinois senator Stephen A. Douglas split Clay's proposal into individual bills that allowed senators to vote or abstain on each.

Signed into law in September 1850, the Compromise of 1850 admitted California as a free state and allowed Utah and New Mexico to make their own decisions regarding slavery. Although slave trading was prohibited in the District of Columbia, slavery itself would be still be allowed there. In addition, interstate slave trading would continue, and a stronger fugitive slave law would be enacted. The Compromise helped stave off civil war for eleven years.

THE GOLDEN WEST: THE CALIFORNIA GOLD RUSH

The gold-induced migration to California created in the American West a dense and economically active population rivaling that of some of the nation's founding states. Such a population demanded faster and better links with the East and the Mississippi Valley, so that the rapid development of a transcontinental rail system was, at least in part, the consequence of the 1848 discovery of gold in California. The rapid exploitation of the mineral wealth of the Sierras also resulted in the creation of a technology and a set of attitudes toward the environment that would come to characterize the development of much of the remainder of the West in the nineteenth century.

By the early 1850s, California was well on its way to a full transition from a Spanish-style subsistence pastoral region to an American resource-extraction region. Intensive agricultural systems were developed to meet the demands of the growing population in and around the mining camps that, by 1852, had spread from the Sutter's Fort area to the north and south along the American River and eastward into the foothills of the Sierras. The small Mexican settlement of Yerba Buena became the city of San Francisco, with an early 1850 population

of nearly 20,000 persons—in a town that eighteen months earlier had held 800. More arrived as each ship docked in San Francisco Bay, which quickly became one of the world's busiest ports. Tents, canvas-walled wood frame structures, hastily nailed-together storage boxes, and here and there a substantial building housed the growing population. What passed for order was maintained by mob rule rather than law, and justice was rendered by vigilante groups. Rents were excessive, as were food prices and the prices of even simple mining equipment like picks, pans, and shovels.

In the gold camps themselves, the squalor, rapid growth, and social disorganization of San Francisco were magnified, particularly as new camps were created. A polyglot ethnic mix continued to be the rule, with substantial numbers of Asians, South Americans, and Indians added to the amalgam of Americans from all regions and walks of life. Few women were present, and those who were ran boarding houses, took in wash, or practiced the world's oldest profession. The population of the gold mining region grew so dramatically that by 1850 California had sufficient population to be admitted to the Union as a state.

GOLD-MINING STAMPS
Two stamps commemorate the western search for gold. One, the California Gold Centennial three-cent stamp (1947–8), celebrates the discovery of gold at Sutter's Mill. The other, the Trans-Mississippi Issue Fifty-Cent Stamp (1898), depicts a western gold prospector.

By the mid-1850s, mining operations in California reached their peak in terms of both productivity and environmental deterioration—the latter resulting from an extractive technology and mindset that held short-term profits to be more important than any kind of sustained yield. In the foothills, hydraulic mining and stamping mills

PANNING FOR GOLD
Hopeful miners search for gold by washing and panning. Though these old-timers, Spriggs, Lamb, and Dillon, were at work in Rockerville, Dakota Territory, in 1889, the basic technique of panning was unchanged since the California Gold Rush.

"THE WHOLE COUNTRY... RESOUNDS TO THE SORDID CRY OF GOLD! GOLD! GOLD!"

SAN FRANCISCO NEWSPAPER, MAY 29, 1848

that crushed and washed rock and gravel (producing massive erosion problems) formed the dominant technology. Nearly all of the mines were run by mining combines, corporate entities who replaced independent miners with employees paid low, albeit steady wages. To the east, in the Sierras themselves, shaft mining in "mother lode" country and separation mills to extract gold from quartzite rock dominated a mining landscape that quickly became fouled with the wastes and by-products of the mining operations. Again the mining combines controlled the production system, giving rise to a social structure of mine owners at the top of the pyramid (along with the wealthy white investors who put up the money), the mine operators and engineers in the middle, and the great mass of the labor force at the bottom. This lowest class consisted of poorer whites, along with

⊹THE MINER'S LIFE⊹

IN 1850, FORTY-NINER William Swain, writing from his claim on the South Fork of Feather River, California, informed his brother: *"George, I tell you this mining among the mountains is a dog's life."* His experience of prospecting echoed that of thousands of other amateur miners who flooded into California during the gold rush. Seeking wealth and luxury, they usually ended up broke and exhausted. But at least they had stories they could tell into their old age —if they lived that long.

FIRST GOLD
This is the first gold nugget found at Sutter's Mill, California, on January 24, 1848.

FEEDING TIME
Hungry miners crowd around a table that is laden with food and utensils. Log cabins stand in the background of this mining camp.

There was gold *"in them thar hills,"* as the saying went; the problem was getting to it. Digging gold out of the Sierra Nevada was a Herculean task that the earliest prospectors typically attacked with tools no more sophisticated than a pickaxe, shovel, pan, and rocker (a rocking box for separating gold from dirt and gravel). Said Swain, *"Gold is found in the most rocky and rough places....[in which] it requires robust labor and hard tugging and lifting to separate the gold from the rock."* Pouring rain in the fall and winter and scorching heat in the summer made the work miserable, as did rampant disease, including dysentery, scurvy, and miscellaneous fever. Unless a sick man had friends to care for him, said miner Cal Gardiner, he was usually *"left to die or recover as heaven might please."*

While living in the diggings (or gold fields), the prospectors resided in tents and hastily assembled log cabins. They subsisted on pork, beans, and whiskey, and governed themselves with a harsh sense of justice: *"Very few ever think of stealing in this country of plenty,"* said miner John Cowden, *"and those who do so are immediately strung up."* The Anglo-American miners were often not just harsh but murderous toward Indians and *"foreigners,"* including Chinese and Mexicans. Ironically, many of the Mexicans were not foreigners, but natives: they had been born in California when it was still part of Mexico.

The miner's life was not only hard but expensive. Prices for food, tools, clothes, and everything else were exorbitant enough to eat up the value of the gold dust the miners so arduously amassed. A weekend's entertainment in town—with all its temptations of saloons, gambling halls, and brothels—could bankrupt the careless miner. One French prospector reported that in San Francisco a woman *"of easy virtue"* charged an ounce of gold just to *"sit near you at a bar or at a card table."* For other services, he said, prices went up: *"A whole night costs from $200 to $400."*

After the gold rush was over, some of the men who had participated looked back on it sourly: *"many curse the day they ever started,"* one reported. But others, whatever the hardships and lack of material rewards, remembered it as a great adventure. Years later, at their fiftieth wedding anniversary, William Swain's wife was still toasting him, *"To my '49er."*

MINING CREW
As gold became harder to find, the individual prospector staking his claim gave way to the organized mining crew, such as this one drifting for gold in Dakota Territory, c. 1876.

some few Asians, Mexicans, and Indians. By 1850 most of those who had come to California to get rich in the gold fields were either reduced to peripheral operations or forced out of the region altogether.

THE SPREAD OF MINING

The growth of corporate mining in California might have spelled disaster for the small miners, but it was a powerful impetus for the diffusion of the extractive industry from California mining fields to other areas. Although a few prospectors had been active in the Great Basin region since soon after the discovery of gold in California in 1848, it was not until 1858 that gold in marketable quantities was discovered in the area of the Sierra's eastern flank near what would become Carson City, Nevada. The following year brought

AMERICAN FLAG
When Nevada was welcomed into the Union on October 31, 1864, a new American flag was devised with thirty-six stars. It was officially adopted in 1865.

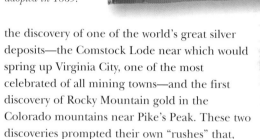

the discovery of one of the world's great silver deposits—the Comstock Lode near which would spring up Virginia City, one of the most celebrated of all mining towns—and the first discovery of Rocky Mountain gold in the Colorado mountains near Pike's Peak. These two discoveries prompted their own "rushes" that, although not as massive as the flood to California,

✦CARSON CITY, NEVADA✦

ORIGINALLY a trading post, Carson City—named after the explorer Kit Carson—was laid out by Abraham Curry in 1858. After the discovery of gold in California (1848), miners and immigrants had poured into the territory, exhausting the supplies of gold in stream beds and outcrops. Many miners traveled eastwards across the Sierra Nevada looking for more opportunities, including the man who was to give his name to America's richest silver mine, Henry Tompkins Paige Comstock.

In 1859 Comstock and others prospecting at Gold Hill on the slopes of Mount Davidson found a thin vein of gold, which turned into bluish quartz rock. Analysis showed it to contain both silver and gold at nearly $4,000 a ton. Almost immediately, some Nevada City businessmen arrived with offers to buy the site, amongst whom was George Hearst (father of William Randolph Hearst).

Comstock, a lazy and shiftless man dubbed "Old Pancake," happily accepted $10,000 for his share.

By 1861 there were more than 10,000 miners and opportunists at the diggings at Virginia City. However, as an already established settlement, Carson City became the area's trading and urban center, a position confirmed when it became the headquarters of the Comstock Mining Company. The city also developed as a center for freight, transportation, and lumber for the underground mines.

In 1861 Congress created the new Nevada Territory, with Carson City as its capital. The first territorial secretary was Orin Clemens, whose young brother Samuel—better known as Mark Twain—accompanied him and wrote about the area's mining in his book Roughing It (1872). Carson City was chartered as a city in 1875, eleven years after Nevada became a state.

MAIL CENTER
Carson City, capital of Nevada Territory, was an overland mail station for Wells, Fargo & Co., whose express office is shown here.

CHINESE MINERS
Around the time of the California Gold Rush, Chinese migration to the United States picked up steam. By 1863, when most white prospectors were gone, Chinese immigrants owned most California placer claims.

provided the initial settlement nuclei of the western Great Basin and of the eastern front of the Rocky Mountain system. And within three years of the Nevada and Colorado finds, prospectors located sufficient quantities of gold and silver in Idaho, Montana, and Arizona to pull miners to those areas as well. Meanwhile, the long-known and well-worked silver mines of New Mexico were subject to the onslaught of an ethnically mixed mining population that began to drive out the miners of Hispanic origin, many of whom had roots in silver mining in the Rio Grande valley that went back to the early seventeenth century.

REGIONAL CENTERS

As each of these mining regions evolved, migration to the region was stimulated, settlements were founded, and the organization of regional centers of economic activity matured. The Comstock

**THE CALIFORNIA GOLD RUSH
1848–1859**

○ mining site

▢ area of Mother Lode 1849

▢ area of Comstock Lode 1859

Californian Trail Routes

— — Lassen's Road

— — Trukee River Road

— — Carson County Route

THE CALIFORNIA GOLD RUSH

The discovery by John W. Marshall of gold on Johann Augustus Sutter's land near Sacramento in 1848 provoked a massive surge in westward migration. California boomed in population, acquiring statehood in 1850.

Lode eventually gave rise to the regional development that culminated in Reno. The Pike's Peak and associated strikes in Colorado provided the requirements for the establishment of an economic and transportation center at Denver. The Idaho fields stimulated the origin and development of smaller cities like Lewiston and Boise. Helena became the focal point of the Montana mineral "improvements." Sleepy Mexican border towns burgeoned into centers of mining activity in southern Arizona; and urban places like Albuquerque, Santa Fe, and Taos in New Mexico, long a part of the Hispanic culture region, found new life with the infusion of a non-Hispanic mining population.

With each new settlement came an increasingly rich cultural and ethnic mix: the predominantly Anglo-German-Scotch/Irish populations from the settled regions of the United States; Asians forced out of the California fields; Irish fleeing the great famine of the mid-1840s in Ireland; and central and eastern Europeans escaping the political turmoil of the European revolutions of 1848. These later rushes to open new mining regions were, in most respects, echoes of the great California Gold Rush. Perhaps the only chief distinction between California and the remainder of the golden West was the number of people involved. While nearly 200,000 prospective miners poured into California from 1849 to 1859, the numbers of those bound for other fields in Nevada, Idaho, Montana, and Arizona were, if sizeable in the aggregate, considerably less than those bound for California.

In 1859 some 10,000 former miners fled the California fields for the new Eldorado in Nevada, to be joined by nearly 20,000 from the East during the next few years. In the same year,

about 20,000 "Fifty-Niners" traveled west from the jumping-off point for the Oregon and California trails in Missouri to arrive in the Front Range of the Colorado Rockies. Traveling in wagons with "Pike's Peak or Bust!" written across their canvas sides, these migrants formed the first major nucleus of a non-Mormon and largely antislavery population between the Missouri River and the Pacific and hence played a crucial role in the West during the great sectional conflict to come.

In 1862, 20,000 gold seekers poured into the massive granite mountains of Idaho north of the Snake River Plain, and some of these probably joined the 30,000 migrants to the gold and silver region of Montana, beginning in 1864. Although nowhere were the numbers of miners comparable to the California gold fields, wherever the Fifty-Niners and others located, they provided the

> "MEN WERE GAMBLING ON ALL SIDES. THEY WERE SHOOTING AND CURSING AND YELLING. THE NOISE AND UPROAR WERE AWFUL."
>
> —MRS. F.A. VAN WINKLE, ON SACRAMENTO IN 1850

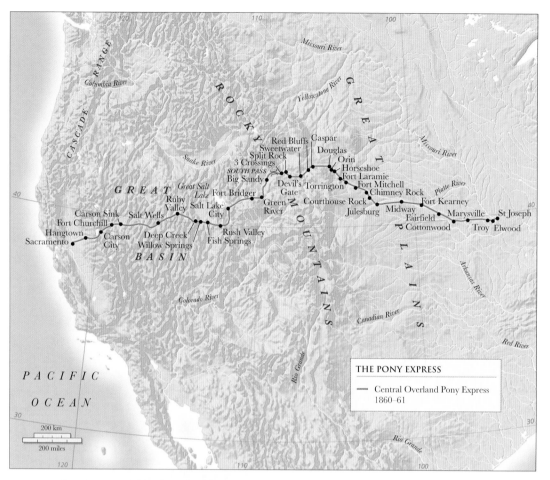

nucleus for an experienced labor force that made the post-Civil War transition to mineral deposits other than precious ones all that much easier and allowed the continuing development of the mineral West: copper in Arizona and Montana; lead in Idaho; iron, coal, and rare earths in Colorado. And just as the mineral migration had brought political organization to California within the framework of the Union, so did it bring about the formal development of political boundaries in the West's other extractive regions: Nevada was organized as a territory separate from Utah in 1861; Colorado was established as a separate territory in 1860; Idaho was separated from Washington and became a separate territory in 1863; Montana split from Dakota Territory in 1864; and Arizona achieved territorial government independent of New Mexico in 1863.

The regional mining populations also formed the earliest centers for western economic development outside the California-Oregon-Utah settlements as they stimulated a host of other economic activities. In the 1850s and 1860s, mining increased the demand for lumber—for railway ties, mine timbers, and sluice boxes—and large-scale timber utilization began in the heavily forested slopes of the Cascades and coastal ranges in the Pacific Northwest. The location of large mining populations in areas like Nevada, Arizona, Idaho, Colorado, and Montana—all places far removed from the centers of agricultural production in the Mississippi valley, or even

THE PONY EXPRESS

Though celebrated in legend, the Pony Express in fact lasted only from April 1860 to October 1861. It used a relay system of riders, a concept based on a long-standing military practice. The route from Saint Joseph, Missouri, to Sacramento, California, spanned a distance of some 1,966 miles, with relay posts about ten miles apart. During its period of operation, it delivered some 35,000 pieces of mail.

HORSES AND WAGONS

Transportation was essential to linking the West to the rest of the country. These members of a survey team led by Ferdinand V. Hayden, photographed in 1871–72, rely on horses and covered wagons.

⊹THE PONY EXPRESS⊹

PONY EXPRESS STAMP
Postmarked with the famous "Running Pony" stamp in San Francisco, this envelope was delivered by Pony Express to Missouri, and from there by regular mail to New York.

AFTER GOLD was discovered in the West, what was previously a trickle of migration became a flood. As miners and fortune hunters rushed westward, mail delivery became an important concern. Contact could only be made by arduous and dangerous overland travel or by sea. A government-subsidized mail service took the sea route via Panama, and a letter from New York took a month to arrive in San Francisco.

In 1858 a stagecoach service was established, making a 2,800-mile, 24-day journey from Tipton, Missouri, south through Texas, and then north through California. A rival stage operator, William Russell, decided to save time by using a route due west from Missouri. In January 1860 he began advertising for riders who would get a letter to Sacramento in 10 days. His advertisement ran:

> YOUNG SKINNY WIRY FELLOWS
> *not over eighteen. Must be expert riders
> willing to risk death daily.*
> Orphans preferred. WAGES: $25 per week.

Russell set up 150–190 stations along the route, between ten and fifteen miles apart. The first rider, Johnny Fry, left St. Joseph, Missouri, on April 3, 1860, and the mail arrived at Sacramento in ten days, as Russell had promised. The routine was for a rider to change horses at each station and hand over the mail after 75 to 100 miles. If another rider was not available, then the first had

to carry on. One unverified legend reports that a teenaged William ("Buffalo Bill") Cody once had to ride 380 miles before handing over his consignment.

The enterprise was short-lived. On October 24, 1861, the continental telegraph was completed, and the legendary Pony Express closed down soon afterwards. Nevertheless it had proved that a central route to California was usable throughout the year.

During its eighteen months, the Pony Express employed between 80 and 100 riders, all required to weigh less than 125 lbs., of whom the youngest was reportedly eleven and the oldest in his mid-forties. They made their quickest run, seven days and seventeen hours, when they delivered President Lincoln's inaugural address to the West Coast.

PONY EXPRESS RIDER
This detail of a watercolor by William H. Jackson captures the romantic image of the short-lived service. Here a Pony Express rider clad in buckskin is pursued by Indians.

---

from the developing agricultural regions of California, Utah, and Oregon—created an enormous demand for food supplies at accessible costs, stimulating the growth of mixed crop/livestock agricultural systems everywhere mining appeared. In areas too dry for traditional American farming systems, the lessons learned from a decade of innovative irrigation agriculture in the Mormon agricultural region of the Wasatch Oasis quickly spread. Along rivers like the South Platte in Colorado, small-scale irrigation works began to appear almost as soon as did the first mining populations. Finally, and perhaps most important, mining and the associated resource utilization of timber land and land for agriculture produced a cyclic economy in the West, a system of "boom-and-bust" still characteristic of much of the West in the twentieth and twenty-first centuries, coupled with an "extractive mentality," that holds resource exploitation to be the prime consideration in western economic systems.

LOOKING EASTWARD

As mineral strikes continued to fuel population expansion and settlement of the West, a series of

economic links were established with the East that, for all practical purposes, made the western United States a colony. In the development of this colonial economic system, the West provided the resources—first furs, then gold and silver, then timber and agricultural products such as beef and wheat—and the financiers of the eastern cities provided the capital investment that made resource development possible. As long as the resources continued to be readily available and the market for them held steady, western economies thrived. But when either resource or market dwindled, depression ensued, followed by a period of withdrawal and abandonment from a ravaged landscape.

This system, begun with the St. Louis-based fur trade, continued in the California gold fields of the 1850s and spread throughout most of the West before the Civil War. It came to be of great significance in the growth of mercantile cities such as San Francisco, Portland, Denver, and others where resource extraction produced a basis for urban location that was different from the stimulus produced by agriculture. Western cities, based on the point location of widely

separated resources, developed much larger market areas (from which they received agricultural products and to which they provided finished goods) than those of their eastern counterparts and were more widely spaced. The great distances between places and the even greater distances between the locations of the raw materials being produced, the locations of their consumption (the markets of the East), and the locations of the manufacturing regions that supplied the equipment necessary to the extractive process all contributed to an enormous demand for the development of a transportation system that would link East and West and, perhaps even more important, would link the separate centers of the West together.

TO LINK A NATION

During the decade of the 1850s, efforts designed to facilitate the maturation of transportation systems were a major part of western economic development. Freighting by large wagons increased along the Santa Fe, California, and other trails, hauling mine equipment and supplies to the mining regions and, in many instances, transporting processed minerals out. The

✦TELEGRAPH✦

BASED on prior experiments by other scientists and collaborations with Leonard Gale and Alfred Vail, American inventor and artist Samuel F. B. Morse devised several models of the electromagnetic telegraph throughout the 1830s, ultimately finding success in 1844 and transmitting the message "What hath God wrought!" from Baltimore to Washington, D.C. By 1852 over 16,500 miles of telegraph wire existed, increasing to 50,000 miles by 1860. On October 24, 1861, telegraph wires were connected in Salt Lake City, linking the East and West coasts. The telegraph allowed for the transmission of news without the time lapse of the Pony Express or the train. In addition, it aided in the creation of small-town newspapers as they now had access to a wealth of information.

The device included a key that allowed an operator at the sending end to tap out a message in code, known as Morse code, that was transmitted via electronic pulses over wires to the "sounder," or receiver.

TELEGRAPH KEY
Alfred Vail made improvements on Samuel Morse's telegraph, including this key with altered spring tension.

movement of people and mail via stagecoach also intensified as stage lines began to extend transport and communication links to even the remotest of the mining regions. The stages, however, could not carry mail quickly enough to satisfy the demand for ever more rapid communication between East and West. That demand stimulated the romantic, if ephemeral, Pony Express, created in 1860 as an express-mail system. The Pony Express lasted for little more than a year before giving way to a more modern form of communication in the fall of 1861 as the Pacific and California State telegraph lines were linked to form the first transcontinental telegraph.

The stagecoach lines, in turn, declined rapidly in the face of public demands for a new transportation technology—a railroad system first linking the Mississippi valley with the Pacific and then linking the regional centers of the West together. Despite the existence of freighter and

stagecoach lines, for most Americans of the 1850s "improved transportation" meant "railroads." In 1849 New York visionary and entrepreneur Asa Whitney published his *A Project for a Railroad to the Pacific*, graced with a small outline map depicting a series of prospective railway routes linking several points in the Mississippi valley with the regional centers of San Francisco and the Willamette Valley on the Pacific. Whitney's proposals for a transcontinental railway found ready acceptance in both public and private sectors. Interest groups in the Missouri cities of St. Louis, St. Joseph, and Springfield, identified as prospective initial points in Whitney's proposal, began jockeying to be named as the starting point for a western railway.

DISASTER IN THE SAN JUANS

Even before the publication of Whitney's promotional tract, there had been attempts to define a railroad route with a Mississippi valley terminus, and once again Thomas Hart Benton and John Charles Frémont assumed center stage. Recognizing that the city that promoted itself most effectively would be the city to receive federal support for the construction of a transcontinental railway, Benton proposed that his son-in-law would lay out a railway route along the 38th parallel of latitude between St. Louis and San Francisco.

Frémont's plan was to traverse the West along the central route across the Great Plains, via the Kansas River; locate a single pass over the Rockies to the valley of the Green River; and from there travel across the Great Basin and the Sierras to California. Frémont knew the Colorado Rockies and had traveled through Colorado's South Park

BILL OF FARE. CAMP DESOLATION
December 25, 1848.

— MENU —
MULE.

SOUP.
Mule Tail.

FISH.
Baked White Mule.
Boiled Gray Mule.

MEATS
Mule Steak, Fried Mule, Mule Chops,
Broiled Mule, Stewed Mule, Boiled Mule,
Scrambled Mule, Shirred Mule,
French-fried Mule, Minced Mule,

DAMNED MULE
Mule on Toast (without the Toast),
Short Ribs of Mule with Apple Sauce
(without the Apple Sauce),

RELISHES
Black Mule, Brown Mule, Yellow Mule,
Bay Mule, Roan Mule,
Tallow Candles.

BEVERAGES
Snow, Snow-Water, Water

between the San Juan-Sawatch ranges and the Front Range during his 1843–44 expedition. His failure to consider the necessity for a second mountain crossing after the first pass across the Colorado Rockies is therefore inexplicable. However, he never got far enough for this curious gap in his planning to matter.

Traveling with many veterans of his previous expeditions, Frémont and his men reached the vicinity of Pueblo, Colorado, where they hired a veteran mountain man, Old Bill Williams, as a guide across the mountains. Williams had trapped in this area for thirty years, and past experience had given Frémont great confidence in the utility of experienced fur trappers as guides. But Williams, perhaps too old for the task, became confused in the welter of stream valleys and passes of the San Juan Mountains and led Frémont into disaster. Attempting to cross the San Juans in the dead of winter, with temperatures at twenty below zero and snow depths of ten feet or more, proved impossible, and Frémont decided to turn back. It was a sensible decision but much too late, and after breaking his party several times to speed a march out of the mountains, Frémont himself determined to go for help at the Taos settlement. Before he could return, many of the men left in the mountains had succumbed to cold, starvation, and exhaustion. Out of an original force of thirty-three men, only twenty-three survived the hunger and snows, and three of these were later killed by Ute Indians when they went back into the mountains in an attempt to retrieve records and scientific equipment.

It was one of the greatest disasters in American exploratory history, but Frémont, in a politically motivated attempt to put a good face on what had been a debacle, later wrote of the expedition's contribution: "The result was entirely satisfactory…[and] convinced me that neither the snow of winter nor the mountain ranges were obstacles in the way of a road." He meant, of course, a railroad, and more specifically a railroad to the Pacific via the 38th parallel, with St. Louis at the eastern end of the line and San Francisco as the western terminus. More people believed his statement than disbelieved it—or at least they so behaved—and the efforts to locate a railroad route to California went forward with increased vigor. The federal government became officially involved in the form of the U.S. Army Corps of Topographical Engineers and the "Great Reconnaissance."

EXPEDITION MENU
This possibly exaggerated list of dinner fare was composed by a member of John C. Frémont's failed fourth expedition, which ended in the San Juan Mountains.

UTE PASS
This crossing at Pike's Peak, Colorado, evolved from a bison hunting trail used by Ute Indians to a wagon road and, later, a route for the Colorado Midland Railway.

"I WILL BUILD A RAILROAD ONE OF THESE DAYS FOR YOU TO GO BACK ON."

—RAILROAD MAGNATE LELAND STANFORD
TO HIS WIFE, AFTER TRAVELING
WEST BY WAGON

THE SPECULATOR

Land speculators, like the one in this comic 1852 painting, capitalized on the discoveries of federal surveyors and helped settle the West.

THE GREAT RECONNAISSANCE

FOLLOWING THE MEXICAN WAR, THE U.S. CORPS OF TOPOGRAPHICAL ENGINEERS LAUNCHED AN AMBITIOUS PROJECT TO SURVEY EVERY PART OF THE WEST. CALLED THE GREAT RECONNAISSANCE, IT SOLIDIFIED THE COUNTRY'S SOUTHERN BOUNDARY AND PREPARED THE WAY FOR THE TRANSCONTINENTAL RAILROAD.

> "[THE TOPOGRAPHIC ENGINEERS ARE] THE EYES OF THE COMMANDING GENERAL...WITH THESE HE CAN SEE THE COUNTRY... WITHOUT THEM HE IS LITERALLY GROPING IN THE DARK."
>
> —JOHN J. ABERT, HEAD OF THE U.S. ARMY CORPS OF TOPOGRAPHICAL ENGINEERS, 1848

BETWEEN THE END of the Mexican War and the beginning of the Civil War, the U.S. Army Corps of Topographical Engineers engaged in the nation's greatest and most comprehensive exploratory effort to date, probing and examining nearly every corner of the West. In over two dozen separate surveys, the members of this elite organization carried the philosophical premise of Manifest Destiny forward into practice and converted the West into a recognizable and usable part of the nation.

The initial efforts of the Corps of Topographical Engineers in the 1850s were in surveying the boundary between the United States and Mexico

following the Mexican War. In this border region, largely unknown and unmapped in scientific terms, the contributions of scientific explorers were far from a simple boundary survey. Rather, the explorations of the Corps in the Southwest represented the final stage of exploration in the service of the nation's imperial objectives. They were also a critical salvo in the battle raging over which part of the United States east of the Mississippi should benefit the most from the development of a transcontinental rail line. In that context, they provided the basis for the final diplomatic agreement, the Gadsden Purchase, that defined the ultimate confines of the nation's expansion southward.

of the Corps of Topographical Engineers, urged that the nation develop a railroad in the borderlands between the United States and Mexico to avoid the harsh winter weather, aid in policing the border, and provide the link with southern California that was, in his view, necessary to retain that region as part of the United States. The proposed path would link a route southwest from New York to Pittsburgh, St. Louis, and Little Rock with a route connecting southern port cities to Vicksburg and on to Little Rock. From here the route would cut across Texas. intersecting the Texas rivers at the head of navigation, cross the Rio Grande south of Santa Fe, and, staying just north of the 32nd parallel, terminate at San Diego. Abert's proposed connection would link both the agricultural and industrial regions east of the Mississippi with the Gulf of Mexico and Texas, and connect with southern California and a north-south rail line linking San Diego with San Francisco. The route offered something for nearly everyone, and in 1849 Abert dispatched Captain Randolph Marcydestined to become one of the

MULTICOLORED CLIFFS

Great Reconnaissance surveyors passed through Wyoming's scenic Green River Valley, later painted by Thomas Moran, 1882.

THE SOUTHERN ROUTE

Those members of the Corps of Topographical Engineers not involved in the boundary surveys were responding directly to the accelerating demand for establishment of a feasible railroad route. In spite of the continued focus of Benton and his associates on the 38th parallel, the army directed its attention to the southern route along the 32nd parallel. Colonel J. J. Abert, commander

EXPLORERS AND SURVEYS

The rapid expansion of the United States created an urgent need to explore and survey the vast new territories. Expeditions to carry out this mission included the "Great Reconnaissance" railroad surveys of the 1850s.

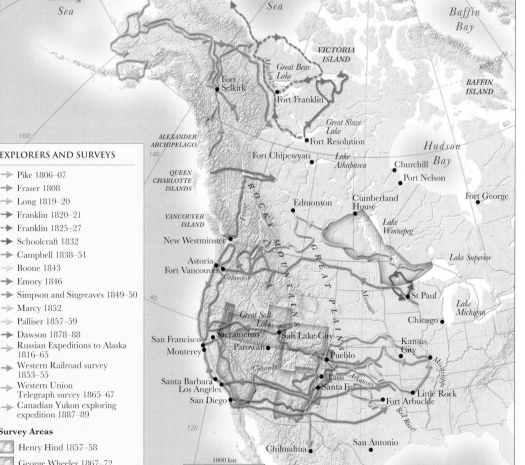

EXPLORERS AND SURVEYS

- Pike 1806–07
- Fraser 1808
- Long 1819–20
- Franklin 1820–21
- Franklin 1825–27
- Schoolcraft 1832
- Campbell 1838–51
- Boone 1843
- Emory 1846
- Simpson and Sitgreaves 1849–50
- Marcy 1852
- Palliser 1857–59
- Dawson 1878–88
- Russian Expeditions to Alaska 1816–65
- Western Railroad survey 1853–55
- Western Union Telegraph survey 1865–67
- Canadian Yukon exploring expedition 1887–89

Survey Areas

- Henry Hind 1857–58
- George Wheeler 1867–72
- Clarence King 1867–73

✦TOPOGRAPHICAL ENGINEERS✦

IN A RELATIVELY short period, the U.S. Army Corps of Topographical Engineers made invaluable contributions in the exploration of the region west of the Mississippi River. The Army Reorganization Act of 1838 established the Topographical Engineers as a unit separate but equal to the regular Corps of Engineers. An elite group of officers, most of the Topographical Engineers—sixty-four of seventy-two—were West Point graduates.

The Topographical Engineers evolved from a long tradition of illustrious service by engineers and surveyors. During the Revolutionary War, George Washington appointed Robert Erskine official surveyor and geographer of the Continental Army. A unit of sixteen topographical engineers was created to do reconnaissance for the War of 1812.

Throughout the 1840s and 1850s, the Topographical Engineers made numerous trips into the territories west of the Mississippi. They suggested transportation routes, surveyed new areas, built canals, and made the West far more livable for settlers. The Civil War divided the unit in 1861, with nine officers going to the Confederate side and eighteen to the Union army. Illness and retirements also plagued the Topographical Engineers, and in 1863 the unit merged with the Corps of Engineers.

DRESS UNIFORMS
The heavy wool uniforms worn by Army officers were often ill-suited to western climates.

Salt Lake, report on the Mormon settlement there, and then head north to Fort Hall. Their exploration began uneventfully over the well-traveled Oregon-California-Mormon Trail to South Pass and, beyond that key junction, south to the fort of fur-trade legend Jim Bridger. Here they engaged Bridger as a guide—confirming the continuing connection between the fur trade and expansion of American geographical awareness of the West. Bridger helped the Army explorers in searching for a pass through the Wasatch suitable for a railroad, but without success. When the party reached Salt Lake, Stansbury concluded what the engineers who laid out the Union Pacific fifteen years later would conclude: the only feasible route lay not along the emigrant trail of the Mormons but farther north, into the Cache Valley.

After wintering in Salt Lake and writing generally favorable reports of the Mormons, Stansbury and Gunnison surveyed the area around the Great Salt Lake and then turned eastward. Rather than following the emigrant trail back to South Pass, Bridger led them on a route considerably south of the South Pass: through the Great Divide Basin of south-central Wyoming; around the northern end of the Sierra Madre and Medicine Bow ranges (both northern extensions of the Colorado Rockies); through the northern end of the Laramie Plains; across the low Laramie Range (a northern extension of the Front Range of the Colorado Rockies), via the pass near the head of Chugwater and Lodgepole creeks; and thence due east to strike the Platte River. This route was a powerful testimony to the geographical knowledge of the fur trade, for it was, with minimal exceptions, the route later followed by

LITHOGRAPH
The Great Reconnaissance collected much data for students of American flora and fauna, like this Smithsonian researcher at work among ornithological specimens.

greatest of the Corps' explorers in the 1850s—westward from Fort Smith, Arkansas, to explore and survey the Texas portion of the proposed right-of-way.

Marcy's explorations discovered routes that were feasible topographically but were disadvantaged by great shortages of wood and water—the two most critical resources necessary for a rail line in the age of wood-burning steam locomotives. During the following two years, other Corps

explorers also surveyed potential routes across Texas to the Rio Grande and into the desert and mountain vastness of New Mexico. While these explorations, led by Lieutenant James Simpson, Captain Lorenzo Sitgreaves, and others, located no more fully satisfactory routes than the southernmost route favored by Marcy, they offered alternative routes directly across New Mexico to the Gila River, the Colorado, and California. Perhaps more important for science, Simpson and Sitgreaves in particular contributed some of the first detailed examinations of the brilliant Southwestern Pueblo culture.

Although the early emphasis of the Corps was on the southern route, as an arm of a federal agency the Topographical Engineers had to be responsive to the demand for exploration of prospective routes in other quarters. In 1849, for example, Captain Howard Stansbury and Lieutenant John Gunnison were instructed to survey the Platte River road across South Pass to

DRAWINGS OF TOADS
These botanical drawings of Southwestern toads were made by U.S. Army surveyor William Emory. Clockwise from the top are the leopard frog of Mexico, the prairie-dwelling crawfish frog, and the Rio Grande leopard frog.

WEAPONS OF THE ARMY

The Model 1842 musket at top, a muzzleloader, was the first standard-issue firearm for U.S. soldiers made from interchangeable parts. At bottom is the 1843 U.S. Cavalry carbine, a breechloader. Both weapons used percussion caps.

the first transcontinental railroad. But Captain Stansbury was injured in a fall from horseback and was unable to publicize his report. His discovery of the optimal central route to the Pacific went unnoticed by nearly everyone, and the argument over the advantages of northern vs. southern vs. central routes continued unabated.

Finally, in 1853, in an attempt to resolve the issue of which was the "most practicable and economical" railroad route to the Pacific, Congress authorized the establishment of a Bureau of Explorations and Surveys, to be staffed with Corps of Engineers personnel and directed by Major William Emory. In addition to the army personnel who would serve as surveyors and "topographers" (the term used for mapmakers or cartographers), civilian scientists and artists were invited to join the surveying parties, ensuring that the results of the surveys would be of broader scope and interest than just the demarcation of suitable transportation lines. The Bureau selected four routes to be surveyed, each route

> "IF UNCLE SAM SHOULD EVER SELL THAT TRACT FOR ONE CENT PER ACRE, HE WILL SWINDLE THE PURCHASER OUTRAGEOUSLY."
>
> —JOURNALIST HORACE GREELEY ON THE UTAH DESERT, 1859

determined more on the basis of political support in Washington than on the reality of physical geography: one route between the 47th and 49th parallels, one along the 38th parallel, a third along the 35th parallel, and the final one along the 32nd parallel. The 41st parallel route, explored by Stansbury and Gunnison and ultimately followed by the Union Pacific, was absent from the surveys.

Appointed to lead the northernmost survey was Isaac Stevens, newly appointed governor of Washington Territory. Stevens's survey was the most involved and faced the greatest number of geographical problems, including several mountain crossings and the negotiation of major river crossings. Two separate surveys, one led by Stevens up the Missouri and across the Continental Divide and the other by George McClellan east across the Cascade Range, were conducted

in 1853–54. Several portions of the route were found to be easier than anticipated: Stevens, for example, had much less difficulty in negotiating the Bitterroot Range than had Lewis and Clark nearly a half-century earlier. But no suitable passes were located across the Cascade Range. Stevens, as might be expected of the new governor of Washington Territory, where a northern route could be expected to terminate, was enthusiastic and said that a northern route "would not present the slightest impediment to the passage of railroad train." Critics of the northern route, meanwhile, maintained that it would prove improbably expensive. One of the members of

→ISAAC STEVENS←

ISAAC STEVENS (1818–1862) served with gallantry in the Mexican War and then worked for the U.S. Coast Survey. After resigning from the army, he was appointed the first (and youngest) governor of the Washington Territory (1853–57), during which time he directed exploration for a northern railway route.

In 1855 Stevens organized the Walla Walla Council, offering homes, livestock, horses, and regular payments to the Yakama (Yakima), Cayuse, Umatilla, Walla Walla, and Nez Perce in exchange for their agreement to move onto reservations. Although Stevens had promised the nations they would have up to three years to vacate their lands, white settlers began to arrive within twelve days of the treaty's signing. The betrayal triggered the Yakima War, as the nations united to attack white settlements over the next two years.

Stevens was subsequently elected territorial delegate to the U.S. Congress (1857–61). During the Civil War, he was promoted to brigadier general of volunteers (1862) and was killed in action.

JOHN JAMES Abert (1788–1863) graduated from West Point in 1811. He left the army and joined the District of Columbia militia as a private soldier at the War of 1812 battle of Bladensburg, Maryland, in 1814. Upon returning to the army as a major later that same year, Abert served as a topographical engineer. He worked on civil engineering projects until 1829, when he took over the Topographical Bureau in Washington, D.C. Abert was instrumental in the evolution of the Bureau into the Corps of Topographical Engineers, of which he assumed leadership upon its establishment in 1838. Through his close association with it, his name became virtually synonymous with the Corps.

Under Abert, the Corps explored the West extensively, mapping the Mississippi River and Great Lakes, performing reconnaissance related to the Mexican War, and surveying the Oregon country. Data brought back from their expeditions advanced American science and prepared the way for the transcontinental railroad. Previously promoted to colonel, Abert remained at the Corps until his retirement in 1861.

Abert's wife, the former Ellen Matlack Stretch, frequently accompanied him on his travels. One of their six children, James William, also graduated from West Point.

Stevens's own party noted, "A road might be built over the tops of the Himaleyah mountains—but no reasonable man would undertake [it]." In an attempt to silence critics, the Washington territorial legislature commissioned another survey, led by Frederick Lander, a civilian engineer. But although Lander laid out a route that would ultimately be used for rail traffic, public (meaning political) opinion was against the northern route.

38TH PARALLEL SURVEY

The 38th parallel survey was led by Captain John Gunnison, a veteran of western exploration and the Corps who had accompanied Stansbury's explorations of 1849. In the minds of many, the logical choice to command this survey was Frémont —in spite of the debacle in the snows in 1848–49. He at least knew the pitfalls of the southern Rocky Mountains crossing. But intense lobbying by Benton went for naught, and Frémont was not appointed. Benton arranged a privately financed expedition with his son-in-law in command, but "the Pathfinder" once again met disaster in the snows of the San Juans, and his expedition ended in failure. It was his last effort as an explorer, but he would be heard from again as the Republican Party's first presidential candidate in the election of 1856 and, later, as a general in the Union Army during the Civil War.

Gunnison, meanwhile, methodically went about the business of his exploration, one that

BIRD SPECIMEN
This Western Grebe was one of the zoological specimens documented in the reports of the Pacific Railroad surveys of 1853–54.

epitomized the work of the Corps on the Railroad Surveys: comprehensive, productive, fraught with danger and even tragedy. Accompanying Gunnison on the first leg of his journey into the southern Colorado Rockies were several veterans of Frémont's ill-fated fourth expedition of 1848–49. For a time at least, they fared better with Gunnison than they had with Frémont. The mountains that had turned Frémont back proved passable, and Gunnison crossed the San Juan Mountains to the Grand (upper Colorado) River, down the Grand to its junction with the Green River, across the Green to the Wasatch, and across that range to the Sevier River of eastern Utah. Throughout most of the route, the party was beset by Indians, but once beyond the Wasatch and in Mormon country, Gunnison felt safe enough to split his command. This was to prove a tragic mistake.

As Gunnison and a relatively small detachment camped in the valley of the Sevier in October 1853, a war party of Paiutes attacked the surveyors' camp, killing the commander and all but four of his men. This was the worst disaster to befall the Corps during the Great Reconnaissance, and it changed the minds of many who had favored the central route. Nevertheless, the survey continued and, under the command of Lieutenant E. G. Beckwith, reinvestigated Stansbury's routes through the Wasatch and then west across the Great Basin by way of the Humboldt River to the Sierra Nevada. Beckwith surveyed several passes

WHIPPLE AT THE COLORADO RIVER
Mojave Indians assisted the survey team of Lieutenant Amiel Whipple as they crossed the Colorado River. Whipple explored the 35th parallel from Little Rock to Los Angeles.

INDIAN ORNAMENTS

This drawing of Indian ornaments and manufactures was published in the reports of Lt. Amiel Whipple's surveys.

BURRO PACK TRAIN

Pack animals, like these miners' burros in a Colorado mountain pass, were often used on western expeditions.

across the Sierras to California, one of which would prove to be the route of the first transcontinental railway. Beckwith had completed what Stansbury's discovery of the pass across the Laramie Range and the route through the Great Divide Basin had begun—the surveying of the route that would become the Union and Central Pacific right-of-way to San Francisco.

The Stansbury-Beckwith route notwithstanding, most Americans viewed the 35th parallel route as the optimum one. Lieutenant Amiel Whipple led a party westward from Fort Smith, Arkansas, along the Canadian River route that was well known by 1853, having been used for two decades as a way to the New Mexican settlements along the Rio Grande north of El Paso. Crossing the Rio Grande at Albuquerque, Whipple surveyed a route westward to the Zuni pueblos and then southwest along the Bill Williams Fork of the Colorado to its junction with the main stream. Whipple then followed the Colorado northward to the site of Needles, California, before swinging westward across the Mojave Desert to San Bernadino.

There were few differences between Whipple's route and that laid out by Simpson and Sitgreaves a few years earlier. He had simply confirmed what majority opinion already held: the best route for a Pacific railroad was through the Southwest but well north of the 32nd parallel route favored by the army. The exploration of that 32nd parallel

⇒GOUVERNEUR⇐ KEMBLE WARREN

CREDITED WITH creating the first accurate map of the area west of the Mississippi River, Gouverneur Kemble Warren (1830–1882) was born in Cold Spring, New York. In 1850 Warren graduated second in his West Point class and was immediately appointed a second lieutenant in the Corps of Topographical Engineers, initially working on surveying the Mississippi Delta, among other projects. Warren mapped potential Pacific Railroad routes in 1853, and in 1855 he served as Chief Topographical Engineer on the Sioux Expedition in the present-day Dakotas, Wyoming, and Montana. From 1856 to 1859, Warren explored the Dakota and Nebraska territories, until he was transferred to the Bureau of Exploration and sent to teach at West Point. Made a major general in the Civil War, Warren is perhaps best known for his vital role in winning the Battle of Gettysburg (1863).

route, led by Lieutenant John Parke and Captain John Pope, had been anticipated by the Mexican boundary surveys in 1853 but were, nevertheless, important in scientific terms. Parke contributed important geographic and geologic information on the Chiricahua Mountains of Arizona; and Pope, surveying the eastern end of the 32nd parallel route through the Guadalupe Mountains of west Texas and southern New Mexico, added a considerable fund of data to ethnography. But in the context of their objective of a railway route, the Parke and Pope surveys did little more than confirm the already enthusiastic claims for the

SIOUX ARTIFACT

This war club was collected by Gouverneur Kemble Warren after the dust cleared at the Blue Water Creek massacre in 1855. Many Lakota Sioux were killed or taken prisoner by General W. S. Harney and his troops.

southernmost road made by the surveyors of the Mexican boundary. However, one chief impediment to that route remained the failure of any of the southern surveys to locate good passes across the southernmost reaches of the Sierra Nevada, and upon that impediment the 32nd parallel route foundered.

RESULTS

By 1855 the work of the Pacific Railroad Surveys was completed and a massive twelve-volume report was generated, but without any conclusion regarding the best route for a transcontinental line. Although Secretary of War Jefferson Davis offered the opinion, as might be expected of a southerner, that the 32nd parallel route was "the most practicable and economical route for a railroad from the Mississippi River to the Pacific Ocean," the fact of the matter was that the failure of the surveys to locate southern passes across the Sierras diminished rather than heightened the case for the southern route. Perhaps the most unexpected result of the surveys was that they located not one but a number of feasible routes for the transcontinental railroad. Indeed, it might be said that the surveys created more confusion than they dispelled. In addition, the survey reports represented a fundamental clash in values between exploration as a scientific venture and exploration as a utilitarian enterprise designed to locate new resources. Yet in spite of the confusion they generated and the conflict they revealed, the reports of the Pacific Railroad Surveys and other exploratory ventures of the Corps of Topographical Engineers in the 1850s were a resounding success. The explorers of the Surveys managed to develop increased scientific and public awareness of the complexity and scale of the American West.

The Great Reconnaissance continued until the Civil War put an end to rmy exploration and assigned other tasks to officers with the word "engineer" in their commissions. But the efforts of men like Emory, Stansbury, Marcy, and Gunnison established the benchmark for scientific exploration and cartography by the military. More than simple reconnaissance, the work of the Topographical

BLUE WATER CREEK MAP

This sketch by Gouverneur Kemble Warren not only maps a waterway but records the U.S. Army's attack on Lakota Sioux chief Little Thunder in 1855.

Engineers was also crucial in a political and economic sense, as the Corps provided a scientific response to the resource orientation of the western economy by offering an inventory of the Western environment. The work of the Corps was pure Humboldtean scientific inquiry and the outcome very near Humboldt's own conception of the ultimate aim of geographical exploration: "to recognize unity in the vast diversity of phenomena." As such, the scientific consequences of the Great Reconnaissance were considerable for earth sciences such as physical geography and geology; life sciences such as paleontology, zoology, and botany; and human sciences such as archaeology: anthropology, and ethnology. Finally, the reconnaissance stamped an indelible mark on the American image of the West, producing a transition from a purely romantic view to a romantic-scientific one. The

ZUNI, NEW MEXICO

This illustration was made by Baldwin Möllhausen, an artist, naturalist, and topographer who was part of the Amiel Whipple survey team. The expedition traveled through Albuquerque and the Zuni Pueblo. Möllhausen's diaries of the trip were later translated from German and published.

⟡BLEEDING KANSAS⟡

BY 1854 SLAVERY had become the nation's most contentious issue. At that time the Kansas Territory had just a few hundred settlers, but the prospect of its becoming a state made it a focus of conflict because of its proximity to Missouri, a slave state, and Iowa, a free state. If Kansas became a slave state, it would give the South two more votes in the Senate; northern abolitionists were equally anxious to prevent slavery in the new territory. Congress mediated by passing the Kansas-Nebraska Act, which allowed territorial residents to determine the slavery issue.

Conflict in "Bleeding Kansas," as the *New York Tribune* named it, originated with the formation of a New England society to finance the emigration of antislavery settlers who established the towns of Lawrence, Topeka, and Osawatomie. Proslavery Missourians promptly founded Leavenworth, Atchison, and Lecompton. In November 1854 and March 1855, proslavery advocates secured the outcome of territorial elections by bringing in bands of "Border Ruffians" from Missouri. After another election again resulted in a proslavery victory, northern antislavery organizations sent their supporters consignments of Sharp's rifles, known as "Beecher's Bibles" after the abolitionist Henry Ward Beecher.

The antislavery faction (called free-soilers or Jayhawkers) drew up a constitution and elected their own legislature in Topeka, leading to further violence. Houses of proslavery families were burned, resulting in a large posse of Border Ruffians ransacking and destroying much of Lawrence in May 1856. John Brown, a fervent abolitionist, then led a party that killed five proslavery men at Pottawatomie Creek, an act that aggravated the bloodshed on both sides. Although the illegal free-soil legislature was dispersed by federal troops in July 1856, internecine warfare continued, and at the Marais des Cygnes massacre of May 1858 some thirty proslavery advocates attacked a group of free-soilers, killing five.

GUNFIGHT IN BLEEDING KANSAS
Violence erupted in 1850s Kansas, where ballot-box stuffing threw elections to proslavery forces. Activists poured into the territory from all over the country.

By August 1858 sufficient free-soilers had arrived to overturn a referendum on the proslavery constitution. Even then President James Buchanan managed to delay Kansas's admission to the Union, which was not achieved until January 29, 1861. In seven years of conflict, the population of "Bleeding Kansas" had grown from a few hundred to over 100,000.

brilliant illustrations and the comprehensive text of the *Pacific Railroad Reports* and other publications emerging from the work of the Corps offered the nation a comprehensive view of the West. And Gouverneur Kemble Warren's masterful cartographic compilation of the results of the Great Reconnaissance provided the first truly scientific and accurate map of the region west of the Mississippi River.

CONFLICTS

Before the more comprehensive view of the West could be properly acted upon, a period of conflict intervened, halting for a time the further development of the region. While the Great Reconnaissance was proceeding, a series of clashes of opposing values began to dominate the West. The emergence of the West as a distinct region with its integrated subregions based on mineral extraction had given rise to several conflicts. The interests of specific settlements, the hinterlands they served, and the regions in which they were located were often pitted against the interests of the nation as a whole. Exploration and resource development placed the interests of science against those of the public, the interests of theory against those of utility. Those who would develop western resources for private gain found

❖THE CIVIL WAR IN THE WEST❖

ALTHOUGH THE CIVIL WAR (1861–65) was decided east of the Mississippi, the campaigns west of that river are noteworthy. They fell into three principal categories: New Mexico, Missouri, and Native American.

NEW MEXICO CAMPAIGN

In February 1861 Texans overrode Sam Houston's views, voting more than three to one to secede from the Union and taking over the federal stores and weapons at San Antonio. Emboldened by the move of Union troops eastwards and the resignations of over 300 federal officers with Southern sympathies, Texan leaders planned a campaign to take the New Mexico Territory, Colorado, and California out of the Union by force.

In summer 1861 Colonel John Baylor led a Texan force to occupy Fort Bliss and Fort Fillmore in New Mexico, announcing on August 1 that southern New Mexico was now the Confederate Territory of Arizona. Henry Sibley won another victory for the Confederates at Valverde on February 21, 1862, and captured Santa Fe the next month.

The only major Union force left was at Fort Union, east of Santa Fe, which was now reinforced by 900 volunteers ("Pikes Peakers") from Colorado. Disobeying orders to defend Fort Union, Colonel Slough, the Pikes Peakers commander, marched out to confront the Texans at Glorietta Pass. In a daring and dangerous maneuver (March 28, 1862), some 400 Pikes Peakers circled around the Texan force, destroying their entire wagon train and driving off their horses. With more Union troops

ABRAHAM LINCOLN
Lincoln, photographed two months before his death in 1865, went to war to preserve the Union.

now hurrying from California, the Confederates were forced to fall back, first to Santa Fe and then into Texas. On July 4, 1862, New Mexico was back in Union hands. Because it ended the Texan plan to win the Southwest, the battle at Glorietta Pass has been called the "Gettysburg of the West."

MISSOURI CAMPAIGN

Although Missouri had elected the proslavery Claiborne Jackson as governor in 1860, his subsequent demand for secession was defeated heavily at a state convention, which voted to unseat him and the entire state legislature. By April 1861, when the guns fired on Fort Sumter, Jackson had organized a sizeable Confederate force to take the large federal arsenal at St. Louis, commanded by Captain Nathaniel Lyon. Lyon surrounded and captured 700 of Jackson's troops and then led his force of German emigrant volunteers to the state capital at Jefferson City. The Confederates retreated south to Springfield, where Lyon launched an attack at Wilson's Creek on August 10, 1861. Lyon was killed, and the defeated Union forces were forced to retire north as the Confederates received reinforcements from Arkansas and Louisiana.

By now the Union had appreciated Missouri's strategic importance, and early in 1862 General Samuel Curtis pushed the Confederate troops south to Pea Ridge in northwest Arkansas. The Union victory there (March 7) was followed by the capture of New Madrid on the Mississippi (March 14). Apart from a Southern raid in 1864, Missouri remained in Union hands for the remainder of the war.

REMAINS OF FORT UNION
Fort Union, New Mexico, whose thick adobe walls housed a force of Colorado volunteers during the Civil War, was abandoned in 1883.

NATIVE AMERICAN CAMPAIGNS

While some Native Americans took sides in the war (the Cherokees fought with the South; Seminole leader Billy Bowlegs supported the Union; the Creeks split their support), many seized the opportunity to avenge the wrongs they had suffered at white hands. The withdrawal of federal troops to the East had left control of western territories in the hands of local untrained militia and inexperienced officials. Consequently, food and payments intended for reservations were often

PEA RIDGE, ARKANSAS
The thwarting of the Rebel attack here in 1862 put Missouri under Union control. Two Confederate generals were killed in the battle.

late or never arrived at all, while the constant incursions of white settlers onto Native American lands aroused deep resentment.

In Minnesota the Santee Sioux were refused food supplies because government officials had delayed payment. The Santee rebelled in 1862, attacking Fort Ridgely and killing settlers throughout western Minnesota. They were joined by the Yankton Sioux, but their rising came to an end in September when federal and militia troops captured 2,000 Sioux. Thirty-eight were hanged in December 1862, the largest mass execution in American history.

Over the next two years there were Indian risings all over the West. The Shoshones fought engagements north of Salt Lake City, while the Apaches under Cochise and Mangas Colorado were defeated at Apache Pass in July 1862. The leading Union commander was Kit Carson, who put down the Mescalero Apaches in 1862, then went on to defeat the Navajos at Canyon de Chelly (northeast Arizona territory) in January 1864. He also led the force against the Kiowas at the battle of Adobe Walls in November 1864.

THE CIVIL WAR

As the slave states of the South seceded from the Union, precipitating the Civil War, the central issue of slavery remained ill-defined in much of the West. Complicating the picture was the Dred Scott decision of 1857, in which the Supreme Court had ruled that Congress could not prohibit slavery in U.S. territories.

THE CIVIL WAR

- Union states
- Confederate states
- ⚡ slavery legal
- **Jan 1861** date of secession from the Union

themselves in opposition to the emergence of the concept of public lands and public land policy as it began to take shape. In many areas the objectives of the military were in conflict with those of the civilian population they were ostensibly supposed to protect, as well as being in opposition to public-interest groups and politicians. The very notion of a continuous development in the West set the concepts of "civilization" and "progress" against the rights of indigenous peoples.

These conflicts flamed up into the relatively minor conflagrations of the Utah War and border warfare in "Bleeding Kansas" and the beginning of major white-Indian military conflicts in the West. They were also part of the broader holocaust of the Civil War. Still, as important as they were, these clashes could not halt but only delay what had already begun. The West had been explored and much of it settled. Although large areas still remained to be discovered in a scientific sense, the vast territory that had been the fiefdom of the St. Louis fur barons only two decades earlier was now sufficiently "known" to allow its inexorable development toward a series of interlocking economic regions. Following the Civil War, those regions would be fully integrated with the restored Union.

"IF YOU PEN AN INDIAN UP ON A SMALL SPOT OF EARTH, AND COMPEL HIM TO STAY THERE, HE WILL NOT BE CONTENTED, NOR WILL HE GROW AND PROSPER."

—CHIEF JOSEPH OF THE NEZ PERCE

INDIAN ATTACK

Conflicts between Indians and whites intensified as the United States increased its presence in the West. On the Santa Fe Trail, the south fork took travelers through a dangerous patch of desert where Kiowa or Comanche attack was possible. Here an "Indian alarm" is raised on the Cimarron River.

SAMUEL BOWLES
*This influential Massachusetts editor wrote
many letters back to his newspaper while
on a Western sojourn in 1865.*

"THE COUNTRY
IS FABULOUSLY
RICH IN GOLD,
SILVER, COPPER,
LEAD...THIEVES,
MURDERERS,
DESPERADOES...
SHARPERS...POETS,
PREACHERS,
AND JACKASS
RABBITS."

—MARK TWAIN ON THE WEST, 1861

THE WEST IN THE AMERICAN MIND, 1865

BY THE CIVIL WAR ERA, THE LANDSCAPE OF THE WEST WAS NO LONGER A MYSTERY. NOW THOROUGHLY MAPPED, THE REGION WAS KNOWN TO HOUSE EXTRAORDINARY NATURAL RESOURCES. FOR AMERICANS WANTING TO TAP THIS WEALTH, THE WEST PROMISED BOUNDLESS POSSIBILITIES.

THE OUTBREAK OF the Civil War (1861–65) ended what was arguably the most important period in the history of the American West, a period of geographical exploration, resource development, settlement, and regional organization. Most important, it was a period during which the image of the West began to take a firm shape in the American mind. By the war's end, the image was solidified. In 1865, Samuel Bowles, the editor and publisher of the Springfield, Massachusetts, *Gazette*, traveled across the West and recorded his impressions of the New West and the new westerners. "The two sides of the Continent," he wrote, "are sharp in contrasts of climate, of soil, of mountains, of resources, of production, of everything." In the newer West, Bowles proclaimed, were mountains broader and higher, valleys richer, mineral deposits more bountiful— "nowhere denser forests, larger trees, nowhere so wide plains, nowhere such majestic

rivers." In the West beyond the Mississippi was "a nature to pique the curiosity and challenge the admiration of the world," a nature destined to "develop a society and a civilization, a commerce and an industry, a wealth and a power" that eventually would contribute to American supremacy. Bowles's nationalistic impressions were neither

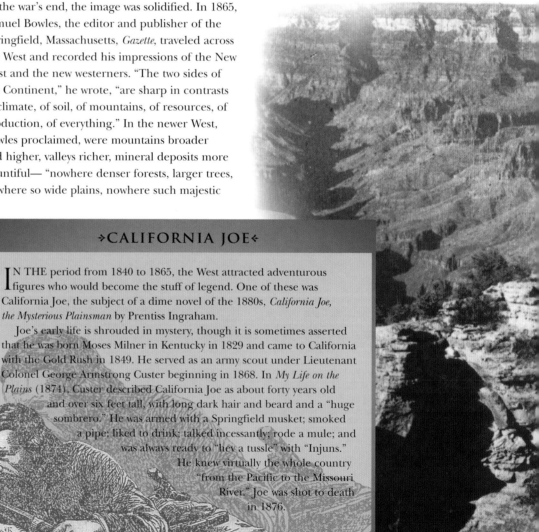

→CALIFORNIA JOE←

IN THE period from 1840 to 1865, the West attracted adventurous figures who would become the stuff of legend. One of these was California Joe, the subject of a dime novel of the 1880s, *California Joe, the Mysterious Plainsman* by Prentiss Ingraham.

Joe's early life is shrouded in mystery, though it is sometimes asserted that he was born Moses Milner in Kentucky in 1829 and came to California with the Gold Rush in 1849. He served as an army scout under Lieutenant Colonel George Armstrong Custer beginning in 1868. In *My Life on the Plains* (1874), Custer described California Joe as about forty years old and over six feet tall, with long dark hair and beard and a "huge sombrero." He was armed with a Springfield musket; smoked a pipe; liked to drink; talked incessantly; rode a mule; and was always ready to "hev a tussle" with "Injuns." He knew virtually the whole country "from the Pacific to the Missouri River." Joe was shot to death in 1876.

unique nor unusual. For Bowles, and for many of his contemporaries, the West by 1865 had come to symbolize America itself. The scope and splendor of the region symbolized the strength and greatness and freedom of the larger national unit. In the West were lands and limitless resources suitable to match the American destiny.

Such a claim had more strength because of the pattern of American settlement—east to west. The West was the last area to be settled in the American expansion, and thus it was the West that stood out most clearly in the American mind as the most dramatic and most American portion of the country. In the East may have been picturesque and pastoral scenery; but in the West was grandeur. Here the power of creation combined with the force of history to create the zenith of national development. By the end of the 1840–65 period, Americans had commenced their ultimate stage of continental expansion, and as they did so the grandest scenes opened before them. For Samuel Bowles, as for most Americans by

the end of the Civil War, the growth of the United States to 1865 had become a drama that would end not on a tranquil note but on a rising crescendo, a series of chords struck from natural abundance and vastness that were unparalleled in the American experience.

COUNTER-IMAGES

But just as the West is and has been a land of environmental extremes, so has it been a region characterized by polarity of opinions about it. By 1865 the reality of the region in terms of its physical, political, economic, and cultural characteristics was precariously balanced against the expectations of Bowles and like thinkers. The American images of the West contained not just elements of wealth, freedom, opportunity, and

*Horace
Greeley*

✦GO WEST, YOUNG MAN✦

HORACE GREELEY (1811–1872), founder of the *New York Tribune*, corresponded with many editors. Among these was John Babstone Lane Soule of the *Terre Haute Express* in Indiana. In an 1851 editorial, Soule wrote, *"Go West, young man,"* and Greeley adopted the phrase in his newspaper, making it famous as the motto for the westward migrations of the time. The phrase has traditionally been attributed to Greeley, even though he was punctilious in crediting Soule.

Some hold that Soule merely adapted an earlier comment of Greeley's: *"If you have no family or friends to aid you, turn your face to the Great West and there build up your home and fortune."* But it was Greeley who added his own gloss when he advised Josiah Bushnell Grinnell, *"Go West, young man, go West and grow up with the country!"*

scenic splendor but the conflicting elements of scarcity, hardship, barrenness, and oppression. Based upon information obtained from migrants who had labored across the deserts and mountains and suffered greatly to reach the Pacific Coast, from miners who had left tor the gold fields of the California El Dorado with great expectations only to meet with abject failure, and from farmers attempting to eke out a subsistence in semiarid or subhumid climates that were beyond the experience of American agriculture, a counter-image of the West as a land of danger and hardship developed. This less-positive image of the West was not the prevailing one in 1865, but it was present as a contrapuntal theme in the nationalistic symphony composed by Bowles and those like him. The negative image would gain strength in some quarters after 1865—largely as the consequence of the combination of experience and increasing scientific awareness of the limitations of arid lands—but in 1865 the popular conviction was still based on the promise of new wealth and opportunity. The next generation would act on that conviction.

**ARTIST
AT WORK**
*Painter Thomas
Moran sketches at Bright
Angel Cove near Yavapai Point,
Grand Canyon, Arizona, c. 1903.*

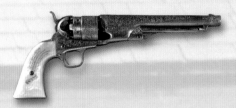

THE WEST SUBDUED

1865–1900

FROM THE END OF THE CIVIL WAR TO
THE TURN OF THE CENTURY, THE WEST WAS
A PLACE OF UNBRIDLED ENERGY AND CONFLICT.
AS MIGRANTS AND INVESTMENT CAPITAL POURED
INTO THE REGION, U.S. MILITARY FORCES FOUGHT THE
LAST OF THE INDIAN WARS. THE TRANSCONTINENTAL
RAILROAD BRIDGED THE CONTINENT, WHILE GAPS
OPENED AMONG PEOPLE OF MANY ETHNICITIES,
INCLUDING HISPANIC, ASIANS, AND AFRICAN
AMERICANS. RANCHING, FARMING, AND OTHER
ENTERPRISES SUBDUED THE WEST, BUT IN POPULAR
MYTHOLOGY IT REMAINED EVER WILD:
A PLACE OF COWBOYS, OUTLAWS,
AND ENDLESS PROMISE.

⇥TIMELINE⇤
1865-1900

The late nineteenth century saw Americans flooding into the West and the closing of the western frontier. Most valuable western land was settled. Indian tribes were confined to reservations as the western Indian Wars drew to an end. Even the cowboy—that mythic symbol of American freedom—became an employee of the large corporations that eventually dominated the region's ranching and farming.

1866–1868
Lakota Sioux leader Red Cloud organizes war parties to harass soldiers, resulting in the U.S. Army's abandonment of three forts on the Bozeman Trail.

1867
The United States purchases Alaska from Russia.

1869
•Congress establishes the Board of Indian Commissioners to promote President Ulysses S. Grant's Peace Policy toward western Indians.
•Wyoming Territory passes a law giving women the right to vote and hold public office.
•May 10. The Golden Spike Ceremony at Promontory Point, Utah, celebrates the completion of the transcontinental railroad.

1872
Congress creates Yellowstone, the first federally administered park, in northwestern Wyoming.

1876
June 25. Lakota Sioux and Northern Cheyenne warriors kill the soldiers of the Seventh Cavalry under Lieutenant Colonel George Armstrong Custer at the Battle of the Little Bighorn.

1877
African-American "Exodusters" found the town of Nicodemus, Kansas.

1879
The federal government creates the U.S. Geological Survey to coordinate geological exploration. Between 1881 and 1894, USGS will be headed by John Wesley Powell.

1881
Oct. 26. The Earp brothers triumph over the criminal Clanton gang at a shoot-out at the O.K. Corral, Arizona.

1882
The Chinese Exclusion Act bars Chinese laborers from entering the United States.

1883
William "Buffalo Bill" Cody presents his first Wild West exposition in Chicago.

1886–1887
Thousands of western cattle die during a severe winter, effectively ending the days of the open range.

1886
Apache leader Geronimo surrenders to U.S. forces for the final time.

1887
The Dawes Severalty Act calls for the division of reservation lands into allotments owned as private property by individual Indians.

1889
Apr. 22. Indian Territory (later Oklahoma) is opened to settlement by non-Indian migrants.

1890
Dec. 29. U.S. soldiers wound or kill at least 200 Lakota Sioux men, women, and children at Wounded Knee South Dakota, which brings the western Indian Wars to a close.

1892
•Naturalist John Muir helps found the Sierra Club to protect western wilderness lands.
•With the support of many western farmers, the Populist Party presidential candidate James B. Weaver receives more than 1 million votes.

1893
Historian Frederick Jackson Turner declares the end of the western frontier in a lecture at the Chicago World's Fair.

1896
The discovery of gold near the mouth of the Klondike River sparks the Klondike Gold Rush.

1898
The United States annexes Hawaii.

THE WESTWARD TORRENT

AFTER SURVIVING THE CRISIS OF THE CIVIL WAR, MANY AMERICANS AGAIN TURNED THEIR ATTENTION TO THE WEST. FROM PIONEER FAMILIES HOPING TO ESTABLISH A HOMESTEAD TO CAPITALISTS EAGER TO BUILD BUSINESS EMPIRES, AMERICANS SAW THE WESTERN REGION AS A LAND OF PROMISE AND PROGRESS, FULL OF EXCITING OPPORTUNITIES.

AFTER THE CIVIL WAR ground to a halt at Appomattox Courthouse, Virginia, on April 9, 1865, a message from God seemed to scroll across the sky. "You are still my chosen people," it said. "You have survived a calamitous internal rift; now go forth and conquer." Millions of Americans embraced this theme as their personal mission. Capital diverted during the war years, innovations suppressed, reforms thwarted, and dreams deferred joined to produce an explosive torrent of energy that would roll across the American West with the force of a tidal wave.

From railroad tycoons to land developers, American entrepreneurs stood poised to invest capital and vigor in the nation's last untamed area. Those who became railroad, mineral, and lumber magnates looked to the American West to provide opportunity and wealth. But others also hung their dreams on the West: settlers who hoped homesteads would bring financial salvation or that elusive goal, happiness; ranchers and miners who visualized vast empires and attendant riches; town builders who aspired to carry westward American civilization as they knew it; women who craved jobs, husbands, or better lives for their families; and former slaves who saw in the West a place free from bigotry and vengeance. Americans—indeed, the world—mythologized the West into a glorious, improbable land of progress, egalitarianism, and promise. Certainly much of the dream had substance. As optimists and promoters hoped, opportunity and growth abounded: migrants streamed westward; the transcontinental railroad spliced the West to the rest of the nation; Alaska and Hawaii joined the West; and the mining, lumber, and cattle industries flourished. But the West was also a place of injustice and discord. As the tentacles

of society spread over the West and tightened their grasp, conflict between migrants and Indians accelerated; the federal government and eastern capitalists enlarged their domination of western development; and questionable business practices and volatile farm conditions bred protest movements such as the Grange and the Populist Party.

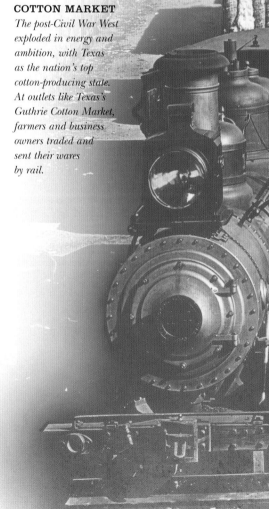

COTTON MARKET
The post-Civil War West exploded in energy and ambition, with Texas as the nation's top cotton-producing state. At outlets like Texas's Guthrie Cotton Market, farmers and business owners traded and sent their wares by rail.

SITTING BULL
Hunkpapa Sioux leader Sitting Bull (Tatanka Yotanka) and his forces joined other Sioux in fighting U.S. forces.

"WHEN I WAS YOUNG I WALKED ALL OVER THIS COUNTRY...AND SAW NO OTHER PEOPLE THAN THE APACHES. AFTER MANY SUMMERS I WALKED AGAIN AND FOUND ANOTHER RACE OF PEOPLE HAD COME TO TAKE IT."

—APACHE LEADER COCHISE, 1866

THE INDIAN WARS

DETERMINED TO ACQUIRE THE HOMELANDS OF WESTERN NATIVE AMERICANS, THE UNITED STATES CONTRIVED BOTH MILITARY AND SOCIAL SOLUTIONS TO THE "INDIAN PROBLEM." WHILE U.S. TROOPS BATTLED TRIBES ACROSS THE WEST, DEFEATED TRIBES WERE PUSHED ONTO RESERVATIONS WHERE THEY WERE REQUIRED TO ADOPT WHITE CUSTOMS.

AS THE RAILROADS advanced, bringing American settlers and foreign immigrants in their wake, the Indian tribes ranging the plains, mountains, and deserts formed an obstacle that had to be destroyed or neutralized. The westward movement scarcely slowed as both the army and the civilian Indian Bureau contended with the problem. Americans and their elected officials debated the virtues of harsh military action versus more benign diplomatic or paternal policies. Whatever their opinions on the "Indian problem," however, no American advocated leaving the West to the exclusive possession of the Indians.

Tribes directly threatened were understandably hostile. Between 1865 and 1890 waves of opposition swelled and surged across the West. Conflict erupted first on the northern Plains, where Indians sometimes starved because of the shrinkage of their lands and because whites—from professional hunters to tourists—brought down whole herds of buffalo for hides, robes, meat, and pure sport, thus depriving Plains Indians of their major resource. At the same time, other Plains Indians, especially

RED CLOUD
In 1866 Lakota Sioux leader Red Cloud (Maqpeya-luta) launched a war against U.S. personnel building forts along the Bozeman Trail.

Sioux who were growing in numbers and force, defied restrictive federal policies. Against the government's demands, they preferred to range widely in pursuit of buffalo and fight wars with enemies to acquire horses and consolidate power.

The year 1865 proved cataclysmic. Sioux, Cheyenne, and Arapaho warriors mounted widespread retaliation for Colonel John M. Chivington's brutal attack on Arapahos and Cheyennes at Sand Creek, in Colorado, the previous year. They burned ranches; leveled stage stations; and killed settlers, especially along the South Platte River. When mutinous Civil War veterans who wanted to go home pursued the Indians, chaos resulted.

RED CLOUD'S WAR

Members of Congress received telling evidence of military deficiencies, yet they continued to underwrite the building of military forts to protect travelers and immigrants on the Bozeman Trail. This road extended through the heart of Sioux buffalo ranges, from Fort Laramie, on the North Platte River in what is now Wyoming, to

APACHES IN CONFERENCE
Even when negotiating for peace, a band of Indian warriors was impressive. Geronimo (standing to right of horse) led his Chiricahua Apaches at an 1886 meeting.

Virginia City, Montana Territory. During 1866 Lakota Sioux leader Red Cloud organized war parties to torment workers and army personnel building at the three guardian forts. Although Colonel Henry B. Carrington and his officers scorned the forays, Red Cloud envisioned a brutal end for Carrington and his men: "In two moons, the command will not have a hoof left."

Red Cloud and his warriors were not to be easily dismissed. During the fall of 1866 he assembled bands of Sioux, as well as Cheyenne and Arapaho allies, in a council on Tongue River, north of Fort Phil Kearny. Although this camp was large, a brash, loud-mouthed Civil War veteran, Captain William J. Fetterman, boasted, "Give me 80 men, and I'll ride through the whole Sioux nation."

On the frigid morning of December 21, 1866, Fetterman seized his chance. At Carrington's orders he rode out to protect a logging train from Sioux onslaught. The impetuous captain disobeyed Carrington's directives and attacked the Sioux. Red Cloud's forces not only killed but scalped and horribly mutilated the bodies of Fetterman and all his 79 men, leaving the dismembered corpses on the snowy ground so that they could not enter the afterworld with whole bodies. The Lakotas called this the Battle of One Hundred Slain, but the army labeled it the "Fetterman Massacre" and vowed reprisal.

Humiliated and increasingly aware of military shortcomings, Congress authorized a rash of treaties with the Apaches, Arapahos, Bannocks, Cheyennes, Kiowas, Sioux, Shoshones, and Navajos. In 1867 a peace delegation signed the Medicine Lodge Treaty with Cheyennes and other tribes of the southern Plains and also initiated talks at Fort Laramie with Sioux leaders. When negotiators promised to abandon the Bozeman Trail and the half-built forts, Red Cloud and others agreed to peace. The Fort Laramie Treaty of 1868 resulted.

⤞THE SAND CREEK MASSACRE⤝

FOR YEARS after the discovery of gold in Colorado (1858), Cheyennes and Arapahos firmly refused to sell their lands and move to reservations. Consequently, in spring 1864, a volunteer force led by Colonel John Chivington began attacking their villages. In negotiations at Fort Weld, tribal leaders were told that if they camped nearby and reported to army posts, they would be safe from attack. On this understanding Black Kettle, a Southern Cheyenne, took his band of 600—of whom two-thirds were women and children—plus some Arapahos and their chief, Left Hand, to Sand Creek near Fort Lyon.

On November 28, 1864, Chivington arrived with a cavalry force. The following morning, ignoring the American flag and white flag of truce atop Black Kettle's tipi, Chivington's men took up positions around the camp and opened fire. While some Cheyennes, including Black Kettle, managed to return fire or escape, thirty warriors and 125 women and children were killed. Left Hand was shot down as he stood with his arms folded. A witness later reported: *"The men used their knives, ripped open women, clubbed little children."*

General Nelson Miles called the massacre the *"foulest and most unjustifiable crime in the annals of America."* Chivington was forced to resign, but any goodwill left between whites and Indians in the region had been destroyed.

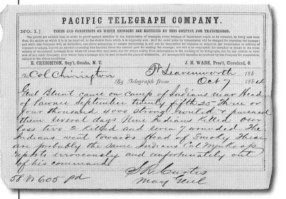

SAND CREEK MESSAGE TO CHIVINGTON
An 1864 telegram reporting a Cheyenne presence near the Pawnee River led to the Sand Creek Massacre, where more than a hundred Cheyenne were killed.

AN AGE OF MASSACRES
Whites as well as Indians suffered massacres. These are survivors of an August 1862 Sioux massacre of white settlers on the Minnesota River.

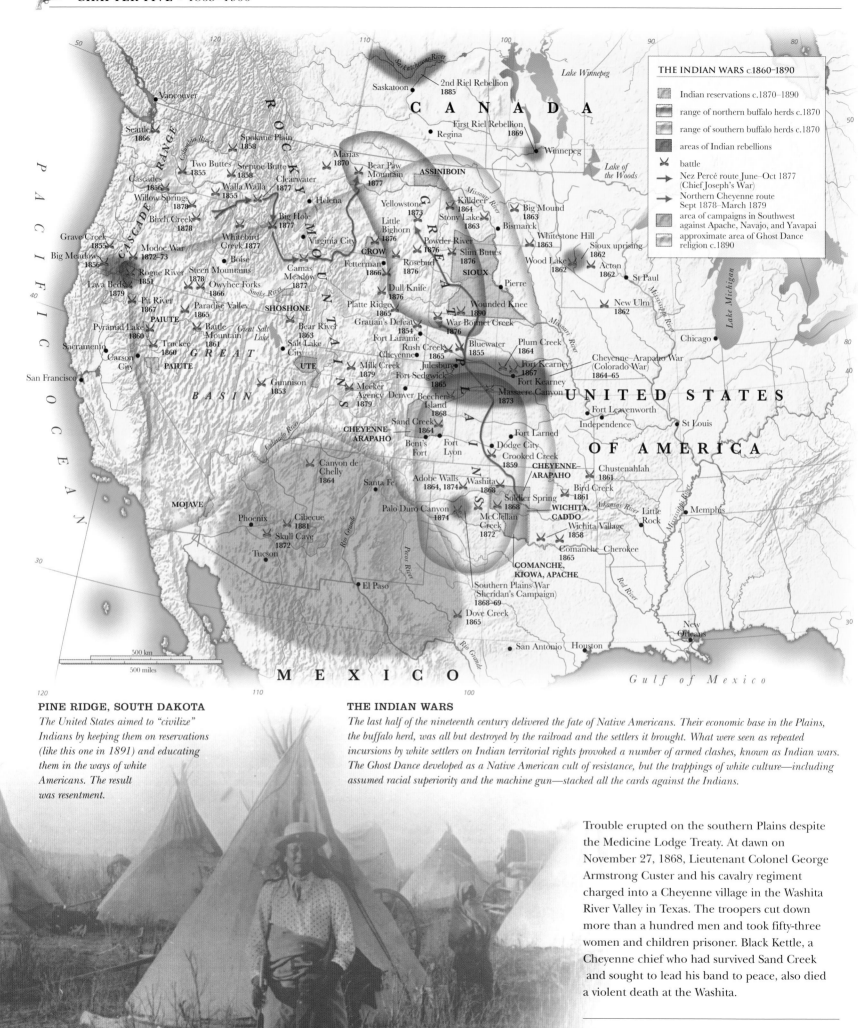

THE INDIAN WARS c.1860–1890

Indian reservations c.1870–1890

range of northern buffalo herds c.1870

range of southern buffalo herds c.1870

areas of Indian rebellions

battle

Nez Percé route June–Oct 1877 (Chief Joseph's War)

Northern Cheyenne route Sept 1878–March 1879

area of campaigns in Southwest against Apache, Navajo, and Yavapai

approximate area of Ghost Dance religion c.1890

CANADA

UNITED STATES OF AMERICA

MEXICO

Gulf of Mexico

PACIFIC OCEAN

ROCKY MOUNTAINS

CASCADE RANGE

GREAT PLAINS

GREAT BASIN

Lake Winnepeg

Lake of the Woods

Lake Michigan

Vancouver

Saskatoon — 2nd Riel Rebellion 1885

First Riel Rebellion 1869

Regina

Winnepeg

Seattle 1866

Spokane Plain 1858

Marias 1870

Bear Paw Mountain 1877

ASSINIBOIN

Killdeer 1864

Big Mound 1863

Two Buttes 1855

Steptoe Butte 1858

Clearwater 1877

Cascades 1856

Walla Walla 1855

Willow Springs 1879

Birch Creek 1878

Helena

Big Hole 1877

Yellowstone 1873

Stony Lake 1863

Bismarck

Whitestone Hill 1863

St Paul

Grave Creek 1855

Modoc War 1872–73

Whitbird Creek 1877

Virginia City

Little Bighorn 1876

CROW

Powder River 1876

Slim Buttes 1876

SIOUX

Sioux uprising 1862

Acton 1862

Big Meadows 1856

Boise

Rosebud 1876

Wood Lake 1862

New Ulm 1862

Rogue River 1851

Steen Mountains 1878

Camas Meadow 1877

Fetterman 1866

Powder River 1876

Lava Beds 1879

Owyhee Forks 1866

Snake River

Dull Knife 1876

Pierre

Pit River 1867

Paradise Valley 1865

SHOSHONE

Platte Ridge 1865

Wounded Knee 1890

Pyramid Lake 1860

Battle Mountain 1861

Great Salt Lake

Bear River 1863

Grattan's Defeat 1854

War Bonnet Creek 1876

PAIUTE

Truckee 1860

Salt Lake City

Fort Laramie

Rush Creek

Bluewater 1855

Plum Creek 1864

Sacramento

UTE

Cheyenne

Milk Creek 1879

Julesburg 1865

Fort Kearney 1867

Chicago

Carson City

PAIUTE

Gunnison 1853

Meeker Agency 1879

Fort Sedgwick 1865

Fort Kearney

Cheyenne–Arapaho War (Colorado War) 1864–65

San Francisco

Denver

Beecher's Island 1868

Massacre Canyon 1873

Fort Leavenworth

Independence

St Louis

Sand Creek 1864

CHEYENNE ARAPAHO

Canyon de Chelly 1864

Santa Fe

Bent's Fort

Fort Lyon

Fort Larned

Dodge City

Crooked Creek 1859

CHEYENNE– ARAPAHO

Chustenahlah 1861

MOJAVE

Adobe Walls 1864, 1874

Washita 1868

Soldier Spring 1868

Bird Creek 1861

Little Rock

Phoenix

Cibecue 1881

Skull Cave 1872

Palo Duro Canyon 1874

McClellan Creek 1872

WICHITA, CADDO

Wichita Village 1858

Memphis

Tucson

Rio Grande

Pecos River

Comanche–Cherokee 1865

COMANCHE, KIOWA, APACHE

El Paso

Southern Plains War (Sheridan's Campaign) 1868–69

Dove Creek 1865

Red River

Arkansas River

Missouri River

Mississippi River

San Antonio

Houston

New Orleans

Columbia River

Colorado River

Saskatchewan River

500 km

500 miles

PINE RIDGE, SOUTH DAKOTA

*The United States aimed to "civilize"
Indians by keeping them on reservations
(like this one in 1891) and educating
them in the ways of white
Americans. The result
was resentment.*

THE INDIAN WARS

*The last half of the nineteenth century delivered the fate of Native Americans. Their economic base in the Plains,
the buffalo herd, was all but destroyed by the railroad and the settlers it brought. What were seen as repeated
incursions by white settlers on Indian territorial rights provoked a number of armed clashes, known as Indian wars.
The Ghost Dance developed as a Native American cult of resistance, but the trappings of white culture—including
assumed racial superiority and the machine gun—stacked all the cards against the Indians.*

Trouble erupted on the southern Plains despite
the Medicine Lodge Treaty. At dawn on
November 27, 1868, Lieutenant Colonel George
Armstrong Custer and his cavalry regiment
charged into a Cheyenne village in the Washita
River Valley in Texas. The troopers cut down
more than a hundred men and took fifty-three
women and children prisoner. Black Kettle, a
Cheyenne chief who had survived Sand Creek
and sought to lead his band to peace, also died
a violent death at the Washita.

INDIAN SCOUT
To fight in unfamiliar regions, the U.S. Army recruited Indians for strategy and fighting. This 1873 photograph by Edweard Muybridge shows Loa-Kum Ar-Nuk of the Warm Springs tribe, recruited as a U.S. scout in California's Modoc War.

PEACE AND WAR

Clearly treaties were incapable of solving long-standing problems. Settlers and miners kept coming, reservations offered a dismal way of life, and simmering hatred befuddled leaders on both sides. In 1869 Congress, ever hopeful of finding a peaceful settlement, created the Board of Indian Commissioners to "civilize" Indians, keep them on reservations, and destroy corruption in the Indian Service. In that year and the next, in what was called his Peace Policy, President Ulysses S. Grant turned to religious groups to staff the reservations. His plan only complicated matters further, for denominations feuded among themselves.

When settlers continued to encroach on their lands, Indians reacted with more violence. The Comanches, who had accepted the Treaty of Medicine Lodge's reservation policy and an assimilation program, relocated in Indian Territory (later Oklahoma) but used their new base to continue to hunt buffalo and conduct raids in Texas. At the same time, in New Mexico and Arizona, Cochise, a daring Chiricahua Apache chief who had once escaped from peace talks gone sour by whipping a knife from his moccasin and slashing through a tent wall, and Victorio, a Mimbreno Apache who often traveled with his wife and five children yet remained elusive, led Apaches in relentless assaults on white settlers and soldiers. Cochise claimed to have killed "ten white men for every Indian slain," but he soon came to realize that whites outnumbered Apaches: "We kill ten; a hundred come in their place."

Despite the overwhelming odds, Cochise and the embittered Victorio continued to oppose the forced relocation of their people to a reservation. The southern Plains provided the backdrop for raids, battles, and slaughter elsewhere. In 1872–73

☙THE APACHE WARS☙

THE APACHE WARS (1861-1886) pitted American troops against the Apaches, a nomadic people living in what is now Arizona and New Mexico. Longtime raiders of their Pueblo neighbors as well as Spanish and Mexican settlements, the Apaches welcomed the American victory over Mexico in 1848, but not the increasing white incursions into their territory. A series of disputes, including the whipping of Mimbreno Apache chief Mangas Colorado by drunken miners, aggravated matters.

In February 1861 the Chiricahua Apache chief Cochise—Mangas Colorado's son-in-law—was wrongfully arrested for abducting a rancher's children. Although he escaped, those with him, including his brother, were kept as hostages. Cochise then took white hostages to bargain for his people's lives. Negotiations failed, and both sides executed their hostages, leading to bitter guerrilla warfare for the next eleven years.

In 1863, Kit Carson campaigned against the Mescalero Apaches near El Paso, forcing them within months to surrender and relocate to Bosque Redondo. That same year, Mangas

AN APACHE PRINCESS
The granddaughter of Chiricahua Apache leader Cochise survived the Apache Wars, in which Cochise led guerrilla raids against U.S. troops from 1861 to 1872.

Colorado, who had been captured by treachery, was killed by prison guards. In 1871 a mercenary force from Tucson attacked an encampment of peaceful Aravaipa Apaches, murdering more than 100. These and other incidents intensified Apache hatred of whites. Meanwhile, Cochise continued his guerrilla raids until he agreed to terms in 1872 (he died two years later). This did not stop other Apache bands from attacking white settlements, and only in 1873, after a lengthy campaign by General George Crook, did many Apaches agree to settle on reservations. Nevertheless, in 1877 Victorio, a Mimbreno Apache, began a campaign (Victorio's Resistance) that lasted until he and more than half his followers were killed in the Battle of Three Peaks (October 1880).

In 1881 Geronimo, a Chiricahua Apache, escaped from his reservation with a small band. Twice returned to the reservation, he nevertheless escaped again and led a raiding campaign until September 1886, when, having been pursued by 5,000 soldiers, he surrendered to General Nelson Miles at Skeleton Canyon, south of Apache Pass, bringing the Apache Wars to an end.

APACHE WARS COUNCIL
Attempts to end the Apache Wars included this March 1886 council between General George Crook (far right) and Apache leader Geronimo (third from left), in the Sierra Madre Mountains.

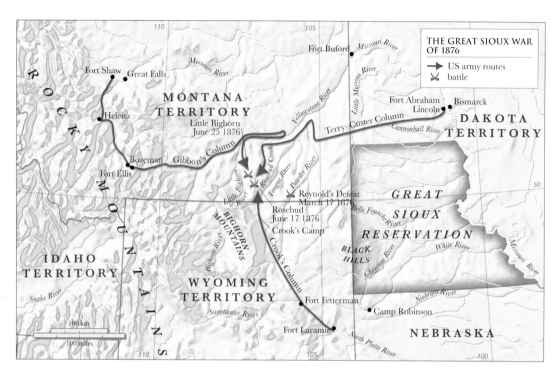

THE GREAT SIOUX WAR OF 1876

→ US army routes
⚔ battle

THE GREAT SIOUX WAR

In 1876, U.S. forces fought Sioux bands for control of the Black Hills of South Dakota. Three columns converged on the Sioux hunting grounds, led by George Crook from the south, John Gibbon from the west, and Alfred Terry from the east. Despite a victory over Terry's subordinate George Armstrong Custer at Little Bighorn on June 25, the Sioux and their Cheyenne allies were ultimately defeated.

ATROCITY

Readers learned of Indian wars through newspaper articles, many of which stirred anti-Indian opinion. This 1886 print depicts a white man entering his house to find his wife and child killed by Indian arrows.

the Modoc War in northern California resulted in national horror. On April 11, 1873, at a peace conference intended to resolve a conflict between Modocs and the United States, Modoc leaders brought the fury of the nation on them by drawing hidden weapons and killing all but one of the white negotiators. Retribution swiftly followed. Fifteen hundred Modocs were relocated about 1,500 miles to the east in Indian Territory. Modoc leader Kintpuash, also known as Captain Jack, and three others died on the gallows; their heads were shipped to the Army Medical Museum in Washington, D.C.

As a result of failed peace talks, newspapers branded Grant's Peace Policy unworkable and wrongheaded. Indians, many reasoned, were neither trustworthy nor rational. In addition, too many agendas tore at policymakers. Congress spoke of peace, military leaders of suppression, religious officials of conversion, reformers of acculturation, and settlers of their continuing fear. More confrontations were inevitable.

RESISTANCE CONTINUES

One of these was the Red River War, which erupted in northwestern Texas in 1874. Cheyennes, Comanches, and Kiowas, angered by the slaughter of buffalo, assaulted hunters, ambushed Texas Rangers, and attacked freight wagons and trading posts. U.S. military forces vanquished the Indians by cutting them off from food supplies. Afterwards the military dispersed Indian leaders to prisons and even an old Spanish fortress in Florida.

Indian resistance continued even though 1874 marked the collapse of the southern Plains tribes and the death of the Apache leader Cochise. Victorio inherited Cochise's mantle. He resisted the U.S. advance at every turn, launched an open war, and led cavalry pursuers in an exhausting race across New Mexico's mountains and deserts. Mexican soldiers ran him down and killed him in 1880.

Meanwhile, on the northern Plains, Grant's hopes for a peaceful settlement were dying. Indian leaders resisted resettlement on reservations and sometimes exploited the chaos to enlarge their own power. Irrepressible

Red Cloud protested the Treaty of Fort Laramie and the boundaries of the Great Sioux Reservation. Substandard supplies, including moldy beef, rancid flour, and moth-infested blankets, further inflamed Sioux peoples. The advance of the Northern Pacific railroad also unsettled Indian leaders.

Then, in 1874, the showy Custer, who had led the attack on the Cheyennes in the Washita River Valley in 1868, again appeared on the scene. His reconnaissance of the Black Hills in South Dakota in 1874 uncovered gold and set off a rush to this heartland of the Great Sioux Reservation. When the Sioux refused to sell or lease the Black Hills, the contest was on.

Although most of the Sioux had settled on reservation land, many remained in the Powder River country to the west, which had been

designated "unceded territory" in the Fort Laramie Treaty of 1868. These groups, owing allegiance to the Hunkpapa chief and holy man Sitting Bull and the superb fighting leader Crazy Horse, prevented Red Cloud and other Indian leaders from parting with the Black Hills. The government therefore ordered these "hunting bands" to report to the reservations by February 1, 1876, or be considered hostile Indians. When they failed to appear, the army took the field.

THE GREAT SIOUX WAR

The "Great Sioux War" of 1876 featured three columns converging on the haunts of the hunting bands in the valleys of the Yellowstone River and its tributaries. General George Crook advanced from the south, General Alfred Terry from the east, and Colonel John Gibbon from the west. Riding with Terry was Custer and the Seventh Cavalry.

Meantime, the bands gained strength as Indians from the reservation rode west to join their brethren in hunting buffalo and fighting off the soldiers. By late June the Sioux and Cheyenne village, containing about 7,000 people and nearly 2,000 fighting men, sprawled for three miles down the valley of Montana's Little Bighorn River. On June 25 Custer divided his regiment and attacked. His immediate command of 210 men fell under the onslaught of overwhelming numbers. No man survived. The balance of the regiment, more than 300 strong, held out for two days until General Terry's approach caused the Indians to withdraw.

In this greatest of Indian victories lay the seeds of defeat. A stunned and angry nation supported a military offensive that drove all the Sioux and Cheyennes either to surrender or flee to Canada. Crazy Horse and his people gave up in the spring

✦CUSTER'S LAST STAND✦

THE BATTLE of the Little Bighorn, known as Custer's Last Stand, was the most stunning Sioux victory in the Great Sioux War of 1876. As U.S. forces converged on the Sioux, General Alfred Terry dispatched Lieutenant Colonel George Armstrong Custer and his Seventh Cavalry to block any move southwards by Chief Crazy Horse. On June 25, 1876, the vainglorious Custer sighted the Sioux village along Montana's Little Bighorn River and decided to attack what he thought was an inferior force. He divided his regiment into four groups. The pack train with escort was to stay where they were, well to the south, while in front of them another detachment under Major Frederick Benteen was to block the Sioux. Custer took two groups north and detached Major Marcus Reno to attack the village's southern side, while he circled around to the other end. When Reno attacked,

CUSTER'S LAST STAND
Many color lithographs of Custer's Last Stand, like this one, appeared after the battle in publications and barroom walls. They recast the event in fanciful, heroic terms.

Gall and his warriors turned Reno's flank, forcing him back to Benteen's position. Some fifty troopers were killed and sixty wounded.

Gall's warriors then joined Crazy Horse, attacking Custer's men on a small hill. A Sioux woman later said, *"The smoke of the shooting and the dust of the horses shut out the hill…but the Sioux shot straight and the soldiers fell dead… [W]hen we came to the hill there were no soldiers living and Long Hair [Custer] lay dead among the rest."*

An Arapaho said: *"He was dressed in buckskin, coat and pants, and was on his hands and knees. He had been shot through the side, and there was blood coming from his mouth…Then the Indians closed in around him, and I did not see any more."*

HUMAN REMAINS
Hundreds of U.S. Army soldiers were killed at Little Bighorn. Remains included this bit of human vertebrae split by a metal arrow.

---

of 1877. Sitting Bull and his dwindling following held out in Canada until starvation forced their surrender in 1881. The government had already seized the Black Hills during the public outrage over the Custer disaster. Conquered and confined to the reservation, the Sioux were now at the mercy

CUSTER'S EXPEDITION
George Armstrong Custer's 1874 expedition to the Black Hills of South Dakota sparked a gold rush and led to his fatal military confrontation with the Sioux.

of government overlords and their programs for transforming all Indians into white people.

Increasingly the reservation seemed the answer to the "Indian problem." Concentrate the Indians on reservations, ran the argument, thus removing them from white travel routes and spreading settlements. There, control and "civilize" them so they could be absorbed into the larger population.

For a time the aim was to establish as many tribes as possible on new reservations in Indian Territory. The Modocs had been moved there

→CHIEF JOSEPH←

AFTER the U.S. government appropriated six million acres of Nez Perce land, Chief Old Joseph refused to sign a treaty that would move his people from the Wallowa Valley in northeastern Oregon onto an Idaho reservation. Following his death in 1871, his son Chief Joseph (1840–1904) continued Nez Perce resistance, winning a court order in 1873 that allowed them to stay in the valley. This was reversed, however, and by 1877 he had reluctantly agreed to move his band to Idaho.

However, when some angry Nez Perce warriors attacked nearby settlements, federal troops retaliated, and Joseph felt he had no choice but to align himself with his prowar brother Ollikut. In the following months, approximately 700 Nez Perce fled towards Canada on a 1,700-mile trek through Idaho, Wyoming, and Montana, defeating U.S. forces in numerous skirmishes along the way. (An admiring William Tecumseh Sherman wrote that they *"fought with almost scientific skill."*) Just thirty miles from the Canadian border, they surrendered at Snake Creek in the Bear Paw Mountains after six days of fighting. In a famous speech, Chief Joseph concluded, *"From where the sun now stands, I will fight no more forever."*

He never saw his homeland again. Joseph and his people were sent first to Kansas, then to Indian Territory, and finally to a non-Nez Perce reservation in northern Washington. In 1904 his doctor reported that Joseph had *"died of a broken heart."*

after their war of 1873. After leading his army during a long, exhausting chase from their Oregon and Idaho homeland, Chief Joseph and his Nez Perces surrendered on the battlefield of Bear Paw Mountain, Montana, only to be packed off to a new home in Indian Territory.

Dull Knife and his Cheyennes had been sent to Indian Territory after the war of 1876, but they quickly resolved to go back home. Many of them had sickened and died from malaria and the substandard rations they had been issued. In the autumn of 1878 Dull Knife and 300 Cheyennes broke for the north. Troops gave chase and tried to intercept them. The flight came to an end at Fort Robinson, Nebraska, where the forlorn people were locked in empty barracks, without food or water, until they would consent to go back. They refused, and on the night of January 9, 1879, they burst free and sought to escape. Many fell under a rain of soldier bullets, and the survivors were rounded up. Finally they were permitted to live with the Sioux on their reservation.

The Utes of Colorado, content with reservations in their mountain homeland, felt increasing pressure from Colorado officials as mineral strikes set off a white invasion. Against this backdrop, in 1879, Utes at the White River Agency killed their agent, utopian crusader Nathan

LAKOTA CAMP

Tensions rose at reservations as Indians were granted substandard lands and pushed to assimilate. The Lakota Sioux camp here is probably on or near Pine Ridge, site of the Wounded Knee massacre.

Meeker, and some of his staff. They also pinned down a military force sent to Meeker's relief. The intercession of Chief Ouray as peacemaker ended the crisis without further bloodshed, but the Utes had to give up their homes for a desert reservation farther west, in Utah.

REFORM

As these white-Indian problems and other scandals sullied the nation's reputation, a growing number of citizens protested escalating mismanagement of the contretemps with native peoples. Reformers deplored the failure of Grant's Peace Policy and the worsening conditions on reservations. In 1881 Indian champion and writer Helen Hunt Jackson published *A Century of Dishonor*, which roundly criticized the U.S. government for failing to fulfill treaties and other promises.

A reform movement gathered strength as eastern women and men founded such organizations as the Women's National Indian Association, the Ladies' National Indian League, the Boston Indian Citizenship Committee, and the most powerful of all, the Indian Rights Association. These groups held annual conferences at Lake Mohonk, New York, to draw public attention to the plight of Native Americans and to propose improvements. Battered from all

"THERE IS NOT AMONG THESE THREE HUNDRED [INDIAN BANDS]... ONE WHICH HAS NOT SUFFERED CRUELLY AT THE HANDS EITHER OF THE GOVERNMENT OR OF WHITE SETTLERS."

—REFORMER HELEN HUNT JACKSON, 1881

sides, Congress adopted legislation intended to answer the Indian question for all time. Reformers hailed the Dawes Severalty Act of 1887 as this ultimate solution. It provided for grants of 160 acres of reservation farmland or 320 acres of grazing land to each head of family.

Advocates hoped the emphasis on family and self-support would break up tribal relationships, do away with the need for rations and even for reservations, and finally assimilate all Indians into American society. To "Americanize the American Indian" was the goal. Despite hopeful beginnings, the Dawes plan led to disaster and despair. Indians who agreed to the plan often received poor lands, while speculators bought the high-yield areas of former reservations. Indians sacrificed their own culture and traditions for white ways that proved meaningless to them.

GERONIMO

By the 1880s greater numbers and superior technology had made the Indian wars more carnage than honorable victory. Still, sporadic resistance marked the final capitulation of Indian tribes across the West. Geronimo and his Apache followers in Arizona were the last to give in. Alternating between refuges in Mexico's Sierra Madre and the miserable desert reservation of San Carlos, Arizona, these most formidable of

⇥HELEN HUNT JACKSON⇤

BORN Helen Maria Fiske in Amherst, Massachusetts, the prolific writer Helen Hunt Jackson (1830–1885) was widowed and lost two sons before marrying William Sharpless Jackson in 1875. Four years later she attended a lecture in Boston by Chief Standing Bear on the government's mistreatment of the Ponca Indians. Profoundly moved, she became, according to one observer, *"a holy terror"* as she worked for Native American rights.

In 1881 Jackson published *A Century of Dishonor*, an indictment of the federal government's policy towards Native Americans. Appointed special commissioner of Indian Affairs, she investigated the conditions of the Mission Indians in Southern California and issued a report calling for massive government reforms. In 1884 she published a novel, *Ramona*, hoping to do for Indians what *Uncle Tom's Cabin* had done for slaves. The reforms of the Dawes Severalty Act resulted in 1887.

AFTER THE MASSACRE
Josephine Meeker and others are held hostage by Ute chief Douglas after the Meeker Massacre and Battle of Milk Creek in 1879. They were later released when the conflict was resolved peacefully.

all Indian fighters pinned down a significant portion of the U.S. Army. General George Crook, employing Apache scouts and mule trains, penetrated the Sierra Madre stronghold in 1883 and forced Geronimo's surrender. But in 1885 he again broke loose from the reservation, and again the troops and Indian scouts campaigned deep into Mexico. Finally, on September 4, 1886, Geronimo surrendered to General Nelson A. Miles. Exiled in Florida and then in Alabama, he ended his years at Fort Sill, Oklahoma, as a farmer and celebrity showman.

THE FINAL ACT

If there were any doubts about which side had triumphed, they were dispelled the following year when Congress opened 2 million acres in Indian Territory, a region that had been reserved for Indians, to non-Indian migrants. On April 22, 1889, 100,000 would-be settlers surged along the lines of troops stationed to hold back "Sooners," people who tried to rush in to claim land before a gun gave the signal at noon. After the gun's report, "Boomers"—people who rushed in legally after this signal—charged forward on everything from horses to bicycles, claiming some 1.92 million acres in a few hours. Within nine weeks 6,000 claimants filed for homesteads. The following year Indian Territory became Oklahoma Territory, headed by an Anglo-American government, although it still contained Indian nations.

Still, some Indians hoped for last-minute salvation from what appeared to them as a white scourge. In 1890 the Teton Sioux of South Dakota, who had watched rations shrink and cattle die from an epidemic, rallied to the teachings of Wovoka, a Paiute shaman. Wovoka promised that rites and ceremonies would bring back the

GHOST DANCE DRESS
The Sioux sought to revitalize their culture through the spiritual Ghost Dance.

old, lost world and its life. When Sioux performed "Ghost Dances," as their white critics termed the rituals, troops grew alarmed and arrived to impose order. Indians who resisted the troops ended up dead, including the intrepid Sitting Bull and eight of his followers. In the terrible bloodletting of Wounded Knee, some 200 men, women, and children fell dead or injured by Hotchkiss cannon operated by soldiers, who tossed the bodies into mass graves and essentially brought the era of Indian conflict to a close.

Only Indians who found some way to adapt to reservation living survived the Indian wars without cultural demoralization. The so-called Five Civilized Tribes of Indian Territory—the Choctaws, Chickasaws, Cherokees, Creeks, and Seminoles—proved especially adept at

---

✦WOUNDED KNEE✦

IN AUTUMN 1890, government attempts to halt the spread of the Ghost Dance religion among the Plains Indians focused on the Teton Sioux of South Dakota. On December 15 that year, Chief Sitting Bull was killed at the Standing Rock Reservation while being arrested. Upon hearing the news, the Miniconjou chief Big Foot took his band of 350 towards the Pine Ridge Reservation in hopes of joining Red Cloud, who advocated peace rather than confrontation. On December 28 a unit of the Seventh Cavalry found the band and ordered them to camp near Wounded Knee Creek.

Ill with pneumonia, Big Foot obeyed the army's instructions, agreeing that his warriors would hand over their weapons the following day. The Sioux camped where they were told, and the army set up four Hotchkiss guns around the camp. On the morning of December 29, surrounded by 500 troopers, the Indians allowed the soldiers to take their weapons, but when one tried to take the gun of a deaf warrior, Black Coyote, a shot rang out. Both sides took this as an

attack, and after some close-quarter fighting, the Sioux tried to take cover. The Hotchkiss guns then opened fire, bullets ripping into tipis and the fleeing Indians. One woman, Louise Weasel Bear, said, *"We tried to run, but they shot us like we were buffalo."*

When it was over, at least 153 Sioux, including Big Foot, lay dead in the snow. The final total of people killed may have been 200 or more, as many of the wounded crawled away to die. Twenty-five soldiers were killed and thirty-nine wounded. The massacre marked the end of the Plains Indian Wars.

BURYING THE SIOUX
About 200 Sioux, including women and children, were killed or injured by U.S. troops at Wounded Knee. The frozen corpses of Sioux were buried early in 1891.

✦THE OKLAHOMA LAND RUSH✦

WHEN PUBLIC clamoring for lands in Indian Territory became impossible to ignore, negotiations began to acquire surplus acreage from the Native Americans. Finally, in March 1889, President Benjamin Harrison declared that 2 million acres would be opened to settlement under the Homestead and Pre-emption laws. When the news was announced, some 100,000 eager farmers, cattlemen, and settlers came from all over the country and, under close cavalry escort, took up positions along the border.

At noon an April 22, 1889, when the army's guns and bugles sounded the start, excited Boomers poured across the border in wagons, on horseback (including four circus midgets riding a single horse), on bicycles, on foot, or packed intolong trains. One claimant wrote to his brother: *"I looked down the line for an instant and it appeared like a huge serpent moving, it was the most people I ever saw together."*

A reporter at the scene noted, *"The horsemen had the best of it from the start. It was a fine race for a few minutes, but soon the riders began to spread out like a fan, and by the time they had reached the horizon they were scattered about as far as eye could see."* Chaos ruled everywhere, and many who were clinging to the roofs and sides of the trains jumped off, risking their lives to be first to a claim. Yet even some of those on horseback arrived to find the land they wanted already claimed by illegal Sooners who had managed to evade federal troops.

Within hours the towns of Guthrie, Oklahoma City, Kingfisher, and Norman had sprung into existence—with many of the best lots taken by federal marshals—and lawyers, estate agents, bankers, financiers, and mortgage agents had set up business in the backs of wagons or on a plank between two trestles. By nightfall all 2 million acres had been claimed.

More of the Indian Territory was opened for settlement by the same method in 1891 and 1892. The largest area of all, the Cherokee Outlet, six million acres on the northern border, was opened in September 1893.

OKLAHOMA LAND RUSH
On September 16, 1893, the 6 million acres of the Cherokee Outlet were opened to 100,000 land-hungry people who hurried to claim them.

blending their own traditions with white ways. A part-Chickasaw woman, born in 1881 in a log house, attended Bloomfield Academy for Native American girls in Kemp and, after graduation, taught a Native American school in Paul's Valley. The Navajos of Arizona and New Mexico also coped by clinging to their cultural heritage and adopting only bits and pieces of white culture. They increased their sheep herds so that Navajo land and population grew.

Like these Indians, many other native people survived and adapted, yet they suffered what one anthropologist termed "cultural neurosis" as a result of having one foot in a widely scorned culture and the other in a culture alien to them. Only time would reveal the destructive consequences of their forced adaptation to a world they were unprepared to understand.

✦GEORGE CROOK✦

A WEST POINT graduate, George Crook (1828–1890) served with distinction in the Civil War. His reputation as an Indian fighter began in 1866, when he campaigned against the Paiutes in Oregon and Idaho. Whereas previous commanders had relied on static forts and outposts, Crook followed a successful course of constant patrolling throughout the territory, a tactic he later used during the Apache Wars. A skillful negotiator, he convinced many Apaches to settle on reservations and helped to pacify the Sioux after the Battle of Little Bighorn.

In 1882 Crook took charge of operations against Geronimo, using mules instead of horses to follow the Apache chief into the Sierra Madre in Mexico. Geronimo returned peacefully, and for a year the Apaches were at peace. When Geronimo again left the reservation, Crook promised him safety and short-term imprisonment if he returned. A reprimand from Washington led Crook to resign. The Lakota chief Red Cloud said of him, *"Crook never lied to us. His words gave the people hope."*

WEST-BOUND TRAINS
*Railroads like the Chicago, Burlington &
Quincy Railroad Company carried dreamers
and schemers to the West.*

"I'VE BEEN
WORKING ON
THE RAILROAD,
ALL THE
LIVE-LONG DAY,
I'VE BEEN
WORKING ON
THE RAILROAD,
JUST TO PASS
THE TIME AWAY."

—FOLK SONG OF WESTERN
RAILWAY WORKERS, C. 1870S

THE RAILROAD WEB

AIDED BY ENORMOUS FEDERAL LOANS AND LAND GRANTS, RAILROAD
COMPANIES BEGAN CONSTRUCTION ON THE FIRST TRANSCONTINENTAL
RAILROAD DURING THE 1860S. WITH FORTUNES TO BE MADE, COMPANIES
SCRAMBLED TO LAY TRACK AS QUICKLY AS POSSIBLE, HIRING LOW-PAID
RECENT IMMIGRANTS TO DO THE BACKBREAKING AND OFTEN
DANGEROUS WORK OF BRIDGING EAST AND WEST.

RAILROADS REVOLUTIONIZED the American West. When Congress adopted the Pacific Railroad Act in 1862, the dream of a transcontinental railroad could at last become reality. Congress nourished—some would say force-fed—its project of a transcontinental rail line by giving railroad companies 170 million acres of public land, worth more than half a billion dollars, as well as loans for every mile of track laid.

The Central Pacific—working its way east from Sacramento, California—and the Union Pacific–building west from Omaha, Nebraska–were the first recipients. States also rushed to help the railroad companies that would bring them settlers and commerce. Individual railroad investors rode the crest of the future by seizing openings created by the nation's wish to be geographically united by a transcontinental railroad. California's Big Four—Charles Crocker, Mark Hopkins, Collis P. Huntington, and Leland Stanford—employed political rhetoric and outright corruption to spur their project, the Central Pacific (CP), which broke ground in January 1863.

As construction boss, Charles Crocker on occasion roared like a "mad bull." He compelled men and machinery onward, relying primarily on Chinese laborers. With a kind face and gentle eyes, Mark Hopkins kept the accounts. He also helped devise ways in which company directors could vote themselves huge fortunes and argued that the CP should continue to issue stock far in excess of its value. Collis P. Huntington lobbied Congress for preferential laws, federal aid, and other favors with a similar lack of scruples. Bribery and outright threats sometimes accompanied his efforts. But it was Leland Stanford, a wholesale grocer elected California's governor, who represented the Central Pacific to the public. With his massive shoulders held high and a hint of a scowl on his high forehead, Stanford used pork barrelling and lobbying to promote the CP—and to bolster his own financial position and political power. Despite their transgressions, the Big Four helped ramrod a technological marvel. The Central Pacific began to blaze the mightiest trail yet across the West.

Soon the Union Pacific (UP) joined in earnest. Hard-driving executive Thomas C. Durant supplied the motivating force. Yet it was not until Major General Grenville M. Dodge resigned from the Union Army in 1866 and took on the job of chief engineer that the UP roadbed began to inch slowly from Omaha, across Nebraska, and toward the Great Salt Lake.

To perform this backbreaking work, the Union Pacific hired recent immigrants. Most of those wielding shovels and swinging picks were Irish, African-American, and Hispanic men. Dodge recruited another Union officer, John Stephen Casement, to discipline laborers into military efficiency. Railroad workers looked like a veritable army, with at least 10,000 on the UP side and another 13,000 laboring for the CP. They toiled with military precision. One observer claimed that a UP gang could haul iron rails off a horse-drawn cart, along the roadbed, and into position in "less than 30 seconds," so that "four rails go down to the minute."

By 1866 Ben Holladay, an untutored adventurer who controlled 5,000 miles of stagecoach routes at his peak and personally goaded on his drivers, recognized that a transcontinental railroad was

KINGS OF WALL STREET
Wall Street financiers promoted railroad building, which yielded multimillions in trade. Major figures included Jay Gould and Sidney Dillon (fourth and fifth from left).

finally imminent. Because Holladay felt certain that railroads would soon push stagecoaches into second place, he had the foresight to sell out for $1.8 million to a New York outfit, the Wells Fargo Express Company, which eventually made its own fortune serving and supplementing railroad lines.

LAYING THE RAILS
In the 1860s, tens of thousands of men, mostly immigrants, laid tracks for the Union Pacific (shown here) and Central Pacific railroads. The standard pace for the work was two miles of track per day.

❯LELAND STANFORD❮

BORN in Watervliet, New York, Amasa Leland Stanford (1824–1893) practiced law in Wisconsin before moving to California in 1852 and becoming a successful merchant. As governor (1861–63), Stanford worked to keep California in the Union and used his political power to secure land grants and state investment in the Central Pacific Railroad, which he had cofounded in 1861. After his term as governor, Stanford became Central Pacific's president, an office he held to the end of his life, and president of the Southern Pacific Company (1885–90). With his wife in 1885 he founded Stanford University in memory of his son, Leland, Jr. That year the California legislature named him to the U.S. Senate, where he served to his death.

Holladay was prophetic, for nothing stopped the UP and CP work gangs. Laborers for both companies tolerated everything from torrential rains to avalanches that obliterated work camps and buried workers alive. Other workers, suspended in wicker baskets, planted explosives in solid rockface and hoped they would be yanked back in time to escape the blasts. Some laborers crept across sheer mountainsides carving ledges for tracks or dangled high above canyons threading wooden trestles from one side to the other. Railroad workers bored tunnels through intimidating rock peaks, such as the Summit Tunnel at Donner Pass in California's Sierra Nevada. Here a 20-foot-high bore worked its way, inches at a time, through 1,659 feet of granite.

Despite their heroism, railroad workers drew low wages and endured poor treatment. Some Union Pacific agents hauled wagonloads of unemployed Irish hands to a distant construction site, promising them fair wages for their work. Once there, the agents told the workers to fight it out to see which ones would get the jobs—at lower wages than promised. The Central Pacific also tried to hold down costs by cutting wages. The company paid white workers thirty-one dollars per month plus room and board; Chinese workers received only thirty-one dollars but no room and board, a monthly savings of one-third to the company.

By 1867 the Central Pacific employed 12,000 Chinese workers, approximately 90 percent of the work force on the road. Superintendent Crocker stated that the "Chinese are skilled in using the hammer and drill; and they proved themselves equal to the best Cornish miner in that work." Yet when Chinese workers struck for higher wages in the spring of 1867, employers denied their

RAIL BY RAIL
The transcontinental railroad was built by pick and shovel and thousands of hands, including Chinese ones. While dynamite had been invented in 1866, it was not in general use in time to carve this trail through the Sierra Nevada.

demands, cut off food supplies, and threatened to bring in 10,000 African Americans. When Chinese workers returned to their jobs, they finished the western portion of the transcontinental railroad, making the Central Pacific largely a Chinese achievement.

In 1868 the race accelerated. The UP laid 425 miles of track, while the CP bored 15 tunnels and built 360 miles of road. Finally, after overlapping each other's grades, laying rail that did not connect, for some 200 miles in Nevada and Utah, and after making numerous other miscalculations, the Union Pacific and Central Pacific lines met on May 10, 1869, at Promontory Point, Utah. Fifteen hundred people gathered to watch officials pound in the final spike. Newly established telegraph lines flashed the news to New York City. A New Yorker could now travel to California in one week rather than several months.

AFTER THE TRIUMPH

This first wild spree of railroad building bequeathed to the West thousands of miles of track, a skeleton for the region's emerging system of commerce and communication. But falling stock values, high

---

✣BUILDING RAILROADS✣

BUILDING A RAILROAD in the mid-nineteenth century comprised four main stages: surveying the route, grading the roadbed, laying the ties and rails, and keeping crews supplied with tools and equipment.

The enterprise's success depended on the surveyors, who coped with Indian attacks, weather, and hunger while they determined the best route to take. Behind them, grading gangs carried out the arduous labor of preparing the roadbed: building up the track on low ground or digging out channels through higher ground, as well as blasting and digging tunnels through mountains and constructing bridges over rivers. With no earth-moving equipment, the crews used plows, horse-drawn scrapers, shovels, picks, and handcarts. When a mountain blocked the route, blasting teams hacked holes in the rock face with cold chisels and sledgehammers, and used gunpowder or, later, the new and volatile nitroglycerine to open up tunnel entrances. If the rock was suitable, more explosives and boring equipment would be used to extend the tunnel, but it was otherwise dug out by teams of men with picks, hacking away while others barrowed out the rock they loosened.

If, as happened often in the mountains, the snows brought blizzards and rock falls, then snow sheds were built. These were enormous, open-ended, hangar-like structures that provided protection for the track and shelter for the crews.

Once the roadbed was graded, crews laid the track, picking ties and rails off long platform cars, placing and hammering them into position, and proceeding forward as the cars moved over the newly laid rails. Each iron rail weighed 700 pounds and needed five men to lift it, walk it forward, and drop it into place. A strong, experienced team could lay two rails on either side every sixty seconds. It was by such crude methods that Central Pacific crews laid ten miles of track in one day, April 28, 1869—a record that still stands.

ALONG "THE LOOP"
To bridge heights, such as the 600-foot elevation difference between the Colorado towns Georgetown and Silver Plume, rail lines sometimes had to twist and turn over themselves in dizzying loops.

FASTER THAN RAILROADS

As fast as railroads were, they were outsped by the telegraph. Recently established telegraph lines, laid in the West by Western Union, were used to transmit news of the completion of the transcontinental railroad.

costs, and bankruptcy prevented other companies from quickly duplicating the feat of the CP and UP. Moreover, it soon became obvious that both had used substandard materials so that rails rusted and ties rotted. Roadbeds sometimes collapsed, and poorly engineered curves threw cars from the track. By the 1880s Dodge looked back on his dream with sadness, describing the road he had helped to build as "two dirt ballasted streaks of rust."

Despite such disillusion, as the nation's economy slowly recovered from the Panic of 1873, western railroad building entered its second great period. During the 1880s feeder lines gradually snaked over the West to connect trunk lines and provide branches. In this decade railroad companies laid some 40,000 miles of track west of the Mississippi River; by 1890, 72,473 miles of track webbed the West.

When investors found themselves bedeviled by high costs and unstable traffic, they attempted to consolidate more and more track under their own control. Speculator Jay Gould bought several lines and tried to create a national railroad system, but in the 1880s his Gould system, based on that of the Missouri Pacific, collapsed. In California, however, the indomitable Big Four, their company having been restyled as the Southern Pacific, enjoyed a monopoly over the state's rail system.

In 1893 the last of the proposed transcontinental lines, the Great Northern, reached Seattle and revealed the financial stability railroad companies could attain. The Great Northern's founder, James J. Hill, rejected speculation and promotion in favor of sound management and conservative financing. A Scots-Canadian, Hill seemed to have little interest in the power wars waged by other railroad magnates. Instead he designed a system to carry wheat, copper, and lumber with efficiency and dispatch.

Fortunes rose and fell on railroads. Crocker alone poured $2.3 million into an opulent Nob Hill mansion in San Francisco. Huntington also lived lavishly, but in addition he and his wife, Arabella Duvall Huntington, organized and endowed California's splendid Huntington Library, Art Collections, and Botanical Gardens. Stanford, along with his wife, Jane Lathrop Stanford, founded, developed, and left to the state of California Stanford University.

But what did the era of railroad construction mean to the average American? For one thing,

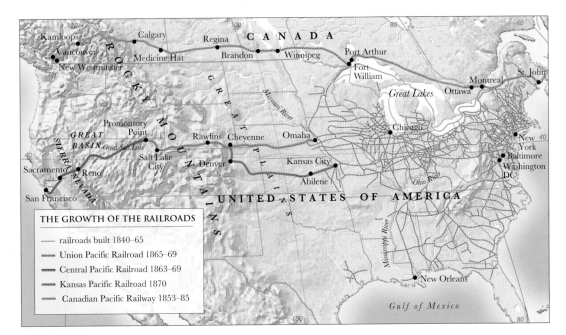

THE GROWTH OF THE RAILROADS

----- railroads built 1840–65

===== Union Pacific Railroad 1865–69

===== Central Pacific Railroad 1863–69

===== Kansas Pacific Railroad 1870

===== Canadian Pacific Railway 1853–85

THE GROWTH OF RAILROADS

Work on completing a transcontinental railroad, linking the already mature network of the East to the Pacific coast, began in 1863, building east from San Francisco, and continued in 1865, building westward from Omaha, Nebraska. The railroads were symbolically linked at Promontory Point with a final, golden spike in 1869.

SELLING THE RAILROAD
Upon the 1869 completion of the transcontinental railroad, the Union Pacific Railroad courted new customers with a flashy advertisement for the Platte Valley Route. The route opened on May 10, 1869 and in 1870, 150,000 took the cross-country journey.

within a few years after the Civil War, railroads connected the East, South, and Midwest to the West. Nine major routes carried trade goods and passengers back and forth at delirious speeds up to forty miles an hour. In 1870 some 150,000 passengers traversed the transcontinental line.

Railroad expansion also swelled the number of migrants streaming to the American West from the East, the South, Canada, and Europe. Not only did railroads make it easier to move a family, stock, and equipment, but railroad companies actively recruited migrants. Settlers were courted for two reasons: to settle on land owned by the companies and to increase the goods railroad lines carried to and from the West.

To achieve these goals, each company established an Immigration Bureau, which advertised the availability of western land throughout Europe, and a Land Department,

which sold parcels of its government land grants to migrants. These settlement programs offered easy credit terms, free transportation for goods and equipment, and the promise of prosperity in the West. They especially promoted the Great Plains, promising opportunities to get rich quickly in an area that many called a "great American desert." Boosters portrayed it as "a flowery meadow" awaiting "diligent labor and economy to ensure an early reward."

During the post-Civil War years, thousands of eastern Europeans took up the challenge. Steamship and railroad companies issued posters, advertisements, and gimmicks that promised riches beyond imagining. Advertisers pictured the Great Plains as a "prairie which is ready for the plow"; they enticed women with jobs such as milkmaid and with a wide choice of husbands.

AMERICA FEVER: THE WORLD GOES WEST

Journalists dubbed the excitement "America Fever." In 1882 more than 105,000 emigrants put Norway, Sweden, and Denmark behind them. Others left Germany, Ireland, England, Wales, Scotland, Holland, Belgium, Austria, Switzerland, Czechoslovakia, Poland, Russia, and Canada for such destinations as Nebraska and the Dakotas. By 1900 immigrants and their descendants accounted for 47 percent of Nebraska's population.

Arriving in the United States, a family might hire a boxcar into which they crammed food, clothing, household implements (from washbasins to stoves), farm equipment, fence posts, one or more dogs, farm animals, children, and themselves. This "emigrant car" made its way slowly across the Middle West and onto the Plains, where it might stand on a siding for a year or two, providing a

CIVILIZATION BY RAIL
As railroads spread, they connected the West to the rest of the United States, making it easier for population and commerce to flourish in many parts of the West. In this 1890 photograph, several people stand before a locomotive in the Black Hills.

❖DEADWOOD, SOUTH DAKOTA❖

DEADWOOD SPRANG up on the steep banks of Deadwood Gulch in 1875, when gold was discovered in the area, resulting in the influx of over 20,000 miners. Located in a canyon in western South Dakota's Black Hills, the town gained notoriety for its one main street lined with saloons and gambling halls, and its colorful characters and their wild—and often violent—ways. In 1876 legendary James Butler "Wild Bill" Hickok, Deadwood's new town marshal and a former soldier, scout, and marksman who had appeared in Buffalo Bill's Wild West show, was shot in the back of the head by Jack McCall in an act of revenge while playing poker at Deadwood's "No.10" saloon. The cards he was holding—a pair of black aces, a pair of black nines, and the nine of diamonds—are still known as the "dead man's hand."

Hickok had arrived in Deadwood with frontierswoman Martha Canary, better known as "Calamity Jane." Famous for her theatrics and drunken antics, Calamity Jane claimed to have been, among other things, an Army scout for General Custer, a teamster transporting supplies to mining camps, a construction worker on the railroad, a nurse, a gambler, and on occasion, a prostitute. She died in 1903 and is buried next to Wild Bill in Deadwood's Mount Moriah Cemetery, also known as "Boot Hill."

Not all of Deadwood's inhabitants, however, were drinkers and gamblers. Henry Weston Smith, a preacher, arrived in town in 1876 determined to bring religion to the hard-living miners. On August 20, 1876, Smith, the first preacher in the area, left a note on his front door saying that he had gone to Crook City and would be back at 2:00 P.M. Instead, his body was found, bloodstained sermon notes and Bible in hand, along the ten-mile route to his destination. It was never determined whether Indians, miners, or another party were responsible for Smith's death. He, too, is buried at Mount Moriah Cemetery.

GOLD MAKES A TOWN
Rough towns like Deadwood, South Dakota, arose after the discovery of gold in the Black Hills. The influx of miners worsened relations with Indians and generated numerous legends.

PROSTITUTES DRINKING
While western towns became more domesticated with the coming of the railroad, old elements remained. This 1890 photograph shows "soiled doves" who entertained the locals in saloons. For years, men outnumbered women in the West.

temporary home for the family as its members scratched a homestead out of the land that had been touted so highly.

Nineteenth-century railroads brought to the West not only people but also eastern products, and with them branches of eastern corporations. Gradually, large eastern enterprises forced many smaller western companies out of business. Sears, Roebuck and Company eventually dominated the mail-order business, while railroad lines carried Schlitz and Pabst beer from Wisconsin to western saloons. Thanks to the railroads, even western families living in remote, rural areas could enjoy a

standard of living similar to that of eastern Americans. Railroads also fundamentally reshaped the West by transplanting eastern values. The railroads brought in settlers who made the Wild West less wild. Although some migrants sought excitement or dissipation, others yearned for a stable life, which would include churches, schools, law enforcement, and all the other trappings defined as civilization.

With the coming of the railroad, then, saloons and brothels retreated first to the side streets and then to the edges of towns. Main Street boasted instead churches, a town hall, and mercantile

establishments. Between 1865 and the mid-1880s, for example, Helena, Montana, garnered a reputation as a raw western town overflowing with drink, gambling, and prostitutes. In fact, prostitution provided the largest single source of employment for Helena's women. They held forth in infamous "hurdy gurdy" halls and such dancing saloons as "Chicago Joe" Welch's Red Light Saloon, or worked out of the "cribs" that lined the back streets. By 1883, when the Northern Pacific arrived, Helena's rebirth had begun, as families and businesspeople launched campaigns against prostitution and demanded restrictive legislation.

U.S. GEOLOGICAL SURVEY

Expedition members at this camp at Red Buttes, 1870, include geologist Ferdinand V. Hayden (seated, second from right).

"TO A GREAT EXTENT, THE REDEMPTION OF ALL THESE LANDS WILL REQUIRE EXTENSIVE AND COMPREHENSIVE PLANS."

—GEOLOGIST JOHN WESLEY POWELL ON ARID LANDS, 1878

WET PLATE CAMERA

Survey photographers faced daunting locations with bulky equipment. This 50- to 70-pound camera was carried on John Wesley Powell's 1872 Grand Canyon expedition.

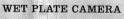

FEDERAL INNOVATIONS

AS RAILROADS TRANSPORTED MORE PEOPLE WESTWARD, THE FEDERAL
GOVERNMENT SPONSORED GEOLOGICAL SURVEYS TO DRAW MAPS,
STUDY RESOURCES, AND GUIDE PLANNING. SCIENTISTS SUCH AS
CLARENCE KING, FERDINAND VANDEVEER HAYDEN, AND JOHN
WESLEY POWELL CONDUCTED DARING EXPLORATIONS AND MADE
RECOMMENDATIONS ABOUT LAND USE. AS A RESULT OF THEIR EFFORTS,
CONGRESS ESTABLISHED THE FIRST NATIONAL PARK, YELLOWSTONE.

AT FIRST the federal government aided development and growth in the West. As Congress ordered troops westward to control Native Americans and clear routes for migrants, it sent civilian scientists and explorers along to draw maps, survey wagon routes, and plot locations of water, grass, animals, and other resources.

Such information soon revealed the need for planning and control. As early as 1864, despite protests, federal officials established Yosemite Park, California, then gave it to the state government to administer. Two years later, Clarence King, a 25-year-old Yale graduate who explored Yosemite as part of the California Geological Survey, conceived the idea of a master survey of the area between the Rockies and the Sierra Nevada. In accepting King's proposal, Congress confirmed the coming of a new era of civilian—rather than military—exploration. When Secretary of War Edwin M. Stanton handed King his commission in 1867, he warned the young surveyor, "The sooner you get out of Washington, the better. [T]here are four major generals who want your place."

King went to Sacramento where he assembled his team, including geologists, topographers, cavalry, a botanist, an ornithologist, and photographer Timothy O'Sullivan. On July 3 the group mounted horses and mules on which they scaled Donner Pass and dipped into the Great Basin. From temporary campsites, experts classified flora and fauna, collected rock and mineral samples, took barometric readings and

NATIVE AMERICAN ANTHROPOLOGY
In 1879, John Wesley Powell, pictured here with Paiute chief Tau-Gu, helped persuade Congress to establish the Bureau of Ethnology. For more than two decades, he oversaw the bureau's sponsorship of anthropological research on Native American languages and tribes.

photographs, made meteorological observations, and surveyed the land. Malaria struck nearly every one of the party in August, and lightning hit King in September, yet they pushed onward. Finally the company stopped to winter in Carson City and Virginia City, Nevada, where it assembled data for its first public report, *The Mining Industry*.

HAYDEN AND POWELL
Geologist Ferdinand Vandeveer Hayden also proved an indefatigable explorer as well as a western promoter whose wild enthusiasms sometimes led to overstatement and hyperbole. In 1869 Hayden guided the U.S. Geological and Geographic Survey of the Territories into Colorado and New Mexico. In 1870 Congress appropriated $25,000 for Hayden to survey Wyoming, and in 1871 it earmarked $40,000 for the Yellowstone River country. Hayden tried to describe such sites as the Mammoth Hot Spring with mere words—"perfectly transparent" and "beautiful ultramarine depth"—but photographer Williams Henry Jackson and landscape artist Thomas Moran, both of whom accompanied Hayden, produced actual images of Yellowstone's fabled Grand Canyon, Firehole Basin, and Tower Falls.

Thus inspired, in 1872 Congress created the first federally administered park, Yellowstone, in northwestern Wyoming. Hundreds of Americans traveled Yellowstone's dazzling canyons and valleys on foot, in covered wagons, or by carriages. They camped out in tents and fished, hunted, and studied plants and animals.

At the same time, Hayden's great rival, John Wesley Powell, explored the Colorado Plateau. A one-armed Civil War veteran with a determined set to his jaw, Powell first caught public attention in 1869 when he floated the length of the Green and Colorado Rivers, losing scientific equipment and some 2,000 pounds of provisions to treacherous whitewater. He and the men who

stuck with him not only survived but became national heroes. In response, the Smithsonian Institution funded a second Colorado River trip in 1871 and subsequent surveys of southern Utah and parts of Nevada.

After Powell completed his geological and topographical work in 1873, he turned with growing apprehension to what he believed to be "the gradual disappearance" of Native Americans. He warned that "the march of humanity cannot be stayed. Whether we desire it or not, the ancient inhabitants of the country must be lost." Along with anthropologist Alice C. Fletcher, photographer John K. Hillers, and stenographer James C. Pilling, Powell recorded what he could of Indian words, customs, and appearance, especially those of the Southern Paiutes. When he exhibited photographs and artifacts at the 1876 Centennial Exhibition, in Philadelphia, he presented a slightly inaccurate, yet still valuable, chronicle of a portion of America's native peoples.

Powell then began to hammer at the government's land-use policy. In his 1878 *Report on the Lands of the Arid Regions of the United States*, he warned that arid zones were incapable of supporting densely settled populations. Rather than being used haphazardly for small farms, he admonished, arid zones must be classified according to potential utilization—such as mineral, irrigable, or ranch—and a plan formulated for each such use.

U.S. GEOLOGICAL SURVEY
The following year Congress combined all the surveys into one—the U.S. Geological Survey. Clarence King served a year as director, but Powell then took over and continued to chide Congress for its land-use programs. In his view, water, the key to western development, had to be regulated by federal dams and canals, which would be controlled by local irrigation districts.

Powell's plan alienated nearly everyone, from settlers who feared restrictions on the size of farms to ranchers who trembled at losing their monopoly on water. Yet Powell was clearly right. Ranchers, farmers, and water companies claimed streams, lakes, and rivers as their own. They diverted water to their land or to people willing to pay for it; those who could not afford water went without. Because Powell's plea for planned usage failed, western states were left to grapple with the problem. In 1879 and 1881 Colorado tried to regulate water by adopting two irrigation acts that established water commissioners and state agencies to enforce claims and allot resources. Other states followed Colorado's lead, but interstate water problems defied state regulation.

ITALIANS OUT WEST
*The West was a patchwork of ethnicities.
Italian fishermen tend their boats at
Monterey, California, in 1889.*

"HOW CAN I CALL

THIS MY HOME,

AND HOW CAN

ANYONE BLAME

ME IF I TAKE MY

MONEY AND GO

BACK TO MY

VILLAGE IN

CHINA?"

—CHINESE IMMIGRANT LEE CHEW
ON AMERICAN MISTREATMENT OF
THE CHINESE

WESTERNERS IN CONFLICT

THE WEST HAD A DIVERSE POPULATION, INCLUDING NATIVE AMERICANS, HISPANICS, AFRICAN AMERICANS, ASIANS, AND WHITES OF MANY ETHNIC AND RELIGIOUS BACKGROUNDS. ALL TOO OFTEN, THE CULTURAL DIFFERENCES AMONG THESE GROUPS BECAME LINKED TO A BITTER AND SOMETIMES VIOLENT COMPETITION FOR LAND AND RESOURCES.

BECAUSE NO PRECEDENT in American history prepared migrants from the East to encounter western inhabitants, nor westerners to meet their eastern neighbors, both sides sallied forth with information derived largely from myth, rumor, and prejudice. Yet railroads, coaches, and wagons spilled settlers onto the western plains by the thousands, causing cultural explosions that still reverberate throughout the United States.

Invading the West were whites of virtually every ethnic and religious background, including domestic workers, teachers, miners, ranchers, lumberers, entrepreneurs, and an ever-increasing contingent of homesteaders. Homesteaders flocked to the American West from the eastern United States, Canada, and Europe. Single and married, men and women, they took advantage of the 1862 Homestead Act, which gave a head of family over age twenty-one 160 acres of land after five years of continuous residence and payment of a filing fee. Later, settlers benefited from the 1873 Timber Culture Act, which gave homesteaders in dry areas 360 acres if they planted trees on forty of those acres.

After sisters Edith Eudora and Ida Mary Ammons joined the hundreds of young, single women taking up claims, they were ecstatic over the opportunities the West offered. Living on a claim near Pierre, South Dakota,

Edith said that hardships "were more than compensated for by its unshackled freedom." Despite her exuberance, western settlement forced people to encounter ideas and cultures different from their own. When the sisters' Indian neighbors made their first visit, Edith and Ida Mary hid trembling in their claim shack. Although they resolved their misconceptions, thousands of other westerners did not.

Generally, white settlers expected their ways and ideas to enthrall and assimilate peoples already living in the West. Such an assumption was naive at best, especially given the wide range of inhabitants. After the Civil War thousands of Indian peoples called the West home, but eastern Indians now lived in the West as well. After they lost their eastern lands to encroaching migrants, these Indians had used the very trails whites had fashioned to travel west.

Largely because their notions of progress, prosperity, society, and family were specific and well ingrained, whites found Indian ways baffling. They branded as wasteful Plains Indians who used horses to roam widely in pursuit of buffalo. Due to their cultural myopia, whites judged Indians who eschewed profit as anomalies, deserving of

AFRICAN-AMERICAN PIONEERS

Freed from slavery, African Americans, such as this woman and child, built homesteads and new lives out West.

⇒ SEWARD'S FOLLY ⇒

ALTHOUGH RUSSIA had claimed the Alaska peninsula for over fifty years, by the 1850s sporadic warfare with the Tlingit Indians combined with over-trapping of the sea otter to make it uneconomic. Further, the Crimean War had raised Russian fears that Britain might attempt to occupy Alaska by force as a natural extension of Canada. They therefore hoped the United States would buy the territory.

William Seward

The opportunity came in 1867 when American fishermen petitioned Secretary of State William Seward for fishing rights in Alaskan waters. When the Russians refused, Seward, a keen expansionist, offered to buy Alaska for $5 million. On the night of March 29, 1867, the Russian ambassador called on Seward and took advantage of his enthusiasm to raise the price to $7.2

million. By morning they had agreed a formal treaty, which Seward put to the Senate the same day. He easily secured Senate approval, but the House of Representatives stalled as many criticized the secrecy of the treaty negotiations. There was also adverse reaction in the press, which described the *"barren, worthless, God-forsaken region"* variously as *"Walrussia," "Seward's Icebox,"* and *"Seward's Folly."*

President Andrew Johnson's impeachment trial further delayed ratification, although some favored the sale because of Russian support for the Union during the Civil War. Once the idea circulated that the acquisition was a natural part of U.S. expansion and could isolate Canada, congressional and public opposition ceased, and the treaty was finally ratified on July 14, 1868.

ESKIMO FAMILY
More native peoples entered the United States with Seward's purchase of Alaska in 1867.

extinction. Nor could whites find much merit in Native Americans' political or social organization. Most Indians lived in groups of several hundred people led by an individual or several individuals assisted by a council of elders. Perhaps most startling of all to whites, most Native American societies practiced plural marriage.

ALASKA

The addition of Alaska to the West added to the mounting cultural confusion. As early as 1867, a Russian minister to the United States approached Secretary of State William H. Seward about the region. Could Seward, he wondered, convince Congress to purchase Alaska from Russia, which regarded the vast area as an economic drawback? Although most Americans mistakenly thought of Alaska as a remote, frozen wasteland, Seward laid

a treaty before Congress in March 1867. Following a pro-Alaska campaign, the Senate ratified the treaty in April 1867. Even though journalists and others derided the action, calling the new acquisition "Seward's Folly" and "Seward's Ice Box," the addition of Alaska enlarged the American West by 586,400 miles, at a cost of about two cents an acre.

The acquisition of Alaska also expanded the West's native population. Such groups as the Kwakiutl, Tlingit, and Nootka, in southern Alaska, lived by fishing for salmon and trading the skins of furbearing animals. Farther north, Eskimos and Aleuts pursued such sea mammals as whales in skin-covered kayaks and open boats, speared seals through holes in the ice and walrus along its edges, or hunted such land animals as caribou and polar bear.

TEACHING NATIVE AMERICANS
Native American children in the West were schooled in the language, customs, values, and religion of the dominant society. These children, with their Native American teacher, are wearing white people's clothing.

Why, many whites wondered, did native peoples allow the West's vast resources to lie essentially undiscovered and unexploited? At the same time, native peoples generally failed to understand white values, especially the profit mentality. Buffalo Bird Woman, a Hidatsa, thought it ridiculous and even sacrilegious that white American farmers exhausted the land to grow more bushels of corn than they could use.

In Arizona a Yavapi woman named Nellie Quail related that after her people identified tracks of Jesus Christ in Arizona's remote Verde Valley, they regarded the place as sacred and attempted to preserve it. During the 1880s a white American heard the story, fenced the area, and began charging entrance fees. Quail failed to understand how anyone could seek profit from a holy site. Similar misinterpretations plagued relations between whites and the West's Spanish-heritage peoples, some of whom qualified as natives. By 1865 thousands of other Hispanics had migrated from Central America and Mexico, filling the Southwest with a rich culture and historical heritage of their own.

Yet most whites turned a jaundiced eye on Hispanic peoples and cultures. Because they looked at the world in different ways, Hispanics and whites disagreed on the definition of progress. On the one hand, Hispanics generally had adapted to seasonal crops and limited markets. They lived slower lives than Yankees, devoted considerable time to family and religious activities, and perceived land as a long-term resource rather than reason for financial speculation. On the other hand, most whites undertook the arduous trip West to find fortunes, or at least to live more prosperous lives than they had in their former homes. Whites intended to take full advantage of land, trade routes, mines, forests, and animals to produce profit.

AFRICAN AMERICANS

African Americans also contributed to the growing proclivity of the West's cultural stew to boil over. Layered in with other cultures were those who, before the Civil War, had gone west as slaves and

---

✦HISPANIC LIFE IN THE SOUTHWEST✦

HISPANIC RESIDENTS of the Southwest retained much of their culture despite the coming of Anglo-Americans after Mexico ceded the region to the United States in 1848. In Arizona, many Hispanic families relied on ranching and agriculture for their livelihood, as they might have in Mexico or Spain. The state's constitution was based largely on Spanish code and rules, and Mexican food, such as chili and tortillas, was commonly available.

Using traditional techniques, skilled craftsmen throughout the region provided necessities for frontier life, including eating utensils, clothes,

shoes, and blankets. The arrival of canned food provided additional raw materials for another traditional craft, tinwork. Tin cans were hammered flat and made into picture frames, candleholders, and other household items.

Although religious, Hispanics in the Southwest were not always able to practice traditional Catholicism because priests were not available. In response to this need, folk Catholicism, which included recognition of local patron saints and many religious holidays, developed. This brand of Catholicism was prevalent in New Mexico. Healing methods, including herbs, rituals, and human

touch, were often combined with religious practices. The social graces ingrained in Hispanic culture also influenced life in the Southwest. There were specific rules of etiquette for almost every situation. For example, an unexpected guest would be invited to dine with the expectation that he would politely decline. Rules also existed for courting, marriage, and other life events.

HISPANIC OWNERS
For generations, from Spanish to Mexican to American times, Hispanic families owned ranches in the Southwest. An example was the Lugo family of Bell, California.

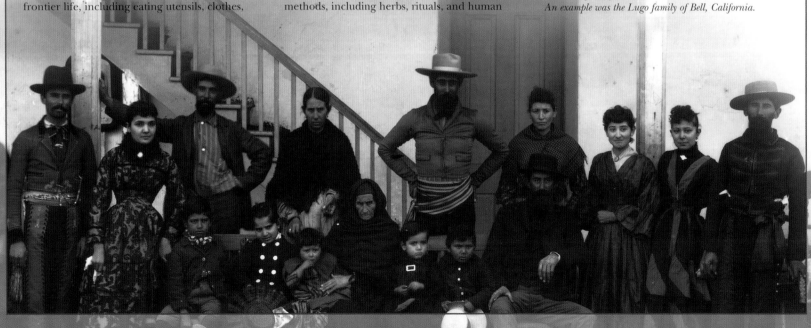

"THE ... GOD OF GLORY HAS WORKED IN ME. I HAVE HAD OPEN AIR INTERVIEWS WITH THE LIVING SPIRIT OF GOD FOR MY PEOPLE; AND WE ARE GOING TO LEAVE THE SOUTH."

—BENJAMIN "PAP" SINGLETON, 1880, ON LEADING "EXODUSTERS" TO KANSAS

free blacks and, after the war, continued to migrate in growing numbers. African-American men soon learned they could make the best money as cowboys, drovers, or soldiers. In 1866 Congress authorized African-American regiments of cavalry and infantry. Despite old horses, inadequate equipment, poor food, and blatant racism, black men rushed to join. They chalked up an excellent record of service with higher rates of reenlistment and lower rates of desertion than white regiments.

Other African Americans moved into riverboat towns and cities where they clustered in low-paying, menial jobs. They worked for a pittance in cash and scraps of food as domestic servants, cooks, laundresses, day laborers, porters, and deckhands. Despite the obstacles, some of them established businesses or entered the professions. Barbering offered upward mobility for black men in many western cities, while a significant number of black women became teachers, boardinghouse owners, and small entrepreneurs.

Former slaves known as Exodusters, after the Biblical exodus of people freed from captivity, traveled up the Missouri River to Kansas or journeyed overland to Oklahoma and Colorado to escape the evils of sharecropping, tenant farming, and antiblack sentiment. In 1870 African Americans in Kansas numbered 17,108. In 1877 Benjamin "Pap" Singleton led a group of Exodusters to Kansas, where they founded Nicodemus. Other African-American communities in Kansas sprang up in Atchison, Kansas City, Lawrence, Leavenworth, Topeka, and Wyandotte. By 1880 black Kansans totaled 43,107.

⇒ BUFFALO SOLDIERS ⇐

BUFFALO SOLDIERS were the black cavalry regiments who served in the West after the Civil War. The name was bestowed by the Comanches and Cheyennes, who thought the soldiers' hair resembled the buffalo's woolly coat.

In July 1866, in response to the need for more troops on the expanding western frontier, Congress approved the establishment of two cavalry and four (later two) infantry regiments composed of African Americans. With the prospect of earning $13 a month plus room, board, and lodging, there was no shortage of volunteers, many of whom had already served with Union forces during the war.

Although many white officers refused postings to the new units, the Ninth Cavalry and Tenth Cavalry were mustered into service. Colonel Edward Hatch took command of the Ninth, which was posted to Texas in June

BLACK COWBOY
African Americans who did not become soldiers could make relatively good money as cowboys. This New Mexican cowboy was known as "Nigger Bob."

1867 and made responsible for protecting stage routes and settlements in the area. Many Texans saw the regiment's presence as an insult due to Texas's support of the Confederacy.

Transferred to New Mexico in 1876, the Ninth Cavalry spent five years engaged against the Apaches before moving north in 1881. After attracting more odium by evicting illegal white settlers from Indian Territory, in 1890 they took part in the Ghost Dance Campaign, although they were not present at the Wounded Knee massacre.

The Tenth Cavalry, under Colonel Benjamin Grierson, met considerable prejudice at Fort Leavenworth. Posted to Fort Riley in 1867, they engaged in successful actions against the Sioux and Cheyennes. During the late 1870s and early 1880s, the Tenth was part of the force that drove the Apache chief Victorio into Mexico. Later, with Lieutenant Henry Flipper, the first black regular army officer, they fought Geronimo, a campaign in which Sergeant William McBrayar won the Congressional Medal of Honor.

The Buffalo Soldiers gained a reputation for courage and gallantry in battle, maintaining the lowest desertion rate in U.S. military history.

Some facets of the African-American migration set off alarm bells in the minds of white westerners. Because black migrants often arrived in large numbers and destitute condition, they elicited harsh treatment from residents anxious about their own ability to survive on the Plains. When economically successful, however, African-American migrants raised the hackles of westerners who feared economic competition from "inferiors" who they believed would accept low pay and poor conditions.

Because the existence of prosperous African Americans planted doubt and trepidation in the minds of other westerners, they have seldom come to the fore in the historical record. Yet they were numerous. Mary Ellen Pleasant arrived in San Francisco during the Gold Rush and became a restaurateur and investor during the 1860s. An

indomitable woman with a penchant for seizing opportunities, Pleasant established elegant restaurants and boardinghouses as well as laundries that offered jobs to black women and men.

ASIANS

Given the qualms and prejudices rippling throughout the West, it is unsurprising that whites mistrusted Indians and Indians mistrusted whites, while whites, Hispanics, and African Americans developed suspicions of each other. Perhaps the one group against whom they could all unite were Asians, who practiced religions, spoke languages, and dressed in ways few westerners had ever seen or heard. Shortly after the Civil War the first significant number of Asians arrived in Hawaii and California. The largest group of migrating Asians

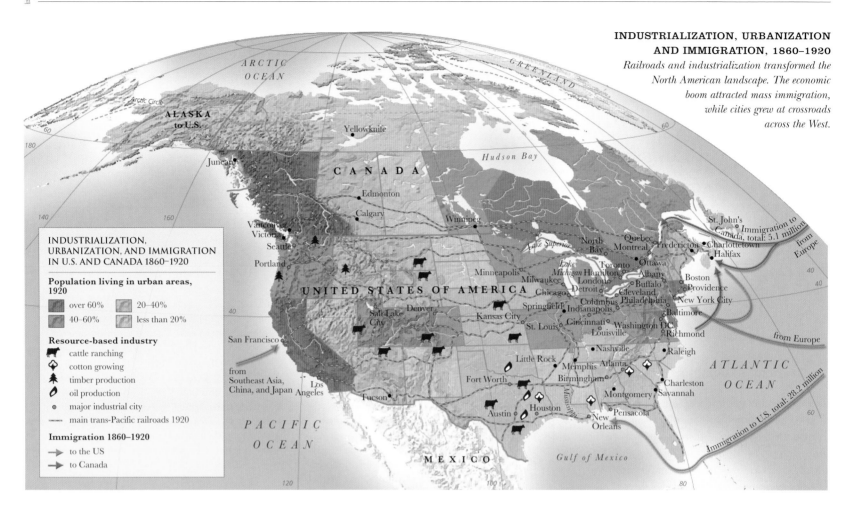

INDUSTRIALIZATION, URBANIZATION AND IMMIGRATION, 1860–1920
Railroads and industrialization transformed the North American landscape. The economic boom attracted mass immigration, while cities grew at crossroads across the West.

INDUSTRIALIZATION, URBANIZATION, AND IMMIGRATION IN U.S. AND CANADA 1860–1920

Population living in urban areas, 1920

- over 60%
- 40–60%
- 20–40%
- less than 20%

Resource-based industry

- cattle ranching
- cotton growing
- timber production
- oil production
- major industrial city
- main trans-Pacific railroads 1920

Immigration 1860–1920

- → to the US
- → to Canada

came from China, primarily as a result of the 1868 Burlingame Treaty, which established reciprocal trade, travel, and immigration between the United States and China.

Of more than 100,000 Chinese who migrated to the continental United States between 1870 and 1877, more than 90 percent were men who worked as miners, railroad builders, factory workers, entrepreneurs, vendors, fishermen, and agriculturalists. By the late 1870s more than 70,000 Chinese men and fewer than 4,000 women lived and worked in California alone.

Asian immigrants helped pioneer other parts of the West as well. Ah Yuen of Evanston, Wyoming, worked as a cook in mining and railroad camps during the 1860s and 1870s, and later held a prominent place in Old Pioneer celebrations. In Warrens, Idaho, a Chinese immigrant named "Polly" married homesteader Charlie Bemis. During the 1880s they built a successful homestead and helped enlarge the Warrens area.

The case of Polly Bemis exposes another misgiving that haunted many westerners: they dreaded the idea of marriage between one cultural group and another. Westerners opposed intermarriage so widely that the late-nineteenth century marked the rise of antimiscegenation

JAPANESE IMMIGRANTS
Tens of thousands of Asians entered the United States in the late nineteenth century. Many, like this Japanese family, adopted American ways, but their presence added to the region's racial uneasiness.

statutes throughout the West. In 1862 Oregon prohibited marriage not only between whites and African Americans, but between whites and "Orientals," also called Mongolians. Three years later Arizona barred blacks, mulattos, Indians, and Mongolians from marrying whites. And in 1885 the Choctaw council passed a law making black-Choctaw marriage a felony.

With westerners' sensitivities strained, the West provided a giant petri dish for racial and ethnic enmity. Other differences among westerners further engendered suspicion and conflict.

In 1867 Martha White McWhirter helped establish the Woman's Commonwealth, a Christian socialist, feminist, and celibate community in Belton, Texas. Although the group achieved autonomy and financial success, it drew searing criticism and disdain from clergy, family members, and neighbors.

Other westerners feared Jewish immigrants, many of whom founded agricultural communities on the Great Plains. In 1882 they organized at Beersheba, Kansas, and Painted Woods, in Dakota Territory. Although some Jewish farm families endured and even prospered, most moved to cities, including Omaha, Nebraska; Grand Forks, North Dakota; Seattle, Washington; and Portland, Oregon. There they established businesses and communities that included the rabbis and temples they had lacked while living in rural areas.

Catholics also elicited their share of suspicion. Many native-born westerners opposed Irish and German Catholic settlers because they viewed them as "Papists" intent on undermining the American system and its values. In truth, numerous Catholic migrants established schools and hospitals throughout the West. The Sisters of the Presentation of the Blessed Virgin Mary made their way in 1888 from Ireland to Dakota Territory, where they founded schools and hospitals for Native Americans.

The high drama and low chicanery of the Indian wars have overshadowed defiant battles among other groups of westerners. A similar, if far less bloody, scenario played out among the federal government, western settlers and entrepreneurs, and Hispanics of the Southwest.

HISPANICS

Like Native Americans, Hispanics witnessed the shrinking of their lands and influence, sometimes through the machinations of their own people, other times at the hands of white migrants who poured into Texas, New Mexico, Arizona, and California. Although white settlers often hoped, as one stated, that under white rule "everything would improve; population would increase; consumption would be greater, and industry would follow," the results were frequently less positive for Hispanics.

Texas soon exploded in controversy and strife. Long before the arrival of whites, Tejanos—or Hispanic Texans—held land under the system of derechos, or rights. In this structure, families and their descendants rather than individuals owned land. But when white migrants arrived they instituted American law and divided family lands among individual heirs. As a result many Hispanic heirs sold their lands or lost them to land-grabbing schemes.

The situation worsened when whites established cattle ranches in Texas. Most Tejanos lacked the necessary funds to erect fences, dig wells, purchase feed, and experiment with improved breeds of cattle. White ranches pushed Tejanos to marginal lands and subsistence-level ranching. By the time large-scale farming replaced ranching in Texas during the 1870s, most Tejanos, who constituted 73 percent of

FAR FROM HOME
Some Native American children were educated at local day schools, but many, like these three girls, attended boarding schools hundreds of miles from home. These girls from the Dakotas were students at Virginia's Hampton Institute.

the state's population, could do little more than provide unskilled labor for these ventures.

Similarly, in New Mexico, many Hispanics lost their lands to newcomers through sale, fraud, or as a result of congressional refusal to give them title to communal farming and grazing lands. The Surveyor General and Court of Private Land Claims confirmed only 24 percent of Hispanic land claims, and the Claims Court confirmed an astonishingly low 6 percent. Consequently, women continued to farm tiny irrigated plots, while their menfolk scoured New Mexico and Colorado for seasonal, poorly paid labor on farms, ranches, railroads, or in mines. Although a small proportion of Hispanics retained power in New Mexico and served in the territorial legislature, most found themselves reduced to poverty and powerlessness.

In California the collapse of large Hispanic-owned ranchos led to the virtual disappearance of jobs for sheepherders, vaqueros, and other skilled rural workers. Typically, whites who purchased former rancho lands established relatively small farms and used family labor or hired white farm workers. California Hispanics sought jobs elsewhere, frequently following harvests around the state in hopes of earning a pittance as field-workers.

The developing western economy gradually created a low-paid, manual, Hispanic work force. Although Hispanics had comprised 62 percent of

⊹CHINATOWN, SAN FRANCISCO⊹

SAN FRANCISCO'S Chinatown was home to tens of thousands of Chinese immigrants in the late 1800s. Also known as "Tangrenbu," the six-block segment of the city—which later expanded to ten blocks—was a respite for Chinese Bay Area immigrants who endured racial intolerance from European immigrants. In Tangrenbu the Chinese were able to live in a manner similar to that of their homeland. They transformed the buildings and open spaces with brightly colored paint, canopies, lanterns, and potted plants. Women rarely ventured out alone, unless they were prostitutes or servants. Men wore the traditional queues (long braids and a shaved forehead), and many immigrants wore traditional dress.

As early as 1838, there were Chinese in Yerba Buena, a Mexican village that became San Francisco in 1849. Many of the first immigrants were merchants and traders who would help bring laborers from China to do work declined by others, such as building railroads, dredging swampland, and doing laundry. Throughout the 1850s, the number of Chinese immigrants increased immensely: 20,000 passed through San Francisco customs in 1852 alone. By 1856 San Francisco's first Chinese-language newspaper, *The Oriental*, listed over thirty general stores in Tangrenbu, as well as butchers, boarding houses, restaurants, doctors, and herb stores.

ETHNIC COEXISTENCE
Even in San Francisco's Chinatown there was ethnic variety, as is suggested by this photograph of a Jewish balloon man at work in the Chinese enclave.

TIBURCIO VÁSQUEZ
Mexican American bandits became folk heroes for fighting Anglo-American domination. In California Vásquez, a notorious robber, was sheltered by local Mexican Americans.

the workers in the Southwest in 1860, this share rose to 80 percent by 1870. And as their population grew, their lives deteriorated. In such border cities as El Paso, Texas, families lived in slums called barrios, devoid of sewers, paved streets, and sidewalks. Women tried to mitigate the harsh conditions by hauling water from rivers or public water pipes and gathering driftwood or loose coal from railroad yards for cooking fuel. Some took paid employment as domestic servants, nursemaids, laundresses, and even prostitutes. Others headed households while husbands and sons ranged over the Southwest, following the crops.

Like Indians, Hispanics resisted. Throughout the post-Civil War years, educated Hispanics who had retained or made fortunes infiltrated the political system. After the Civil War, when Estevan Ochoa profited from his freighting, mining, and sheep-raising businesses, he successfully ran for mayor of Tucson, Arizona. In California in the 1890s, Don Romualdo Pacheco served as state senator and lieutenant governor, and Don Ignacio Sepulveda sat on the superior court bench in Los Angeles. Besides helping themselves, these individuals tried to help other Hispanic people. But even in Tucson, where a Spanish-speaking elite dominated, approximately 80 percent of employed Hispanics fell at the bottom of the economic ladder.

HISPANIC RESISTANCE

Many Hispanic workers tried to improve their lot. Using the few evening hours left after a twelve-to-fourteen–hour day in factory or field, they attended night schools to improve their English and learn

MANUAL LABOR IN ARIZONA

In California and the Southwest, Hispanics constituted a large portion of the population. Although some were prosperous business owners and politicians, many Hispanics were low on the economic ladder. In places like Arizona, where this horse and pack- burro caravan traveled, Hispanics often made their living by manual labor.

vocational skills. Thousands of others, women and men alike, organized or joined labor unions, which staged strikes and vitriolic protests.

Others fought back with physical force. Tejano leader Juan Cortina, renowned in Mexican ballads, resisted white land encroachments first in the Cortina "wars" of 1859–61. Some said that Cortina, son of a Tejano rancher, was little more than a ruthless caudillo, or chieftain, but others characterized him as a man of the people, a true folk hero. Through the 1870s, by pronunciamentos and personal action, Cortina led Hispanic defiance against white Texans and especially against the Texas Rangers. Joaquín Murieta, California's Robin Hood, assumed an even greater mythical stature. John Rollin Ridge, a Cherokee journalist, enlarged and spread bandit Murieta's story. Reportedly beaten, forced to witness his wife's rape, and thrown out of California's mines by whites, Murieta supposedly retaliated through thievery and bloodshed. Actually, he was probably a composite character representing a variety of outlaws who were more social bandits than career criminals. Driven outside of the law by conditions beyond their control, the Joaquín Murietas of the Southwest set out to extract justice for their people.

Arizona and New Mexico also suffered armed revolt during this era. Land feuds of the 1880s provoked Hispanic ranchers to form Las Gorras Blancas—the White Caps—in 1888. Resentful and feeling that their backs were against an unyielding wall, the White Caps burned crops, threatened white landowners, and retaliated where they could, such as riding against white ranchers who had fenced a public grazing area for their exclusive use.

A few whites protested the shoddy treatment of Hispanics. In an 1883 letter, poet Walt Whitman harangued Americans to "appreciate the splendor and sterling value" of Spanish-heritage peoples in the American Southwest. To Whitman, no group of people demonstrated a "grander" spirit of religion, loyalty, patriotism, courage, and honor.

Most Americans ignored the problem, however, choosing instead to romanticize the Spanish-heritage peoples of the Southwest. In spite of the realities of barrio life, an 1890 article in *Harper's Monthly* depicted "Texo-Mexicans" as "picturesque foreign waifs" who rendered Texas "fertile in vivid contrast and rich local coloring. " In 1891 another writer called New Mexico's adobe communities "a picture, a romance, a dream, all in one."

Meanwhile, many Hispanics lived on the edge, fearful of lynchings and riots. Vicious riots against Hispanics occurred in Beeville, Texas, in 1894 and in Laredo five years later, illuminating a problem that nineteenth-century leaders and reformers had not yet recognized and tackled.

⇢JOAQUÍN MURIETA⇠

THE FULL TRUTH about Joaquín Murieta (or Murietta; 1829?-1853?) will probably never be known. While there is general agreement that a man of that name led a band of outlaws in California in the early 1850s, fact has become confused with fiction since the 1854 publication of John Rollin Ridge's *The Life and Adventures of Joaquin Murieta*, portraying a dashing, romantic figure avenging wrong.

What is not in doubt is that the Foreign Miners Tax forced many Mexicans and Chinese off their mining claims in California. Among these was Joaquín Murieta, whose real name, by some accounts, was Joaquín Carillo. Whether from bitterness at being forced off his claim or whether, as legend says, from anger over his brother's murder or his wife's rape, Murieta led a gang intent on wreaking vengeance on American mining communities, burning houses and killing miners and prospectors. In 1852 the outlaws began to rob stagecoaches, and Murieta

reportedly killed a sheriff trying to capture him.

Because so many of the state's most notorious gang leaders shared the name Joaquín, in 1853 the California legislature authorized Harry Love to capture the "gang of robbers commanded by the five Joaquins." Love's posse found Murieta in a canyon and shot him as well as many of his band. The bandit's head was cut off, as was the hand of a confederate, "Three-Fingered Jack," as proof of their apprehension. Whether the head really was that of Murieta is still disputed, but both appendages were displayed in sideshows for many years afterward.

GOLD RUSH BOOM TOWNS
Sheep Camp, Alaska, was one of the boom towns that sprang up as a result of the Klondike Gold Rush.

"WHILE THE LIFE WAS HARD AND IN SOME WAYS EXACTING, YET IT WAS FREE AND WILD AND CONTAINED THE ELEMENTS OF DANGER WHICH MY NATURE CRAVED."

—NAT LOVE, 1907, ON BEING A COWBOY

DEVELOPMENT RUN RAMPANT

AMERICANS HAD LONG IMAGINED THE WEST AS A HAVEN FOR SMALL ENTREPRENEURS. BUT INDEPENDENTLY OWNED FARMS, RANCHES, AND MINES FOUND IT HARD TO COMPETE WITH THE LARGE COMPANIES THAT OVERTOOK THESE INDUSTRIES. EVEN THE FAMOUSLY SELF-RELIANT COWBOY WAS OFTEN THE EMPLOYEE OF A BIG BUSINESS.

THE WEST increasingly fell victim to the aspirations of post-Civil War America: limitless growth, unstoppable progress, and unimaginable prosperity. When Congress passed the Homestead Act in 1862, it had envisioned a region of family farms, but much of the West proved inhospitable to small farmers. In spite of the excitement of taking up western land, homesteading was a demanding business. Raging fires swept through fields and killed animals, torrential downpours caused destructive floods, and cyclones carried away entire barns. Winter

blizzards were so dense that men wore ropes around their waists to guide them from house to barn and back, while in the summer hordes of grasshoppers darkened the sky and ate crops to the ground.

Many migrants left to return to former homes or try their luck elsewhere. Others stayed, believing that hardship was, as one Dakota woman said, "a natural part of life," and hoped that conditions would improve. Indeed, homesteading grew better for some. In the late 1880s a Norwegian minister's wife remarked that "as time passed people's circumstances improved."

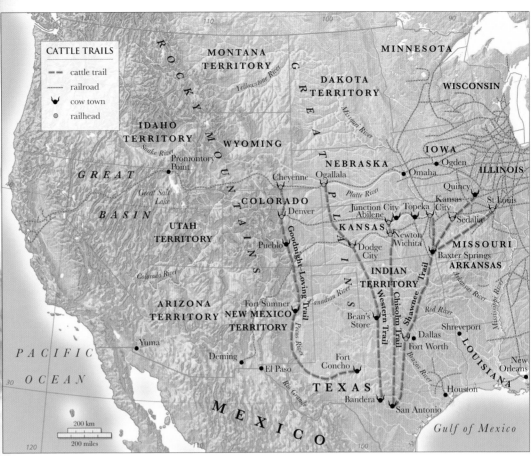

CATTLE DRIVE

Driving herds of cattle from Texas to be sold on the auction block in Abilene, Kansas, was an ongoing venture in the 1870s. It involved cowboys, ranchers, and cattle buyers, some of them unscrupulous.

CATTLE TRAILS

The cattle industry of Texas and the Southwest developed from an infrastructure established under the Spanish, focusing on a triangle straddling the Rio Grande. Transcontinental railroads shifted the focus away from ports to railheads such as Kansas City. Meanwhile, the growth of population on the West Coast created new markets. Between 1866 and 1886 some 10 million Texan longhorns were driven across the trails to Kansas and Missouri or along the Pecos to the western markets.

Seldom was the situation rosy in the homesteaders' West, however. Through mass purchases and corrupt practices, eight of every nine acres of federal land intended for homesteaders fell into the hands of speculators, railroads, and state governments. Similar procedures also undermined the intent of the Desert Land Act of 1877. Corporate farmers, cattle ranchers, and lumber companies escalated their holdings and swelled their profits, often to the detriment of small farmers.

CATTLE DRIVES AND COWBOYS

Large-scale ventures received other boosts as well. The disappearance of buffalo on the Great Plains created a void that begged to be filled. Although several entrepreneurs recognized the opportunity, Joseph G. McCoy, a cattle dealer in Springfield, Illinois, seized it. In 1867 he formed a partnership with his brother's company, which shipped cattle to New York and New Orleans. McCoy had resolved to drive cattle from Texas to a railhead in Abilene, Kansas, without losing huge numbers to Native Americans or "Texas fever."

He personally convinced Abilene officials that a "long drive" was possible, oversaw construction of a stockyard, and haggled with railroad companies for a payment of $5 for each cattle car his company shipped from Abilene.

Thirty-five thousand steers went on the auction block in Abilene during McCoy's first year of operation, and 75,000 the following year. Abilene sprouted into a dusty and violent town, which

THE CHUCK WAGON

Cowpunchers take their meal around the chuck wagon c. 1875–80. Enduring low rations of beans and coffee was a minor problem compared to keeping cattle together and moving in one direction.

welcomed an influx of cowboys, ranchers, and cattle buyers each spring. Sporting flowing hair and buckskins with fringes, Joe McCoy became mayor of Abilene. Nearly a western icon himself, he claimed to have watched infamous gambler and gunfighter Wild Bill Hickok clear the town with a couple of well-placed shots.

In the meantime, ranchers pounced on McCoy's scheme. Railroad advertising assured them of fortune at the end of the trail if they drove more and more cattle to Abilene each season. By 1870 a steer that cost $9 in Texas and $4 in trail expenses brought as much as $28 in Abilene. Ranchers tried but failed to hold the line against unstable markets and high interest rates on loans to purchase cattle. During the Panic of 1873, scores of ranchers joined the ranks of the bankrupt.

During the late 1870s and early 1880s, recovery began. According to a Texas woman rancher, "It was once again exciting to turn my herd toward the trail." As profits escalated, American and European investors sank huge sums into the cattle industry. Some capitalists bought inexpensive

✦COWBOY GEAR✦

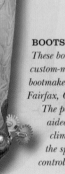

Cowboy, c. 1887

COWBOYS adopted much of their equipment from the Spanish/Mexican vaqueros who preceded them. Two crucial accessories were a bandanna and hat. In addition to absorbing sweat, bandannas were worn over the nose and mouth during dust storms. The high-crowned, wide-brimmed hat gave shade from the sun, kept dust out of the eyes, and kept rain from running down the back. While wide-brimmed straw hats (sombreros) were common in the South, hats in the North, with slightly narrower brims, were made of strong felt to resist harsher weather. In 1865 John B. Stetson produced his popular "Boss of the Plains" hat with a flat, high crown and four-inch brim. Another popular type, the ten-gallon hat, with a high, rounded crown, came from the vaqueros, who used to put decorative braids ("galons") around their hats.

Chaps, heavy leather trousers worn to protect the legs from cattle horns and spiked thickets, got their name from "chaparreras," the Spanish word for the garment. Stovepipe boots—with 17-inch tops and 2-inch heels to catch and hold the stirrups securely—were necessary for the long days (12–14 hours) spent in the saddle.

The lariat, a rawhide noose for snaring a steer, was essential. So was the heavy Western saddle designed for long hours on horseback. The pommel, a strong, upright horn, provided protection as well as a solid tie-point when roping cattle. The rear cantle was high enough to give support but low enough to allow easy dismounting.

BOOTS
These boots were custom-made by the bootmaker Blucher in Fairfax, Oklahoma. The pointed toes aided in climbing and the spurs in controlling horses.

COWBOY HAT
A high-crowned, wide-brimmed hat gave shade and protection from dust and rain.

SADDLE
The cowboy's saddle, like this example from Texas in the 1850s, was designed for long hours on horseback. It had a high pommel (horn) at the front, a cantle at the back, long stirrups, and flaps to protect the cowboy's legs from the horse's sweat.

government land, hired experienced ranchers as advisers, and produced unheard-of profits. Others, notably the Swan Land and Cattle Company of Wyoming, borrowed $3.75 million in the East to purchase a hundred-mile swath of small ranches. Swan officials merged the ranches into a corporate monolith, which boasted more than 100,000 head of cattle.

From the long drive to the Swan Company, the scene was set for the emergence of a new American folk hero, the cowboy. This bold breed learned their skills from Mexican vaqueros, or "buckaroos," as many pronounced it. With rope in hand and beneath him a well-trained cutting horse—a horse that separates a cow from a herd—the cowboy took on cantankerous 1,000-pound Texas longhorns and forced them across trails fraught with danger. Cowboys were usually in their teens and twenties; older men were hesitant to spend months "biting the dust" raised by cattle hooves, eating a diet consisting largely of bacon and beans, and fighting off would-be cattle thieves.

Despite the job's drawbacks and its wages of $25–$35 a month, men of all backgrounds chose to be cowboys: Confederate and Union veterans, farmers, sons of titled English families, Hispanics, and African Americans. By the 1870s African Americans had become a common sight on the trail, where they might fare well or badly at the hands of their fellow cowboys. In the mid-1870s, Texas cowboy Charles A. Siringo joined forces with an African-American cowboy named Gabe. During the spring of 1876, as they worked their way up the Chisholm Trail from Texas through Oklahoma to Kansas, the mustachioed and daring-eyed Siringo shared everything he had with Gabe. Only a few years later, however, Poll Allen, the leading cowboy with John Husley's Texas Twenty-Two Ranch, made it clear he hated blacks. When Husley hired a black cowboy in 1878, Allen ran the man off by taking potshots at him.

Despite such obstacles, some black cowboys became legendary. Emanuel Organ, known as Texas's greatest black cowboy during the 1870s, sometimes survived only by finding water in cow tracks and sleeping on frozen ground with a thin bedroll as protection. Organ was still in the saddle six months before he died—at the age of 90. Texas also produced black cowboy Willie M. "Bill" Pickett, who went from Oklahoma's 101 Ranch to rodeo fame and later to ranching on his own. Pickett became the first cowboy to gain fame for bulldogging cattle, or seizing a steer's horns and twisting its neck until it falls; some experts even credit Pickett with inventing the technique.

While nineteenth-century ranching achieved a glamorous image, it also reverberated across the West in less-than-romantic ways. Large-scale ranchers overgrazed grass down to bare dirt, wildly overstocked their herds, and used water until supplies reached near-scarcity. Anxious to protect their herds from rustlers, ranchers broke up the range by stringing barbed-wire fences around their property and government-owned grazing lands. The disastrous winter of 1886–87 revealed the folly of such actions. Thousands of cattle died far from feed or snared in snowdrift-covered fences. In May 1887 the Swan Land and Cattle Company of Wyoming went bankrupt. Other companies survived only by restricting herds and growing hay as feed.

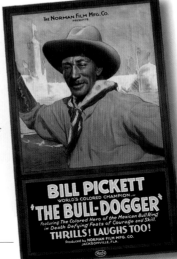

BILL PICKETT
Pickett was an African-American cowboy and rodeo star who pioneered a steer-wrestling technique called bulldogging.

The days of the open range and long drives had ended. By the late 1880s cowboys spent most of their time rounding up cattle and digging postholes for the miles of fencing. They also watched the size of their herds decline and sheep slip into their midst. As cattle herds shrank, Mormons in Utah and southern Idaho, Basques in Nevada, Hispanics in New Mexico, and Scots in Washington and Montana introduced sheepraising. They sold the wool to eastern textile factories and the meat to western slaughterhouses.

Sheep raisers drew the wrath of cattle ranchers and stock raisers who claimed that sheep ripped open the land with their sharp hoofs, destroyed vegetation with their close cropping, and fouled pastures so that cattle refused to graze on them. Ranchers resorted to extreme tactics

to run off sheep herders. As one Montana rancher threatened, "If you take your sheep to Powder River bring your coffin along. You will need it."

Other sheep herds fell at the hand of night riders—called gunnysackers for the masks they wore—who left slaughtered sheep and herd dogs in their wake. Near Rifle, Colorado, gunnysackers drowned approximately 4,000 sheep. Others set flocks on fire, dynamited them, or drove them over cliffs. Only a determination to use their share of the West—and the considerable profits from raising sheep—gave sheep herders the will to resist. By 1900 almost 25 million sheep foraged in Arizona, California, Colorado, New Mexico, Utah, and Wyoming.

FARMING

Like ranching, farming also had to turn corporate to survive. After the Panic of 1873, the bankrupt Northern Pacific railroad set out to recover its losses by coaxing more farmers to the Plains. The company supplied Oliver Dalrymple, a master wheat farmer from Minnesota, with 4,500 acres of prime land in the Red River Valley in present-day North Dakota. Dalrymple launched a bonanza farm (a huge farm clearly intended to make money) by hiring scores of workers and bringing in railroad cars stuffed with agricultural machinery. When Dalrymple exceeded the Northern Pacific's wildest fantasies, eastern investors took note. They elbowed out small farmers by quickly buying up most of the 300-mile-long valley so that in 1878 bonanza farms

CALIFORNIA ORANGES
California produce made big profits for investors but supplied low wages for the labor force that harvested it, like these Los Angeles orange pickers, 1895.

AGRICULTURAL TRADE
St. Paul-based L.L. May & Co. and Seattle-based Lilly, Bogardus & Co. sold agricultural products.

checkerboarded the area. In other parts of the West the presence of cheap labor facilitated large-scale farming. In California, Hispanic, Japanese, and Chinese workers cleared the land; built roads; dug drainage and irrigation ditches; and planted, weeded, and harvested crops for less than half the pay of white laborers. In 1881 Asian harvesters earned 80 cents while whites collected $1.50.

MINING AND LUMBER

Besides ranching and farming, mining also went big time during the late nineteenth century. With their mining pans, sacks of gold dust, and turbulent experiences in the "diggings," the lives of miners appeared nearly as exciting as cowboys. In reality, the number of individual miners decreased. Although prospectors found gold and silver from Colorado to Alaska between 1866 and 1896, these surface minerals played out rapidly.

In Colorado the most important mining boom of the 1870s took place in California Gulch. Leadville, Creede, and Cripple Creek followed. Unheard-of wealth resulted for the fortunate. Storekeeper Horace Austin Warner Tabor grubstaked former shoemaker August Rische and former steelworker George Hook for a return of one-third of whatever they discovered. Although Rische and Hook seemed unlikely to succeed as miners, they struck silver on Frayer Hill at a point that appealed to them because it lay in the shade of a pine tree. Tabor's original investment amounted to about $50, but he sold his share for $1 million, which financed a claim-buying spree. After Tabor married his second wife, Elizabeth "Baby Doe" Tabor, in 1883, the couple became Leadville benefactors, even building an 800-seat, $40,000 theater in 1879, which they named—what else?—the Tabor Opera House.

Farther north, in Alaska, prospectors unearthed gold in the southeastern panhandle as early as 1872. Yet it was the rich strikes twenty-four years later that set off a frenzy reminiscent of the California Gold Rush. In 1896 miners spotted fragments of gold in Bonanza Creek near the mouth of the Klondike River, in Canada's Klondike Territory. Two years later others found gold in the hills above Nome, on Alaska's far western edge. Even Nome's sandy beaches contained gold.

Impoverished by a deep depression at home, gold seekers flooded Alaska, reaching Nome directly by ship and the Klondike through its Alaskan gateways. The Klondike proved a comparatively orderly rush because of the Canadian North West Mounted Police, but prospectors faced daunting obstacles in getting there. Most started out in Dyea and braved the steep, treacherous Chilkoot Pass rather than follow the easier but longer way from Skagway through White Horse Pass.

Women as well as men rushed to Alaska and the Klondike to share in the wealth. Married and single women came from all over the world to take on work as saloon girls and prostitutes, as cooks and boardinghouse keepers, and as miners. Like male miners, women often found disappointment and frustration at the end of the trail. When Georgia White reached Dawson City in the Klondike during the spring of 1898, she reported that it was "very hard to get work" and that "many disgusted men were selling outfits."

Unfortunately for individual prospectors, mineral wealth lying far beneath the surface

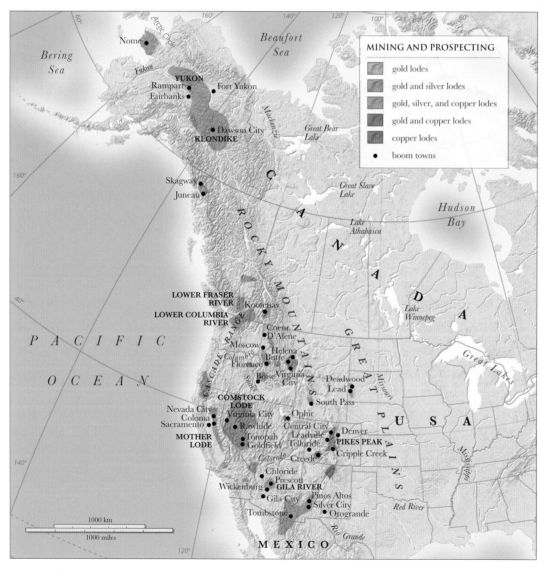

MINING AND PROSPECTING

The rush to mine gold in Alaska and the Klondike in the late nineteenth century was one part of a far-flung process of exploiting the West's mineral reserves. In Canada and the United States, the richness of western mineral resources drove governments to consolidate territories and promoted the growth of large, well-capitalized mining companies equipped with the necessary machinery and manpower.

DAWSON CITY GOLD
With the discovery of gold on Bonanza Creek in 1896, Dawson City swiftly became the largest city in Canada west of Winnipeg. Like other Klondike gold rush cities, it was supported by its mining, supply industry, gambling, and racy public image.

demanded large mining companies with capital, machinery, and know-how. Across the West, Eastern and British capitalists supplied the funds to sink mine shafts, build crushing mills, and hire miners willing to burrow deep into the earth. The rewards proved enormous: Idaho's Bunker Hill and Sullivan Mine alone held deposits of silver and lead worth $250 million. Meanwhile, mines in Colorado, Idaho, and Montana yielded huge amounts of lead and zinc. The Tri-State District of southwest Missouri, southeastern Kansas, and northeastern Indian Territory contained even greater deposits of those minerals. By mining a billion dollars worth of lead and zinc in a fifty-year period, the Tri-State District established itself as the world's leading supplier.

In 1875 Montana miners developed the world's richest copper mine—the Anaconda—near Butte, while Arizona miners established the rich Copper Queen mine at Bisbee. When the nation's first electric-generating plant opened in New York City in 1882, it was clear that eastern businesses in need of copper wire would provide an ever-increasing demand for western copper.

Fossil fuels provided another source of power and profit. Mine smelters and other businesses shouted for more and more coal. As railroads expanded, they demanded immense amounts of coal, and mines in present-day Oklahoma, Kansas, Colorado, and other western areas spewed out millions of tons to supply them.

In the Pacific Northwest, stands of magnificent trees beckoned large-scale entrepreneurs. After the Civil War, lumber companies erected numerous sawmills along streams, rivers, and falls. Soon the crack of falling trees became a common sound. Forest after forest went to supply the nation with siding for houses and other buildings, shingles, fence posts, telegraph poles, firewood, and railroad ties, leaving behind barren hillsides prickly with stumps of once mighty trees.

Gradually, lumber interests devised ways—often devious and at the government's expense—to increase their holdings. When the Timber and Stone Act of 1878 offered for sale 160 acres of land unfit for farming and valuable "chiefly for timber," lumber company officials set out to recruit immigrants wherever they could find them—in cities, along waterfronts, and in cheap boardinghouses. They herded these men to claim timber lands, then transferred the deeds to company ownership. For their help immigrants received $5 or a meal. By 1900 misuse of the Timber and Stone Act caused nearly 3.6 million acres to fall into the hands of claimants, mostly lumber magnates.

The growth of corporate industry in the West also spawned a number of support enterprises, such as slaughtering, meat processing, logging, milling, and smelting. As early as 1868, San Francisco had fifteen iron works and machine shops. The city's Levi-Strauss Company supplied sturdy clothing, while banks, insurance companies, schools, hospitals, and wholesalers and retailers provided a variety of services.

Towns and cities also grew rapidly. By 1900 almost 30 percent of people in the Great Plains area were urban dwellers. Those who chose urban areas wanted to obtain schools for their children, find a more lucrative source of income, enter a trade or profession, or escape demanding farm or ranch work. But because each town or city usually sprang up as the offshoot of a specific function, such as serving as a railhead, many developed too quickly for proper planning to occur.

Near chaos often resulted. As one young California woman said, "False-front store buildings rubbed elbows with tar paper shacks, while pigs and chickens roamed the streets… criminals too…it isn't safe to be out at night unarmed." From St. Louis to Los Angeles, from San Diego to Seattle, urban dwellers longed for wells and sanitary facilities, board sidewalks and nightlamps, fire and police departments, and increased constraint of gambling and prostitution.

The West's economic flowering undoubtedly brought profit. Entrepreneurs and investors, farmers and merchants, railroads and steamships reaped huge returns. But other westerners benefited as well. Because neither western towns, farms, mining and lumbering camps, nor businesses could survive without women's labor, they took up paid employment outside their homes. A growing number of women, especially whites, worked as clerks in shops and offices; as operatives in factories, mills, and canneries; as journalists and writers; as seamstresses and milliners; as teachers and school superintendents; and as nurses and doctors.

Some westerners believed, however, that large-scale development was inimical to their interests. As early as the 1860s, Mormon leader Brigham Young urged his followers in Utah to reject imports from "the states" and to act as stewards for the Utah environment. Young ordered members of the Mormon church—also known as the Church of Jesus Christ of Latter-Day Saints—to establish textile, iron, beet sugar, and cotton production facilities. After the Panic of 1873 further demonstrated the instability of the nation's economy, 400 investors in Brigham City founded the United Order of Enoch and other similar organizations to bring together workers, experts, and resources under boards of managers. After Young died in 1877, the Mormon church reluctantly allowed its members to dig silver mines, lay railroad track, and expand trade. Church officials realized that if they failed to exploit Utah's resources, the many gentiles, or non-Mormons, pouring into Utah would happily do so.

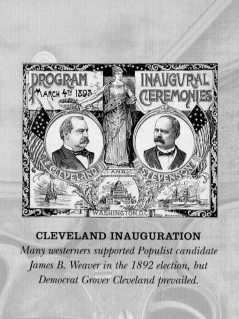

CLEVELAND INAUGURATION
Many westerners supported Populist candidate James B. Weaver in the 1892 election, but Democrat Grover Cleveland prevailed.

"THE FORCES OF REFORM THIS DAY ORGANIZED WILL NEVER CEASE TO MOVE FORWARD, UNTIL EVERY WRONG IS RIGHTED."

—PLATFORM OF THE PEOPLE'S
(OR POPULIST) PARTY, 1892

PROBLEMS AND POLITICS

THE WEST'S RAPID DEVELOPMENT PROMPTED FEVERED REACTIONS FROM THE PUBLIC. APPALLED BY THE DESTRUCTION OF WILDERNESS LANDS, CONSERVATIONISTS SPURRED THE FEDERAL GOVERNMENT TO ESTABLISH A NATIONAL PARK SYSTEM, WHILE WANING PROFITS AND WAGES IN THE WEST DROVE WORKERS TO FORM UNIONS AND FARMERS TO JOIN THE POPULIST PARTY.

AS SOME WESTERNERS pocketed their gains from economic development and others opposed growth, western resources suffered. Settlers themselves helped scar the West by fabricating a web of roads and railroad lines, punctuated with homes, barns, and other buildings. Those who farmed used sod plows that ripped into the deep roots of buffalo and mesquite grasses and sliced the Plains sod into layers. Gradually, natural grass cover disappeared, wind and rain eroded topsoil, and deep gullies etched their way into the earth.

TECHNOLOGY AND THE ENVIRONMENT

At the same time, increasingly sophisticated technology wounded the West. As commercial fisheries drove Chinese fishing families off the Pacific Northwest coastline, they brought with them improved nets, boats, and heavy equipment that trapped destructive numbers of abalone and snared such marine mammals as seals and sea lions.

Corporate farmers in California planted wheat on every available inch of land and destroyed all natural vegetation in their paths. Farmers also developed the technology to tap streams, rivers, and lakes to irrigate these crops. Tulare Lake in west central California, which once covered 760 square miles, shriveled to 36 square miles. Fish no longer bred in its water, and waterfowl disappeared from its shores.

Also in California, hydraulic strip-mining swept tons of soil and rock into rivers and choked canyons with debris that resulted in spring floods. When underground mining took over, companies stripped millions of feet of timber from the land to use as mine supports and fuel for their smelters. The air was soon fouled with smoke.

Even as economic development set the stage for ecological chaos, a conservation movement

CUTTING TREES

As trees were felled on a large scale, naturalists spoke out and the federal government began conservation programs. Here tree cutters stand inside the trunk of a redwood in 1892.

gathered momentum in the United States. During the 1870s, Ellen Swallow Richards, who received a Ph.D. in chemistry from the Massachusetts Institute of Technology, helped pioneer two new fields of study: home economics and environmental science.

The warnings and protestations of naturalist John Muir further alerted Americans to the risks enveloping the West. An irascible Scotsman who neither loved the wilderness nor hated civilization as much as most people think, Muir first came to public attention through the tireless exertions of his mentor, Jeanne Carr, of Oakland, California. When Muir wrote to Carr that "I owe all my best friends to you," he was not exaggerating. With Carr providing him advice and contacts, Muir set out to protect the West's trees and mountains from the tumultuous technology that was sweeping over the region, often leaving permanent destruction in its wake. Speaking in favor of what would later be termed conservation, Muir argued that "to obtain a hearing on behalf of nature from any other standpoint than that of human use is impossible." Along with the men and women of the Sierra Club, Muir especially championed those forest monarchs, the giant California redwoods.

THE FEDERAL GOVERNMENT AGAIN

The federal government—the single most powerful force in the nation—stepped into the breach. At the urging of Muir and professional forester Gifford Pinchot—whose mother was also a staunch environmentalist—the government, beginning in 1901, initiated a massive preservation program that eventually made it the largest single landowner in the West.

Such definitive action set off a national controversy. Many people believed that American resources would renew themselves over time, but others maintained that precious water, soil, animals, minerals, and trees would disappear in the foreseeable future. The latter group of individuals goaded the government to control and manage whatever resources the West had left. Meanwhile, objections emerged from westerners themselves. Some complained that federal control of resources would slow growth and diminish the influence of state and local governments. Ranchers refused to pay grazing fees and threatened with bodily harm the federal agents who tried to collect them. Protesters set fire to forest reserves in Colorado and Wyoming.

In addition to opposing conservation, westerners had a cornucopia of other complaints. When the Panic of 1873 and the droughts and farm problems of the 1880s and 1890s hit farmers, they flocked to the Farmers' Alliance, the Populist Party, and the Grange (or Patrons of Husbandry).

⇢POPULIST PARTY⇠

FORMALLY KNOWN as the People's Party of America, the Populist Party supported agrarian causes and criticized an increasingly industrialized society. It was born out of Farmers' Alliances that were formed in the late 1870s in the Midwest and the South. In June 1890, Kansas formed the first state-level People's Party.

The party proved surprisingly strong in the 1890 elections, with Democratic and/or Alliance candidates winning over forty contests. Two Populists won Senate seats that year (in Kansas and South Dakota). These successes planted the seeds for the establishment of a National People's Party in 1892. Based on the belief that governmental power reflects the power of the people, the party platform called for government control of transportation and communication systems, the direct election of senators, the elimination of poverty, and free coinage of silver. Populist presidential candidate James B. Weaver garnered 1 million popular and 22 electoral votes in the 1892 election. Just four years

POPULIST PYTHON

A cartoonist in 1900 satirizes the Populist Party as a python with the head of William Jennings Bryan swallowing the Democratic Party donkey.

later, in 1896, the Democratic Party effectively absorbed Populism, and the national movement collapsed with the defeat (repeated in 1900 and 1908) of Democratic presidential candidate William Jennings Bryan. Some state-level movements remained alive for the next few years.

These organizations provided a forum for airing charges against railroads, supporting the temperance cause, and advocating women's suffrage. Populists urged direct election of senators, a graduated income tax, regulation of monopolies and utilities, and government control of currency. They held rallies, marches, and speeches, and sent representatives to Washington, D.C., to plead for reform.

Political humorist Josh Billings remarked that "wimmin is everywhere" in the farm protest movement, and indeed they were. A mother of eleven and a farm woman, Luna E. Kellie, of Nebraska, served as secretary, bookkeeper, and a speaker for the Farmers' Alliance. She wrote Populist songs and edited the Populist newspaper, *Prairie Home*, on her dining room table. A mother of four who won admittance to the Kansas bar in 1885, Mary Elizabeth Lease, of Kansas, gave more than 160 speeches supporting Populist programs in 1890. Journalists widely reported her warning Kansas farmers to "raise less corn and more hell."

From conservationists to farmers, men to women,   wage workers to urban inhabitants, westerners complained. Workers resisted poor wages and dangerous conditions. During the 1880s, Chinese fruit pickers in Santa Clara County, California, staged a strike for better working conditions and higher wages.

But most strikes and labor organizations excluded workers of color. In Cripple Creek, Colorado, white miners drove out Hispanics, Chinese, Japanese, and others because they

> "THE GREAT COMMON PEOPLE OF THIS COUNTRY ARE SLAVES, AND MONOPOLY IS THE MASTER. THE WEST AND SOUTH ARE BOUND AND PROSTRATE BEFORE THE MANUFACTURING EAST."
>
> —POPULIST LEADER MARY ELIZABETH LEASE TO KANSAS FARMERS, 1890

feared they would work for low wages and cause the entire wage structure to fall. Miners and other skilled workers also refused to admit as members of their unions such southern Europeans as Slavs, Italians, and Greeks, as well as women. In Montana the Butte Miners Union, the largest local mining union in the West, imposed a closed shop on Butte mines, meaning that owners could hire only union members. Labor reformers also tended to overlook children. Commonly parents

hired out their children to people in need of domestic or field workers. Hispanic children worked in sun-parched fields as migrant laborers. In mining regions, ten-year-old boys who descended into mine tunnels suffered tuberculosis, impaired vision, weakened limbs, disabling accidents, and silicosis, a chronic lung disease caused by breathing silica dust.

As a result of protests, strikes, and rallies, westerners sometimes saw change. Certain territories and states granted women the right to vote. Wyoming Territory did so in 1869; Utah followed in 1870, Washington Territory in 1883, Colorado in 1893, and Idaho in 1896. On the federal level, Congress adopted the Interstate Commerce Act in 1887, which created the Interstate Commerce Commission and attempted to bring farmers some relief by regulating railroad rates and practices.

U.S. EXPANSION AND IMPERIALISM

Through the Spanish-American War and the annexation of Hawaii in 1898, active interventionism in Latin American and East Asian affairs entered U.S. foreign policy. It continued throughout the twentieth century.

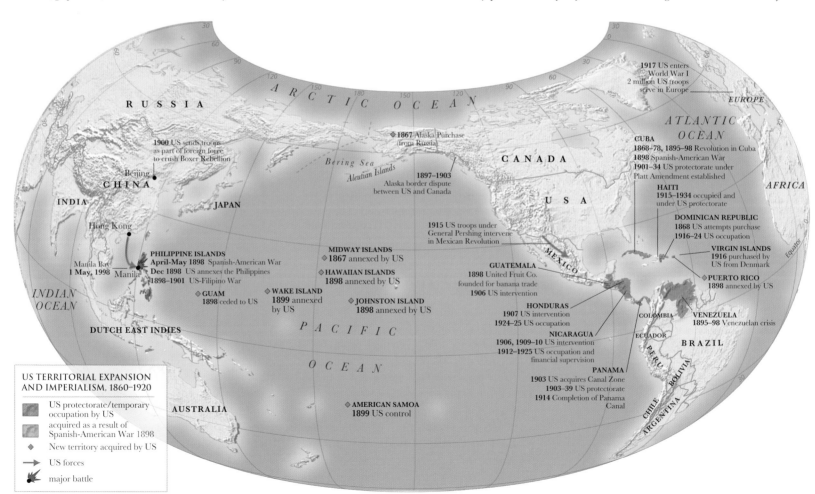

1917 US enters World War I 2 million US troops serve in Europe

1900 US sends troops as part of foreign force to crush Boxer Rebellion

1867 Alaska Purchase from Russia

1897–1903 Alaska border dispute between US and Canada

CUBA
1868–78, 1895–98 Revolution in Cuba
1898 Spanish-American War
1901–34 US protectorate under Platt Amendment established

HAITI
1915–1934 occupied and under US protectorate

DOMINICAN REPUBLIC
1868 US attempts purchase
1916–24 US occupation

VIRGIN ISLANDS
1916 purchased by US from Denmark

1915 US troops under General Pershing intervene in Mexican Revolution

MIDWAY ISLANDS
1867 annexed by US

GUATEMALA
1898 United Fruit Co. founded for banana trade
1906 US intervention

PUERTO RICO
1898 annexed by US

PHILIPPINE ISLANDS
April–May 1898 Spanish-American War
Dec 1898 US annexes the Philippines
1898–1901 US-Filipino War

Manila Bay
1 May, 1998 Manila

HAWAIIAN ISLANDS
1898 annexed by US

WAKE ISLAND
1899 annexed by US

JOHNSTON ISLAND
1898 annexed by US

HONDURAS
1907 US intervention
1924–25 US occupation

VENEZUELA
1895–98 Venezuelan crisis

GUAM
1898 ceded to US

NICARAGUA
1906, 1909–10 US intervention
1912–1925 US occupation and financial supervision

PANAMA
1903 US acquires Canal Zone
1903–39 US protectorate
1914 Completion of Panama Canal

AMERICAN SAMOA
1899 US control

RUSSIA · CHINA · INDIA · JAPAN · Hong Kong · DUTCH EAST INDIES · AUSTRALIA · CANADA · USA · MEXICO · COLOMBIA · ECUADOR · PERU · BRAZIL · BOLIVIA · CHILE · ARGENTINA · EUROPE · AFRICA

ARCTIC OCEAN · Bering Sea · Aleutian Islands · PACIFIC OCEAN · INDIAN OCEAN · ATLANTIC OCEAN · Equator

US TERRITORIAL EXPANSION AND IMPERIALISM, 1860–1920

- US protectorate/temporary occupation by US
- acquired as a result of Spanish-American War 1898
- ◆ New territory acquired by US
- → US forces
- major battle

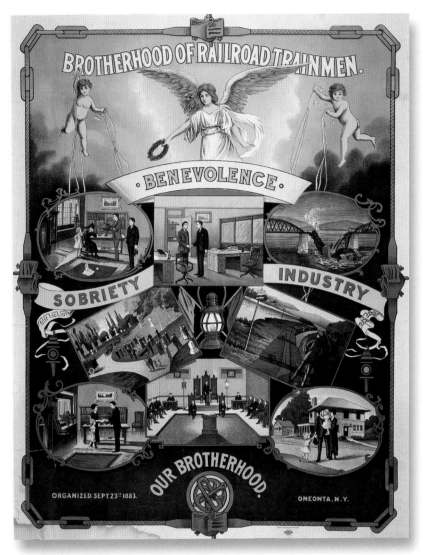

THE LAST reigning monarch of the Hawaiian Islands, Queen Liliuokalani (1838–1917) was born Lydia Kamakameha in Honolulu and married the son of an American sea captain in 1862. Educated in the western tradition, she succeeded to the throne upon the death of her brother, King Kalakaua, in January 1891 and immediately proposed a new constitution for Hawaii in an attempt to protect native Hawaiians from encroaching American interests.

After failing to obtain adequate support for her constitution, Liliuokalani attempted to rule by edict, upon which a group of American revolutionaries led by Sanford Dole deposed her, established the Republic of Hawaii (1894), and pressed for annexation by the United States. Although President Grover Cleveland supported Liliuokalani's efforts to regain her throne, Hawaii's geographical significance finally led Congress to annex it in 1898. Gracious in defeat, the queen spent her remaining years working to preserve Hawaiian culture and established the Liliuokalani Trust for orphaned and destitute Hawaiian children.

A skillful musician, Liliuokalani wrote many songs, of which her best known is "Aloha Oe."

RAILROAD UNION

Dangerous working conditions and low wages led workers to form unions. Membership was promoted by advertising like this 1915 poster for the Brotherhood of Railroad Trainmen, which had been founded in 1883.

ALASKA

The federal government also responded to entreaties from Alaskan settlers. At first it had followed precedent by classifying Alaska as "Indian country" and directing the U.S. Army to administer it. Army officials established a number of coastal forts to suppress alcohol, regulate the fur trade, and settle infrequent conflicts with Native Alaskans. But in 1881 settlers in and around Juneau sent a delegate to Washington, D.C., to demand a governor and a court system from Congress, which finally approved the request in 1884.

Other changes followed for Alaska settlers. In 1897 Congress created the office of Surveyor General for the District of Alaska and, the following year, extended homesteading laws to the region. In the 1900 Civil Code for Alaska, Congress revised the Organic Act of 1884 and established such posts as Fort Gibbon, on the Yukon, and Fort Davis, near Nome, to regulate and protect the horde of gold seekers who appeared after the gold strikes.

Moreover, the idea of establishing national parks continued to gain popularity with the American public. In 1890 feminist Fay Fuller, wearing bloomers and sturdy boy's shoes, forced Americans to think about western wilderness areas when she climbed Mt. Rainier, in Washington. The same year Congress reclaimed Yosemite from California and declared it a national park; and enacted the Forest Reserve Act, which allowed presidents to withdraw timber lands from public use.

Presidents Benjamin Harrison, Grover Cleveland, and William McKinley responded enthusiastically. Under McKinley, in 1898 Gifford Pinchot took over direction of the Division of Forestry in the Department of Agriculture. Pinchot staffed the division with professionally trained foresters, instituted grazing fees in national forests, and encouraged presidents to withdraw even more land from public use. Although many western senators and representatives bitterly criticized Pinchot and called him a "petty despot" and a "Czar," these anticonservationists failed to understand the vast damage that western land, forests, and other resources had already sustained.

The federal government also flexed its muscle in Hawaii. Trade ships, New England missionaries, and sugar commerce had provided an early and strong bond between the Hawaiian Islands and the United States, but not until 1887 did Hawaiian sugar planters—mostly Americans—initiate a successful revolution against native rulers. This uprising resulted in a liberal constitution and American control of the government until Queen Liliuokalani came to the throne in 1891 and replaced the 1887 constitution with a document putting rule squarely in her own hands.

Queen Liliuokalani's reassertion of native authority disappointed many Americans who hoped for annexation of Hawaii to the United States. But early in 1893 the U.S. minister to Hawaii, John L. Stevens, ordered U.S. Marines to protect American lives and property there. Stevens used these troops to support a revolution led by Sanford B. Dole. On February 1, 1894, Stevens declared Hawaii a protectorate of the United States. As Hawaii's first president, Dole urged annexation by the United States.

In response to protests regarding the way the new government had come to power, President Grover Cleveland initiated a series of investigations. On July 4, 1894, American leaders in Hawaii declared a republic. Nearly a month later President Cleveland recognized the new government but refused to annex the islands. His successor, William McKinley, held no such scruples. After recognizing Hawaii's strategic importance during the Spanish-American War, which began in 1898, McKinley convinced Congress to approve annexation that same year.

"YES, WILD BILL WITH HIS OWN HANDS HAS KILLED HUNDREDS OF MEN. OF THAT I HAVE NOT A DOUBT."

—WRITER GEORGE WARD NICHOLS ON WILD BILL HICKOK, 1867

"WAIT FOR THE WAGON" SHEET MUSIC

Along with plays, dime novels, and shows, sheet music for the parlor piano shaped popular ideas about the West. This music is for a minstrel show c. 1840–60.

MYTHOLOGIZING THE WEST

SOME WHO CAME WESTWARD FOUND THEIR DREAMS OF PROSPERITY FULFILLED; OTHERS ENCOUNTERED ONLY DISAPPOINTMENT, BUT SUCH MIXED EXPERIENCES HAD LITTLE EFFECT ON THE REGION'S IMAGE. MYTHOLOGIZED IN DIME NOVELS, WILD WEST SHOWS, AND THE LEGENDS OF LARGER-THAN-LIFE OUTLAWS AND LAWMEN, THE GOLDEN WEST REMAINED A LAND OF OPPORTUNITY IN THE POPULAR MIND.

D URING THE LATE nineteenth century, few Americans recognized the realities of the American West. Instead most saw the region as little more than a romantic fabrication, a painted stage set for drama. More than any other region of the country, the West captured the popular imagination.

Beginning in the late 1860s, dime novels began to appear. Through them cavorted courageous men, virtuous women, and "hostile," "bloodthirsty," and "savage" Indians. In 1869 Ned Buntline (the pen name for Edward Judson) published *Buffalo Bill: King of the Border Men.* Buntline portrayed western scout William F. Cody as the heroic Buffalo Bill, who killed thousands of buffalo, protected women, and drove off attacking Indians to provide food and safety for settlers.

Other men appeared as heroes in the thousands of dime novels that followed. In an 1890s thriller, eight men hid several "white maidens" in a grotto and fought off "savages" to protect the women's lives and virtue. Gradually, though, women in these western sagas came to act on their own. When

Deadwood Dick, a popular hero of the 1890s, found himself held at gunpoint by a woman who insisted that he marry her, his wife lunged at the woman, who "fell back, with a blade run through her heart–dead!" Another of the dime novel's capable women threw sandbags out of a hot-air balloon on the heads of Sioux Indians and brandished her revolver until they dispersed.

BUFFALO BILL

In 1891, showman William F. "Buffalo Bill" Cody (center rear, wearing cowboy hat) took part in a meeting of Indian chiefs and U.S. officials at Pine Ridge, South Dakota. Cody had once been a scout for the U.S. Cavalry.

↦DIME NOVELS↤

DIME NOVELS paid little regard to accuracy but much to sensation and excitement. While the most popular related the adventures of characters in the Wild West, others included costume romances, war stories, working-girl narratives, historical adventures, and detective stories, all aimed at young, working-class readers and sold at newsstands and dry-goods stores.

The genre was established in 1859, when Beadle and Adams issued *Malaeska, the Indian Wife of the White Hunter*, the first of "Beadle's Dime Novels." A tragic story of an Indian woman married to a white man who dies, the 128-page paperback sold over 300,000 copies in a year. It is calculated that Beadle and Adams sold over 5 million of their little books in four years.

While their sensationalism had little basis in reality, dime novels embedded certain figures into American mythology. In *Ragged Dick* (1867), Horatio Alger introduced moral tales of poor boys becoming wealthy by hard work and perseverance. These, however, were never as popular as the adventures featuring such Wild West notables as Jesse James and Calamity Jane.

Publishers employed writers like Ned Buntline (E. Z. C. Judson), who, from 1869 onwards, glamorized "Buffalo Bill" Cody in a wildly improbable and exciting series. J. R. Coryell created the equally famous but fictitious Nick Carter, who appeared in over 1,000 titles, while Edward L. Wheeler wrote yarns about the real-life Indian fighter Richard W. Clarke ("Deadwood Dick").

Dime novels were the staple diet of American popular literature until they were slowly superseded in the early 1900s by pulp magazines and the Western novels of writers such as Zane Grey and Max Brand (Frederick Faust). Until then, readers could enjoy heart-pounding moments such as this one, provided by Wheeler in *Deadwood Dick's Doom* (c. 1899): an armed Deadwood Dick cries, "You lie, you brute! and if you but lay a hand on that girl I'll bore a hole in your thick skull!"

WESTERN ACES
Dime novels, so called because of their ten-cent price, remained popular into the early twentieth century. This example, Western Aces, *dates from 1936.*

Dime novelists also cast Native American men and women in stock roles. They characterized the men as either good Indians—truthful, reliable, and capable of speaking correct English—or as bad Indians—hostile, barbaric, and incapable of adopting white ways. They portrayed women as beautiful, kind, and endearing Indian princesses or as ugly, filthy, overworked squaws.

THE WILD WEST SHOW

Cody, the Iowa native and Nebraska resident whom Buntline had made famous as Buffalo Bill, realized that the widespread fascination with the American West constituted a business opportunity. He decided to take the West and his own heroic image and transform them into a combination circus and stage play. In 1883 Cody presented his first Wild West exposition in Chicago before the wondering eyes of 42,000 people. As his show grew in popularity, Cody took it to Europe, where the stars played before kings and queens. Roping, riding, shooting, mock battles, and American Indian chiefs all contributed to the excitement.

A young woman from Greenville, Ohio, achieved fame in Cody's arena. Annie Moses, who renamed herself Annie Oakley, had learned to shoot in the woods around her home. As a young woman, Annie beat her future

✦ BUFFALO BILL'S WILD WEST SHOW ✦

WILLIAM F. CODY (1846–1917) had led an adventurous life as Pony Express rider, army scout, Indian fighter, and buffalo hunter before the dime-novel writer Ned Buntline (E. Z. C. Judson) made him famous across the country as "Buffalo Bill." In 1872 Buntline cashed in on Cody's popularity, putting him on the New York stage in *The Scouts of the Plains.* Cody further added to his reputation by returning to the West to rejoin the Fifth Cavalry during the Sioux War of 1876.

In 1883 Cody created the Wild West Show (originally entitled the Wild West, Rocky Mountain, and Prairie Exhibition), and although similar rival shows soon appeared, his was the most famous. A glamorized depiction of the thrills and excitement of the romantic West as Americans saw it—or wanted to see it—the show attracted audiences across America and, later, across the world. Posters advertised "actual scenes, genuine characters" from the West.

Cody's show was half circus and half pageant, with audiences delighting in expert horsemen, rope tricks, and marksmen, all interspersed with thrilling reenactments of Indians attacking the Deadwood

ANNIE OAKLEY
Born in Ohio as Annie Moses, the "peerless lady wing-shot" Oakley was one of the main attractions of Buffalo Bill's Wild West Show for seventeen seasons.

1895 poster promoting Buffalo Bill's Wild West Show

Stage or the death of Custer at the Little Bighorn, still a recent memory. In 1885 Cody featured the famous Sioux chief Sitting Bull and also brought in Annie Oakley, the sharpshooter who was as brilliant a shot as legend says. Distinguished guests at the show had cigarettes shot out of their mouths at twenty yards, and Oakley's name is still given to punch-marked complimentary theater tickets (from her trick of perforating a playing card before it hit the ground).

"Buffalo Bill" Cody, c. 1875

In 1887 Cody took his show to Europe, where it was rapturously received. Performances included a private staging for Queen Victoria and her court. London made Cody particularly welcome, and the patronage of the Prince of Wales meant that one night the "passengers" in the famous Deadwood Stage scene comprised four European monarchs visiting London for Victoria's Jubilee.

The Wild West Show remained an attraction for another twenty years before changing tastes forced its merger with another Western show in 1909. It ended up going bankrupt in 1915.

other paintings and sculpture American Indians stood mighty and proud as "noble savages."

GUNFIGHTERS

Virtually every mythmaker, from dime novelists to artists to journalists, exalted western gunfighters and disseminated their stories. In 1864 Jesse James started his career much like Joaquín Murieta—retaliating against Union soldiers who had tortured his stepfather and abused his pregnant mother. Jesse first rode with his brother Frank James, accompanied also by William "Bloody Bill" Anderson, who had led irregulars against Union soldiers near the end of the Civil War. Jesse and Frank soon went on to rob banks, stagecoaches, and railroads. With partners Jim Cole and Bob Younger, they gunned down lawmen, vigilantes, and other victims until Missouri bounty hunter Bob Ford shot Jesse in the back on April 3, 1882. Within six months, Frank turned himself in.

The growing western myth also idealized other gunfighters, including Wyatt Earp, John "Doc" Holliday, and Ike Clanton, all of whom shot it out at the O.K. Corral in Tombstone, Arizona, on October 26, 1881. In that notorious and bloody battle, Earp, his brothers, and Holliday faced Ike and Billy Clanton and the McLaury brothers. When the smoke cleared, two of the Earps had been wounded and Holliday had his holster shot off, but Billy Clanton and the McLaurys lay dead.

According to reports, hundreds of other fabled lawmen and gunfighters roamed the West. On the side of the law, ex-Chicago police detective Allan Pinkerton organized a team of sleuths who claimed, "We never sleep." Pinkerton's National Detective Agency pursued the most renowned gunslingers of the day, from the James Gang to Butch Cassidy's Wild Bunch. Pat Garrett, sheriff of Lincoln County, New Mexico, also gained fame, notably for tracking and killing Billy the Kid in 1881.

Billy, also known as Henry McCarty and William Bonney, was a prime example of the western gunfighter. A vain yet intelligent young man, he killed far fewer than the twenty-one men of legend. He laid the groundwork for his reputation during the brutal Lincoln County War of 1877–78, a conflict between a reigning business monopoly, which supplied nearby Fort Stanton, and an aspiring one. Billy owed his notoriety less to outlaw exploits than to imaginative newspaper stories and even to the man who killed him. In his *An Authentic Life of Billy the Kid*, Garrett embellished the outlaw's feats, perhaps to add luster to his own prowess as a lawman.

Throughout this mythologizing of the American West, Native Americans were persistently portrayed as a source of trouble, fear, and death. An occasional African American played a bit part

husband, sharpshooter Frank Butler, in a shooting match. Shortly after they married, Frank decided to manage his wife's career instead of performing. It was Frank who persuaded Bill Cody to give Annie a spot in his show. Within months, adoring audiences called Annie Oakley "Little Miss Sure Shot" and thought of her as an archetypal western woman even though she had never lived in the West.

Western artists also presented their own particular visions of the West in drawings, watercolors, and paintings. Frederic Remington and George Caleb Bingham created a world of visual beauty inhabited by people who looked much like those in nineteenth-century novels, plays, and Wild West shows. In Remington's *Sign Language* (1889), Native Americans appeared as inferior beings obviously destined for extinction, but in

→OUTLAWS OF THE OLD WEST←

FOLLOWING THE CIVIL WAR, former soldiers accustomed to fighting and little else were drawn to the West, where vigilante groups often comprised the only law. The growing spread of ranching meant cattle were there to be stolen; new towns meant there were banks to be robbed; and land disputes could be settled by the party with the most gunmen. Against this background, some outlaws achieved legendary status.

Bob, Jim, and Cole Younger with sister

Jesse James

Jim Murphy, Sam Bass, and crony Seaborn Barnes (left to right)

SAM BASS

The career of Sam Bass (1851–1878) as an outlaw was short and violent. With Joel Collins, he formed a gang that robbed stagecoaches, and, in September 1877, held up a Union Pacific train, stealing $60,000. The gang split up, and Collins and two others were killed a few weeks later, while Bass returned to Texas. The following year, with a new gang, he robbed four trains, causing numerous posses to be sent after him. He planned to rob the bank at Round Rock, but gang member Jim Murphy warned the Texas Rangers, and Bass and his men were caught in a gun battle. Bass escaped, though badly wounded, and was captured outside the town the following day. He died on his twenty-seventh birthday.

BUTCH CASSIDY AND THE WILD BUNCH

Born Robert LeRoy Parker in Utah, Butch Cassidy (1866–1909) took up rustling with a Mike Cassidy, whose name he took later. After serving a two-year sentence in Wyoming (1894–96), he began a career in robbery, eventually becoming leader of the Wild Bunch, a violent gang that attracted such outlaws as the Sundance Kid (Harry Longbaugh) and Kid Curry (Harvey Logan). For five years they stole cattle and robbed trains and banks, operating together or in smaller, independent groups.

The gang made their last train holdup near Wagner, Montana, on August 24, 1901, then rode south to Texas. Cassidy and the Sundance Kid left for South America with Etta Place and made an unsuccessful attempt at ranching. They finally returned to robbery, and it is generally believed they were killed by Bolivian soldiers in 1909.

The Wild Bunch, a.k.a. the Hole-in-the-Wall Gang, including Butch Cassidy (seated, right) and the Sundance Kid (seated, left)

CATTLE ANNIE AND LITTLE BRITCHES

For two years in Indian Territory, the teenaged Anna McDoulet (Cattle Annie) and Jennie Stevens (Little Britches), both born in 1879, acted as spies for Bill Doolin's gang, stole horses, and sold whiskey to the Osage and Pawnee Indians. Thrilled at being on the wrong side of the law, they escaped capture by wearing men's clothing and informed the Doolin Gang when lawmen were in the area. Both were apprehended in 1895 and sentenced to short terms of imprisonment. Cattle Annie was released on health grounds after a few months and is thought to have died of consumption in New York. Little Britches left prison in October 1896, but her life thereafter is unknown.

Outlaw girls Cattle Annie (left) and Little Britches, c. 1880

THE JAMES-YOUNGER GANG

Probably the most famous outlaws of the Old West were two sets of brothers who carried out armed robberies over a ten-year period. Jesse James (1847–1882) and his brother Frank (1843–1915) began raiding Union farms and settlements with Confederate guerrillas during the Civil War. On February 13, 1866, they robbed their first bank at Liberty, Missouri, killing a bystander and getting away with a reported $62,000.

The Younger brothers were Cole (Thomas Coleman, 1844–1916), Jim (James Henry, 1848–1902), John (1851–1874), and Bob (Robert Ewing, 1853–1889). Cole and Jim, who had fought with Quantrill's Raiders during the Civil War, joined forces with the James brothers in 1866, then were joined by John, Bob, and others. Averaging around twelve men, the gang roamed the country, robbing banks from Iowa to Texas, and, from 1873, also robbing trains. They were given tacit support by many southerners who saw them as taking revenge on Yankee banks and institutions.

In 1874 John Younger was killed by Pinkerton detectives. Two years later an attempted bank robbery at Northfield, Minnesota, proved disastrous. After a shootout, the Younger brothers were captured, though the James brothers escaped. They hid out for three years, then returned to train robbing in 1879 with a new gang. Robert Ford, a bounty hunter, shot Jesse James in 1882, and Frank James surrendered soon afterwards. Despite three trials for robbery and murder, he was acquitted and returned to his family home, where he died in the same room where he was born.

The Younger brothers went to prison, where Bob died in 1889. Cole and Jim were paroled in 1901, but Jim committed suicide the following year. To the end, Cole maintained his innocence.

as a soldier or cowboy, a Hispanic as a pesky bandit, an Asian as a worker on the railroad or a cook; but, like Native Americans, they were flat, predictable characters.

THE END OF THE OLD WEST

In 1890 the U.S. Census Bureau declared the saga of the West finished: the region had achieved a population density of an average of two people per square mile and was thus considered "settled." This proclamation encouraged Americans to believe that the Old West teetered on the brink of extinction. Three years later University of Wisconsin historian Frederick Jackson Turner reaffirmed Americans' anxieties about a vanishing frontier when he delivered his now-famous address "The Significance of the Frontier in American History" on the grounds of the World Fair in Chicago, while Buffalo Bill Cody's Wild West extravaganza played outside its gates.

Americans clutched at the romanticized West for fear of what its disappearance might mean. To them the growth of farming, mining, lumbering, and industry equaled progress with a capital P. Poor wages and bad working conditions were lamentable but necessary byproducts of progress; the forced removal of Indians also seemed unavoidable. Whites continued to think of the West in unambiguous terms: heroes defeating villains, right overcoming wrong, and fulfillment outweighing disappointment.

This interpretation made its way around the world. Consequently, people continued to come from as far away as Asia, seeking a better life in this region of prosperity and opportunity. When migrants arrived they often discovered that deceit, corruption, disappointment, and prejudice also pervaded the West. Although they told their stories loudly and widely, others persisted in migrating, lured by a region that, despite its difficulties, still promised more than their homelands.

A Norwegian milkmaid working in South Dakota during the 1890s affirmed this point. She wrote home that she worked "from dawn-to-dusk," turning her hand "to whatever task came along." Yet she declared that she never labored as arduously or with as little reward as she had in Norway. Thus, although the post-Civil War West may have had its problems and failings, the Old West was unquestionably a golden West for many people across the spectrum.

THE EVER-GOLDEN FRONTIER
While the frontier was considered closed by 1900, dreams for a better life in the West persisted. Towns like Raton, New Mexico (pictured c. 1887), which bloomed as a railroad repair stop, exemplified the promise of the West.

"UP TO OUR OWN DAY AMERICAN HISTORY HAS BEEN IN A LARGE DEGREE THE HISTORY OF THE COLONIZATION OF THE GREAT WEST."

—HISTORIAN FREDERICK JACKSON TURNER, "THE SIGNIFICANCE OF THE FRONTIER IN AMERICAN HISTORY," 1893

THE CONTEMPORARY WEST

1900 TO PRESENT

THE TWENTIETH CENTURY SAW THE BIRTH OF A
NEW WEST IN WHICH FRONTIER CONDITIONS
GAVE WAY TO AN URBAN CIVILIZATION, EVEN AS
THE OLD WEST LIVED ON IN MYTH. NEW FORMS OF
TRANSPORTATION, INCLUDING THE CAR AND THE
AIRPLANE, SHRANK DISTANCES, WHILE FEDERAL
SUPPORT AND PRIVATE ENTERPRISE INVIGORATED
THE WESTERN ECONOMY. AFTER THE GREAT
DEPRESSION AND WORLD WAR II, THE NEW WEST
EMERGED AS A MULTICULTURAL, POLITICALLY
POWERFUL REGION OF HIGH-TECH INDUSTRY
AND LONG-STANDING CONFLICTS.

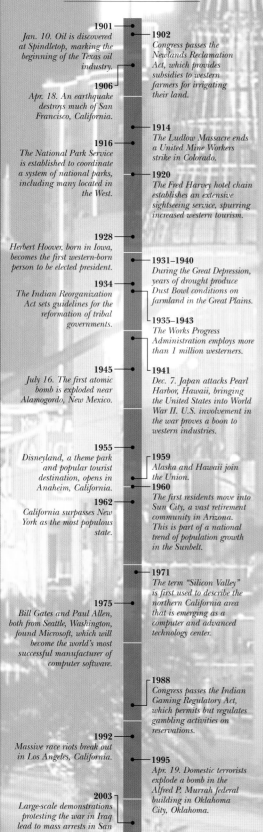

⇥TIMELINE⇤
1900 TO PRESENT

The American West emerged in the twentieth century as one of the nation's most vibrant regions. With the help of the federal government, westerners built an array of industries that survived the Great Depression to fuel economic growth after World War II. The region's prosperity drew a multicultural work force to the West, while its natural beauty made it a leading tourist destination.

1901
Jan. 10. Oil is discovered at Spindletop, marking the beginning of the Texas oil industry.

1902
Congress passes the Newlands Reclamation Act, which provides subsidies to western farmers for irrigating their land.

1906
Apr. 18. An earthquake destroys much of San Francisco, California.

1914
The Ludlow Massacre ends a United Mine Workers strike in Colorado.

1916
The National Park Service is established to coordinate a system of national parks, including many located in the West.

1920
The Fred Harvey hotel chain establishes an extensive sightseeing service, spurring increased western tourism.

1928
Herbert Hoover, born in Iowa, becomes the first western-born person to be elected president.

1931–1940
During the Great Depression, years of drought produce Dust Bowl conditions on farmland in the Great Plains.

1934
The Indian Reorganization Act sets guidelines for the reformation of tribal governments.

1935–1943
The Works Progress Administration employs more than 1 million westerners.

1945
July 16. The first atomic bomb is exploded near Alamogordo, New Mexico.

1941
Dec. 7. Japan attacks Pearl Harbor, Hawaii, bringing the United States into World War II. U.S. involvement in the war proves a boon to western industries.

1955
Disneyland, a theme park and popular tourist destination, opens in Anaheim, California.

1959
Alaska and Hawaii join the Union.

1960
The first residents move into Sun City, a vast retirement community in Arizona. This is part of a national trend of population growth in the Sunbelt.

1962
California surpasses New York as the most populous state.

1971
The term "Silicon Valley" is first used to describe the northern California area that is emerging as a computer and advanced technology center.

1975
Bill Gates and Paul Allen, both from Seattle, Washington, found Microsoft, which will become the world's most successful manufacturer of computer software.

1988
Congress passes the Indian Gaming Regulatory Act, which permits but regulates gambling activities on reservations.

1992
Massive race riots break out in Los Angeles, California.

1995
Apr. 19. Domestic terrorists explode a bomb in the Alfred P. Murrah federal building in Oklahoma City, Oklahoma.

2003
Large-scale demonstrations protesting the war in Iraq lead to mass arrests in San Francisco, California.

THE NEW WEST

AT THE DAWN OF THE TWENTIETH CENTURY, THE OLD WEST BEGAN TO
GIVE WAY TO A NEW WEST. THIS WEST WAS MORE URBAN, ETHNICALLY
DIVERSE, AND SYMPATHETIC TO CONSERVATIONISM. IT WAS LESS
ISOLATED FROM THE REST OF THE NATION BUT RETAINED ITS REGIONAL
DISTINCTIVENESS. DURING THE CENTURY, THE WESTERN ECONOMY
GREW THROUGH BOTH FEDERAL SUPPORT AND PRIVATE ENTERPRISE.

IN 1902 THE NOVELIST Frank Norris
spoke for many of his generation when in a
mournful dirge he wrote: *Suddenly we have
found that there is no longer any Frontier…And the
Frontier has become so much an integral part of our
conception of things that it will be long before we shall
all understand that it is gone. We liked the Frontier; it
was romance, the place of the poetry of the Great March,
the firing-line where there was action and fighting.*

His lament was not unique. Indeed,
millions of Americans bemoaned what
they perceived to be not only the passing
of an era but a profound transformation
of American society. No longer were they a
pioneering people on an ever-expanding
dynamic frontier; instead there was a new
generation of sedate urban dwellers. And
with these physical changes they feared
the spiritual changes that would come in
their wake, particularly a decline of the
values associated with the frontier, such
as individualism, freedom, self-reliance,
manliness, and courage.

But if frontier conditions diminished
after 1890, of course the West did not
disappear, nor selected areas within it that
retained frontier characteristics. Rather, the
twentieth century saw the West emerge steadily
as an urban civilization. It was still characterized
by wide, open spaces, to be sure, but these were
increasingly punctuated by clusters of towns and
cities containing the bulk of the population. By
the end of the twentieth century, the majority of
westerners lived in urban areas that had come to
be characteristic of the region.

How did this New (post-1890) West differ from
the Old (pre-1890) West? Although the Old West

SALT LAKE CITY, UTAH

*The bustle of Main Street in 1908 indicates the city's
rapid growth. To address growth-related problems, a
vice district and a beautification program were created.*

contained many free lands available for farming,
much of the New was semiarid, with few areas
suitable for the kind of agriculture familiar to
easterners. The Old had a sparse population
thinly dispersed over extensive open spaces; the
New sprouted towns and cities. And even though
most of the people in the Old were of western
and northern European backgrounds, with the
exception of Native Americans, this was not true
of the New. Its burgeoning cities had a diverse
mix of peoples—not only central and southern
Europeans, but Hispanics, Asians, and African
Americans, among others. In the Old West many
pioneers took pride in their geographic isolation,
which enabled them to build a new society without
too much outside interference. The New West
was not as isolated. In fact, it was quite closely
integrated into the nation's transportation and
communications network, and consequently it lost
some of its regional distinctiveness. Old Westerners
assumed that the region's vast natural resources
were inexhaustible, and so tended to be exploitative
and wasteful. New Westerners, on the other hand,
became increasingly conscious that the bounties
of nature in their region were shrinking and

ESKIMOS

*In the early twentieth century, many native Alaskan tribes
were relocated to new villages as whites settled the area.
These Eskimos, photographed in the 1910s, wait on a
dock with their children and baggage.*

needed to be conserved and replenished. More
than previous generations, New Westerners came
to believe in the need for environmental balance
and the use of science to achieve it.

Of course, a region as vast as the West was not
uniform but contained within it subregions that
differed greatly in their environmental and cultural
characteristics. West of the 98th meridian, new
settlers in the northern reaches encountered
the Great Plains—a treeless expanse of flatlands
where the annual rainfall was sparse, often no
more than ten inches annually, in contrast to the

✦EARTHQUAKES✦

THE SAN ANDREAS fault, extending approximately 800 miles through California, is the zone separating the North American and Pacific tectonic plates, making California prone to seismic activity. San Fernando, Coalinga, Lomo Prieta, Morgan Hill, and Northridge all experienced earthquakes registering above 6.0 on the Richter Scale in the latter half of the twentieth century. The 1906 San Francisco earthquake, however, remains the best known of all California quakes.

Registering 8.3 on the Richter Scale, the April 18 earthquake and ensuing fire virtually destroyed the city and resulted in more than 700 deaths. According to an eyewitness account from a police sergeant, *"Davis Street split right open in front of me. A gaping trench...about six feet deep and half* full of water suddenly yawned between me and the east side of the street." Ferry building ticket clerk and telegraph operator Thomas Chase remembered, *"Buildings along First Street from Howard to Market crumbled like card houses. One was brick. Not a soul escaped. Clouds of that [dust] obliterated the scene of destruction. The dust hung low over the rubble in the street."* A third account from *Examiner* editor P. Barrett noted, *"... we had found ourselves staggering and reeling. It was as if the earth was slipping gently from under our feet. Then came a sickening swaying of the earth that threw us flat upon our faces...We could not get on our feet...Big buildings were crumbling as one might crush a biscuit in one's hand."*

The fire that followed the earthquake raged for three days. After the cataclysm, rebuilding began almost immediately. Within eighteen months the city offered more office space than ever, as well as a brand new City Hall.

AFTERMATH
A few battered structures in the financial district survived the 1906 San Francisco earthquake and fire. They included the Kohl Building, the Merchants' Exchange Building, and the Mills Building.

RADIO
An Inuit family gathers to take in a 1926 radio broadcast from a Zenith set. By June 30 of that year, Alaska had two AM radio stations, one based in Juneau and the other in Anchorage. The radio soon became indispensable in American households.

Native Americans such as the Pueblos, Navajos, and Apaches long before whites ever settled North America, and settled by Spaniards before the British established colonies on the East Coast. Its cultural life differed from other parts of the West, with old established Native American, Spanish, and Mexican cultures.

California constituted another distinct subregion of the West. It was a highly diversified state, not only geographically—with subregions of its own—but demographically, with a great mix of peoples from differing ethnic, racial, and cultural backgrounds. It differed from the more humid Pacific Northwest states of Oregon, Washington, and Idaho where smaller, homogeneous populations gave that area a less hectic cast. And many Americans after 1900 also came to consider noncontiguous areas such as Alaska and Hawaii as part of the West, both with significant. populations of native peoples.

SWEEPING CHANGES
Although westerners in 1900 could not foresee all of the great changes that would sweep the region during the next 100 years, not all of the influences were unfamiliar. As in the nineteenth century, the federal government was to play a major role in shaping the life of the area. At that time federal authorities had distributed lands and encouraged

humid East where the norm was thirty-five inches yearly or more. The soil was dry, and the weather tended to extremes of heat in summer and cold in winter. During much of the year, strong winds blew across the Plains, which encompassed Kansas, Nebraska, Montana, the Dakotas, and parts of eastern Colorado, eastern New Mexico, western Texas, and Oklahoma. This extensive area had been occupied by widely dispersed Native American tribes such as the Sioux, Mandans, and Comanches before white settlement. In 1900 most of this region had just recently acquired statehood.

West of the Great Plains was the Rocky Mountain area. In Utah, Montana, Colorado, and Wyoming newcomers encountered the majestic Rockies, often 10,000 feet and higher, that defined much of the surrounding landscape. At the turn of the century, these lands were heavily dependent on extractive industries like mining and not hospitable to intensive settlement. This area differed from the Southwest, comprising Texas, New Mexico, Arizona, and parts of Oklahoma and Nevada. A region of little rain and semiarid grasslands and deserts, it had been occupied by the building of roads and railroads. In the twentieth century Congress authorized huge new irrigation and reclamation projects to recover arid lands. Instead of railroads, the federal government constructed scores of airports. No less important was a vast network of military bases and installations that poured large sums of federal monies into many western localities.

As in the nineteenth century, development of the region was also a result of vigorous private enterprise. Indeed, private entrepreneurs did much to spread new technologies that were to shape the contours of the twentieth-century West. Some of these technologies, such as jet travel, lessened the previous geographic isolation of the West. Others, such as air conditioning, revolutionized lifestyles and settlement patterns.

The growth of computer technology and electronics also changed the economy of the West as it became less dependent on natural resources. The increasing diversity of peoples from all over the globe did much to transform life as the West gradually developed a multicultural society. All of these changes came so rapidly that the mind-set of many westerners lagged behind. They still

regarded themselves as highly individualistic, self-sufficient, and independent folk and viewed government as an evil even as they became more dependent on governmental services. The fact remained that after 1900 the West was a very different place than it had been in previous years.

> "WE HAD OUR FRONTIER. WE SHALL DO ILL INDEED IF WE FORGET AND ABANDON ITS STRONG LESSONS."
>
> —WRITER EMERSON HOUGH ON THE SIGNIFICANCE OF THE AMERICAN FRONTIER, 1918

JA RANCH

This ranch, called by the initials of the original owner, John Adair, is the oldest ranch in the Texas panhandle. Founded in 1876, it once encompassed nearly 1 million acres. Although smaller today, it is run as a working cattle ranch by the Adairs' descendants.

FORD MODEL T
Fifteen million of these cars were on the road from east to west coast at the height of their popularity. The Model T cost $600 in 1913.

"IN UTAH WE HIT A PRAIRIE DOG HOLE IN THE ROAD WITH SUCH FORCE THAT A TIE BOLT CAME OUT OF THE TIE ROD CONNECTING THE FRONT WHEELS."

—ALICE HUYLER RAMSEY, ON DRIVING WESTWARD AS SHE BECAME THE FIRST WOMAN TO MOTOR COAST TO COAST, IN 1909

THE TRANSPORTATION REVOLUTION

THE AUTOMOBILE, THE AIRPLANE, AND THE PANAMA CANAL ALL CONTRIBUTED TO THE WEST'S RAPID GROWTH IN THE FIRST DECADES OF THE TWENTIETH CENTURY. ASIDE FROM PROMOTING AN ECONOMIC BOOM, THESE INNOVATIONS IN TRANSPORTATION BOUND THE WEST MORE CLOSELY TO THE EAST, BOTH GEOGRAPHICALLY AND CULTURALLY.

THROUGHOUT the history of the West before 1890, newcomers had tried to conquer distance, had hoped to span the wide, open spaces and lessen their sense of isolation. From the days of Coronado and his horses to the stagecoaches of Wells Fargo to the mid-century dreams of Leland Stanford for a transcontinental railroad, westerners had tried mightily to bridge the great distances between East and West. By 1900 the major transcontinental railroads had just been completed, bringing East and West together: the Great Northern; the Northern Pacific; the Union Pacific; and the Atchison, Topeka and Santa Fe. Only five days of comfortable travel separated the Atlantic Coast from the Pacific rim, bringing an end to more than three centuries of western isolation. But transportation development became even more intense between 1900 and 1930.

THE AUTOMOBILE
The opening of the century coincided with the invention of the automobile. Westerners avidly took to this new mode of transport that bound communities within the region more closely to each other. It did much to tie remote hinterlands directly to neighboring towns and cities. By 1912 automobile associations such as the American Automobile Association and the California Automobile Association were loudly campaigning for a transcontinental highway.

In 1912 they sponsored an exciting automobile race from New York City to Los Angeles along what they euphemistically designated as the Lincoln Highway. Millions of Americans followed the progress of the lumbering autos over a congeries of paved and unpaved roads. With Henry Ford's development of the Model T, not only wealthy people but average wage earners could tool about in cars.

STREETCARS AND AIRPLANES
Within cities life was changed by horse-drawn or electric streetcars that enabled urban dwellers to move about their communities with an ease that previous generations could only have imagined. Transportation in the West was also greatly affected by the ompletion of the Panama

Canal in 1914. For westerners it opened up new markets not only in the East but in Europe. Farmers and businesspeople had a new window on the world.

As if these advances in transportation were not sufficiently revolutionary, the invention of the airplane by the Wright Brothers in 1903 also had a profound impact on the West. It knit the subregions of the West together as never before, and westerners adapted it to their needs with enormous enthusiasm. No wonder that by 1930 the number of registered pilots in the West and the number of airplanes in the region was three times as great as in other parts of the United States.

Indeed, more profound changes occurred in transportation development during the first three decades of the twentieth century than westerners had experienced in the previous three centuries. The impact of these changes was far-ranging, for transportation was the key to rapid growth. It provided new markets and bound the West more closely to the national economy. It brought large numbers of new settlers and facilitated the migration of a needed labor force. It lessened cultural isolation and hastened the flow of newspapers, magazines, and educational activities. By the 1920s innovations in communications such as radio reinforced the impact of the developments in transportation.

CURTISS PLANES

As a pilot and aircraft designer, Glenn Curtiss was an aviation pioneer. Some of his aviation "firsts," such as the first takeoff from and landing on water (1911), occurred at his aviation school in San Diego, California. These Curtiss planes were photographed in New York.

⋟THE PLANES OF RYAN AIRCRAFT⋞

BORN in Parsons, Kansas, T. Claude Ryan (1898–1982) was five years old when the Wright Brothers made the first successful flight in a motor-powered airplane. He soon made his name as an aviation pioneer in his own right. In San Diego, California, in 1922, he founded a flying service that grew into Ryan Airlines, the nation's first year-round, regularly scheduled, daily passenger airline. In 1926 the company began designing and making its own planes. However, the company fell into financial straits, and Ryan sold out to his partner, B. F. Mahoney, though he stayed on as manager. Ryan's fortunes changed in February 1927 with an unusual telegram: *"Can you construct Whirlwind engine plane capable flying nonstop between New York and Paris? Stop. If so please state cost and delivery date."* It was from pilot Charles Lindbergh, seeking a company to build a plane in which he could attempt to fly from New York to Paris and win a $25,000 prize.

The result was the Spirit of St. Louis, a custom-built Ryan NYP that was a modified version of a Ryan mail plane known as the M-2. Among the modifications, the wingspan had to be increased and the cockpit had to be moved back to allow for a larger fuel tank. In this plane, in May 1927, Lindbergh made the first solo nonstop transatlantic flight.

Ryan later founded a new business, the Ryan Aeronautical Company, which designed the Ryan ST (Sport Trainer) in 1934 and went on to build military trainers used in World War II.

HAIL, LINDBERGH!

This music honoring the flight of Lindbergh was composed by Margaret G. Banfield in 1927.

LINDBERGH'S PLANE

Charles Lindbergh made the first solo nonstop transatlantic flight in the Spirit of St. Louis, *a modified version of a Ryan mail plane. It was nearly twenty-eight feet long.*

> "OIL IS LIKE A WILD ANIMAL. WHOEVER CAPTURES IT HAS IT."
>
> —CALIFORNIA-BASED OIL BARON J. PAUL GETTY

A GROWING ECONOMY, 1900-1930

BY 1920 MODERN TECHNOLOGY HAD REVOLUTIONIZED MANY OF THE WEST'S TRADITIONAL ENTERPRISES WHILE ALSO CREATING NEW ONES, MOST NOTABLY THE OIL INDUSTRY AND THE FILM BUSINESS. WITH THE HELP OF FEDERAL DAM-BUILDING PROGRAMS, FARMING ALSO FLOURISHED AS AGRIBUSINESS CONCERNS LEARNED HOW BETTER TO MANAGE THE REGION'S PRECIOUS WATER SUPPLY.

AS RESIDENTS of the newest region to be settled, westerners often felt like colonists. They were aware of their economic dependence on the capital, manufactured goods, and markets of the eastern United States and of Europe. They had little influence in national affairs because as yet the West was sparsely settled, containing no more than 12 percent of the nation's population. They felt a sense of cultural inferiority because they depended largely on imports from the East for their books, art, music, theater, and architecture.

Perhaps in no one sphere did westerners feel their colonial status more keenly than in economic affairs. In the period from 1900 to 1930, westerners tried mightily to overcome the shortage of investment capital that was impeding their growth. First, they tried to attract eastern investors like the

A. P. GIANNINI
Giannini used Bank of Italy funds to help rebuild San Francisco's small businesses after the 1906 earthquake.

Guggenheim family or capitalists in Scotland, England, and France. Second, they tried to build up their own financial institutions, such as banks and mortgage companies. A. P. Giannini, for example, founded the Bank of Italy in San Francisco in 1904 and encouraged the formation of thousands of small business enterprises throughout California.

But private capital was not sufficient to develop an area as large as the West. The most important source of new investment funds, perhaps, was the federal government. It proved to be the largest and most significant investor in facilitating the growth of the region. Federal funds poured into the West in a myriad of ways. One was the encouragement of western farmers and cattle growers through subsidies, low-cost loans and credit, road building, and scientific research. The Agricultural Extension

CABLE RIGGER
In 1934, a worker participates in the construction pf Boulder Dam. Also known as Hoover Dam, the structure was built to divert water from the Colorado River.

Act of 1914 and the Highway Acts of 1916 and 1922 were major sources of help. Federal irrigation and reclamation programs constituted another major effort. These included the Newlands Act of 1902 and an extensive program of dam construction throughout the semiarid West, culminating in the building of Hoover Dam in Nevada, beginning in 1928. By establishing the National Park System in 1916, which encouraged tourism, the federal government virtually gave a new industry to the West, particularly in the 1920s, when automobiles made many majestic western sites accessible to millions of visitors.

MILITARY INSTALLATIONS

Another important source of federal capital was in the rapidly expanding network of military installations. Most of the old Army posts used during the nineteenth-century Indian wars had largely disappeared by 1900. In their place new facilities sprang up that dwarfed their predecessors. During the First World War the army undertook a rapid expansion of its training camps in the West, and many of these continued to function—if on a smaller scale—during the 1920s. Meanwhile, in 1919 the Navy moved fully one-half of the nation's fleet to the Pacific Coast and established major new bases in San Diego, San Francisco, and Seattle. The fledgling air force built dozens of new airfields throughout the West, beginning with the San Diego Naval Air Station in 1913; March Field near Riverside, California, in 1918; and Randolph Field in San Antonio, Texas, in 1928. These military facilities quickly became a very important part of local western economies.

IRRIGATION DITCH
A ditch, gated to control water flow, irrigates alfalfa crops. Even today the American West is dotted with these relatively simple and efficient water-distribution systems.

GOOSE CREEK OIL FIELD
This Galveston Bay oil field was the site of the first offshore drilling project in Texas. Consistently rich wells were sporadic here until 1917, when drilling increased and the well called Sweet 16 spouted 35,000 barrels a day.

AGRICULTURE

Significant changes swept western agriculture during these years. In the nineteenth century most western farmers strove for self-sufficiency, trying to produce enough for themselves and their families. That was the true meaning of a homestead: to realize the Jeffersonian dream of a nation of small, independent yeoman farmers. But even though some westerners continued to pursue this ideal in the twentieth century, the reality came to be very different. For one thing, most of the semiarid areas of the West were not suitable for self-sufficient farming. For another, changing technology and shifting world markets significantly affected agriculture in the West. Commercial agriculture—production for market—replaced self-sufficiency. As in industry, big units often attained greater economic efficiency than small ones. Vast farms came into being that could be likened to factories in the fields, operated by large corporations that hired gangs of laborers and used expensive, complex machines. This type of farming soon became known as agribusiness, directed by large landowners or impersonal corporations.

Western farmers thus came to produce enormous quantities of specialized crops for world markets. During these years the West became the world's largest wheat grower. New urban markets in the United States fostered the expansion of fruit and vegetable production in California, Colorado, and other western states. Fruit became a specialty of California and the states of the Pacific Northwest. Cotton was grown in large quantities in California, Arizona, and New Mexico, especially during and after World War I. Rocky Mountain states like Utah, Colorado, and Idaho became major producers of beet sugar, while Hawaii specialized in sugarcane.

How could the new breed of western farmers raise large quantities of varied crops on arid lands? The transformation of what Americans

---

✦THE BUSINESS OF FRUIT✦

BY THE start of the twentieth century, fruit and vegetables began to replace wheat and barley as the key California crops. Oranges, in particular, proved to be a remarkably successful crop for California. The first commercial orange groves were planted in California in the mid-1800s, and just a century later, the state boasted approximately 20 million orange trees on 250,000 acres. Other fruit grown in California included grapes, peaches, cherries, apricots, and pears.

California was not the only West Coast state with agricultural riches. Oregon has proved fertile ground for apples, cherries, and pears, not to mention an abundance of berries, including strawberries and cranberries. Not to be outdone, Washington State has consistently produced outstanding pears, cherries, apricots, strawberries, peaches, and, of course, apples. In fact, between 1905 and 1915, large-scale commercial orchards became common in the Pacific Northwest. In 1908, 1 million apple trees were planted in Washington, which was the number one apple producer by 1917. In British Columbia, too, the fruit business boomed in the early twentieth century.

The agriculture industry was no stranger to controversy. The poor wages and treatment of migrant workers, who provided an additional labor pool to farmers, led to protests. With little or no access to health or social services, migrant workers were at the mercy of their employers. In the second half of the century, the efforts of farmworkers, led by César Chávez, to unionize and press for reform gained national attention.

ADVERTISEMENT
This 1917 ad for Adams California Fruit Chewing Gum traded on the reputation that California fruit had for delightful flavor.

ORANGES
These Washington oranges are going through a "Stamm washer" at a fruit-packing facility in Lamanda Park, California, in 1923. The conveyor belt closely resembles those used today.

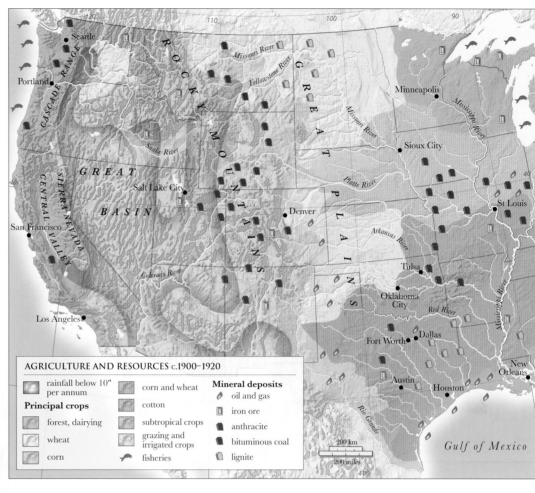

AGRICULTURE AND RESOURCES c.1900–1920

				Mineral deposits	
	rainfall below 10" per annum		corn and wheat	oil and gas	
Principal crops			cotton	iron ore	
	forest, dairying		subtropical crops	anthracite	
	wheat		grazing and irrigated crops	bituminous coal	
	corn		fisheries	lignite	

200 km
200 miles

AGRICULTURE AND RESOURCES

Growth in the West in the early twentieth century brought changes, including the breaking up of the Great Plains into mixed farms, the conversion of cattle pasture to farmland, and the establishment of national parks in the Rockies.

in the nineteenth century viewed as the Great American Desert into a twentieth-century Great American Garden was achieved by considerable ingenuity–and by the application of technology. Two methods were particularly important. One was irrigation and reclamation, the other dry farming. In both cases, water was the key to agricultural expansion.

Between 1900 and 1930 the movement to bring water to the arid West took on many of the characteristics of a crusade. Among the leaders of this crusade were some of the great engineers of the period, such as John P. Smythe, Elwood P. Mead, and Frederick H. Newell. These men advocated the irrigation and reclamation of vast areas in the West so as to turn deserts into productive farms. Their vision attracted the cooperation of political leaders in Congress. In 1902 the lawmakers enacted the Newlands Act, which provided federal subsidies for western farmers to irrigate dry farmlands. In addition, Congress created the Reclamation Service. Headed by Frederick H. Newell, it was soon

WASHINGTON WHEAT FIELD

After achieving statehood in 1889, Washington experienced rapid economic growth caused largely by wheat and cattle farming in its eastern part. The population boomed from 75,000 to 1.2 million by the start of World War I.

spending millions of dollars to build dams throughout the West. Newell's dream was to create thousands of new small family farms, but in practice the dream was rarely realized. New areas of the West did come under cultivation, but they were mostly farmed by wealthy individuals or large corporations.

Western localities organized themselves to distribute their scarce water resources. Many western states followed the lead of California, where under the Wright Act of 1887, communities were allowed to organize irrigation districts in which users could undertake equitable water distribution.

Although irrigation and reclamation was the most important method to make arid lands productive, western farmers also used the technique of dry farming, especially on the Great Plains. This was a sophisticated method whereby farmers conserved moisture in the soil by preventing evaporation. Requiring considerable skill and understanding of scientific agricultural techniques, dry farming helped wheat growers on the Great Plains to boost their production by "storing" water to be used in years of scarce rainfall.

✦DRILLING FOR OIL✦

ALTHOUGH EARLY TEXAN wells had produced some oil, self-taught geologist Patillo Higgins believed more could be found below the underground salt dome at Jefferson County's Spindletop Hill. In 1892 he set up a company and began drilling the following year, sinking three unsuccessful shallow shafts. In 1899 Anthony Lucas, an expert in salt-dome formations, drilled down to 575 feet and in 1900 sank another drill on an adjoining site.

With the traditional cable-tool technique, heavy metal drill bits bored through rock, while water, pumped down the inside of the drilling rod, forced the cuttings (rock debris) to the surface. Lucas's major difficulty was drilling through sand; the sides of the shaft constantly collapsed. But when experts pumped mud down the hole rather than water, this flushed out the cuttings and consolidated the drill walls. The technique soon became common practice.

A heavier rotary bit was then used in a four-inch pipe, and on January 10, 1901, mud bubbled up, forcing the thousand-foot pipe out of the ground. A few minutes later a stream of oil shot 100 feet into the air. It took nine days to cap the jet—and the oil age had arrived in Texas. Soon there were six wells operating at Spindletop. Hitherto worthless land now sold for $20,000 and was sold again within fifteen minutes for $50,000. The population of the local town, Beaumont, grew from 10,000 to 50,000 as 500 corporations set up business there.

The first well produced 100,000 barrels a day, more than all the other wells in the country combined. Although Spindletop's production gradually declined, by 1985 its fields had produced over 153 million barrels of oil.

OILMEN
These drillers in Blue Ridge were part of the Texas oil industry that began at Spindletop in 1901.

MINING AND PETROLEUM

Along with agriculture, extractive industries continued to be developed in the West, with mining an important source of income between 1900 and 1930. If gold and silver were the exotic metals of the nineteenth century, other minerals came to be sources of wealth in the twentieth century. Western states like Arizona, Montana, Colorado, Utah, and New Mexico became the nation's leading producers of copper, titanium, manganese, and other metals used for industrial production. Like agriculture, mining became a large-scale enterprise, requiring huge investment in complicated machinery and elaborate scientific methods. Although tens of thousands of small-scale miners continued to operate throughout the West, most of the production came from big corporations like Phelps Dodge, Anaconda, and Kennecott. In the nineteenth century, mines had been underground, but the new technology of the early twentieth century used surface mining of large, open pits. The Bingham copper mine near Salt Lake City was one of the largest in the world, but similar operations were underway near Tombstone, Arizona, and Silver City, New Mexico.

It was during these years that westerners discovered another major natural resource in their region—petroleum. Before 1900 the market for oil was largely limited to lighting for kerosene lamps. But the invention of automobiles, airplanes, and diesel engines for ships and railroads, and many new industrial uses created extensive new markets for petroleum. And as westerners scoured their region, they found enormous reserves of oil under the ground in California, Texas, and Oklahoma. These states were the major producers during this period, but other western states, such as Kansas and New Mexico, also struck oil. Discovery of the great

HALIBUT
A 200-pound fish hangs near the water in the Pacific Northwest, where fisheries boomed between 1900 and 1930.

Spindletop field in Texas in 1901 set off a boom that created a new generation of millionaires in the west. Tens of thousands of small producers, as well as major corporations such as Standard Oil, Texaco, Sinclair, and Chevron, came to exercise an important influence as production and refining of petroleum grew into one of the most profitable of the West's new industries.

LUMBER, FISHING, AND RANCHING

The Pacific Northwest lacked oil, but it contained some of the most valuable stands of timber in the world. From the great Redwoods of northern California to the forests of fir and spruce in Washington and Oregon, these three states developed the lumber industry as a major source of income. Although small operators were active during these years, large corporations came to account for an appreciable share of total production. Most important was the Weyerhaeuser company, founded by Fred Weyerhaeuser, who came to the Pacific Northwest from Wisconsin at the turn of the century to organize what became the largest lumber company in the world. Other major producers, such as Pope and Talbot, also became mainstays of the industry, with extensive integrated operations including mills, finishing plants, and ships.

COPPER MINE
The Bingham copper mine near Salt Lake City, Utah, photographed c. 1909, used surface mining techniques to became one of the world's largest copper mines.

BELL RANCH
Named for a bell-shaped butte within its borders, this New Mexico cattle ranch was created from a land grant originally awarded in 1824. The ranch lands were parceled and sold in 1947.

For the states on the Pacific Coast, fisheries came to be an important source of income. Alaska, Washington, and Oregon specialized in catching salmon, for which there were great markets in the nation's rapidly growing cities. Between 1900 and 1930, California caught and processed millions of pounds of sardines yearly. Much of the catch was canned for food consumption, but significant quantities were also used by farmers for fertilizer. The fisheries of California attracted a colorful array of ethnic groups, as Chinese, Japanese, Portuguese, Italians, and Hawaiians fished for shrimp, abalone, and tuna.

Of course, in the minds of most Americans, the West has always been associated not so much with fish as with the cattle and sheep industries. Yet after 1900 livestock were less important in the western economy than they had been in the nineteenth century. As the open range declined, cattle growers used fenced lands, scientific breeding, and special feeds to produce premium animals that they shipped to the great slaughtering and packing houses in Omaha, Kansas City, and Chicago. These years also saw the rise and decline

of sheep growing in the West. Production of wool was particularly important in New Mexico, Wyoming, and Nevada between 1900 and 1915, but declined thereafter, partly as a result of growing demand for synthetic fibers like rayon. Cattle growers viewed the sheepherders as their enemies, since they competed for increasingly scarce range lands in the West. Indeed, range "wars" between these protagonists were not uncommon.

MANUFACTURING

Although westerners strove mightily to diversify their economy between 1900 and 1930, they were not too successful in development of manufacturing. The West accounted for only 5 percent of the national total of manufacturing dollars. Enterprising entrepreneurs did establish some small-scale industries. In 1913 Donald Douglas began the fabrication of airplanes in southern California. Claus Spreckels, the Sugar King, built a string of sugar refineries in California. Chevron constructed new oil refineries in the northern and southern parts of the state. The Colorado Fuel and Iron Company built one of

the few steel fabricating facilities in the West in Pueblo, Colorado. The Wheeler-Osgood Sash and Door Company in Tacoma, Washington, was one of the most modern in the nation and also a notable manufacturer of furniture. Many eastern companies established branches in the West to serve the growing region, including General Motors, Ford, Chrysler, B.F. Goodrich, and the Swift Company of Chicago, which built a meat-packing plant in Portland, Oregon. Shipbuilding and repair added to manufacturing income. Moran's shipyard in Seattle garnered an important Navy contract when it bid successfully to build the American battleship *Nebraska*.

TOURISM

As railroads made the West more accessible, westerners sought to exploit the spectacular beauty of the region by encouraging tourism. To attract visitors they built new resorts and a galaxy of world-class luxury hotels, including the Coronado del Mar in San Diego. Its 750 elegant rooms were covered with more than seventeen acres of fine carpet, and its beautiful gardens were modeled after those surrounding the French palace at Versailles. The hotel offered a private railroad spur for those of its guests who came in their own personal railroad cars.

In San Francisco the Fairmont boasted that it was in a class of its own. The Brown Palace Hotel in Denver, famous for its breathtaking interior atrium, was one of the finest in the Rocky Mountain area. Colorado Springs became the

---

⇝ THE HARVEY GIRLS ⇜

WHEN FRED HARVEY (1835–1901) established his first railway restaurant in Topeka, Kansas (1876), eating establishments were generally abysmal, with poor service and little provision for travelers. Harvey changed that with a chain of restaurants set up along the route of the Santa Fe Railway. His success depended on providing good food for travelers in clean and comfortable surroundings, but equally important was his innovation of well-trained, efficient waitresses dressed in black-and-white uniforms: the Harvey Girls.

From the 1880s onward, and especially in the first part of the twentieth century, Harvey Houses and Harvey Girls were famous across the Southwest, from Kansas to California. Harvey set strict standards: His waitresses had to be unmarried, between eighteen and thirty years old, and of good moral character. Once hired, they undertook not to get married for at least a year, lived in dormitories, and were chaperoned by house mothers who enforced a 10 P.M. curfew. The pay was $17.50 a month, with free room,

board, and uniforms, and employment began with a thirty-day training course at Topeka. Most Harvey Girls were recruited from good homes in the East, and their civilizing influence is said to have played an important role in the taming of the West.

The popular movie musical *The Harvey Girls* (1946) ends with Judy Garland falling in love with saloon keeper John Hodiak. Many Harvey Girls experienced similar happy endings. Legend has it that some 20,000 of them became the wives of cowboys, ranchers, and railroadmen. The essayist Elbert Hubbard reported that 4,000 babies born to former Harvey Girls were named Fred, Harvey, or both. Perhaps Will Rogers said it best: Fred Harvey "kept the West in food and wives."

HARVEY GIRLS
These Harvey Girls were trained and ready to wait on customers at the Harvey House in Hutchinson, Kansas, in 1926.

home of an entire new resort complex, with the luxurious Broadmoor Hotel as its centerpiece. At the Grand Canyon in 1904, the Fred Harvey hotel and restaurant chain built the Bright Angel Lodge and the El Tovar Hotel to accommodate guests from around the world. In the Southwest the Camelback Inn in Tucson featured a unique desert atmosphere to attract eastern dudes. Many smaller cities encouraged businesspeople to build fine tourist accommodations, of which the Del Monte in Monterey, California, was a good example. By the time of World War I, Yellowstone National Park boasted seven hotels, with the Mammoth Hot Springs as the most lavish.

Western tourism was greatly boosted by Fred Harvey, the outstanding Inn Keeper of the West. An Englishman who came to the United States in 1875, he and the company he founded constructed a chain of excellent restaurants and hotels throughout the West between 1886 and 1920. The food and service at many of the company's establishments were often directly attached to an Atchison, Topeka and Santa Fe railroad station. Even in remote areas, its high quality of food and service became legendary. In addition, the Fred Harvey chain bolstered tourism by building gift shops near its hotels and restaurants that featured Native American arts and crafts, including jewelry, rugs, and pottery.

In many ways the company educated unknowing easterners about the rich Native American and Hispanic cultures of the Southwest. By 1920 it had inaugurated extensive sightseeing services throughout the region, replete with elegant automobiles for tourists.

The organization of the National Park Service in 1916 boosted western tourism by making the region's beautiful attractions accessible not only to the wealthy few but to millions of ordinary Americans. Director Steve Mather undertook a rapid expansion of the system in the 1920s. During that decade about 50 million cars were added to America's automobile fleet, and the federal

GLACIER CLIMB

A group of men and women trek up the cracked surface of Paradise Glacier in Mount Rainier National Park, Washington. The National Park Service attracted millions of visitors to its parks after its founding in 1916.

SIGHTSEEING

Twentieth-century tourists navigate a tunnel cut through a California sequoia. In a nod to the invention that jumpstarted the tourism industry, California companies still offer Model T rides through Yosemite National Park.

›TOM MIX‹

BORN IN MIX RUN, Pennsylvania, Tom Mix (1880-1940) served as an army sergeant and Texas Ranger, and joined a Wild West Show in 1906. Hired to round up cattle for the Selig Company's film *Ranch Life in the Great Southwest* (1910), he was given a small part, and the studio retained him thereafter. For six years Mix appeared in over 100 Selig one- and two-reelers, directing, writing, and producing many of them. Filled with action and stunts (most of which he did himself), his films became highly popular. In 1917 Mix moved to the Fox studio, where he and his horse Tony became even better known. By this time the film western had gained a wide audience, and *The Untamed* (1920) made Tom Mix its leading promoter. In 1927 and 1928, he was the country's top box-office draw.

Mix realized that audiences wanted excitement, romance, and humor, elements that he expertly incorporated into such films as *Sky High* (1921), *Riders of the Purple Sage* (1925), and *The Last Trail* (1927). He left Fox in 1928, taking Tony on a three-year stint with the Ringling Brothers Circus, then returned to make some sound westerns for Universal before retiring, having made over 300 films. While there was little subtlety in Mix's movies, his heroic and virtuous American cowboy established the pattern for the western film hero.

Riders of therple

government and most states embarked on an extensive road-building program. Instead of thousands of visitors yearly in the national parks, the numbers rose to millions. Yosemite in California, Yellowstone in Montana, Mount Rainier in Washington, and Mesa Verde in Colorado were among the most popular. By 1929 the total number of visitors was nearly 10 million. Most did not stay in fancy hotels or expensive accommodations. To serve these throngs, businessmen and women built auto courts—the predecessors of motels—and camp sites where visitors could "rough it."

Of the many migrants to the West, some came mainly to restore their health. Contemporary physicians considered the warm dry climates, high altitudes, and fresh air of the West beneficial for people suffering from diseases such as tuberculosis, asthma, and arthritis. The destinations of the "lungers" (those afflicted with respiratory problems) varied, but California, Colorado, Arizona, and New Mexico were favorite locations. These health seekers were also responsible for establishing excellent medical and health-care facilities in their new homes. President Theodore Roosevelt was perhaps symbolic of a whole group of talented individuals who came to regain their health in the West and developed a lifelong love for the region.

HOLLYWOOD

Those tourists who did not come to improve their health or to view the natural beauties of the West often came to see Hollywood, which in these years was emerging as the movie capital of the world. Hollywood did not establish itself as a major moving-picture production center until the post-World War I decade. Its promise grew because, apart from a mild climate, California was

attractive to some of the early major movie producers, such as George K. Spoor and William Zelig. These men were often the target of patent infringement suits by Thomas Edison and others. In Hollywood they escaped legal harassment by periodically disappearing across the nearby Mexican border. By 1914 they and other important movie producers, such as Samuel Goldwyn, Lewis Selznick, Adolph Zukor, William Fox, Jack Warner, and Louis B. Mayer, had developed the "star" system, which brought moviegoers into theaters by the millions. In this period Mary Pickford, Douglas Fairbanks, and Charles Chaplin were big attractions. In the 1920s Rudolph Valentino, Clara Bow, and Mae West became heartthrobs for millions more.

Being in the West, Hollywood did much to romanticize the nineteenth-century West with highly successful "westerns" that featured stars like Tom Mix, Ed "Hoot" Gibson, and William S. Hart. These movies fed American nostalgia for a simpler age and strengthened the image of the cowboy as

a national hero. At the same time such films often fostered negative stereotypes of Native Americans, Hispanics, African Americans, and Asians.

MOVIE STARS

The moving-picture phenomenon ushered in an era of stardom for showstoppers like Mae West, left, and Charlie Chaplin, above. These stars commonly glorified the Old West in their films, as in Chaplin's The Gold Rush *(1925).*

THEODORE ROOSEVELT
The twenty-sixth U.S. president thought it was important to protect the common worker from the power of the wealthy.

"LEAVE IT AS IT IS. YOU CANNOT IMPROVE ON IT...WHAT YOU CAN DO IS TO KEEP IT FOR YOUR CHILDREN, YOUR CHILDREN'S CHILDREN, AND FOR ALL WHO COME AFTER YOU."

—U.S. PRESIDENT THEODORE ROOSEVELT, ON PRESERVING THE GRAND CANYON, 1903

POLITICS AND PEOPLE, 1900-1930

THE PROGRESSIVE ERA RALLIED MANY WESTERNERS AGAINST THE EXPLOITATION OF THE REGION'S LAND AND PEOPLE. CONSERVATIONISTS CONDEMNED THE MISUSE OF THE AREA'S WATER SOURCES AND TIMBERLANDS. LABORERS BECAME MORE OUTSPOKEN, STRIKING FOR BETTER WAGES AND WORKING CONDITIONS. MEANWHILE, WOMEN AND MINORITIES CHANGED THE DEMOGRAPHICS OF THE WEST.

THE ECONOMIC GROWTH of the West between 1900 and 1930 gave the region a somewhat greater visibility in politics. Aware of their great dependency on eastern capital and manufactures, westerners eagerly joined a national protest against the excessive power of large corporations, a protest that was an important part of the progressive reform movement. Many westerners were prominent in progressive politics. Hiram Johnson became the reform governor of California in 1910, the vice-presidential candidate of the Progressive Party in 1912, and a U.S. senator after 1918. He had built much of his early career in fighting the Southern Pacific Railroad as a symbol of corporate power in California. Henry Teller of Colorado was a prominent, influential Democrat in the United States Senate who was often viewed as representing western miners.

Franklin K. Lane, a former city attorney for San Francisco, became Woodrow Wilson's secretary of the interior. Judge Ben Lindsey of Denver won national fame as a pioneer in the treatment of juvenile delinquents. Of Progressives in the U.S. Senate, William Borah of Idaho, Arthur Capper of Kansas, George Norris of Nebraska, Edward P. Costigan of Colorado, and Bronson Cutting of New Mexico were often in the news.

Western concern over corporate power was partly due to labor problems that arose during this period. In the mining and timber areas of the West, workers were often restless and exploited. In response, in 1905 some of the lowest-paid workers organized the Industrial Workers of the World (IWW), a militant labor union. Led by Big Bill Haywood, the IWW advocated violence and the overthrow of the capitalist system. In many communities it inspired fear and opposition. Initially that did not dampen the union's ardor, but it encountered increasing opposition. Some of the bitter strikes during this period included the Ludlow, Colorado, coal strike of 1914, which was brutally broken by Pinkerton guards hired by the coal companies. Violent strikes by miners in Coeur d'Alene, Idaho; copper miners in Butte, Montana, and Bisbee, Arizona; gold miners in Cripple Creek, Colorado; and lumber workers in Everett, Washington, added to the pattern of labor violence and anti-union activity in the West. Strong opposition to the IWW by the federal government during and after the First World War and by large corporations led to its decline by 1920.

THE TEAPOT DOME SCANDAL
A cartoon ridicules Secretary of the Interior Albert Fall, who took a bribe to lease oil reserves in Teapot Dome, Wyoming, to a businessman. Fall was convicted in 1929.

CONSERVATION

Among the widely discussed political issues in these years were those relating to the conservation of the West's diminishing natural resources. Westerners were divided on this question. Some were avid followers of distinguished naturalist John Muir, who advocated preservation of large nature areas and reduction or prohibition of access for development and settlement. Muir's opposition to the flooding of the beautiful Hetch Hetchy Valley near San Francisco in 1911 for a water reservoir reflected his general position. Other westerners agreed with Gifford Pinchot, President Theodore Roosevelt's director of the Forest Service in 1905, who, while believing that western resources should be conserved, also favored limited settlement and development. A third view was represented by U.S. Senator—and later Secretary of the Interior—Albert Fall of New Mexico, who opposed any kind of restrictions on exploitation and development of natural resources by private individuals, whether they included oil, timber, or wildlife. By 1930 these divergent views had received wide publicity. Western consciousness over the need for conservation of the region's water, timber, minerals, fish, and wildlife was considerably greater than it had been at the opening of the century.

Between 1900 and 1930 the West was transformed from a frontier area into an urban civilization. Technological changes, economic development, significant increases in population,

FIRE PATROL
A U.S. Forest Service fire patrol, shown sometime between 1910 and 1923, rolls along a stretch of railroad. The Forest Service was established in 1905 to provide citizens with good water and timber, but it has since been expanded to conserve forests, grasslands, and other environments as well as to provide services such as recreation.

⟡WAR BOND DRIVES⟡

SINCE THE AMERICAN REVOLUTION, the U.S. government has issued bonds to pay for its war efforts, and drives encouraging Americans to buy them have combined financial prudence with support for the armed forces.

Between June 1917 and April 1919, the sale of Liberty Bonds raised more than $20 billion from Americans eager to demonstrate their patriotism. Boisterous parades promoted the sale of bonds. In San Francisco in September 1918, 10,000 people paraded with an effigy of the Kaiser nailed into a coffin. In the coming weeks, San Francisco bond-drive events included an appearance by movie star Mary Pickford, an aria by French tenor Lucien Muratore, and a patriotic "community sing."

Oklahoma responded to a draft-resistance movement by meeting or exceeding the state's quotas. Those who could afford to buy bonds but didn't were called "slackers" and had to ride in the "slacker wagon."

The bond-drive tradition continued in World War II. Called Defense Savings Bonds when they began to be issued in May 1941, they were renamed War Bonds following Pearl Harbor (December 1941). Firms promoted payroll-deduction programs, volunteers sold bonds door to door, and film stars toured the country selling bonds. The campaign sold more than $185 billion of War Bonds.

POSTERS
Posters, like these from World War I, were a mainstay of the effort to sell bonds.

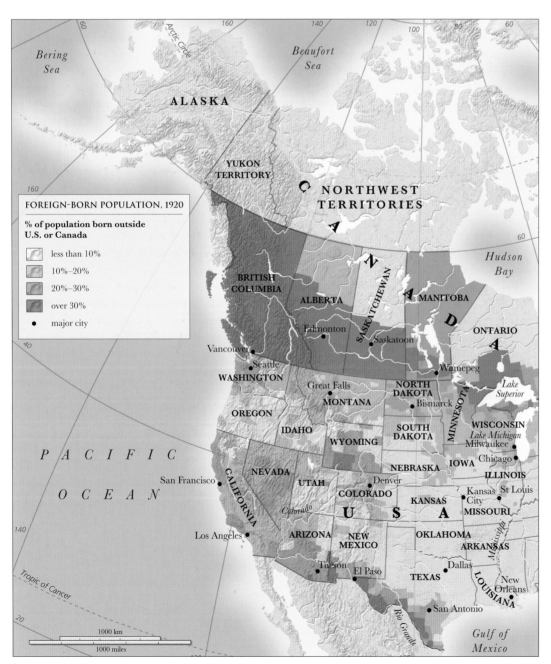

FOREIGN-BORN POPULATION, 1920

% of population born outside U.S. or Canada

- less than 10%
- 10%–20%
- 20%–30%
- over 30%
- ● major city

and the rise of towns and cities all combined to produce a complex civilization that nineteenth-century westerners would have found unfamiliar. In this process World War I also played a role.

WORLD WAR I

To be sure, the First World War did not affect the West as profoundly as the second would. In the first place, the war between 1914 and 1918 was fought mainly in Europe. Americans in the Northeast and Middle West thus were more concerned about it than those in the West, to whom it appeared more remote. And of course the United States was directly involved for only eighteen months, from 1917 to 1918. Nevertheless, the war left its imprint on the course of western growth.

The most visible economic impact of the war was to stimulate shipbuilding on the Pacific Coast. Shipyards in San Francisco and Seattle hired about 100,000 new workers. Other industries were also stimulated. The Pacific Coast fisheries expanded to supply the growing military market. California fishermen doubled their catches of sardines and increased their production of tuna. Rising meat prices benefited western cattle growers. Meanwhile, the sudden need for millions of uniforms for the American Expeditionary Force (AEF) brought a boom in the planting of cotton in California and Arizona. Increased industrial production nationwide stimulated the demand for western minerals. Western copper production grew appreciably while metals like titanium, used in steel alloys, were in great demand.

FOREIGN-BORN POPULATION, 1920
By 1920 many areas of the West had a substantial foreign-born population. Some ethnic groups concentrated in certain areas, such as the Chinese in San Francisco.

"THESE INDIANS ARE IN A MOST DEPLORABLE STATE OF BARBARISM, AND...NOTHING BUT FORCE WILL INDUCE THEM TO PERMIT THEIR CHILDREN TO BE EDUCATED AND ADOPT THE WAYS OF CIVILIZATION."

—SUPERINTENDENT OF INDIAN SCHOOLS ESTELLE REEL, 1900

RACE RIOTS

Smoke rises from the ruins of African-American homes after the Tulsa race riots of 1921. A white girl's rape charge against a black youth triggered a mob that burned and looted the black section of town.

PAWNEE SCHOOL

This boarding school for Pawnee Indians, established with federal funds in Pawnee, Oklahoma, was intended to incorporate young native Americans into white culture. Because of their heritage, these children, photographed c. 1910, were deemed unfit for higher education.

Wartime mobilization resulted in sporadic food shortages and brought considerable prosperity to western farmers, particularly wheat and grain growers. Demand for timber also sprouted as the U.S. army built dozens of new camps to train recruits. That led to a temporary mini-boom for the lumber industry in the Pacific Northwest. Throughout the West, its citizens rallied to the wartime cause with great enthusiasm. They planted victory gardens and actively supported war- bond drives. Sometimes the patriotism was accompanied by nativism and intolerance, reflected in extreme anti-German sentiments, and hatred of aliens, radicals, antiwar activists, and dissenters.

But the war-induced boom was short-lived, and between 1919 and 1921 it was followed by a postwar

bust. When the federal government abruptly cancelled its war contracts early in 1919, a severe depression ensued. The shipbuilding industry on the Pacific Coast was especially hard hit, but farmers, fishermen, cattle growers, and miners were also affected. Plummeting prices brought increasing unemployment, bankruptcy, and economic suffering. These conditions worsened as returning war veterans searched for civilian jobs.

The sudden depression aggravated labor-management tensions. Many westerners were frightened by the Seattle general strike in February 1919, when Mayor Ole Hanson threatened to call on troops to break the work stoppage. Postwar tensions also led to the suppression of political radicals. In the fall of 1919, members of the American Legion attacked the offices of the IWW in Centralia, Washington, using violence to break up that union. In Longview, Texas, a serious race riot broke the peace. Many Americans, including westerners, began to feel disillusionment about American entry into the war and about the Treaty of Versailles, which brought an uncertain peace.

MINORITIES

All of these social, economic, and political changes had a particularly important impact on minorities in the West. Throughout its history the West had been a multicultural society, including the first Americans—American Indians—and attracting people from all over the globe. Most minorities found a better life in the West than in the countries they had left, enjoying greater freedom, economic opportunity, and mobility and less social stratification. In the twentieth century, however, population movements came not so much from Europe and Asia as from other regions in the United States. These migrations included not only a greater proportion of women than in the nineteenth century, but also Hispanics, African Americans, and some Asians.

American Indians were among the most distinctive minorities in the West. Between 1900 and 1930 the majority lived on isolated reservations in remote areas where they had little contact with other Americans. The largest tribes included the Sioux in South Dakota, the Cherokees in Oklahoma, and the Pueblos and Navajos in New Mexico and Arizona. Most Indians lived in dire poverty. Until 1924 they did not even enjoy the full benefits of American citizenship. The Bureau of Indian Affairs forced many Indian

⊹SPANISH FLU⊹
PANDEMIC

THE "SPANISH INFLUENZA" virus swept the globe in 1918 as World War I was nearing its end. It got its name when Spain, a neutral country, publicized the flu's devastating effects, which combatant nations were reluctant to admit. Contemporary conditions encouraged its spread, with returning soldiers bringing it back home and refugees taking it across the world.

The first instances in the United States took place at Fort Riley, Kansas, in March 1918, when a soldier reported fever, a sore throat, and a headache. By midday there were a hundred similar cases, rising to 500 the next week, with forty-eight fatalities. For a few months the disease slackened. But September 1918 brought a dreadful resurgence, and by the end of the year the death toll in Kansas alone was 12,000.

The flu's virulence was frightening, and while many died quickly, others suffered slowly as liquid built up in their lungs. Army Surgeon General Dr. Victor Vaughan wrote: "Every bed is full, yet others crowd in. The faces wear a bluish cast, a cough brings up the blood-stained sputum."

Scare stories pervaded the country, many of them based on fact. One report told of four women playing bridge one evening and three dying the next morning. Schools were closed, quarantines imposed, and masks worn; but the disease's speed defeated all efforts.

In October 1918 more than 195,000 Americans died, and a shortage of coffins and morticians meant bodies were sometimes left in gutters or stacked on front porches. Then, for no known reason, the disease slowed. The following year saw thousands more dying, but the pandemic had run its course. Over the period 1918–19, more than 40 million people died worldwide, including more than 600,000 in the United States.

RED CROSS NURSES

During the pandemic of 1918, two Red Cross nurses demonstrate the care of influenza patients using a person on a stretcher.

parents to send their children away to government boarding schools in an effort to wean them away from their ancestral languages and cultures, and to teach them trades. Others lost their lands in a land-allotment system outlined in the Dawes Act of 1887 that they did not fully understand. Life for most American Indians in the West was very bleak indeed. The federal policy of seeking rapid assimilation, however rational it was in theory to government administrators, often resulted in despair and suffering for the Indians.

The numbers of Hispanics who came to the United States between 1900 and 1930 were small compared to those in later times. Perhaps no more than 100,000 made the migration during this period. The first wave came during the Mexican Revolution from 1911 to 1917 to escape the turmoil in their land. During the First World War approximately 50,000 more Mexicans came to alleviate farm-labor shortages in the West. In California, Arizona, New Mexico, and Texas they helped in harvesting crops and maintaining road beds for the railroads. During these years the urban barrios (Hispanic concentrations) in the border areas between the United States and Mexico grew, particularly in San Antonio, El Paso, Tucson, Phoenix, and Los Angeles. Smaller numbers joined an older Hispanic population in New Mexico that constituted one-half of the state's population and gave it a distinct character and culture.

Relatively few African Americans settled in the West between 1900 and 1930, totaling no more than 20,000. In California a small African-American community arose in the Watts district of Los Angeles, while farther north in Oakland a similar neighborhood developed. Many of these residents worked as Pullman car porters on the transcontinental trains of the Union Pacific or Atchison, Topeka and Santa Fe railroads. Smaller numbers were scattered throughout the West in Oregon, Washington, Texas, Kansas, and Oklahoma. Everywhere African Americans lived in segregated communities and were excluded from many occupations and public facilities. Such segregation also extended to public schools and recreational facilities.

Small clusters of Asian Americans existed throughout the West. The Chinese Americans who lived in the West were descendants of the more than 60,000 workers who came between 1848 and 1882 as miners and to help build western railroads. Under the Chinese Exclusion Act of 1882, no new immigrants from China were admitted. Chinese Americans were not integrated into American society but lived in self-contained communities. They had their own newspapers and

cultural institutions and developed a vibrant subculture that was not very visible to most Americans. The largest Chinatown was in San Francisco, but smaller communities were scattered throughout the West in cities such as Los Angeles, Seattle, and Portland and in numerous smaller towns. Many Chinese Americans operated small businesses such as laundries and restaurants. During these years anti-Chinese prejudice was not as virulent as it had been in the nineteenth century, yet Chinese Americans were still excluded from most spheres of American life.

Between 1890 and 1924, about 75,000 Japanese came to the West, most settling on the Pacific Coast. They were remarkably successful as fruit and vegetable growers, fishermen, nurserymen, landscape gardeners, and shop owners. Many faced considerable prejudice in California, where the state legislature enacted the Alien Land Act of 1913 to prevent them from owning land. The measure did not prove to be successful because of loopholes. In 1905-7 San Francisco attempted to segregate Japanese children in the public schools, but after strong diplomatic protests by the Japanese government and the

SUFFRAGE JOURNAL

Founded in 1917, The Woman Citizen was a weekly publication whose goal was to further the cause of women's rights, particularly the right to vote. Every U.S. congressman received a copy free of charge.

intervention of President Theodore Roosevelt, the city rescinded its policy. Nevertheless, Japanese Americans kept largely to themselves to avoid discrimination and lived in tight-knit ethnic neighborhoods, mostly in San Francisco, Los Angeles, Seattle, and Portland. Other Asians in the West included more than 10,000 Filipinos, many of whom worked in California as household servants or field laborers. Immigrants from India worked on large California farms where they, like most other Asians in the West, lived a self-contained existence.

WOMEN

The growing number of women in the West after 1900 changed the demographic characteristics of the population. In the nineteenth century many parts of the West had been settled by single, young, white males. But the migration between 1900 and 1930 changed that pattern as many of the newcomers came in family groups. The balance between men and women thus became more equal and similar to patterns in the rest of the nation. Many western states followed the example of Wyoming and Utah territories in 1869 and 1870 by extending voting rights to women well before the Nineteenth Amendment granted national woman suffrage in 1920. And since Spanish law had a greater influence in the West than elsewhere in the United States, many western

WOMEN AT THE POLLS

These women in Cheyenne, Wyoming, are petitioning for votes in 1888. Illustrations like these, appearing in eastern newspapers, quashed the idea that western suffragists were not civilized, well-bred women.

SCHOOLHOUSE

This one-room log schoolhouse, photographed around 1900, was typical of many in the West at the turn of the twentieth century. About a thousand single New England women emigrated to the West and South before the Civil War to teach school.

states, such as California, Texas, and New Mexico, provided for community property laws whereby a married woman was entitled to an equal share of a married couple's property.

During World War I, women secured more job opportunities than in peacetime, but for most these gains proved to be temporary. Throughout most of the period from 1900 to 1930, 90 percent of women stayed in the home. Yet enterprising women operated ranches and farms throughout the West and constituted a majority of the teachers in the public schools and in the nursing profession. Those women who entered the job market found their opportunities somewhat limited, although the changing economy provided some new employment options in service industries. These included a variety of clerical, office, and bank jobs. By 1930 the position of women in the West was similar to that elsewhere in the nation.

PUEBLO PAINTING
Buffalo Mother, Buffalo Dance *is a painting by Awa Tsireh, a groundbreaking Pueblo artist of the early twentieth century.*

"MAKE THEM LAUGH, MAKE THEM CRY, AND BACK TO LAUGHTER...I AM A SERVANT OF THE PEOPLE. I HAVE NEVER FORGOTTEN THAT."

—FILM ACTRESS MARY PICKFORD, KNOWN AS "AMERICA'S SWEETHEART"

GLORIA SWANSON
Swanson's movie career hit its peak in the 1920s after a series of collaborations with legendary director Cecil B. DeMille. Her lavish costumes added to the public perception of movie actors as royalty.

THE 1920S

THE IMPORTANCE OF THE AUTOMOBILE FOR WESTERN LIFE FIRST BECAME CLEAR IN THE 1920S, AS CITIES SPRAWLED OUTWARD TO ACCOMMODATE A STEADY STREAM OF IMMIGRANTS HEADING WEST. THE DECADE ALSO SAW THE FLOWERING OF A REGIONAL ART AND LITERATURE, AS WELL AS THE BEGINNINGS OF HOLLYWOOD'S INFLUENCE ON POPULAR CULTURE IN THE WEST AND ELSEWHERE.

1928 CAMPAIGN BANNER

The first president born west of the Mississippi, Iowa native Herbert Hoover was elected during boom times in 1928, only to find himself in office when the Great Depression struck. He was soundly defeated in his reelection bid in 1932.

THE DECADE OF THE 1920s brought growth and prosperity to some parts of the West but hardships to others. Farmers on the Great Plains experienced difficult times as agricultural prices plummeted and farm debts increased. Many mining operators in the Rocky Mountain area faced increasing global competition and shrinking profits. That was also true of those in the Southwest, although the enormous expansion of oil production brought prosperity to parts of Texas, Oklahoma, and New Mexico. California experienced great population increases during the 1920s and a significant expansion of its economic base. The fortunes of the Pacific Northwest, on the other hand, were more closely tied to the ups and downs of its timber and fishing industries, and the region had much more moderate—and haphazard—growth.

A deepening agricultural depression on the Great Plains spawned political radicalism there. North Dakota became a hotbed of political protests. Under the leadership of A. A. Townley and a later governor and U.S. senator, William Langer, the protesters organized the Nonpartisan League in 1915 as an agrarian reform party opposed to large railroad and grain-milling corporations. In the 1920s the Nonpartisan League dominated North Dakota politics and enacted a socialist program. That included hail insurance for farmers and state ownership of grain elevators, flour mills, packing houses, and some banks. The program became immensely popular and spread into neighboring states,

CHARLOTTE ANITA WHITNEY

Suffragist Whitney, pictured here with lawyer John F. Neylan, was a social worker by trade who went on to help found the Communist Labor Party. She was convicted under California's anti-syndicalism law.

notably Minnesota, Idaho, Colorado, Oregon, Washington, Montana, and South Dakota, in each of which the Nonpartisan League elected state legislators.

Elsewhere in the West, politicians tended to reflect a middle-of-the-road or moderate stance. California governors William D. Stephens, Friend Richardson, and C. C. Young were all political moderates. This was also true in Texas and Wyoming, where Miriam "Ma" Ferguson and Nellie Tayloe Ross became the first women to be elevated to governorships following their husbands, "Pa" Ferguson and William B. Ross.

Nativism and antiradical feelings found direct expression in western politics of the 1920s. During the decade the Klu Klux Klan gained considerable influence in several state legislatures and even helped to elect governors. The organization was especially strong in Texas, Oklahoma, Colorado, and Oregon.

Many western states also enacted anti-syndicalism laws that prohibited membership in any organization that advocated the violent overthrow of the U.S. government, such as the Industrial Workers of the World or the Communist Party of America. California was especially energetic in administering these laws and indicted more than 500 people, including the well-known activist Charlotte Anita Whitney.

Nowhere in the West was the increase of population as dramatic as in southern California in the 1920s. There San Diego and Los Angeles grew significantly, contributing to the doubling of the state's population to more than 6 million. Many of the newcomers came from the Middle West. This decade also witnessed a larger influx of Mexican citizens than ever before. From 1919 to 1929, more than 250,000 persons born in Mexico or born to Mexican parents came to California, many as migratory field laborers.

What made western cities distinctive was their urban sprawl. In that regard Los Angeles was the prototype of a number of rapidly growing urban centers in the West. Before the First World War, cities had, to some extent, been shaped by the directions taken by railroads. But the western cities of the 1920s were given much of their form by automobiles that made travel to outlying areas practical. During the 1920s

localities and states greatly extended roads and streets, leading to a wide dispersal of people and the building of highways.

CULTURAL LIFE

In the 1920s, Hollywood emerged as the world's preeminent motion-picture production center. But western cultural life developed even greater distinctiveness during the decade with a movement emphasizing regionalism—focusing on the distinctive characteristics of the West. Several literary centers arose where writers, artists, and musicians gathered for inspiration and mutual support. Their vision was to develop a distinctive voice for the West in the broader context of national culture.

One of these centers was in Carmel, California, where Robinson Jeffers, a charismatic poet, and other talented individuals such as George Sterling, Eugene Manlove Rhodes, and R. Carey McWilliams visited. A celebration of Native American and Hispanic cultures in the Southwest inspired another group of literati to settle in Santa Fe, New Mexico, where Mary Austin, Witter Bynner, Harvey Fergusson, and Stanley Vestal wrote about the distinctiveness of the West in terms of its peoples and majestic natural environment. In Texas J. Frank Dobie celebrated the special mystique that had grown up around the cowboy. On the Plains the great novelist Ole Rölvaag chronicled the special hardships that the settlers of the treeless plains encountered. What drew these varied authors together was their belief that writers should find inspiration in their native soil— in their case, the American West.

The regional movement also did much to vitalize western art. In the 1920s several new art institutes were established in southern California to promote regional painting, including the Otis Institute and the Los Angeles Art Center School. The Southwest Museum of Los Angeles gathered one of the finest collections of aboriginal Native American arts and crafts anywhere. San Francisco established the de Young Memorial Museum in 1926, reflecting the increasing cultural maturity of the West. A number of painters who sought to reflect California's particular ambiance emerged in this period, including Dong Kingman, Tom Craig, Millard Sheets, and William Clapp.

Another noted art center was Taos, New Mexico, where spectacular scenery and local Native American and Hispanic cultures drew a distinguished group of painters who portrayed New Mexico and the Southwest. The Taos Society of Artists was founded by Bert Phillips, Ernest L. Blumenschein, and several others in 1915 but expanded greatly in the 1920s. Dozens of other painters seeking new directions came, including Walter Ufer, E. Irving Couse, Victor Higgins, Robert Henri, and Oscar Berninghaus. Santa Fe hosted a group of post-Impressionist and abstract artists, among them Andrew Dasburg, Marsden Hartley, John Sloan, Raymond Jonson, and John Marin. After World War II one of the twentieth century's greatest painters, Georgia O'Keeffe, moved to Abiquiu, New Mexico, where she used the Southwest as inspiration for her work.

The regional movement brought about the first national recognition of Native American artists. Their use of symbolism, delicate colors, and individual styles was greatly admired by cubist and abstract painters. Native American artists

---

⇸TAOS, NEW MEXICO⇷

THE ARTIST COLONY at Taos was founded in 1898 when Ernest Blumenschein and Bert Phillips entered the village seeking a blacksmith to fix a broken wagon wheel. Blumenschein would later recall his initial impressions of Taos, "[T]he drama of the vast spaces, the superb beauty and serenity of the hills, stirred me deeply. I realized I was getting my impressions from nature, seeing it for the first time with my own eyes, uninfluenced by the art of any man." Another artist, Joseph Sharp, who had been spending a few months out of the year in Taos, had already sung the village's praises, but Blumenschein and Phillips were nevertheless overcome. Blumenschein remained in Taos for a few months before returning to New York, and went back to the village annually until relocating there in 1919. Phillips, meanwhile, made Taos his home immediately.

Other artists soon followed suit, and on July 19, 1915, Oscar Berninghaus, Eanger Irving Couse, W. Herbert Dunton, Blumenschein, Phillips, and Sharp founded the Taos Society of Artists. Drawing inspiration from the scenery and Native American culture, the Society organized a show at the Palace of the Governors in Santa Fe, followed by a traveling exhibition in 1917. Robert Henri arrived in Taos in 1916, drawing other artists to the village, including John Sloan, George Bellows, and Randall Davey. With the arrival of heiress and patron of the arts Mabel Dodge, an intellectual salon setting was born. Painters Georgia O'Keeffe and Marsden Hartley, photographers Ansel Adams and Paul Strand, and writers D. H. Lawrence and Willa Cather were all introduced to the wonders of Taos at Dodge's invitation in the 1920s. Later artists included the post-World War II "Taos Moderns," whose work was more abstract than that of the realists who had established the first artists' colony in Taos.

Perhaps O'Keeffe summed up the feelings of the artists who settled in Taos, New Mexico, when she stated, "If you ever go to New Mexico, you will itch to return for the rest of your life."

Norman S. Chamberlain
Corn Dance, Taos Pueblo
Oil on canvas, 1934

Eanger Irving Couse
Elkfoot of the Taos Tribe
Oil on canvas, 1909

> "THE WORST OF US IS NOT WITHOUT INNOCENCE, ALTHOUGH BURIED DEEPLY IT MIGHT BE... I TRY TO...SPEAK TO THAT INNOCENCE."
>
> —ANIMATOR WALT DISNEY

Fred Kabotie, Ma-Pe-Wi (Velino Shije Herrera), and Awa Tsireh, encouraged by well-known painter John Sloan, were featured in a special New York City exhibit in 1920 that aroused much favorable comment in the art world and was a precursor to similar art shows later in the decade.

HOLLYWOOD

In the realm of popular culture, Hollywood soared in importance during the 1920s. This was the golden age of the silent film, when stars like Greta Garbo, Theda Bara, Harold Lloyd, Pola Negri, and Gloria Swanson enthralled millions of fans who followed not only their films but their private lives, as portrayed in movie and celebrity magazines. Movies became big business as each week 60 million Americans paid about $400 million for admission to theaters. To meet the demand, businesspeople built more than 20,000 new theaters during the decade—some, like the Roxy in New York, lavish and extravagant. Audiences grew even larger after 1927, when

WALT AND MICKEY

Animator Walt Disney poses with his creation Mickey Mouse, the cartoon rodent who made him famous. Mickey made his debut in Steamboat Willie, *released on November 18, 1928, at the Colony Theater in New York. It was the first cartoon with synchronized sound.*

⊹WILLA CATHER⊹

THE VIRGINIA-BORN Willa Sibert Cather (1873–1947) was nine when her family moved to Nebraska, where she came to know the immigrant farmers who feature in much of her work. Graduating from the University of Nebraska in 1895, she became an English teacher, published several stories and poetry, and from 1906 to 1912 was managing editor for *McClure's Magazine* in New York.

Following her first novel, *Alexander's Bridge* (1912), Cather visited the Southwest and subsequently published her best-known book, *O Pioneers!* (1913). In 1922 she won the Pulitzer Prize for *One of Our Boys*, while *A Lost Lady* (1923) received two movie treatments. Other Cather works include *My Antonia* (1918); *My Mortal Enemy* (1926); and her last novel, *Sapphira and the Slave Girl* (1940).

A common thread in Cather's books was the moral effect that contact with nature could have on an individual. Unlike other authors of the time, she did not romanticize pioneer life, but this restraint only made her writing more memorable. For many readers she elegized the quiet heroism of the West's pioneer farmers.

producers introduced films with sound. Al Jolson starred in the first of these successful ventures, *The Jazz Singer*. The new technology also inspired a brilliant young animator, Walt Disney, who in 1928 invented the immortal Mickey Mouse, starring that year in *Steamboat Willie*. Mickey was soon joined by his female counterpart, Minnie, and many other popular animated characters.

The first three decades of the twentieth century were a spectacular era in western growth. During that period, westerners diversified their economy and built an extensive transportation system. They increased their population and built new cities. They raised their political visibility in national affairs. And they developed a vibrant and distinctive regional culture. But the Great Depression of the 1930s brought a halt to this dynamic period of expansion.

COWBOY DANCE
The residents of Anson, Texas, held an annual cowboy dance during the Depression era that recalled old western traditions.

THE WEST IN THE GREAT DEPRESSION

THE ECONOMIC SORROWS OF THE DEPRESSION WERE KEENLY FELT IN THE WEST, PARTICULARLY IN THE GREAT PLAINS, WHERE DROUGHTS TURNED ONCE FARMABLE LANDS INTO THE DUST BOWL. WESTERNERS, HOWEVER, FOUND SOME RELIEF FROM NEW DEAL PROGRAMS, WHICH INFUSED THE REGION WITH MUCH-NEEDED CAPITAL FOR THE CONSTRUCTION OF DAMS AND OTHER PUBLIC WORKS. MEANWHILE, THE FEDERAL GOVERNMENT LAUNCHED A NEW POLICY TOWARD NATIVE AMERICANS.

"IT'S NOT THE SUFFERING OF BIRTH, DEATH, LOVE THAT THE YOUNG REJECT, BUT THE SUFFERING OF ENDLESS LABOR WITHOUT DREAM, EATING THE SPARE BREAD IN BITTERNESS."

—IOWA-BORN AUTHOR MERIDEL LESUEUR, DURING THE GREAT DEPRESSION

DUST BOWL
This farmer walks with his sons in a howling dust storm in Cimarron County, Oklahoma, in 1935. The climatic disaster known as the Dust Bowl lasted ten years. It was caused by a series of four droughts combined with record-breaking heat and constant winds.

THE GLAMOUR OF HOLLYWOOD in the 1920s masked some problems in the West during that decade. Many small farmers on the Great Plains and cattle ranchers in the Southwest had never recovered from the post-World War I slump in their markets. Global competition dampened their profits—and those of miners in the region. New oil discoveries after 1927 caused a glut that plunged that industry into a deep depression. Nor did minority groups such as Hispanics—many of whom were engaged in migratory field labor—share in the prosperity of white-collar city dwellers. Further, a shortage of investment capital in the West slowed the economic diversification so many westerners desired. Thus, the West as a region was vulnerable when the stock-market crash of 1929 brought the entire nation into the Great Depression.

THE GREAT DEPRESSION, 1929–1933

Unemployment	Families receiving benefit	Migration	Population change, 1929–33
less than 10%	less than 10%	from the Great Plains	decrease
11–15%	11–15%	from Appalachia	0–10% increase
16–25%	over 15%	Black migrants from the South	10–20% increase
over 25%	area affected by drought	other	over 20% increase

THE GREAT DEPRESSION

The stock-market crash of 1929 shattered millions of dreams and left many North Americans destitute. Farmers were particularly hard hit, as banks withdrew funding; so were black people in both cities and rural areas. The Roosevelt administration devised a series of relief programs known as the "New Deal" in an attempt to restart the economy.

Like a majority of Americans, in 1932 westerners voted overwhelmingly for Franklin D. Roosevelt and change, hoping that the New Deal he promised would alleviate the economic crisis. In addition to depression conditions, in the 1930s the West suffered from some of the most severe climatic conditions in a century.

Extremes of cold and heat plagued the Great Plains, with temperatures ranging from 120 degrees to 50 degrees below 0 in a single year. Droughts beset the Plains and other parts of the West, along with swarms of grasshoppers and locusts that devoured crops. By 1935 these natural conditions made parts of the West such as Kansas, Nebraska, Oklahoma, Colorado, and New Mexico particularly sensitive to high winds that accelerated serious soil erosion. As the best topsoils were blown away, the combination of winds and drought created the Dust Bowl, which was devastating to man and beast. The toll on the inhabitants of the region was enormous, leading to death, destruction, economic ruin, and a massive exodus of small farmers known as Okies and Arkies. Immortalized in John Steinbeck's novel *The Grapes of Wrath* (1939), tens of thousands of these destitute westerners took to the road in their old jalopies, most often on Route 66, traveling to California where they hoped—often in vain—for a better life.

THE NEW DEAL

Meanwhile, a variety of New Deal programs attempted to improve conditions for people in the West, as in the rest of the nation. One of the most popular was the Civilian Conservation Corps (CCC), a work program for unemployed young men between the ages of eighteen and twenty-five. Housed in old army camps, the volunteers received room and board in addition to one dollar per day. The CCC was mainly engaged in outdoor conservation projects such as reforestation, forest fire prevention, and flood control. It was particularly popular with Native American young men who adapted well to this kind of work. Westerners also benefited from many new public works and dam- building projects that were sponsored by the Public Works Administration (PWA), including Boulder Dam on the Nevada-Arizona border (1931–35) and Grand Coulee (1934–41) and Bonneville Dams (1933–38) in the Pacific Northwest. These large-scale construction projects hired thousands of new workers, not enough to eliminate mass unemployment but enough to alleviate it.

A larger number of westerners came into contact with the Works Progress Administration (WPA), created in 1935 to provide temporary work relief programs in thousands of communities. WPA workers repaired streets, painted school rooms, repaired public buildings such as post offices, and were involved in scores of small-scale projects. Cultural programs were a significant part of the WPA. They put unemployed writers to work to compile a series of guidebooks for many western states, some of which books turned out to be the best available. The WPA also hired unemployed musicians to give concerts in schools and community centers and offer free music lessons. The program pioneered in gathering hitherto unrecorded musical songs and chants of the Hispanic people of New Mexico.

In the sphere of art, the WPA hired unemployed artists throughout the West and used them to create murals and paintings in post offices and public buildings. In addition, the WPA encouraged distinctive western regional artisans, such as the Hispanic wood carvers in the villages of northern New Mexico and Native American painters and potters. The WPA Historical Records program hired unemployed individuals to record and preserve not only the historical records in their community but historic buildings as well. Between 1935 and 1943, the WPA employed more than 1 million people in the West. At the same

---

✦THE OKIES✦

DURING THE GREAT DEPRESSION of the 1930s, high winds across the western plains turned thousands of acres of farmland into a dust bowl. The protective layer of grass that had covered it for centuries had been plowed up by homesteaders, and there was nothing to prevent the topsoil being swept away by the wind.

When a seven-year drought began in 1931, followed by dust storms in 1932, thousands of small farmers from Texas, Oklahoma, and Arkansas ("Okies" and "Arkies") packed up their belongings and set out west. They were enticed by advertisements that boasted: "Plenty of jobs for everyone in California."

Many of the overloaded automobiles and trucks broke down as they crossed the brutal Arizona desert. In his novel *The Grapes of Wrath* (1939), John Steinbeck describes the migrants' route: *"66 is the path of a people in flight, refugees from dust and shrinking land, from the thunder of tractors and invasion, from the twisting winds that howl up out of Texas, from floods that bring no richness to the land and steal what little richness is there."*

Overwhelmed by the number of arrivals, California officials turned back many at the border. Migrants who completed the journey found that employers were using the influx of desperate workers to beat down wages, employing the police or vigilantes to deal with those who protested. The term "Okies" came into popular use when a Californian journalist saw cars in the migrant camps bearing the Oklahoma license plate "OK" and scribbled the word "Okies" on the back of a photograph, which was subsequently published with that title. Okies became the common term for all migrant workers, even though Oklahoma farmers comprised only about 20 percent of the migrants.

In 1936 it was estimated that nearly 3 million people had entered California, and nearly half a million people in Los Angeles county were on relief. Only with the outbreak of World War II and consequent full employment were many of the Okies able to leave relief camps and live decent lives again.

REFUGEES
These refugees from the Dust Bowl wait aboard their truck as a flat tire is fixed in June 1939.

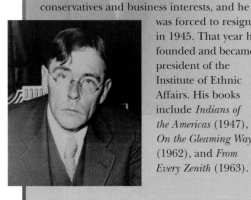

⊁JOHN COLLIER⊰

BORN IN ATLANTA, John Collier (1884-1968) was an anthropologist and social worker whose involvement in Native American affairs began in the early 1920s. He served as executive secretary of the American Indian Defense Association from 1923 to 1933 and championed the Pueblo Indians in their fight to retain their land (1924). Editor of *American Indian Life* from 1926, Collier was appointed Commissioner of Indian Affairs in 1933, in which capacity he implemented the Indian Emergency Conservation Work Program (a version of the Civilian Conservation Corps). In 1934 he introduced the Indian Reorganization Act, which sought to end federal policies of assimilation and allotment. He also helped to establish the Inter-American Institute of the Indian in Mexico City (1940) and the National Congress of American Indians (1944).

Collier's pro-Indian policies met with considerable opposition from western conservatives and business interests, and he was forced to resign in 1945. That year he founded and became president of the Institute of Ethnic Affairs. His books include *Indians of the Americas* (1947), *On the Gleaming Way* (1962), and *From Every Zenith* (1963).

time the National Youth Administration (NYA) provided subsidies and work-study programs that allowed thousands of high school and college students to finish their educations.

NATIVE AMERICANS

No group of westerners felt the influence of New Deal programs more keenly than Native Americans. Under the leadership of John Collier, director of the Bureau of Indian Affairs, the federal government reversed its previous policies of forcing Indians to assimilate into American society. Instead Collier emphasized cultural pluralism and self-determination: Indians should rule themselves and practice their own cultural traditions. Thus, the bureau encouraged tribal self-government and the use of native languages, religions, music, and crafts. Collier abolished most Indian boarding schools, which had wrenched many children from their parents, and established schools on reservations. There the children could live at home with their families in familiar social and cultural surroundings. Where possible he hired teachers and bureau administrators who were Native Americans. However, not all Indians were supportive of Collier's policies. In particular, the Navajo tribe opposed his efforts to reduce their livestock herds in the interest of soil conservation.

ENVIRONMENTAL POLICIES

Some New Deal programs directly affected the western environment. The major force behind many New Deal conservation programs was Secretary of the Interior Harold L. Ickes, who viewed himself as the champion of the West. He believed the government could serve as protector of the West's natural resources against greedy private exploiters, whether they sought land, timber, water, minerals, or fish and game. New Deal agencies planted millions of trees to protect against fierce winds and soil erosion. The Forest Service and the National Park Service intensified their efforts to protect and expand national forests and parks. The Department of Agriculture greatly enlarged its soil conservation programs by paying subsidies to those farmers who practiced sound conservation policies. The Bureau of Reclamation inaugurated hundreds of new irrigation and reclamation projects designed to protect fragile lands and reclaim arid or exhausted soil. These policies represented some of the best thinking about conservation in the 1930s, although in later years environmentalists questioned their wisdom in certain cases.

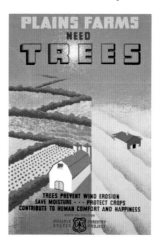

CONSERVATION POSTER
Joseph Dusek's poster, which encourages planting trees to conserve soil, was the result of a New Deal art project.

GRAND COULEE DAM
Located on the Columbia River in Washington state, the Grand Coulee began construction in 1933. This 550-foot-tall behemoth was a popular project taken on by Franklin D. Roosevelt's Public Works Administration.

Ickes was also concerned about protecting western grasslands. From the time of the first settlements in the West, cattle growers had been allowed to graze their animals freely on open range lands owned by the federal government. That practice not only deprived the national treasury of revenue but contributed to the rapid deterioration of large grazing areas. To remedy this alarming trend, Congress enacted the Taylor Grazing Act of 1934, under which the Interior Department no longer allowed cattle growers to use public lands unless they secured licenses and paid moderate fees. More important, the act established the Grazing Service, which restricted access to some lands altogether in the hope of protecting areas that had been overgrazed for decades.

By the end of the 1930s, New Deal programs had left a significant mark on the West. Although President Roosevelt failed to end mass unemployment or resolve many other problems of the Great Depression, he alleviated some of the suffering of millions while steering the government toward making a huge investment in the West. The infusion of such funds was an important element in developing the region and its economy, and in improving the quality of life of many of its citizens.

ATOMIC BOMB
In the Manhattan Project, scientists in New Mexico developed the two atomic bombs dropped on Japan in August 1945.

"LOS ANGELES WAS JUST A BEEHIVE, TWENTY-FOUR HOURS A DAY...THE DEFENSE PLANTS WERE MOVING FULL TIME, SHIPYARDS AND ALL THE REST."

—WORLD WAR II VETERAN DON MCFADDEN, RECALLING WARTIME LOS ANGELES

WORLD WAR II

WITH THE BOMBING OF PEARL HARBOR, THE WEST ENTERED ONE OF ITS MOST DYNAMIC PERIODS. THE WORLD WAR II YEARS TRANSFORMED THE REGION, MAKING IT A NEXUS FOR MANUFACTURING AND SCIENTIFIC RESEARCH WHILE ACCELERATING WESTERNERS' MIGRATION FROM RURAL AREAS TO URBAN CENTERS. THE ATOMIC BOMB, DEVELOPED IN NEW MEXICO, CHANGED WARFARE FOREVER.

BY 1939, on the eve of World War II, the West had slowly recovered from the Great Depression, partly because of increased national defense expenditures. In California, aircraft factories and shipyards were rapidly expanding production and hiring thousands of new workers. Farmers and cattle growers throughout the West saw rising prices for their products as the United States exported increasing quantities of food to Great Britain. American rearmament caused shortages of metals, benefiting mineral producers throughout the Rocky Mountain and Southwest areas. Similarly, oil men and women profited from the petroleum shortages that developed as Texas and the mid-continent region attempted to meet not only

GOING HOME

World War II uprooted vast numbers of Americans, sending troops to war and increasing the population of western cities with war-oriented industries. In 1945, after the war, these home-bound GIs board a C-54 transport plane in Long Beach, California.

American but British needs. After 1939 the majority of westerners were increasingly concerned about foreign rather than domestic affairs, although most were loath to support U.S. involvement in the conflict. If the West had not grown significantly in the decade after 1929, it had recovered from some of the ravages brought by the depression.

The recovery of the West took a new turn with the Japanese attack on Pearl Harbor in December 1941 and the entry of the United States into World War II. Unlike World War I, the conflict in 1941 was also fought in the Pacific area

and therefore involved the West much more intensely. National mobilization profoundly affected every aspect of western life. It energized the economy, led to massive government support of science, muted political rivalries in the interest of national unity, disrupted the lives of those who went off to join the armed forces or work in war factories, and recruited even film and radio personalities to support the war effort. During World War II, westerners were united in a common cause as they have not been before or since.

World War II served as an important stimulus to the western economy. It led to the establishment of huge aircraft factories in southern California and expansion of those in Seattle. Industry leaders like Donald Douglas, Howard Hughes, the Boeing Airplane Company, North American Aviation, and Reuben Fleet of Consolidated Aircraft employed in excess of 450,000 workers who built more than 100,000 planes in wartime. These included Boeing's famous B-17 bomber; B-25 bombers; the legendary North American P-51 fighter; and, later in the war, the Boeing B-29 bomber that rained bombs—including atomic weapons—on Japan. General Jimmy Doolittle used North American B-25s in his famous raid over Tokyo in 1942, launched from an aircraft carrier in the Pacific.

Wartime pressures revolutionized shipbuilding as well. A former road and dam builder, Henry J. Kaiser used prefabrication methods to build thousands of Liberty ships—10,000-ton merchant vessels—some of which he completed in less than four days. More than

400,000 workers toiled around the clock in his shipyards in Los Angeles; Richmond, California; and Portland, Oregon. Stimulated by government orders, new factories sprang up in California, Utah, and Oregon to produce steel and aluminum, while the government built the world's largest magnesium plant near the sleepy little town of Las Vegas, Nevada. Everywhere in the West new military installations, weapon test sites, air fields, and supply depots invigorated local economies.

WARTIME SCIENCE

The war also invigorated scientific research in the West. Before 1940 most scientific research in the United States was conducted east of the Mississippi River. But between 1941 and 1945 the West became one of the most important science centers in the nation. That was due in part to the establishment of a new scientific laboratory in Los Alamos, New Mexico, to develop and build the world's first atomic bomb. Led by the brilliant physicist Robert Oppenheimer and his associate, Enrico Fermi, the Los Alamos facility gathered the greatest concentration of scientific talents in the history of the world. Work at Los Alamos was supplemented by Ernest O. Lawrence of the University of California at Berkeley, who had built one of the first atom smashers in the world, and by plutonium production facilities in a vast new federal laboratory in Hanford, Washington.

Meanwhile, pioneering research in rocketry was being conducted by J.C. Lauritsen

PEARL HARBOR

The destroyer USS Shaw takes a deadly hit during the Japanese surprise attack on the morning of December 7, 1941. Eighteen ships were destroyed, overturned, or sent to the bottom of the harbor that day.

⇥LOS ALAMOS AND THE ATOMIC BOMB⇤

BY THE START OF WORLD WAR II, scientists had discovered that nuclear fission and an atomic chain reaction could unleash unimaginable results. In August 1939, Albert Einstein wrote President Franklin Roosevelt warning that Germany might become capable of developing nuclear fission. In 1941 British scientists calculated that the isotope of uranium 235 could produce an explosion equivalent to several thousand tons of TNT.

Initially three government-sponsored laboratories around the country conducted studies into nuclear weaponry, but the need for a central facility was clear. In late 1942 General Leslie Groves chose J. Robert Oppenheimer to be scientific director of a new laboratory at Los Alamos, New Mexico. In December 1942 in Chicago, Enrico Fermi produced the first self-sustaining chain reaction, convincing Oppenheimer and others that a nuclear weapon was theoretically possible.

The organization of Los Alamos was unusual. General Groves saw it as a military laboratory, but the leading scientists who manned it adamantly refused to wear uniforms or accept military commissions. A batch of younger physicists, enlisted as part of the Special Engineer Detachment (SED), did wear uniforms and took part in a formal parade. According to one scientist's wife, while the normal military staff put on a good display,

"the newly arrived SED boys were terrible. They couldn't keep in step. Their lines were crooked...They waved at friends and grinned...one general even called them a disgrace to the army."

Early arrivals found that housing and washing facilities were not ready, and families who could not get into the crowded dormitories on campus were forced to live pioneer lives on nearby dude ranches. But conditions gradually improved, and the laboratory's effect on the community was marked: between January 1943 and January 1945, the population of Los Alamos rose from 1,500 to 5,700.

In its first year, the laboratory designed a uranium-235 weapon triggered by firing one part of a critical mass into another. However, it was feared this technique could lead to early detonation. In the second year, therefore, the laboratory worked on the more difficult problem of implosion—the uniform compression of plutonium to a super-critical mass. This proved to be the solution.

It was realized from the beginning that the implosion bomb would have to be tested, and a site in the Jornado del Muerto desert near Alamogordo, New Mexico, was selected; Oppenheimer named it "Trinity" from a poem by John Donne. Here, on July 16, 1945, the first atomic bomb was successfully exploded, creating a mushroom-shaped cloud that rose to 35,000 feet; its force was equivalent to 20,000 tons of TNT. A month later similar bombs devastated Hiroshima and Nagasaki, ending World War II and introducing the Atomic Age.

MUSHROOM CLOUD

A telltale mushroom cloud rises on the horizon at a nuclear testing site. The dust within the cloud forms from material vaporized by a nuclear explosion, and returns to the earth as radioactive fallout.

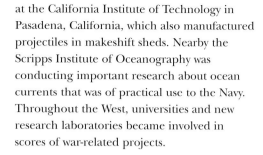

at the California Institute of Technology in Pasadena, California, which also manufactured projectiles in makeshift sheds. Nearby the Scripps Institute of Oceanography was conducting important research about ocean currents that was of practical use to the Navy. Throughout the West, universities and new research laboratories became involved in scores of war-related projects.

SOCIAL IMPACT

In addition to its economic and scientific effects, World War II had an important social impact on the West. It accelerated urbanization in parts of the West, such as California. As people streamed to areas with a concentration of war-oriented factories, cities such as San Diego doubled in size while others, such as Los Angeles, San Francisco, Seattle, and Portland, grew appreciably. Some smaller towns experienced a boomtown syndrome. Richmond, California, home to the Kaiser shipyards, grew from 20,000 to 180,000 in just three years. On the other hand, some communities in the Great Plains, Rocky Mountains, and Southwest areas lost population as men and women left to join the armed forces or work in factories on the West Coast.

Not only did cities grow, but they reflected increasing racial and ethnic diversity. The shortage of labor during the war resulted in some relaxation of discriminatory practices. More than 200,000 African Americans, most from the South, came west in search of job opportunities, predominantly in the shipyards. Under what was called the bracero agreement between the United States and Mexico, about 150,000 Mexicans yearly came to the West to provide the field labor needed to harvest crops and to maintain roadbeds on the railroads. American-born Hispanics distinguished themselves in the armed forces, as did the more than 25,000 Indians who served in the military. Private Ira Hayes, a Pima Indian, earned the Congressional Medal of Honor for his heroism at Iwo Jima. In the Pacific war, the Navajo Code Talkers—a special communications unit that transmitted secret military messages in the Navajo language that the Japanese were unable to decipher—performed valuable service. In many different ways, the war opened up new opportunities for minorities.

Discrimination did continue. The federal government unjustly incarcerated about 120,000 Japanese and Japanese Americans in detention camps throughout the West. Even so, some volunteered as farm laborers while others joined a famous regiment that distinguished itself in the Italian military campaigns.

SHIP CONSTRUCTION
Miss Eastine Cowner, formerly a waitress, is shown here in 1943 working as a scaler at the Kaiser shipyards in Richmond, California. She is helping to build the ship SS. George Washington Carver. Many civilians, particularly women, took jobs in factories and shipyards to aid the war effort.

HOLLYWOOD GOES TO WAR

Hollywood played an important role in the conflict. All of the major movie studios geared their films to promote patriotism and national unity. Most filmmakers made special training pictures for the armed forces. Frank Capra directed the *Why We Fight* series, which was designed to acquaint millions of draftees with the issues that had brought Americans into the conflict. Walt Disney effectively used animated characters, such as Mickey Mouse and Donald Duck, to promote war programs. The motion-

picture colony also established the Hollywood Canteen, a community center for servicemen and women that was hosted by well-known movie stars. Many of these personalities, particularly Bob Hope, did a great deal to maintain military morale by entertaining troops around the globe. Radio personalities promoted war causes as Jack Benny, Burns and Allen, Abbott and Costello, and Fred Allen used their talents to bolster the national effort.

THE HOLLYWOOD CANTEEN
Actresses Marlene Dietrich and Rita Hayworth serve food at this legendary club for servicemen that opened in October 1942, a month before this photo was taken.

⇥NAVAJO CODE TALKERS⇤

DURING WORLD WAR II, the U.S. need for an unbreakable code in battlefield communications was crucial. No matter how complex American codes were, the Japanese continually deciphered them. Furthermore, it sometimes took as long as two and a half hours to send and decode messages.

In 1942 Philip Johnston, an engineer and World War I veteran, learned of army efforts to use Native American languages as a code. Johnston, whose parents had been missionaries among the Navajos, was one of only about forty fluent speakers of Navajo. He convinced the authorities that the Navajo language, which had never been written down, had unique advantages, making it possible to encode, transmit, and decode a three-line English message in twenty seconds.

In May 1942, twenty-nine Navajos enlisted as Marine Corps Radio Operators and proceeded to develop an innovative alphabet, a dictionary, and a code. Military terms were assigned Navajo terminology with an English equivalent. For example:

minesweeper – *"beaver"* – cha
destroyer – *"shark"* – ca-lo
submarine – *"iron fish"* – besh-lo
amphibious – *"frog"*- chal

In time, more than 400 Navajos were recruited as radio operators; all had to memorize the Navajo dictionary and code words. After completing their training, Code Talkers were sent to Marine units in the Pacific, where their code proved impossible for the Japanese to crack, playing a vital role in the U.S. victory. During the first forty-eight hours of the Battle of Iwo Jima, Code Talkers sent and received more than 800 messages without error.

CODE TALKERS
These code talkers, working for a Marine regiment based in the Pacific, give orders by radio using their own Navajo language.

THE WAR AND THE WEST

World War II left a deep imprint on the West. It brought greater diversification to what had been a colonial economy based on raw materials. The effects of that change were visible in the manufacturing and service sectors and in the growing network of military installations.

A region that had played only a small role in American science before 1941 now became one of the science centers of the nation. Before the war the West was a region of few cities, but by 1945 it boasted numerous new urban centers, including Phoenix, Tucson, Las Vegas, Albuquerque, and San Diego.

World War II also increased the role of minorities in the life of the West, bringing in greater numbers of African Americans and Mexican Americans, and raising the communal consciousness of Native Americans. If many westerners before 1940 felt that they lived in a colony dependent on the older East, the war stimulated their self-confidence and bred a new self-image in which they viewed themselves as pioneering pacesetters for the rest of the nation.

SEGREGATION
African-American student G. W. McLaurin sits apart from other students as a 1948 University of Oklahoma class is in session.

"IT WAS NOT AN EASY TASK ATTRACTING TALENT TO A LABORATORY… NEAR A TOWN OF NOT YET 5000 SITUATED IN A SMALL RURAL VALLEY NOTED MAINLY FOR ITS WINE, ROSES, CATTLE, AND GRAVEL."

—SCIENTIST DUANE SEWELL ON
THE EARLY DAYS AT LAWRENCE
LIVERMORE LABORATORY, 1950s

THE WEST, 1945–1960

THE POST-WAR ECONOMY OF THE WEST CONTINUED TO SURGE, FUELED BY THE FEDERAL GOVERNMENT'S COLD WAR FUNDING OF MILITARY BASES AND DEFENSE INDUSTRIES. A BOOM IN TOURISM ALSO ENRICHED THE REGION. LURED BOTH BY NATIONAL PARKS AND THE MODERN ATTRACTIONS OF LAS VEGAS AND DISNEYLAND, MILLIONS CAME TO SEE THE WEST AS THE NATION'S PLAYGROUND.

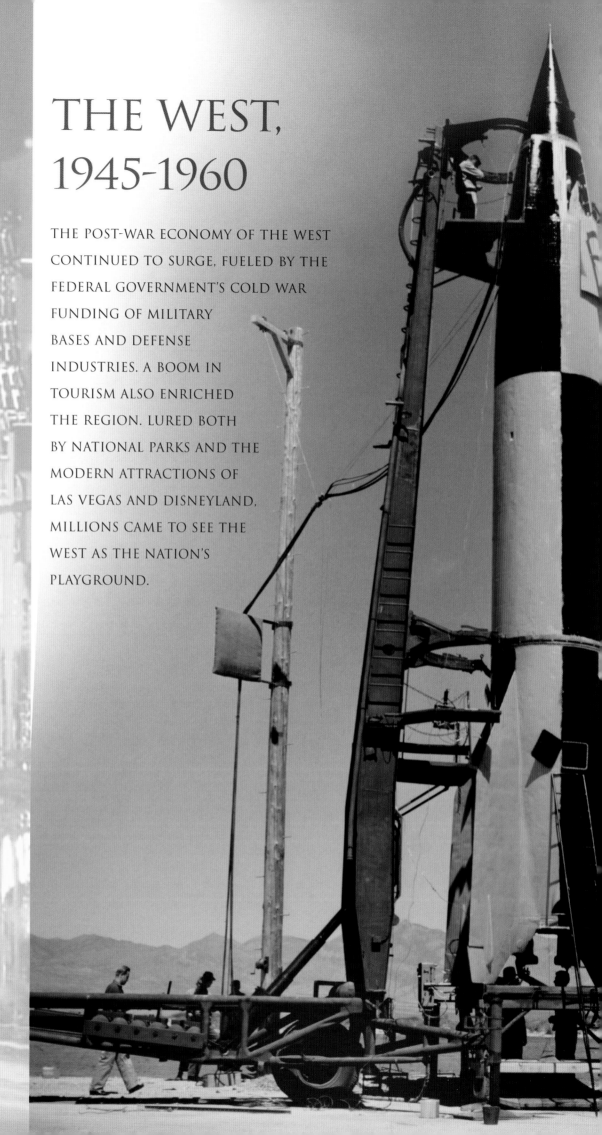

A FRESH, OPTIMISTIC ATTITUDE colored much of western life between 1945 and 1960. This period witnessed another wave of population growth, one that was truly spectacular in the broad context of the western experience. The economy had recovered from the doldrums of the Great Depression and was robust and vital. Federal intervention in western growth was even more notable than in the prewar era as the government spent lavishly on water and highway projects. Yet even these were dwarfed by the huge military expenditures of federal agencies that touched every region of the West. The cold war between the United States and the Soviet Union stimulated growth. Although the United States was officially at peace during this era, the Korean War and preparations for possible wars elsewhere dominated national policies at home and abroad. Related to the nation's domestic and international concerns was an energy boom in the West. Rapidly growing cities created new markets for natural gas, oil, and coal while the military

buildup expanded demand for minerals such as uranium and copper. This large-scale development of energy resources created increasing environmental concerns, laying the foundations for a new environmental conservation movement. That concern was sharpened by the rapid growth of western cities that placed additional pressures on existing resources.

MILITARY EXPANSION

Although the United States and the Soviet Union confronted each other throughout the world, the cold war had a particularly important influence

on the West. In many ways the United States did not undertake a large-scale demobilization after World War II, as after previous conflicts. Rather, it maintained or established new military installations, many of them in the West. With American occupation of Japan and a new emphasis on the importance of the Far East in American diplomacy, the naval establishments along the Pacific Coast became more significant than ever. Not only was one-half of the U.S. Navy stationed in the Pacific, but the navy greatly expanded its shore installations to support the fleet. Congress developed San Diego and San

V-2 ROCKET
Workers test a V-2 missile at the White Sands Proving Ground in New Mexico. Several of these German weapons of World War II were brought home by the U.S. Army to serve as prototypes for rocket production.

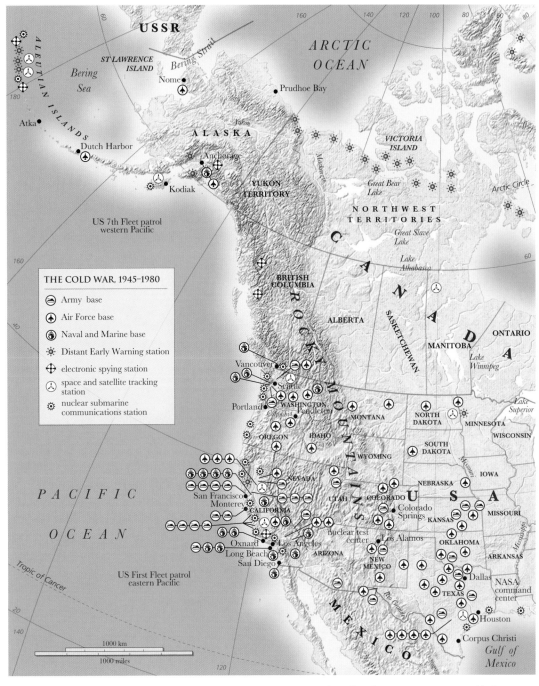

THE COLD WAR
With the post-World War II emergence of a global struggle between the U.S.-led and Soviet-led blocs, western North America acquired a new importance. Its vastness and

remoteness from East Coast power centers were ideal for research and development programs, and it had a developed infrastructure created to conduct the war against Japan in the Pacific.

✦BREAKING THE SOUND BARRIER✦

ON OCTOBER 14, 1947, Charles Elwood ("Chuck") Yeager flew a rocket-powered research plane, the Bell X-1, at a speed of over 660 miles per hour, breaking the sound barrier (Mach 1) for the first time. Born in 1923, Yeager was a World War II hero who had shot down thirteen enemy aircraft (five in a single day). He then became a flight instructor and test pilot, and in 1947 the newly created U.S. Air Force assigned him to fly the experimental X-1.

The problem with supersonic flight lay in the effect of shock waves on an aircraft as it approached Mach 1, causing violent shaking and loss of control. (A Mach number represents the ratio of the speed of an aircraft to the speed of sound; at 20,000 feet, Mach 1 is 660 miles per hour.) Extensive wind-tunnel tests proved inadequate, because pressure waves rebounding across the tunnel made accurate measurement impossible. Only in real flight could the answer be found.

The streamlined Bell X-1, with a bullet-shaped nose and a short, 28-foot wing span, was slung beneath a B-29 plane and released in flight. Yeager tested its airworthiness on eight trips before his historic attempt at the sound barrier. On the morning of the flight, the support team presented him with a raw carrot, a pair of glasses, and a length of rope to commemorate his trouble with a horse the day before. Two broken ribs added to his problems when, later, he carried out the most difficult part of the procedure: climbing down the ladder from the bomb bay of the B-29, thousands of feet in the air, and wriggling sideways into the small cockpit of the X-1.

Released from the B-29 high above Muroc Army Air Base (later Edwards Air Force Base), California, Yeager accelerated until the instruments showed he had reached .965 on the Machmeter. The needle faltered and then jumped to a reading of 1.06. Observers below, hearing the sonic boom, thought he had been killed, but then his voice came through: *"It's smooth as glass up here."*

He later wrote: *"There was no buffet, no jolt, no shock. Above all, no brick wall to smash into. I was alive."*

In 1952 Yeager set another record flying at 1,650 mph, more than twice the speed of sound. He was celebrated in Tom Wolfe's *The Right Stuff* (1979).

BELL X-1
In 1947, with Chuck Yeager as pilot, "Glamorous Glennis," nicknamed in honor of his wife, became the first airplane to fly faster than sound.

---

force established major missile bases in locations as varied as the Great Plains—in the Dakotas–but also in Colorado, the White Sands Missile Range in New Mexico, and Vandenberg Air Force Base in California.

The development of new sophisticated weapons also stimulated selected spheres of science. During these years the West became one of the most exciting centers for scientific research in the world. Much of this activity was related to national security. Western universities received large grants from the federal government to undertake thousands of studies that enabled them to hire many of the best scientists in the nation. The expansion of Stanford University and the University of California, especially its branch at Berkeley, was spectacular, but most western universities received lavish grants to expand their scientific research activities. At the same time the new Atomic Energy Commission created new nuclear research laboratories of its own, including those at Los Alamos, New Mexico; Lawrence Livermore, California; Arco (near Idaho Falls), Idaho; and Hanford, Washington. These were often supplemented by weapons laboratories such as those at Rocky Flats in Denver or the Sandia Corporation in Albuquerque. In addition, the Department of Defense underwrote expensive weapons research programs conducted by private corporations such as Martin Marietta in Denver; Thiokol in Utah; Boeing in Seattle;

Francisco Bay into extensive home bases, complete with supply depots, hospitals, repair facilities, and training schools. The U.S. Marines similarly expanded their operations in the West, building Camp Pendleton in California into one of their largest operations centers. The army maintained large training camps throughout the West, adding considerably to the incomes of scores of communities.

But perhaps the largest increase of military bases in the West was due to the expansion of the air force. Before World War II the United States Air Force (then known as the U.S. Army Air Corps) possessed no more than about 1,200 planes and was twelfth in world rankings. By contrast, between 1945 and 1960 the United States maintained the largest air force in the world with more than 20,000 aircraft, missiles, and rockets. That required new military bases throughout the West. Moreover, the testing of

new air weapons—especially the missiles developed in the 1950s—was facilitated by the wide, open spaces that the West, more than any other region in the nation, could provide. In a symbolic gesture, Congress decided in 1956 that the new Air Force Academy, to train future officers for the service in much the same manner as West Point and Annapolis served, respectively, the Army and Navy, should be located in the West, in Colorado Springs.

NEW WEAPONS

The 1950s not only saw the development of jet aircraft but also inaugurated a new age of rockets and missiles. These weapons were developed in the West, where secrecy in remote areas and test ranges was easier to establish than in the East. Not only was population density lower in many parts of the West, but the federal government owned large tracts of land in the region. Thus, the air

SALT LAKE CITY
A lamppost-lined street suggests the pleasant prosperity many people experienced in the 1950s. The postwar period brought improvements to Salt Lake City, including a new airport terminal and a water-treatment system.

SHOOTING STAR
A Lockheed P-80A, also known as the Shooting Star, *flies over the Southwest. Placed into service in 1945, this aircraft was the first operational U.S. turbojet fighter. Production was slowed after the end of World War II.*

485004

and an intricate web of aerospace companies in southern California, including North American Aviation and Lockheed. Indeed, California garnered 40 percent of all federal aerospace and development contracts in the United States and more than two-thirds of those awarded west of the Mississippi River. One-third of all workers engaged in missile industries were in California, totaling more than 1 million people. The Atomic Energy Commission was extremely active in the 1950s, developing a more powerful nuclear weapon with the H-bomb, promoted by Edward Teller of Lawrence Livermore Laboratory. Between 1946 and 1960 the commission carried out a series of extensive nuclear tests in the Nevada desert and Pacific atolls to study the pervasive effects of radiation.

The many scientific projects spawned by the cold war led to the infusion of federal monies that contributed significantly to the economic boom in the West. Federal expenditures for national security in the region exceeded $150 trillion in the years between 1945 and 1960. Much of this investment triggered new private scientific and technological enterprises related to aerospace and electronics industries, creating hundreds of thousands of new jobs. Between 1945 and 1969

the number of scientists and engineers in the region tripled, exceeding 400,000 persons. The West emerged as the nation's major aircraft and missile manufacturing center, emphasizing not only production but also research and development.

If San Diego and Los Angeles built the most spectacular technological and scientific complexes, other western cities were not far behind. Salt Lake City, Denver, Phoenix, Tucson, Albuquerque, and Seattle each created impressive new centers for research and development. Many of the spectacular weapons in the decade were made in the West, including North American Aviation's B-70 bomber and X-15 supersonic plane; Boeing's Minuteman Missile; Rockedyne's Hound Dog air- to-surface missiles; and Douglas's Thor Able booster rockets. Many of these companies benefited from their proximity to the research facilities of the Jet Propulsion Laboratory in Pasadena, California. In Phoenix, Motorola became the largest employer in the area during the 1950s, while Tucson prospered because of the large payrolls brought by the Hughes

Aircraft and Goodyear Aircraft companies. The expansion of federal military installations and weapons development centers contributed to the postwar economic boom in the West. Wherever western population growth was greatest, it was usually due to establishment of new federal military bases. This was true of the areas around Atomic Energy Commission operations in New Mexico and Idaho; Vandenberg Air Force Base in California; the Air Force Academy and the headquarters of the North American Air Defense Command in Colorado Springs; the Ogden, Utah, Supply Depot; and Hill Air Force Base, the largest employer in Utah. In western states with sparse populations, federal expenditures were particularly important. Air force bases such as the Minuteman Missile Complex in central Montana or Malstrom

MILITARY GEAR
In 1955 Camp Pendleton Marines compare the gear of World War II soldiers, left, at 58 pounds per man, with new streamlined gear, right, weighing 40 pounds less.

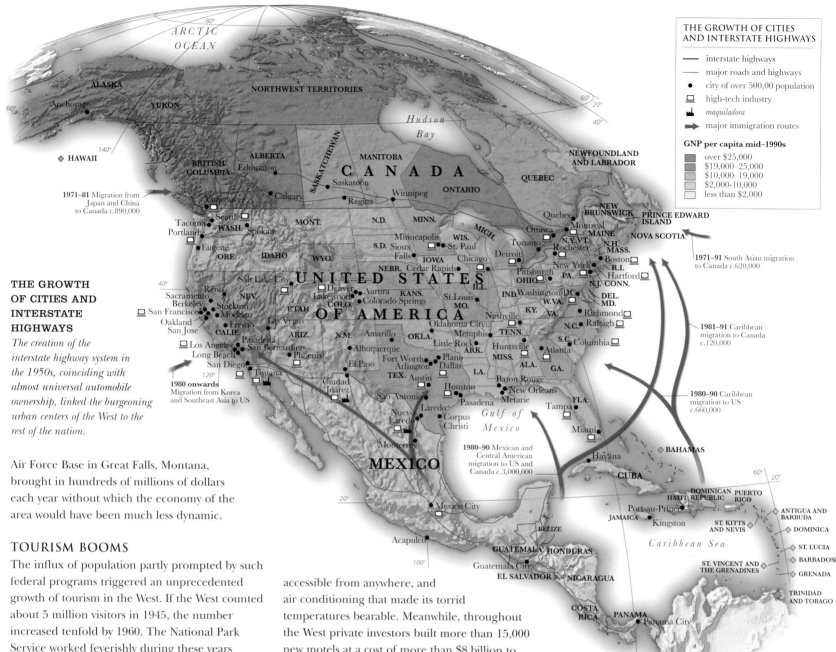

THE GROWTH OF CITIES AND INTERSTATE HIGHWAYS

The creation of the interstate highway system in the 1950s, coinciding with almost universal automobile ownership, linked the burgeoning urban centers of the West to the rest of the nation.

Air Force Base in Great Falls, Montana, brought in hundreds of millions of dollars each year without which the economy of the area would have been much less dynamic.

TOURISM BOOMS

The influx of population partly prompted by such federal programs triggered an unprecedented growth of tourism in the West. If the West counted about 5 million visitors in 1945, the number increased tenfold by 1960. The National Park Service worked feverishly during these years to develop its many sites to accommodate the throngs. The Tourist Rush was no less significant than the Gold Rush of 1849 in bringing large numbers of people to the West.

Yosemite, Yellowstone, Mesa Verde, and Grand Canyon became especially popular attractions. But many others came to drink, carouse, and gamble in Las Vegas, Nevada, making it the entertainment center of America. Ever since Bugsy Siegel, a notorious gangster, built the first luxury hotel on the Strip—the Sands—Las Vegas attracted celebrities, big-name entertainers, and millions of people who lost themselves in a fantasyland for adults. The population of Las Vegas rose from 15,000 in 1945 to 130,000 in 1960, making it the fastest-growing city in the West. Perhaps this growth would not have been quite as spectacular had it not coincided with the invention of jet airplanes that made Las Vegas

accessible from anywhere, and air conditioning that made its torrid temperatures bearable. Meanwhile, throughout the West private investors built more than 15,000 new motels at a cost of more than $8 billion to accommodate the large numbers of visitors. Along with federal expenditures, tourism became a major source of income for the West.

If Las Vegas became America's favorite playground for adults, Disneyland emerged as the nation's most popular destination for children. Conceived by Walt Disney, the animator who gave birth to Mickey Mouse, Donald Duck, and other cartoon characters, Disneyland opened as a fantasyland and recreational complex at Anaheim, California, in 1956. With exhibits and activities arranged around fairy tales and historical and cartoon characters, Disneyland appealed to the young—and not so young—imaginations as no other theme park in the United States. Almost immediately it became a major mecca for American and foreign tourists, attracting several millions yearly. It became a major asset to the expanding tourist complex of southern California.

RETIRING TO THE WEST

The West also became a pacesetter with another major service industry—retirement communities for senior citizens. As Americans lived longer, they sought living spaces in mild climates and attractive natural surroundings such as the West offered. In these years private developers like Del Webb built entire cities for the elderly such as Sun City, Arizona. In California, Ross Cortese founded Rossmour Leisure World in Seal Beach, an elaborate complex of varied living accommodations. Designed to provide many amenities like golf courses and swimming pools, these retirement villages offered houses, apartments, and medical facilities to people over fifty-five.

NEW DAMS

The great influx of people to the West placed great strains on its fragile water resources. After all, much of the area west of the 98th meridian was semiarid, with an annual rainfall of less than ten inches and with limited reserves of ground water. To provide water for the millions of newcomers, the federal government expanded its dam-building programs in the region, spending more than $100 billion for irrigation and reclamation projects, a cost second only to its military outlays. Among the biggest projects was the Central Arizona program, to carry water from the Colorado River to the Phoenix and Tucson areas. Expansion of the Hoover Dam in Nevada supplied the increasing power needs of Los Angeles and the cities of the Southwest. The Department of the Interior also completed the Bonneville and Grand Coulee dams in the Pacific Northwest, where they supplied nearly one-half of all the power used in that region. Federal aid to the Central Valley Project in California allowed transfer of water from the northern part of the state to the more populous, and more arid, south. But the building of massive dams also brought problems. Often it destroyed scenic areas, displaced long-time residents, or created new agricultural-producing areas at the same time that the federal government was also concerned with farm surpluses. Nor did the Bureau of Reclamation always consider the long-term effects of the salt that irrigation waters deposited on the land. All of these, and other considerations, led to controversies over dam building in the West. Most bitter were those swirling about Hell's Canyon in Idaho and other sites in that state where private developers opposed federal efforts to monopolize dam building on the Snake River. In Colorado and Arizona, environmentalists successfully opposed plans to dam the Grand Canyon. In Congress a battle raged over creation of a Missouri Valley Authority—along the pattern of the Tennessee Valley Authority—when it became clear that it would displace many Indian tribes. Eventually only a portion of the project was implemented by the Bureau of Reclamation.

⇾LAS VEGAS CASINOS⇽

THE LAS VEGAS of the twenty-first century would make Bugsy Siegel—builder of the first luxury resort on "the Strip"—proud. Today the Strip, or Las Vegas Boulevard, bustles with big, glitzy casino hotels. While the El Rancho and the Hotel Last Frontier preceded Siegel's Flamingo Hotel, these western-themed ranches were not the elaborate creations that Siegel envisioned. Backed with funds from crime kingpin Meyer Lansky, Siegel set about creating a hotel that would attract the crème de la crème of Hollywood. Opening on December 26, 1946, Siegel's luxurious oasis in the desert set high standards for the dozens of casinos-resorts that would follow in the next three decades, including the Sands, the Riviera, the Desert Inn, the Mirage, and the MGM Grand.

The 700-room Caesar's Palace, an opulent ode to ancient Rome, opened in 1966, and Circus Circus—the first resort geared toward families—in 1972. The 1990s saw the development of mega-resorts with elaborate themes, the first being the medieval Excalibur which opened in 1990 featuring over 4,000 rooms and a fire-breathing dragon. Las Vegas tourists can even travel the world in simulated fashion, visiting ancient Egypt (Luxor), Paris (Paris), Venice (The Venetian), Tuscany (Bellagio), or New York City (New York New York).

Despite the over-the-top attractions that have made Las Vegas more family-friendly, it remains at heart a gambler's paradise, although the odds of leaving "Sin City" ahead of the game are slim. Like so many others, Andrés Martinez experienced Las Vegas's wrath:

"The next hour and a half was an anguishing blur. Instead of going back to the baccarat pit, I tried blackjack again, then craps, roulette, pai gow poker, anything…Blackjack had been particularly harsh all evening…I was running out of casino games to turn to."

SLOT MACHINES
These seemingly endless rows of slots are found at Las Vegas's New York New York Casino.

⇾DAMS⇽

IN THE twentieth-century West, dams have commonly been built to provide water for irrigation, generate electrical power, and control flooding. A dam can do all these things by concentrating a river's water at a certain point to create a reservoir or lake. The water surface in the reservoir is at a higher level than that of the original riverbed, so gravity can be used to divert water from the reservoir through canals to lands that need it. Hydroelectric power is generated when reservoir water is released through a channel called a penstock, where it spins a turbine that turns a generator and produces electrical current. To protect communities from flooding, floodwaters can be stored in the reservoir and released gradually over time. Dams may also have unintended consequences: providing a place for recreational swimming and boating, but also flooding or desiccating valued areas.

Whatever their purposes, dams must be built to survive under enormous stresses, including gravity, earthquakes, and water pressure. Dams are classified by how they are constructed to withstand forces. The strongest and most massive type of dam is a gravity dam, usually built of concrete on a rock foundation and relying on its own weight to resist the thrust of water. An example is the Grand Coulee Dam on the Columbia River in Washington. Arizona's Bartlett Dam is another type, a buttress dam, which depends on a series of vertical supports or buttresses. Other types include embankment dams and arch dams.

GLEN CANYON DAM
This dam located on Arizona's Lake Powell controls water flow through the Grand Canyon. The discharge of water through the eight turbines of the dam's power plant produces electricity for the area.

The struggle over Dinosaur National Monument was especially fierce. In 1956 Congress enacted the Colorado River Storage Project Act, intended to provide water for the southwestern states. Designed to store water for the upper basin states (Wyoming, Colorado, Utah, and Nevada), the plan was also to ensure adequate supplies for those in the lower basin (Arizona, Nevada, and California). In the process the Bureau of Reclamation planned a whole series of dams, including one to be built in Dinosaur National Monument. The possible destruction of that beautiful, historic area aroused such opposition from environmentalists that the bureau ultimately abandoned the proposal.

GROWING CITIES

To some extent federal efforts to assure more water for the West were related to the rapid growth of the region's cities. The years between 1945 and 1960 witnessed spectacular increases in the populations of the region's town and metropolitan areas. Older cities like San Diego, Los Angeles, San Francisco, Denver, Portland, and Seattle grew by 30 percent or more. The spurt was even more dramatic in Phoenix, Tucson, Las Vegas, Houston, Dallas, and Albuquerque, each of which more than doubled in population.

Western cities took on distinctive characteristics as metropolitan areas with central cities surrounded by rings of suburbs. That was largely due to their growth in an era of widespread automobile ownership, which tended to bring the dispersal of population. The various neighborhoods of these cities were often connected by strips of highways and freeways. The federal government did much to accelerate this pattern. The Interstate Highway Act of 1956 granted massive federal aid to the states to build a system of connecting highways that bound cities more closely to each other, although it often destroyed existing neighborhoods and a sense of community.

The introduction of jet air travel in the 1950s further accelerated urban growth. The federal government assumed most of the cost of building new airports. Such improvements in transportation —along with the important influence of television—ended the former isolation of many western communities and integrated them more closely into national life.

ENERGY

Much of this dynamic growth was due to more intensive energy development during these years. Newcomers to the cities needed not only jobs and employment but energy, whether for transportation, heating and cooling, or electric power. The surge of population growth thus created new markets for energy producers, including uranium, oil, natural gas, and coal. Since the West contained all of these resources, the millions of additional consumers inspired another minerals boom in the West.

The development of the atomic bomb in 1945 ushered in a period of hope that nuclear energy would have many peacetime applications. The most immediate expression of this hope in the 1950s was the construction of nuclear energy plants to generate power. Private utilities built such facilities throughout the West, but required uranium to fuel them. The Atomic Energy Commission also bought uranium to make bombs and exercised a monopoly over the sale of the mineral. Uranium was found overseas and also in Utah and New Mexico. The expectation that nuclear plants could supplant other forms of energy prompted a brief uranium mining boom in the Grants, New Mexico, and Moab, Utah, areas between 1950 and 1957. Like other mining rushes, the boom collapsed when supply became much greater than demand.

More stable was natural gas, which came to be the major source of energy for consumers in western cities. A byproduct of petroleum, natural gas was produced in Texas, Oklahoma, New Mexico, and other western states and distributed by pipeline to cities throughout the nation. Since it was cheap, clean-burning, and easy to transport, many consumers preferred it over coal. In these years strip coal-mining operations were popular in the West. Large amounts of coal were still needed for power plants and manufacturing establishments. New technologies in mining technology made it possible—and cheaper—to mine coal above the ground rather than in underground mines. Coal deposits in Colorado, Utah, Wyoming, Montana, North Dakota, and New Mexico could be readily removed by huge power shovels that tore rocks, soil, and trees from the surface, leaving behind piles of rubble. Environmentalists were appalled. Moreover, fragmented or chipped coal left behind was carried off by rains and polluted river systems, endangering plants and wildlife. But the demand for this coal was steady, and it was low in sulfur content and burned more cleanly than eastern coal. Most of this type of mining was done by private companies operating on federally owned lands. Opposition grew steadily by 1960 and succeeded in limiting the scope of strip-mining operations.

Petroleum continued to be a major product of some western states, but the expanding market for petroleum products did not create the big boom for which westerners had hoped. Increasingly the United States relied on oil imports from the Middle East, because production costs were cheaper there. Western oil producers tried to cut their production costs by resorting to off-shore drilling rigs that searched for oil under the ocean floor, particularly off California, and the Gulf Coast. Smaller oil producers in the interior thus faced greater difficulties in competing with large corporations that imported cheaper crude petroleum, although refiners suffered less.

Between 1945 and 1960 the colonial dependence of the West on the East diminished. In part this was due to the phenomenal growth of the West during these years, which gave the region greater economic and political power in national affairs. It was also because of increased federal intervention in development of the West. Pennsylvania Avenue was taking the place of Wall Street in providing investment capital for the West, whether through expenditures for national security and military installations or through projects to bring water to arid regions. By these means the federal government did a great deal to shape the configurations of western life in this period.

LAKEWOOD PARK
This community in the unincorporated part of Los Angeles County, photographed in 1950, was the largest planned housing development in history, with 17,150 homes.

SOCIAL CHANGE

Like the rest of the nation, the West during these years developed a multicultural society. The numbers of African Americans and Spanish-speaking people in the West increased considerably. Asian Americans, although not immigrating in large numbers in the 1950s, moved more rapidly into the mainstream of American society. Between 1945 and 1950, Native Americans displayed greater racial consciousness and solidarity in their struggle to claim equal rights as American citizens.

Before World War II, African Americans in the West had totaled less than 1 percent, but the black population more than tripled between 1945 and 1960. Many of the newcomers came from the South, where sharecropping was declining. Almost 1 million settled in urban areas where job opportunities were available, mainly Los Angeles, Oakland, Denver, Houston, and Dallas. More than 800,000 African Americans had served in the armed forces during World War II, and many of these veterans were unwilling to submit quietly to the racial discrimination to which they had been subjected in prewar years. The civil-rights movement of the 1950s thus had repercussions in those parts of the West with sizable African-American populations. Protests, sit-ins, picketing, and integration of public facilities were especially visible in urban areas like Los Angeles, San Francisco, Portland, Denver, Houston, and Phoenix.

Spanish-speaking communities in the West grew rapidly during this era. Immigration from Mexico increased as at least 4 million came to the United States. The barrios of east Los Angeles became home to the largest concentration of Mexican-born people outside Mexico City. Texas and California had the largest Hispanic population, but Arizona, New Mexico, and Colorado also saw significant increases. Many of the migratory field workers who came to work on American farms did not return to Mexico but swelled the barrios of the Pacific Northwest, Utah, Montana, and other western states. During the 1950s one of the most prominent civil rights organizations for Hispanics was the League of United Latin American Citizens (LULAC, founded in 1929), led by George I. Sánchez, which fought in the courts to bring down discriminatory barriers.

Although Asians had lived in the United States for several generations, it was only in the 1950s that they began to move into the mainstream of American society. Japanese Americans had suffered the humiliation of internment during World War II, but most Americans of this era sought to rectify that injustice. Japanese Americans did not return to the ethnic ghettos in which they had lived before 1940 but came to reside

SEEKING ADMISSION
Six blacks seek enrollment in the University of Oklahoma in 1948: George McLaurin, Mozeal A. Dillon, Helen Holmes, Mauderie Hancock Wilson, James Bond, and Ivor Tatum.

in integrated neighborhoods. They found that American society lowered barriers in employment, education, and the professions that had limited their opportunities in earlier years. Although the removal of prejudicial practices against Chinese Americans was slower, the reverberations of the civil rights movement led to lessening of discrimination as well. Chinese communities, however, as represented by Chinatowns in San Francisco and Los Angeles, resiliently retained their Chinese lifeways.

This was a turbulent period for Native Americans. New commissioners of the Bureau of Indian Affairs between 1945 and 1960 reversed the New Deal emphasis on self-determination and began to call for the termination of Indian reservations. They urged an end to tribal organization and resettlement and integration of Indians in big cities. The first phase of this termination policy proved disastrous for those Indians who participated, for they were not prepared for the culture shock that awaited them. Many of the larger tribes resisted the policy of forced integration. The resistance movement, led by the Congress of American Indians and by a group of young Indians who were veterans of World War II, advocated greater self-determination, cultural nationalism, and civil rights. Young activists included Mel Thom of the National Indian Youth Council, who urged a more activist, aggressive stance. Through their campaigns they won the right of Indians to vote and hold office—as in New Mexico in 1948—rights that had previously been denied them. More than in earlier years, Indians now sought a place in the American political process to secure greater equality.

CAMPAIGN HAT
This modified cowboy hat was worn to the 1992 Republican convention by a delegate supporting Texan George Bush.

"THE AMERICAN WEST IS JUST ARRIVING AT THE THRESHOLD OF ITS GREATNESS AND GROWTH... THE FUTURE OF THE AMERICAN WEST NOW IS BOTH FABULOUS AND FACTUAL."

—PRESIDENT LYNDON B. JOHNSON, 1963

THE WEST AFTER 1960

DECADES OF ECONOMIC GROWTH BROUGHT THE WEST A HUGE BOOST IN POPULATION, WHICH IN TURN GAVE THE REGION MORE POWER IN NATIONAL POLITICS. BUT THERE WERE ALSO AREAS OF CONFLICT, FROM THE CIVIL DISCORD OF THE 1960s TO LATER DISPUTES OVER HOW TO USE THE WEST'S RESOURCES WHILE PROTECTING THE ENVIRONMENT.

AFTER 1960, as the West underwent a demographic revolution, the region assumed an increasingly important role in American life. Population in the region more than tripled, from about 16 million in 1945 to about 80 million in 2000. This growth represented the greatest increase of population in the region's history. To be sure, the movement of people westward was not an isolated phenomenon. It was part of a larger trend in which Americans moved in large numbers from the East and Middle West to the South—as well as the West. One contemporary observer, Kevin Phillips, dubbed these areas offering warm climates and informal lifestyles as the Sunbelt, extending from the states of the Deep South and along the Gulf, and then cutting a swath westward to include the Southwest, the border areas between the United States and Mexico, and on to California.

The emergence of the Sunbelt had major implications for the West. It greatly stimulated economic growth of the region. It increased western influence in national politics and in American culture, particularly popular culture. It boosted the expansion of western cities. It brought large numbers of minorities to the region who provided greater cultural diversity. However, this expansion exacted a price. The pressure of so many people on fragile environments in the West created manifold ecological problems for several landscapes, polluting streams, ravaging forests, and harming fish and wildlife. Also, since much of the West is a desert region of limited rainfall, the paucity of water resources to sustain the teeming millions increasingly loomed as a major problem, and as a potential barrier to massive future growth. These implications raised major

questions about western attitudes towards growth, future development, and ecological balance in the twenty-first century.

Most newcomers to the West settled in towns and cities, which continued their substantial growth during these years. Ironically, cities in the desert grew more spectacularly than in any other portion of the West. Phoenix and Tucson transformed themselves from sleepy towns of about 100,000 in 1960 to vast metropolitan areas with more than 1 million people each. It is doubtful that they would have grown so quickly had it not been for the invention of air conditioning and the launching of irrigation projects that provided needed water. No less striking was the emergence of Las Vegas, Nevada, as a great metropolitan area encompassing more

than 500,000 permanent residents—with more than 10 million visitors yearly. As one of America's favorite tourist attractions, it developed its unique status not only because of air conditioning and water resources, but because the improvement and cheapening of jet travel made it easily accessible from anywhere in the United States, while its glitz gave it a distinctive allure.

Other cities in the West also continued to expand. The Los Angeles area maintained a torrid pace as the Mecca of the Pacific Coast—almost doubling from 5 to 9 million. Other cities in California experienced even greater increases, notably San Jose and Sacramento. The urban West near the end of the century included a number of substantial metropolitan areas, such as Denver, Seattle, Salt Lake City, Albuquerque, El Paso, Dallas, and Houston. Nor should the expansion of the largest centers obscure the rapid growth of dozens of smaller and midsized cities, such as Boise, Idaho; Billings, Montana; and Bismarck, North Dakota.

The scores of urban clusters in the West near the end of the century dramatized the transformation of the region during those hundred years. In 1900, with a sparse and widely dispersed population, the West was just passing out of the frontier stage. A century later the majority of its people were living in densely populated cities with a familiar mix of problems, including pollution, crime, and traffic congestion.

HAIGHT STREET

A tie-dye-clad biker poses in front of a purple building in this famously psychedelic section of San Francisco. Haight Street was a counterculture mecca in the 1960s.

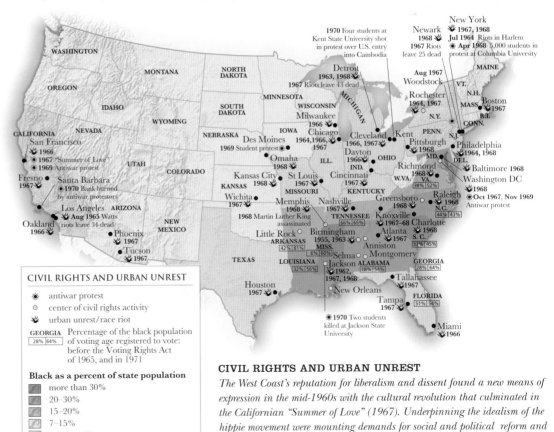

CIVIL RIGHTS AND URBAN UNREST

The West Coast's reputation for liberalism and dissent found a new means of expression in the mid-1960s with the cultural revolution that culminated in the Californian "Summer of Love" (1967). Underpinning the idealism of the hippie movement were mounting demands for social and political reform and explosive tensions within urban communities, especially among poor blacks.

✦THE WATTS RIOTS✦

ALTHOUGH THE CIVIL RIGHTS ACT of 1964 was intended to introduce a new era in race relations, some states, including California, brought in legislation to block many of its housing provisions. This led to deep resentment, especially in the black Watts neighborhood of Los Angeles, which had high unemployment, a high crime rate, and poor housing.

On August 11, 1965, a white policeman pulled over a black man on suspicion of drunken driving. A crowd gathered, arguments began, and police reinforcements were met by stones and bottles. The following day gangs of youths lined the intersection of Avalon Boulevard and Imperial Highway, throwing stones at passing cars driven by whites. Police attempts to disperse the crowd by driving through the streets with red lights and sounding sirens had little effect, as did suggestions to seal off the area. Local councilors and human-rights activists failed to calm matters as rioters began looting liquor and firearms stores and setting vehicles ablaze.

By August 13, because police had stopped fire crews entering for their own safety, buildings that had been set on fire were left to burn down. As rioting and looting continued, the National Guard, brought in on the 14th, was forced to return rioters' gunfire. A European journalist reported that the scene looked like Germany during the last months of World War II.

At the end of six days, thirty-four people were dead, almost all of them black; more than 1,000 were injured; and $35 million worth of property had been destroyed. A commission of inquiry headed by former CIA director John McCone found numerous economic and social causes for the riots and recommended improvements in education, housing, and health care. One result of this was the March 1972 opening of the King/Drew Hospital, now one of the most efficient and effective hospitals in the country.

NEWSPAPER
This newspaper, the official organ of the black militant Black Panther party, began publication in 1967, as racial tensions increased in the aftermath of the Watts riots.

STORES BURNING
Three stores are destroyed by fire on Avalon Boulevard on August 13, two days after rioting began in Watts. Property damages reached tens of millions of dollars.

MIGRANT WORKERS
Migrant farmworkers in the American West, such as these, photographed in 1974, have traditionally suffered low pay, ill treatment, and unsanitary conditions.

As western cities grew, they also came to attract people of a wide range of ethnic, racial, and cultural backgrounds. The increased migration of African Americans to the West led to the rise of substantial concentrations in the Watts district of Los Angeles; Oakland; Dallas; Houston; and elsewhere. No less significant was the rapid increase of Spanish-speaking Americans and the expansion of barrios in many cities. East Los Angeles continued to have the largest concentration of Mexicans outside Mexico City. Houston, San Antonio, El Paso, San Diego, Albuquerque, and Denver numbered large concentrations of Spanish-speaking people. Civil wars in Central America prompted migrations from Nicaragua and El Salvador.

In these years a sizable number of new Asian immigrants also settled in the West. They included not only immigrants from China and Japan, but from southeast Asia. After American intervention in Vietnam in the 1960s and 1970s, refugees from that country and from Laos, Thailand, Korea, and Taiwan streamed into the west. By 1990 the Los Angeles public schools were teaching in more than 52 different languages to accommodate children of the newcomers. The West had always had an attraction for people around the world, but the ethnic and racial diversity it developed by the late twentieth century was greater than at any other period of its history.

NATIVE AMERICANS

Native Americans could not remain immune to many of the changes swirling about them. After the disastrous experience of termination policy in the 1950s, the federal government returned to a policy of encouraging self-determination. President Lyndon Johnson with his Great Society programs and President Richard Nixon with the Indian Reform Act of 1972 encouraged economic development on the reservations. Not all of these programs were successful. Oil and gas leases brought in some income. The record of manufacturing operations was mixed. But they did motivate individual tribes to initiate their own enterprise. Many began to emphasize tourism and gambling. Federal programs improved housing conditions on various reservations.

Nevertheless, less than one-half of Native Americans in the West lived on reservations. Significant numbers moved to western towns and cities where employment opportunities were more readily available. The clash of cultures that such moves entailed brought major divisions within Native American communities throughout the region. Traditionalists, who wanted to maintain their distinct cultures, challenged assimilationists. Among the former, Russell Means of the American Indian Movement and many leaders of the Sioux nation in South Dakota sought to resist the intrusion of American culture in their lives. In a symbolic gesture, in 1969 Means and his followers occupied Alcatraz Island in San Francisco Bay to emphasize their position. On the other hand, a large tribe like the Navajo Nation in Arizona and New Mexico, led by Peterson Zah, did not necessarily favor assimilation but was open to adapting elements of the dominant culture where it seemed practical, as in the field of education.

At the opening of the twentieth century, many observers had predicted the extinction or assimilation of Native Americans in the West. By 2000, however, the number of Native Americans had actually increased tenfold to 2.5 million, and tribal cultures and identities were vibrant and distinctive. No less important were the attitudinal changes of many Americans towards Indians. In 1900 many had little appreciation of Indian cultures and had negative stereotypes of Indians. By 2000, however, most Americans had a fuller understanding of the complexities and achievements of the Native American civilizations in their midst, and greater empathy for the traumas of Indian removal endured by most Native Americans before 1900. In the 1970s and afterward, such changing attitudes were clearly reflected in popular culture, particularly in Hollywood movies such as Little Big Man (1970) and Dances With Wolves (1990).

ECONOMY AND POLITICS

Whatever their ethnic background, all westerners were affected by economic changes in the region. After 1960, manufacturing industries such as steel and machine tools declined. Since the West,

⟶CESAR CHAVEZ⟵

BORN NEAR YUMA, Arizona, César Estrada Chávez (1927–1993) labored as a migrant farmworker from the age of ten. He joined the U.S. Navy in 1945, serving in the western Pacific, and married in 1948. Like other migrant farmworkers, he was always on the move, looking for work.

In 1952 Chávez joined the self-help group Community Service Organization (CSO), becoming its national director in the late 1950s. In 1962 he founded the National Farm Workers Association (NFWA), which in 1965 joined the Agricultural Workers Organizing Committee in a boycott against Delano grape growers. In 1966 Chávez amalgamated the two unions into the United Farm Workers (UFW), and through his efforts, the nonviolent "La Huelga" (Spanish for strike) received much public support.

The five-year boycott forced most winegrowers to sign UFW contracts. However, when the contracts expired in 1973, many owners opted for the Teamsters' Union instead, causing 10,000 Californian farmworkers to walk out in protest. Chávez sought a new grape boycott, and by 1975 some 17 million Americans supported him. That year California's Agricultural Labor Relations Act enabledUFW members to achieve better pay.

In 1988 Chávez conducted a 36-day "Fast for Life" to protest the pesticide poisoning of grape workers and their children. In 1994 his widow accepted a posthumous Medal of Freedom for her late husband.

BOYCOTT POSTER
César Chávez organized boycotts to support the United Farm Workers (UFW).

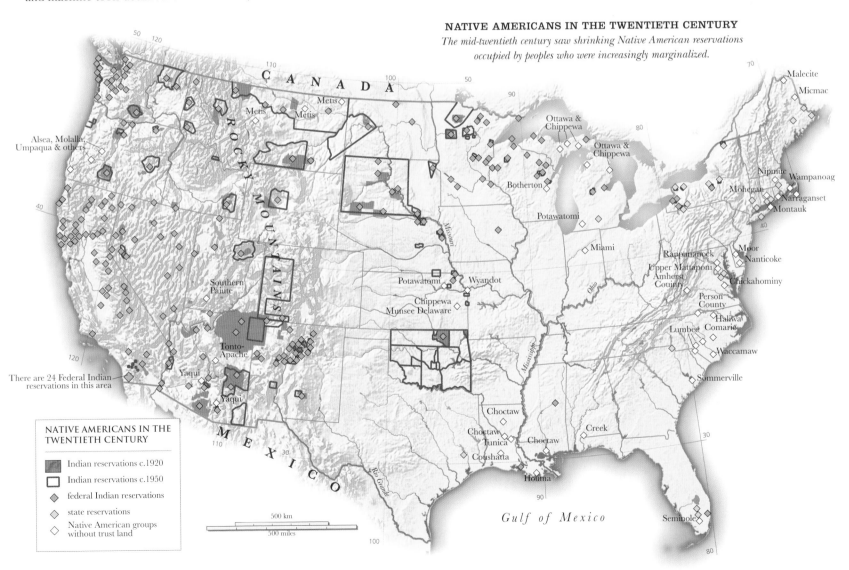

NATIVE AMERICANS IN THE TWENTIETH CENTURY
The mid-twentieth century saw shrinking Native American reservations occupied by peoples who were increasingly marginalized.

NATIVE AMERICANS IN THE TWENTIETH CENTURY

- Indian reservations c.1920
- Indian reservations c.1950
- federal Indian reservations
- state reservations
- Native American groups without trust land

500 km
500 miles

AIM ACTIVIST

The American Indian Movement (AIM) occupied the Pine Ridge Reservation town of Wounded Knee, South Dakota, in 1973. This AIM member rejoices at news of the cease-fire between AIM militants and federal forces.

unlike the East, had never developed an extensive network of manufacturing, it was less affected by this change. Instead the West was especially receptive to newer industries such as electronics, computers, medical and scientific research, and advanced technology. Most visible was the emergence of Silicon Valley in California during the 1970s, a complex of hundreds of computer chip and advanced technology firms in a ninety-mile corridor between San Francisco and San Jose. Although this was the largest concentration of such advanced technology companies in the West, other cities in the region developed similar clusters, notably Denver, Austin, Phoenix, Tucson, Albuquerque, Salt Lake City, Seattle, and Portland. At the same time western service industries expanded rapidly. Among major sources of income, tourism and federal military facilities still ranked high. On the other hand, federal dam building declined by the 1980s, although federal welfare payments increased. With the growth of its population, western financial institutions as well as medical services grew at an unprecedented scale.

The substantial growth of population in the West and increased economic power gave the West greater clout in national politics. Every decade after 1960 the West profited from Congressional redistricting and made substantial gains in the House of Representatives. The growing influence of the West was also visible in the White House. Of the nine presidents serving from 1961 to 2003, six had been born west of the Mississippi or had settled there: Lyndon B. Johnson, Richard Nixon,

SUNSET BOULEVARD

This legendary Los Angeles byway, the subject of many a song and film, stretches twenty-seven miles from downtown to the Pacific.

Ronald Reagan, George H. W. Bush, Bill Clinton, and George W. Bush. Indeed, the West contributed more chief executives in these years than any other region. The western presence was also more prominent in the federal judiciary. Former governor Earl Warren of California served as a strong chief justice of the United States Supreme Court (1953–69), with Sandra Day O'Connor from Arizona gaining prominence in 1988 as the first woman to be appointed to the Supreme Court. Their selection also reflected the changing composition of the major political parties in the West. Republicans made substantial gains in many western states. Although the West was not necessarily conservative, westerners tended to favor middle-of-the-road positions, in contrast to many Democratic liberals from the Northeast.

The tripling of the West's population in a single generation placed enormous strains on the western environment. A bevy of environmental groups, such as the Sierra Club and the National Wildlife Federation, conducted successful national campaigns to educate the

CAMPAIGN BUTTONS
Ronald Reagan and George H. W. Bush, both transplants to the West, and western-born Lyndon B. Johnson all were elected president. Bush's son George W. Bush would also win the office.

American public about the dangers that rapid western settlement posed for the environment. Beginning with Lyndon Johnson's administration, Congress responded to these concerns by enacting laws to regulate purity of water, protect wildlife, restrict strip mining, and improve air quality. Stringent regulation of nuclear power plants addressed other concerns of environmentalists. But some issues became sources of increasingly bitter conflict during the last two decades of the century. These included battles to limit timber cutting on federal lands; to restrict grazing by private cattle ranchers; to limit off-shore oil drilling; and to create expanded wilderness areas and wildlife refuges for endangered species such as the spotted owl. Many westerners viewed these proposals as a deliberate effort of easterners and wealthy individuals to preserve the West as a pristine playground for their self-indulgence and enjoyment. Instead some westerners favored development of the region's resources to provide jobs for people in industries such as logging, fishing, mining, and livestock.

These conflicts came to a head in periodic outbursts of western opposition to environmental groups, such as the Sagebrush Rebellion in the late 1970s, when the Nevada legislature enacted resolutions defying the prohibition of grazing on federal lands where it had been permitted, not only in Nevada but throughout the West. In a less strident manner, western Congressional delegations worked to strike a balance between total withdrawal of western resources on the one hand and unregulated, unbridled exploitation by private individuals and corporations on the other. In many ways the issue was not unique to the years after 1960, but had characterized western development for more than a century.

⋄SILICON VALLEY⋄

THE EMERGENCE of Silicon Valley as a technological epicenter began decades before the rise of the personal computer industry. It can be attributed in large part to Frederick Terman, who was determined to make his alma mater, Stanford University, the equivalent of MIT. As a member of Stanford's faculty, Terman encouraged his students to establish technology companies in the community. Terman even invested in the endeavors of his students, including Hewlett-Packard, founded in 1939 by William Hewlett and David Packard. As Stanford's dean of engineering following World War II, Terman focused the schoolws energies on new research opportunities, obtained military contracts to fund faculty research, and developed the Stanford Industrial Park (currently Research Park), which offered long-term leases to technology companies. Tenants included Varian Associates, General Electric, Eastman Kodak, and, in 1956, Shockley Semiconductor Laboratory. Shortly thereafter, a group of employees left Shockley and established Fairchild Semiconductor Corporation. Fairchild, in turn, spawned further spin-offs in the 1960s, including National Semiconductor and Intel.

Military funding waned in the late 1960s and early 1970s, and venture capitalists began to finance start-ups. The 1980s and 1990s saw a shift in focus from semiconductors to personal computers, then computer software, and finally the Internet boom. Successful businesses included Apple, Oracle, Sun Microsystems, and Yahoo. By the early twenty-first century, the boom was over. Between 2001 and 2002, Silicon Valley lost 127,000 jobs, or 9 percent of its workforce. But millionaires can still be made in Silicon Valley if the right deal and technology find each other.

ORACLE HEADQUARTERS
The office complex of software giant Oracle, located in Redwood City, California, gleams in the sunlight. The company was founded here in 1977.

COWBOY BOOTS
This glazed-porcelain tribute to the fabled western footwear was created in 1980 by artist William Wilhelmi.

"I THINK EVERY AMERICAN HAS A BIT OF THE FRONTIER IN HIM, A FEELING FOR IT."

—WESTERN AUTHOR LOUIS L'AMOUR, 1987

DREAM AND REALITY

IN THE AMERICAN MIND, THE WEST HAS OFTEN BEEN SEEN AS A UTOPIA—AN UNTAINTED WILDERNESS WHERE EVERY INDIVIDUAL IS A COWBOY FREE TO DETERMINE HIS OWN DESTINY. BUT THE REAL WEST WAS AND IS A MORE COMPLEX, MULTICULTURAL SOCIETY, CHARACTERIZED BY SCARCITY AND CONFLICT AS WELL AS ABUNDANCE AND PROMISE.

THROUGHOUT ITS HISTORY, the West has had at least two images. One has been as a perception in the minds of millions of people in the United States and, indeed, around the world. This was a perception of an idyllic society, a society that provided an escape from the harsh realities that individuals faced in their everyday lives. It represented the realization of utopian dreams. Yet the real West was often very unlike the idyllic image conjured up in imaginations of peoples from a wide variety of cultures. The dream and the reality have both been central to the roles of the West in American society.

The West of reality was more turbulent and troublesome than the West of the imagination. The real West was characterized by successive waves of settlers vying with each other for wealth and power, clashing in ethnic and social conflicts, and achieving success in some cases but failure in others. As an intensely human experience, western settlement contained within itself manifold human dimensions, ranging from triumph to tragedy. Even before Europeans discovered the American

West, the "West" as a distant and little-known region had an imaginative existence in the minds of people around the world. From ancient times until the present, people around the world viewed the West as a land of riches—a land where fortunes were to be made. In the twentieth century the lure was no less great, as investments in the underdeveloped portions of the American West promised to bring great returns. Moreover, from the fifteenth century until today, Europeans and Americans viewed the West as a major gateway to the perceived riches of the Far East—to China, Japan, India, and the Indies, which conjured up visions of unprecedented riches. In the second half of the twentieth century such a vision also worked in reverse as Japanese investors made major real-estate investments in the American West.

The West of myth embodied human yearnings for perfection—for a land where happiness was eternal. It represented an ideal world without the disorder, the ambiguity, the uncertainty, and the limitations of the daily

world of our experience. The West also represented an ultimate wilderness, a Garden of Eden. In the increasingly technological society of the twentieth century, many individuals around the globe yearned for wide, open spaces, for sparsely settled areas untrammeled by civilization. Throughout the twentieth century the West provided hope for such images. Moreover, the idea of a wilderness that could provide redemption was deeply ingrained in the cultures of western civilization and Christianity. In the eighteenth century, great preachers like Jonathan Edwards had likened life's journey to a pilgrimage through wilderness. "There are many mountains, rocks, and rough places that we must go over in the way," Edwards had thundered in one of his sermons. "[W]hat better end can you propose to your journey than to obtain heaven?" Although nineteenth-century thinkers secularized this version of the wilderness, they did not completely expunge the concept of a redeeming wilderness from American perceptions.

The West of the imagination also included a pronounced emphasis on individualism. At a time when many individuals felt greater constraints in living in urban, congested, technological societies, the West—in theory—beckoned as a land where individuals were still

GOLDEN GATE BRIDGE
Construction began on this famous San Francisco landmark on January 5, 1933. For Asian immigrants to the West, this bridge stood for the same ideals of freedom as the Statue of Liberty.

supreme. The American cowboy was the living symbol of that individualism, reflecting freedom of action. Never mind that the cowboy was the creation of generations of mythmakers, from Buffalo Bill and his Wild West shows to the writers of pulp westerns, movies, and television scripts. The image was firmly fastened in the minds of millions of Americans and people around the world. The individualism personified by the American cowboy was reinforced by the masculinity that many writers accorded him—at least until the middle of the twentieth century, when the role of women finally began to receive more attention. Until then, however, both fiction and nonfiction authors tended to view the West as the preserve of men—especially white Anglo males. Characteristics associated with men, such as virility, physical strength, courage, daring, endurance, and self-reliance, were attributed to the American cowboy, who came to represent a role model to successive generations. Various manifestations of cowboy life, such as attire, were widely emulated throughout the world. By wearing jeans, boots, cowboy hats, and bolo ties, people who did not even live in the West could vicariously act out their fantasies.

LAND OF OPPORTUNITY

Unlimited opportunity was another aspect of the western myth. From its first settlement, the West represented an alternative to the highly stratified, class-ridden societies of Europe, Latin America, and the Far East. To the teeming millions in those areas, the West represented a large contrast—a region where individuals could make their mark, where opportunities were limited only by the abilities of individuals. That perception was bound up with visions of vast wealth. From the days of the Spanish explorers who were drawn by visions of the Seven Cities of Cíbola, settlers were drawn to the West by visions of perceived riches. Often they were not disappointed: the North American continent proved to be a veritable storehouse of underexploited riches, including valuable minerals, wildlife, timber, and agricultural products. For individuals brought up on the teachings of the Bible, it did not take too many flights of imagination to believe they had stumbled onto a veritable Garden of Eden.

But wealth was not the only magnet that drew humanity westward. The idea of freedom in a new environment was another attraction. Although Europeans sought such freedom for themselves, frequently they denied it to others, such as African Americans or Native Americans. Throughout the centuries, religious or political freedom became a major aspect of the western image. In the nineteenth and twentieth centuries, the opportunity

◈ROSWELL◈ AS POPULAR MYTH

ONE OF the more unusual legends to take root in the modern West concerns an extraterrestrial spacecraft that supposedly crashed near Roswell, New Mexico, in 1947. In July of that year, the story goes, the U.S. Air Force recovered wreckage of the flying saucer, along with remains of dead aliens, and, behind an elaborate cover-up, has since been housing and studying them—perhaps at a top-secret site called Area 51 at Groom Lake near Rachel, Nevada.

Bizarre as this story is, it has had a long and healthy life, particularly since the 1970s, when the Roswell story began to bloom in the popular imagination, and the 1980s, when Robert Lazar, a man who claimed to have worked at Area 51, spoke of seeing alien spaceships at that site, "produced by an alien intelligence, with alien materials." Other allegedly eyewitness testimony and even a purported film of an alien autopsy have been brought forward to bolster the case. In 1994, in response to Congressional and General Accounting Office inquiries, the air force conducted an investigation and concluded that the thing recovered near Roswell in July 1947 was debris from one of their own balloon-borne research projects. Nevertheless, the "Roswell incident" and Area 51 have become part of the culture, creating an unexpected tourist trade in these parts of the West.

"UFO Crash Site" sign near Roswell, New Mexico

to build experimental societies—from Fourier's utopias in Indiana in the 1840s to the Mormons in the mid-nineteenth century to Haight-Ashbury in the 1960s—drew people to the West.

THE FRONTIER MYTH

Despite social inequalities in the West, the region projected an image of an egalitarian society, a place where social classes had had less time to harden than in older regions. The image of the West as an egalitarian society was greatly strengthened by the nineteenth-century American historian Frederick Jackson Turner, whose theories

⊹TURNER THESIS⊹

IN HIS 1893 ESSAY "The Significance of the Frontier in American History," historian Frederick Jackson Turner (1861–1932) argued that the frontier was not a physical area or region but rather a continuous process of development across the continent. The "Turner thesis" (or "frontier thesis") proposed that as the frontier moved westward, the struggles of pioneers to develop their new land engendered deep-seated ideals of self-reliance and democratic egalitarianism. According to Turner, this created a lasting—if not permanent—"dominant individualism" in the American character.

The Turner thesis became accepted by many historians, and though others historians disagreed, his views long remained influential. He included many caveats, but popular understanding tended to ignore these. The notion of the frontier influenced everything from Walt Disney's Frontierland to President John F. Kennedy's "New Frontier" platform.

Over the last thirty-five years, many academics have rebutted Turner's views. In 1968 Yale's Howard Lamar criticized him for his apparent separation of modern America from the America of the past. Others thought he had overlooked the roles of Native Americans, Mexicans, and women in the country's history. Later scholars argued that Turner's theory was racist, since it emphasized the "triumph" of Europeans over the "uncivilized" aboriginal inhabitants.

New Western Historians like Patricia Nelson Limerick suggested the word "frontier" itself was nationalistic and racist, since it had come to mean "the area where white people are scarce." Others felt Turner had overlooked universal social factors—i.e., the conflict between rich and poor, between whites and other races, and even between men and women. These views led in turn to a reaction in support of Turner and new versions of the view that the "frontier" or "borderland" had indeed played a significant part in America's development.

The arguments will continue, but as Martin Ridge of the Huntington Library has said: "Today, historians, whether defenders or critics of Turner's ideas, still feel compelled to confront them."

Frederick Jackson Turner

about the influence of the frontier on successive generations of Americans had an enormous impact. One of his dicta was that the frontier was the great social equalizer in American society and a major factor in making equality a prime goal of the American body politic. Until the middle of the twentieth century, Americans viewed their national character as being embodied in the West of myth. Westerners were considered quintessential Americans, although only if viewed in a narrow cultural focus that minimized the role of women and minorities.

After 1950, American cultural perceptions broadened. The image of the West came to include a larger segment of American society, containing groups that previously had been only shadowy figures. These included Native Americans, themselves divided into hundreds of distinctive civilizations with unique cultural characteristics. In the mosaic of the American national character, Hispanics represented another important strand, along with Asians and African Americans. Similarly, an appreciation of the role of women in development of the West surfaced only at the end of the twentieth century. In short, the myth

WOTAN'S THRONE
This distinctively shaped rock formation is seen from the South Rim of the Grand Canyon. The butte was named by U.S. Geological Survey scientist François Matthes.

of the West as representative of American character was just that—a myth focusing mainly on men and on Anglo and European cultural influence.

LAND OF HOPE

Whatever ambiguities different people perceived in the West of myth, in one way or another the West retained its image of hope and optimism, its promise of a better life and a better future. Millions of people who went west found portions of their dreams represented there, whether in the form of a plot of land, a leisurely lifestyle, a sense of freedom, or simply proximity to the region's awesome scenery. The link between the dream and the reality was not completely broken.

And yet there remained real differences between the West of reality and the West of dreams. In the twentieth century the West became no longer a wilderness but a highly urbanized society. Instead of emphasizing individuals, the West since 1900 was preeminent in developing mass culture. Despite its symbolic ties to masculinity, the West after 1900 has focused increasingly on gender equality. The large influx of population placed enormous pressures on its diminishing natural resources. Instead of unlimited plenitude, reality revealed increasing limitations and even scarcity—of water, timber, land, and fish and wildlife. That meant the placing of boundaries on the limitless opportunity that had been the hallmark of the western image. The great increase of western population set limits to the freedom that was associated with the West, replacing it with congestion and conformity. As the West became more settled, social stratification hardened. Corporate capitalism and the growth of inner cities resulted in a degree of social complexity that made the West similar to older regions. Nor did many westerners feel that they had arrived in a promised land. Alienation, rootlessness, and geographical mobility were typical of the region.

Still, more than most sections of the United States, the West developed into a multicultural society. Proximity to Mexico led to the influx of millions of Mexicans into the United States, particularly in the borderlands stretching from Texas to California. Moreover, since the Pacific Coast faced the Orient, increasing numbers of Asians—Chinese, Japanese, East Indians, Vietnamese, and Malaysians—migrated to the region as Congress relaxed immigration laws. African Americans moved in ever-larger numbers to the West after 1940 in search of better economic opportunities. Native Americans migrated from reservations to urban areas, seeking to escape high unemployment rates in remote areas. In a city like Los Angeles, the public schools had children speaking more than 300 different languages. Southern California reflected the nation's great cultural diversity with a myriad of cultures, religions, and lifestyles.

At the beginning of the twenty-first century, then, Americans continued to perceive two Wests. One was the West of myth—a land where dreams and hopes of a better life could be realized. That West was enshrined in books, television, movies, and art. The other was the West of reality. It was a highly urbanized region with the same social, economic, and environmental problems as the rest of the nation. Often the twain did not meet. Yet the American yearning for progress and improvement suggested that the West of myth was not likely to fade quickly, and that it would perform the same function of providing hope in the future as it had in the past.

SELECT BIBLIOGRAPHY

CHAPTER 1:
THE WEST BEFORE COLUMBUS. PREHISTORY TO 1500 A.D.

D'Azevedo, Warren L., ed. *Great Basin.* Vol.11 of *Handbook of North American Indians*, edited by William C. Sturtevant. Washington, D.C., 1986.

DeMallie, Raymond J., ed. *Plains.* Vol. 13 of *Handbook of North American Indians*, edited by William C. Sturtevant. Washington, D.C., 2001.

Driver, Harold. *Indians of North America.* Chicago, 1961.

Fagan, Brian M. *Ancient North America: The Archaeology of a Continent.* New York, 1995.

Heizer, Robert F., ed. *California.* Vol. 8 of *Handbook of North American Indians*, edited by William C. Sturtevant. Washington, D.C.,1978.

Kirch, Patrick Vinton. *Feathered Gods and Fishhooks: Prehistory and Archaeology of Hawaii.* Honolulu, 1997.

Orme, Antony R., ed. *The Physical Geography of North America.* New York, 2002.

Ortiz, Alfonso, ed. *Southwest.* Vols. 9 and 10 of *Handbook of North American Indians*, edited by William C. Sturtevant. Washington, D.C., 1979, 1983.

Sullivan, Lawrence E., ed. *Native American Religions: North America.* New York, 1989.

Suttles, Wayne, ed. *Northwest Coast.* Vol. 7 of *Handbook of North American Indians*, edited by William C. Sturtevant. Washington, D.C., 1990.

Swanton, John R. *Indian Tribes of North America.* Smithsonian Institution, Bureau of American Ethnology, Bulletin 145. Washington, D.C., 1952.

Walker, Jr., Deward E., ed. *Plateau.* Vol. 12 of *Handbook of North American Indians*, edited by William C. Sturtevant. Washington, D.C., 1998.

Washburn, Wilcomb E., ed. *History of Indian-White Relations.* Vol. 4 of *Handbook of North American Indians*, edited by William C. Sturtevant. Washington, D.C., 1988.

CHAPTER TWO:
SPAIN IN THE WEST. 1500–1800

Bolton, Herbert E. *Coronado: Knight of Pueblos and Plains.* Albuquerque, N. Mex.,1949.

———. *Rim of Christendom: A Biography of Eusebio Francisco Kino, Pacific Coast Pioneer.* New York, 1936.

Brooks, James F. *Captives and Cousins: Slavery, Kinship, and Community in the Southwest Borderlands.* Chapel Hill, N.C., 2002.

Chávez, Thomas E. *Spain and the Independence of the United States: An Intrinsic Gift.* Albuquerque, N. Mex., 2002.

Chipman, Donald E. *Spanish Texas, 1519–1821.* Austin, Tex., 1992.

Cook, Warren L. *Flood Tide of Empire: Spain and the Pacific Northwest, 1543–1819.* New Haven, Conn., 1973.

Crosby, Harry W. *Antigua California: Mission and Colony on the Peninsular Frontier, 1697–1768.* Albuquerque, N. Mex., 1994.

Forbes, Jack D. *Apache, Navaho, and Spaniard.* 2nd ed. Norman, Okla., 1994.

Gerhard, Peter. *The North Frontier of New Spain.* Rev. ed. Norman, Okla., 1993.

Gutiérrez, Ramón A. *When Jesus Came, the Corn Mothers Went Away: Marriage, Sexuality, and Power in New Mexico, 1500–1846.* Stanford, Calif., 1991.

Jackson, Jack. *Los Mesteños: Spanish Ranching in Texas, 1721–1821.* College Station, Tex., 1986.

John, Elizabeth A. H. *Storms Brewed in Other Men's Worlds: The Confrontation of Indians, Spanish, and French in the Southwest, 1540–1795.* 2nd. ed. Norman, Okla., 1996.

Kelsey, Harry. *Juan Rodríguez Cabrillo.* San Marino, 1986.

Kessell, John L. *Spain in the Southwest: A Narrative History of Colonial New Mexico, Arizona, Texas, and California.* Norman, Okla., 2002.

Kessell, John L., Rick Hendricks, Meredith D. Dodge, and Larry D. Miller, eds. *The Journals of don Diego de Vargas, New Mexico, 1691–1704.* 6 vols. Albuquerque, N. Mex., 1989–2002.

Lyon, Eugene. *The Enterprise of Florida: Pedro Menéndez de Avilés and the Spanish Conquest of 1565–1568.* Gainesville, Fla., 1976.

Powell, Philip Wayne. *Soldiers, Indians, and Silver: The Northward Advance of New Spain, 1550–1600.* Berkeley, Calif., 1952.

Pupo-Walker, Enrique, and Frances M. López-Morillas, eds. *Castaways: The Narrative of Alvar Núñez Cabeza de Vaca.* Berkeley, Calif., 1993.

Simmons, Marc. *The Last Conquistador: Juan de Oñate and the Settling of the Far Southwest.* Norman, Okla., 1991.

Teja, Jesús F. de la. *San Antonio de Béxar, A Community on New Spain's Northern Frontier.* Albuquerque, N. Mex., 1995.

Weber, David J. *The Spanish Frontier in North America.* New Haven, Conn., 1992.

Weddle, Robert S. *The French Thorn: Rival Explorers in the Spanish Sea, 1682–1762.* College Station, Tex., 1991.

Wood, Peter H. "La Salle: Discovery of a Lost Explorer." *American Historical Review* 89 (April 1984): 294–323.

CHAPTER THREE:
THE WINDS OF CHANGE. 1800–1840

Allen, John L. *Passage through the Garden: Lewis and Clark and the Image of the American Northwest.* Urbana, Ill., 1975.

———. ed. *North American Exploration.* Volume 3 of *A Continent Comprehended.* Lincoln, Nebr., 1997.

Cook, Warren L. *Floodtide of Empire: Spain and the Pacific Northwest, 1543–1819.* New Haven, Conn., 1973.

DeConde, Alexander. *This Affair of Louisiana.* New York, 1976.

Dippie, Brian W. *Catlin and His Contemporaries: The Politics of Patronage.* Lincoln, Nebr., 1990.

Flores, Dan L., ed. *Jefferson and Southwestern Exploration: The Freeman and Custis Accounts of the Red River Expedition of 1806.* Norman, Okla., 1984.

Gallagher, Marsha and David C. Hunt, *Karl Bodmer's America.* Lincoln, Nebr., 1984.

Goetzmann, William H. *Army Exploration in the American West.* New Haven, Conn., 1959.

———. *Exploration and Empire: The Explorer and the Scientist in the Winning of the West.* New York, 1966.

Goetzmann, William H. and Glyndwr Williams. *The Atlas of North American Exploration: From the Norse Voyages to the Race to the Pole.* New York, 1992.

Jackson, Donald. *Thomas Jefferson and the Stony Mountains: Exploring the West from Monticello.* Urbana, Ill., 1981.

———, ed. *The Journals of Zebulon Montgomery Pike with Letters and Related Documents.* 2 vols. Norman, Okla., 1966.

———, ed. *The Letters of the Lewis and Clark Expedition with Related Documents, 1783–1854.* 2 vols. Urbana, Ill., 1978.

Karamanski, Theodore. *Fur Trade and Exploration: Opening the Far Northwest, 1821–1852.* Norman, Okla., 1983.

McKelvey, Susan Delano. *Botanical Exploration of the Trans-Mississippi West, 1790–1850.* Jamaica Plain, Mass., 1956.

Meinig, Donald W. *The Great Columbia Plain: A Historical Geography, 1805–1910.* Seattle, 1968.

———. *The Shaping of America: A Geographical Perspective on 500 Years of History.* Vol. 2: *Continental America, 1800–1857.* New Haven, Conn., 1993.

Moulton, Gary E., ed. *The Journals of the Lewis and Clark Expedition,* 13 vols. Lincoln, Nebr., 1983–2001.

Ronda, James P. *Astoria and Empire.* Lincoln, Nebr., 1990.

———. *Lewis and Clark among the Indians.* Lincoln, Nebr., 1984.

Stephanson, Anders. *Manifest Destiny: American Expansion and the Empire of Right.* New York, 1995.

Van Alystyne, Richard W. *The Rising American Empire.* New York, 1960.

Weber, David J. *The Spanish Frontier in North America.* New Haven, Conn., 1992.

Wishart, David J. *The Fur Trade of the American West, 1807–1840: A Geographical Synthesis.* Lincoln, Nebr., 1979.

CHAPTER FOUR:
THE EAGLE SCREAMS. 1840–1865

Faragher, John Mack. *Women and Men on the Overland Trail.* New Haven, Conn., 1979.

Frémont, John Charles. *The Exploring Expedition to the Rocky Mountains.* Washington D.C., 1988.

Johnson, Overton, William H. Winter, and Angela Firkus. *Route across the Rocky Mountains.* West Lafayette, Ind., 2000.

Jordan, Terry G. *North American Cattle Ranching Frontiers.* Albuquerque, N. Mex., 1993.

Madsen, Brigham D. *Exploring the Great Salt Lake: The Stansbury Expedition of 1849–50.* Salt Lake City, 1988.

Mattes, Merrill J. *The Great Platte River Road: The Covered Wagon Mainline Via Fort Kearny to Fort Laramie.* Lincoln, Nebr., 1987.

May, Dean. *Utah, A People's History.* Salt Lake City, 1987.

Meinig, Donald W. *Continental America, 1800–1867.* Vol. 2 of *Shaping America.* New Haven, Conn., 1994.

Nevins, Allan. *Frémont, Pathmarker of the West*. Lincoln, Nebr., 1992.

Norris, L. David, Odie B. Gaulk, and James C. Milligan. *William H. Emory: Soldier-Scientist*. Tucson, Ariz., 1998.

Parkman, Francis, and Bernard Rosenthal. *The Oregon Trail*. Oxford, 2000.

Ronda, James P. *Beyond Lewis & Clark: The Army Explores the West*. Tacoma, Wash., 2003.

Smith, Duane A. *Mining America: The Industry and the Environment, 1800–1980*. Lawrence, Kans., 1987.

Stansbury, Howard. *Exploration of the Valley of the Great Salt Lake (Exploring the American West)*. Reprint, Washington, D.C., 1988.

Stegner, Wallace. *The Gathering of Zion: The Story of the Mormon Trail*. New York: 1964.

Unruh, Jr., John D. *The Plains Across: The Overland Emigrants and the Trans-Mississippi West, 1840–1860*. Urbana, Ill., 1979.

Utley, Robert M. *The Indian Frontier of the American West, 1846–1890*. Albuquerque, N. Mex., 1983.

Weber, David. *Richard H. Kern: Expeditionary Artist in the Far Southwest, 1848–1853*. Albuquerque, N. Mex., 1985.

CHAPTER FIVE:
THE WEST SUBDUED, 1865–1900

Arrington, Leonard J., and Davis Bitton. *The Mormon Experience: A History of the Latter-day Saints*. New York, 1979.

Butler, Anne M. *Daughters of Joy, Sisters of Misery: Prostitutes in the American West, 1865–90*. Urbana, Ill., 1985.

Fite, Gilbert C. *The Farmers' Frontier, 1865–1900*. New York, 1966.

Jordan, Terry G. *North American Cattle-Ranching Frontiers: Origins, Diffusion, and Differentiation*. Albuquerque, N. Mex., 1993

Lamar, Howard R. *The Far Southwest, 1846–1912: A Territorial History*. 1966; Albuquerque, N. Mex., 2000.

Myres, Sandra L. *Western Women and the Frontier Experience, 1800–1915*. Albuquerque, N. Mex., 1982.

Nugent, Walter. *Into the West: The Story of Its People*. New York, 1999.

Paul, Rodman W. *The Far West and the Great Plains in Transition, 1859–1900*. New York, 1988.

Paul, Rodman W., and Elliott West. *Mining Frontiers of the Far West, 1848–1880*. Rev. ed. Albuquerque, N. Mex., 2001.

Prucha, Francis Paul. *The Great Father: The United States Government and the American Indians*. 2 vols. Lincoln, Nebr., 1984.

Riley, Glenda. *Women and Indians on the Frontier, 1825–1915*. Albuquerque, N. Mex., 1984.

Taylor, Quintard. *In Search of the Racial Frontier: African Americans in the American West, 1528–1990*. New York, 1998.

Utley, Robert M. *Cavalier in Buckskin: George Armstrong Custer and the Western Military Frontier*. Rev. ed. Norman, Okla., 2001.

West, Elliott. *Growing Up with the Country: Childhood on the Far Western Frontier*. Albuquerque, N. Mex., 1989.

CHAPTER SIX:
THE CONTEMPORARY WEST, 1900 TO PRESENT

Etulain, Richard W. *Re-Imagining the Modern American West: A Century of Fiction, History, and Art*. Tucson, Ariz., 1996.

Etulain, Richard W., Pat Devejian, Jon Hunner, and Jacqueline Etulain Partch, eds. *The American West in the Twentieth Century: A Bibliography*. Norman, Okla., 1994.

Fernlund, Kevin J., ed. *The Cold War American West, 1945–1989*. Albuquerque, N. Mex., 1998.

Lamar, Howard R. *The New Encyclopedia of the American West*. New Haven, Conn., 1998.

Lowitt, Richard. *The New Deal and the West*. Bloomington, Ind., 1984.

McWilliams, Carey. *Southern California Country: An Island on the Land*. New York, 1946.

Malone, Michael P., and Richard W. Etulain. *The American West: A Twentieth-Century History*. Lincoln, Nebr., 1989.

Milner, Clyde A., II, Carol O'Connor, and Martha A. Sandweiss, eds. *The Oxford History of the American West*. New York, 1994.

Nash, Gerald D. *The American West in the Twentieth Century: A Short History of an Urban Oasis*. Albuquerque, N. Mex., 1977.

———. *The American West Transformed: The Impact of the Second World War*. Bloomington, Ind., 1985.

———. *The Federal Landscape: An Economic History of the Twentieth-Century West*. Tucson, Ariz., 1999.

Pomeroy, Earl. *The Pacific Slope: A History of California, Oregon, Washington, Idaho, Utah, and Nevada*. New York, 1966.

ABOUT THE CONTRIBUTORS

JOHN LOGAN ALLEN is Professor and Chair of the Department of Geography and Recreation at the University of Wyoming. His teaching and research interests include the exploration of North America, particularly the American West, and the human impact on natural environments. Among his publications are *North American Exploration*, 3 vols. (1997); *Atlas of World Geography*, 2nd ed. (2000); and *Atlas of World Politics*, 5th ed. (2001).

RICHARD W. ETULAIN is Professor Emeritus of History at the University of New Mexico. Specializing in the history and literature of the American West, he is the author or editor of more than forty books. Among his recent volumes are *The Hollywood West* (co-edited with Glenda Riley, 2001) and *New Mexican Lives* (2002). He is the author of a forthcoming biography of Calamity Jane and a general history of the American West.

JOHN L. KESSELL is Professor Emeritus of History at the University of New Mexico. A founding editor of the Vargas Project, he has specialized in the Spanish borderlands. His latest book is *Spain in the Southwest: A Narrative History of Colonial New Mexico, Arizona, Texas, and California* (2002).

GERALD D. NASH was Distinguished Emeritus Professor of History at the University of New Mexico (UNM). A leading scholar of the American West, he was associated with UNM from 1961 to 1995. He wrote a dozen books focusing on the twentieth-century West, including *The Federal Landscape: An Economic History of the Twentieth-Century West* (1999). His last book was *A Brief History of the American West Since 1945*, published in 2000, the year of his death.

GLENDA RILEY is Alexander M. Bracken Professor of History at Ball State University, Muncie, Indiana. She is an expert in the history of American women, particularly in the West, and in the history of the early American republic. She has published extensively on the subject of frontier women. Her books include *Women and Indians on the Frontier, 1825–1915* (1984) and *Women and Nature: Saving the Wild West* (1999).

JAMES P. RONDA is Barnard Professor of Western American History at the University of Tulsa. The author of such books as *Lewis and Clark among the Indians* (1984) and *Astoria and Empire* (1990), he was a guest scholar and principal consultant for the July 2003 Library of Congress exhibition commemorating the Lewis and Clark expedition. He also authored *Lewis and Clark: The Army Explores the West*, due for publication in 2003.

ROBERT M. UTLEY served for twenty-five years in various capacities with the U.S. National Park Service and other federal agencies. Since his retirement, he has devoted himself to historical research and writing, and specializes in the history of the American West. His many books include *Lone Star Justice: The First Century of the Texas Rangers* (2002) and *Cavalier in Buckskin: George Armstrong Custer and the Western Military Frontier* (Oklahoma, 1988, 2001).

W. RAYMOND WOOD is Professor Emeritus at the University of Missouri-Columbia. His research interests center on the Ozark Highlands of the midcontinent and on the Great Plains of North America, including both prehistoric studies and ethnohistory, especially of the Plains village peoples. His publications include *An Atlas of Early Maps of the American Midwest*, Part II (2001), and *Archaeology on the Great Plains* (editor, 1998).

INDEX

Page numbers in *italics* refer to maps or illustrations.

ACKNOWLEDGMENTS

Dorling Kindersley and Hydra Publishing extend special thanks to: Robert M. Utley; W. Raymond Wood; John L. Kessell; James P. Ronda; John Logan Allen; Glenda Riley; the late Gerald D. Nash; Robert W. Etulain; Ellen Nanney, Smithsonian Institution; Amy Pastan, for photo research; Jemal Creary, Corbis; Ralph Eubanks, Prints and Photographs Division, Library of Congress; Erin Pauwels and Lauretta Dives, Picture Desk; Dale G. Miller, Kirsten van der Veen, Daria Wingreen, Leslie Overstreet, and Ronald Brashear, Smithsonian Institution Libraries; Jake Homiak, Paula Fleming, Becky Malinsky, and Pam Wintle, Smithsonian Institution's National Anthropological Archives; Felicia Pickering, Smithsonian's National Museum of Natural History; Robert Johnston, Smithsonian American Art Museum; Jennifer Robertson, National Portrait Gallery; Douglas Mudd, Channon Perish, and Susan Strange, Smithsonian's National Museum of American History, Behring Center; David Sterling, *Smithsonian Magazine*; and David Burgevin, Smithsonian's Office of Imaging and Printing Services. For editorial contributions: Melinda Corey, Elin Woodger, Norman Murphy, Michele Camardella, Karin Beuerlein, Liz Sonneborn, Deborah Rhodes. For the index: Chris Carruth.

PICTURE CREDITS

Key: l =left, r = right, c = center, t = top, b = bottom.

Abbreviations:
DK = DK Picture Library
LC = Library of Congress
NAA = National Anthropological Archives, Smithsonian Institution
NARA = National Archives and Records Administration
NASM = National Air & Space Museum, Smithsonian Institution
NMAH = National Museum of American History, Behring Center, Smithsonian Institution (AC=Archives Center; ND=Numismatics Division; PHD=Photo History Division)
NMAI = National Museum of the American Indian, Smithsonian Institution
NMNH = National Museum of Natural History, Smithsonian Institution
NPM = National Postal Museum, Smithsonian Institution
SAAM = Smithsonian American Art Museum
SI = Smithsonian Institution
SIL = Smithsonian Institution Libraries
USDA = United States Department of Agriculture

Endpapers "Street view in Corinne, Box Elder County, Utah," William H. Jackson, 1869, NARA. 1 "Owen Brown, Ruth Thompson, Jason Brown, in front of log house, c. 1880s," NMAH-PHD. 2/3 Ellsworth, Kansas, c. 1890s, NAA. 4/5 *Grand Cañon of the Colorado*, William H. Jackson, SAAM 1994.91.85. 6/7 NARA. 8-9 *Among the Sierra Nevada Mountains, California*, Albert Bierstadt, SAAM 1977.107.1. 9 tr (&10 l) NMAI 26.119.630. 10-11 *Alaskan Coast Range*, Albert Bierstadt, SAAM 1967.136.7. 12 l LC-USZ62-44648. 12/13 t NAA. 12/13 b NMNH. 13 tr NMNH. 13 br NMNH. 14 t *Te-ah'–ke-ra-lée-re-coo, The Cheyenne, a Republican Pawnee, Pawnee*, George Catlin, SAAM 1985.66.107. 14/15 NAA. 15 t NMAI 5.65. 16 tl *Iron Bluff, 1200 Miles above St. Louis*, George Catlin, SAAM 1985.66.389. 16-17 *Hopi Mesa, c.* 1872, John K. Hillers, SAAM 1994.91.77. 17 tl, c NMNH. 18 bl LC-USZ62-51066. 18/19 NMNH—Photo by Ed Castle. 19 bl NMNH. 19 br LC-USZ62-113079. 20 tr NMNH. 20 c NMAI 82.322.7879. 20 b *Canon de Chelle, Walls of the Grand Canon about 1200 Feet in Height Wheeler Survey)*, 1873, Timothy H. O'Sullivan, SAAM 1994.91.134. 20/21 t NAA. 21 b NMNH. 22 t *Coo-coo-coo, The Owl, an Aged Chief*, 1836, George Catlin; SAAM 1985.66.232. 22/23 *Hidatsa Village, Earth-covered Lodges on the Knife River, 1810 Miles above St. Louis*, 1832, George Catlin, SAAM 1985.66.383. 23 *Cherokee Phoenix*. 24 t NAA. 25 t NMNH. 25 b NAA. 26 t NMNH. 26 b NMAI 22.8647. 26-7 NAA. 27 t NMAI 2.1673. 27 b NAA. 28 t DK. 28 b *Buffalo Chase in Winter Indians on Snowshoes*, 1832-33, George Catlin, SAAM 1985.66.416. 28-9 NARA. 29 r NMNH. 30 1 *A Corner of Zuni, from the portfolio The North American Indian*, 1903, Edward S. Curtis, SAAM 1988.5.11. 31 tr DK. 31 b "Women Grinding Corn (Pueblo Zuni)" Plate 6 from *Report of an Expedition Down the Zuni and Colorado Rivers by the United States Army Corps of Engineers*, by Captain L. Sitgreaves, Publisher: Washington, R. Armstrong, 1853, SIL. 32 tl *George Catlin*, 1849, William Fisk, NPG.70.14. 32 tr "Drawing of Native Peoples suffering from smallpox" from *Historia general de las cosas de Nueva España por el m.p.r. fr. Bernardino de Sahagnú, de la Orden de los frayles menores de la Servancia*, Publisher: México, D.F., P. Robredo, 1938, SIL. 33 tr DK. 33 b NAA. 34 tl *Bird's Eye View of the Mandan Village, 1800 miles above St. Louis*, 1837-39, George Catlin, SAAM 1985.66.502. 34 b NMAI. 34/5 *Wichita Lodge, Thatched with Prairie Grass, Wichita*, 1834-35, George Catlin, SAAM 1985.66.492. 35 tr NMAI. 36/7 b *Buffalo Dance, Mandan*, 1835-37, George Catlin, SAAM 1985.66.440. 37 tl DK. 37 r *Buffalo Chase, a Surround by the Hidatsa*, 1832-33, George Catlin, SAAM 1985.66.409. 38 tr NMNH. 38 b NMNH. 38/9 NAA. 39 tl Cornell University. 39 tr © Russ Finely/Finley-Holiday Films. 40 b NAA. 41 tl NMAI. 41 tr NMNH. 41 cr DK. 41 br NMNH. 41 bl NMNH. 42 tl *Mark Twain* (Samuel Langhorne Clemens), John White Alexander, NPG.81.116. 42/43 *Shoshone Falls, Snake River, Idaho, View across the Top of the Falls Wheeler Survey)*, Timothy H. O'Sullivan, SAAM 1994.91.141. 44 bl NMAI 24.2139. 44 tr NAA. 45t NMNH. 45 b *The Chief's Canoe*, before 1927, Belmore Browne, SAAM 1964.18.1. 46 tl © Bettmann/CORBIS, #BE047692. 46 tr NMAI 9.8095. 47 tl LC. 47 r DK. 48 t NMAI 41393. 48 b *Mandan Scalping an Enemy*, 1835-37, George Catlin, SAAM 1985.66.498. 49 tl NMNH. 49 r © Bettmann/CORBIS, #BE039841. 50 © Russ Finley/Finley-Holiday Films, 1984. 51 t NMAI. 51 b NMAI 11.1739. 52 tr NMAI 5.3776. 52 NMNH. 53 NMAI. 54/5 "Spaniards Landing in the New World" from *Our Country: A household history for all readers, from the discovery of America to the present time of 1877-1879*, by Benson John Lossing © CORBIS, #43743. 55 Comb Morion, favored headgear of Spanish conquistadors, DK. 56 The Art Archive/Museo Historico Nacional Buenos Aires/Dagli Orti, PD# AA366955. 56/57 © Bettmann/CORBIS, #E192. 57 NMAH—ND. 58 tl DK. 58 tr The Art Archive/Museo Ciudad Mexico/Dagli Orti, PD# AA373457. 58 bl Frontispiece from *Relation de Alvar Nunez CaBeca de Vaca reprint, The narrative of Álvar Núñez Cabeza de Vaca*, translated by Buckingham Smith, 1851, Publisher: Washington, SIL. 59 tl The Art Archive/Album/Joseph Martin, PD# AA346764. 59 c The Art Archive/National Palace Mexico City/Dagli Orti, PD# AA379971. 60 tl © CORBIS, #IH107866. 60/61 *Pueblo Scene*, c. 1920, Forman G. Hanna, SAAM 1994-91.62. 61 t © George H. H. Huey/CORBIS, #AX931447. 61 b DK. 62 t The Art Archive/Navy Historical Service Vincennes France/Dagli Orti, PD# AA364971. 62 b "Rio Grande Near Frontera" from *Report on the United States and Mexican Boundary Survey, made under the Direction of the Secretary of the Interior, by William H. Emory, 1857-1859*, Volume I, Publisher: Washington: A.O.P. Nicholson, printer 1857-59, SIL. 63 t © Stapleton Collection/CORBIS, #AABR002459. 63 b "Entrée des Espagnols dans" from *Histoire de la conquête de la Floride, ou, Relation de ce qui s'est passé dans la découverte de ce païs par Ferdinand de Soto composée en espagnol par l'Inca Garcillasso de la Vega; & traduite en françois par Sr. Pierre Richelt*, Publisher: A Leide: Chez Pierre van der Aa,1731, SIL. 64 t LC-USZ62-105386. 64 b The Art Archive/New York Public Library/Harper Collins Publishers, PD# AA328808. 64/65 DK. 65 t © Archivo Iconografico, S.A./Corbis, #CS005446. 66 t DK. 66 bl © Bettmann/CORBIS, #SF9478. 66 br The Art Archive/The Art Archive, PD# AA334156. 67 t The Art Archive/Bibliothèque des Arts Décoratifs Paris/Dagli Orti, PD# AA393161. 67 b LC-USZ62-69898. 68 tl Illustration of Gaspar Pérez de Villagrá from the frontispiece of *History of New Mexico by Gaspar Pérez de Villagrá, Alcalá, 1616*, translated by Gilberto Espinosa, Publisher: The Quivera Society, Los Angeles, 1933, SIL. 68 tr The Art Archive/National Museum of Sculpture Valladolid/Dagli Orit (A), PD# AA348290. 68 br © Richard T. Norwitz/Corbis, #IH211409. 69 t "First Baptism in Upper California, July 22nd, 1769 from *The American Indian (Uh-nish-in-na-ba)*, by Elijah Middlebrook Haines, Publisher: Chicago, The Mas-sin-na'-gan Co., 1888, SIL. 69 b The Art Arhive/Museo de America Madrid/Dagli Orti, PD# AA392915. 70 t The Art Archive/Museo Nacional del Virreinato Tepotzotlàn Mexico/Dagli Orti, PD# AA383058. 70/71 The Art Archive/Museo Nacional Bogota/Dagli Orti, PD# AA366136. 71 b LC-USZ62-121191. 72 t © David Muench/Corbis. 72 c The Art Archive/University Library Coimbra, PD# AA335700. 72 b LC-USZ6-823. 73 l NAA. 73 br The Art Archive/National History Museum Mexico City/Dagli Orti, PD# AA381305. 74 The Art Archive/Queretaro Museum Mexico/Dagli Orti (A), PD# AA346908. 74 b The Art Archive/Queretaro Museum Mexico/Dagli Orti, PD# AA383084. 75 tl NMAH-ND. 75 bl LC-USZC4-6437. 76 tl NMNH. 76/7 © Russ Finley/Finley-Holiday Films. 77 NARA. 78 t LC-USZC4-8924. 78/79 b "The Plaza and Church of El Paso" from *Volume 1 of Report on the United States and Mexican boundary survey, made under the direction of the secretary of the Interior, by William H. Emory, major First Cavalry, and United States commissioner*, Publisher: Washington: A.O.P. Nicholson, printer, 1857-59, SIL. 79 © Bettman/Corbis. 80 tl The Art Archive/Biblioteca Nacional Mexico/Dagli Orti, PD #AA392072. 80 tr NPM. 80 b LC-USZ62-73350. 82 t "Inscription of Don Diego de Vargas on El Morro, New Mexico" from *The Mercurio Volante of Don Carlos De Siguenza y Gongora*, Publisher: Los Angeles: The Quivira Society, 1932, SIL. 82/83 LC-USZC4-5666. 83 t *Nino Jesus*, 18th century, Unknown artist, SAAM 1996.91.52. 84 t "Governor Vargas" from *First expedition of Vargas into New Mexico, 1692*, by Diego de Vargas, translated by J. Manuel Espinosa, Publisher: The University of New Mexico Press, 1940, SIL. 84 c *Our Lady of Guadalupe*, c. 1780-1830, attributed to Pedro Antonio Fresquis, SAAM 1986.65.113. 85 b LC-D428-229. 86 b NMNH. 87 t The Art Archive/National Archives Mexico/Dagli Orti, PD# AA381322. 87 b LC-USZC4-5664. 88 The Art Archive/British Library/British Library, PD# AA333699. 90 t NMAH-ND. 90 b The Art Archive/Museo del Prado Madrid/Album/Joseph Martin, PD# AA346746. 91 tr (Detail), Courtesy of Museum of New Mexico, Neg. No. 149804. 91 c The Art Archive/Museo del Prado Madrid/Album/Joseph Martin, PD# AA348016. 91 b LC-USZC4-2032. 92 The Art Archive/Harper Collins Publishers, PD# AA332465. 93 © George H.H. Huey/Corbis, #AX931531. 94 b "Military Plaza-San Antonio, Texas" from Emory, SIL. 94/95 "Fall of the River Niagara, that is to be seen betwixt the Lake Ontario and that of Erie," from *A new discovery of a vast country in America: extending above four thousand miles, between New France and New Mexico*, by L. Hennepin, Publisher M. Bentley, J. Tonson, H. Bonwick, T. Goodwin, and S. Manship,1698, SIL. 95 bl The Art Archive/Bibliothèque des Arts Décoratifs Paris/Dagli Orit (A), PD# AA359506. 95 br Frontispiece from Hennepin, SIL. 96 t DK. 96/97 *Comanche Moving Camp, Dog Fight en Route*, 1834-35, George Catlin, SAAM 1985.66.466. 98 t NMAH-AC. 98/99 NMAH-PH. 100 b "San Carlos" from *The beginnings of San Francisco from the expedition of Anza, 1774, to the city charter of April 15, 1850; with biographical and other notes*, by Zoeth Skinner Eldredge, Vol. I, Publisher: Zoeth Skinner Eldredge,1912, SIL. 101 tr The Art Archive/Navy Historical Service Vincennes France/Dagli Orti, PD# AA384566. 101 b The Art Archive/Navy Historical Service Vincennes France/Dagli Orti, PD# AA383183. 102 DK. 103 tr NMAH. 103 bl "Fr. Francisco Hermenegildo Garcés" from Haines, SIL. 104 NMAH. 104/105 The Art Archive/Navy Historical Service Vincennes France/Dagli Orti, PD# AA364969. 105 t NMAH. 105 c Plate II, "Yuma Indians from California"from *Report upon the Colorado River of the West: explored in 1857 and 1858 by Lieutenant Joseph C. Ives, Corps of Topographical Engineers*, Publisher: Washington Government Printing Office, 1861, SIL. 105 b Courtesy of National Society Sons of the American Revolution, Louisville, Kentucky. 106/7 *Old Mesilla Plaza*, 1885-1886, Leon Trousset, SAAM 1951.13. 108 t The Art Archive/Napoleonic Museum Rome/Dagli Orti, PD# AA370281. 108 c The Art Archive/Private Collection/Dagli Orti, PD# AA386718. 108 b The Art Archive/Musée Carnavalet Paris/Marc Charmet, PD# AA329797. 109 © G.E. Kidder Smith/Corbis, #GE002637. 110 b © Stapleton Collection/Corbis, #AABR002661. 111 t "The Taking of Quebec by the English" from Hennepin, SIL. 111 b © Corbis, #IH158429. 112 NAA. 112/113 © Philip James Corwin/Corbis, #JC002217. 114/15 "The Great Explorers" 1890-1909 reproduction of original artwork by Frederic Remington, LC-USZC4-7161. 115t Eighteenth-century compass, DK. 116 *William Henry Drayton*, 1783, B. B. Ellis, after Benoit Louis Prevost, after Pierre Eugène Du Simitière, NPG.75.71. 116/17 *Grand Canyon of the Yellowstone and Falls*, 1885, F. Jay Haynes, SAAM 1993.77.1. 117 tr *Declaration of Independence* 1818, James Barton Longacre, NPG.80.129. 118 b "Making a Portage" from *The Great Fur Land or Sketches of Life in the Hudson's Bay, Territory*, by H. M. Robinson, Publisher: Toronto: Coles Pub. Co., 1879, SIL, Photo by Ed Castle. 118/19 © Historical Picture Archive/CORBIS, #HT009818. 119 © Hulton-Deutsch Collection/CORBIS, #HU062137. 120 t © CORBIS, #CB056980. 120 b NMAI 9.7038. 121 t © Stapleton Collection/

CORBIS, #AAEE001081. 121 b The Art Archive/British Library/British Library, PD# AA341093. 122 l NMNH. 122 c NMNH. 122 tr NMAI. 123 t Courtesy of Anchorage Museum of History and Art. 123 b Courtesy of University of Alaska. 124 t *Encampment of Crow Indians*, 1908, Joseph Henry Sharp, SAAM 1985.66.362,159. 124/125 *River Bluffs, 1320 miles above St. Louis*, 1832, George Catlin, SAAM 1985.66.399. 125 t LC. 126 t NMNH. 126 b *Blackfoot Camp Scene*, n.d., Edwin Willard Deming, SAAM 1985.66.362,337. 126/27 NMAH. 127 tr NMAH. 127 tl NMAH. 127 b NMNH. 128 t The Art Archive/Chateau de Blerancourt/Dagli Orti, PD# AA364883. 128 b NMAH. 128/29 t LC-DIG-ppmsca-01659. 129 b *Thomas Jefferson*, 1805, Gilbert Stuart, NPG.82.97. 130 tl © Gianni Dagli Orti/CORBIS, #IH187791. 130 tr NPM, Photo by James O'Donnell. 130 bl Plate 153 from *Flora borealiamericana, sistens caracteres plantarum quas in America septentrionali collegit et detexit* Andreas Michaux, Publisher: Parisiis [Paris] et Argentorati [Strasbourg]: Typis Caroli Crapelet, apud fratres Levrault, anno XI—1803, SIL. 130 bc Plate 103 from Michaux, SIL. 130 br Plate 10 from Michaux, SIL. 131 NMAH-AC. 132 t The United States Capitol. 132 b NMAH. 133 l © Bettmann/CORBIS, #BE043512. 133 r © Gianni Dagli Orti/CORBIS, #IH182965. 134 NPS. 135 t (Detail) Courtesy of Scotts Bluff National Monument, NPS. 135 b Title Page from *Voyages from Montreal, on the river St. Laurence, through the continent of North America, to the Frozen and Pacific Oceans: in the years 1789 and 1793*, by Alexander Mackenzie, Esq., Publisher: New-York: Printed and sold by G.F. Hopkins, at Washington's Head, no. 118, Pearlstreet, 1802, SIL. 136 t *Meriwether Lewis*, 1803/7, Charles Balthazar Julien Fébret de Saint-Mémin, NPG.74.39.420. 136 c *William Clark* (detail), 1832, George Catlin, NPG.71.35. 136 b NMAH. 137 t "A Canoe striking on a Tree" from *A journal of the voyages and travels of a Corps of Discovery, under the command of Captain Lewis and Captain Clarke*, by Patrick Gass, Publisher: Philadelphia: printed for Mathew Carey 1808, SIL. 138 tc NMAH. 138 bl Courtesy of Missouri Historical Society Archives, Clark Family Papers. 138/39 t LC–G4126.S12. 138/39 b "Captin Clark and his men shooting Bears" from Gass, SIL. 140 t NMNH, Photo by Dale Hrabak. 140/41 © Dewitt Jones/Corbis, #DJ001812. 141 t NMAH–ND. 142 l *Grand Canon, Colorado River, Near Paria Creek, Looking West (Wheeler Survey)*, 1872, William Bell, SAAM 1994.91.10. 142 b *Big Bend on the Upper Missouri, 1900 Miles above St. Louis*, 1832, George Catlin, SAAM 1985.66.390. 143 r Courtesy of Missouri Historical Society Archives, Clark Family Papers. 144 LC-USZ62-78235. 145 tl *DeWitt Clinton*, 1816, John Wesley Jarvis, NPG.65.53. 145 cr *John Jacob Astor*, c. 1825, John Wesley Jarvis, NPG.78.204. 145 b NMNH. 146 *The Grand Canyon of the Yellowstone*, 1893-1901, Thomas Moran, SAAM 1928.7.1. 147 LC-USZC4-6294. 148 tl © Raymond Gehman/CORBIS, #AY003960. 148/49 LC-USZC4-849. 149 bl NAA. 149 br Courtesy of

Jedediah Strong Smith Society. 150 t NAA. 150/51 *Mandan Attacking a Party of Arikara, 1832-33*, George Catlin, SAAM.1985.66.464. 151 t NAA. 151 b Courtesy of University of California, Berkeley, The Bancroft Library. 152 tl LC-USZ62-112764. 152 b NAA. 152/53 c "Crossing of the Platte—Mouth of Deer Creek" from *Exploration and survey of the valley of the Great Salt Lake of Utah: including a reconnoissance of a new route through the Rocky Mountains, by Howard Stansbury, Captain, Corps of Topographical Engineers, U.S. Army*, Publisher: Philadelphia: Lippincott, Grambo & Co., 1852, SIL. 153 r *Zebulon Montgomery Pike*, Unidentified Artist, NPG.80.15. 154 t NPM. 154/55 b *The Fur Traders*, 1938, Elizabeth Davey Lochrie, SAAM 1985.8.26. 156 tl *Mountain Hemlock (Tsuga Mertensiana)*, c. 1938, Mary Vaux Walcott, SAAM. 1970.355.605. 156 c *Cholla Opuntia Whipplei*, 1938, Mary Vaux Walcott, SAAM.1970.355.369. 156 b *The North American sylva; or, A description of the forest trees of the United States, Canada, and Nova Scotia*, by Thomas Nuttall, Publisher: Philadelphia, Smith & Wistar, 1849, SIL. 156/57 *Mouth of the Platte River, 900 Miles above St. Louis*, 1832, George Catlin, SAAM 1985.66.369. 158 tl SI. 158/59 b "Arrival of Caravans at Sante Fe" from *Commerce of the prairies; or, The journal of a Santa Fé trader*, by Josiah Gregg, Publisher: New York, H.G. Langley1844, SIL. 159 t "La Ciudad de Santa Fe" from *Military reconnaissance of the Arkansas Rio del Norte and Rio Gila, by W.H. Emory…constructed under the orders of Col. J.J. Abert…1847; drawn by Joseph Welch, Abert's report of 1846-47—New Mexico Expedition*, Publisher: SI, 1847, SIL. 160 tl NMAH-AC. 160 tr *Sam Houston*, 1858, Unidentified artist, NPG.77.263. 160 b NMNH. 161 tr LC, Photo by Ed Castle. 161 bl NMAH-ND. 162 Courtesy of Scotts Bluff National Monument, NPS. 162/63 Courtesy of Woolaroc Museum, Bartlesville, Oklahoma. 164 b LC-USZC4-683. 165 t *John Quincy Adams*, c. 1844, George Caleb Bingham, NPG.69.20. 165 b Courtesy of Scotts Bluff National Monument, NPS. 166/67 "Main Street, Atchison, Kansas, 1860s," © Bettmann/Corbis, #F4235. 167 r *Three Crossings Station*, (detail), William H. Jackson, Courtesy of Scotts Bluff National Monument, NPS. 168/69 *Westward the Course of Empire Takes Its Way*, 1861, Emanuel Gottlieb Leutze, SAAM 1931.6.1. 169 r Texas. 170 tl SIL. 170 tr NMAH-ND. 170 b NAA. 171 br NPM. 172 t SIL. 172 bl *John Charles Frémont*, 1861, Mathew B. Brady, NPG.83.284.5. 172 bc *Jessie BentonFrémont*, c. 1863, Unidentified photographer, NPG.81.M95. 172 br *Thomas Hart Benton*, c. 1861, Ferdinand Thomas Lee Boyle, NPG.66.1. 174 l Courtesy of U.S. Department of the Interior, U.S. Geological Survey. 174c Courtesy of Peabody Museum of Salem, Photo by Chip Clark. 174 tr Courtesy of the US Naval Academy Museum, Private Collection, Photo by Chip Clark. 175 tr NMAH, Photo by Joe Goulait. 175 b *Memoirs of My Life*, John C. Frémont, Published Chicago & NY, 1886,. Vol. 3, SIL. 176 tl Courtesy of Scotts Bluff National Monument, NPS. 176 b NMAH-AC. 177 b SIL. 178 t "Fort Laramie" from *Exploration and survey of the valley of the Great Salt*

Lake of Utah, including a reconnoissance of a new route through the Rocky Mountains, by Howard Stansbury, captain, Corps topographical engineers, U.S. Army, Publisher: Philadelphia, Lippincott, Grambo & Co., 1852, SIL. 178 b NMAH. 179 Courtesy of Scotts Bluff National Monument, NPS. 180 tl NMAH. 180 tr LC-USZC4-2630. 180 bl NMAH. 180/81 NMAH. 181 tl LC-USZC4-2630. 182 tr "Yerba Buena in the Spring of 1837" from Eldredge, 1912, SIL. 182 b *The expedition of theDonner party and its tragic fate*, Published: Los Angeles, Grafton Publishing Corporation, 1920, SIL. 182 br LC-USZ62-27607. 183 bl *Scotophis emoryi* from *Notes of a military reconnoissance, from Fort Leavenworth, in Missouri, to San Diego, in California, including parts of the Arkansas, Del Norte, and Gila Rivers*, by W. H. Emory, Washington: Wendell and Van Benthuysen, printers, 1848, SIL. 183 br Cooper-Hewitt, National Design Museum. 184 NAA. 185 l © Bettmann/CORBIS, #BE06281. 185 tr Texas. 186 tl NAA. 186 bl NMNH. 186/87 "Brownsville, Texas" from *Report on the United States and Mexican Boundary Survey…by William H. Emory, major First Cavalry, and United States commissioner, vol. 1, Published: Washington: C. Wendell, printer, 1857-58*, SIL. 187 tr Courtesy of West Point Museum Art Collection, United States Military Academy. 188 t "Gunnison's Island Eastern Shore Looking North, Great Salt Lake" from Stansbury, 1852, SIL. 188 b © Bettmann/CORBIS, #BE053563. 189 "Bowery, Mint & President's House—Great Salt Lake City" from Stansbury, 1852, SIL. 190 tl NAA. 190/91 NMAH-PHD. 191 tl LC. 191 r *Daniel Webster Addressing the United States Senate*, 1860, Eliphalet Brown, Jr., NPG.80.226. 192 tl NPM, Photo by James O'Donnell. 192 tr NPM, Photo by James O'Donnell. 192-3 b LC-USZ62-7120. 193 tl NAA. 193 tr NMAH-ND. 193 br © CORBIS, #NA002863. 194 t NMAH. 195 b LC-USZ62-20161. 194/95 NAA. 196 t DK. 196 b NAA. 197 tl NPM. 197 br Courtesy of Scotts Bluff National Monument, NPS. 198 tl NMAH. 198 br SIL, Photo by Ed Castle. 199 NAA. 200 *The Speculator*, 1852, Francis William Edmonds, SAAM 1976.114. 200/01 *Cliffs of the Upper Colorado River, Wyoming Territory*, 1882, Thomas Moran, SAAM 1936.12.4. 202 tl *Regulations for the Uniform and Dress of the Army of the US*, June 1857, SIL, Photo by Ed Castle. 202 bl Plate 36 from Emory, 1857-59, SIL. 202/03 NMNH. 203 tr NMAH. 203 c NMAH. 203 br *Isaac Stevens*, 1861, J. H. Bufford, NPG.82.41. 204 tl Courtesy of West Point Museum Collection, United States Military Academy Museum. 204 tr "Long-necked Grebe, Plate XXXVIII" from Volume XII, *Reports of Explorations and Surveys…made under the direction of the Secretary of War, in 1853-4. Volume I-XII*, Publisher: Washington; Thomas H. Ford, Printer, 1855 and 1860, SIL, Photo by Ed Castle. 204 b "Rio Colorado Near the Mojave Villages" Plate 2 from Volume III, Part 1, *Reports of Explorations and Surveys…*SIL, Photo by Ed Castle. 205 tl " Indian Ornaments and Manufactures" from Volume III, Part 3, *Reports of Explorations and Surveys…* SIL, Photo by Ed Castle. 205 NAA. 206 tl NARA.

206 tr NARA. 206 b NMNH. 206/07 "Zuni" from *Diary of a journey from the Mississippi to the coasts of the Pacific with a United States government expedition*, by Baldwin Möllhausen, Vol. II,Published: London: Longman, Brown, Green, Longmans & Roberts, 1858, SIL. 207 tr © Bettmann/CORBIS, #BE049310. 208 tl *Abraham Lincoln*, 1865, Alexander Gardner, NPG.81.M1. 208 tr © CORBIS, #IH158601. 208 b © Tom Bean/CORBIS, #TB003424. 209 "Indian Alarm on the Cimarron River" from Gregg, SIL. 210 tl *Samuel Bowles*, c. 1870, Napoleon Sarony, NPG.78.286. 210 bl NAA. 210/11 NAA. 211 tr *Horace Greeley*, c. 1850, Unknown photographer, NPG.77.9. 212/13 "A mother buys nostrums from the trader; in the Dakotas, c. 1900," NMAH-AC. 213 Colt-Paterson revolver; NMAH. 214 l Colt-Paterson revolvers in case; NMAH. 214/15 LC-USZ62-29471. 216 tl NAA. 216 c NAA. 216/17 NAA. 217 tl © CORBIS, #NA015673. 217 c LC-USZ62-11024. 218 b NARA. 219 tl NAA. 219 tr NARA. 219 b NAA. 220 t NAA. 220/21 NARA. 221 tl *George Armstrong Custer*, c. 1863, unidentified photographer, NPG.82.53. 221 tr NMNH. 221 b NMAH. 222 t NAA. 222/23 LC-DIG-ppmsc-02527. 223 t *Eminent Women*, detail of Helen Maria Fiske Hunt Jackson, 1884, Eugene L'Africain after photographs, NPG 81.51. 224 c NMAI 2.8574. 224 br NAA. 225 t © Bettmann/CORBIS, #BPA2# 5155. 225 b Courtesy of Arizona Historical Society, Tucson. 226 tl NMAH. 226/27 The Art Archive, PD# AA350383. 227 tr *Kings of Wall Street* (detail), 1882, Buek and Lindner lithography company and published by Root and Tinker, NPG.73.14. 227 br *Millionaires of the United States* (detail), 1884, Franklin Square lithography company, NPG.85.54. 228 NMAH-PHD. 228/29 SIL. 229 NMAH-AC. 230 tl NMAH-AC. 230/31 LC-USZ62-11783. 231 l The Art Archive/Bill Manns, PD# AA392451. 231 r The Art Archive/National Archives, Washington DC. 232 tl NAA. 232 r NMAH. 232 bl NMAH. 234 tl NMAH. 234/35 SI. 235 t *William Henry Seward*; 1853, Francis D'Avignon after daguerreotype by Jeremiah Gurney, NPG.72.68. 235 b LC-USZ62-71633. 236 t SI. 236 b Courtesy of Seaver Center for Western History Research, Natural History Museum of Los Angeles County. 237 t NMAH. 237 b The Art Archive, PD# AA392426. 238 t Courtesy of Bishop Museum. 239 t NAA. 239 b LC-G403- 0265-C. 240 t NAA. 240/41 NAA. 241 Courtesy of Robert B. Honeyman, Jr. Collections, Bancroft Library, Berkley, California. 242 tl LC-USZ62-36829. 242/43 The Art Archive/Bill Manns, PD# AA392473. 243 b The Art Archive/Bill Manns, PD# AA392410. 244 tl LC-DIG-ppmsc-02638. 244 cl DK. 244 cc DK. 244 cr DK. 244 br Bill Pickett movie poster, 1923, Ritchey Lithographic Corporation, NPG 84.113. 245 tl SI-Archives. 245 tr SIL-Horticulture. 245 b LC-USZ62-78372. 246/47 *Sourdough gold, the log of a Yukon adventure*, by Mary Lee Caldwell Davis, Publisher: Boston, W.A. Wilde co., 1933, SIL. 248 tl NMAH. 248/49 LC-USZ62-110711. 249 r LC-USZC4-1473. 251 tl NMAH. 251 tr *Liliuokalani*, c. 1891, Menzies Dickson, NPG.80.320. 252 t DK.

252 b NMAH-AC. 252/53 LC-USZ62-17608. 253 t NMAH-AC. 254 t LC-USZC4-1393. 254 tr *William Frederick Cody ("Buffalo Bill")*, c. 1875, José Maria Mora, NPG.77.155. 254 br Courtesy of Denver Public Library. 255 tl The Art Archive/National Archives, Washington DC, PD# AA389810. 255 tc The Art Archive/ National Archives, Washington DC, PD# AA 389813. 255 tr *Jesse Woodson James*, 1870?, Unknown artist, NPG.88.206. 255 cl The Art Archive/Bill Manns, PD# AA392406. 255 b *The Wild Bunch*, 1900, John Swartz, NPG.82.66. 256/57 NMAH-PH. 258/59 "Horse Wrangler" © David Stoecklein/Corbis, #PE-264-0003. 259 "Las Vegas Strip at night," DK. 260/61 LC-USZ62-107801. 261 LC-C2688-600. 262 NMAH-PHD. 262/63 LC-USZ62-60681. 263 LC-USZ62-99483. 264 t NMAH. 264/65 NASM. 265 tl NMAH. 265 c NASM. 266 SIL. 266 c The Bancroft Library. University of California, Berkeley. 266/67 LC-USZ62-54627. 267 tr LC-USZ62-77427. 267 c LC-USZC4-4838. 268 tr NMAH-Archives Center. 268 bl LC-USZ62-97470. 268/69 USDA. 270 tr LC-ppmsc 01692. 270 bl LC-USZ62-38628. 270 br LCPP006A-15668. 270/71 LC-USZ62-121049. 271 b Courtesy of Kansas State Historical Society. 272 LC-USZ62-100874. 273 tl LC-USZ62-58968. 273 tr LC-USZC4-1177. 273 c *Sir Charles Spencer Chaplin*, 1915-16, Berkshire Poster Co., T/NPG.84.114.87. 273 b LC-USZ62-119963. 274 NMAH. 274/75 LC-USZ62-107556. 275 LC-USZ62-130058. 276 LC-USZC4-8012. 276 tr NMAH. 277 t LC-USZ62-33788. 277 b NMAH-PHD. 278 bl LC-USZ62-126995. 278 br NMAH. 279 t LC-USZ62-2235. 279 b NARA 48-RST-7B-113. 280 *Buffalo Mother, Buffalo Dance*, 1917-25, Awa Tsireh, SAAM 1979.144.17. 280/81 *Gloria May Josephine Swanson*, 1978 from c. 1921 negative, Nickolas Muray, T/NPG.78.192.93. 281 t NMAH. 281 b The Bancroft Library. University of California, Berkeley. 282 t *Corn Dance, Taos Pueblo*, 1934, Norman S. Chamberlain, SAAM 1964.1.77. 282 b *Elk-Foot of the Taos Tribe*, 1909, Eanger Irving Couse, SAAM 1910.9.5. 283 t LC-USZ62-8912. 283 b *Walter Elias Disney*, 1933, Edward Steichen, NPG.82.87. 284 *Cowboy Dance*, 1941, Jenne Magafan, SAAM 1962.8.46. 284/85 LC-USZ62-11491. 286 © Bettmann/Corbis, #BE060387. 287 tl LC-USZ62-111222. 287 tr DK. 287 b LC-USZC2-815. 288 NMAH. 288/89 © Bettmann/Corbis, #U781919ACME. 289 NARA 295978. 290 SI. 291 tl LC-USW3-028673. 291 tr © Corbis, #NA005595. 291 b LC-USZ62-113250. 292 LC-USZ62-116927. 292/93 © Corbis, #IH064029. 294 t NASM. 294 b DK. 295 t Courtesy of Lockheed Martin Corporation. 295 b © Bettmann/Corbis, #U1276131INP. 297 bl DK. 297 br DK. 298 © Bettmann/Corbis, #U1148153INP. 299 LC-USZ62-84494. 300 t NMAH. 300 DK. 301 DK. 303 t LC-USZC4-2420. 304 l DK. 304 tr © Bettmann/Corbis, #BE022778. 305 tl NMAH. 305 tc NMAH. 305 tr NMAH. 305 b © Ed Kashi/Corbis, #ZK001177. 306 t *Cowboy Boots*, 1980, William Wilhelmi, SAAM 1981.107A-B. 306/07 DK. 307 © AINACO/Corbis, #AN001287. 308 t © Bettmann/Corbis, #BE036876. 308/09 DK.